The Marx Revival

The planet is in deep trouble because of capitalism, and Karl Marx, freed from the chains of 'real socialism', is being rediscovered all around the world as the thinker who provided us with its most insightful critique. *The Marx Revival* is the best, most complete, and most modern guide to Marx's ideas that has appeared since the fall of the Berlin Wall. Written by highly reputed international experts, in a clear form accessible to a wider public, it brings together the liveliest and most thought-provoking contemporary interpretations of Marx's work. It presents what he actually wrote in respect of twenty-two key concepts, the areas that require updating as a result of changes since the late-nineteenth century, and the reasons why it is still of such relevance in today's world. The result is a collection that will prove indispensable both for specialists and for a new generation approaching Marx's work for the first time.

Marcello Musto is Associate Professor of Sociology at York University. He has published worldwide in more than twenty languages and his most recent titles are *Another Marx: Early Manuscripts to the International* (2018), *The Last Years of Karl Marx: An Intellectual Biography* (2020), and *Travels with Marx: Destinations, Reflections and Encounters* (2020).

The Marx Revival
Key Concepts and New Interpretations

Edited by
Marcello Musto
York University

CAMBRIDGE
UNIVERSITY PRESS

University Printing House, Cambridge CB2 8BS, United Kingdom

One Liberty Plaza, 20th Floor, New York, NY 10006, USA

477 Williamstown Road, Port Melbourne, VIC 3207, Australia

314–321, 3rd Floor, Plot 3, Splendor Forum, Jasola District Centre, New Delhi – 110025, India

79 Anson Road, #06-04/06, Singapore 079906

Cambridge University Press is part of the University of Cambridge.

It furthers the University's mission by disseminating knowledge in the pursuit of education, learning, and research at the highest international levels of excellence.

www.cambridge.org
Information on this title: www.cambridge.org/9781107117921
DOI: 10.1017/9781316338902

© Cambridge University Press 2020

This publication is in copyright. Subject to statutory exception and to the provisions of relevant collective licensing agreements, no reproduction of any part may take place without the written permission of Cambridge University Press.

First published 2020

A catalogue record for this publication is available from the British Library.

ISBN 978-1-107-11792-1 Hardback
ISBN 978-1-107-54216-7 Paperback

Cambridge University Press has no responsibility for the persistence or accuracy of URLs for external or third-party internet websites referred to in this publication and does not guarantee that any content on such websites is, or will remain, accurate or appropriate.

Contents

About the Editor	page x
List of Contributors	xi
Preface	xvii
Acknowledgements	xx
Note on the Text	xxi

1 Capitalism   1
MICHAEL R. KRÄTKE

1.1 Capitalism and Its History	1
1.2 Capitalism: What Is in a Word?	3
1.3 The Basic Features of Modern Capitalism	6
1.4 Value, Money, Competition	8
1.5 Exploitation and Accumulation	11
1.6 The Historical Emergence and Development of Capitalism	16
1.7 Marx's Critique of Modern Capitalism	19

2 Communism   24
MARCELLO MUSTO

2.1 Critical Theories of the Early Socialists	24
2.2 Equality, Theoretical Systems, and Future Society: Errors of the Precursors	26
2.3 Where and Why Marx Wrote about Communism	30
2.4 The Limits of the Initial Formulations	33
2.5 Communism as Free Association	37
2.6 Common Ownership and Free Time	41
2.7 Role of the State, Individual Rights, and Freedoms	45

3 Democracy   51
ELLEN MEIKSINS WOOD

3.1 Marx's Critique of Democracy	51
3.2 The Changing Meanings of Democracy	53
3.3 Marx on 'Bourgeois Democracy'	58
3.4 From Politics to Political Economy	62
3.5 The Political Limits of Capitalist Democracy	65

4 Proletariat — 70
MARCEL VAN DER LINDEN

- 4.1 The Revolutionary Subject — 70
- 4.2 Defining the Proletariat — 72
- 4.3 Excluding the Lumpenproletariat — 75
- 4.4 Excluding Chattel Slaves — 79
- 4.5 Problematic Consequences — 84
- 4.6 A Final Word — 87

5 Class Struggle — 92
ALEX CALLINICOS

- 5.1 Genealogy — 92
- 5.2 Theoretical Articulation — 94
- 5.3 Politics — 98
- 5.4 Assessment — 103

6 Political Organization — 108
PETER HUDIS

- 6.1 The Philosophical Basis of Marx's Concept of Organization — 108
- 6.2 Marx on Political Organization before and during the 1848 Revolutions — 109
- 6.3 *Capital*, the First International, and the Paris Commune — 114
- 6.4 Two Concepts of Organization: Marx versus Lassalle on the Party — 118
- 6.5 Marx versus Post-Marx Marxism on Organization — 122

7 Revolution — 126
MICHAEL LÖWY

- 7.1 Revolutionary Praxis: The Early Writings — 126
- 7.2 Revolution as Self-Emancipation: The First International and the Paris Commune — 131
- 7.3 The Late Marx: Germany and Russia, Centre and Periphery — 134
- 7.4 After Marx — 136

8 Work — 141
RICARDO ANTUNES

- 8.1 Work as a Vital Human Activity — 141
- 8.2 Labour as an Alienated Activity — 143
- 8.3 Labour, Value-Theory, Fetishism, and Associated Work — 145
- 8.4 Work Today — 153

9 Capital and Temporality — 157
MOISHE POSTONE

- 9.1 Reconceptualizing Marxism — 157
- 9.2 History and Domination — 159
- 9.3 Critique and Historical Specificity — 161
- 9.4 The Dialectic of Temporal Mediation — 166

	Contents	
	9.5 The Dual Crisis of Capital	171
	9.6 An Adequate Critical Theory for Today	174
10	Ecology	177
	JOHN BELLAMY FOSTER	
	10.1 Marx and the Earth	177
	10.2 Western Marxist Criticisms of Marx on Nature	178
	10.3 The Rediscovery of Marx's Ecology	181
	10.4 The Emergence of Marxian Ecological Praxis	191
11	Gender Equality	197
	HEATHER A. BROWN	
	11.1 Marx, Gender, and Feminism	197
	11.2 Marx's Early Writings on Gender Equality and Emancipation	198
	11.3 Political Economy, Gender, and the Transformation of the Family	200
	11.4 The Dialectics of the Pre-capitalist Family	206
	11.5 The Importance of Dialectical Intersectionality	209
12	Nationalism and Ethnicity	212
	KEVIN B. ANDERSON	
	12.1 Refuting a Legend	212
	12.2 Poland and the European Democratic Revolution	213
	12.3 Race, Class, and Slavery during the American Civil War	218
	12.4 Ireland: Struggling against both National and Ethnic Oppression	224
	12.5 Reflections for the Twenty-First Century	228
13	Migration	232
	PIETRO BASSO	
	13.1 The Forced Emigration of Rural Producers	232
	13.2 The Slave Trade and the Super-Exploitation of Black Slaves in the Colonies	234
	13.3 Migration in and from Europe	236
	13.4 Global Labour Market and Industrial Reserve Army	237
	13.5 A Process That Is Not Natural but Social-Historical	239
	13.6 British Proletarians and Irish Proletarians	241
	13.7 Yesterday, Today, Tomorrow	244
14	Colonialism	247
	SANDRO MEZZADRA AND RANABIR SAMADDAR	
	14.1 Capitalism as a World Force and Colonialism	247
	14.2 Capitalism, Colonialism, Transition	251
	14.3 Colonial Relations, Class Question, and the Peasantry	252
	14.4 Slavery	258
	14.5 The Colonized as the Political Subject	261

Contents

15 State — 266
BOB JESSOP
- 15.1 Are There Essential, Permanent, Stable Elements? — 266
- 15.2 Three Essential Theories of the State and State Power — 268
- 15.3 The State as a Social Relation — 274
- 15.4 Marx and State Theory Today — 279

16 Globalization — 285
SEONGJIN JEONG
- 16.1 Globalization in Marx's Words — 285
- 16.2 The Dialectics of Progress — 286
- 16.3 The World Market and Critique of Political Economy — 289
- 16.4 The World Market and the State — 290
- 16.5 Uneven and Combined Development on a World Scale — 292
- 16.6 International Value and Exploitation — 293
- 16.7 World Market Crisis — 296
- 16.8 From World Market to World Revolution — 298

17 War and International Relations — 302
BENNO TESCHKE
- 17.1 A Belated Discovery — 302
- 17.2 The General Problem of International Relations in Marx's Thought — 304
- 17.3 The Early Wager: The Universalization of Capitalism — 307
- 17.4 From Logic to History: The Impact of 1848 and the Crimean War — 309
- 17.5 Historicism as Theory — 314

18 Religion — 320
GILBERT ACHCAR
- 18.1 Marx's Engagement with Religion — 320
- 18.2 Marx' Left-Hegelian Critique of Religion — 321
- 18.3 Towards a Materialist Interpretation of Religion — 327
- 18.4 The Marxian Political Attitude on Religion — 331

19 Education — 338
ROBIN SMALL
- 19.1 Marx's Contribution on Education — 338
- 19.2 The Political Economy of Education — 339
- 19.3 Education, the State, and Society — 342
- 19.4 Marx's Curriculum — 344
- 19.5 Teachers and Their Work — 346
- 19.6 Marx and Education Today — 348

20 Art — 351
ISABELLE GARO
- 20.1 Art and Alienation — 351

Contents

	20.2 Art and the Critique of Political Economy	355
	20.3 The Contemporary Relevance of Marx's Analysis of Art	360
21	**Technology and Science**	363
	AMY E. WENDLING	
	21.1 Science and Technology in Marx's Research	363
	21.2 Communist Machines in the *Grundrisse*	366
	21.3 Technology and Contradiction in *Capital*	368
	21.4 The Use of Marx's Account of Technology	373
22	**Marxisms**	376
	IMMANUEL WALLERSTEIN	
	22.1 Different Versions of Marxism	376
	22.2 Engels' Marxism	377
	22.3 Soviet Marxism	380
	22.4 US Hegemony and the Cold War	384
	22.5 The World Revolution of 1968	387
	22.6 Collapse of the Communisms	389
	Index	393

About the Editor

Marcello Musto is Associate Professor of Sociological Theory at York University (Toronto – Canada). He is author of: *Ripensare Marx e i marxismi. Studi e saggi* (Carocci, 2011); *Another Marx: Early Manuscripts to the International* (Bloomsbury, 2018); *Karl Marx. Biografia intellettuale e politica 1857–1883* (Einaudi, 2018); *The Last Years of Karl Marx: An Intellectual Biography* (Stanford University Press, 2020); and *Travels of Karl Marx: Destinations, Reflections and Encounters* (Europa Editions, 2020). Among his edited volumes there are: *Karl Marx's Grundrisse: Foundations of the Critique of Political Economy 150 Years Later* (Routledge, 2008); *Marx for Today* (Routledge, 2012); *Workers Unite! The International 150 Years Later* (Bloomsbury, 2014); *The International After 150 Years: Labour Versus Capital, Then and Now* (with George Comninel and Victor Wallis, Routledge, 2015); *Marx's Capital after 150 Years: Critique and Alternative to Capitalism*, (Routledge, 2019); *Karl Marx's Life, Ideas, Influences: A Critical Examination on the Bicentenary* (with Shaibal Gupta and Babak Amini, Palgrave, 2019); and *The Routledge Handbook of Marx's 'Capital': A Global History of Translation, Dissemination and Reception* (with Babak Amini, Routledge, forthcoming 2021). His articles appeared in many journals, including the *International Review of Social History*, *Science & Society*, *Critique*, *Review of Radical Political Economics*, *Socialism and Democracy*, *Economic & Political Weekly*, and *Contemporary Sociology*. His writings – available at www.marcellomusto.org – have been published worldwide in more than twenty languages. He is also the editor (with Terrell Carver) of the Series *Marx, Engels, Marxisms* (Palgrave).

Contributors

Gilbert Achcar is Professor of Development Studies and International Relations at School of Oriental and African Studies, University of London (UK). His books include: *Perilous Power: The Middle East and U.S. Foreign Policy* (with Noam Chomsky, Routledge, 2007), *The Arabs and the Holocaust: The Arab-Israeli War of Narratives* (Macmillan, 2010), *Marxism, Orientalism, Cosmopolitanism* (Haymarket, 2013), *The People Want: A Radical Exploration of the Arab Uprising* (University of California Press, 2013), and *Morbid Symptoms: Relapse in the Arab Uprising* (Stanford University Press, 2016).

Kevin B. Anderson is Professor of Sociology at University of California, Santa Barbara (USA). Among his books there are: *Lenin, Hegel, and Western Marxism: A Critical Study* (University of Illinois Press, 1995) and *Marx at the Margins: On Nationalism, Ethnicity, and Non-Western Societies* (University of Chicago Press, 2010). Among his edited volumes there are: *The Rosa Luxemburg Reader* (with Peter Hudis, Monthly Review, 2004), *Dunayevskaya-Marcuse-Fromm Correspondence* (with Russell Rockwell, Lexington, 2012), and *Karl Marx* (with Bertell Ollman, Routledge, 2012).

Ricardo Antunes is Professor of Sociology at the University of Campinas (Brazil). He is author of: *Adiós al trabajo? Ensayo sobre las metamorfosis y la centralidad del mundo del trabajo* (Cortez, 2001), *The Meanings of Work: Essay on the Affirmation and Negation of Work* (Brill, 2013), and *O novo proletariado de serviço na era digital* (Boitempo, 2018). Among his edited volumes there are: *Riqueza e Miséria do Trabalho no Brasil*, volumes I, II, III, and IV (Boitempo, 2014, 2013, 2014, and 2019).

Pietro Basso is Associate Professor of Sociology at Ca' Foscari University of Venice (Italy). He is the author of: *Modern Times, Ancient Hours: Working Lives in the Twenty-First Century* (Verso, 2003) and *Le racisme européen. Critique de la rationalité institutionnelle de l'oppression* (Syllepse, 2016). Among his edited volumes there are:

Razzismo di stato. Stati Uniti, Europa, Italia (Angeli, 2010) and *The Science and Passion of Communism: Selected Writings of Amadeo Bordiga 1912–1965* (Brill, 2019).

Heather A. Brown is Assistant Professor of Political Science at Westfield State University (Massachusetts, USA). She is the author of *Marx on Gender and the Family: A Critical Study* (Brill, 2012).

Alex Callinicos is Professor of European Studies at King's College London (UK). His books include: *The Revolutionary Ideas of Karl Marx* (Bookmarks Publications, 1983), *Against Postmodernism* (Polity Press, 1989), *An Anti-Capitalist Manifesto* (Polity, 2003), *The Resources of Critique* (Polity, 2006), *Imperialism and Global Political Economy* (Polity, 2009), and *Deciphering* Capital: *Marx's* Capital *and Its Destiny* (Bookmarks Publications, 2014).

John Bellamy Foster is Professor of Sociology at the University of Oregon (Eugene, USA). Among his books there are: *The Vulnerable Planet* (1994), *Marx's Ecology* (2000), *Ecology Against Capitalism* (2002), *Naked Imperialism* (2006), *The Ecological Revolution: Making Peace with the Planet* (2009), *The Great Financial Crisis* (with Fred Magdoff, 2009), *The Ecological Rift* (with Brett Clark and Richard York, 2010), and *The Endless Crisis* (with Robert W. McChesney, 2012), all published by Monthly Review Press. He has also written *Marx and the Earth* (with Paul Burkett, Brill, 2016).

Isabelle Garo teaches at the Lycée Chaptal (Paris, France). She is the author of: *Marx. Une critique de la philosophie* (Seuil, 2000), *L'idéologie ou la pensée embarquée* (La Fabrique, 2009), *Foucault, Deleuze, Althusser et Marx. La politique dans la philosophie* (Démopolis, 2011), *Marx et l'invention historique* (Syllepse, 2012), *L'or des images. Art, monnaie, capital* (La Ville Brûle, 2013), and *Communisme et stratégie* (Amsterdam, 2019). She also co-edited *Marx politique* (with Jean-Numa Ducange, La Dispute, 2015).

Peter Hudis is Professor of Philosophy and Humanities at Oakton Community College (Des Plaines, IL, USA). He is author of: *Marx's Concept of the Alternative to Capitalism* (Brill, 2012) and *Frantz Fanon, Philosopher of the Barricades* (Pluto, 2015). He has edited: *The Rosa Luxemburg Reader* (with Kevin B. Anderson, Monthly Review Press, 2004), *The Letters of Rosa Luxemburg* (Verso, 2011), and *The Complete Works of Rosa Luxemburg*, volumes 1, 2, and 3 (Verso, 2013, 2015, and 2019).

List of Contributors

Seongjin Jeong is Professor of Economics at Gyeongsang National University (Jinju, Republic of Korea). He is the author of: *Marx and the Korean Economy* (Chaekgalpi, 2005), *Marx and Trotsky* (Hanul, 2006), and *Marx and the World Economy* (Hanul, 2015). Among his edited volumes there are: *Marxist Perspectives on South Korea in the Global Economy* (with Martin Hart-Landsberg and Richard Westra, Routledge, 2016) and *Varieties of Alternative Economic Systems: Practical Utopias for an Age of Global Crisis and Austerity* (with Richard Westra and Robert Albritton, Routledge, 2017).

Bob Jessop is Distinguished Professor of Sociology at Lancaster University (UK). Among his books there are: *The Capitalistic State: Marxists Theories and Methods* (Martin Robertson, 1982), *Nicos Poulantzas: Marxist Theory and Political Strategy* (Macmillan, 1985), *State Theory: Putting the Capitalist State in Its Place* (Polity, 1990), *The Future of the Capitalist State* (Polity, 2002), *State Power: A Strategic-Relational Approach* (Polity, 2007), and *The State: Past, Present, Future* (Polity, 2016). Among his edited volumes there are: *Karl Marx's Social and Political Thought: Critical Assessments*, volumes 1, 2, 3, and 4 (Routledge, 1990) and *Karl Marx's Social and Political Thought: Critical Assessments*, volumes 5, 6, 7, and 8 (with Wheatley Russell, Routledge, 1999).

Michael R. Krätke is Professor of Sociology at Lancaster University (UK). He is the author of: *Kritik der Staatsfinanzen: zur politischen Ökonomie des Steuerstaats* (VSA Verlag, 1984) and *Kritik der Politischen Ökonomie heute. Zeitgenosse Marx* (VSA Verlag, 2017).

Michael Löwy is Emeritus Research Director at the French National Center for Scientific Research (Paris, France). Among his books there are: *Morning Star: Surrealism, Marxism, Anarchism, Situationism, Utopia* (University of Texas Press, 2000), *Romanticism Against the Tide of Modernity* (with Robert Sayre, Duke University Press, 2001), *The Theory of Revolution of the Young Marx* (Brill, 2003), *Fire Alarm: Reading Walter Benjamin's 'On the Concept of History'* (Verso, 2005), *La Cage d'acier: Max Weber et le marxisme wébérien* (Éditions Stock, 2013), and *Rosa Luxemburg, l'étincelle incendiaire* (Le Temps des Cerises, 2018).

Marcello Musto is Associate Professor of Sociological Theory at York University (Toronto, Canada). He is the author of: *Another Marx: Early Manuscripts to the International* (Bloomsbury, 2018) and *The Last Years of Karl Marx: An Intellectual Biography* (Stanford University Press, 2020).

Sandro Mezzadra is Associate Professor of Political Theory at the University of Bologna (Italy). He is the author of: *La condizione postcoloniale. Storia e politica nel presente globale* (Ombre Corte, 2008), *In the Marxian Workshops: Producing Subjects* (Rowman & Littlefield, 2018), and *The Politics of Operations: Excavating Contemporary Capitalism* (Duke University Press, 2019). Among his books there are: *Border as Method, or, the Multiplication of Labor* (with Brett Neilson, Duke University Press, 2013).

Moishe Postone was Professor of History at the University of Chicago (USA). He authored: *Time Labor and Social Domination* (Cambridge University Press, 1993), *Marx est-il devenu muet* (La Tour-d'Aigues, 2003), and *Deutschland, die Linke und der Holocaust Politische Interventionen* (ça ira, 2005). He also edited: *Bourdieu: Critical Perspectives* (with Craig J. Calhoun and Edward LiPuma, Polity Press, 1993) and *Catastrophe and Meaning* (with Eric Sentner, University of Chicago Press, 2003).

Ranabir Samaddar is Distinguished Chair in Migration and Forced Migration Studies, Calcutta Research Group (Kolkata, India). Among his books there are: *Memory, Identity, Power: Politics in the Junglemahals, 1890–1950* (Orient Longman, 1998), *The Marginal Nation: Transborder Migration from Bangladesh to West Bengal* (Sage, 1999), and *Karl Marx and the Postcolonial Age* (Palgrave MacMillan, 2017). He also co-edited: *Beyond Kolkata: Rajarhat and the Dystopia of Urban Imagination* (with Ishita Dey and Suhit K. Sen, Routledge, 2014).

Robin Small is Emeritus Professor at the University of Auckland (New Zealand). He is the author of: *Marx and Education* (Ashgate, 2005), *Nietzsche and Rée: A Star Friendship* (Oxford University Press, 2005), *Karl Marx: The Revolutionary as Educator* (Springer, 2013), and *Friedrich Nietzsche: Reconciling Knowledge and Life* (Springer, 2016). He is also the editor of: *A Hundred Years of Phenomenology: Perspectives on a Philosophical Tradition* (Ashgate, 2001).

Benno Teschke is Professor of International Relations at the University of Sussex (Brighton, UK). He is the author of *The Myth of 1648: Class, Geopolitics and the Making of Modern International Relations* (Verso, 2003).

Marcel van der Linden is Honorary Fellow at the International Institute of Social History (Amsterdam, the Netherlands). His books include: *Western Marxism and the Soviet Union: A Survey of Critical Theories and Debates since 1917* (Brill, 2007) and *Workers of the World:*

Essays toward a Global Labor History (Brill, 2008). Among his edited books there are: *Beyond Marx: Theorising the Global Labour Relations of the Twenty-First Century* (with Karl Heinz, Brill, 2014), *Capitalism: The Reemergence of a Historical Concept* (with Jürgen Kocke, Bloomsbury, 2016), and *Marx's* Capital: *An Unfinishable Project?* (with Gerald Hubmann, Brill, 2018).

Immanuel Wallerstein was Professor of Sociology at Yale University (New Haven, USA). Among his books there are: *World–Systems Analysis: An Introduction* (Duke University Press, 2004), *The Modern World-System*, volumes I, II, III, and IV (Academic Press, 1974, 1980, 1989, and University of California Press, 2011), *The Capitalistic World-Economy* (Cambridge University Press, 1979), *Historical Capitalism with Capitalist Civilization* (Verso, 1983), *Unthinking Social Science: The Limits of Nineteenth-Century Paradigms* (Polity Press, 1991), *Race, Nation, Class: Ambiguous Identities* (with Etienne Balibar, Verso, 1991), *After Liberalism* (The New Press, 1995), and *Does Capitalism Have a Future?* (with Randall Collins, Michael Mann, Georgi Derluguian, and Craig Calhoun, Oxford University Press, 2013).

Amy E. Wendling is Professor of Philosophy at Creighton University (Omaha, USA). She is the author of: *Karl Marx on Technology and Alienation* (Palgrave-Macmillan, 2009) and *The Ruling Ideas: Bourgeois Political Concepts* (Lexington Books, 2012).

Ellen Meiksins Wood was Professor of Political Theory at York University (Toronto, Canada). Among her books there are: *The Retreat from Class: A New 'True' Socialism* (Verso, 1986), *Democracy against Capitalism: Renewing Historical Materialism* (Cambridge University Press, 1995), *The Origin of Capitalism* (Verso, 2002), *Empire of Capital* (Verso, 2003), and *Citizens to Lords: A Social History of Western Political Thought*, volumes 1 and 2 (Verso, 2008 and 2012).

Preface

Scornful neglect and intemperate hostility, haughty dismissal and marginal course adoption, selective co-optation and selective bowdlerization: these are some of the strategies adopted by establishment intellectuals over the years in response to the challenge of the thinker born two hundred years ago in Trier. Yet, here we are at the beginning of the third decade of the twenty-first century, and it sometimes seems that Karl Marx's real ideas have never been as topical, or as commanding of respect and interest, as they are today.

Since the latest crisis of capitalism broke out in 2008, Marx has been back in fashion. Contrary to the predictions after the fall of the Berlin Wall, when he was consigned to perpetual oblivion, Marx's ideas are once more the object of analysis, development, and debate. Many have begun to ask new questions about a thinker who was often wrongly identified with 'actually existing socialism' and then curtly brushed aside after 1989. Prestigious newspapers and journals with a wide readership have described Marx as a highly topical and far-sighted theorist. Almost everywhere, he is now the theme of university courses and international conferences. His writings, reprinted or brought out in new editions, have reappeared on bookshop shelves, and the study of his work, after twenty years of virtual silence, has gathered increasing momentum, sometimes producing important, ground-breaking results. The years 2017 and 2018 have brought further intensity to this 'Marx revival', thanks to many initiatives around the world linked to the 150th anniversary of the publication of *Capital* and the bicentenary of Marx's birth.

Of particular value for an overall reassessment of Marx's oeuvre was the resumed publication in 1998 of the *Marx-Engels-Gesamtausgabe* (MEGA²), the historical-critical edition of the complete works of Marx and Engels. Twenty-eight volumes have already appeared, and others are in the course of preparation. These volumes contain new versions of some of Marx's works (like *The German Ideology*), all his preparatory manuscripts of *Capital* from 1857 to 1881, all the letters he sent and received during his life, and approximately two hundred notebooks containing excerpts from his reading and reflections to which they gave rise. The latter form the workshop of his critical theory, showing us the complex itinerary of his thought and the sources on which he drew in developing his ideas.

These priceless volumes of the MEGA² edition – many available only in German and therefore still confined to small circles of researchers – show us an author very different from the one that numerous critics, or self-styled followers, presented for such a long time. The publication of previously unknown materials of Marx, along with innovative interpretations of his work, has opened up new research horizons and demonstrated, more clearly than in the past, his capacity to examine the contradictions of capitalist society on a global scale and in spheres beyond the conflict between capital and labour. It is no exaggeration to say that, of the great classics of political, economic, and philosophical thought, Marx is the one whose profile has changed the most in the opening decades of the twenty-first century.

Research advances, together with the changed political conditions, suggest that the renewal in the interpretation of Marx's thought is a phenomenon destined to continue. Recent publications have shown that Marx went deeply into many issues – often underestimated, or even ignored, by scholars of his work – which are acquiring crucial importance for the political agenda of our times. Among these are the ecological question, migration, the critique of nationalism, individual freedom in the economic and political sphere, gender emancipation, the emancipatory potential of technology, and forms of collective ownership not controlled by the state.

Furthermore, Marx undertook thorough investigations of societies outside Europe and expressed himself unambiguously against the ravages of colonialism. He also criticized thinkers who used categories peculiar to the European context in their analysis of peripheral areas of the globe. He warned against those who failed to observe the necessary distinctions between phenomena and, especially after his theoretical advances in the 1870s, he was highly wary of transferring interpretive categories across completely different historical or geographical fields. All this is more evident today, despite the scepticism still fashionable in certain academic quarters. Thus, thirty years after the fall of the Berlin Wall, it has become possible to read a Marx very unlike the dogmatic, economistic, and Eurocentric theorist who was paraded around for so long.

Of course, one can find in Marx's massive literary bequest a number of statements that suggest that the development of the productive forces is leading to dissolution of the capitalist mode of production. But it would be wrong to attribute to him any idea that the advent of socialism is a historical inevitability. Indeed, for Marx, the possibility of transforming society depended on the working class and its capacity, through struggle, to change the world.

If Marx's ideas are reconsidered in the light of changes that have occurred since his death, they prove highly useful for an understanding of capitalist society but also shed light on the failure of socialist experiences in the twentieth century. For Marx, capitalism is not an organization of society in which human beings, protected by impartial legal norms capable of guaranteeing justice and equity, enjoy true freedom and live in accomplished democracy. In reality, they are degraded into mere objects, whose primary function is to produce commodities and profit for others. But if communism aims to be a higher form of society, it must promote the conditions for 'the full and free development of each individual'. In contrast to the equation of communism with 'dictatorship of the proletariat', which many of the 'communist states' espoused in their propaganda, it is necessary to look again at Marx's definition of communist society as 'an association of free human beings'.

This book – which contains contributions by noted international scholars – presents a Marx in many ways different from the one familiar from the dominant currents of twentieth-century socialism. Its dual aim is to reopen for discussion, in a critical and innovative manner, the classical themes of Marx's thought, and to develop a deeper analysis of certain questions to which relatively little attention has been paid until now. It is hoped that the volume will therefore help to bring Marx closer both to those who think everything has already been written about his work and to a new generation of readers who have not yet been seriously confronted with his writings.

It goes without saying that we cannot today simply rely on what Marx wrote a century and a half ago. But nor should we lightly discount the content and clarity of his analyses or fail to take up the critical weapons he offered for fresh thinking about an alternative society to capitalism.

Marcello Musto

Acknowledgements

The editor would like to thank Babak Amini and George Comninel for their editorial help. I would also like to express my gratitude to Patrick Camiller, who has revised Chapter 2, and to Emma Willert who prepared the index.

The editor and publisher are also grateful to the Faculty of Liberal Arts & Professional Studies, York University, Toronto, Canada, for the financial support it provided to this work.

Note on the Text

Marx's writings have been generally quoted from the fifty-volume *Marx Engels Collected Works* (MECW) (Moscow/London/New York: Progress Publishers/Lawrence and Wishart/International Publishers, 1975–2005). Citations from the *Grundrisse* and from the three volumes of *Capital* have been often taken from Penguin editions. Moreover, sometimes, the reader is referred to single works translated into English not included in MECW.

Texts that have not yet been translated into English are often referenced to the *Marx-Engels-Gesamtausgabe* (MEGA^2) (Berlin: Dietz/Akademie/De Gruyter, 1975–), of which sixty-seven of the planned 114 volumes have so far appeared in print. In a few cases, authors have cited single editions in German of writings still not published in the MEGA^2.

As regards the secondary literature, quotations from books and articles not published in English have been translated for the present volume. All the names of journals and newspapers are indicated first in English translation, followed by the name in original language in square brackets. Indications of birth and death dates of authors and historical figures have been provided the first time they are mentioned in each chapter of the book.

1 Capitalism

Michael R. Krätke

1.1 Capitalism and Its History

Today Marx enjoys worldwide fame as the incomparable theorist of capitalism and its most penetrating critic. The term itself, however, rarely appears in his writings. French socialists were already using it in the 1840s and 1850s, but only to denote certain aspects of what we would now understand by capitalism. When Pierre Leroux (1797–1871) spoke of capitalism in his pamphlet against political economy *Malthus and the Economists, or Will There Always Be Poor People?* (1848), he was highlighting the unprecedented power of capitalists, and more specifically industrialists, in modern times.[1] Louis Blanc (1811–82) occasionally employed the term in various editions of his book *The Organization of Work* (1850), referring to 'the appropriation of capital by some to the exclusion of others'.[2] And Pierre-Joseph Proudhon (1809–65), in his *The General Idea of the Revolution in the Nineteenth Century* (1851), had the same idea in mind when he pointed to the power of capitalists in the Parisian housing market.[3]

In Germany, it was Johann Karl Rodbertus (1805–75), a fervent critic of classical political economy, who first wrote of 'capitalism' in the sense of a 'social system'.[4] Albert Schäffle (1831–1903), a liberal-conservative professor of political economy and one of the early 'academic socialists [*Kathedersozialisten*]', became the first to counterpose capitalism to socialism in the title of a book: *Capitalism and Socialism* (1870). The socialists were right, he admitted, alluding to Marx: 'the present economy is characterized by the capitalist mode of production', that is, by the hegemony of 'capitalism'.[5]

---

[1] Cf. P. Leroux, *Malthus et les économistes, ou y aura-t-il toujours des pauvres?* (Boussac: Imprimerie de Pierre Leroux, 1849), p. 179.
[2] L. Blanc, *L'Organisation du Travail* (Paris: Bureau du nouveau monde, 1850), p. 162.
[3] P.-J. Proudhon, *The General Idea of the Revolution in the Nineteenth Century* (New York: Haskell Hause Publishers, 1969), p. 223.
[4] J. K. Rodbertus, *Zur Erklärung und Abhülfe der heutigen Creditnoth des Grundbesitzes* (Berlin: Verlag von Hermann Bahr, 1868), p. XIV.
[5] A. Schäffle, *Kapitalismus und Socialismus* (Tubingen: Verlag der H. Laupp'schen Buchhandlung, 1870), p. 116.

Political economists of the classical era, like Adam Smith and David Ricardo, were long familiar with the terms *capital* and *capitalist* but not with *capitalism*. Marx himself used the word no more than five times in passing, and only in manuscripts that remained unpublished during his lifetime. In the *Economic Manuscript of 1861–63*, capitalism features just once, in a context where it could signify either the boundless drive of capitalists to enrich themselves and make more capital or the total process of capital accumulation.[6] In his first draft for *Capital*, volume II, written in 1865, he wrote of the 'drive of capitalism [*Trieb des Kapitalismus*]' and emphasized that it 'develops completely only on the base of this [capitalist] mode of production'.[7] It is clear what he meant by this: the drive of capitalism is nothing but the propensity of capitalists to accumulate capital beyond all limits, instead of consuming their wealth and enjoying the spoils of their entrepreneurial activities; it is a drive to create ever larger amounts of capital, to expand the scale of production and increase the productivity of labour, and potentially to bring about the ever greater 'overproduction' of commodities.[8] In a further note written in 1877, which Engels incorporated in his edition of *Capital*, volume II (1885), Marx again used the term capitalism equivocally, referring either to 'capitalist production' or to the 'compelling motive' of capitalists to enrichment or accumulation as opposed to 'personal consumption'.[9]

In 1875, in the completely different context of his 'Conspectus of Bakunin's *Statism and Anarchy*', Marx used 'capitalism' in the now familiar sense, as a shorthand term for the 'capitalist mode of production',[10] which is how he continued to characterize the modern economy until his death. In his letter to the editors of the Russian journal *Otechestvennye Zapiski* (*Patriotic Notes*), written in 1877 but published by Engels only after Marx's death, he tried to correct the reading of the chapter on 'primitive accumulation' in *Capital*, volume I, that some of his Russian followers had embraced. In this chapter, he had not offered more than a 'historical sketch of the genesis of capitalism in Western Europe', and he now defended himself against a critic who wanted to turn this into a 'historico-philosophical theory of general development'.[11] In his drafts of a letter to the Russian socialist Vera Zasulich, written in 1881, he spoke

---

[6] Cf. K. Marx, *Zur Kritik der politischen Ökonomie (Manuskript 1861–1863)*, MEGA², vol. II/3.3, p. 1114.
[7] K. Marx, 'Das Kapital, Zweites Buch. Der Cirkulationsprozeß des Kapitals. [Manuskript I]', MEGA², vol. II/4.1, p. 358.
[8] Cf. Ibid. [9] Cf. K. Marx, *Capital*, volume II, MECW, vol. 36, p. 125.
[10] K. Marx, 'Conspectus of Bakunin's *Statism and Anarchy*', MECW, vol. 24, p. 499.
[11] K. Marx, 'Letter to Otechestvenniye Zapiski', MECW, vol. 24, pp. 199–200.

of the 'capitalist system' (as he did, incidentally, in the French and second German editions of *Capital*, volume I) but not of capitalism.[12]

It is easy to understand why Marx considered the term capitalism to have been corrupted by its use in a predominantly moralizing sense that covered only particular aspects of the economic system. The aim he set himself was to identify and explain the fundamentals, the basic elements, and core processes of the capitalist mode of production. Not content with highlighting or condemning some of the most striking aspects of the modern industrial economy, he wanted to analyze its whole fabric or 'inner structure', its 'laws of motion', and the logic of its development. His theory was intended to cover both the whole and the constituent parts of the capitalist system, making it possible to trace both the origins and the long-term development of the modern (Western) economy and society.

In the German-speaking world, it was Werner Sombart (1863–1941) who conferred the dignity and weight of an academic concept on the term capitalism[13] in his book *Modern Capitalism* (1902). He himself regarded it as a sympathetic continuation of Marx's work, and it caused quite a sensation in the academic world as well as helping decisively to establish the term in everyday language. Although 'capitalism' had entered French and German dictionaries as early as the 1860s and 1870s, in the English-speaking world it was rather hesitantly introduced to the wider public during the 1880s.[14]

1.2 Capitalism: What Is in a Word?

In the 1840s, when Marx was just becoming familiar with political economy, he described his object of study as the bourgeois mode of production, bourgeois relations of production, or the mode of production of the bourgeoisie. In the *Grundrisse*, he named it the 'mode of production based upon capital', the mode of production 'dominated by capital', or the 'mode of production of capital'. From 1861 onwards, he used the terms capitalist mode of production, capitalist relations of production, or even capitalist production as a shorthand. In *Capital*, volume I, he similarly referred to the 'capitalist mode of production'. Already in the opening

---

[12] K. Marx, 'Drafts of the Letter to Vera Zasulich', MECW, vol. 24, pp. 349, 353, 357, and 'Letter to Vera Zasulich', MECW, vol. 24, p. 370.

[13] W. Sombart, *Der moderne Kapitalismus. Historisch-systematische Darstellung des gesamteuropäischen Wirtschaftslebens von seinen Anfängen bis zur Gegenwart* (Munich: DTV, 1987), esp. pp. 1–64.

[14] Cf. M. E. Hilger, 'Kapital, Kapitalist, Kapitalismus', in: O. Brunner et al. (eds), *Geschichtliche Grundbegriffe*, vol. 3 (Stuttgart: Klett-Cotta, 1982), pp. 339–454, and the first study on the history and usage of the term by R. Passow, *Kapitalismus. Eine begrifflich-terminologische Studie* (Jena: Gustav Fischer, 1918).

sentence of the first chapter, he made it clear that his object of study was not only the capitalist economy, but the wider framework of the 'societies in which the capitalist mode of production prevails'.[15] Accordingly, one can and will find that Marx's economic analysis of modern capitalism dealt with much more than just 'relations of production' or 'relations of exchange'. He focused on and investigated the various forms of praxis (or action and interaction) – the various forms of labour, the forms of exchange, the forms of organization, the forms of competition – as well as the various forms of thought that determine the basic categories shared by both practical agents and scientific observers (the political economists) living in capitalism. His theory of capitalism, as outlined in *Capital* and other writings, has a wider scope than any other economic theory: it deals with far more than just the 'mode of production' or the 'relations of production' in capitalism, and with more than the complete economic system. The wider structure of modern 'bourgeois' society, the social relations among its members at the level of the individual firm or household or marketplace, their relations of domination and authority, their conflicts and struggles, their relations of cooperation and competition: all this belongs to the general theory of capitalism that Marx envisaged. In fact, his critical theory of capitalism was inspired and informed by the research programme that he had outlined together with Engels in *The German Ideology*. In accordance with what they called the 'materialist conception of history', the capitalist economy would inevitably shape and pervade modern society and create an all-encompassing 'capitalist regime'.

For the classical economists, the great classes of modern society (capitalists, landowners, workers) were given, as were markets, money, manufactures, or banking. For Marx, however, the class structure of modern society was different from all previous structures of social inequality; its quite specific characteristics had to be studied with care, not taken for granted. Only in the last (unfinished) chapter of *Capital*, volume III, do we find so much as a fragment in which he explicitly asks the question: 'What makes a class?'[16] The answer to this question, not given by Marx, would be highly complex. For he regarded the 'classes of modern society' as classes based on the 'capitalist mode of production'.[17] First, it was necessary to understand all the essential features of this mode of production; only then could one answer the question and explain the relations

---

[15] K. Marx, *Capital*, volume I (London: Penguin, 1976), p. 125.
[16] K. Marx, *Capital*, volume III, MECW, vol. 37, p. 871.   [17] Ibid, p. 872.

and interactions (including the pattern of 'class struggles') among those features.

From the 1840s on, Marx called his theory of the capitalist mode of production a 'critique of political economy'. Throughout his economic writings, from the first manuscripts of the early 1840s to the last drafts penned in the early 1880s, he elaborated the first and the most salient critique of the classical political economists. With a few exceptions highlighted and praised by Marx, they lacked a sense of history and were prone to see the capitalist mode of production as the natural order of economic affairs, or the economic order most adequate to 'human nature'. In stark contrast to this view, Marx considered capitalism as a historically specific economic order, an economic system that had a beginning and would eventually come to an end. Any true theory of capitalism had to reveal and to demonstrate its historical specificities as an economic and societal order; any critic of capitalism had to focus on what was specific to the capitalist epoch and that epoch alone.

Accordingly, Marx refrained from dealing with production or labour or exchange in general and mocked those economists – German economists in particular – who indulged in such exercises. To expatiate about the few characteristics 'which all stages of production have in common' could provide nothing more than vacuous generalities and the kind of 'abstract moments' with which no 'real historical stage of production can be grasped'.[18] Such a way of proceeding could only blur, and eventually erase, the historical specificities of modern capitalism. However, to make these specific features stand out clearly, it was necessary to overcome an obvious difficulty: the basic categories pertaining to the capitalist mode of production – commodity, exchange, money, markets, trade, even capital, and wage labour, as well as landed property, real estate, credit, and banking – had been used (and the respective economic relations had existed in one form or another) long before the era of modern capitalism. Actually, they had existed in various combinations, albeit not in the same forms or the same combinations that occurred in the modern era. The task in theorizing modern capitalism was therefore to lay bare what was distinctive about these relations, and corresponding categories, in the capitalist economic and social order.

Marx did deal briefly with 'the commodity as such', with 'money as such' or in general, to mention two of the most famous examples from *Capital*. He also presented some thoughts about the process of human labour in general. But the real thrust of his exposition and argument was

---

[18] K. Marx, *Grundrisse: Foundation of the Critique of Political Economy* (London: Penguin, 1973), p. 88.

always that the economic categories 'bear a historical imprint'.[19] Taking this into account, he sought to identify and map out the specific, even unique, characteristics that commodities, money, market exchange, wage labour, production, consumption, economic growth, and so on assumed in modern capitalism. There could be no theory of capitalism without some causal or functional 'laws'. But, for Marx, all such laws or tendencies could be general only in the sense that they were valid for all kinds of capitalism within the capitalist world economy, both throughout its past history and for as long as the capitalist epoch endured. The general 'laws' of the capitalist economic order remained *historical* laws, in contrast to suprahistorical or ahistorical 'laws of nature', or to the 'natural' economic order or 'state of nature' of economic life that many classical, and neo-classical, economists had in mind.

1.3   The Basic Features of Modern Capitalism

In *Capital* Marx gave short summaries of what, in his view, were the crucial features of capitalism as an economic system. At the end of *Capital*, volume III, in the last section dealing with 'The Revenues and Their Sources', he briefly described some of the main elements that differentiated capitalism from all other historical 'modes of production'. The first characteristic he emphasized was that all production was production of commodities; all products were produced as commodities and assumed the commodity form. Commodity production as such was much older and more widespread than capitalism. What distinguished capitalism, however, was 'that being a commodity [was] the dominant and determining characteristic of its products'.[20] In the capitalist mode of production, every product is turned into a commodity, every kind of production transformed into commodity production, once the basic means and conditions of production, of any production, have been transformed into commodities. The crucial role here is reserved for human labour power. Once this is transformed into a commodity, every product of human labour becomes a potential commodity. In capitalism, commodity production becomes universal, the 'general form of production'.[21]

It should be noted that in this summary Marx explicitly made the key distinction between the production of 'commodities' and 'commodities as the product of capital'. Both seem to coexist in the capitalist mode of production, and both are essential to grasp the specific character of

---

[19] Marx, *Capital*, volume I, p. 273. [20] Marx, *Capital*, volume III, p. 866.
[21] Ibid, p. 869.

capitalism as a mode of production. In the last chapter of the first draft for *Capital*, volume I, he explained further the specific features of the 'commodity as product of capital'. Such commodities are different: (1) they are mass products, not single products, and are clearly products of social, organized labour on a large scale; (2) they are produced for a mass market, not for single customers; and (3) they represent the value of capital used in their production plus the surplus-value created in the same process. For their producers and for their owners, these commodities are only important insofar as they bear a certain amount of value and of surplus-value to be realized on the market.[22] Hence, the most accurate formula for modern capitalism would not be 'production of commodities by means of commodities', but rather 'production of commodities as the product of capital by means of commodities as the product of capital'. Commodities and commodities as the product of capital enter the market and have to pass through the process of circulation. As Marx put it, there are several definite processes 'through which the products must pass and in which they assume definite social characteristics',[23] turning them into commodities as the product of capital.

The second feature that marks the capitalist mode of production is the rule of capital – to be distinguished from the rule of capitalists. In capitalism, and only in capitalism, all commodity production is just a means to a dominant, overarching end, the production of surplus-value. This is the 'direct aim and determining motive of production'.[24] As Marx emphasized, capital – or the capital/wage labour relationship – is the dominant relation of production in capitalism. All capitalist production is production of value and, in particular, of surplus-value. Once produced and realized, surplus-value permits and compels the formation of new capital, so that, in the end, capital produces capital, and ever more capital. In the second part of his summary, therefore, Marx briefly recapitulated his concept of capital as a historically specific relation of production. Capital, as he emphasized in his magnum opus, is 'not a thing, but a social relation between persons which is mediated through things'.[25]

The one relation between persons that Marx invoked in his summary was the relation between capital and wage labour, or between capitalists as bearers and owners of capital and wage labourers as bearers of wage labour and owners of their only commodity, their labour power. Capital, in order to become and remain capital, has to be valourized, its value has to be enhanced, its amount has to grow. Hence, capital should be understood not as a thing, but as an ongoing process in time and space, the

---

[22] Cf. Marx, *Capital*, volume I, pp. 949–70.   [23] Marx, *Capital*, volume III, p. 866.
[24] Ibid, p. 867.   [25] Marx, *Capital*, volume I, p. 932.

process of surplus-value production and appropriation, of surplus-value realization, and of the accumulation of capital or the transformation of surplus-value into new capital (expanded reproduction of capital on a social scale). The reproduction of wage labourers as wage labourers is a necessary part of this overall production.[26]

Marx's summary is very short indeed. Were we to settle for this, his concept of capitalism would boil down to just two components: commodity production and the capital/wage labour relationship. But of course there is much more, and Marx's summary actually directs us towards a number of key points for a proper understanding of his theory of modern capitalism.

1.4 Value, Money, Competition

If capitalism tends to become the 'absolute form'[27] of commodity production, as Marx told us, it follows that capitalism will turn into a mode of production completely 'based upon value'.[28] It is only in capitalism that the relations of production and exchange (or market relations), in principle all economic relationships, become completely pervaded and dominated by the specific relationship between economically active persons that Marx denoted as the 'value' relation. Value was a basic concept for Marx. Without it, neither commodity exchange and money nor capital were conceivable. One could not grasp the concept of surplus-value without it. What is most striking about Marx's theory, however, is the link between value and capitalism. As Marx argued throughout the three volumes of *Capital*, the forms of value can exist simply through the market exchange of commodities. But the true substance of value – social labour as a socially valid abstraction (or 'abstract labour') – only comes into full existence and only acquires practical economic relevance thanks to the development of the distinctively capitalist mode and methods of production – that is, in a regime of industrial mass production. Moreover, only if many capitals are always and everywhere freely competing with one another and are able to move freely between industries, is it possible that the value of every commodity will be determined, as Marx assumed, by the average amount of social labour necessary to reproduce it under the technological conditions that prevail on average in every industry.

In contrast to many of the classical economists, Marx did not assert that value relations reigned supreme in precapitalist times and lost their importance under the conditions of modern capitalism. In his view, it was not until the capitalist mode conquered all spheres of production that

---

[26] Cf. Marx, *Capital*, volume III, pp. 868ff.   [27] Ibid., p. 630.   [28] Ibid., p. 839.

the 'law of value' became fully valid for all market transactions involving commodities and commodities as products of capital.

It is true that the famous forms of value – from the simple form of value to the form of money as analyzed by Marx in the first chapter of *Capital*, volume I – emerged and even fully developed long before the rise of modern capitalism. However, it is in modern capitalism that they first impinge upon everyone's thoughts and actions and assume the 'fixed quality of natural forms of social life', or, as categories, acquire the quality of 'socially valid, and therefore objective'[29] forms of thought. Only in modern capitalism does the dual character of commodity-producing human labour become dominant: on the one hand, useful, concrete labour productive of useful things or use-values; on the other hand, abstract social labour, based upon the social equality of all market producers and productive of things for exchange or values. Once value and the value-producing quality of social labour have been firmly established, the social division of labour in the historical form of a division of labour among private producers creating commodities for a market can be extended and intensified beyond all traditional limits. For now, the regulative law of value brings about social coherence among independent producers – all the accidents and irregular fluctuations of market exchanges notwithstanding.

When and where value prevails, so does money. It is only in capitalism, however, that money as a social relation prevails. Capitalism is the first historical economic order – and the first societal order – in which all commodity exchanges turn into a fully fledged process of 'commodity circulation' that is eventually dominated by 'money circulation'.[30] Economic interactions become fully monetized, at all times mediated by monetary transactions. Everyday life, far beyond the realm of market actions, is pervaded by money as both means and motive of economic action. In capitalist societies, everybody becomes a money owner and money user; money proves to be the nerve of all social relations. On the other hand, capitalism takes up the monetary system it encountered as a given in its earliest stages and drives its historical development into something different. First, it spawns a fully fledged money system, one in which money tends to be eventually replaced with credit, so that the first complete credit system in history comes into being and capitalism turns into a credit economy in all respects. Second, money circulation becomes

---

[29] Marx, *Capital*, volume I, pp. 168–9.
[30] It should be kept in mind that the analysis of 'simple circulation' in the first section of *Capital*, volume I, is just the first step in an analysis that Marx continues later, in volumes II and III. Simple circulation does not disappear, but is reduced to one moment in the general circulation dominated by capital.

dominated by the movements of capital. The circulation – or, more specifically, the circuits and turnovers – of capital determine the circulation of money in a capitalist economy, and the circulating money turns out to be, more and more, just another form of capital, money capital. *Capital*, volume II, is largely devoted to analysis of this major change and its implications.

Capitalism is the first economic order dominated by money in all respects, and it is with money that the movement of capital begins and ends. In its most elementary and most superficial form, capital may be regarded as just a process in time leading from one amount of money to an increased amount of money (M – M'), whatever the source or reason for that increase. In market terms, as Marx puts it in *Capital*, volume I, the process appears as a series of exchanges, of money against commodities and of commodities against money, more money: M – C – M'. Already in its elementary form, this process shows two salient characteristics of capital: (1) its continuous 'metamorphosis' as it moves from one form of value, the commodity, to another one, money, and back; and (2) a change in the amount of value involved. Even before capitalism, capitalists were seeking to enrich themselves and to enhance the value of their capital.

It is only in modern capitalism, however, that this enrichment turns into a systematic and in principle endless venture. Every single capitalist might go bankrupt, individual capitals can and do lose their value or disappear altogether. But capital as a social relation, capital in general, will survive as long as the process of value enhancement – and hence enrichment of capitalists – continues. Once money has fully developed and exists independent of particular exchanges related to particular commodities, once money has gained the character of 'money as money', as Marx put it,[31] the pursuit of wealth changes. Those eager to enrich themselves are now able to acquire abstract social wealth (value) in an abstract and durable form (money). There is no limit to this accumulation of abstract wealth. So the pursuit of wealth, the acquisition of ever larger amounts of abstract wealth in the form of money, becomes an end in itself and turns into an endless process with no intrinsic measure or goal. Capitalists gain a new rationale and an overarching motive for all their economic actions – the valorization of capital, the transformation of a given amount of wealth, in monetary form, into an endless movement involving the enhancement and growth of abstract wealth or value.

What makes modern capitalists different from anyone else who tries to amass a fortune or to enrich himself? They try, successfully, to enter the

---

[31] Marx, *Capital*, volume I, pp. 227ff.

process of value creation itself, that is, to take control of the production of commodities and to assume command over other people's social labour in order to produce more value. Accordingly, under the control and command of capital owners, the process of commodity production and value creation is transformed into a specifically capitalist production process. In this kind of production, the goal is endless enhancement of the original capital producing value and ever more value in order to turn capital into more and larger capital. It follows that capitalists turning to commodity production in order to valourize their capital will pursue the endless production of ever-increasing masses of commodities and ever-increasing amounts of value, controlling ever larger production processes and commanding ever larger quantities of social labour.

1.5 Exploitation and Accumulation

How can the production of commodities turn into a process of valourization that continually increases the value of capital? Marx found the key to an answer in the concept of surplus-value and the process of exploitation of wage labourers. Assuming that wage labourers are hired by capitalists who pay them the going wage and do not cheat them, they are able – at least above a certain level of productivity – to produce a higher value than that of their wages during the time period for which they cede control of their labour power to a capitalist. Again, assuming that all wage labourers produce commodities at their social-value and that their wages are equal to the value of their labour power, a considerable part of the value product of their daily or weekly labour turns out to be surplus-value. In order to appropriate that surplus-value (and to valourize his capital) every capitalist has to organize the process of commodity production in his particular field or branch as effectively and as efficiently as possible. Every capitalist has to put the wage labourers he hires to work, as effectively and as efficiently as possible. In order to make them produce surplus-value and ever more of it, he has to change the whole labour process. First, he must make the wage labourers work longer hours and/or perform more work – or work of a greater intensity or complexity – in the same period of time. Second, he must raise the productivity of their labour, so that they produce larger quantities of commodities in the same period of time. Accordingly, Marx's analysis of the production process under the regime of capital focused upon the methods by which capitalists try to augment the surplus-value production of their employees. Inventing and applying these methods of 'absolute' and 'relative' surplus-value production in ever more astute and systematic ways, capitalists change the world of commodity production. Capital becomes 'industrial capital', while wage labourers become a modern working class of industrial or factory workers.

As they follow their urge to increase the production of surplus-value and to exploit their wage labourers more efficiently, capitalists bring forth a new mode of industrial production: the world of manufactures and of large-scale industry or the factory system. They develop everything to the extreme: the specialization of workers and tools, the division of labour inside the manufactures and factories, the use of machinery, the specialization of machinery, the subordination of workers to whole systems of machinery, the development of factories into whole industrial complexes and industrial districts. Capitalists prolong the working day systematically, intensify labour beyond all limits, and enhance labour productivity by all possible means. They become inventive and innovative, they make use of the insights of modern science and technology, they start to integrate technology and science into the industrial system, they organize and reorganize the production processes in an endless frenzy. Industrial mass production in the factory system was at the centre of Marx's understanding of capitalism as a historically specific mode of production. He was fascinated by the 'revolutionary impact' of modern large-scale industry on all traditional handicrafts, manufactures, and domestic industries, and he foresaw the tendencies towards automation and the mechanization of agriculture.

In Marx's view, industrial capitalism owed its unprecedented dynamic to two driving forces. The first was the ongoing struggle between capitalist employers seeking to exploit their workers as efficiently as possible and wage labourers resisting by all possible means this drive to maximize the exploitation of their labour power – a struggle partly fought out through new inventions, the application of new machinery, reorganizations of the labour process, and the replacement of workers' skills and experience with all sorts of mechanical or automatic devices. The second was the struggle that capitalists fought with one another, in an ever-raging process of competition on markets and beyond markets. Marx did not join the chorus of contemporary critics of competition, nor did he follow those who extolled its virtues. As capital could only exist as many capitals owned by many capitalists (although capital in general and the capitalist class had a reality of their own), competition among them was inevitable.

For the advancement of technological and organizational changes in the industrial system, the never-ending competition between industrial capitalists was crucial. Whoever exploited his workers better, whoever was more innovative and more able to introduce and apply advanced technologies, whoever was quicker and smarter at reorganizing whole plants and factories, would emerge as the winner. Whoever performed best on the market and whoever was able to shift large amounts of capital most swiftly between branches of industry would win.

Thanks to the conflict between capitalists and wage labourers and to the competition among capitalists, modern industrial capitalism became the most dynamic, volatile, innovative, and progressive mode of production in history, but also the most disruptive and in many respects the most destructive. The dynamic of capitalism could unfold once it had pervaded social production in all its width, length, and depth, transforming it into industrial mass production and conquering, as well as transforming, the markets. This is a key insight of Marx's theory of capitalism: it defines its overpowering intrinsic dynamic, its 'revolutionary' character propelling economic and social change on an unprecedented scale and at unprecedented speed. It is easy to see where the full impact of the dynamic of industrial capital comes from. The outcome of the valourization process is a quantum of surplus-value that is appropriated by the capitalists engaged in industrial production. They use their increased wealth in different ways. In Marx's view, the choice for capitalists was obvious: they could spend the additional wealth and stop acting as capitalists or they could act as capitalists and transform the surplus-value they had gained into additional capital.

Turning surplus-value into newly accumulated capital is the logical outcome of the valourization process. So the pursuit of abstract wealth in capitalism turns into an unlimited and endless process of capital accumulation, as capital brings forth ever more capital. Accumulation does include reproduction of the material components of industrial capital, of the money invested, but also of capital as a social relation. Capitalists come out of the process as wealthier and more powerful agents, owning more or larger capital, while wage labourers come out of it impecunious and propertyless as before, dependent on the class of capitalists for jobs and incomes and even more under the domination of ever larger capitals. For capitalists, accumulation of capital has no intrinsic end or measure. No capital can ever be big enough. There is only one external measure for the amount of capital a capitalist can hold, and that is the size of the capital wielded by his competitors. As every capitalist accumulates in order to keep up with his competitors' rate of accumulation, accumulation will continue at an accelerated pace. This 'accelerated' process of accumulation where all capitalists reorganize the production processes they control and run a race against each other, introducing new technologies and replacing machinery in their plants at ever higher speed, forms the (planned) culmination of Marx' analysis of the accumulation process in *Capital*, volume I.[32] In this process, capital is

---

[32] Marx, *Capital*, volume I, pp. 711ff.

not only reproduced on an ever-expanding scale; it also undergoes constant changes that are measurable in terms of both technology and value.

Two further epochal changes flow from the intrinsic dynamic of modern capitalism. Capitalists, in their pursuit of ever more abstract wealth, are bound to push beyond all borders, to disregard and dissolve all traditional boundaries, to disrupt and destroy everything that might come in their way. The higher the prospective gain – the potential rate of profit – the more ruthlessly capitalists are prepared to tear down all barriers to the movement of capital. Capital and capitalists spread out in all directions, expanding markets and the range and scope of production, entering into new fields of production, and appropriating natural resources, land, and labour power wherever they find them. What Marx called in the *Grundrisse* the 'propagandistic tendency' inherent in modern capitalism materializes in the expansion of the capitalist mode of production from one region or territory to another, in the making of a world market. 'The tendency to create the *world market* is directly given in the concept of capital itself.'[33] Capital strives to produce at the largest possible level, for the whole world, and to exploit all the resources of the world. The competing capitalists of many countries expand the market range and the range of production beyond all regional and national borders. They thereby transform capitalism into a world system – not only of trade and exchange, but ultimately of production and reproduction – that will eventually encompass the whole globe and turn all people and all countries into parts of one and the same order. The permanent drive to expand existing markets and open up new and larger ones, as well as to press forwards into new industrial branches and areas, gives one boost after another to the intrinsic drive to increase labour productivity and the exploitation of human labour power.

Capitalism displays historically specific forms of motion and follows historically specific trajectories of development. Many of these forms of motion were first described and investigated by Marx. The most striking examples may be found in *Capital,* volume II, where Marx analyzed the different forms of the circuit of capital and the form and mechanism of its periodic turnover.[34] These specific forms of motion pertain to every individual industrial capital. For social capital as a whole – the capital of a whole country, for instance – he found another historically specific form, the modern economic cycle, or business cycle, which he dubbed the industrial cycle.

This phenomenon, extensively studied by Marx from the late 1840s onwards, stands out as the one overarching feature of modern industrial

---

[33] Marx, *Grundrisse*, p. 408.   [34] Cf. Marx, *Capital,* volume II, pp. 31–155.

capitalism. It is the factory system and its tremendous capacity to expand the scale of production at short notice, together with the increasing dependence on the world market, that give rise to this specific form of motion. In *Capital*, volume I, Marx argued that 'the life of industry becomes a series of periods of moderate activity, prosperity, overproduction, crisis and stagnation'.[35] This cycle of rapid expansions, gluts and contractions of industrial output and markets is repeated endlessly. This characteristic path of modern industry, which 'takes the form of a decennial cycle (interrupted by smaller oscillations)'[36] depends on many preconditions. They are the formation and constant reformation of an industrial reserve army – a surplus population of unemployed or underemployed workers – or the development of a credit system that allows individual capitalists to make use of portions of the total social capital, independent of the rate and amount of accumulation that they are able to realize on their own. The characteristic form of the industrial cycle, as Marx saw it, is therefore closely linked to cycles of employment and unemployment as well as to credit and investment cycles. Capitalism, according to Marx, is the first historical mode of production to move forwards in this peculiar cyclical pattern of growth. Capitalism as a whole moves in such periodic cycles because it generates not only partial, but also general crises of overproduction of commodities and overaccumulation of capital. General crises – a contested phenomenon in Marx's time as in ours – are the decisive, determining moment of the industrial cycle. Since capitalism moves from crisis to crisis, since the crises occur on an ever larger scale and turn into 'world market crises', the industrial cycle should be treated as a crisis cycle.

Last but not least, in *Capital*, volume III, Marx saw capitalism as a 'bewitched and distorted world [*verzauberte und verkehrte Welt*]'[37] which the economic actors perceived through the lens of very peculiar economic forms. They were bedevilled by a strange kind of fetishism or by a variety of 'insane', 'absurd', or 'illusionary forms' of thought. Such mundane forms of economic thought reappeared in the categories of political economy, and the political economists as well as actual capitalists and workers lived under the spell of mystifications. From the very beginning, with his famous analysis of the fetishism of the world of commodities, Marx tried to decipher the mysterious characters inherent in the forms of economic interaction in capitalism. One famous example – which, much to his dismay, was widely neglected by his followers – was the fact that the wage form gave the value of the commodity labour power

---

[35] Marx, *Capital*, volume I, p. 580. [36] Ibid, p. 785.
[37] Marx, *Capital*, volume III, p. 814.

the appearance of something quite different, the value of labour or the price of labour. In this form and in the economic parlance and thought shared by capitalists and workers, the very fact of exploitation becomes blurred and actually disappears from the consciousness of the parties involved in it. The mysterious forms, from the commodity form, or value form, to the money form and many others, constitute a whole world of 'mystifications'.

Marx did not content himself with the analysis of commodity fetishism in the first chapter of *Capital*, volume I, but continued the endeavour through all three volumes. In particular, he took great pains to show how and why capital, the dominant production relation of modern capitalism, turned into a very mysterious 'thing' or being, which political economists as well as practical economic agents found it very difficult to understand. Already in the initial analysis of capital as it appears in the circulation of commodities and money, he deciphered it as 'the capital fetish' or 'value-creating value'[38] even as an 'automatic subject'.[39] And, at the end of volume III, Marx brought his analyses of the mysterious forms and appearances together and tried to present them as elements of a particular kind of religion of everyday life, pertaining to modern capitalism. In the so-called trinity formula, which condenses the production and distribution relations of modern capitalism in the interaction of capital profit, land rent, and labour wages, he captured the very core of this religion or ideology of everyday life, which only exists in modern capitalism – 'the bewitched, distorted and upside-down world haunted by *Monsieur le Capital* and *Madame La Terre* who are at the same time social characters and mere things'.[40] These false appearances, the recurring 'reification' of relations and 'personification' of things, the world of mystifications, belong to the very essence of modern capitalism, as Marx saw it.

1.6 The Historical Emergence and Development of Capitalism

Marx's theory of capitalism was meant to be a general theory, but he did not conceive of it as a theory of pure capitalism, beyond and irrespective of time and space. Although Marx already distinguished between the 'prehistory' and 'contemporary history' of capitalism in the *Grundrisse*,

---

[38] Marx, *Capital*, volume III, p. 968.
[39] Marx, *Capital*, volume I, p. 255. To take such formulations literally, thereby reproducing rather than criticizing the false appearances of the capital fetish, has been a hallmark of several alleged reinterpretations of Marx in recent times.
[40] Marx, *Capital*, volume III, p. 969.

and, although he decided to concentrate on the latter, we find a large number of historical elements in Marx's *Capital*, and they are by no means mere digressions or illustrations. Because of its intrinsic dynamic, the capitalist economy and society should be regarded not as a 'solid crystal, but [as] an organism capable of change, and constantly engaged in a process of change'.[41] Capitalism did undergo rapid development, sometimes real transformations. Its contemporary history cannot be regarded as an endlessly repeated process of reproduction and expanded reproduction of the same basic structures. This is why a number of the general laws that Marx postulated for the capitalist epoch are not just 'laws of motion', but laws of development and change.

Capitalism, Marx insisted, was not a state of nature, nor could it be understood as an autopoietic system creating its own preconditions and necessary components. Money, markets, division of labour, even world trade, wage labour, and landed property were all prerequisites of capitalism that existed long before it. The general theory, properly constructed, should therefore provide clues, even first equations, for an investigation of the history of capitalism. And historical reflections were necessary now and then in order to grasp the peculiarities of modern capitalism.

Capital, volume I, in the chapters on 'so-called primitive accumulation', Marx's historical sketch of the emergence of capitalism in Western Europe, did not have the form of a narrative, but followed, and exemplified, the basic logic laid out in his general theory. Capitalism presupposed as one of its core institutions the capital/wage labour relationship. For this to be established, the producers or workers had to be separated from all means of production and subsistence that allowed them to survive as independent producers, and the means of production and subsistence had to be appropriated and monopolized in the hands of a class of capital owners and a class of landowners. Using the examples mainly of England and Scotland, Marx wanted to show how this happened in reality, rather than in the legends dear to the classical economists and the apologetics of modern capitalism; it was a history of violence, plunder, and crime, based on law-breaking and the extirpation of old laws, traditions, and customs.[42]

We find in *Capital* many more ideas about the origins and historical development of capitalism in Western Europe.[43] The sections on 'commercial capital', on 'interest-bearing capital and financial markets', and on 'landed property and ground-rent'[44] all provide longer

---

[41] Marx, *Capital*, volume I, p. 93.   [42] Ibid, pp. 873ff.
[43] See in particular the chapters that Marx wrote in 1864–65, as first drafts for the planned volumes II and III, as well as in his later manuscripts devoted to these volumes.
[44] These three parts correspond respectively to chapters 16–20, 21–36, and 37–47.

and shorter historical sketches of the rise and transformation of commercial capital, credit and banking, and landed property and agriculture. In these sections, Marx's aim was to draw out what distinguished the older forms of commerce, credit, or agriculture from the modern, capitalist ones, and to identify what transformations had been necessary to integrate commerce, credit, and agriculture into the economic system of modern capitalism.[45]

Marx was well aware of the variety of capitalisms in his time, as he was of the changes taking place in the most advanced capitalist countries. England, the homeland of industrial capitalism, had been his model for the study of industrial development, the most developed country that showed 'to the less developed, the image of its own future'.[46] But, from the 1860s onwards, industrial development began to forge ahead in other parts of the world, challenging Britain's supremacy on the world market. For future editions of *Capital*, Marx already made up his mind to treat the United States as exemplifying the highest degree of capitalist development; it, not England, was going to be the capitalist 'model country' of the future.[47] As long as the development of capitalist production remained incomplete, its laws and tendencies could not become predominant.

In all three volumes of *Capital*, Marx spelled out various laws and tendencies of capitalism. In volume I, these were primarily laws and tendencies of industrial development, pertaining to modern manufacture and to mass production in the factory system. Subsequently, he established several laws or intrinsic tendencies of capitalist accumulation. Then, at the end, he tried to bring it all together in one general law of capitalist accumulation. That law, the culmination of Marx's theory as expounded in *Capital*, volume I, has been the subject of many debates since 1867. It is a rather complicated law indeed, a summary of many tendencies, linking together the amount and the growth of social wealth, the 'extent and energy' of the growth, or accumulation, of capital and the development of the proletariat (the class of wage labourers, including the active labour army, the industrial reserve army, and the pauperized sections). So, what we find is more like a bundle of interconnected tendencies that Marx assembled into a single 'law'. However, the 'absolute general law of capitalist accumulation' was stated with quite a lot of

---

[45] Actually, these draft chapters from the manuscript written in 1845–46 only reflect the level of knowledge that Marx had at that time. As he continued his studies of the history of capitalism in the following years, there is much more to be found in his later manuscripts and notebooks.

[46] Marx, *Capital*, volume I, p. 91.

[47] When studying the United States during the years of the Civil War, Marx became aware that at least three conflicting varieties of capitalism coexisted there within the same geographical and political context.

reservations and provisos; 'like all other laws', he added, 'it is modified in its working by many circumstances, the analysis of which does not concern us here.'[48] But one remark has attracted the greatest attention – and, subsequently, the heaviest criticism. 'It follows', Marx wrote, 'that in proportion as capital accumulates, the situation of the worker, be his payment high or low, must grow worse.'[49] In other words, the social and economic inequality between capitalists and workers – and also the workers' dependence and subjection to the rule of capital, hence the inequality of social power – will increase in the course of capitalist development. A rise in wages, even a continuous one, is fully compatible with such a claim, as long as the growth of capital outpaces it. Unfortunately, Marx tried to crown his argument with another shorthand formula, claiming that the 'accumulation of wealth' would inevitably go together with an 'accumulation of misery'[50] – a claim that misled many to interpret his law as a 'law of immiseration'.

On the other hand, Marx owes his periodical rediscovery and media fame to the fact that many of the tendencies he investigated have reasserted themselves again and again. He is, for example, repeatedly credited as the discoverer and first analyst of the tendency to 'concentration and centralization' of capital (which he observed and included in his theory of accumulation), the development of the factory system and the tendency to automation, the industrialization of agriculture, the spread of globalization and the making of a capitalist world economy, the rise of associated capital and the rise of managers, the acceleration of circulation, the technological revolutions, and the rise of financial markets and the modern credit system.

1.7 Marx's Critique of Modern Capitalism

In assessing the strengths and weaknesses of Marx's critique of capitalism, we should recall the fact, stunning for many, that he never hesitated or ceased to praise the achievements of the capitalist mode of production. In stark contrast to the prevailing mood among fellow socialists, Marx did not hide his admiration for the practical businessmen who had successfully changed the world of commerce, industry, and finance in the frenzied pursuit of their narrow self-interest. In the words of the *Manifesto of the Communist Party*: 'The bourgeoisie, historically, has played a most revolutionary part.'[51] It has 'created more massive and more colossal productive forces than have all preceding generations together',[52] and it

---

[48] Marx, *Capital*, volume I, p. 798. [49] Ibid, p. 799. [50] Ibid, p. 198.
[51] K. Marx and F. Engels, *Manifesto of the Communist Party*, MECW, vol. 6, p. 486.
[52] Ibid, p. 489.

'cannot exist without constantly revolutionizing the instruments of production, and thereby the relations of production, and with them the whole relations of society'.[53] Capitalism, in Marx's view, had proven to be a 'powerhouse' of innovation, of technological development, of organizational changes, and scientific discoveries. He never stopped acclaiming the 'civilizing tendencies' inherent in the capitalist mode of production, although, in 1848, as in later years, he never ignored or denied the social evils, the destruction and degradation, that its rule inflicted upon human beings and nature.

What Marx rejected outright was the contemporary 'false critique' of political economy (and capitalism), the varieties of romantic, reactionary, or utopian and naïve anti-capitalism that prevailed in numerous quarters. In sharp contrast to the moralizing critique widely popular in his day, he did not criticize capitalism as a system of injustice or condemn it as the source of all evils. He saw capitalism not as a wrong track leading mankind astray from its 'true' destination, but as a necessary and largely progressive stage in human history. So, it is highly unlikely that he would ever have supported any of the critiques of capitalism that centre on exorbitant profits, soaring inequalities of income and wealth, perennial insecurity, uncontrolled power of money and finance, growth without limits, rampant globalization that devastates traditional social worlds, or ever harsher competition forcing everybody into a rat race to the bottom.

Marx saw all these aspects very clearly and took them as inevitable consequences of capitalist development. But his critique of capitalism operated at a different level. The strongest argument in his general theory is that the inner logic of capitalism, as an economic system, impels it to weaken, undermine, and eventually destroy the very preconditions of its existence. Capitalism will come to an end because of its inherent tendencies to self-destruction. Marx was quite sure of this, although he never entered into speculations about how the end would come and never hypothesized an imminent collapse of the capitalist system. As Marx put it in an often quoted sentence from *Capital* referring to the development of large-scale industry and the ongoing industrialization of agriculture: 'Capitalist production ... only develops the techniques and the degree of combination of the social process of production by simultaneously undermining the original sources of all wealth – the soil and the worker.'[54]

What about the inner 'contradictions' of the capitalist mode of production? One might think that someone like Marx, who sought to lay bare the 'inner contradictions' of capitalism – from the simplest and most general

---

[53] Ibid, p. 487.   [54] Marx, *Capital*, volume I, p. 638.

(such as the 'contradiction' between use-value and exchange-value as the two sides of the commodity) to the most complex – would see them as key weaknesses, even breaking points, in its fabric.[55] Not quite. In *Capital*, as in other works, the famous 'contradictions' served Marx to locate and grasp the inner dynamic of capitalism and to pinpoint the origin of ongoing changes. Real contradictions cannot be abolished – at least not within the existing framework of commodity exchange or capitalism – but they, or rather the conflicting parties involved, will find or create a new 'form within which they have room to move'.[56] The contradictions of capitalism must and will develop: the 'development of the contradictions of a given historical form of production is the only way in which it can be dissolved',[57] and it is exactly this development of the intrinsic contradictions that Marx uses as an analytical tool.

Marx tried to show how capitalism, by following its intrinsic logic at various points, could and would eventually undermine itself. Already in the *Grundrisse*, he gave a special place to one law of capitalist development, the law of the tendential fall in the rate of profit. This is 'the most important law from the historical standpoint',[58] because it shows how and why (industrial) capitalism will undermine itself. Capital relentlessly develops all productive forces, but 'the historical development of capital itself, when it reaches a certain point, suspends the self-realization of capital, instead of positing it. Beyond a certain point, the development of the powers of production becomes a barrier for capital',[59] because the fall of the general rate of profit will slowly stifle capital accumulation, and the frenzy to accumulate, to innovate, to introduce new technologies will wither away. Despite several attempts (in 1857–58, 1864–65, and later), Marx failed to establish the falling rate of profit as a law connected to technological changes that industrial capital keeps pushing through. If it were the case, as Engels suggested, that he did establish the famous law flawlessly, the consequence might be (as Marx himself indicated) that capitalists would lose the drive for technological change, competition would lose its edge, the rates of accumulation and growth would decline, and capitalism would sink into long-lasting stagnation.

A similar argument may be derived from the phenomenon of crises and cycles and the manner in which Marx treated it. He clearly saw recurrent crises as strong supporting evidence that capitalists could not handle or govern the productive and market forces they were constantly unleashing and that capitalism as an economic and societal system was out of

---

[55] Cf. D. Harvey, *Seventeen Contradictions and the End of Capitalism* (London: Profile Books, 2015).
[56] Marx, *Capital*, volume I, p. 98.　[57] Ibid, p. 619.　[58] Marx, *Grundrisse*, p. 748.
[59] Ibid, p. 749.

everybody's control, including that of the capitalist 'ruling class'. Capitalists did not run capitalism and did not govern competition, especially not the global competition that raged on the world market. Periodically, the whole capitalist system, not despite but because of the tremendous productive powers it created, spiralled into turmoil and disarray – at a heavy cost for workers, for the whole society, and for nature. On the other hand, Marx saw crises in capitalism as moments of necessary catharsis, when the devaluation and destruction of capital created new space and allowed for a new start. So, crises did not necessarily spell doom for capitalism, even if, as Marx assumed, they became increasingly severe and wreaked ever greater devastation in the long run. In both respects, the inner contradictions of capitalism played a role, but only as analytical clues to grasp the phenomenon at hand.

The most fundamental critique of the capitalist regime we can find in Marx is different from his argument about its self-destructive tendencies. It does support the previous point, though, because those tendencies can only unfold as a consequence of the underlying distortion of the relationship of human beings to their own social life. In capitalism, everybody, including the capitalist, lives under the rule of capital, or, as most people would experience it, under the regime of 'market laws' that impose themselves through the sheer pressure of competition. Bending to this pressure, everyone obeys a force that is obviously not a force of nature, but a force of society, like the 'law of value'. In the capitalist epoch, this kind of domination of people's actions and thoughts by something they have produced and shaped themselves – the market regime, money, capital – is aggravated by the mystifications that reign supreme in the religion of everyday life that capitalism brings forth. This is why capitalism is not only the rule of capital, which is personal and impersonal, but an order where the factual and practical constraints of an economy that nobody controls weigh upon the lives and minds of all, an 'iron cage' of universal and impersonal bondage, as Max Weber would have called it.[60]

References

Blanc, Louis (1850), *L'Organisation du Travail*, Paris: Bureau du nouveau monde.
Harvey, David (2015), *Seventeen Contradictions and the End of Capitalism*, London: Profile Books.

---

[60] Max Weber, *The Protestant Ethic and the Spirit of Capitalism* (London: Routledge, 1992), p. 181.

Hilger, Marie-Elisabeth (1982), 'Kapital, Kapitalist, Kapitalismus', in: O. Brunner et al. (eds), *Geschichtliche Grundbegriffe*, vol. 3, Stuttgart: Klett-Cotta, pp. 339–454.

Kocka, Jürgen (2016), *Capitalism: A Short History*, Princeton, NJ: Princeton University Press.

Kocka, Jürgen, and Marcel van der Linden, eds (2016), *Capitalism: The Reemergence of a Historical Concept*, London: Bloomsbury.

Leroux, Pierre (1849), *Malthus et les économistes, ou y-aura-t-il toujours des pauvres?*, Boussac: Imprimerie de Pierre Leroux.

Marx, Karl (1973), *Grundrisse: Foundations of the Critique of Political Economy (Rough Draft)*, London: Penguin.

(1976), *Capital*, volume I, London: Penguin.

(1978), *Zur Kritik der politischen Ökonomie (Manuskript 1861–63)*, MEGA^2, vol. II/3.3.

(1997), *Capital*, volume II, MECW, vol. 36.

(1998), *Capital*, volume III, MECW, vol. 37.

(1989), 'Conspectus on Bakunin's *Statism and Anarchy*', MECW, vol. 24, pp. 485–526.

(1989), 'K. Marx: Drafts of the Letter to Vera Zasulich', MECW, vol. 24, pp. 346–69.

(1989), 'K. Marx: Letter to Vera Zasulich', MECW, vol. 24, pp. 370–1.

(1989), 'Letter to Otechestvenniye Zapiski', MECW, vol. 24, pp. 196–201.

(2011), 'Das Kapital, Zweites Buch. Der Cirkulationsprozeß des Kapitals. [Manuskript I]', MEGA^2, vol. II/4.1, pp. 139–384.

Marx, Karl, and Engels, Friedrich (1976), *Manifesto of the Communist Party*, MECW, vol. 6, pp. 477–517.

Passow, Richard (1918), *Kapitalismus. Eine begrifflich-terminologische Studie*, Jena: Gustav Fischer.

Proudhon, Pierre-Joseph (1969), *The General Idea of the Revolution in the Nineteenth Century*, New York: Haskell Hause Publishers.

Rodbertus, Johann Karl (1868), *Zur Erklärung und Abhülfe der heutigen Creditnoth des Grundbesitzes*, Berlin: Verlag von Hermann Bahr.

Schäffle, Albert (1870), *Kapitalismus und Socialismus*, Tubingen: Verlag der H. Laupp'schen Buchhandlung.

Sombart, Werner (1987), *Der moderne Kapitalismus. Historisch-systematische Darstellung des gesamteuropäischen Wirtschaftslebens von seinen Anfängen bis zur Gegenwart*, Munich: DTV.

2 Communism

Marcello Musto

Translated by Patrick Camiller

2.1 Critical Theories of the Early Socialists

In the wake of the French Revolution, numerous theories began to circulate in Europe that sought both to respond to demands for social justice unanswered by the French Revolution and to correct the dramatic economic imbalances brought about by the spread of the Industrial Revolution. The democratic gains following the capture of the Bastille delivered a decisive blow to the aristocracy, but they left almost unchanged the inequality of wealth between the popular and the dominant classes. The decline of the monarchy and the establishment of the republic were not sufficient to reduce poverty in France.

This was the context in which the 'critical-utopian' theories of socialism,[1] as Karl Marx and Friedrich Engels (1820–1895) defined them in the *Manifesto of the Communist Party* (1848), rose to prominence. They considered them 'utopian'[2] for two reasons: first, their exponents, in different ways, opposed the existing social order and furnished theories containing what they believed to be 'the most valuable elements for the enlightenment of the working class';[3] and, second, they claimed that an alternative form of social organization could be achieved simply through the theoretical identification of new ideas and principles, rather than through the concrete struggle of the working class. According to Marx and Engels, their socialist predecessors had believed that

---

[1] K. Marx and F. Engels, *Manifesto of the Communist Party*, MECW, vol. 6, p. 514.
[2] This term had been used by others before Marx and Engels. See, for example, J.-A. Blanqui, *History of Political Economy in Europe* (New York: G. P. Putnam and Sons, 1885), pp. 520–33. M. L. Reybaud, *Études sur les Réformateurs contemporains ou socialistes modernes: Saint-Simon, Charles Fourier, Robert Owen* (Paris: Guillaumin, 1840), pp. 322–41, was the first to group these three authors under the category of modern socialism. Reybaud's text circulated widely and helped to spread the idea that they were 'the entire sum of the eccentric thinkers whose birth our age has witnessed', p. vi.
[3] Marx and Engels, *Manifesto of the Communist Party*, p. 515.

historical action [had] to yield to their personal inventive action, historically created conditions of emancipation to fantastic ones, and the gradual spontaneous class organization of the proletariat to an organization of society specially contrived by these inventors. Future history resolve[d] itself, in their eyes, into the propaganda and the practical carrying out of their social plans.[4]

In the most widely read political text in human history, Marx and Engels also took issue with many other forms of socialism both past and present, grouping them under the headings of 'feudal', 'petty-bourgeois', 'bourgeois', or – in disparagement of its 'philosophical phraseology' – 'German' socialism.[5] In general, these theories could be related to one another either in terms of an aspiration to 'restore the old means of production and exchange, and with them the old property relations and the old society' or in terms of an attempt to 'cramp the modern means of production and exchange within the framework of the old property relations' from which they had broken. For this reason, Marx saw in these conceptions a form of socialism that was both 'reactionary and utopian'.[6]

The term 'utopian', as opposed to 'scientific' socialism, has often been used in a misleading and intentionally disparaging way. In fact, the 'utopian socialists' contested the social organization of the age in which they lived, contributing through their writings and actions to the critique of existing economic relations.[7] Marx had considerable respect for his precursors:[8] he stressed the huge gap separating Saint-Simon (1760–1825) from his cruder interpreters;[9] and, while he regarded some of Charles Fourier's (1771–1858) ideas as extravagant 'humorous sketches',[10] he saw 'great merit' in the realization that the transformative aim for labour was to overcome not only the existing mode of distribution, but also the 'mode of production'.[11] In Owen's theories, he saw many elements that were

---

[4] Ibid. [5] Ibid, pp. 507–13. [6] Ibid, p. 510.

[7] V. Geoghegan, *Utopianism and Marxism* (Berne: Peter Lang, 2008), pp. 23–38, where it is shown that the 'utopian socialists saw themselves as social scientists', p. 23. The Marxist-Leninist orthodoxy, for its part, employed the epithet 'utopian' in a purely derogatory sense. Cf. the interesting criticism, partly directed at Marx himself, in G. Claeys, 'Early Socialism in Intellectual History', *History of European Ideas* 40 (7): (2014), which finds in the definitions of 'science' and 'scientific socialism' an example of 'epistemological authoritarianism', p. 896.

[8] See E. Hobsbawm, 'Marx, Engels and Pre-Marxian Socialism', in: E. Hobsbawm (ed.), *The History of Marxism. Volume One: Marxism in Marx's Day* (Bloomington: Indiana University Press, 1982), pp. 1–28.

[9] K. Marx and F. Engels, *The German Ideology*, MECW, vol. 5, pp. 493–510. Engels, who held Saint-Simon in high regard, in *Socialism: Utopian and Scientific* went so far as to assert that 'almost all the ideas of later Socialists that are not strictly economic are found in him in embryo', MECW, vol. 25, p. 292.

[10] K. Marx, *Capital*, volume I (London: Penguin, 1976), p. 403.

[11] K. Marx, 'Outlines of the Critique of Political Economy [*Grundrisse*]. Second Instalment', MECW, vol. 29, p. 97.

worthy of interest and anticipated the future. In *Value, Price and Profit* (1865), he noted that, already at the beginning of the nineteenth century, in *Observations on the Effect of the Manufacturing System* (1815), Owen had 'proclaimed a general limitation of the working day as the first preparatory step to the emancipation of the working class'.[12] He had also argued, like no one else, in favour of cooperative production.

Nevertheless, while recognizing the positive influence of Saint-Simon, Fourier, and Owen on the nascent workers' movement, Marx's overall assessment of their ideas was negative. He thought that they hoped to solve the social problems of the age with unrealizable fantasies, and he criticized them heavily for spending much of their time on the irrelevant theoretical exercise of building 'castles in the air'.[13]

Marx did not take exception only to proposals that he considered wrong or impractical. Above all, he opposed the idea that social change could come about through *a priori* meta-historical models inspired by dogmatic precepts. The moralism of the early socialists also came in for criticism.[14] In his 'Conspectus on Bakunin's *Statism and Anarchy*' (1874–1875), he reproached 'utopian socialism' with seeking 'to foist new illusions onto the people instead of confining its scientific investigations to the social movement created by the people itself'.[15] In his view, the conditions for revolution could not be imported from outside.

2.2 Equality, Theoretical Systems, and Future Society: Errors of the Precursors

After 1789, many theorists contended with one another in outlining a new and more just social order, over and above the fundamental political changes that had come with the end of the *Ancien Regime*. One of the commonest positions assumed that all the ills of society would cease as soon as a system of government based on absolute equality among all its components had been established.

This idea of a primordial, and in many respects dictatorial, communism was the guiding principle of the Conspiracy of Equals that developed in 1796 to subvert the ruling French Directorate. In the *Manifesto of the Equals* (1795), Sylvain Maréchal (1750–1803) argued that 'since all have the same faculties and the same wants', there should be 'the same education [and] the same nourishment' for all. 'Why', he asked, 'should not the like portion and the same quality of food suffice for each according

---

[12] K. Marx, *Value, Price and Profit*, MECW, vol. 20, p. 110.
[13] Marx and Engels, *Manifesto of the Communist Party*, p. 516.
[14] See D. Webb, *Marx, Marxism and Utopia* (Aldershot: Ashgate, 2000), p. 30.
[15] K. Marx, 'Conspectus on Bakunin's *Statism and Anarchy*', MECW, vol. 24, p. 520.

to their wants?'[16] The leading figure in the conspiracy of 1796, François-Noël Babeuf (1760–1797), held that application of 'the great principle of equality' would greatly extend the 'circle of humanity' so that 'frontiers, customs barriers and evil governments' would 'gradually disappear'.[17]

The vision of a society based on strict economic equality re-emerged in French communist writing in the period after the revolution of July 1830. In *Travels in Icaria* (1840), a political manifesto written in the form of a novel, Étienne Cabet (1788–1856) depicted a model community in which there would no longer be 'property, money, or buying and selling', and human beings would be 'equal in everything'.[18] In this 'second promised land',[19] the law would regulate almost every aspect of life: 'every house [would have] four floors'[20] and 'everyone [would be] dressed in the same way'.[21]

Relations of strict equality are also prefigured in the work of Théodore Dézamy (1808–1850). In the *Community Code* (1842), he spoke of a world 'divided into communes, as equal, regular and united as possible', in which there would be 'a single kitchen' and 'one common dormitory' for all children. The whole citizenry would live as 'a family in one single household'.[22]

Similar views to those circulating in France also took root in Germany. In *Humanity as It Is and as It Should Be* (1838), Wilhelm Weitling (1808–1871) foresaw that the elimination of private property would automatically put an end to egoism, which he simplistically regarded as the main cause of all social problems. In his eyes, 'the community of goods' would be 'the means to the redemption of humanity, transforming the earth into paradise' and immediately bringing about 'enormous abundance'.[23]

All the thinkers who projected such visions fell into the same dual error: they took it for granted that the adoption of a new social model based on strict equality could be the solution for all the problems of society; and they convinced themselves, in defiance of all economic laws, that all that was necessary to achieve it was the imposition of certain measures from on high, whose effects would not later be altered by the course of the economy.

---

[16] S. Maréchal, 'Manifesto of the Equals or Equalitarians', in: P. Buonarroti (ed.), *Buonarroti's History of Babeuf's Conspiracy for Equality* (London: H. Hetherington, 1836), p. 316.

[17] F.-N. Babeuf, 'Gracchus Babeuf à Charles Germain', in: C. Mazauric (ed.), *Babeuf Textes Choisis* (Paris: Éditions Sociales, 1965), p. 192.

[18] É. Cabet, *Travels in Icaria* (Syracuse, NY: Syracuse University Press, 2003), p. 81.

[19] Ibid, p. 4.   [20] Ibid, p. 54.   [21] Ibid, p. 49.

[22] T. Dézamy, 'Laws of the Community', in: P. E. Cocoran (ed.), *Before Marx: Socialism and Communism in France, 1830–48* (London: The MacMillan Press Ltd, 1983), pp. 188–96.

[23] W. Weitling, *Die Menschheit, wie sie ist und wie sie sein sollte* (Bern: Jenni, 1845), p. 50.

Alongside this naïve egalitarian ideology, based on an assurance that all social disparities among human beings could be eliminated with ease, was another conviction equally widespread among the early socialists: many believed that it was sufficient to theoretically devise a better system of social organization in order to change the world. Numerous reform projects were therefore elaborated in minute detail, setting out their authors' theses for the restructuring of society. The priority, in their eyes, was to find the correct formulation, which, once discovered, citizens would then willingly accept as a matter of common sense and gradually implement in reality.

Saint-Simon was one of those who clung to this conviction. In 1819, he wrote in the periodical *The Organizer* [*L'Organisateur*]: 'The old system will cease to operate when ideas about how to replace existing institutions with others ... have been sufficiently clarified, pooled and harmonized, and when they have been approved by public opinion.'[24] However, Saint-Simon's views about the society of the future are surprising, and disarming, in their vagueness. In the unfinished *New Christianity* (1824), he stated that the 'political disease of the age' – which caused 'suffering to all workers useful to society' and allowed 'sovereigns to absorb a large part of the wages of the poor' – depended on the 'feeling of egoism'. Since this had become 'dominant in all classes and all individuals',[25] he looked ahead to the birth of a new social organization based on a single guiding principle: 'all men must behave with one another as brothers'.[26]

Fourier declared that human existence was grounded upon universal laws, which, once activated, would guarantee joy and delight all over the earth. In his *Theory of the Four Movements* (1808), he set out what he unhesitatingly called the most 'important discovery [among] all the scientific work done since the human race began'.[27] Fourier opposed advocates of the 'commercial system' and maintained that society would be free only when all its components had returned to expressing their passions.[28] The main error of the political regime of his age was the repression of human nature.[29]

---

[24] C. H. Saint-Simon, 'L'Organisateur: prospectus de l'auteur', in: C. H. de Saint-Simon, *Œuvres complètes*, vol. III (Paris: Presses Universitaires de France, 2012), p. 2115.

[25] C. H. Saint-Simon, 'Le nouveau christianisme', in: C. H. de Saint-Simon, *Œuvres complètes*, vol. IV (Paris: Presses Universitaires de France, 2012), p. 3222.

[26] Ibid, p. 3216.

[27] C. Fourier, *The Theory of the Four Movements* (Cambridge: Cambridge University Press, 1996), p. 4.

[28] Ibid, pp. 13–14.

[29] This is the exact opposite of the theory developed by Sigmund Freud, who, in 'Civilization and Its Discontents', in: S. Freud (ed.), *Complete Psychological Works*, vol. 21 (London: Hogarth Press, 1964), pp. 59–148, argued that a non-repressive

Alongside radical egalitarianism and a quest for the best possible social model, a final element common to many early socialists was their dedication to promoting the birth of small alternative communities. For those who organized them, the liberation of these communes from the economic inequalities existing at the time would provide a decisive impetus for the spread of socialist principles and make it easier to argue in their favour.

In *The New Industrial and Societal World* (1829), Fourier envisaged a novel community structure in which villages would be 'replaced with industrial phalanges of roughly 1800 persons each'.[30] Individuals would live in phalansteries, that is, in large buildings with communal areas where they could enjoy all the services they needed. According to the method invented by Fourier, human beings would 'flutter from pleasure to pleasure and avoid excesses'; they would have brief spells of employment, 'two hours at the most', so that each would be able to exercise 'seven to eight attractive kinds of work in the course of the day'.[31]

The search for better ways of organizing society also spurred on Owen, who, over the course of his life, founded important experiments in workers' cooperation. First at New Lanark, Scotland from 1800 to 1825, then at New Harmony in the United States from 1826 to 1828, he tried to demonstrate in actual practice how to realize a more just social order. In *The Book of the New Moral World* (1836–1844), however, Owen proposed the division of society into eight classes, the last of which 'will consist of those from forty to sixty years complete', who would have the 'final decision'. What he envisaged, rather naïvely, was that in this gerontocratic system everyone would be able and willing to assume their due role in the governance of society 'without contest, his fair, full share of the government of society'.[32]

In 1849, Cabet, too, founded a colony in the United States, at Nauvoo, Illinois, but his authoritarianism gave rise to numerous internal conflicts. In the laws of the 'Icarian Constitution', he proposed as a condition for the birth of community that, 'in order to increase all the prospects of success', he should be appointed 'sole and absolute Director for a period of ten years, with the power to run it on the basis of his doctrine and ideas'.[33]

---

organization of society would involve a dangerous regression from the level of civilization attained within human relations.

[30] C. Fourier, *Le nouveau monde industriel et sociétaire*, in C. Fourier, *Œuvres complètes*, vol. VI (Paris: Éditions Anthropos, 1845), p. 15.

[31] Ibid, pp. 67–69.

[32] R. Owen, *The Book of the New Moral World* (New York: G. Vale, 1845), p. 185.

[33] É. Cabet, *Colonie icarienne aux États-Unis d'Amérique: sa constitution, ses lois, sa situation matérielle et morale après le premier semestre 1855* (New York: Burt Franklin, 1971), p. 43.

The experiments of the early socialists – whether the lovingly devised phalansteries, the sporadic cooperatives, or the eccentric communist colonies – proved so inadequate that their implementation on a wider scale could not be seriously contemplated. They involved a derisory number of workers and often very limited participation of the collective in policy decisions. Moreover, many of the revolutionaries (non-English ones, in particular) who devoted their efforts to building such communities did not understand the fundamental changes in production that were taking place in their age. Many of the early socialists failed to see the connection between the development of capitalism and the potential for social progress for the working class. Such progress depended on the workers' capacity to appropriate the wealth they generated in the new mode of production.[34]

2.3　Where and Why Marx Wrote about Communism

Marx set himself a completely different task from that of previous socialists; his absolute priority was to 'reveal the economic law of motion of modern society'.[35] His aim was to develop a comprehensive critique of the capitalist mode of production, which would serve the proletariat, the principal revolutionary subject, in the overthrow of the existing social-economic system.

Moreover, having no wish to inculcate a new religion, Marx refrained from promoting an idea which he considered theoretically pointless and politically counterproductive: a universal model of communist society. For this reason, in the 'Postface to the Second Edition' (1873) of *Capital*, volume I (1867), he made it clear that he had no interest in 'writing recipes for the cook-shops of the future'.[36] He also outlined what he meant by this well-known assertion in the 'Notes on Wagner's *Treatise*

---

[34] According to R. Rosdolsky in *The Making of Marx's 'Capital'* (London: Pluto Press, 1977), the Romantic socialists, unlike Marx, 'were totally incapable of grasping the "course of modern history", i.e., the necessity and historical progressiveness of the bourgeois social order which they criticized, and confin[ed] themselves to moralistic rejection of it instead', p. 422.

[35] K. Marx, *Capital*, volume I (London: Penguin, 1976), p. 92.

[36] Ibid, p. 99. Marx made this point in reply to a review of his work in *Positive Philosophy (La Philosophie Positive)*, in which the Comtean sociologist Eugène de Roberty (1843–1915) had criticized him for not having indicated the 'necessary conditions for a healthy production and just distribution of wealth', see K. Marx, *Das Kapital. Kritik der politischen Ökonomie. Erster Band, Hamburg 1872*, MEGA², vol. II/6, pp. 1622–3. A partial translation of de Roberty's review is contained in S. Moore, *Marx on the Choice between Socialism and Communism* (Cambridge, MA: Harvard University Press, 1980), pp. 84–7, although Moore wrongly claimed that the purpose of *Capital* was 'to find in the present the basis for predicting the future', p. 86.

on Political Economy' (1879–80), where, in response to criticism from the German economist Adolph Wagner (1835–1917), he categorically stated that he had 'never established a "socialist system"'.[37]

Marx made similar declarations in his political writings. In *The Civil War in France* (1871), he wrote of the Paris Commune, the first seizure of power by the subaltern classes: 'The working class did not expect miracles from the Commune. They have no ready-made utopias to introduce by a decree of the people.' Rather, the emancipation of the proletariat had 'to pass through long struggles, through a series of historic processes, transforming circumstances and men'. The point was not to 'realize ideals', but 'to set free elements of the new society with which old collapsing bourgeois society itself is pregnant'.[38]

Finally, Marx said much the same in his correspondence with leaders of the European workers' movement. In 1881, for instance, when Ferdinand Domela Nieuwenhuis (1846–1919), the leading representative of the Social Democratic League in the Netherlands, asked him what measures a revolutionary government would have to take after assuming power in order to establish a socialist society, Marx replied that he had always regarded such questions as 'fallacious', arguing instead that 'what is to be done ... at any particular moment depends, of course, wholly and entirely on the actual historical circumstances in which action is to be taken'. He contended that it was impossible 'to solve an equation that does not comprise within its terms the elements of its solution'; 'a doctrinaire and of necessity fantastic anticipation of a future revolution's programme of action only serves to distract from the present struggle.'[39]

Nevertheless, contrary to what many commentators have wrongly claimed, Marx did develop, in both published and unpublished form, a number of discussions about communist society which appear in three kinds of text. First, there are those in which Marx criticized ideas that he regarded as theoretically mistaken and liable to mislead socialists of his time. Some parts of the *Economic and Philosophic Manuscripts of 1844* and *The German Ideology*; the chapter on 'Socialist and Communist Literature' in the *Manifesto of the Communist Party*; the criticisms of Pierre-Joseph Proudhon in the *Grundrisse*, the *Urtext*, and the *Contribution to the Critique of Political Economy*; the texts of the early

---

[37] K. Marx, 'Marx's Notes (1879–80) on Wagner', in T. Carver (ed.), *Texts on Method* (Oxford: Basil Blackwell, 1975), pp. 182–3.

[38] K. Marx, *The Civil War in France*, MECW, vol. 22, p. 335.

[39] K. Marx to F. Domela Nieuwenhuis, 22 February 1881, MECW, vol. 46, p. 66. The vast correspondence with Engels is the best evidence of his consistency in this regard. In the course of forty years of collaboration, the two friends exchanged views on every imaginable topic, but Marx did not spend the least time discussing how the society of the future should be organized.

1870s directed against anarchism; and the theses critical of Ferdinand Lassalle (1825–1864) in the *Critique of the Gotha Programme* (1875) belong to this category. To these should be added the critical remarks on Proudhon, Lassalle, and the anarchist component of the International Working Men's Association scattered throughout Marx's vast correspondence.

The second kind of text is the militant writings and political propaganda written for working-class organizations. In these, Marx tried to provide more concrete indications about the society for which they were fighting and the instruments necessary to construct it. This group comprises the *Manifesto of the Communist Party*, the resolutions, reports, and addresses for the International Working Men's Association – including *Value, Price and Profit* and *The Civil War in France* – and various journalistic articles, public lectures, speeches, letters to militants, and other short documents such as the *Programme of the French Workers' Party*.

The third and final group of texts, which are centred around capitalism, contain Marx's lengthiest and most detailed discussions of the features of communist society. Important chapters of *Capital* and the numerous preparatory manuscripts, particularly the highly valuable *Grundrisse*, contain some of his most salient ideas on socialism. It was precisely his critical observations on aspects of the existing mode of production that prompted reflections on communist society, and it is no accident that in some cases successive pages of his work alternate between these two themes.[40]

A close study of Marx's discussions of communism allow us to distinguish his own conception from that of twentieth-century regimes, who, while claiming to act in his name, perpetrated a series of crimes and atrocities. In this way, it is possible to relocate the Marxian political project within the horizon that corresponds to it: the struggle for the emancipation of what Saint-Simon called 'the poorest and most numerous class'.[41]

---

[40] Rosdolsky argued in *The Making of Marx's 'Capital'* that, while it is true that Marx rejected the idea of the 'construction of completed socialist systems', this does not mean that Marx and Engels developed 'no conception of the socialist economic and social order (a view often attributed to them by opportunists), or that they simply left the entire matter to [their] grandchildren ... On the contrary, such conceptions played a part in Marx's theoretical system ... We therefore constantly encounter discussions and remarks in *Capital*, and the works preparatory to it, which are concerned with the problems of a socialist society', pp. 413–14.

[41] C. H. Saint-Simon and B.-P. Enfantin, 'Religion Saint-Simonienne: Procès', in: C. de Saint Simon and B.-P. Enfantin, *Oeuvres de Saint-Simon & D'Enfantin*, vol. XLVII (Paris: Leroux, 1878), p. 378. In other parts of their work, the two French proto-socialists use the expression 'the poorest and most laborious class'. See, for example, idem, 'Notre politique est religieuse', ibid, vol. XLV, p. 28.

Marx's notes on communism should not be thought of as a model to be adhered to dogmatically,[42] still less as solutions to be indiscriminately applied in diverse times and places. Yet these sketches constitute a priceless theoretical treasure, still useful today for the critique of capitalism.

2.4 The Limits of the Initial Formulations

Contrary to the claims made by a certain type of Marxist-Leninist propaganda, Marx's theories were the result not of some innate wisdom, but of a long process of conceptual and political refinement. Intense study of economics and many other disciplines, together with observation of actual historical events, particularly the Paris Commune, was extremely important for the development of his thoughts on communist society.

Some of Marx's early writings – many of which he never completed or published – are often surprisingly regarded as syntheses of his most significant ideas,[43] but, in fact, they display all the limits of his initial conception of post-capitalist society.

---

[42] An example of this genre is the anthology K. Marx, F. Engels, and V. Lenin, *On Communist Society* (Moscow: Progress, 1974), which presents the texts of the three authors as if they constituted a homogenous opus of the Holy Trinity of communism. As in many other collections of this type, Marx's presence is altogether marginal: even if his name appears on the cover, as the supreme guarantor of the faith of 'scientific socialism', the actual extracts from his writings (19 pages out of 157) are considerably shorter than those of Engels and Lenin (1870–1924). All we find here of Marx the theorist of communist society comes from the *Manifesto of the Communist Party* and the *Critique of the Gotha Programme*, plus a mere half-page from *The Holy Family* and a few lines on the dictatorship of the proletariat from the letter of 5 March 1852 to Joseph Weydemeyer (1818–1866). The picture is the same in the diffuse anthology edited by the Finnish communist O. W. Kuusinen, *Fundamentals of Marxism-Leninism: Manual*, second rev. (Moscow: Foreign Languages Publishing House, 1963). In part 5, on 'Socialism and Communism', Marx is quoted only eleven times, compared with twelve references to the work of Nikita Khrushchev (1894–1971) and the documents of the Communist Party of the Soviet Union and fifty quotations from the works of Lenin.

[43] See R. Aron, *Marxismes imaginaires. D'une sainte famille à l'autre* (Paris: Gallimard, 1970) which pokes fun at the 'Parisian para-Marxists', p. 210, who 'subordinated *Capital* to the early writings, especially the economic-philosophical manuscripts of 1844, the obscurity, incompleteness and contradictions of which fascinated the reader', p. 177. In his view, these authors failed to understand that 'if Marx had not had the ambition and hope to ground the advent of communism with scientific rigour, he would not have needed to work for thirty years on *Capital* (without managing to complete it). A few pages and a few weeks would have sufficed', p. 210. See also, M. Musto, 'The Myth of the "Young Marx" in the Interpretations of the *Economic and Philosophic Manuscripts of 1844*', *Critique*, 43 (2) (2015), pp. 233–60. For a description of the fragmentary character of the *Economic and Philosophic Manuscripts of 1844* and the incompleteness of the theses contained in them, see M. Musto, *Another Marx: Early Manuscripts to the International* (London: Bloomsbury, 2018), pp. 42–45.

In the *Economic and Philosophic Manuscripts of 1844*, Marx wrote of these matters in highly abstract terms, since he had not yet been able to expand his economic studies and had had little political experience at the time. At some points, he described 'communism' as the 'negation of the negation', as a 'moment of the Hegelian dialectic': 'the positive expression of the annulled private property'.[44] At others, however, inspired by Ludwig Feuerbach (1804–1872), he wrote that:

> communism, as fully developed naturalism, equals humanism, and as fully developed humanism equals naturalism; it is the genuine resolution of the conflict between man and nature and between man and man – the true resolution of the strife between existence and essence, between objectification and self-confirmation, between freedom and necessity, between the individual and the species.[45]

Various passages in the *Economic and Philosophic Manuscripts of 1844* were influenced by the theological matrix of Georg Wilhelm Friedrich Hegel's (1770–1831) philosophy of history: for example, the argument that 'the entire movement of history [had been] communism's actual act of genesis'; or that communism was 'the riddle of history solved', which 'knew itself to be this solution'.[46]

Similarly, *The German Ideology*, which Marx wrote with Engels and was intended to include texts by other authors,[47] contains a famous quotation that has sown great confusion among exegetes of Marx's work. On one unfinished page, we read that, whereas in capitalist society, with its division of labour, every human being 'has a particular, exclusive sphere of activity', in communist society:

> society regulates the general production and thus makes it possible for me to do one thing today and another tomorrow, to hunt in the morning, fish in the afternoon, rear cattle in the evening, *criticize after dinner*, just as I have a mind, without ever becoming hunter, fisherman, shepherd or *critic*.[48]

---

[44] K. Marx, *Economic and Philosophic Manuscripts of 1844*, MECW, vol. 3, p. 294. D. Bensaid, 'Politiques de Marx', in: K. Marx and F. Engels (eds), *Inventer l'inconnu, textes et correspondances autour de la Commune* (Paris: La Fabrique, 2008) affirmed that in its initial phase 'Marx's communism is philosophical', p. 42.

[45] Marx, *Economic and Philosophic Manuscripts of 1844*, p. 296.   [46] Ibid, p. 297.

[47] On the complex character of these manuscripts and details of their composition and paternity, see the recent edition K. Marx and F. Engels, *Manuskripte und Drucke zur Deutschen Ideologie (1845–1847)*, MEGA², vol. I/5. Some seventeen manuscripts are printed there in their fragmentary form as abandoned by the authors, without the semblance of a completed book. For a critical review, prior to publication of MEGA², vol. I/5, of this much-awaited edition – and in favour of the greatest fidelity to the originals – see T. Carver and D. Blank, *A Political History of the Editions of Marx and Engels's 'German Ideology Manuscripts'* (New York: Palgrave Macmillan, 2014), p. 142.

[48] Marx and Engels, *The German Ideology*, p. 47. The words written by Marx are indicated in italic.

Many authors, both Marxist and anti-Marxist, have ingenuously believed that this was the main feature of communist society for Marx – a view they could hold because of their relative unfamiliarity with *Capital* and various important political texts. Despite the plethora of analysis and discussion regarding the manuscript of 1845–46, they did not realize that this passage was a reformulation of an old – and rather well-known – idea of Charles Fourier's,[49] which was taken up by Engels but rejected by Marx.[50]

Despite these evident limitations, *The German Ideology* represented indubitable progress over the *Economic and Philosophic Manuscripts of 1844*. Whereas the latter was informed by the idealism of the Hegelian Left – the group of which he had been part until 1842 – and lacked any concrete political discussion, the former now maintained that 'it is possible to achieve real liberation only in the real world and by real means'. Communism, therefore, should not be regarded as 'a state of affairs to be established, an ideal to which reality will have to adjust itself, [but as] the real movement which abolishes the present state of things'.[51]

In *The German Ideology*, Marx also drew a first sketch of the economy of future society. Whereas previous revolutions had produced only 'a new distribution of labour to other persons',[52]

Communism differs from all previous movements in that it overturns the basis of all earlier relations of production and intercourse, and for the first time consciously treats all naturally evolved premises as the creations of hitherto existing men, strips them of their natural character and subjugates them to the power of

---

[49] See Fourier, *Le nouveau monde industriel et sociétaire*.
[50] The only words that belong to Marx – 'criticize after dinner', 'critical critics', and 'or critic' – actually express his disagreement with the romantic, utopian-inclined views of Engels. We owe the rediscovery and accessible presentation of this important detail to the rigorous philological labours of Wataru Hiromatsu (1933–1994), the editor of the two-volume work with German and Japanese *apparatus criticus*: W. Hiromatsu (ed.), *Die deutsche Ideologie* (Tokyo: Kawade Shobo-Shinsha, 1974). Two decades later, T. Carver wrote that this study made it possible to know 'which words were written in Engels' hand, which in Marx's, which insertion can be assigned to each author, and which deletions', *The Postmodern Marx* (Pennsylvania: Pennsylvania State University Press, 1998) p. 104. Cf. the more recent Carver and Blank, *A Political History of the Editions of Marx and Engels's 'German Ideology Manuscripts'*, pp. 139–40. Marx was referring sarcastically to the positions of other Young Hegelians he had derided and sharply combatted in a book published a few months earlier, *The Holy Family, or Critique of Critical Criticism: Against Bruno Bauer and Company*. According to Carver, *The Postmodern Marx*, 'the famous passage on communist society from *The German Ideology* cannot now be read as one continuous train of thought agreed jointly between two authors'. In the few words he contributed, Marx was 'sharply rebuking Engels for straying, perhaps momentarily, from the serious work of undercutting the phantasies of Utopian socialists', ibid, p. 106. Still, Marx's marginal insertions were integrated seamlessly into Engels's initial text by early twentieth-century editors, thereby becoming the canonical description of how human beings would live in communist society 'according to Marx'.
[51] Marx and Engels, *The German Ideology*, pp. 38, 49.   [52] Ibid, p. 52.

the united individuals. Its organization is therefore essentially economic, the material production of the conditions of this unity.[53]

Marx also stated that 'empirically, communism is only possible as the act of the dominant peoples "all at once" and simultaneously'. In his view, this presupposed both 'the universal development of productive forces' and 'the world intercourse bound up with them'.[54] Furthermore, Marx confronted for the first time a fundamental political theme that he would take up again in the future: the advent of communism as the end of class tyranny. For the revolution would 'abolish the rule of all classes with the classes themselves, because it is carried through by the class which no longer counts as a class in society, which is not recognized as a class, and is in itself the expression of the dissolution of all classes, nationalities'.[55]

Marx continued, together with Engels, to develop his reflections on post-capitalist society in the *Manifesto of the Communist Party*. In this text, which, in its profound analysis of the changes effected by capitalism, towered above the rough and ready socialist literature of the time, the most interesting points on communism concern property relations. Marx observed that their radical transformation was 'not at all a distinctive feature of communism', since other new modes of production in history had also brought that about. For Marx, in opposition to all the propaganda claims that communists would prevent personal appropriation of the fruits of labour, the 'distinguishing feature of communism' was 'not the abolition of property generally, but the abolition of bourgeois property',[56] of 'the power to appropriate the products of society ... to subjugate the labour of others'.[57] In his eyes, the 'theory of the communists' could be summed up in one sentence: 'the abolition of private property'.[58]

In the *Manifesto of the Communist Party*, Marx also proposed a list of ten preliminary benchmarks to be achieved in the most advanced economies following the conquest of power. They included 'abolition of property in land and application of all rents of land to public purposes';[59] the centralization of credit in the hands of the state, by means of a national bank ...; the centralization of the means of communication and transport in the hands of the state ... free education for all children in public

---

[53] Ibid, p. 81. [54] Ibid, p. 49. [55] Ibid, p. 52.
[56] Marx and Engels, *Manifesto of the Communist Party*, p. 498. [57] Ibid, p. 500.
[58] Ibid, p. 498.
[59] Ibid, p. 505. The English translation that Samuel Moore (1838–1911) produced in 1888 in cooperation with Engels, and which is the basis for the MECW edition, renders the German *Staatsausgaben* [state expenditure] as the less statist, more generic 'spending for public purposes'.

schools', but also 'abolition of all right of inheritance', a Saint-Simonian measure that Marx later firmly rejected.[60]

As in the case of the manuscripts written between 1844 and 1846, it would be a mistake to regard the measures listed in the *Manifesto of the Communist Party* – drafted when Marx was just thirty – as his finished vision of post-capitalist society.[61] The complete maturation of his thought would require many more years of study and political experiences.

2.5 Communism as Free Association

In *Capital*, volume I, Marx argued that capitalism was a 'historically determined'[62] social mode of production in which the labour product was transformed into a commodity, with the result that individuals had value only as producers, and human existence was subjugated to the act of the 'production of commodities'.[63] Hence 'the process of production' had 'mastery over man, instead of being controlled by him'.[64] Capital 'care[d] nothing for the length of life of labour power' and attached no importance to improvements in the living conditions of the proletariat. Capital 'attains this objective by shortening the life of labour-power, in the same way as a greedy farmer snatches more produce from the soil by robbing it of its fertility'.[65]

In the *Grundrisse*, Marx recalled that in capitalism, 'since the aim of labour is not a particular product [with a relation] to the particular needs of the individual, but money ... the industriousness of the individual has no limits'.[66] In such a society, 'the whole time of an individual is posited as labour time, and he is consequently degraded to a mere labourer, subsumed under labour'.[67] Bourgeois ideology, however, presents this as if the individual enjoys greater freedom and is protected by impartial legal norms capable of guaranteeing justice and equity. Paradoxically, despite the fact that the economy has developed to such a level that it can allow the whole

---

[60] In the International Working Men's Association, this provision was supported by M. Bakunin (1814–1876) and opposed by Marx. See 'Part 6: On Inheritance', in: M. Musto (ed.), *Workers Unite! The International 150 Years Later* (New York: Bloomsbury, 2014), pp. 159–68.

[61] Their 'practical application' – as the preface to the German edition of 1872 reminded readers – 'will depend ... everywhere and at all times on the obtaining historical conditions, and, for that reason, no special stress is laid on the revolutionary measures proposed at the end of Section II'. By the early 1870s, the *Manifesto of the Communist Party* had become a 'historical document', which its authors felt they no longer had 'any right to alter', in Marx and Engels, *Manifesto of the Communist Party*, p. 175.

[62] Marx, *Capital*, volume I, p. 169. [63] Ibid., p. 172. [64] Ibid., p. 175. [65] Ibid., p. 376.

[66] K. Marx, 'Outlines of the Critique of Political Economy [*Grundrisse*]. First Instalment', MECW, vol. 28., p. 157.

[67] Marx, 'Outlines of the Critique of Political Economy [*Grundrisse*]. Second Instalment', p. 94.

society to live in better conditions than before, 'the most developed machinery now compels the labourer to work for a longer time than the savage does, or than the labourer himself did when he was using the simplest, crudest implements'.[68]

By contrast, Marx's vision of communism was of 'an association of free individuals [*ein Verein freier Menschen*], working with the means of production held in common, and expending their many different forms of labour-power in full self-awareness as one single social labour force'.[69] Similar definitions are present in many of Marx's writings. In the *Grundrisse*, he wrote that post-capitalist society would be based upon 'collective production [*gemeinschaftliche Produktion*]'.[70]

In the *Economic Manuscripts of 1863–1867*, he spoke of the 'passage from the capitalist mode of production to the mode of production of associated labour [*Produktionsweise der assoziierten Arbeit*]'.[71] And in the *Critique of the Gotha Programme*, he defined the social organization 'based on common ownership of the means of production' as 'cooperative society [*genossenschaftliche Gesellschaft*]'.[72]

In *Capital*, volume I, Marx explained that the 'ruling principle' of this 'higher form of society' would be 'the full and free development of every individual'.[73] In *The Civil War in France*, he expressed his approval of the measures taken by the Communards, which 'betoken[ed] the tendency of a government of the people by the people'.[74] To be more precise, in his evaluation of the political reforms of the Paris Commune, he asserted that 'the old centralized Government would in the provinces, too, have to give way to the self-government of the producers'.[75] The expression recurs in the 'Conspectus of Bakunin's *Statism and Anarchy*' (1874–1875), where he maintained that radical social change would 'start with self-government of the communities'.[76] Marx's idea of society, therefore, is the antithesis of the totalitarian systems that emerged in his name in the twentieth century. His writings are useful for an understanding not only of how capitalism works, but also of the failure of socialist experiences until today.

In referring to so-called free competition, or the seemingly equal positions of workers and capitalists on the market in bourgeois society, Marx

---

[68] Ibid.   [69] Marx, *Capital*, volume I, p. 171, translation modified.
[70] Marx, 'Outlines of the Critique of Political Economy [*Grundrisse*]. First Instalment', p. 96.
[71] K. Marx, *Ökonomische Manuskripte 1863–1867*, MEGA², vol. II/4.2, p. 662. Cf. P. Chattopadhyay, *Marx's Associated Mode of Production* (New York: Palgrave, 2016), esp. pp. 59–65 and 157–61.
[72] K. Marx, *Critique of the Gotha Programme*, MECW, vol. 24, p. 85.
[73] Marx, *Capital*, volume I, p. 739.   [74] Marx, *The Civil War in France*, p. 339.
[75] Ibid, p. 332.
[76] Marx, 'Conspectus of Bakunin's *Statism and Anarchy*', vol. 24, p. 519.

stated that the reality was totally different from the human freedom exalted by apologists of capitalism. The system posed a huge obstacle to democracy, and he showed better than anyone else that the workers did not receive an equivalent for what they produced.[77] In the *Grundrisse*, he explained that what was presented as an 'exchange of equivalents' was, in fact, appropriation of the workers' 'labour time without exchange'; the relationship of exchange 'completely disappeared' or it became a 'mere semblance'.[78] Relations between persons were 'actuated only by self-interest'. This 'clash of individuals' had been passed off as the 'the absolute form of existence of free individuality in the sphere of production and exchange'. But, for Marx, 'nothing could be further from the truth', since 'in free competition, it is capital that is set free, not the individuals'.[79] In the *Economic Manuscripts of 1863–1867*, he denounced the fact that 'surplus labour is initially pocketed, in the name of society, by the capitalist' – the surplus labour that is 'the basis of society's free time' and, by virtue of this, the 'material basis of its whole development and of civilization in general'.[80] And in *Capital*, volume I, he showed that the wealth of the bourgeoisie was possible only 'by converting the whole lifetime of the masses into labour time'.[81]

In the *Grundrisse*, Marx observed that in capitalism 'individuals are subsumed under social production', which 'exists outside them as their fate'.[82] This happens only through the attribution of exchange-value conferred on the products, whose buying and selling takes place *post festum*.[83] Furthermore, 'all social powers of production' – including scientific discoveries, which appear as 'alien and external' to the worker[84] – are posited by capital. The very association of the workers, at the places and in the act of production, is 'operated by capital' and is therefore 'only formal'. Use of the goods created by the workers 'is not mediated by exchange between mutually independent labours or products of labour', but rather 'by the circumstances of social production within which the individual carries on his

---

[77] On these questions, see E. M. Wood, *Democracy against Capitalism* (Cambridge: Cambridge University Press, 1995), esp. pp. 1–48.
[78] Marx, 'Outlines of the Critique of Political Economy [*Grundrisse*]. First Instalment', p. 386.
[79] Marx, 'Outlines of the Critique of Political Economy [*Grundrisse*]. Second Instalment', p. 38.
[80] K. Marx, *Economic Manuscript of 1861–1863*, MECW, vol. 30, p. 196.
[81] Marx, *Capital*, volume I, p. 667.
[82] Marx, 'Outlines of the Critique of Political Economy [*Grundrisse*]. First Instalment', p. 96.
[83] Ibid, p. 108.
[84] Marx, 'Outlines of the Critique of Political Economy [*Grundrisse*]. Second Instalment', p. 84.

activity'.[85] Marx explained how productive activity in the factory 'concerns only the product of labour, not labour itself',[86] since it is 'confined to a common place of work under the direction of overseers, regimentation, greater discipline, consistency, and a posited dependence on capital in production itself'.[87]

In communist society, by contrast, production would be 'directly social', 'the offspring of association distributing labour within itself'. It would be managed by individuals as their 'common wealth'.[88] The 'social character of production [*gesellschaftliche Charakter der Produktion*]' would 'from the outset make the product into a communal, general one'; its associative character would be 'presupposed' and 'the labour of the individual ... from the outset taken as social labour'.[89] As Marx stressed in the *Critique of the Gotha Programme*, in post-capitalist society, 'individual labour no longer exists in an indirect fashion but directly as a component part of the total labour'.[90] In addition, the workers would be able to create the conditions for the eventual disappearance of 'the enslaving subordination of the individual to the division of labour'.[91]

In *Capital*, volume I, Marx emphasized that, in bourgeois society, 'the worker exists for the process of production, and not the process of production for the worker'.[92] Moreover, in parallel to exploitation of the workers, there developed exploitation of the environment. In contrast to interpretations that reduce Marx's conception of communist society to the mere development of productive forces, he displayed great interest in what we would now call the ecological question.[93] He repeatedly denounced the fact that 'all profess in capitalist agriculture is a progress in the art, not only of robbing the worker but of robbing the soil'. This threatens both of 'the original sources of all wealth – the soil and the worker'.[94]

In communism, the conditions would be created for a form of 'planned cooperation' through which the worker 'strips off the fetters of his individuality and develops the capabilities of his species'.[95] In *Capital*, volume II, Marx pointed out that society would then be in a position to 'reckon in advance how much labour, means of production and means of subsistence it can spend, without dislocation', unlike in capitalism 'where any

---

[85] Marx, 'Outlines of the Critique of Political Economy [*Grundrisse*]. First Instalment', p. 109.
[86] Ibid, p. 505.   [87] Ibid, pp. 506–07.   [88] Ibid, pp. 95–96.   [89] Ibid, p. 108.
[90] Marx, *Critique of the Gotha Programme*, p. 85.   [91] Ibid, p. 87.
[92] Marx, *Capital*, volume I, p. 621.
[93] An extensive new literature has sprung up in the past twenty years on this aspect of Marx's thought. One of the most recent contributions is K. Saito, *Karl Marx's Ecosocialism: Capital, Nature, and the Unfinished Critique of Political Economy* (New York: Monthly Review Press, 2017), esp. pp. 217–55.
[94] Marx, *Capital*, volume I, p. 638.   [95] Ibid, p. 447.

kind of social rationality asserts itself only *post festum*' and 'major disturbances can and must occur constantly'.[96] In some passages of *Capital*, volume III, too, Marx clarified differences between a socialist mode of production and a market-based one, foreseeing the birth of a society 'organized as a conscious association'.[97] 'It is only where production is under the actual, predetermining control of society that the latter establishes a relation between the volume of social labour time applied in producing definite articles, and the volume of the social want to be satisfied by these articles.'[98]

Finally, in his marginal notes on Adolph Wagner's *Treatise on Political Economy*, Marx made it clear that in communist society 'the sphere [volume] of production' will have to be 'rationally regulated'.[99] This will also make it possible to eliminate the waste due to the 'anarchical system of competition', which, through its recurrent structural crises, not only involves the 'most outrageous squandering of labour power and the social means of production',[100] but is incapable of solving the contradictions stemming essentially from the 'capitalist use of machinery'.[101]

2.6 Common Ownership and Free Time

Contrary to the view of many of Marx's socialist contemporaries, a redistribution of consumption goods was not sufficient to reverse this state of affairs. A root-and-branch change in the productive assets of society was necessary. Thus, in the *Grundrisse* Marx noted that 'to leave wage labour and at the same time to abolish capital [was] a self-contradictory and self-negating demand'.[102] What was required was 'dissolution of the mode of production and form of society based upon exchange value'.[103] In the address published under the title *Value, Price and Profit*, he called on workers to 'inscribe on their banner' not 'the

---

[96] K. Marx, *Capital*, volume II (London: Penguin, 1978), p. 390.
[97] K. Marx, *Capital*, volume III (London: Penguin, 1981), p. 799.
[98] Ibid, p. 186. See B. Ollman (ed.), *Market Socialism: The Debate among Socialists* (London: Routledge, 1998).
[99] Marx, 'Marx's Notes on Wagner', p. 188. [100] Marx, *Capital*, volume I, p. 667.
[101] Ibid, p. 562.
[102] Marx, 'Outlines of the Critique of Political Economy [*Grundrisse*]. First Instalment', p. 235.
[103] Ibid, p. 195. According to P. Mattick, *Marx and Keynes* (Boston: Extending Horizons Books, 1969) p. 363: 'For Marx, the law of value "regulates" market capitalism but no other form of social production.' Therefore, he held that 'socialism was, first of all, the end of value production and thus also the end of the capitalist relations of production', p. 362.

conservative motto: "A fair day's wage for a fair day's work!" [but] the revolutionary watchword: "Abolition of the wages system!"'[104]

Furthermore, the *Critique of the Gotha Programme* made the point that, in the capitalist mode of production, 'the material conditions of production are in the hands of non-workers in the form of capital and land ownership, while the masses are only owners of the personal condition of production, of labour power'.[105] Therefore, it was essential to overturn the property relations at the base of the bourgeois mode of production. In the *Grundrisse*, Marx recalled that 'the laws of private property – liberty, equality, property – property in one's own labour and the ability to freely dispose of it – are inverted into the propertylessness of the worker and the alienation of his labour, his relation to it as alien property and vice versa'.[106] And, in 1869, in a report of the General Council of the International Working Men's Association, he asserted that 'private property in the means of production' served to give the bourgeois class 'the power to live without labour upon other people's labour'.[107] He repeated this point in another short political text, the 'Preamble to the Programme of the French Workers' Party', adding that 'the producers cannot be free unless they are in possession of the means of production' and that the goal of the proletarian struggle must be 'the return of all the means of production to collective ownership'.[108]

In *Capital*, volume III, Marx observed that, when the workers had established a communist mode of production, 'private property of the earth by single individuals [would] appear just as absurd as private property of one human being by another'. He directed his most radical critique against the destructive possession inherent in capitalism, insisting that 'even an entire society, a nation, or even all simultaneously existing societies taken together, are not the owners of the earth'. For Marx, human beings were 'only its possessors, its usufructuaries, and they have to bequeath it [the planet] in an improved state to succeeding generations, like good heads of the household [*boni patres familias*]'.[109]

A different kind of ownership of the means of production would also radically change the lifetime of society. In *Capital*, volume I, Marx unfolded with complete clarity the reasons why in capitalism 'the

[104] Marx, *Value, Price and Profit*, p. 149.
[105] Marx, *Critique of the Gotha Programme*, p. 88.
[106] Marx, 'Outlines of the Critique of Political Economy [*Grundrisse*]. Second Instalment', p. 88.
[107] K. Marx, 'Report of the General Council on the Right of Inheritance', MECW, vol. 21, p. 65.
[108] K. Marx, 'Preamble to the Programme of the French Workers' Party', MECW, vol. 24, p. 340.
[109] Marx, *Capital*, volume III, p. 911.

shortening of the working day is ... by no means what is aimed at, in capitalist production, when labour is economized by increasing its productivity'.[110] The time that the progress of science and technology makes available for individuals is in reality immediately converted into surplus-value. The only aim of the dominant class is the 'shortening of the labour-time necessary for the production of a definite quantity of commodities'. Its only purpose in developing the productive forces is the 'shortening of that part of the working day in which the worker must work for himself, and the lengthening ... the other part ... in which he is free to work for nothing for the capitalist'.[111] This system differs from slavery or the *corvées* due to the feudal lord, since 'surplus labour and necessary labour are mingled together'[112] and make the reality of exploitation harder to perceive.

In the *Grundrisse*, Marx showed that 'free time for the few' is possible only because of this surplus labour time of the many.[113] The bourgeoisie secures growth of its material and cultural capabilities only thanks to the limitation of those of the proletariat. The same happens in the most advanced capitalist countries, to the detriment of those on the periphery of the system. In the *Manuscripts of 1861–1863*, Marx emphasized that the 'free development' of the dominant class is 'based on the restriction of development among the working class'; 'the surplus labour of the workers' is the 'natural basis of the social development of the other section'. The surplus labour time of the workers is not only the pillar supporting the 'material conditions of life' for the bourgeoisie; it also creates the conditions for its 'free time, the sphere of [its] development'. Marx could not have put it better: 'the free time of one section corresponds to the time in thrall to labour of the other section'.[114]

Communist society, by contrast, would be characterized by a general reduction in labour time. In the 'Instructions for the Delegates of the Provisional General Council', composed in August 1866, Marx wrote in forthright terms: 'A preliminary condition, without which all further attempts at improvement and emancipation must prove abortive, is the limitation of the working day.' It was needed not only 'to restore the health and physical energies of the working class', but also 'to secure them the possibility of intellectual development, sociable intercourse, social and political action'.[115] Similarly, in *Capital*, volume I, while noting

---

[110] Marx, *Capital*, volume I, p. 437. [111] Ibid, p. 438. [112] Ibid, p. 346.
[113] Marx, 'Outlines of the Critique of Political Economy [*Grundrisse*]. Second Instalment', p. 93.
[114] Marx, *Economic Manuscript of 1861–1863*, pp. 192, 191.
[115] K. Marx, 'Instructions for the Delegates of the Provisional General Council. The Different Questions', MECW, vol. 20, p. 187.

that workers' 'time for education, for intellectual development, for the fulfilling of social functions, for social intercourse, for the free play of the vital forces of his body and his mind' counted as pure 'foolishness' in the eyes of the capitalist class,[116] Marx implied that these would be the basic elements of the new society. As he put it in the *Grundrisse*, a reduction in the hours devoted to labour – and not only labour to create surplus-value for the capitalist class – would favour 'the artistic, scientific, etc., development of individuals, made possible by the time thus set free and the means produced for all of them'.[117]

On the basis of these convictions, Marx identified the 'economy of time [and] the planned distribution of labour time over the various branches of production' as 'the first economic law [of] communal production'.[118] In *Theories of Surplus Value* (1862–1863), he made it even clearer that 'real wealth' was nothing other than 'disposable time'. In communist society, workers' self-management would ensure that 'a greater quantity of time' was 'not absorbed in direct productive labour but ... available for enjoyment, for leisure, thus giving scope for free activity and development'.[119] In this text, so too in the *Grundrisse*, Marx quoted a short anonymous pamphlet entitled *The Source and Remedy of the National Difficulties, Deduced from Principles of Political Economy, in a Letter to Lord John Russell* (1821), whose definition of well-being he fully shared: that is, 'A nation is truly rich if the working day is six hours rather than twelve. Wealth is not command over surplus labour time [real wealth] but *disposable time*, in addition to that employed in immediate production, for every individual and for the whole society.'[120] Elsewhere in the *Grundrisse*, he asks rhetorically: 'What is wealth if not the universality of the individual's needs, capacities, enjoyments, productive forces? ... What is it if not the absolute unfolding of man's creative abilities?'[121] It is evident, then, that the socialist model in Marx's mind did not involve a state of generalized poverty, but rather the attainment of greater collective wealth.

---

[116] Marx, *Capital*, volume I, p. 375.
[117] Marx, 'Outlines of the Critique of Political Economy [*Grundrisse*]. Second Instalment', p. 91.
[118] Marx, 'Outlines of the Critique of Political Economy [*Grundrisse*]. First Instalment', p. 109.
[119] Marx, *Economic Manuscript of 1861–1863*, p. 390.
[120] Marx, 'Outlines of the Critique of Political Economy [*Grundrisse*]. Second Instalment', p. 92.
[121] Marx, 'Outlines of the Critique of Political Economy [*Grundrisse*]. First Instalment', p. 411.

2.7 Role of the State, Individual Rights, and Freedoms

In communist society, along with transformative changes in the economy, the role of the state and the function of politics would also have to be redefined. In *The Civil War in France*, Marx was at pains to explain that, after the conquest of power, the working class would have to fight to 'uproot the economical foundations upon which rests the existence of classes, and therefore of class rule'. Once 'labour was emancipated, every man would become a working man, and productive labour [would] cease to be a class attribute'.[122] The well-known statement that 'the working class cannot simply lay hold of the ready-made state machinery and wield it for its own purposes' was meant to signify, as Marx and Engels clarified in the booklet *Fictitious Splits in the International*, that 'the functions of government [should] become simple administrative functions'.[123] And in a concise formulation in his 'Conspectus on Bakunin's *Statism and Anarchy*', Marx insisted that 'the distribution of general functions [should] become a routine matter which entails no domination'.[124] This would, as far as possible, avoid the danger that the exercise of political duties generated new dynamics of domination and subjugation.

Marx believed that, with the development of modern society, 'state power [had] assumed more and more the character of the national power of capital over labour, of a public force organized for social enslavement, of an engine of class despotism'.[125] In communism, by contrast, the workers would have to prevent the state from becoming an obstacle to full emancipation. It would be necessary to 'amputate ... the merely repressive organs of the old governmental power, [to wrest] its legitimate functions from an authority usurping pre-eminence over society itself, and restore [them] to the responsible agents of society'.[126] In the *Critique of the Gotha Programme*, Marx observed that 'freedom consists in converting the state from an organ superimposed upon society into one completely subordinate to it', and shrewdly added that 'forms of state are more free or less free to the extent that they restrict the "freedom of the state"'.[127]

In the same text, Marx underlined the demand that, in communist society, public policies should prioritize the 'collective satisfaction of needs'. Spending on schools, healthcare, and other common goods would 'grow considerably in comparison with present-day society and

---

[122] Marx, *The Civil War in France*, pp. 334–5.
[123] K. Marx and F. Engels, 'Fictitious Splits in the International', MECW, vol. 23, p. 121.
[124] Marx, 'Conspectus on Bakunin's Book *Statehood and Anarchy*', p. 519.
[125] Marx, *The Civil War in France*, p. 329.   [126] Ibid, pp. 332–3.
[127] Marx, *Critique of the Gotha Programme*, p. 94.

grow in proportion as the new society develop[ed]'.[128] Education would assume front-rank importance and – as he had pointed out in *The Civil War in France*, referring to the model adopted by the Communards in 1871 – 'all the educational institutions [would be] opened to the people gratuitously and ... cleared of all interference of Church and State'. Only in this way would culture be 'made accessible to all' and 'science itself freed from the fetters which class prejudice and governmental force had imposed upon it'.[129]

Unlike liberal society, where 'equal right' leaves existing inequalities intact, in communist society 'right would have to be unequal rather than equal'. A change in this direction would recognize, and protect, individuals on the basis of their specific needs and the greater or lesser hardship of their conditions, since 'they would not be different individuals if they were not unequal'. Furthermore, it would be possible to determine each person's fair share of services and the available wealth. The society that aimed to follow the principle 'From each according to their abilities, to each according to their needs'[130] had before it this intricate road fraught with difficulties. However, the final outcome was not guaranteed by some 'magnificent progressive destiny' (in the words of Giacomo Leopardi [1798–1837]), nor was it irreversible.

Marx attached a fundamental value to individual freedom, and his communism was radically different from the levelling of classes envisaged by his various predecessors or pursued by many of his epigones. In the *Urtext*, however, he pointed to the 'folly of those socialists (especially French socialists)' who, considering 'socialism to be the realization of [bourgeois] ideas ... purport[ed] to demonstrate that exchange and exchange value, etc., were originally ... a system of the freedom and equality of all, but [later] perverted by money [and] capital'.[131] In the *Grundrisse*, he labelled it an 'absurdity' to regard 'free competition as the ultimate development of human freedom'; it was tantamount to a belief that 'the rule of the bourgeoisie is the terminal point of world history', which he mockingly described as 'an agreeable thought for the parvenus of the day before yesterday'.[132]

In the same way, Marx contested the liberal ideology according to which 'the negation of free competition [was] equivalent to the negation of individual freedom and of social production based upon individual

---

[128] Ibid, p. 85. [129] Marx, *The Civil War in France*, p. 332.
[130] Marx, *Critique of the Gotha Programme*, p. 87.
[131] Marx, 'Outlines of the Critique of Political Economy [*Grundrisse*]. First Instalment', p. 180.
[132] Marx, 'Outlines of the Critique of Political Economy [*Grundrisse*]. Second Instalment', p. 40.

freedom'. In bourgeois society, the only possible 'free development' was 'on the limited basis of the domination of capital'. But that 'type of individual freedom' was, at the same time, 'the most sweeping abolition of all individual freedom and the complete subjugation of individuality to social conditions which assume the form of objective powers, indeed of overpowering objects ... independent of the individuals relating to one another'.[133]

The alternative to capitalist alienation was achievable only if the subaltern classes became aware of their condition as new slaves and embarked on a struggle to radically transform the world in which they were exploited. Their mobilization and active participation in this process could not stop, however, on the day after the conquest of power. It would have to continue, in order to avert any drift towards the kind of state socialism that Marx always opposed with the utmost tenacity and conviction.

In 1868, in a significant letter to the president of the General Association of German Workers, Marx explained that, in Germany, 'where the worker is regulated bureaucratically from childhood onwards, where he believes in authority, in those set over him, the main thing is to teach him to walk by himself'.[134] He never changed this conviction throughout his life and it is not by chance that the first point of his draft of the Statutes of the International Working Men's Association states: 'The emancipation of the working classes must be conquered by the working classes themselves.' And they add immediately afterwards that the struggle for working-class emancipation 'means not a struggle for class privileges and monopolies, but for equal rights and duties'.[135]

Many of the political parties and regimes that developed in Marx's name used the concept of the 'dictatorship of the proletariat'[136] in an instrumental manner, distorting his thought and moving away from the direction he had indicated. But this does not mean we are doomed to repeat the error.

References

Aron, Raymond (1970), *Marxismes imaginaires. D'une sainte famille à l'autre*, Paris: Gallimard.

---

[133] Ibid. [134] 'K. Marx to J. B. von Schweitzer, 13 October 1868', MECW, vol. 43, p. 134.
[135] K. Marx, 'Provisional Rules of the Association', MECW, vol. 20, p. 14.
[136] H. Draper has shown that Marx used the term only seven times, mostly in a radically different sense from the one falsely attributed to him by many of his interpreters or by those who have claimed to be continuing the tradition of his thought. See *Karl Marx's Theory of Revolution. Volume 3: The Dictatorship of the Proletariat* (New York: Monthly Review Press, 1986), pp. 385–6.

Babeuf, François-Noël (1965), 'Briser les chaînes', in: C. Mazauric (ed.), *Babeuf Textes Choisis*, Paris: Éditions Sociales, pp. 187–240.
— (1965), 'Gracchus Babeuf à Charles Germain', in: C. Mazauric (ed.), *Babeuf Textes Choisis*, Paris: Éditions Sociales, p. 192.
Bensaid, Daniel (2008), 'Politiques de Marx', in: Karl Marx and Friedrich Engels, *Inventer l'inconnu, textes et correspondances autour de la Commune*, Paris: La Fabrique, pp. 11–103.
Blanqui, Jérôme-Adolphe (1885), *History of Political Economy in Europe*, New York, London: G. P. Putnam and Sons.
Cabet, Étienne (1971), *Colonie icarienne aux États-Unis d'Amérique: sa constitution, ses lois, sa situation matérielle et morale après le premier semestre 1855*, New York: Burt Franklin.
— (2003), *Travels in Icaria*, Syracuse, NY: Syracuse University Press.
Carver, Terrell (1998), *The Postmodern Marx*, Pennsylvania: Pennsylvania State University Press.
Carver, Terrell, and Blank, Daniel (2014), *A Political History of the Editions of Marx and Engels's 'German Ideology Manuscripts'*, New York: Palgrave Macmillan.
Chattopadhyay, Paresh (2016), *Marx's Associated Mode of Production*, New York: Palgrave.
Claeys, Gregory (2014), 'Early Socialism in Intellectual History', *History of European Ideas* 40 (7): 893–904.
Dézamy, Théodore (1983), 'Laws of the Community', in: Paul E. Cocoran (ed.), *Before Marx: Socialism and Communism in France, 1830–48*, London: The MacMillan Press Ltd, pp. 188–96.
Draper, Hal (1986), *Karl Marx's Theory of Revolution. Volume 3: The Dictatorship of the Proletariat*, New York: Monthly Review Press.
Engels, Friedrich (1987), *Socialism: Utopian and Scientific*, MECW, vol. 25, pp. 244–312.
Fourier, Charles (1845), *Le nouveau monde industriel et sociétaire*, in: C. Fourier (ed.), *Œuvres complètes de Ch. Fourier*, vol. VI, Paris: Éditions Anthropos.
— (1996), *The Theory of the Four Movements*, Cambridge: Cambridge University Press.
Freud, Sigmund (1964), 'Civilization and Its Discontents', in: S. Freud, *Complete Psychological Works*, vol. 21, London: Hogarth Press.
Geoghegan, Vincent (2008), *Utopianism and Marxism*, Berne: Peter Lang.
Hiromatsu, Wataru, ed. (1974), *Die deutsche Ideologie*, Tokyo: Kawade Shobo-Shinsha.
Hobsbawm, Eric (1982), 'Marx, Engels and Pre-Marxian Socialism', in: Eric Hobsbawm (ed.), *The History of Marxism. Volume One: Marxism in Marx's Day* (Bloomington: Indiana University Press), pp. 1–28.
Kuusinen, Otto Wille, ed. (1963), *Fundamentals of Marxism-Leninism: Manual*, second rev., Moscow: Foreign Languages Publishing House.
Maréchal, S. (1836), 'Manifesto of the Equals or Equalitarians', in: Philippe Buonarroti (ed.), *Buonarroti's History of Babeuf's Conspiracy for Equality* (London: H. Hetherington), pp. 314–17.

Marx, Karl (1975), 'Marx's Notes (1879–80) on Wagner', in: Terrell Carver (ed.), *Texts on Method*, Oxford: Basil Blackwell, pp. 179–219.
  (1975), *Economic and Philosophic Manuscripts of 1844*, MECW, vol. 3, pp. 229–348.
  (1976), *Capital*, volume I, London: Penguin.
  (1978), *Capital*, volume II, London: Penguin.
  (1981), *Capital*, volume III, London: Penguin.
  (1984), *Value, Price and Profit*, MECW, vol. 20, pp. 101–49.
  (1986), *The Civil War in France*, MECW, vol. 22, pp. 307–59.
  (1986), 'Outlines of the Critique of Political Economy [*Grundrisse*]. First Instalment', MECW, vol. 28.
  (1986), 'Outlines of the Critique of Political Economy [*Grundrisse*]. Second Instalment', MECW, vol. 29.
  (1987), *Das Kapital. Kritik der politischen Ökonomie. Erster Band, Hamburg 1872*, MEGA², vol. II/6.
  (1988), *Economic Manuscript of 1861–1863*, MECW, vol. 30.
  (1988), *Letters 1868–70*, MECW, vol. 43.
  (1993), *Letters 1880–83*, MECW, vol. 46.
  (2010), *Critique of the Gotha Programme*, MECW, vol. 24, pp. 75–99.
  (2010), 'Conspectus on Bakunin's *Statism and Anarchy*', MECW, vol. 24, pp. 485–526.
  (2012), *Ökonomische Manuskripte 1863–1867*, MEGA², vol. II/4.2.
Marx, Karl, and Engels, Friedrich (1976), *The German Ideology*, MECW, vol. 5, pp. 19–539.
  (1976), *Manifesto of the Communist Party*, MECW, vol. 6, pp. 477–517.
  (2018), *Manuskripte und Drucke zur Deutschen Ideologie (1845–1847)*, MEGA², vol. I/5.
Marx, Karl, Engels, Friedrich, and Lenin, Vladimir (1974), *On Communist Society*, Moscow: Progress.
Mattick, Paul (1969), *Marx and Keynes*, Boston: Extending Horizons Books.
Moore, Stanley (1980), *Marx on the Choice between Socialism and Communism*, Cambridge, MA: Harvard University Press.
Musto, Marcello (ed.) (2014), *Workers Unite! The International 150 Years Later*, New York: Bloomsbury.
  (2015), 'The Myth of the "Young Marx" in the *Interpretations of the Economic and Philosophic Manuscripts of 1844*', *Critique*, vol. 43 (2): 233–60.
  (2018), *Another Marx: Early Manuscripts to the International*, London: Bloomsbury.
Ollman, Bertell (ed.) (1998), *Market Socialism: The Debate among Socialists*, London: Routledge.
Owen, Robert (1845), *The Book of the New Moral World*, New York: G. Vale.
Reybaud, M. Louis (1840), *Études sur les Réformateurs contemporains ou socialistes modernes: Saint-Simon, Charles Fourier, Robert Owen*, Paris: Guillaumin.
Rosdolsky, Roman (1977), *The Making of Marx's 'Capital'*, London: Pluto Press.

Saint-Simon, Claude Henri (2012), 'L'organisateur: prospectus de l'auteur', in: *Œuvres complètes*, vol. III, Paris: Presses Universitaires de France, pp. 2115–16.

(2012), *Le nouveau christianisme*, in: C. H. Saint-Simon, *Œuvres complètes*, vol. IV, Paris: Presses Universitaires de France, pp. 3167–226.

Saint-Simon, Claude Henri, and Enfantin, Barthélémy-Prosper (1878), 'Religion Saint-Simonienne: Procès', C. H. Saint-Simon and B.-P. Enfantin, in: *Oeuvres de Saint-Simon & D'Enfantin*, vol. XLVII, Paris: Leroux.

Saito, Kohei (2017), *Karl Marx's Ecosocialism: Capital, Nature, and the Unfinished Critique of Political Economy*, New York: Monthly Review Press.

Webb, Darren (2000), *Marx, Marxism and Utopia*, Aldershot: Ashgate.

Weitling, Wilhelm (1845), *Die Menschheit, wie sie ist und wie sie sein sollte*, Bern: Jenni.

Wood, Ellen Meiksins (1995), *Democracy against Capitalism*, Cambridge: Cambridge University Press.

3 Democracy

Ellen Meiksins Wood

3.1 Marx's Critique of Democracy

'The Marxist critique of bourgeois democracy', wrote Ernest Mandel, 'starts from the idea that this democracy is formal because the workers do not have the material means to exercise the rights which the bourgeois constitutions formally grant all citizens'.[1] So, for instance, 'Freedom of the press is just a formality when only the capitalists and their agents are able to get together the millions of dollars needed to establish a daily newspaper.' These observations neatly sum up a standard Marxist critique of 'bourgeois democracy'.[2] They do not imply that Marxism is in principle opposed to the rights and freedoms associated with 'liberal democracy'. They simply suggest that the 'bourgeois' form of democracy is bogus, or at least inadequate and incomplete, because it fails to confront the fundamental inequalities of class power which determine political outcomes, even while it may allow for workers' organizations that can partially redress the balance.

Yet to define the Marxist critique in this way is not to say very much. The question we are canvassing here is not how a socialist democracy might be conceived by Karl Marx, but rather what Marx has to teach us about the kind of capitalist democracy in which we live; and on this score there is much more to be said. The proposition that political processes in 'bourgeois democracy' are, for better or worse and to greater or lesser degrees, affected by class inequalities is, as far as it goes, hard to dispute; but it is scarcely enough to distinguish Marxism from other accounts of how liberal democracy works in capitalist societies marked by huge disparities of wealth. If Marxism had nothing more to tell us than that political processes are shaped by differences of wealth, there would be

---

[1] E. Mandel, 'On Workers' Democracy', *The Militant*, 33–4: 6 (August 22, 1969).
[2] For an account of how, indeed, 'bourgeois rights' and civil liberties can be seen as important from a Marxist point of view, see N. Geras, 'The Controversy About Marx and Justice', *New Left Review*, 150: 47–85 (1985).

little point in turning to Marxist analysis for illumination on the workings of contemporary democracy.[3] Nor is it even enough to say that Marx went far beyond his contemporaries – or, for that matter, political analysts in our own time – in exposing the realities of class power and their effects on politics. There must be more to Marx's understanding of democracy to justify the claim that it has something truly distinctive and valuable to teach us even now and, indeed, now more than ever.

Marx's great insight was not simply that democracy in 'bourgeois' society was compromised by the inequalities of class power. If anything, he was keenly aware that there had never before, at least since ancient Greek democracy, existed a form of society in which inequalities of wealth had *less* effect on political outcomes than they did in societies with certain civic rights and liberties that we associate with liberal democracy – the kinds of rights and liberties that allow the labouring classes to form their own organizations and exercise their 'freedom of the press', to create and disseminate their own newspapers. Never before had working-class organizations, exercising 'bourgeois' freedoms of speech and association, had such direct and significant effects in the political domain. Without that conviction, he would hardly have been urging working-class movements to take advantage of the available possibilities in their own political struggles. It was never Marx's purpose to belittle the importance of these liberal rights and liberties or their usefulness to working classes. On the contrary, he was from the start a passionate defender of such liberties; and his socialism emerged out a growing realization that the liberties he sought to defend required something more than democratic legal forms and political rights abstracted from the realities of social power.[4] But nor was it his intention simply to demonstrate that the political effects of inequality were actually worse than they looked. The distinctive force of his critique must be found somewhere else.

Had Marx lived to see the modern welfare state, promoted and sustained by workers' movements and the social democratic parties representing them, he would still have regarded the socialist struggle as far from complete; but there was nothing in his view of liberal democracy that would have forced him to deny the possibility of such achievements. There is nothing particularly mysterious about how modern liberal democracy has been able to sustain advances of this kind. What requires explanation is why, even with enfranchised working-class majorities, social reforms have not advanced further, why social inequities have

---

[3] See, for example, A. Gelman, L. Kenworthy, and Y.-S. Su, 'Income Inequality and Partisan Voting in the United States', *Social Science Quarterly*, 91 (5): 1203–19 (2010).

[4] K. Marx, 'On the Jewish Question', MECW, vol. 3, p. 168.

remained so intractable, why economic inequalities have not diminished but grown deeper, why the social gains of the welfare state are, as we have learned with particular emphasis in the neo-liberal era, so vulnerable and precarious. For centuries, since classical antiquity, dominant classes feared and resisted political democracy. It seemed to them self-evident that granting political rights to the labouring majority would threaten inequalities of property and privilege. Yet, even though working-class struggles have made great advances, modern democracy has proved unfounded the fear that private property and inequality would be gravely endangered. In fact, economic inequalities are once again increasing. Whatever other explanations are on offer, it is surely worth asking what there is about modern democracy that has made it so consistent, both in theory and in practice, with the grossest inequalities of wealth and power.

An answer can be found in Marx's analysis of capitalism. It is here, even more than in his expressly political writings, that he exposed the limits of liberal democracy, which have less to do with who wields political power and how, or in whose particular interests, than with the scope of political power, what falls within its reach and what remains beyond its boundaries. It soon becomes clear that the complex relation between political and economic power in capitalism demands a redefinition of democracy not only to correct the imbalances of class inequality, but also to extend the reach of democratic power, including 'liberal' democratic principles of civil rights and liberties.

3.2   The Changing Meanings of Democracy

Let us first consider the conventional meaning of democracy. Literally, it means the rule or power of the people, the *demos*, which in its original Greek usage meant the 'people', not simply as a political category, but as something like a social class. Aristotle, for instance, defined democracy as a constitution in which 'the sovereign authority is composed of the poorer classes, and not of the owners of property'.[5] This 'democratic' constitution, of course, excluded slaves; and women too were denied the rights of citizenship. But the possession of political rights by the free labouring poor was enough to constitute a democratic polity, in contrast to an oligarchy, 'where those who have property are the sovereign authority'; and each form of polis would pursue the particular interests and the particular conception of justice upheld by its dominant social group.

This is the sense in which democracy would be understood for centuries thereafter, and for that reason it long remained an object of fear and

---

[5] Aristotle, *The Politics of Aristotle* (London: Oxford University Press, 1946), p. 115.

loathing among dominant classes. Yet eventually the designation 'democratic' would become the highest praise in the political vocabulary, which even the rich could happily claim for themselves. This transformation was, to be sure, a consequence of long and bitter popular struggles by those deprived of democratic rights; but it also entailed a change of meaning that would have been incomprehensible in ancient Greece or even early modern Europe.

The meaning of the word democracy was, first, transformed by the US 'Founding Fathers', who effectively redefined both its parts – the *demos*, or people, and the *kratos*, or power. At first, they were not at all inclined to describe their preferred form of government as a democracy. They called their chosen form of state a republic, in explicit opposition to democracy as it was then understood. But in the heat of constitutional debates, they made a rhetorical shift: they began to describe their 'republic' as a 'representative democracy'.[6] In the process, the *demos* lost its class meaning and became a political category rather than a social one; and *kratos* was made compatible with the *alienation* of popular power, the opposite of what it had meant to the ancient Athenians. This was so not simply because the very idea of *representative* democracy would have been alien to Greek democrats, for whom the essence of democracy was direct and active citizenship, a share for the *demos* in public deliberations. More important is how representation itself was conceived by Federalist leaders like James Madison (1751–1836) and Alexander Hamilton (1757–1804). The object of representation for the 'Founding Fathers' was not to give a political voice to the majority, but rather to *distance* an already enfranchised people as much as possible from political power. As in ancient Greece, slaves and women were excluded; but, unlike Athenian democracy, the US redefinition was meant to dilute or to filter popular power, including the power of male citizens who constituted the 'people', the political nation, with the intention of placing a protective screen of representatives between the private citizen and public power.[7]

By the nineteenth century, democracy would be increasingly identified with *liberalism*, shifting the focus away from the idea of popular power towards the limitation of state power by civil liberties and constitutional rights. Democracy came to be treated as an extension of constitutional principles rather than as an expansion of popular power. Even while

---

[6] The idea of 'representative democracy' as it relates to the US Constitution is generally traced to the Federalist Papers, especially no. 10, written by Madison in 1787, and no. 35, written by Hamilton in 1788 (A. Hamilton, J. Madison, and J. Jay, *The Federalist Papers* [New York: New American Library, 1961]).

[7] This was the key point of Madison's argument in Federalist 10 that the new constitution would guard against the effects of a 'majority faction'.

accepting that political progress might, and perhaps even should, inevitably include the extension of the franchise, liberalism tended to place the emphasis not on the elevation of the common people, the *demos*, to new heights of social power, but rather on the limitation of political power, protection against tyranny, and on the liberation of the individual citizen – from the state, from communal regulation, from traditional bonds and identities.[8] The heroes in this story were not the Levellers, or the Chartists, or trade unionists, or socialists, or suffragettes, or any of the others who have for centuries struggled for people's power. Instead, the heroes of this historical narrative were the propertied classes who, in pursuit of their own class interests, typically against intrusions by an overweening monarchical state, brought us advances such as the Magna Carta and the so-called Glorious Revolution of 1688 in England.

The emphasis on civil rights and liberties did not mean that democracy could be claimed to exist without an extension of the franchise. Although the word 'democracy' would certainly be used to characterize states with less than universal suffrage (a state might be described as a 'democracy' even where half the population – notably women – were excluded), it generally implied a more inclusive franchise, beyond the traditional limits of wealth or noble birth. What distinguished modern forms of 'liberal democracy' were that political rights no longer had the same salience as they did in ancient Greece. In the ancient world, political and economic power were so inextricably connected that, when the common people did achieve political rights, as they had in ancient Greek democracy, they would be freed from the most common forms of exploitation – such as slavery, serfdom, or debt-bondage – which depended on the legal or political subordination of labouring classes to legally and politically privileged classes. To grant peasants and other direct producers a share in political power was at the same time and inseparably to weaken drastically the exploitative power of wealthier, appropriating classes. Producing classes in the ancient democracy not only had unprecedented political rights, but at the same time, and for the same reason, an unprecedented degree of freedom from exploitation in the form of tax and rent. So the significance of democracy was political and economic at the same time.

This was no longer true in modern democracy. By the nineteenth century, at least in the more well-developed capitalist economies, the power of economic exploitation no longer depended on direct coercive power derived from legal or political standing. Capitalists and workers

---

[8] The liberal limitation of popular political power, even in the context of expanded political participation, is especially evident in John Stuart Mill's (1806–73) *On Liberty*, which asserted the need for protection against 'the tyranny of the majority' (J. S. Mill, *On Liberty* [Indianapolis: Hackett Publishing Co., 1978]).

could, and eventually would, be free and equal in juridical terms; and, unlike slaveholders or feudal lords, the capitalist employer's power to appropriate the surplus labour of workers did not require the workers' legal or political subordination. This meant that, while dominant classes would continue to fear that their interests and property would be endangered by an extension of the franchise, and while universal political rights were never freely granted by dominant classes but required long and bitter struggles, it became possible for the rich and powerful, however grudgingly and belatedly, to accept the inclusion of the working classes in the political nation.

The abstraction of political rights from social inequalities and economic domination would be acknowledged in a different way by workers themselves. Although the battle for political rights was far from over in the nineteenth century, by the second half of the century, especially in England, where there existed a mass proletariat, industrial capitalism was sufficiently advanced that capital had gained control of the workplace and the labour process.[9] The establishment of a more or less separate economic sphere, with its own system of power, was now complete. The struggle for a democratic franchise by working-class movements began, after the defeat of the Chartists, to give way increasingly to industrial struggles. When the franchise finally came, as important as that was, it no longer seemed to hold quite the same promise it once had in the eyes of campaigners for universal suffrage; and the main issues for the working class would increasingly be concentrated in the workplace, in the confrontation between workers and employers over the terms and conditions of work. While the socialist left might lament this development as a decline in working-class consciousness, the transfer of struggle away from the political domain to 'the point of production' reflected a reality of capitalism and its distinctive configuration of power.

Capitalism had made it possible for the first time in history to conceive of political rights as having little bearing on the distribution of social and economic power; and it was possible to imagine a distinct political sphere in which all citizens were formally equal, a political sphere abstracted from the inequalities of wealth and economic power outside the political domain. Political progress, or even the progress of democracy, could be conceived in terms that were socially indifferent, with an emphasis on political and civil rights that regulated the relations between citizen and state, not the maldistribution of social and economic power among citizens, who in the abstract sphere of politics were equal.

---

[9] These developments are superbly detailed in E. P. Thompson, *The Making of the English Working Class* (Harmondsworth: Penguin, 1968).

This formally separate political sphere had as its corollary and its necessary condition an equally separate 'economy', which became the subject of a new mode of theorizing, the 'science' of economics.[10] The classical political economists were not, of course, the first in history to reflect on the processes of production, appropriation, and distribution, which are the primary subjects of the economic discipline; but never before the advent of capitalism had it been possible to conceive of these processes as abstracted from 'non-economic' relations and practices, operating according to their own distinct laws, the purely 'economic' laws of the market. It had never been possible before to conceptualize an 'economy' with its own forms of coercion, to which political categories seemed not to apply. The 'laws' of supply and demand, the production and distribution of goods, or the formation of wages and prices, could, for the purposes of economic 'science', be treated as impersonal mechanisms; and human beings in the economic sphere could be perceived as abstract factors of production, whose relations to each other were very different from the relations of power, domination, and subordination that defined the political sphere, the sphere of rulers and subjects or citizens and states.

The abstraction of the political sphere from economic inequality and domination, then, characterized both classical political economy and liberal political philosophy. But there was something more. Capitalism had made possible not only a neat division of labour between discrete and autonomous 'sciences', but also a view of the world in which 'economic' forms of power and coercion are not recognized as power and coercion at all. In the political domain, it might be necessary to limit excesses of power or to safeguard democratic liberties; but the political principles of liberty and checks on power did not belong in the 'economy'. Indeed, a free economy was one in which economic imperatives were given free rein. The essence of the capitalist 'economy' is that a very wide range of human activities, which in other times and places were subject to the state or to communal regulation of various kinds, have been transferred to the economic domain, subjected not only to the hierarchies of the workplace, but also to the compulsions of the market, the relentless requirements of profit maximization and constant capital accumulation, none of which are subject to democratic freedom or accountability.

---

[10] For more on the formal separation of political and economic spheres, see E. M. Wood, *Democracy against Capitalism* (Cambridge: Cambridge University Press, 1995), pp. 19–48.

3.3 Marx on 'Bourgeois Democracy'

When Marx launched his public career as a journalist in 1842, his first concern was to defend the very civil liberties that constitute modern liberal democracy, and above all the freedom of the press, against intrusions by the state. Although Marxism would come to be associated with a contempt for 'bourgeois democracy', Marx himself never abandoned a conviction that, whatever their limits, 'bourgeois' freedoms were worth gaining and preserving. But he very early recognized the inadequacies of formal political and civil rights abstracted from social and economic realities. He very soon began to confront the 'social question' in his journalistic articles; and, when he set out to theorize more formally about the state, he sought ways to combine the struggle for purely political democracy with social struggles that challenged the injustices and inequalities left intact by formal democracy.

In works like 'On the Jewish Question', he sought to construct a political theory that went beyond the Hegelian opposition of 'state' and 'civil society', a theory of the state that would expose the social realities underlying the formal universality and neutrality of the political sphere. The modern state, wrote Marx, had become a 'real' state when it was transformed from a private affair of the ruler and his servants and turned into a public affair of the people, the result of a political revolution 'which overthrew this sovereign power and raised state affairs to become affairs of the people, which constituted the political state as a matter of general concern, that is, as a real state'.[11] At the same time, this transformation of the state deprived civil society of any political character. In the middle ages, public and private spheres had not been so clearly separated. Organizations in 'civil society' – corporate entities, guilds, and estates – had a public dimension. But with the decline of feudalism and of its intermediate bodies between the private life of citizens and the public domain of the state, civil society was transformed into a sphere of private economic egoism: 'Throwing off the political yoke meant at the same time throwing off the bonds which restrained the egoistic spirit of civil society. Political emancipation was at the same time the emancipation of civil society from politics, from having even the semblance of a universal content.'[12] The general interest, in other words, was confined to an abstract political sphere, estranged from the everyday life of real human beings, who in the day-to-day world of civil society inhabited a sphere of egoistic and conflicting private interests. 'Human emancipation will only be complete', Marx wrote, when 'only when man has recognised and organised his [own powers] as social forces, and consequently no longer separates social power

---

[11] Marx, 'On the Jewish Question', p. 166.   [12] Ibid.

from himself in the shape of political power, only then will human emancipation have been accomplished'.[13] Marx was here, in abstruse philosophical terms, identifying the formal separation of economic and political that is unique to capitalism, which permits the confinement of 'democracy' to an abstract political domain while leaving inequalities of wealth and the structures of class power untouched in the 'economy'.

It soon became clear to Marx that theorizing on the state could take him only so far in his quest for a more complete understanding of *human* – as against formally *political* – emancipation. A dissection of 'civil society' itself was required, and this would compel him to undertake what became his life's work, his critique of political economy and an analysis of capitalism. The foundations can already be found as early as his *Economic and Philosophic Manuscripts of 1844*;[14] but before his critique of political economy truly reached its maturity, in 1857–8 in the *Grundrisse* and finally in *Capital*, he actively participated in and continued to comment on contemporary political events, in ways that would have wide-ranging implications for the Marxist understanding of 'bourgeois democracy'.

The *Manifesto of the Communist Party*,[15] co-authored with Friedrich Engels, is, of course, the best known of Marx's political writings; and what stands out for our purposes is the narrative of bourgeois progress that lies at its heart. There is no mistaking the importance these young revolutionaries attached to the advances achieved by the bourgeoisie, however contradictory the consequences were. The progress they ascribed to the bourgeoisie's revolutionary victories was material and political at the same time. Just as capitalism had immeasurably advanced the forces of production, the bourgeoisie had destroyed traditional structures of prescriptive hierarchy and privilege, leaving the political arena open to working-class struggles and to a final confrontation between capital and labour. Just as the material advances of capitalism were inseparable from the exploitation of wage labourers, yet at the same time laid the foundations for socialism, the bourgeois republic in 1848 remained an instrument of the dominant class, yet at the same time provided new tools of struggle for the working class.[16] The formal rights and liberties of the bourgeois republic allowed for political organizations of unprecedented kinds, including a variety of socialist parties, which created a wholly new terrain of struggle.

---

[13] Ibid.
[14] K. Marx, *Economic and Philosophic Manuscripts of 1844*, MECW, vol. 3, pp. 229–346.
[15] K. Marx and F. Engels, *Manifesto of the Communist Party*, MECW, vol. 6, pp. 477–519.
[16] For a discussion of the extent to which some leftist critics have turned away from the idea of class, see E. M. Wood, *The Retreat from Class: A New 'True' Socialism* (London: Verso, 1986).

Almost three decades later, in a work that more clearly spells out his aspirations for a socialist democracy, he continued to emphasize the importance of 'bourgeois' rights and liberties in achieving that ultimate democratic goal. In the *Critique of the Gotha Programme*, Marx raised questions about the German workers' party programme, including its 'democratic' demands. The party, he told us, demands a 'free state'; but the German state was all too free, in the sense that an overbearing bureaucratic state, lacking precisely the kinds of 'bourgeois' democratic limits imposed on other modern states, freely imposed its will on the people. True freedom 'consists in converting the state from an organ superimposed upon society into one completely subordinate to it, and even today forms of state are more free or less free to the extent that they restrict the "freedom of the state"'.[17] To completely 'subordinate the state to society' would, of course, require revolutionary transformations of the underlying social relations, the structure of class power that dominates all spheres of social life, inside and outside the state; but Germany had hardly begun to restrict the freedom of the state. The German workers' party asserts its various democratic demands without acknowledging that 'all those pretty little gewgaws rest on the recognition of the so-called sovereignty of the people and hence are appropriate only in a *democratic republic*'.[18]

The implication is clearly that workers' parties in states without the bourgeois freedoms and popular sovereignty enjoyed by the Swiss or the Americans might do well to devote their revolutionary zeal to achieving them, as a prelude to a truly socialist transformation; but even if Marx could envisage circumstances in which that avenue was blocked and more revolutionary methods were immediately required, he could still foresee that the mechanisms of 'bourgeois democracy' might have something to teach a truly socialist society, even after the transitional 'dictatorship of the proletariat'.[19] 'What transformation', Marx asked,

will the state undergo in communist society? In other words, what social functions will remain in existence there that are analogous to present state functions? This question can only be answered scientifically, and one does not get a flea-hop nearer to the problem by a thousand-fold combination of the word 'people' with the word 'state'.[20]

---

[17] K. Marx, *Critique of the Gotha Programme*, MECW, vol. 24, p. 94.   [18] Ibid, p. 95.
[19] For a lengthy discussion of this much debated concept see H. Draper, *Karl Marx's Theory of Revolution, Volume III: The 'Dictatorship of the Proletariat'* (New York: Monthly Review Press, 1986), in particular pp. 175–325.
[20] Marx, *Critique of the Gotha Programme*, p. 95.

Much has been said about Marx's conviction that the state in socialist society will wither away; but his formulation of the question in the *Critique of the Gotha Programme* suggests that he foresaw a socialist democracy in which some kind of public power still exists, and that even the most democratic state will remain a state, which will require restrictions on its 'freedom', something very like the forms, if not the substance, of bourgeois democracy.

In *The Eighteenth Brumaire of Louis Bonaparte*, Marx composed one of the most complex and incisive analyses of a particular political event, the *coup d'état* of Louis Napoleon (1808–73) in 1851, replacing a bourgeois republic with a dictatorship. Marx brilliantly navigated all the complexities of this episode, with all its conflicting interests and parties, while situating rapidly moving events in their larger historical context, with an intricate analysis of the social forces in play. He traced the degeneration of a republic into a dictatorship in profoundly illuminating ways. The work is a model of political analysis and deserves to be regarded as a classic. But it is not a theory of the capitalist state, and much confusion has been generated by various commentaries that treat 'Bonapartism', as described in *The Eighteenth Brumaire of Louis Bonaparte*, as the essence of the capitalist state. The independence of the Bonapartist dictatorship as it stood above the warring factions, we are told, typifies the 'relative autonomy' of the capitalist state, which derives its independence from the conflicts among various class 'factions' that inevitably characterize capitalism. Or else it is suggested that the degeneration of the bourgeois republic into a dictatorship reflects the inevitable tendency of capitalist democracy to limit democratic freedoms in order to sustain the power of capital, which is inevitably threatened by the very democratic forms it has engendered.

But the society Marx is so effectively dissecting in *The Eighteenth Brumaire of Louis Bonaparte* is scarcely capitalist at all, and the very characteristics of 'Bonapartism' that have been singled out as the essence of the capitalist state derive from the *non*-capitalist features of the Bonapartist state. At its heart is, as Marx tells us, an immense bureaucratic and military organization, an 'parasitic body', in which the '*material interests* are interwoven in the closest fashion. Here it finds posts for its surplus population and makes up in the form of state salaries for what it cannot pocket in the form of profit, interest, rents, and honorariums.'[21] The 'bourgeoisie', then, is not fundamentally capitalist. Its economic interests are too firmly rooted in the state; and the whole parasitic structure in which its material interests lie predates the

---

[21] K. Marx, *The Eighteenth Brumaire of Louis Bonaparte*, MECW, vol. 11, p. 139.

revolution. 'All revolutions perfected this machine instead of breaking it. The parties, which alternately contended for domination regarded the possession of this huge state structure as the chief spoils of the victor.'[22] The class on which this structure rests, whose labour produces the material benefits derived from possession of the state, under Louis Bonaparte no less than in the pre-Revolutionary absolutist state, is not a capitalist proletariat but 'the most numerous class of French society ... the *small-holding peasants*'.[23]

3.4 From Politics to Political Economy

Whatever else we may learn from *The Eighteenth Brumaire of Louis Bonaparte*, it does not reveal the secrets of capitalist democracy, nor did Marx claim that it did. But if this remarkable study of a 'bourgeois republic' in decline has little to do with the capitalist state, it is worth reflecting for a moment on why its incomparable insights into the passage from more democratic governance to tyranny have so little to tell us specifically about capitalist democracy. It may help to explain why Marx felt compelled to address fundamental questions about the politics of capitalism, and the problem of democracy, in a new language of political economy, and not the old discourse of political philosophy or the kind of incisive political journalism at which he excelled. There is no doubt that democracy in capitalist societies can degenerate into far less democratic forms, and that, even if we leave aside the most dramatic examples of capitalist dictatorship from our own recent history, the maintenance of democratic rights and freedoms requires constant vigilance and struggle. But *The Eighteenth Brumaire of Louis Bonaparte* is not a guide to capitalist democracy precisely because the material interests of capital do *not* reside in the state and capitalism does *not* inevitably require the dissolution of democracy in order to maintain the class power of capital. It is a social order that can, unlike any other system before it, sustain some kind of democracy without fundamentally threatening class domination.

In every other society before capitalism, access to political rights was inextricably associated with economic power; and democracy by definition meant restrictions not only on the powers of the state, but on the powers of appropriation, the economic power that gave dominant classes access to the labour of direct producers. This remained true of the Bonapartist state, with its reliance on the state as an instrument of appropriation from the peasantry. In contrast, it is a – indeed *the* – defining characteristic of

[22] Ibid, p. 186.   [23] Ibid, p. 187.

capitalism that political and economic power are no longer bound together in this way.

A society such as this, in which the legal and political forms of democracy can be secure while the dominant class remains equally secure in its hold on property and access to the labour of others, is hard to explain in the language of political analysis. It requires the kind of political economy that Marx undertook in the *Grundrisse* and *Capital*. It would, then, be a mistake to understand Marx's critique of political economy as just a transfer of analysis from the state to 'civil society' or as an abandonment of politics for 'economics'. His analysis of capitalism does not simply represent a technical improvement on classical political economy. It remaps the whole social terrain, not only the 'economy', but the political domain. While Marx certainly offered alternative accounts of market mechanisms, the technicalities of wages, price, and profit, what is most revolutionary about his analysis of capitalism is its understanding of capitalism as a system of social relations. Capital, Marx told us, is not simply a quantity of material goods or instruments of production. It is 'a social relation of production', and the economic categories of political economy are not just things or factors of production, but expressions of certain specific social relations.

One major effect of this approach was to shed new light on the boundaries and relations between the 'economic' and the 'political'. While Marx certainly acknowledged that capitalism had created a historically unprecedented formal separation between these two spheres – the historical conditions that enabled the 'science' of economics as well as the modern idea of formal democracy – his account of the 'economy' as a system of social relations had significant implications for how that formal separation should be understood. Just as the limitations of classical political economy are exposed by Marx's critique, the limited vision of liberal democracy is starkly revealed once we scrutinize it in Marx's terms.

In his mature work on political economy, notably the *Grundrisse* and *Capital*, Marx refined and elaborated the principles of historical materialism established in earlier works such as *The German Ideology*. Those principles do not begin with an abstract division between 'political' and 'economic', state and civil society, or 'base' and 'superstructure'. The 'material' is itself social. It is constituted by 'practical activity' and social relations, the relations among human agents and between them and nature, in the process of obtaining the basic conditions of existence and social reproduction. In *Capital*, volume III, Marx told us more about the nature of material relations and how they affect the conditions of social organization, both 'economic' and 'political': 'the specific economic form in which unpaid surplus labour is pumped out of direct producers ... reveals the innermost secret, the hidden basis of the entire social structure';[24] and here there is a fundamental difference between capitalism and all preceding social forms.

In pre-capitalist forms,

> in which the direct labourer remains the 'possessor' of the means of production and labour conditions necessary for the production of his own means of subsistence, the property relationship must simultaneously appear as a direct relation of lordship and servitude, so that the direct producer is not free; a lack of freedom which may be reduced from serfdom with enforced labour to a mere tributary relationship ... Under such conditions the surplus-labour for the nominal owner of the land can only be extorted from them by other than economic pressure, whatever the form assumed may be.[25]

In other words, in every society before the development of capitalism, wherever exploitation existed, the capacity to extract surplus labour from direct producers depended on one form or another of direct coercion, on the military, political, and jurisdictional powers of the exploiting class. In most such societies, peasants were the main direct producers, and they remained in possession of the means of production, the land. The ruling classes that exploited them did so mainly by monopolizing political and military power – either through a centralized state, which extracted peasant surpluses in the form of some kind of tax or corvée labour; or they had some other kind of hold on military and jurisdictional power – such as feudal lordship – which enabled them to extract surpluses from peasants who were in a dependent condition, such as serfs or peons, and were forced to forfeit surplus in the form of rent to their overlords. Economic and political power, then, were fused; and there was always a more or less clear division between rulers and producers, between those who had political power and those who did the society's labour.

The primary difference between capitalism and all preceding social forms rests, for Marx, on its specific mode of exploitation and a distinctive relation between economic and 'extra-economic' power. The exploitative powers of capital do not depend directly on political or military force. Capitalists certainly need the state to support them, but their exploitative powers are purely economic. They can rely on economic compulsions, the propertylessness of workers who are forced to sell their labour power for a wage just to obtain access to the means of production. Political and economic powers are not fused in the way they once were. It is for this reason that there exists in capitalism, as in no other system before it, a distinct 'economic' sphere – formally separate from the 'political' domain – with its own system of compulsion and coercion,

[24] K. Marx, *Capital*, volume III, MECW, vol. 37, pp. 777–8.   [25] Ibid, pp. 776–7.

its own forms of domination, its own hierarchies, which fall outside the scope of democratic freedom as it is commonly conceived.

The most immediately obvious manifestations are capital's control of the workplace and its unprecedented control of the labour process. No feudal lord could regulate the peasant's labour as closely as the processes of work in capitalism are commanded by the dominance of capital and the requirements of capital accumulation, even where the rights of labour are most firmly entrenched and protected by powerful trade unions. Beyond the direct control exercised by capital in the workplace, there are the compulsions of the market through which capital allocates labour and resources. These compulsions of profit maximization and constant capital accumulation, which subordinate human needs, ecological sustainability, and even the organization of time to the requirements of profit, are truly systemic imperatives; and every sphere of life that comes within their field of force, every sphere of life that is commodified, falls outside the reach of democratic control or accountability. The systemic imperatives of capitalism do not require the legal or political dependence of workers; and the power of capital, together with, and through the medium of, market imperatives, dictates increasing aspects of human existence, even in the presence of universal political rights and legal equality.

3.5 The Political Limits of Capitalist Democracy

Today's conventional conceptions of democracy, or democratic rights and liberties, rely on the formal separation of political and economic spheres in capitalism, which permits the formal abstraction of political democracy from social inequalities and economic domination. To devise a conception of democracy and democratic accountability that encompasses new forms of economic power and coercion requires an understanding of capitalism unavailable either to liberal political philosophy or to classical political economy, or indeed to modern economics or political science. It requires us to return to Marx. While he acknowledged, as a 'real appearance', the formal separation of political and economic spheres specific to capitalism, he sought to go beyond that appearance to the underlying substance of the capitalist system, not simply as a separate economic mechanism, but as a total system of social relations, a new configuration of social power.

Marx's analysis of capitalism as a system of social relations, and not just a mechanism of production and distribution, makes it clear that the capitalist system has created new spheres of power and new forms of domination which fall outside the scope of democratic freedom as it is commonly conceived. His analysis makes it clear that there now exists a distinct 'economic' sphere – formally separate from the 'political' domain – with its own system of compulsion and coercion, its own forms of domination, its own hierarchies. The basic condition of the capitalist system is the naked exposure of all individuals to market imperatives – by means of the dispossession that compels people to sell their labour power for a wage; by means of the 'privatization' of any social goods and services that stand between people and dependence on the market; and so on.[26] In the *political* sphere – the sphere where human beings operate as citizens rather than as workers or capitalists – it is possible for them to exercise their rights as citizens without intruding on the power of capital in the economic sphere. Even in capitalist societies with a tradition of strong state intervention, the fundamental economic powers of capital can be left largely intact by the extension of political rights.

This also means that political change has no immediate consequences in the transformation of society, and the translation of political power into economic and social gains is mediated in historically unprecedented ways. With so much of human life governed by the structures, processes, and principles of the capitalist economy, it is not enough to say that popular movements of one kind or another could, in principle, take hold of the state apparatus by peaceful electoral means and could, if they chose, then effect major social transformations. It is undeniable that socialist or social democratic parties have brought about significant improvements in the life conditions of a capitalist society; but these have proved precarious. Even with secure possession of political power and the strongest political will, there remains a massive gulf between political and economic change. Controlling and transforming the 'economy', with its own structure of power and compulsion, requires a massive effort quite distinct from and beyond possession of the state.

But, even if a thorough social transformation seems a distant prospect, to acknowledge that capitalism is not just an economic mechanism, but a distinctive configuration of social power suggests an immediate political program: the extension of familiar 'bourgeois' democratic principles into domains as yet untouched by them. Political and civil rights as they are understood in today's 'liberal democracies' are aimed above all at limiting the power of the state and protecting individual rights and freedoms against arbitrary power. If capitalism has created its own distinct structure of power, we have to find ways of conceptualizing democratic liberties and

---

[26] For a discussion of this dispossession see G. Kennedy, *Diggers, Levellers, and Agrarian Capitalism: Radical Political Thought in Seventeenth Century England* (Lanham: Lexington Books, 2008).

rights that encompass these other forms of power too. While working-class struggles have established certain limited rights against the powers of capital, above all the right to form unions, we have hardly begun to apply democratic principles to capital and the compulsions of the market.

This is not just a question of creating safety nets, nor is it simply a question of regulating markets. Nor is it even only – as important as this is – a matter of correcting the gross inequalities that the capitalist market inevitably reproduces. To assert our autonomy, not only in relation to state power, but also in relation to the power of capital, means bringing democracy not just to the workplace, but also to spheres of life where it is now excluded by market imperatives. It means recognizing that the market is not simply a sphere of freedom, opportunity, and choice, but a domain of power, which imposes its imperatives on every sphere of human life and compels us to act in ways damaging to our own well-being and to the environment, in the interests of profit maximization and capital accumulation. The market is, in other words, a limitation on our democratic freedoms. A democratic challenge to this form of domination, this limitation of our freedom, means *detaching* as much of human life as possible from the compulsions of the market – that is, in other words, it means to decommodify.

Today, all advanced capitalist countries and many developing countries enjoy universal political rights. They have what we call democracy.[27] But much of what governs our everyday lives has been put outside the reach of democratic accountability, governed instead by the power of capital and capitalist economic imperatives. It is one of the paradoxes of our time that every day governments everywhere are deliberately putting more and more of our lives out of democratic reach, to be ruled by market imperatives. Markets have intruded even into social services that have previously been protected from them.[28] The consequence of increasing commodification has been not only to narrow the scope of democratic governance, but also to increase inequality and all the social ills that follow from it.[29]

---

[27] To the extent to which even formal democracy can be seen to be failing in a society like the United States, see N. Wood, *Tyranny in America: Capitalism and National Decay* (London: Verso, 2004).

[28] For instance, the National Health Service in the UK has increasingly been subjected to market principles, beginning with New Labour; while, in the United States, health reform has strengthened the sway of the market by further empowering private insurance companies.

[29] On the overall deleterious effects of social inequality, see, for example, R. Wilkinson and K. Pickett, *The Spirit Level: Why Greater Equality Makes Societies Stronger* (New York: Bloomsbury Publishing, 2011).

If democracy has anything to do with power – how, by whom, and over what it is exercised – it must be redefined to include a whole range of human activities that now fall outside its reach. And if democracy has to do with *checks* on arbitrary power, it must embrace the assertion of rights and liberties against not only the powers of the state, but also against those forms of arbitrary power lodged in the 'economic' sphere. Our freedoms in a capitalist democracy are constrained far more by the economic imperatives of the market than by the actions of the state, and markets are subject to no democratic accountability. Democracy requires, at the very least, that our liberties be protected by checking the 'freedom' of the economy just as we check the 'freedom' of the state.

It would be a major democratic advance if the principles of 'bourgeois democracy', its liberal rights and freedoms, were extended into the economic domain from which capitalism has excluded them – if, for example, what are now called social and economic rights were treated as no less basic entitlements than are civic and political rights in a liberal democracy. But we should have no illusions about the possibility of compelling the market to operate according to principles other than its natural imperatives, however much we 'regulate' it. Wherever the market prevails, so will the compulsions of profit maximization; and to extend rights and liberties into the economic spaces from which they are excluded requires that the provision of certain basic goods and services is not dependent on the maximization of profit. The extension of democracy, in other words, requires decommodification. But a truly democratic 'economy', in which power really did belong to the people, would – by definition – mean the end of capitalism.

References

Aristotle (1946), *The Politics of Aristotle*, London: Oxford University Press.

Draper, Hal (1986), *Karl Marx's Theory of Revolution, Volume III: The 'Dictatorship of the Proletariat'*, New York: Monthly Review Press.

Gelman, Andrew, Kenworthy, Lane, and Su,Yu-Sung (2010), 'Income Inequality and Partisan Voting in the United States', *Social Science Quarterly*, 91 (5): 1203–19.

Geras, Norman (1985), 'The Controversy about Marx and Justice', *New Left Review*, 150: 47–85.

Hamilton, Alexander, Madison, James, and Jay, John (1961), *The Federalist Papers*, New York: New American Library.

Kennedy, Geoff, (2008), *Diggers, Levellers, and Agrarian Capitalism: Radical Political Thought in Seventeenth Century England*, Lanham: Lexington Books.

Mandel, Ernest (1969), 'On Workers' Democracy', *The Militant*, 33–4 (22 August): 6–7.

Marx, Karl (1975), *Economic and Philosophic Manuscripts of 1844*, MECW, vol. 3, pp. 229–346.

(1975), 'On the Jewish Question', MECW, vol. 3, pp. 146–74.

(1979), *The Eighteenth Brumaire of Louis Bonaparte*, MECW, vol. 11, pp. 99–209.

(1989), *Critique of the Gotha Programme*, MECW, vol. 24, pp. 75–99.

(1998), *Capital*, volume III, MECW, vol. 37.

Marx, Karl, and Engels, Frederick (1976), *Manifesto of the Communist Party*, MECW, vol. 6, pp. 477–519.

Mill, John Stuart (1978), *On Liberty*, Indianapolis: Hackett Publishing Co.

Thompson, E. P. (1968), *The Making of the English Working Class*, Harmondsworth: Penguin.

Wilkinson, Richard G., and Pickett, Kate (2011), *The Spirit Level: Why Greater Equality Makes Societies Stronger*, New York: Bloomsbury Publishing.

Wood, Ellen Meiksins (1986), *The Retreat from Class: A New 'True' Socialism*, London: Verso.

(1995), *Democracy against Capitalism*, Cambridge: Cambridge University Press.

Wood, Neal (2004), *Tyranny in America: Capitalism and National Decay*, London: Verso.

4 Proletariat

Marcel van der Linden

4.1 The Revolutionary Subject

In his mid-twenties, Karl Marx arrived at the conclusion that the proletariat is the only social force that is capable of transcending capitalism. His 'A Contribution to the Critique of Hegel's Philosophy of Right' (1844) characterizes the proletariat as

> a class *in* civil society which is not a class *of* civil society, an estate which is the dissolution of all estates, a sphere which has a universal character by its universal suffering and claims no *particular right* because no *particular wrong*, but *wrong generally*, is perpetrated against it.

The proletariat is the 'all-round antithesis' to existing society, which is 'the *complete loss* of man and hence can win itself only through the *complete re-winning of man*'.[1]

Gradually, the nature of proletarian self-emancipation became clearer to him. In *The German Ideology* (1845–46), he asserts that the abolition of bourgeois society will require the collective appropriation of all productive forces. This can only be effected through

> a revolution, in which, on the one hand, the power of the earlier mode of production and intercourse and social organisation is overthrown, and, on the other hand, there develops the universal character and the energy of the proletariat, which are required to accomplish the appropriation, and the proletariat moreover rids itself of everything that still clings to it from its previous position in society.[2]

These passages from Marx articulate at least four trends. *First*, the notion of classes and class struggles, which date back to the eighteenth-century debates. During the decades preceding the 1789 French Revolution, social analysts such as Quesnay, Turgot, and others began to distinguish two or three social classes. In Britain, Hume, Ferguson, and others

---
[1] K. Marx, 'A Contribution to the Critique of Hegel's Philosophy of Right: Introduction', MECW, vol. 3, p. 186; translation corrected.
[2] K. Marx and F. Engels, *The German Ideology*, MECW, vol. 5, p. 88.

developed similar distinctions almost at the same time. A possible explanation for this discovery of social classes is the growth of national states, combined with expanding trading circuits, and the increasing income differences that resulted from this. In addition, the rise of manufacturers and factories gradually made it impossible for journeymen and other skilled workers to become independent entrepreneurs themselves. Just like the French and British authors before, the early Marx did not distinguish between 'classes' and 'estates'. In the *Critique of Hegel's Philosophy of Right*, for example, the proletariat was still called an 'estate'. But this confusion did not last long. In *The Poverty of Philosophy* (1847) the proletariat had already become a 'class'.

Second, Marx was probably influenced by Lorenz von Stein (1815–90), who in 1842 had published a book on *The Socialism and Communism of Contemporary France*, which foreshadowed much of Marx's class theory. Von Stein thought that the rising industrial society made workers either obstinate and malicious or transformed them into dull instruments and servile subordinates. He considered personal and hereditary property as the root cause of this decline of the working classes, since it resulted in the dominant power of some and the unfreedom of others.[3] With observations like these, von Stein anticipated some major arguments of historical materialism; but,

unlike Marx, he did not postulate an inexorable proletarian revolution which would ultimately resolve societal contradictions. Instead, he proposed a fundamentally reformist political strategy in which the state guides the distribution of economic resources in a form that would prevent the class polarises envisioned by Marx.[4]

Third, Marx had been deeply impressed by the rebellion of Silesian weavers in 1844. In his 'Critical Notes on the Article: "The King of Prussia and Social Reform. By a Prussian"'[5] he pointed out that, in the Silesian weavers' rebellion,

the proletariat at once, in a striking, sharp, unrestrained and powerful manner, proclaims its opposition to the society of private property. The Silesian rebellion *begins* precisely with what the French and English workers' uprisings *end*, with consciousness of the nature of the proletariat. The action itself bears the stamp of this *superior* character. Not only were machines, these rivals of the workers, destroyed, but also *ledgers*, the titles to property. And while all other movements

---

[3] L. von Stein, *Der Socialismus und Communismus des heutigen Frankreichs. Ein Beitrag zur Zeitgeschichte* (Leipzig: Wigand, 1842), Part I.
[4] J. Singelmann and P. Singelmann, 'Lorenz von Stein and the Paradigmatic Bifurcation of Social Theory in the Nineteenth Century', *British Journal of Sociology*, 37 (3) (1986), 431.
[5] K. Marx, 'Critical Notes on the Article: "The King of Prussia and Social Reform. By a Prussian"', MECW, vol. 3, p. 201.

were aimed primarily only against the *owner of the industrial enterprise*, the visible enemy, this movement is at the same time directed against the banker, the hidden enemy.

Robin Blackburn (1940–)[6] has rightly observed that much of this article 'is still written in the old philosophical jargon and concerns an argument about the nature of the German revolution. But Marx concludes from the weavers' revolt that the proletariat is the "active agent" of the revolution.'

Fourth and the last, Friedrich Engels published his *The Condition of the Working Class in England: From Personal Observation and Authentic Sources* in 1845. Basing himself on Manchester's textile industry, Engels suggested how manufacture 'centralises property in the hands of the few', and therefore how the working population becomes centralized, as '[a] manufacturing establishment requires many workers employed together in a single building, living near each other and forming a village of themselves in the case of a good-sized factory.'[7]

In combination, these influences brought Marx to his analysis of human history as a history of class struggles that would culminate in the class struggle to end all class struggles – that is, the proletarian revolution. Marx's approach has forever changed the way in which we think about historical developments and radical politics. Marx was quick to admit that many important elements of his theory of revolution had been anticipated by others. In 1852, he wrote to Joseph Weydemeyer (1818–1866):

> Now as for myself, I do not claim to have discovered either the existence of classes in modern society or the struggle between them. Long before me, bourgeois historians had described the historical development of this struggle between the classes, as had bourgeois economists their economic anatomy. My own contribution was 1. to show that the *existence of* classes is merely bound up with *certain historical phases in the development of* production; 2. that the class struggle necessarily leads to the *dictatorship of the* proletariat; 3. that this dictatorship itself constitutes no more than a transition to the *abolition of all classes* and to a *classless society*.[8]

4.2 Defining the Proletariat

Neither in his early nor in his later work did Marx use the term 'working class' frequently. He preferred the notion of the proletariat, an ancient Roman conception, probably dating from the sixth century BCE. It

---

[6] R. Blackburn, 'Marxism: Theory of Proletarian Revolution', *New Left Review*, 97: 6 (1976).
[7] F. Engels, *The Condition of the Working Class in England: From Personal Observation and Authentic Sources*, MECW, vol. 4, p. 325.
[8] 'K. Marx to J. Weydemeyer, 5 March 1852', MECW, vol. 39, pp. 62, 65.

describes a relatively large, but not well-defined, group of free, poor citizens, whose 'offspring [*proles*]' could serve the empire as soldiers.[9]

During the late eighteenth and early nineteenth centuries, the word 'proletariat' made a comeback. Initially, it was used in a general sense to describe the estate of people without property, beyond honour. The workers were only a part of this amorphous mass. According to the French nobleman Adolphe Granier de Cassagnac, writing in the 1830s, the proletariat formed 'the lowest rank, the deepest stratum of society', which consisted of four groups: 'the workers, the beggars, the thieves and public women':

> The worker is a proletarian, because he works in order to live and earns a wage; the beggar is a proletarian, who does not want to work or cannot work, and begs in order to live; the thief is a proletarian, who does not want to work or beg, and, in order to make a living, steals; the prostitute is a proletarian, who neither wants to work, nor beg, nor steal, and, in order to live, sells her body.[10]

A few years later, Heinrich Wilhelm Bensen (1798–1863) distinguished seven categories of proletarians: apart from three groups of workers he also noted 'the poor, who are bereft of support from the public purse', 'the common soldiers', 'gypsies, prostitutes, bandits etc.', and 'the small servants of religious and secular origin'.[11]

Gradually a differentiation was made that could have one of two outcomes: either the workers declared that they were *not* proletarians, but a separate class or estate, or they identified with the proletariat and started to see the other groups, who had previously also been considered as proletarians, to be 'less' and 'different'. The German communist workers in London, with whom Marx and Engels were associated, favoured the second outcome. In the *Manifesto of the Communist Party*, which Marx and Engels were instructed to write for these workers on the basis of common discussions, 'the modern working class – the proletarians'[12] were seen as a unity. The thieves, beggars, and prostitutes were now devaluated as a lower stratum, the lumpenproletariat, the

> 'dangerous class', the social scum, that passively rotting mass thrown off by the lowest layers of old society, [which] may, here and there, be swept into the

---

[9] R. Zaniewski, *L'Origine du prolétariat romain et contemporain. Faits et théories* (Louvain and Paris: Editions Nauwelaerts and Béatrice Nauwelaerts, 1957), pp. 15–53.
[10] A. Granier de Cassagnac, *Histoire des classes ouvrières et des classes bourgeoises* (Paris: Desrez, 1838), p. 30.
[11] H. W. Bensen, *Die Proletarier. Eine historische Denkschrift* (Stuttgart, 1847), p. 344.
[12] K. Marx and F. Engels, *Manifesto of the Communist Party*, MECW, vol. 6, p. 490.

movement by a proletarian revolution; its conditions of life, however, prepare it far more for the part of a bribed tool of reactionary intrigue.[13]

This exclusion of the 'immoral' part of the lower classes was combined with further demarcations. For Marx, it was self-evident that chattel slaves did not belong to the proletariat. Quite early, the European labour movements had already distanced themselves from their bonded brothers and sisters. The famous London Corresponding Society (LCS), which E. P. Thompson[14] called 'a new kind of organization' of a working-class nature, in 1792 redefined its constituency under the influence of the slave revolution on Saint-Domingue. In the early months of that year, the LCS declared the equality among all, 'black or white, high or low, rich or poor', but by August the 'black or white' disappeared from the society's agenda, once the news from the Caribbean reached the British Isles. 'Race had thus become a tricky and, for many, in England, a threatening subject, one that the leadership of the LCS now preferred to avoid.'[15] Marx later was to reduce chattel slavery to 'an anomaly in relation to the bourgeois system itself', which 'can exist at individual points within the bourgeois system of production', although 'only because it does not exist at other points'.[16]

Marx equally marked the proletariat off from the petty bourgeoisie. The *Manifesto of the Communist Party* declares: 'Of all the classes that stand face to face with the bourgeoisie today, the proletariat alone is a really revolutionary class. The other classes decay and finally disappear in the face of Modern Industry.'[17]

The lower middle class, the small manufacturer, the shopkeeper, the artisan, the peasant, all these fight against the bourgeoisie, to save from extinction their existence as fractions of the middle class. They are therefore not revolutionary, but conservative ... If by chance they are revolutionary, they are so only in view of their impending transfer into the proletariat ... they desert their own standpoint to place themselves at that of the proletariat.[18]

Thus, the boundaries of the proletariat were delimited on all sides. The class struggle is seen to be waged mainly between capitalists, landowners, and wage earners. The other, intermediate classes are historically less

---

[13] Marx and Engels, *Manifesto of the Communist Party*, p. 494. Quite interestingly, in *Capital*, volume I, Marx implicitly referred to Granier de Cassagnac's classification and talked about 'vagabonds, criminals, prostitutes, in a word, the "dangerous" classes'. K. Marx, *Capital*, volume I, MECW, vol. 35, p. 637.
[14] E. P. Thompson, *The Making of the English Working Class* (London: Victor Gollancz: 1963), p. 23.
[15] P. Linebaugh and M. Rediker, *The Many-Headed Hydra: Sailors, Slaves, Commoners, and the Hidden History of the Revolutionary Atlantic* (Boston: Beacon Press, 2000), p. 274.
[16] K. Marx, 'Outlines of the Critique of Political Economy [*Grundrisse*]. First Instalment', MECW, vol. 28, p. 392.
[17] Marx and Engels, *Manifesto of the Communist Party*, p. 494.   [18] Ibid.

important and play no independent political role; they 'decay and finally disappear in the face of Modern Industry'.[19] In his later writings, Marx tried to further substantiate this thesis. His critique of political economy is partly an attempt to circumscribe as precisely as possible the historical nature and social boundaries of the proletariat. In *Capital*, volume I, he finally defines the pure proletarian as the worker who 'as a free man can dispose of his labour power as his own commodity', and 'on the other hand has no other commodity for sale'.[20]

The ongoing process of capital accumulation will, according to Marx, let the number of these doubly-free workers grow, both absolutely and relatively. For, the larger the capitals, the more workers they need. 'Accumulation of capital is, therefore, increase of the proletariat.'[21] Capitalist production 'reproduces to an ever increasing extent the class of wage labourers, into whom it transforms the vast majority of direct producers'.[22] The proletariat is recruited 'from all classes of the population':

The lower strata of the middle class – the small tradespeople, shopkeepers, and retired tradesmen generally, the handicraftsmen and peasants – all these sink gradually into the proletariat, partly because their diminutive capital does not suffice for the scale on which Modern Industry is carried on, and is swamped in the competition with the large capitalists, partly because their specialised skill is rendered worthless by new methods of production.[23]

Consequently, as the precise moment of revolutionary change approaches, capitalist society will be increasingly split up into two large hostile camps.

It is argued here that Marx's delimitations of the proletariat did not always follow logically from his critique of political economy – moral impulses, political cogitations, and wishful thinking probably played an important role in his considerations. Accordingly, significant contradictions were unavoidable while historical facts had to be denied. The examples of the lumpenproletariat and the chattel slaves can arguably corroborate this contention.

4.3   Excluding the Lumpenproletariat

The 'lumpenproletariat' makes its initial appearance in the early writings of Marx and Engels, where they discussed the ancient Roman Empire. The notion turns up for the first time in *The German Ideology* (1845–46),

---

[19] Ibid.   [20] Marx, *Capital*, volume I, p. 179.
[21] Marx, *Capital*, volume I, MECW, vol. 36, p. 609.
[22] K. Marx, *Capital*, volume II, MECW, vol. 36, p. 40.
[23] Marx and Engels, *Manifesto of the Communist Party*, p. 494.

in a passage discussing the issue of the Plebeians, who, 'midway between freemen and slaves, never succeeded in becoming more than a proletarian rabble [*Lumpenproletariat*]'.[24] However, as a contemporary concept, the lumpenproletariat makes its first appearance during the years 1848–51, when Marx analyzed French revolutionary and counter-revolutionary trends. Marx was struck by his observation of the workers' actions and reactions on both sides of the barricades – an apparent absurdity that he could only explain by valuing those on the good side as 'real' proletarians and devaluing those on the wrong side as pseudo-proletarians.[25]

When, in 1851, the workers were again divided and, some of them, supported Louis Bonaparte (1808–1873), Marx found some justification for his analysis. In *The Eighteenth Brumaire of Louis Bonaparte* (1851–52), he included in the lumpenproletariat not only 'decayed *roués*' of aristocratic descent and 'ruined and adventurous offshoots of the bourgeoisie', but also

vagabonds, discharged soldiers, discharged jailbirds, escaped galley slaves, rogues, mountebanks, *lazzaroni*, pickpockets, tricksters, gamblers, *maquereaus*, brothel keepers, porters, *literati*, organ-grinders, rag-pickers, knife grinders, tinkers, beggars – in short, the whole indefinite, disintegrated mass, thrown hither and tither, which the French term *la bohème*.[26]

This characterization begs an analytical and empirical question of which social groups Marx could have precisely meant. It seems that he attempts to lump together a range of the following groups.

(i) *Displaced peasants*. The *Manifesto of the Communist Party* dissertates about the 'passively rotting mass thrown off by the lowest layers of old society'.[27] Probably, this is a reference to those formers peasants, who, through enclosures or other measures, were robbed of their means of existence, migrated to the cities, and became the unskilled part of the modern proletariat. If this is what Marx meant, then

---

[24] Marx, *The German Ideology*, p. 84.
[25] This led to a certain ambivalence: the 'wrong' workers *were* and *were not* proletarians. Hal Draper pointed this out and observed 'a certain ambivalence on the question whether the lumpenproletariat is to be regarded as a part of the proletariat or not' (H. Draper, 'The Concept of the "Lumpenproletariat" in Marx and Engels', *Economies et Sociétés*, VI [12]: 2294 [1972]). In *The Class Struggles in France* (1850), one can for instance read that the counter-revolutionary Mobile Guards 'belonged for the most part to the *lumpenproletariat*, which in all big towns forms a mass sharply differentiated from the industrial proletariat'. Just a few lines later, Marx writes, however, that 'the Paris proletariat was confronted with an army, drawn from its own midst'. K. Marx, *The Class Struggles in France, 1848 to 1850*, MECW, vol. 10, p. 62.
[26] K. Marx, *The Eighteenth Brumaire of Louis Bonaparte*, MECW, vol. 11, p. 149.
[27] Marx and Engels, *Manifesto of the Communist Party*, p. 494.

the difference between a recent ex-peasant who is becoming a proletarian rather than a lumpenproletarian seems to be a matter of attitude rather than of relation to the means of production: the proletarian has become more resigned to selling his labour power. Displaced peasants could also feature as 'people without a definite trade, vagabonds, gens sans feu et sans aveu', but again one would expect such people to turn into proletarians over time.[28]

(ii) *Displaced proletarians*. A second group is made up of urban workers without means of existence – men and women who have lost their jobs, or are too old or too sick to find employment. It is true, of course, that Marx did not include this group in the lumpenproletariat in *Capital*,[29] but it is likely to assume that the long-term unemployed and other proletarians at the lowest level of existence did resort to crime and prostitution. Cowling is justified in saying,

> Marx is ambivalent about how easy it would be for a proletarian thrown out by one branch of industry to find employment in another. Some of his writing about the worker as a mere appendage of the machine suggests that one might turn easily from the appendage of one machine into the appendage of another; on the other hand, there are suggestions that people become so distorted by one machine that they are not suitable to work with another. Again, there may be problems about accepting factory life at all, which mean that one has to start life in a factory young, although perhaps moving to another factory might not be so difficult. Perhaps this ambiguity corresponds to real life in the mid nineteenth century: one factory might involve more training or more distortion of the person or worse conditions than another; the demand for hands would be greater at one time than another. Any difficulties would surely lead some proletarians towards lumpen expedients.[30]

(iii) *Self-employed*. Marx's third category consists of 'porters, *literati*, organ-grinders, rag-pickers, knife grinders, tinkers'.[31] These groups have in common that they are self-employed and that their occupations are unlicenced. Similarly, one can wonder if unemployed often performed these activities. Historical studies can attest to this.[32]

(iv) *Dubious professions*. Finally, we have the mountebanks, tricksters, gamblers, brothel keepers, and prostitutes. What unites them is not a specific type of labour relation, but presumably the immoral nature of their work. 'What is going on here seems to be that Marx is

---

[28] M. Cowling, 'Marx's Lumpenproletariat and Murray's Underclass: Concepts Best Abandoned?' in M. Cowling and J. Martin (eds), *Marx's Eighteenth Brumaire: (Post) Modern Interpretations* (London: Pluto Press, 2002), p. 230.
[29] Marx, *Capital*, volume I, pp. 637–8.
[30] Cowling, 'Marx's Lumpenproletariat and Murray's Underclass', p. 231.
[31] Marx, *The Eighteenth Brumaire*, p. 149.
[32] For example, see G. S. Jones, *Outcast London: A Study in the Relationship between Classes in Victorian Society* (Oxford: Clarendon Press, 1971), part I.

including an assortment of occupations which command widespread dislike to make the lumpenproletariat seem less reputable rather than engaging in any kind of serious social (or socialist) analysis.'[33]

Apart from these deductions, the very complexity of Marx's analysis poses some empirical challenges. The historical sociologist Mark Traugott (1947–) has made a careful and detailed study of six battalions (comprising 3,845 individuals) of the 'lumpenproletarian' Mobile Guard in 1848. He has concluded that the social composition of the workers on the wrong side of the barricades does not confirm Marx's hypothesis of the lumpenproletarian:

> First, if self-reported occupations tell us anything at all, the Mobile Guard consisted in the main of workers in artisanal trades requiring relatively high levels of skill and training. This is not to deny the presence of a scattering of occupations that fit descriptions of the lumpenproletariat. If, unsurprisingly, no Mobile Guardsman listed his previous occupation as pimp, beggar, or thief, one does find listed a handful of itinerant peddlers, a single ragpicker, several street musicians, a magician, a mountebank, and a number for whom 'no profession' is specified. But even if one were to adopt a broad definition of lumpenproletarian status that included tinkers, scrap-metal dealers, market porters, and literati of all kinds, one could come up with only eighty-three such individuals or 3.0 percent of the total sample.[34]

Marx's concrete analysis of the French situation was thus misleading. Besides, the social groups considered by Marx as lumpenproletarians have certainly not always been reactionaries. Victor Kiernan[35] has, for instance, argued that the London lumpenproletariat after periods of seeming resignation could break out like a cyclone; and, once in movement, its actions were characterized by 'above all, audacity, spontaneity, disregard of the arbitrary chalk-lines within which society coops up its fowl; a cheerful conviction that the law is an ass'. Usually, such waves of militancy followed in the wake of protests by 'ordinary' workers: 'It was when those who normally had jobs suffered acute spells of unemployment, and showed signs of mutinying, that the stragglers joined in, and might go further.' More in general, 'lumpenproletarians' have often been a driving force in social struggles.[36] Naturally, this doesn't make them

---

[33] Cowling, 'Marx's Lumpenproletariat and Murray's Underclass', p. 232.
[34] M. Traugott, *Armies of the Poor: Determinants of Working-Class Participation in the Parisian Insurrection of June 1848* (Princeton, NJ: Princeton University Press, 1985), pp. 76–7. See also P. Caspard, 'Aspects de la lutte des classes en 1848: le recruitement de la garde nationale mobile', *Revue historique*, 511: 81–106 (1974).
[35] V. Kiernan, 'Victorian London – Unending Purgatory', *New Left Review*, 76: 82 (1972).
[36] F. Bovenkerk, 'The Rehabilitation of the Rabble: How and Why Marx and Engels Wrongly Depicted the Lumpenproletariat as a Reactionary Force', *The Netherlands Journal of Sociology*, 20 (1) (1984), 13–41.

a new vanguard, as has sometimes been suggested.[37] It underlines, however, that the 'lumpenproletariat' is not an analytical, but a moral category.[38]

This concept's untenability becomes particularly clear in the Global South. Vic Allen has rightly claimed that in

> societies in which bare subsistence is the norm for a high proportion of all the working class, and where men, women, and children are compelled to seek alternative means of subsistence, as distinct from their traditional ones, the *lumpenproletariat* is barely distinguishable from much of the rest of the working class.[39]

Fuzzy concepts like 'the informal sector' are an expression of such social conditions under which (semi-)proletarian households combine numerous activities to ensure their survival.[40]

4.4 Excluding Chattel Slaves

The contrast between 'free' wage labour and slavery is a recurring theme in Marx's *oeuvre*. As an expert on European antiquity and as a contemporary to the American Civil War, Marx was very much aware of the slavery problem. *Capital*, volume I was published two years after the abolition of slavery in the United States in 1865 and twenty-one years before it was officially proclaimed in Brazil. Marx considered slavery a historically backward mode of exploitation that would soon be a thing of the past, as 'free' wage labour embodied the capitalist future. He compared the two labour forms in several writings. He certainly saw similarities between them – both produced a surplus product and 'the wage labourer, like the slave, must have a master who puts him to work and rules over him'.[41] At the same time, he distinguished some differences that overshadowed all the common experiences they shared.

(i) *Ownership of labour power*. Labour power can, according to Marx,

> appear upon the market as a commodity, only if, and in so far as, its possessor, the individual whose labour power it is, offers it for sale, or sells it, as a commodity. In

---

[37] For example, F. Fanon, *The Wretched of the Earth* (Harmondsworth: Penguin, 1967); compare the critique in P. Worsley 'Frantz Fanon and the "Lumpenproletariat"', *The Socialist Register* 1972: 193–230.

[38] In the late nineteenth and early twentieth centuries the 'lumpen' concept became a foundation for socialist eugenics (M. Schwartz, '"Proletarier" und "Lumpen": Sozialistische Ursprünge eugenischen Denkens', *Vierteljahrshefte für Zeitgeschichte*, 42: 537–70 [1994]).

[39] V. Allen, 'The Meaning of the Working Class in Africa', *Journal of Modern African Studies*, 10 (2): 188.

[40] For example, see J. Breman, *Wage Hunters and Gatherers: Search for Work in the Urban and Rural Economy of South Gujarat* (Delhi: Oxford University Press, 1994), 3–130.

[41] K. Marx, *Capital*, volume III, MECW, vol. 37, p. 384.

order that he may be able to do this, he must have it at his disposal, must be the untrammeled owner of his capacity for labour, i.e., of his person.[42]

The future wage labourer and the money owner 'meet in the market, and deal with each other as on the basis of equal rights, with this difference alone, that one is buyer, the other seller; both, therefore equal in the eyes of the law'.[43] In other words, the workers have to 'own' their labour power and have to offer it themselves on the market as a commodity. But why should that be so? History has given us many instances where workers' labour power was offered on the market, although not by the workers themselves. Child labour, where the parents or guardians of the child receive the wages, is one clear example. The slaves-for-hire, who lived in various parts of the Americas and Africa in the eighteenth and nineteenth centuries, can be given as another example. A Brazilian study describes the situation of these slaves (so-called *ganhadores*), whose owners had sent them into the city to earn wages, as follows:

> The *ganhadores* moved about freely in the streets looking for work. It was a common, although not general, practice for slaveowners to permit their slaves to live outside the master's home in rented rooms, sometimes with former slaves as their landlords. They only returned to the master's house to 'pay for the week', that is, to pay the weekly (and sometimes daily) sum agreed upon with their masters. They were able to keep whatever exceeded that amount.[44]

(ii) *Duration of the labour relation.* The crucial distinction between 'free' wage earners and slaves is, according to Marx, the duration of their labour relation. The wage-labourer

> should sell it [his labour-power] only for a definite period, for if he were to sell it rump and stump, once for all, he would be selling himself, converting himself from a free man into a slave, from an owner of a commodity into a commodity.[45]

Ordinarily, one may call such a transaction (i.e., the piecemeal 'sale' of a commodity, without change of ownership) *letting* and not sale – an obvious thought that was expressed a long time ago.[46] The difference

---

[42] Marx, *Capital*, volume I, p. 178.   [43] Ibid.

[44] J. J. Reis, '"The Revolution of the Ganhadores": Urban Labour, Ethnicity and the African Strike of 1857 in Bahia, Brazil', *Journal of Latin American Studies*, 29: 359 (1997). Marx was aware of the existence of slaves-for-hire but he did not draw any theoretical conclusions from this. See, for example, Marx, *Capital*, volume III, p. 464: 'Under a slave system, the labourer has a capital value, namely, his purchase price. And when he is hired out, the hirer must pay, in the first place, the interest on this purchase price and, in addition, replace the annual wear and tear on the capital.'

[45] Marx, *Capital*, volume I, p. 178.

[46] F. Oppenheimer, *Die soziale Frage und der Sozialismus. Eine kritische Auseinandersetzung mit der marxistischen Theorie* (Jena: G. Fischer, 1912), p. 120. Marx saw the analogy between wage labour and the hiring process. For instance, compare his remark that 'The

between selling and letting seems insignificant, but it is not. If A sells a commodity to B, then B becomes the owner instead of A. But if A hires out a commodity to B, then A remains the owner and B only gains the right to use the commodity for a certain period of time. The commodity's 'substance' remains with A, while B gets the usufruct.

If wage labour is based on hiring, and not on buying labour power, then the crucial difference between a wage labourer and a slave is not the 'definite period'[47] during which the labour power is alienated, but the *letting* of labour power is one thing, and its *sale* another. Why did Marx not concede this? Presumably, because it would put a different complexion on the creation of value. After all, the substance (the value) of the wage earner's labour power would then not be appropriated by the capitalist, but it would remain the property of the worker. Engels thought that house renting is 'a transfer of already *existing*, previously *produced* value, and that therefore 'the total sum of values possessed by the landlord and the tenant *together* remains the same as it was before'.[48] Following this argument, a wage labourer would not be capable of producing surplus-value if the wage relationship were a form of hiring/letting.

(iii) *Fixed versus variable capital*. Because the duration of the labour relationship is seen as the main difference between the wage earner and the slave, the former represents variable capital and the latter fixed (constant) capital. The wage labourer embodies 'that part of capital' which

both reproduces the equivalent of its own value, and also produces an excess, a surplus-value, which, given the circumstances, may itself vary more or less. This part of capital is continually being transformed from a constant into a variable magnitude. I therefore call it the variable part of capital, or, shortly, *variable capital*.[49]

Chattel slaves are, according to Marx, economically indistinguishable from cattle or machines: 'The slave-owner buys his labourer as he buys his horse.'[50] The slave's purchase price is his capital-value, and this has to be depreciated over a number of years.[51] But how is it justified to define only wage labour as variable capital, because 'that part of capital' can be 'more or less' according to circumstances? Is the same not true for commodity-producing slave labour? Slave prices could fluctuate enormously and slaves could be sold at any time.

price of the labour power is fixed by the contract, although it is not realized till later, like the rent of a house.' Marx, *Capital*, volume I, p. 185.
[47] Marx, *Capital*, volume I, p. 178.
[48] F. Engels, *The Housing Question*, MECW, vol. 23, p. 320.
[49] Marx, *Capital*, volume I, p. 219.   [50] Ibid, p. 272.
[51] Marx, *Capital*, volume III, p. 464.

(iv) *Creation of value and surplus-value.* If a wage labourer produces commodities, then these commodities are 'at the same time, use values and values', and therefore 'the process of producing them must be a labour process, and at the same time, a process of creating value'.[52] But the same is obviously true for slaves growing cane sugar, tobacco, or indigo. They were also producing commodities, just like wage earners. Therefore, slaves must have created value as well. Marx could not admit this, because slaves were fixed capital, and only capital is capable of creating value.

Concurrently, the wage labourer's labour power is a source of 'more value than it has itself':[53] because

labour pre-exists in the form of wage labour, and the means of production in the form of capital – i.e., solely because of this specific social form of these two essential production factors – does a part of the value (product) appear as surplus value and this surplus value as profit (rent), as the gain of the capitalist.[54]

Again, Marx thought that this was not true for the slave's labour. The slave owner has paid cash for his slave and therefore 'the returns from the labour of the slave ... merely represent the interest on the capital invested in this purchase'.[55] Historically, however, the Caribbean sugar plantations based on slave labour were often extremely profitable, because the produced sugar had much more value than the capital invested by the planters (ground rent, depreciation of the slaves, depreciation of the sugar cane press, etc.). Can one really maintain that only wage labour reproduces the equivalent of its own value and produces an excess amount of value (a surplus-value)? Or is the chattel slave 'a source not only of value, but of more value than itself'?

(v) *Rate of profit.* According to Marx, the profit rate is tangentially declining, given the ongoing increase of labour productivity:

Since the mass of the employed living labour is continually on the decline as compared to the mass of objectified labour set in motion by it, i.e., to the productively consumed means of production, it follows that the portion of living labour, unpaid and congealed in surplus value, must also be continually on the decrease compared to the amount of value represented by the invested total capital.[56]

Naturally, the end of this development – the collapse of capitalism – will have been reached as soon as variable capital is reduced to zero, and total capital consists only of constant capital. Paradoxically though it may seem, if we are to believe Marx, this future situation had already become

---

[52] Marx, *Capital*, volume I, p. 196.   [53] Ibid., p. 204.
[54] Marx, *Capital*, volume III, p. 868.   [55] Ibid., p. 618.   [56] Ibid., p. 211.

a reality in the Caribbean slave plantations during the eighteenth century, with almost complete lack of variable capital and formidable capital accumulation.

Inconsistencies like these reveal that Marx's value-theoretical approach of privileging productive wage labour was not well founded. Slaves and 'free' wage earners are more similar than is often acknowledged. Under capitalism many intermediary and transitional forms between both modes of exploitation have existed – the *ganhadores* are just one example. What is more, slaves and 'free' wage labourers have in many cases done the same work for the same capitalist (e.g., on Brazilian coffee plantations or in factories in the US South).[57] Evidently, the slave's labour power is forever the property of the slave holder, while the labour power of the wage labourer is made available to the capitalist for short periods of time. Yet, it is unclear why in the former case no value and surplus-value is created. It is high time to broaden the labour theory of value in such a way that it would embrace the slave and other unfree workers' labour power with an equal measure of applicability.

Marx was apparently not completely convinced of his own analysis. Contrary to his own argument, he often indicated that he considered chattel slavery as a capitalist mode of exploitation all the same. His wavering was apparent from his statement, quoted earlier that slavery is 'an anomaly in relation to the bourgeois system itself', which 'can exist at individual points within the bourgeois system of production', but 'only because it does not exist at other points'.[58] In the first volume of *Capital*, while discussing slavery in the US South, Marx noticed:

But in proportion, as the export of cotton became of vital interest to these states, the overworking of the negro and sometimes the using up of his life in 7 years of labour, became a factor in a calculated and calculating system. It was no longer a question of obtaining from him a certain quantity of useful products. It was now a question of *production of surplus-value itself*.[59]

In *Capital*, volume III, Marx wrote about the slave economy:

The entire surplus labour of the labourers, which is manifested here in the surplus product, is extracted from them directly by the owner of all instruments of production, to which belong the land and, under the original form of slavery,

---

[57] See M. Hall and V. Stolcke, 'The Introduction of Free Labour on São Paulo Coffee Plantations', *Journal of Political Science of Peasant Studies*, 10 (2–3): 170–200 (1983); T. S. Whitman, 'Industrial Slavery at the Margin: The Maryland Chemical Works', *Journal of Southern History*, 59 (1): 31–62 (1993).

[58] Marx, 'Outlines of the Critique of Political Economy [*Grundrisse*]. First Instalment', p. 392

[59] Marx, *Capital*, volume I, p. 244. Emphasis added.

the immediate producers themselves. Where the capitalist outlook prevails, as on American plantations, *this entire surplus-value is regarded as profit.*[60]

And in the *Grundrisse,* he argued: 'That we now not only describe the plantation-owners in America as capitalists, but that they *are* capitalists, is due to the fact that they exist as anomalies within a world market based upon free labour.'[61]

Chattel slaves were thus an integral part of capitalism and produced surplus-value, although this was impossible because they embodied fixed, and not variable, capital.

4.5 Problematic Consequences

The exclusion of lumpenproletarians and chattel slaves was not well thought out. One gets the impression that Marx *first* proclaimed the double-free wage earners as the revolutionary subject on philosophical grounds, and *then* collected some arguments that were partly of an ad hoc nature. The outcome was a theory of the working class fraught with empirical and logical inconsistencies – not only with respect to excluded groups like the lumpenproletariat and chattel slaves, but also when it comes to the 'real' proletariat in a narrow sense.

First, most 'proletarian' movements in Marx's time were *not* based on the double-free wage earners that he was thinking of. The Silesian weavers, who in 1844 revealed to Marx the revolutionary potential of the proletariat, were not 'workers' in the Marxian sense. They were self-employed cottagers representing 'embryonic forms' of capitalist wage labour: 'they owned the means of production and only obtained the raw materials from the merchant-wholesaler'. This is not to deny, of course, that these weavers – who happened to be mainly women[62]

lived in constant dependency on the merchant-wholesaler. Whenever the price for cloth fell, the losses were passed on to the weavers in the form of wage cuts. An overabundance of labour and a shortage of capital on the part of the workers meant that the merchant capitalists were in a position to dictate almost at will the level of wages and the working conditions.[63]

---

[60] Marx, *Capital,* volume III, p. 790. Emphasis added.
[61] Marx, 'Outlines of the Critique of Political Economy [*Grundrisse*]. First Instalment', p. 436.
[62] G. Notz, 'Warum der Weberaufstand kein Weberinnenaufstand war', in U. Bitzegeio, A. Kruke, and M. Woyke (eds), *Solidargemeinschaft und Erinnerungskultur im 20. Jahrhundert. Beiträge zu Gewerkschaften, Nationalsozialismus und Geschichtspolitik* (Bonn: Verlag J. H. W. Dietz Nachf, 2009).
[63] C. von Hodenberg, 'Weaving Survival in the Tapestry of Village Life: Strategies and Status in the Silesian Weaver Revolt of 1844', in J. Kok (ed.), *Rebellious Families: Household Strategies and Collective Action in the Nineteenth and Twentieth Centuries*

The worker-communists of the Communist League in London, upon whose request Marx and Engels authored the *Manifesto of the Communist Party*, were mostly semi-proletarianized journeymen working in artisanal shops and in putting-out or sweating systems.[64] The social basis of German Social Democracy in Marx's time can perhaps best be characterized as a 'popular movement of small producers'.[65] The social basis of the Paris Commune was somewhat similar.[66] Also, Marx very much overestimated the British workers' concentration in large workshops.[67] Historical research indicates that, during the nineteenth century, workers, who were employed by large factories of the large-scale industries, played a less significant role in the labour movements than the self-employed and artisans.[68]

Second, Marx overestimated the speed and size of proletarianization. It was, for example, wishful thinking when Marx and Engels asserted, in the *Manifesto of the Communist Party*, that in 'existing society, private property is already done away with for nine-tenths of the population; its existence for the few is solely due to its non-existence in the hands of those nine-tenths'.[69] This was a clear exaggeration: 'This situation did around 1848 not even exist in advanced England, let alone in France and Germany.'[70] In the meantime, full proletarianization very much progressed in the advanced capitalist countries – although there existed counter-tendencies, such as the resurgence of share cropping and self-

---

(New York and Oxford: Berghahn, 2002), p. 41; *Aufstand der Weber. Die Revolte von 1844 und ihr Aufstieg zum Mythos* (Bonn: Dietz, 1997), ch. 2.

[64] A. Brandenburg, *Theoriebildungsprozesse in der deutschen Arbeiterbewegung, 1835–1850* (Hannover: SOAK-Verlag, 1977).

[65] T. Welskopp, *Das Banner der Brüderlichkeit. Die deutsche Sozialdemokratie vom Vormärz bis zum Sozialistengesetz* (Bonn: Dietz, 2000), pp. 60–228.

[66] R. V. Gould, *Insurgent Identities: Class Community, and Protest in Paris from 1848 to the Commune* (Chicago: University of Chicago Press, 1995), ch. 6; indications already in J. Rougerie, 'Composition d'une population insurgée: l'example de la Commune', *Le Mouvement Social*, 48: 31–47 (1964).

[67] R. Samuel, 'The Workshop of the World: Steam Power and Hand Technology in Mid-Victorian Britain', *History Workshop Journal*, 3 (1): 6–72 (1977).

[68] On the one hand, Marx considered workers as 'true' proletarians who were not qualified, on the other hand, he sometimes excluded workers from the proletariat who should have been included according to his own analysis. When Marx, for instance, discussed the relative surplus population in *Capital*, volume I, he regarded prostitutes as an important part of the actual lumpenproletariat. Marx, *Capital*, volume I, p. 637. Elsewhere, especially in the *Theories of Surplus Value* (e.g., K. Marx, *The Economic Manuscript of 1861–63*, MECW, vol. 31, pp. 21–2), Marx claimed that prostitutes, if they worked for a brothel keeper, perform (unproductive) wage labour, like actors or musicians, and thus were, by implication, part of the proletariat in the narrow sense of the word.

[69] Marx and Engels, *Manifesto of the Communist Party*, p. 500.

[70] M. Mauke, *Die Klassentheorie von Marx und Engels* (Frankfurt/Main: Europäische Verlagsanstalt, 1970), p. 118.

employment.[71] Yet, the worldwide capitalist expansion in Africa, Asia, and Latin America has only to a very limited extent resulted in the growth of a 'pure' proletariat: 'in class terms, the pattern of capitalist development on the periphery was incapable of following the full "proletarianizing" logic of that of the centre'.[72]

Third, Marx underestimated capitalism's ability to incorporate the proletariat. Marx, as we have seen, considered the proletariat as 'a class *in* civil society which is not a class *of* civil society'. Gradually, however, the proletariat has become a part of civil society. At least three influences, not foreseen by Marx, probably played a role in this process. (i) The *political incorporation* of the proletariat, partly also resulting from the efforts of labour movements. For the British case, Bert Moorhouse (1894–1954)[73] has argued that 'the majority of the ruling class believed that incorporation was necessary to bind the masses to the prevailing system but also wanted such integration to be constrained and channeled so that, though institutional forms might change, and could be promoted as having changed, the differential distribution of power in society would remain unaltered'. (ii) The *incorporation of proletarians as consumers*. It is true that Marx in the *Grundrisse* has drawn our attention to the capitalist's attempts to spur the workers 'on to consumption, to endow his commodities with new attractions, to talk the workers into feeling new needs, etc.',[74] but nowhere did he evince to have understood the huge implications of the proletariat's golden chains.[75] (iii) *Technological changes of labour processes* have had a double consequence: '(1) a drastic (and continuing) reduction in the production-worker component, and (2) a vast proliferation of job categories in the distribution and service sectors of the economy.'[76]

---

[71] M. Wells, 'The Resurgence of Sharecropping: Historical Anomaly or Political Strategy?', *American Journal of Sociology*, 90 (1): 1–29 (1984); G. Steinmetz and E. O. Wright, 'The Fall and Rise of the Petty Bourgeoisie: Changing Patterns of Self-Employment in the Postwar United States', *American Journal of Sociology*, 94 (5): 973–1018 (1989); D. Bögenhold and U. Staber, 'The Decline and Rise of Self-Employment', *Work, Employment and Society*, 5: 223–39 (1991).

[72] K. Post, *Revolution's Other World: Communism and the Periphery, 1917–39* (Houndmills: Macmillan, 1997), p. 5; also S. Amin and M. van der Linden (eds), *'Peripheral' Labour? Studies in the History of Partial Proletarianization* (Cambridge: Cambridge University Press, 1996).

[73] H. F. Moorhouse, 'The Political Incorporation of the British Working Class: An Interpretation', *Sociology*, 7: 346 (1973).

[74] Marx, 'Outlines of the Critique of Political Economy [*Grundrisse*]. First Instalment', p. 217.

[75] M. A. Lebowitz, *Following Marx: Method, Critique and Crisis* (Leiden and Boston: Brill, 2009), p. 308.

[76] P. Sweezy, 'Marx and the Proletariat', *Monthly Review*, 19 (7): 37 (1967); R. Edwards, 'Sweezy and the Proletariat', in S. Resnick and R. Wolff (eds), *Rethinking Marxism:*

4.6 A Final Word

Marx's theory of the proletariat is in need of serious reconsideration. Its theoretical demarcation of the proletariat with regard to other subaltern groups (the self-employed and chattel slaves) is inconsistent; the concrete class analyses based on this theory have, to a significant extent, been refuted by empirical historical research; and its forecast of the growth of the proletariat has only been confirmed partly by later developments.

Arguably, we need a new conceptualization of the proletariat that is based on inclusion rather than exclusion. Such a conceptualization can be achieved in two ways. One option is to do away with the idea of 'anomalies' and consider all forms of market-oriented labour (including unfree labour) as variations of capital-positing labour. This is the position advocated by Jairus Banaji and Rakesh Bhandari. It implies that the differences between chattel slaves, sharecroppers, and wage earners are only of a gradual nature since all of them work for capital and labour under economic and/or non-economic compulsion:

> Finding the essence of wage-labour in capital-positing activity not only allows a change in the extension of the concept and thereby a challenge to the apologetic Eurocentric occlusion of slavery and colonialism in the writing of the history of capitalism, it also allows us to throw into relief the way in which wage-labour in whatever form is enslaved.[77]

Another option is to broaden the concept of the proletariat to include all commodified labour. From this perspective, the proletariat consists of all carriers of labour power whose labour power is sold or hired out to employers (including individuals, corporations, and institutions) under economic or non-economic compulsion, regardless of whether these carriers of labour power are themselves selling or hiring out their labour-power; and regardless of whether these carriers themselves own means of production.[78] Naturally, all aspects of this provisional definition require further reflection. Nevertheless, this conceptual demarcation indicates the common class-basis of all subaltern workers: the *coerced* commodification of their labour power.

Struggles in Marxist Theory: Essays for Harry Magdoff and Paul Sweezy (Brooklyn: Autonomedia, 1985).

[77] R. Bhandari, 'The Disguises of Wage-Labour: Juridical Illusions, Unfree Conditions and Novel Extensions', *Historical Materialism,* 16 (1): 96 (2008); 'Slavery and Wage Labor in History', *Rethinking Marxism,* 19 (3): 396–408 (2007); J. Banaji, *Theory as History: Essays on Modes of Production and Exploitation* (Leiden and Boston: Brill, 2010).

[78] M. Van der Linden, *Workers of the World: Essays toward a Global Labor History* (Leiden and Boston: Brill, 2008), ch. 2.

According to both approaches, all constituents of this redefined proletariat share their exploitation by employers and the commodification of their labour power. Therefore, they share a common class interest in the transcendence of capitalism. Recent historical research has, for instance, revealed concrete cases of struggles conducted jointly by slaves and 'free' wage earners.[79] At the same, the short- and medium-term interests of segments of this new broad-spectrum proletariat can diverge strongly. This redefinition of the proletariat comes at a price though. If we accept that not only 'free' wage earners are integral parts of capitalism, but also chattel slaves and other groups of workers, then both variable capital ('free' labourers) and fixed capital (slaves) are capable of producing value and surplus-value. A new theory of value will then become necessary.[80]

References

Allen, V. L. (1972), 'The Meaning of the Working Class in Africa', *Journal of Modern African Studies*, 10 (2): 169–89.

Amin, Shahid, and van der Linden, Marcel, eds (1996), *'Peripheral' Labour? Studies in the History of Partial Proletarianization*, Cambridge: Cambridge University Press.

Banaji, Jairus (2010), *Theory as History: Essays on Modes of Production and Exploitation*, Leiden and Boston: Brill.

Bensen, Heinrich W. (1847), *Die Proletarier. Eine historische Denkschrift*, Stuttgart.

Bhandari, Rakesh (2007), 'Slavery and Wage Labor in History', *Rethinking Marxism*, 19 (3): 396–408.

—— (2008), 'The Disguises of Wage-Labour: Juridical Illusions, Unfree Conditions and Novel Extensions', *Historical Materialism*, 16 (1): 71–99.

Blackburn, Robin (1976), 'Marxism: Theory of Proletarian Revolution', *New Left Review*, 97: 3–35.

Bögenhold, Dieter, and Staber, Udo (1991), 'The Decline and Rise of Self-Employment', *Work, Employment and Society*, 5: 223–39.

Bovenkerk, Frank (1984), 'The Rehabilitation of the Rabble: How and Why Marx and Engels Wrongly Depicted the Lumpenproletariat as a Reactionary Force', *The Netherlands Journal of Sociology*, 20 (1): 13–41.

Brandenburg, Alexander (1977), *Theoriebildungsprozesse in der deutschen Arbeiterbewegung, 1835–1850*, Hannover: SOAK-Verlag.

Breman, Jan (1994), *Wage Hunters and Gatherers: Search for Work in the Urban and Rural Economy of South Gujarat*, Delhi: Oxford University Press.

Caspard, Pierre (1974), 'Aspects de la lutte des classes en 1848: le recrutement de la garde nationale mobile', *Revue historique*, 511: 81–106.

---

[79] See Linebaugh and Rediker, *The Many-Headed Hydra*.

[80] Note that from a logical point of view: 'The labour theory of *surplus* value is ... unnecessary to the moral claim Marxists make when they say that capitalism is exploitative.' G. A. Cohen, *History, Labour and Freedom: Themes from Marx* (Oxford: Clarendon Press, 1988), p. 214.

Cohen, G. A. (1988), 'The Labour Theory of Value and the Concept of Exploitation', in G. A. Cohen (ed.), *History, Labour and Freedom: Themes from Marx*, Oxford: Clarendon Press.
Cowling, Mark (2002), 'Marx's Lumpenproletariat and Murray's Underclass: Concepts Best Abandoned?', in Mark Cowling and James Martin (eds), *Marx's Eighteenth Brumaire: (Post)Modern Interpretations*, London: Pluto Press, pp. 228–42.
Draper, Hal (1972), 'The Concept of the "Lumpenproletariat" in Marx and Engels', *Economies et Sociétés*, VI (12): 2285–312.
Edwards, Richard (1985), 'Sweezy and the Proletariat', in Stephen Resnick and Richard Wolff (eds), *Rethinking Marxism: Struggles in Marxist Theory: Essays for Harry Magdoff and Paul Sweezy*, Brooklyn: Autonomedia, pp. 99–114.
Engels, Frederick (1975), *The Condition of the Working Class in England: From Personal Observation and Authentic Sources*, MECW, vol. 4, pp. 295–583.
—— (1988), *The Housing Question*, MECW, vol. 23, pp. 317–91.
Fanon, Frantz (1967), *The Wretched of the Earth*. Preface Jean-Paul Sartre, Harmondsworth: Penguin.
Gould, Roger V. (1995), *Insurgent Identities: Class Community, and Protest in Paris from 1848 to the Commune*, Chicago: University of Chicago Press.
Granier de Cassagnac, Adolphe (1838), *Histoire des classes ouvrières et des classes bourgeoises*, Paris: Desrez.
Hall, Michael, and Stolcke, Verena (1983), 'The Introduction of Free Labour on São Paulo Coffee Plantations', *Journal of Political Science of Peasant Studies*, 10 (2–3): 170–200.
Herrnstadt, Rudolf (1965), *Die Entdeckung der Klassen. Die Geschichte des Begriffs Klasse von den Anfängen bis zum Vorabend der Pariser Julirevolution 1830*, Berlin: VEB Deutscher Verlag der Wissenschaften.
Jones, Gareth Stedman (1971), *Outcast London: A Study in the Relationship between Classes in Victorian Society*, Oxford: Clarendon Press.
Kiernan, Victor (1972), 'Victorian London – Unending Purgatory', *New Left Review*, 76: 73–90.
Lebowitz, Michael A. (2009), *Following Marx: Method, Critique and Crisis*, Leiden and Boston: Brill.
Linebaugh, Peter, and Rediker, Marcus (2000), *The Many-Headed Hydra: Sailors, Slaves, Commoners, and the Hidden History of the Revolutionary Atlantic*, Boston: Beacon Press.
Marx, Karl (1975), 'A Contribution to the Critique of Hegel's Philosophy of Right: Introduction', MECW, vol. 3, pp. 175–87.
—— (1975), 'Critical Notes on the Article: "The King of Prussia and Social Reform. By a Prussian"', MECW, vol. 3, pp. 189–206.
—— (1978), *The Class Struggles in France, 1848 to 1850*, MECW, vol. 10, pp. 45–145.
—— (1979), *The Eighteenth Brumaire of Louis Bonaparte*, MECW, vol. 11, pp. 99–209.
—— (1986), 'Outlines of the Critique of Political Economy [*Grundrisse*]. First Instalment', MECW, vol. 28.
—— (1989), *The Economic Manuscript of 1861–63*, MECW, vol. 31.

(1996), *Capital*, volume I, MECW, vol. 35.
(1997), *Capital*, volume II, MECW, vol. 36.
(1998), *Capital*, volume III, MECW, vol. 37.
Marx, Karl, and Fredrick Engels (1975), *The German Ideology. Critique of Modern German Philosophy According to Its Representatives Feuerbach, B. Bauer and Stirner, and of German Socialism According to Its Various Prophets*, MECW, vol. 5, pp. 19–539.
(1976), *Manifesto of the Communist Party*, MECW, vol. 6, pp. 477–519.
(1983), *Letters, 1852–55*, MECW, vol. 39.
Mauke, Michael (1970), *Die Klassentheorie von Marx und Engels*, Frankfurt/Main: Europäische Verlagsanstalt.
Moorhouse, H. F. (1973), 'The Political Incorporation of the British Working Class: An Interpretation', *Sociology*, 7: 341–59.
Notz, Gisela (2009), 'Warum der Weberaufstand kein Weberinnenaufstand war', in Ursula Bitzegeio, Anja Kruke, and Meik Woyke (eds), *Solidargemeinschaft und Erinnerungskultur im 20. Jahrhundert. Beiträge zu Gewerkschaften, Nationalsozialismus und Geschichtspolitik*, Bonn: Verlag J. H. W. Dietz Nachf, pp. 97–118.
Oppenheimer, Franz (1912), *Die soziale Frage und der Sozialismus. Eine kritische Auseinandersetzung mit der marxistischen Theorie*, Jena: G. Fischer.
Post, Ken (1997), *Revolution's Other World: Communism and the Periphery, 1917–39*, Houndmills: Macmillan.
Reis, João José (1997), '"The Revolution of the Ganhadores": Urban Labour, Ethnicity and the African Strike of 1857 in Bahia, Brazil', *Journal of Latin American Studies*, 29: 355–93.
Rougerie, Jacques (1964), 'Composition d'une population insurgée: l'example de la Commune', *Le Mouvement Social*, 48: 31–47.
Samuel, Raphael (1977), 'The Workshop of the World: Steam Power and Hand Technology in Mid-Victorian Britain', *History Workshop Journal*, 3 (1): 6–72.
Schwartz, Michael (1993), '"Proletarier" und "Lumpen": Sozialistische Ursprünge eugenischen Denkens', *Vierteljahrshefte für Zeitgeschichte*, 42: 537–70.
Singelmann, Joachim, and Singelmann, Peter (1986), 'Lorenz von Stein and the Paradigmatic Bifurcation of Social Theory in the Nineteenth Century', *British Journal of Sociology*, 37 (3): 431–52.
Steinmetz, George, and Wright, Erik Olin (1989), 'The Fall and Rise of the Petty Bourgeoisie: Changing Patterns of Self-Employment in the Postwar United States', *American Journal of Sociology*, 94 (5): 973–1018.
Sweezy, Paul (1967), 'Marx and the Proletariat', *Monthly Review*, 19 (7): 25–42.
Thompson, E. P. (1963), *The Making of the English Working Class*, London: Victor Gollancz.
Traugott, Mark (1985), *Armies of the Poor: Determinants of Working-Class Participation in the Parisian Insurrection of June 1848*, Princeton, NJ: Princeton University Press.
Van der Linden, Marcel (2008), *Workers of the World: Essays toward a Global Labor History*, Leiden and Boston: Brill.

Von Hodenberg, Christina (1997), *Aufstand der Weber. Die Revolte von 1844 und ihr Aufstieg zum Mythos*, Bonn: Dietz.
— (2002), 'Weaving Survival in the Tapestry of Village Life: Strategies and Status in the Silesian Weaver Revolt of 1844', in Jan Kok (ed.), *Rebellious Families: Household Strategies and Collective Action in the Nineteenth and Twentieth Centuries*, New York and Oxford: Berghahn, pp. 39–58.
Von Stein, Lorenz (1842), *Der Socialismus und Communismus des heutigen Frankreichs. Ein Beitrag zur Zeitgeschichte*, Leipzig: Wigand.
Wells, Miriam J. (1984), 'The Resurgence of Sharecropping: Historical Anomaly or Political Strategy?', *American Journal of Sociology*, 90 (1): 1–29.
Welskopp, Thomas (2000), *Das Banner der Brüderlichkeit. Die deutsche Sozialdemokratie vom Vormärz bis zum Sozialistengesetz*, Bonn: Dietz.
Whitman, T. Stephen (1993), 'Industrial Slavery at the Margin: The Maryland Chemical Works', *Journal of Southern History*, 59 (1): 31–62.
Worsley, Peter (1972), 'Frantz Fanon and the "Lumpenproletariat"', *The Socialist Register* 1972: 193–230.
Zaniewski, Romuald (1957), *L'Origine du prolétariat romain et contemporain. Faits et théories*, Louvain and Paris: Editions Nauwelaerts and Béatrice Nauwelaerts.

5   Class Struggle

Alex Callinicos

5.1   Genealogy

The class struggle is probably the idea most closely identified with Karl Marx – above all thanks to the opening lines of the *Manifesto of the Communist Party*:

The history of all hitherto existing society is the history of class struggles.

Freeman and slave, patrician and plebeian, lord and serf, guild-master and journeyman, in a word, oppressor and oppressed, stood in constant opposition to one another, carried on an uninterrupted, now hidden, now open fight, a fight that each time ended, either in a revolutionary reconstitution of society at large, or in the common ruin of the contending classes.[1]

But the class struggle is also a concept for which Marx denied paternity: thus he wrote to Joseph Weydemeyer (1818–66) on 5 March 1852: 'as for myself, I do not claim to have discovered either the existence of classes in modern society or the struggle between them. Long before me, bourgeois historians had described the historical development of this struggle between the classes, as had bourgeois economists their economic anatomy.'[2] By 'bourgeois historians' Marx had in mind especially the liberal intellectuals of Restoration France, who started to interpret the political struggles of European history in terms of deeper social antagonisms. François Guizot (1787–1874) wrote in 1828: 'Modern Europe was born from the struggle of the various classes of society.'[3] Adolphe Blanqui (1798–1854) prefaced his *Histoire de l'économie politique* (1837) with a passage that may have influenced Marx when writing the *Manifesto of the Communist Party*:

In all the revolutions, there have always been but two parties opposing each other; that of the people who wish to live by their own labour, and that of those who would live by the labour of others ... *Patricians and plebeians, slaves and freemen,*

---

[1] K. Marx and F. Engels, *Manifesto of the Communist Party*, MECW, vol. 6, p. 382.
[2] 'K. Marx to J. Weydemeyer, 5 March 1852', MECW, vol. 39, p. 62.
[3] F. P. G. Guizot, *History of Civilization in Europe* (London: Harmondsworth, 1997), p. 130.

guelphs and ghibelines, red roses and white roses, cavaliers and roundheads, are only varieties of the same species.[4]

Analytically, however, the most important influence was that of David Ricardo (1772–1823). In the aforementioned letter to Weydemeyer, Marx quoted the opening lines of Ricardo's *On the Principles of Political Economy and Taxation*:

> The produce of the earth – all that is derived from its surface by the united application of labour, machinery, and capital, is divided among three classes of the community; namely, the proprietor of the land, the owner of the stock or capital necessary for its cultivation, and the labourers by whose industry it is cultivated.[5]

Ricardo formulated a rigorous and generalized version of the labour theory of value, according to which the value of commodities is determined by the labour required to produce them. He argued, furthermore, that wages and profits are inversely related, thereby positing an antagonism of interests between labour and capital. As Marx wrote in *The Economic Manuscript of 1861–63*, 'Ricardo exposes and describes the economic antagonism of classes – as shown by the intrinsic relations – and ... consequently political economy perceives, discovers the root of the historical struggle and development.'[6] From *The Poverty of Philosophy* (1847) onwards, Ricardo was the key reference point for Marx's critique of political economy.

Nevertheless, one can detect another, more abstract source for Marx's treatment of the concept of class struggle, namely Hegel's notion of contradiction as constitutive, 'the root of all movement and life' rather than 'an accident, an abnormality as it were, a momentary fit of sickness'.[7] Thus, in *The Poverty of Philosophy*, Marx targeted what he regarded as Proudhon's tendency to separate out the 'good' and 'bad' sides of every phenomenon, whereas: 'What constitutes dialectical movement is the coexistence of two contradictory sides, their conflict and their fusion into a new category. The very setting of the problem of eliminating the bad side cuts short the dialectic movement.'[8] A prime example of the positive and productive role of

---

[4] Quoted in R. Raico, 'Classical Liberal Roots of the Marxist Doctrine of Classes', in Y. Maltsev (ed.), *Requiem for Marx* (Auburn, AL: Praxeology Press, 1993), p. 191. The author is grateful to Diego Costa for this reference. See also, on Restoration liberalism, A. Callinicos, *Social Theory: A Historical Introduction* (Cambridge: Polity, 2007), pp. 57–66.
[5] D. Ricardo, 'On the Principles of Political Economy and Taxation', in P. Sraffa (ed.), *The Works and Correspondence of David Ricardo*, vol. I (Cambridge: Cambridge University Press, 1951–2), p. 5.
[6] K. Marx, *The Economic Manuscript of 1861–63*, MECW, vol. 31, p. 392.
[7] G. W. F. Hegel, *The Science of Logic* (Cambridge: Cambridge University Press, 2010), p. 382.
[8] K. Marx, *The Poverty of Philosophy. Answer to the Philosophy of Poverty by M. Proudhon*, MECW, vol. 6, p. 168.

contradiction is the class struggle, understood in terms that show the influence of both Ricardo and the liberal historians:

> The very moment civilization begins, production begins to be founded on the antagonism of orders, estates, classes, and finally on the antagonism of accumulated labour and immediate labour. No antagonism, no progress. This is the law that civilization has followed up to our days. Till now the productive forces have been developed by virtue of this system of class antagonisms.[9]

This conception of class struggle as a driving force of historical development and progress plays a strategic role in Marx's explanatory theory and his version of socialism. A key difference between Marx and the Utopian socialists is that he welcomed the class struggle as not simply a symptom of the antagonisms of the capitalist mode of production, but as the source of the solution of these antagonisms, through proletarian revolution.

5.2 Theoretical Articulation

The concept of class struggle is integrated into Marx's theory at two levels: first, his general theory of history, and, second, the critique of political economy culminating in *Capital*. If we take the theory of history first, the class struggle operates together with (but subordinated to) the tendency of the development of productive forces to come into conflict with the relations of production. This is already clear in the letter to Weydemeyer of 5 March 1852, where Marx continued the passage cited earlier, thus:

> My own contribution was 1. to show that the *existence of classes* is merely bound up with *certain historical phases in the development of production*; 2. that the class struggle necessarily leads to the *dictatorship of the proletariat*; 3. that this dictatorship itself constitutes no more than a transition to the *abolition of all classes* and to a *classless society*.[10]

Clause 1 implicitly subordinates the class struggle to the development of the productive forces. More than twenty-five years later, there is a similarly elliptical version of the same thought in Marx's and Friedrich Engels's circular letter to August Bebel (1840–1913) and others of 17–18 September 1879. 'For almost 40 years we have emphasized that the class struggle is the *immediate* motive force of history [*nächste treibende Macht der Geschichte*] and, in particular, that the class struggle between bourgeoisie and proletariat is the great lever of modern social revolution.'[11]

---

[9] Marx, *Poverty of Philosophy*, p. 132.
[10] 'Marx to Weydemeyer, 5 March 1852', MECW, vol. 39, pp. 62, 65.
[11] K. Marx and F. Engels to August Bebel, Wilhelm Liebknecht, Wilhelm Bracke and Others (Circular Letter). 17–18 September, MECW, vol. 45, p. 408; italics added.

These passages make clear that Louis Althusser (1918–90) was oversimplifying dangerously when he claimed that Marx and Engels affirmed in the *Manifesto of the Communist Party*: 'The class struggle is the motor of history.'[12] They should probably be interpreted in the light of Marx's famous summary of his theory of history in the 1859 preface to *A Contribution to the Critique of Political Economy*. The *fundamental* driving force of historical transformation is understood here as the tendency of the productive forces to develop and thereby to come into conflict with the prevailing relations of production – that is, the relations of economic control over these productive forces. The conflict between the forces and relations of production gives rise to an intensification of the class struggle and this creates the conditions for a social revolution that, by replacing the existing relations of production with new ones that permit a further development of the productive forces, inaugurate a different mode of production.

This theory of history is often dismissed as 'technological determinist', but this is only so if social revolution is treated as inevitable.[13] In the opening passage of the *Manifesto of the Communist Party*, Marx and Engels wrote that the class struggle 'each time ended, *either* in a revolutionary reconstitution of society at large, *or* in the common ruin of the contending classes.'[14] This suggests a degree of indeterminacy: is it the course of the class struggle that selects which of these alternatives actually prevails? The relatively open character of the 1859 preface itself is indicated by its importance for Antonio Gramsci (1891–1937) in his *Prison Notebooks*, which sought to develop a much fuller account of the role played by political and ideological superstructures in social revolution. But, in any case, it seems reasonably clear that for Marx the class struggle plays an executive role, acting, not as the fundamental source of historical transformations, but as the means through which they are effected.[15]

Let us turn, secondly, to the more complex understanding of the class struggle in *Capital* (1867). The structure of this work is articulated through an analysis of the production, circulation, and distribution of surplus-value, which form the subject matter of, respectively, the three volumes. By demonstrating that the source of the capitalist's profits lie in the extraction of surplus-value from wage labourers producing

---

[12] L. Althusser, *Réponse à John Lewis* (Paris: Maspero, 1973), p. 26.
[13] See, for example, Althusser's critique of the 1859 preface in *Sur la reproduction* (Paris: Presses Universitaires de France, 1995), pp. 243–52.
[14] Marx and Engels, *Manifesto of the Communist Party*, p. 382; italics added.
[15] The most powerful case for this interpretation of historical materialism, and of the place of the class struggle within it, is offered in G. A. Cohen, *Karl Marx's Theory of History – A Defence* (Oxford: Clarendon, 1978); see also G. A. Cohen, *History, Labour, and Freedom: Themes from Marx* (Oxford: Oxford University Press, 1988), pp. 14–20.

commodities Marx made exploitation, and hence class antagonism, constitutive of capitalism. This put the class struggle implicitly (and sometimes explicitly) at the centre of *Capital*. The process through which surplus-value is created and extracted from workers in production is necessarily a process of class struggle. This comes out most clearly in the famous chapter 10 of *Capital*, volume I, 'The Working Day'. Here Marx portrayed the extremes that British capitalists sought to go in order to lengthen working hours and thereby to increase the amount of absolute surplus-value they extracted from their workers. But he also showed the forms of resistance that workers developed, culminating in political movements that succeeded in winning legislation that restricted the working day.

But it is a sign of the complexity of Marx's treatment of the class struggle that he sought to contextualize this struggle, pointing in the first place that the workers' intervention solved the collective action problem that had confronted capitalists, since they had a common interest in preventing the destruction of labour power produced by excessively long working hours but were unable to do so individually because of the pressure of competition from their rivals. Second, state-imposed restrictions on the working day encouraged capitalists to shift towards the production of relative surplus-value, which involves raising the rate of exploitation through a higher productivity of labour achieved through the introduction of new, more advanced means of production.

The concept of relative surplus-value underlines one of Marx's most important themes, the accumulation of capital as a process in which rival capitals respond to competitive pressures by investing in expanded and more efficient production, thereby developing the productive forces. But it also allows Marx to portray the process of technological innovation as itself a form of class struggle. Thus he wrote in *Capital*, volume I: 'It would be possible to write quite a history of the inventions, made since 1830, for the sole purpose of supplying capital with weapons against the revolts of the working class. At the head of these in importance, stands the self-acting mule, because it opened up a new epoch in the automatic system.'[16] In the much more extensive discussion of technology in the *Economic Manuscript of 1861–63*, Marx used the name the workers gave to this key labour-saving innovation in the cotton industry – the iron man – to symbolize the domination of dead over living labour:

Here too past labour – in the automaton and the machinery moved by it – steps forth as acting apparently in independence of [living] labour, it subordinates labour instead of being subordinate to it, it is the iron man confronting the man of flesh and blood. The subsumption of his labour under capital – the absorption

---

[16] K. Marx, *Capital*, volume I, MECW, vol. 35, p. 439.

of his labour by capital – which lies in the nature of capitalist production, appears here as a technological fact.[17]

The peculiarly intense development of the productive forces under capitalism plays, as one would expect, an important role in Marx's account of economic crises. Setting out the famous 'Law of the Tendency of the Rate of Profit to Fall' in part 3 of *Capital*, volume III, Marx argued that the competitive struggle among capitalist forms encourages them to invest increasingly heavily in means of production. This reduces their costs of production per unit, but it also tends to lead to a rising organic composition of capital – that is, the ratio between capital invested in means of production and capital invested in the employment of labour power. But, since, according to the labour theory of value that Marx inherited from Ricardo, labour is the source of new value, a rising organic composition of capital implies a fall in the rate of profit. This process, in which rising productivity finds expression in falling profitability, is the capitalist determination of the transhistorical tendency for the forces of production to come into conflict with the relations of production.[18]

So, Marx, unlike contemporary neo-Ricardian economists as well as some Marxists, did not see economic crises as arising directly from the conflict between capital and labour – for example, because of an increase in wages that brings down the rate of profit.[19] Marx's more complex theory of profit allowed for the possibility, ruled out by Ricardo, that profits and wages could rise simultaneously. In *Capital*, volume I, he wrote that 'the rate of accumulation is the independent, not the dependent, variable; the rate of wages, the dependent, not the independent, variable'.[20] In other words, fluctuations in wages reflect those in the rate of capital accumulation, regulated in particular by changes in the reserve army of labour as workers are drawn into or expelled from the productive process. Marx indeed argues in *Value, Price and Profit* that 'the very development of modern industry must progressively turn the scale in favour of the capitalist against the working man, and that consequently the general tendency of capitalistic production is not to raise, but to sink the average standard of wages'.[21]

---

[17] Marx, *Economic Manuscript of 1861–63*, p. 30.
[18] See K. Marx, *Capital*, volume III, MECW, vol. 37, p. 248, and the discussion of Marx's theory of crises in A. Callinicos, *Deciphering* Capital*: Marx's* Capital *and Its Destiny* (London: Bookmarks, 2014), ch. 6.
[19] See, for example, I. Steedman, *Marx after Sraffa* (London: NLB, 1977), A. Negri, *Marx beyond Marx: Lessons on the* Grundrisse (South Hadley, MA: Bergin & Garvey, 1984), P. Armstrong, J. Harrison, and A. Glyn, *Capitalism since World War II: The Making and Breakup of the Great Boom* (London: Fontana, 1984).
[20] Marx, *Capital*, volume I, p. 615.
[21] K. Marx, *Value, Price and Profit*, MECW, vol. 20, p. 148.

5.3 Politics

The fact that the class struggle under capitalism is not the originator of crises did not diminish its importance for Marx. The idea that 'crises are always but momentary and forcible *solutions* of the existing contradictions' implies that there is no tendency for capitalism to break down economically (contrary to theorizations offered by later Marxists such as Rosa Luxemburg and Henryk Grossman).[22] Consistent with Marx's overall theory of history, the class struggle in capitalism acts as the executor of structural tendencies. This is very clear in chapter 32 of *Capital*, volume I, 'Historical Tendency of Capitalist Accumulation', where Marx showed the increasing socialization of production as occurring in the context of the ever greater concentration and centralization of capital, thanks to which 'grows the mass of misery, oppression, slavery, degradation, exploitation; but with this too grows the revolt of the working class, a class always increasing in numbers, and disciplined, united, organized by the very mechanism of the process of capitalist production itself', leading to the overthrow of capital.[23]

But this 'revolt of the working class' that overcomes the conflict between the forces and relations of production is not an instantaneous act. Marx conceived the class struggle as itself a process undergoing stages. This idea is already present in his writings of the 1840s. This Marx traced in *The Poverty of Philosophy* the development of the workers' movement from 'partial combinations' to wage-specific economic battles, through the development of permanent trade unions, to the formation of political organization:

> Large-scale industry concentrates in one place a crowd of people unknown to one another. Competition divides their interests. But the maintenance of wages, this common interest which they have against their boss, unites them in a common thought of resistance – *combination*. Thus combination always has a double aim, that of stopping competition among the workers, so that they can carry on general competition with the capitalist. If the first aim of resistance was merely the maintenance of wages, combinations, at first isolated, constitute themselves into groups as the capitalists in their turn unite for the purpose of repression, and in the face of always united capital, the maintenance of the association becomes more necessary to them than that of wages ... In this struggle – a veritable civil war – all the elements necessary for a coming battle unite and develop. Once it has reached this point, association takes on a political character.

---

[22] Marx, *Capital*, volume III, p. 248; italics added. Compare R. Luxemburg, 'The Accumulation of Capital: A Contribution to the Economic Theory of Imperialism', in P. Hudis and P. Le Blanc (eds), *Complete Works of Rosa Luxemburg*, vol. II (London: Verso, 2015) and Henryk Grossman, *The Law of Accumulation and Breakdown of the Capitalist System* (London: Pluto, 1992).

[23] Marx, *Capital*, volume I, p. 750.

Economic conditions had first transformed the mass of the people of the country into workers. The combination of capital has created for this mass a common situation, common interests. This mass is thus already a class as against capital, but not yet for itself. In the struggle, of which we have noted only a few phases, this mass becomes united, and constitutes itself as a class for itself. The interests it defends become class interests. But the struggle of class against class is a political struggle.[24]

In delineating this trajectory (which he also outlined in the *Manifesto of the Communist Party*), Marx was generalizing from the experience of the British workers' movement, from militant trade unionism to Chartism, which Engels had already closely studied in *The Condition of the Working Class in England*.[25] The significance of Chartism was that, by campaigning for manhood suffrage, it transformed British factory labourers' economic grievances into a political movement that, Marx believed, represented a direct challenge to bourgeois domination of the state. The significance for Marx of this transition from economic to political survived the defeat of Chartism in 1848. Thus, he and Engels sought in the debates with Mikhail Bakunin (1814–76) and his supporters in the International Working Men's Association (IWMA) to insist on the necessity of working-class political action. Marx clarifies the specificity of political struggle in a letter to Friedrich Bolte (1896–1959) on 23 November 1871:

every movement in which the working class comes out as a *class* against the ruling classes and attempts to coerce them by pressure from without is a political movement. For instance, the attempt in a particular factory or even a particular trade, to force a shorter working day out of the individual capitalists by strikes, etc., is a purely economic movement. The movement to force through an eight-hour *law*, etc., however, is a *political* movement. And in this way, out of the separate economic movements of the workers there grows up everywhere a *political* movement, that is to say a movement of the *class*, with the object of achieving its interests in a general form, in a form possessing general, socially binding force ... Where the working class is not yet far enough advanced in its organization to undertake a decisive campaign against the collective power, ie, the political power, of the ruling classes, it must at any rate be trained for this by continual agitation against, and a hostile attitude towards the policies of the ruling classes.[26]

This text also underlines one of the abiding themes of Marx's treatment of the class struggle in capitalism, namely its transformative effect on the working class itself. Workers, through organizing to defend their

---

[24] Marx, *Poverty of Philosophy*, pp. 210–11.
[25] Marx and Engels, *Manifesto of the Communist Party*, pp. 492–4; A. Gilbert, *Marx's Politics: Communists and Citizens* (Oxford: Martin Robertson, 1981), ch. III.
[26] 'K. Marx to F. Bolte, 23 November 1871', MECW, vol. 44, p. 258.

collective economic interests, progressively overcome their fragmentation and passivity, shaping themselves into a political subject capable not simply of resisting capital, but of replacing it altogether. In the 1840s, this view of the effects of class struggle on working-class consciousness and organization set Marx and Engels apart from other socialist and communist tendencies, which saw strikes and trade unions as symptoms of the dysfunctional character of bourgeois society, lacking any positive content of their own. Thus, in breaking with the Communist League in 1850, they declared: 'we say to the workers: You have 15, 20, 50 years of civil war to go through to alter the situation and to train yourselves for the exercise of power'.[27] As we have seen, Marx understood workers' trade union struggles as 'a veritable civil war': these struggles had for him a significance that transcended their specific objectives, through helping to give workers the consciousness, confidence, and self-organization required for them to become a collective political subject.

When initially formulated in the second half of the 1840s, this conception of the class struggle suffered from a serious contradiction. In *The Poverty of Philosophy*, Marx embraced the content of Ricardo's version of classical political economy, including the so-called iron law of wages, according to which, thanks to Thomas Robert Malthus's (1766–1834) law of population, real wages tend towards the level of bare physical subsistence. This theory was used by economists and many socialists to argue that trade union struggles were futile. Marx accepted the theory but rejected this conclusion. Rather than ignoring the apparent contradiction, he embraced it, for example, in the lecture 'Wages' he gave in Brussels in December 1847:

> All these objections of the bourgeois economists are ... correct, but only correct from their point of view. If in the associations it really were a matter only of what it appears to be, namely the fixing of wages, if the relationship between labour and capital were eternal, these combinations would be wrecked on the necessity of things. But they are the means of uniting the working class, of preparing for the overthrow of the entire old society with its class contradictions. And from this standpoint the workers are right to laugh at the clever bourgeois schoolmasters who reckon up to them what this civil war is costing them in fallen, injured, and financial sacrifices. He who wants to beat his adversary will not discuss with him the costs of the war.[28]

Marx subsequently moved to a more stable position. In the *London Notebooks* of 1850–53, he developed a critique of various aspects of

---

[27] K. Marx, 'Meeting of the Central Authority September 15, 1850', MECW, vol. 10, p. 626.
[28] K. Marx, 'Wages', MECW, vol. 6, p. 436.

Ricardo's political economy, including the theory of wages.[29] Already in the articles he wrote for the *New-York Daily Tribune* about the Preston textile workers' lockout of 1853–54, Marx stressed that the fluctuations in wages and profits caused by the business cycle gave workers the opportunity at least temporarily to improve their position. But his rejection of the iron law of wages was most fully developed over a decade later, in *Value, Price and Profit*, Marx's contribution to a debate at the General Council of the IWMA in May 1865. In response to the argument of the Owenite, John Weston, that trade union struggles were economically futile, Marx argued that the division of new value between wages and profits was, in principle, indeterminate:

> But as to profits, there exists no law which determines their minimum. We cannot say what is the ultimate limit of their decrease. And why cannot we fix that limit? Because, although we can fix the minimum of wages, we cannot fix their maximum. We can only say that, the limits of the working day being given, the maximum of profit corresponds to the physical minimum of wages; and that wages being given, the maximum of profit corresponds to such a prolongation of the working day as is compatible with the physical forces of the labourer. The maximum of profit is therefore limited by the physical minimum of wages and the physical maximum of the working day. It is evident that between the two limits of the maximum rate of profit and immense scale of variations is possible. The fixation of its actual degree is only settled by the continuous struggle between capital and labour, the capitalist constantly tending to reduce wages to their physical minimum, and to extend the working day to its physical maximum, while the working man constantly presses in the opposite direction.
>
> The matter resolves itself into a question of the respective powers of the combatants.[30]

Marx concluded that trade union struggles were economically rational, since, in the right conditions, they could increase both real wages and even the relative wage (the share of new value taken by workers). As he was to argue more fully in *Capital*, volume I, however, the capitalists retained the ultimate sanction of responding to higher wages by introducing labour-saving technology and laying workers off, thereby increasing the industrial reserve army and shifting the balance of power in their favour. This underlined the necessity of political action directed at the system itself, but did not imply that 'the working class ought to renounce their resistance against the encroachments of capital ... By cowardly giving way in their everyday conflict with capital, they would certainly disqualify themselves for the initiating of any larger movement.'[31]

---

[29] See, *Globalization and the Critique of Political Economy: New Insights from Marx's Writings* (London: Routledge, 2015), pp. 101–4.
[30] Marx, *Value, Price and Profit*, pp. 145–6.   [31] Ibid, p. 148.

Here again we see Marx stressing the educative role of the class struggle in training workers to becoming a governing class. He also developed a more nuanced understanding of the relationship between class struggle and forms of politics apparently unrelated to class. This can be seen, for example, in his shifting attitude to the national question, most notably with respect to Ireland. In the late 1860s, Marx came to the conclusion that it was in the interest of the British working class to support the cause of Irish independence. He wrote to Ludwig Kugelmann (1828–1902) on 29 November 1869:

> Every movement of the working class in England itself is crippled by the dissension with the Irish, who form a very important section of the working class in England itself. The *primary condition* for emancipation here – the overthrow of the English landed oligarchy – remains unattainable, since its positions cannot be stormed here as long as it holds its strongly-entrenched outposts in Ireland.[32]

The second element of Marx's argument – that Irish independence would undermine the foundations of class domination in Britain itself ('Ireland lost, the British "Empire" is gone, and the class war in England, till now somnolent and chronic, will assume acute forms', he told Laura (1845–1911) and Paul Lafargue (1842–1911) on 5 March 1870) – was mistaken.[33] Liberal and Unionist administrations implemented substantial land reform in Ireland in the late nineteenth and early twentieth centuries, helping to create a substantial class of prosperous Catholic peasants – a development that helped to ensure that, when southern Irish independence eventually came in 1922–23, it left the British Empire largely unshaken. But the idea – most fully developed in a slightly later letter to Sigfrid Meyer (1840–72) and August Vogt (1830–83) of 9 April 1870 – that Irish subjection to Britain fostered quasi-racial divisions between native Protestant British workers and Catholic Irish migrants within the metropolis itself, and thereby constituted 'the *secret of the impotence of the English working class*, despite its organization', represented an important intellectual breakthrough.[34] This insight was capable of generalization in different directions. On the one hand, it drew attention to the mechanisms of divide-and-rule that could help reproduce capitalist society and keep workers in a subordinate position; on the other, it pointed towards Lenin's argument that the Communist movement should support the right of self-determination of oppressed nations as a means of uniting the working class internationally and rallying broader forces against imperialism.

---

[32] 'K. Marx to L. Kugelmann, 29 November 1869', MECW, vol. 43, p. 389.
[33] 'K. Marx to L. and P. Lafargue, 5 March 1870', MECW, vol. 43, p. 449.
[34] 'K. Marx to S. Meyer and A. Vogt, 9 April 1870', MECW, vol. 43, p. 474.

5.4 Assessment

The most problematic aspect of Marx's conception of class struggle is his tendency to view it not simply as an evolutionary process, but as one that must be understood teleologically. He stated this most explicitly in the chapter on the 'Historical Tendency of Capitalist Accumulation' in *Capital*, volume I: 'capitalist production begets, with the inexorability of a law of Nature [*mit der Notwendigkeit eines Naturprozesses*], its own negation'.[35] But the same propensity arguably underlay Marx's relative indifference to the problem of political organization. Thus, he wrote in the *Manifesto of the Communist Party* of the 'organization of the proletarians into a class, and, consequently into a political party'.[36] But the specific form taken by this 'party' is quite indeterminate.[37]

This attitude is understandable enough given Marx's historical circumstances. His practical political experience embraced different organizational forms, from secret underground revolutionary groups such as the Communist League, to the IWMA, a broad coalition of different socialist tendencies and British trade unionists. Moreover, he sought to conceptualize socialist revolution as a process of working-class self-emancipation; this encouraged him to stress the significance of elemental mass movements in comparison with the conspiracies of communist sects. But the emergence of mass working-class parties, often declaring their allegiance to Marx's own ideas, meant that the problem of organization could not be ignored by later Marxists, most notably the generation of Lenin and Luxemburg. Gramsci magisterially linked addressing this problem to the effort to develop a more elaborated understanding of what he insisted on treating as the plurality of superstructures constituting the realms of 'civil' and 'political' society.[38]

A theory of class struggle moreover implies a theory of class structure. Notoriously, Marx's fullest treatments of actual class relations are to be found in his political writings on France; he left open their relationship to the more abstract theory of class structure implicit but undeveloped in *Capital*.[39] The work of the contemporary Marxist sociologist Erik Olin Wright (1947–2019) is notable for the sustained effort it undertakes to

---

[35] Marx, *Capital*, volume I, p. 751.
[36] Marx and Engels, *Manifesto of the Communist Party*, p. 493.
[37] See, for example, 'K. Marx to F. Freilgrath, 29 February 1860', MECW, vol. 41, pp. 82, 87.
[38] See, for example, A. Gramsci, *Quaderni del carcere*, V. Gerratana (ed.) (Turin: Einaudi, 1975); vol. II, pp. 751–64, vol. III, pp. 1555–652.
[39] Explorations of this relationship will be found in S. Ossowski, *Class Structure in the Social Consciousness* (London: RKP, 1963), part 1 and N. Poulantzas, *Political Power and Social Classes* (London: NLB, 1973).

integrate a rigorously articulated theory of class rooted in Marx's political economy with systematic study of empirical trends.[40]

The lacunae Marx left behind do not diminish the significance of his theory of class struggle. Even if he did not originate the idea of class struggle itself, its integration into his theory of history and critique of political economy gave it far greater analytical depth. Later Marxist historians would also greatly extend its range. Some of the most impressive achievements have been by the school of British Marxist historians that emerged after the Second World War – Christopher Hill (1912–2003), Rodney Hilton (1916–2002), Eric Hobsbawm (1917–2012), and Edward P. Thompson (1924–93), among others. Thompson's famous *The Making of the English Working Class* (1963) transformed the terrain of the Industrial Revolution, which had provided Engels and Marx with their own starting point. Another work by a historian of the same generation (although not, like the others, associated with the Communist Party of Great Britain), Geoffrey de Ste Croix's (1910–2000) *The Class Struggle in the Ancient Greek World* (1981), demonstrated the fertility of Marx's ideas as a source of historical interpretation, in this case of classical antiquity.

Of course, the theory of class struggle has constantly been criticized, from Max Weber (1864–1920) to Michel Foucault (1926–84), for its allegedly partial and reductive character. The influence of poststructuralism in the past generation has tended to demote class to one of a multiplicity of antagonisms – gender, race, sexual orientation, nationality, and so on – each with its own specific character irreducible to any of the others.[41] It can be no part of any Marxist response to deny the existence or the importance of non-class antagonisms. But it is still open to Marxists to argue that class and class struggle, because they are rooted in the structure of production, has a more fundamental explanatory role.

This is, for example, the line taken by de Ste Croix. He anchors the Marxist conception class in exploitation: '*Class* (essentially a relationship) is the collective social expression of the fact of exploitation, the way in which exploitation is embodied in a social structure.' He then goes to argue that Weber's alternative conceptualization of class largely in terms of status as descriptive rather than explanatory:

---

[40] For example, E. O. Wright, *Class Structure and Income Determination* (New York: Academic Press, 1979), *Classes* (London: Verso, 1985), and *Class Counts* (Cambridge: Cambridge University Press, 1997).

[41] Some of the most effective critiques have been influenced by Weber: F. Parkin, *Marxism and Class Theory: A Bourgeois Critique* (London: Tavistock, 1979), and M. Mann, *The Sources of Social Power*, vol. I (Cambridge: Cambridge University Press, 1986).

The 'status groups' and even the 'classes' of Weber are not necessarily (like Marx's classes) in any *organic relationship* with one another and consequently they are not dynamic in character but merely lie side by side, so to speak, like numbers in a row. Class in Marx's sense ... is essentially a relationship, and the members of any one class are necessarily related *as such*, in different degrees, to those of other classes. The members of a Weberian class or status group *as such*, on the other hand, need not have any necessary relationship to the membership of any other class or status group *as such*; and even where a relationship exists ... it will rarely involve anything more than efforts by *individuals* to rise up in the social scale – a feature of human society so general and obvious that it hardly helps us to *understand* or *explain* anything except in the trite and innocuous way.[42]

This argument is capable of much fuller development and extension. For example, Foucault developed a historical account of the specifically 'modern' forms of power-knowledge that he sought to describe using concepts such as the disciplines, security, and governmentality.[43] But this account presupposes an understanding of the development of capitalism that Foucault effectively helped himself to from Marx (all the while abusing Marxism). Spelling out the connections, which Foucault completely failed to do, might well reinstate the explanatory centrality of Marx's critique of political economy.

Indeed, the era in which poststructuralism has flourished is, what it is now commonplace to call, neo-liberalism. One way of characterizing this version of capitalism is to say that it represents a very one-sided form of class struggle, in which capital has been remarkably successful in removing many of the obstacles that had previously limited the scope of the processes of exploitation and competition. These processes of class struggle also have gendered, racial, and imperial dimensions. Their effects have been greatly to weaken and to fragment the organized workers' movement in the North. But another aspect of the same process has been the massive extension of industrial capitalism in Asia, above all thanks to China's incorporation in the world market, which has led to a substantial growth in the global working class, although the associated forms of organization and consciousness still remain inchoate. One of the main thrusts of contemporary Marxist political economy has been to decode the particular forms taken by these transformations, to puzzle out how they have proved possible, and to explore their political implications. Even non-Marxists such as Thomas Piketty (1971–) have offered their own version of this diagnosis, in Piketty's case, analyzing the growth

---

[42] G. de Ste Croix, *The Class Struggle in the Ancient Greek World* (London: Duckworth, 1981), pp. 43, 90.

[43] For example, M. Foucault, *Security, Territory, Population: Lectures at the Collège de France, 1978*, M. Senellart (ed.) (Basingstoke: Palgrave Macmillan, 2007).

in economic inequality in recent decades.[44] This suggests that Marx's theory of class struggle continues to offer at least some guidance to the present, even if many would doubt if it offers any means of escape from it. It remains to be seen whether they are right.

References

Althusser, Louis (1973), *Réponse à John Lewis*, Paris: Maspero.
(1995), *Sur la reproduction*, Paris: Presses Universitaires de France.
Armstrong, Philip, Harrison, John, and Glyn, Andrew (1984), *Capitalism since World War II: The Making and Breakup of the Great Boom*, London: Fontana.
Balibar, Étienne (1995), *The Philosophy of Marx*, London: Verso.
Callinicos, Alex (2007), *Social Theory: A Historical Introduction*, Cambridge: Polity.
(2014), *Deciphering* Capital*: Marx's* Capital *and Its Destiny*, London: Bookmarks.
Cohen, G. A. (1978), *Karl Marx's Theory of History – A Defence*, Oxford: Clarendon.
(1988), *History, Labour, and Freedom: Themes from Marx*, Oxford: Oxford University Press.
Draper, Hal (1978), *Karl Marx's Theory of Revolution*, vol. 2, New York: Monthly Review Press.
Eagleton, Terry (2011), *Why Marx Was Right*, New Haven, CT: Yale University Press.
Foucault, Michel (2007), *Security, Territory, Population: Lectures at the Collège de France, 1978*, Michel Senellart (ed.), Basingstoke: Palgrave Macmillan.
Gilbert, Alan (1981), *Marx's Politics: Communists and Citizens*, Oxford: Martin Robertson.
Gramsci, Antonio (1975), *Quaderni del carcere*, Valentino Gerratana (ed.), Turin: Einaudi.
Grossman, Henryk (1992), *The Law of Accumulation and Breakdown of the Capitalist System*, London: Pluto.
Guizot, F. P. G. (1997), *History of Civilization in Europe*, London: Harmondsworth.
Harvey, David (2010), *A Commentary on Marx's* Capital, London: Verso.
Hegel, G. W. F. (2010), *The Science of Logic*, Cambridge: Cambridge University Press.
Luxemburg, Rosa (2015), 'The Accumulation of Capital: A Contribution to the Economic Theory of Imperialism', in Peter Hudis and Paul Le Blanc (eds), *Complete Works of Rosa Luxemburg*, vol. II, London: Verso.
Mann, Michael (1986), *The Sources of Social Power*, vol. I, Cambridge: Cambridge University Press.
Marx, Karl (1976), 'The Poverty of Philosophy. Answer to the Philosophy of Poverty by M. Proudhon', MECW, vol. 6, pp. 105–212.
(1976), 'Wages', MECW, vol. 6, pp. 415–37.

---

[44] T. Piketty, *Capital in the 21st Century* (Cambridge, MA: Harvard University Press, 2014).

et al. (1978), 'Meeting of the Central Authority September 15, 1850', MECW, vol. 10, p. 625–30.
(1985), *Value, Price and Profit*, MECW, vol. 20, pp. 101–49.
(1989), *The Economic Manuscript of 1861–63*, MECW, vol. 31.
(1994), *The Economic Manuscript of 1861–63*, MECW, vol. 34.
(1996), *Capital*, volume I, MECW, vol. 35.
(1998), *Capital*, volume III, MECW, vol. 37.
Marx, Karl, and Engels, Fredrick (1976), *Manifesto of the Communist Party*, MECW, vol. 6, pp. 477–519.
(1983), *Letters, 1852–55*, MECW, vol. 39.
(1985), *Letters, 1860–1864*, MECW, vol. 41.
(1988), *Letters, 1868–70*, MECW, vol. 43.
(1989), *Letters, 1870–73*, MECW, vol. 44.
Negri, Antonio (1984), *Marx beyond Marx: Lessons on the* Grundrisse, South Hadley, MA: Bergin & Garvey.
Ossowski, Stanislaw (1963), *Class Structure in the Social Consciousness*, London: RKP.
Parkin, Frank (1979), *Marxism and Class Theory: A Bourgeois Critique*, London: Tavistock.
Piketty, Thomas (2014), *Capital in the 21st Century*, Cambridge, MA: Harvard University Press.
Poulantzas, Nikos (1973), *Political Power and Social Classes*, London: NLB.
Pradella, Lucia (2015), *Globalization and the Critique of Political Economy: New Insights from Marx's Writings*, London: Routledge.
Raico, Ralph (1993), 'Classical Liberal Roots of the Marxist Doctrine of Classes', in Yuri Maltsev (ed.), *Requiem for Marx*, Auburn, AL: Praxeology Press, pp. 189–220.
Sraffa, Piero (ed.) (1951–2), *The Works and Correspondence of David Ricardo*, eleven vols, Cambridge: Cambridge University Press.
de Ste Croix, Geoffrey (1981), *The Class Struggle in the Ancient Greek World*, London: Duckworth.
Steedman, Ian (1977), *Marx after Sraffa*, London: NLB.
Thompson, E. P. (1980), *The Making of the English Working Class*, Harmondsworth: Penguin.
Wright, Eric O. (1979), *Class Structure and Income Determination*, New York: Academic Press.
(1985), *Classes*, London: Verso.
(1997), *Class Counts*, Cambridge: Cambridge University Press.

6 Political Organization

Peter Hudis

6.1 The Philosophical Basis of Marx's Concept of Organization

Although Karl Marx was actively involved in revolutionary organizations throughout his life and developed some of his most important ideas while participating in them, his contribution to political organization is one of the least discussed aspects of his body of work. Even while he was still alive, many of Marx's followers (as well as his critics) held that his organizational contributions paled in comparison with those of other leading socialists and communists of the time. This view became far more widespread in the twentieth century, when Leninist conceptions of political leadership and party building became predominant in the Marxist movement. The fact that Marx, unlike Lenin (1870–1924), never developed a theory of organization may be part of the reason for the general neglect of his work as an organizational activist and thinker. But it can hardly explain all of it, since it is certainly possible to have a distinctive *concept* of organization while refraining from developing an explicit organizational *theory*.[1] The tendency to neglect the former makes it harder to grasp the *internal coherence* of Marx's overall project of human emancipation. The *basis* of Marx's concept of organization is discernable as early as 1843:

We develop new principles for the world out of the world's own principles. We do not say to the world: cease your struggles, they are foolish, we will give you the true watchword of the struggle. We merely show the world what it is really fighting for, and consciousness is something that it *has* to acquire, even if it does not want to. The reform of consciousness consists *only* in making the world aware of its own consciousness ... in *explaining* to it the meaning of its own actions.[2]

---

[1] See J. Cunliffe, 'Marx, Engels and the Party', *History of Political Thought*, 2 (2): 349 (1981): 'There could be no theory of the "party" as an immutable organizational form [in Marx] because there was no place for one given the principle of self-emancipation of the class and the rejection of sectarianism.' I nevertheless differ from his claim that this infers that Marx lacked a *concept* of organization.

[2] K. Marx, 'Letters from *Deutsch-Französische Jahrbücher*', MECW, vol. 3, p. 144.

Marx was here expressing a key insight of Hegelian dialectics: that the object generates its own categories of knowledge. The task of the theoretician is not to *impose* upon the object of investigation an arbitrary plan or schema, but rather capture and explicate its *self-movement*. Marx elaborated upon this later in 1843, as follows: 'Revolutions require a passive element, a material basis ... It is not enough for thought to strive for realization, reality must also strive towards thought.'[3] He now identified the force *within* the material realm that could realize the idea of freedom without turning away from philosophy *tout court*. On these grounds, he took issue with what he called 'the practical political party', which embraces reality at the expense of philosophy, and 'the party originating from philosophy', which fails to grasp the actual movement of history.[4] He was looking for a party of a *new* type that surmounts the one-sidedness of both tendencies.

To be sure, these early writings refer to the party in a broad sense – as an organized embodiment of ideas – rather than an instrument for securing state power. Nevertheless, they serve as the basis of the concept of organization that he developed for the rest of his life. Political parties for Marx were about much more than the exercise of power or domination. They are forms for intervening in reality on the basis of ideas that have proven their historical objectivity. For this reason, he often referred to 'the party' even when it consisted of no more than he and Friedrich Engels.[5]

6.2 Marx on Political Organization before and during the 1848 Revolutions

Marx's discovery of the proletariat as the revolutionary class had direct *organizational* ramifications, since he immediately sought to make contact with workers. Upon arriving in the Paris at the end of 1843 he met with 'materialist communists' (most of whom were artisans) and rank-and-file workers. He voiced his enthusiasm in a letter to Ludwig Feuerbach (1804–72): 'You would have to attend one of the meetings of the French workers to appreciate the pure freshness, the nobility which burst forth from these toil-worn men.' In them he saw the work of 'history preparing the practical element for the emancipation of mankind.'[6]

Subsequently, Marx spent six weeks in England in the summer of 1845, where he met with Chartist leaders and agreed to the idea of forming an international organization of democratic working-class forces for the

---

[3] K. Marx, 'Contribution to the Critique of Hegel's Philosophy of Right: Introduction', MECW, vol. 3, p. 183.
[4] Ibid, p. 180. [5] 'K. Marx to F. Lassalle, 12 November 1858', MECW, vol. 40, p. 354.
[6] 'K. Marx to L. Feuerbach, 11 August 1844', MECW, vol. 3, p. 355.

exchange of information. This led to the September 1845 formation (in London) of the Society of Fraternal Democrats. Marx did not attend its founding meeting. But this hardly reflected a lack of interest in organization. He was now pursuing the idea of forming an international organization for the exchange of information based on *communist* principles. This resulted, in February 1846, in his co-founding (along with Engels and the Belgian communist Philippe Gigot [1819–60]) of the Communist Correspondence Committees (CCCs). He spelt out its mission to Pierre-Joseph Proudhon (1809–65):

> [It will consist of] a constant interchange of letters which will be devoted to discussing scientific questions ... the chief aim our correspondence, however, will be to put the German socialists in touch with the French and English socialists ... It will be a step made by the social movements in its *literary* manifestation to rid itself of the barriers of *nationality*.[7]

The CCCs soon emerged as an incipient political party – especially when Chartists and German exiles living in England were brought on board. Chartist leader Julian Harney (1817–97) agreed to join it; so did members of the League of the Just (Marx had earlier met their German members in London in 1845). The CCCs was hardly a monolithic group: sharp differences emerged between Marx and Wilhelm Weitling (1808–71) at the start of 1846, which led Weitling to leave the group. Yet, as early as 1846, the basic features of Marx's concept of organization was embodied in the group, insofar as it emphasized the need for independent proletarian organization, internationalism, and for a group based on definite revolutionary *ideas*.[8]

But what specific ideas were at issue? Communists at the time were few in number, and they tended to be artisans, not industrial workers – especially in backward Germany, where the former outnumbered the latter five to one. The material conditions did not permit a 'strong and organized Communist Party' to directly push for proletarian revolution. Instead, as Marx argued in a circular to G. A. Köttgen (1805–82), it was necessary to ally with the progressive bourgeoisie to promote democracy – the condition best suited for developing proletarian consciousness: 'push forward the bourgeois petitions for freedom of the press, a constitution, and so on. When this has been achieved, a new era will dawn for communist propaganda. Our means

---

[7] 'K. Marx to P. Proudhon, 5 May 1846', MECW, vol. 38, pp. 38–9.
[8] 'The Communist Correspondence Committees reveals a distinguishing feature of the Marx-Engels team at the very outset – a recognition of the need to organize to make ideas influential.' See A. H. Nimtz, Jr., *Marx and Engels: Their Contribution to the Democratic Breakthrough* (Albany: State University of New York Press, 2000), p. 31.

will be increased, the antithesis between bourgeois and proletarian will be sharpened.'[9]

The specific *form* of this broader class alliance depends on a number of factors. Overemphasizing the power and democratic impulses of the bourgeoisie can lead the workers' movement into reformism and opportunism. Underemphasizing its power and democratic impulses can lead it into adventurism and sectarianism. Everything depends on a proper view of the historical conditions in which the movement finds itself. The 'Marx party' – as many refer to his group by 1846[10] – developed organizational perspectives on the basis of ideas that were *adequate* to its object.

By 1847, Marx's influence was considerable enough for the League of the Just to ask Marx to join it – in exchange for it giving up its conspiratorial, secret nature. Marx agreed, and the Brussels CCCs became a League branch. At its London Congress of June 1847 (which Marx did not attend), it changed its name to the Communist League. Marx was named a member of its central authority.

During this period, Marx also lectured at the German Workers' Educational Society and helped form the German Workers' Society[11] and Brussels Democratic Association (of which he became vice-president). These commitments consumed much time and energy, since Marx often found it necessary to take issue with those who argued for an immediate communist insurrection while bypassing alliances with the forces agitating for a democratic republic. This did not prevent him, however, from completing the book that he considered the programmatic basis of much of his organizational work – *The Poverty of Philosophy*, which criticized Proudhon's effort to apply Ricardo's quantitative determination of labor time to socialism. For Marx, political organization needed the direction provided by such comprehensive theoretical works.

The clearest expression of this is the *Manifesto of the Communist Party*, which the Communist League assigned Marx to write at the end of 1847. It contains several distinct organizational concepts: (1) While it critiques theoreticians who invent visions of the future out of their heads, it does not oppose articulating the goal itself. Communists 'merely express, in

---

[9] K. Marx and F. Engels, 'Letter from the Brussels Communist Correspondence Committee to G.A. Köttgen', MECW, vol. 6, pp. 55–6.
[10] For a fuller discussion of this issue, see M. Rubel, 'Le parti proletarian', in *Marx critique du marxisme* (Paris: Payot, 1974), pp. 183–92.
[11] This *Brussels* German Workers' Society should not be confused with the Cologne German Workers' Society, founded by Andreas Gottschalk (1815–49) at the end of 1847. Although Marx also participated in it, he developed major differences with Gottschalk over the latter's rejection of the need for an alliance with the democratic bourgeoisie.

general terms' the '*ultimate* results'[12] of the 'future of that movement'[13] based on 'the actual relations springing from existing class struggles'.[14] There is not a hint in it that intellectuals must import socialist consciousness *to* the workers from the outside. (2) It nowhere speaks of a single party to lead; instead, 'The Communists do not form a separate party opposed to other working-class parties.'[15] (3) Although the Communist League commissioned it, its name nowhere appears in it – not even in the title. It is the *Manifesto of the Communist Party* – *not* the Communist League. It appears that Marx thought of 'party' in a more elevated sense than the requirements of a particular organization. He meant 'party' in the 'eminent historical sense' – as the set of principles and practices that revolutionaries need to take responsibility for given the specific contours of the movement of history.[16]

This implies that any particular organization is ephemeral – it has to *earn* its right to exist, and if it fails to do so or has outlived its time, it needs to go under. Marx never made a fetish of organization. This underlines all of his organizational practice – especially during the all-important revolutions of 1848. Although it is not possible here to delineate Marx's activities during 1848–50, five crucial points must be noted.

First, shortly after the revolution began in France, in February 1848, and Germany (in March), Marx moved to Cologne and set to work to issue a new periodical – the *Neue Rheinische Zeitung*. This daily served as the organizing centrr for communist agitation. So crucial did he view it that Marx suggested as early as the spring of 1848 that the Communist League, which was weak in Germany, dissolve and its functions become assumed by the publication. Although the League remained in existence, the bulk of Marx's energies throughout 1848–9 centred on the *New Rhenish Newspaper* [*Neue Rheinische Zeitung*].

Second, its subtitle was *Organ of Democracy*. Given the weakness of the proletarian movement at the time, its central task, Marx argued, was demanding the expansion of democratic liberties through an alliance with the progressive elements of the bourgeoisie and petty-bourgeoisie. This did not imply a *compromise* with the latter forces, since Marx referred to the *New Rhenish Newspaper* as the *extreme left wing* of the democracy. Nor did he 'depart somewhat' from the *Manifesto of the Communist Party*'s emphasis on an independent proletarian party.[17] Instead, at issue was the

---

[12] K. Marx and F. Engels, *Manifesto of the Communist Party*, MECW, vol. 6, p. 497; emphasis added.
[13] Ibid, p. 518.   [14] Ibid, p. 498.   [15] Ibid, p. 497.
[16] See 'K. Marx to F. Freiligrath, 29 February 1860', MECW, vol. 41, p. 87.
[17] J. Molyneux makes this claim in *Marxism and the Party* (London: Pluto Press, 1978), p. 22.

role of workers as *subject* of revolution. Where that subject is too weak to stand on its own it needs to advance its cause within the broader democratic movement. This does not, however, involve downplaying proletarian subjectivity, but rather enabling it to properly function given the historical context. For by agitating for broad-based democratic liberties, the workers will be best equipped, Marx held, to press for their independent class interests as the franchise is widened. As Marx declared in its final issue of 19 May 1849, its 'last word will always and everywhere be: the emancipation of the working class!'[18]

Third, as the counter-revolution obtained the upper hand (following the June days of 1848 in France and the suppression of the uprising in Vienna), Marx argued that the proletariat must seek out new allies in the *peasantry*. Wilhelm Wolff (1809–64), one of Marx's closest friends and of peasant origin himself, did instrumental work in organizing peasants on behalf of the Marx party at the end of 1848 and 1849. At the same time, Marx became even more searing in his critique of the liberal bourgeoisie, writing:

> The bourgeoisie in *France*, however, *headed* the counter-revolution only after it had broken with all obstacles to the rule of its own class. The bourgeoisie in *Germany* meekly joins the *retinue* of the absolute monarchy and of feudalism before securing even the first conditions of existence necessary for its own freedom and its rule ... History presents no more *shameful and pitiful* spectacle than that of the *German bourgeoisie*.[19]

This recalls Marx's statement of 1843 that 'we [Germans] ... never found ourselves in the company of freedom except once – on the *day of its burial*'.[20] Marx did not have to wait for the final defeat of the 1848 revolutions to single out the treachery of the property-owning classes.

Fourth, Marx responded to the consolidation of the counter-revolution by placing greater emphasis on the need for revolutionary parties to be steeped in *theory*. In September 1848, he delivered a series of lectures to the First Vienna Workers' Association on wage labour and capital, followed by talks on the same subject to the Brussels Workers' Society (in November 1848) and the German Workers' Educational Society (in September 1849). Meanwhile, the *New Rhenish Newspaper* serialized the text of these lectures that became *Wage Labor and Capital*. Considerable resistance to this emphasis on theory soon emerged in the Communist League. August Willich (1810–78) and Karl Schapper (1812–70), who broke from Marx in 1850 over their advocacy of an armed insurrection

---

[18] K. Marx and F. Engels, 'To the Workers of Cologne', MECW, vol. 9, p. 467.
[19] K. Marx, 'The Victory of the Counter-Revolution in Vienna', MECW, vol. 7, p. 504.
[20] Marx, 'Contribution to the Critique of Hegel's Philosophy of Right', p. 183.

(led by themselves!) in Germany, argued that such appeals to 'intellect' should be set aside for the sake of 'agitating the masses'. Marx responded,

> In their view, indeed revolution consists merely in the overthrow of the existing government; once this aim has been achieved, '*the* victory' has been won ... These gentlemen also abhor thinking, unfeeling thinking ... as though any thinker, Hegel and Ricardo not excepted, had ever attained the degree of unfeelingness with which this sentimental drivel is poured over the heads of the public![21]

Fifth, Marx's work on political organization in this period is summed up in his March 1850 'Address to the Communist League'. It evaluates the experience of the 1848 revolutions and their aftermath by underlining the 'treacherous role' played by bourgeoisie, the importance of workers finding allies in the rural proletariat, and the need to continue the revolution 'in permanence'. He wrote, 'While the democratic petty bourgeoisie wish to bring the revolution to a conclusion as quickly as possible ... it is our interest and our task to make the revolution permanent.' This must be done, he insisted,

> By taking up their position as an independent party as soon as possible and by not allowing themselves to be misled for a single moment by the hypocritical phrases of the democratic petty-bourgeois into refraining from the independent party of the proletariat. Their battle cry must be: The Revolution in Permanence.[22]

This clarion call did not mean that the time had come to take communist measures. The treachery displayed by the bourgeoisie and petty-bourgeoisie does not mean that the working class suddenly has the ability to take matters into its own hands. He knew it was still not strong enough to seize political power – let alone introduce a communist economy. He was putting forth a perspective that he hoped would guide them in future struggles even as they faced the immediate task of widening the democratic franchise.

6.3   *Capital*, the First International, and the Paris Commune

With the revolutions in full retreat by 1851–52, Marx moved to disband the League at the end of 1852. It played its role in a historic moment that had now subsided. But, while the ephemeral expression of the party vanishes, the party itself – in the eminent historical sense – does not. As he wrote in 1860, 'The League, like the *société des saisons* in Paris and a hundred other societies, was simply an episode in the history of a party that is everywhere springing up naturally out of the soil of modern

---

[21] K. Marx and F. Engels, 'Review, May to October 1850', MECW, vol. 10, p. 530.
[22] K. Marx, 'Address of the Central Authority of the League, March 1850', MECW, vol. 10, pp. 281, 287.

society.'[23] As much as Marx involved himself in political parties, he was just as willing to let them die.

Marx retreated to the British Museum to research political economy and work on what became his greatest theoretical work, *Capital*. He belonged to no party or grouping in the 'wholly ephemeral sense'[24] from 1852 to 1864. Yet this did not mean a retreat from organization as such. Throughout this period, Marx referred to his work for 'the party' – by which he meant responsibility for the body of thought he had committed himself to since his break from bourgeois society. Referring to the *Grundrisse*, he wrote, 'I owe it to the Party that the thing shouldn't be disfigured by the kind of heavy, wooden style.'[25] When his *Contribution to the Critique of Political Economy* was about to come off the press in 1859, he proclaimed 'I hope to win a scientific victory for our party.'[26]

Marx understood from the inception of his political career that spontaneous forms of organization are a *necessary* but *insufficient* condition for liberation. Needed as well is an organizational expression *of ideas* that can provide direction for 'the future of that movement'.[27] Although he referred to the latter as 'the party', he clearly did not mean by it a group[28] that seeks to dominate or control spontaneous struggles from the outside. Likewise, he did not consider 'ephemeral' parties that arise from the masses as of secondary importance. As the masses produce new organizational formations, radicals – including *Marx* – are obligated to join and *engage* them with their ideas. For Marx, *proletarian* parties are not sects; they must embody 'the self-conscious, independent movement of the immense majority in the interests of the immense majority'.[29]

The greatest proof of this is Marx's involvement in the International Working Men's Association (IWMA). He neither founded it nor aspired for supreme leadership over it – although his impact on it was immense. It arose from British and French workers expressing solidarity with the Polish national liberation struggle (in a meeting of July 1863) and subsequent events in support of the North in the US Civil War. After workers in Paris positively responded to a call to form an organization uniting all working people, the IWMA was formed (in London) in September 1864. Marx participated on behalf of German workers and was appointed to

---

[23] 'K. Marx to F. Freiligrath, 20 February 1860', MECW, vol. 41, p. 82; cf. footnote 16.
[24] Ibid, p. 81. [25] 'K. Marx to F. Engels, 12 November 1858', MECW, vol. 40, p. 354.
[26] 'K. Marx to J. Weydemeyer, 1 February 1859', MECW, vol. 40, p. 377.
[27] Marx and Engels, *Manifesto of the Communist Party*, p. 518.
[28] Of course, formal, organized parties of revolutionaries – such as the Communist League – *are* needed. But these too are ephemeral: they come and go based on the contingencies of the historical moment. No single particular organizational form or expression, according to Marx, has universal applicability.
[29] Marx and Engels, *Manifesto of the Communist Party*, p. 495.

a committee to draft its bylaws and write its inaugural address, and served on its general council.

Although not as daring as the *Manifesto of the Communist Party* when it came to spelling out communist principles, the clarity of the inaugural address – which proclaimed 'To conquer political power has therefore become the great duty of the working class'[30] – propelled Marx to the leadership of the IWMA. By the time of the Geneva Congress of 1866, he admitted that for all intents and purposes he was its head.[31] Yet he took care not to present himself as any leader maximum. The IWMA was an organization *of*, not *for*, the working class. As he wrote in 1866, 'It is the business of the International Working Men's Association to combine and generalize the *spontaneous movements* of the working classes, but not to dictate or impose any doctrinary system whatever.'[32]

The European working-class movements at the time were highly diverse – ranging from trade unionists to Proudhonists opposed to unions, and from radical democrats to communists. All were part of the IWMA. Anti-capitalist currents were never dominant in it, although their influence increased over time. Marx's work in it involved a complex series of balancing acts, as he struggled to maintain organizational unity in the face of numerous internal conflicts. Yet the multi-tendency character of the IWMA, which for the first time enabled working people to cross national barriers and work together in a single organization, was a sign not of its weakness, but of its strength. Marx argued, 'Before the foundation of the International all the different organizations had been societies founded by some radicals among the ruling classes for the working classes, but the International was established by the working men for themselves.'[33]

The greatest test of the IWMA came with the Paris Commune of 1871. It did not initiate the commune, which was completely spontaneous; but, once it arose, it threw its resources into solidarity with it. Within ten days of the uprising, Marx was assigned to issue an address to the people of Paris. After sending out dozens of letters to sections of the IWMA urging them to send aid to the commune, Marx commenced writing *The Civil War in France*. It singles out its central contribution as placing 'the whole initiative hitherto exercised by the State ... into the hands of the

---

[30] MECW, vol. 20, p. 12.
[31] See K. Marx to F. Engels, 13 March 1865: 'The International Association takes up an enormous amount of time, and I am in fact the head of it', MECW, vol. 42, p. 130.
[32] K. Marx, 'Instructions for the Delegates of the Provisional General Council. The Different Questions', MECW, vol. 20, p. 190.
[33] K. Marx, 'Record of Marx's Speech on the Seventh Anniversary of the International', MECW, vol. 22, pp. 633–4.

Commune. It compelled the "old centralized government" to "give way to the self-government of the producers."[34] All of this was achieved without a single party or political tendency monopolizing power. Whereas earlier revolutions were 'forced to develop, what absolute monarchy had commenced, the centralization and organization of state power, and to expand the circumference and the attributes of the state power',[35] the Paris Commune, in contrast, sought to *dismantle* the machinery of the state through decentralized, democratic control of society by the freely associated populace.

Marx was by no means uncritical of the commune. He took issue with its failure to march on Versailles and disarm the counter-revolutionary forces that ultimately crushed it. But nowhere did he say that it failed because it lacked a centralized 'vanguard party' to lead to the struggle. On the contrary, he called the commune the proper political form or 'lever for uprooting the economical foundations upon which rests the existence of classes, and therefore of class rule'.[36] This 'expansive political form' was one that the Marx party – although a minority in the commune – directly helped advance, mainly through the efforts of Léo Frankel (1844–96) and Elisabeth Dmitrieff (1850–1910).

The defeat of the commune, and the harsh repression that accompanied it throughout Europe, radically altered the objective situation. For Marx, the decentralized, federal structure of the IWMA no longer suited the needs of the time. In response, at the London Conference in September 1871, he strongly supported the resolution of Édouard Vaillant (1840–1915) to transform the IWMA into a political party. Marx stated,

> Considering, that against this collective power of the propertied classes the working class cannot act, as a class, except by constituting itself into a political party, distinct from, and opposed to, all old parties formed by the propertied classes; That this combination of the working class into a political party is indispensable in order to ensure the triumph of the social revolution and its ultimate end – the abolition of classes.[37]

In endorsing this resolution of a supporter of Louis August Blanqui (1805–81), Marx was not endorsing his view that a proletarian party should consist of a small nucleus of professional revolutionaries. Marx

---

[34] K. Marx, *The Civil War in France. Address of the General Council of the International Working Men's Association*, MECW, vol. 22, p. 332.
[35] K. Marx, 'Drafts of *The Civil War in France*', MECW, vol. 22, p. 484.
[36] Marx, *The Civil War in France*, p. 334.
[37] K. Marx and F. Engels, 'Resolution of the Conference of Delegates of the of the International Working Men's Association Assembled at London from 17th to 23rd September 1871', MECW, vol. 22, p. 427.

had a much more expansive conception of the party in mind, grounded in the basic principles of the IWMA. Those principles, he argued, now needed to be adapted to changing circumstances by promoting a greater connection between the economic and political dimensions of working-class struggle.[38]

Although Marx stressed that the focus on a proletarian political party was consistent with the founding principles of the IWMA, which held that the social and political emancipation of the working class is inseparable, the resolution adopted at the 1871 London Conference (and reaffirmed at the 1872 Hague Congress) *did* represent a new and somewhat radical point of departure – one that the IWMA proved unable to bring to fruition. This was due, at least in part, to opposition to the new perspective from within the IWMA. Many of the British trade unionists objected to it, on the grounds that it shifted the IWMA's focus away from the economic struggle. The anarchist followers of Mikhail Bakunin (who were admitted to the IWMA in 1869) also objected, stating 'We reject and repulse at any price all compromise whatever with a purely political party.'[39] Matters were hardly resolved when Bakunin and his followers were expelled from the IWMA for wanting to establish a secret society within it, in violation of democratic norms. The IWMA was now coming apart at the seams. In light of the growing acrimony, Marx proposed that the general council be moved to New York – a move that amounted to its demise. Despite the time and energy that Marx devoted to organizations – and none consumed more of his than the IWMA – he was fully willing to let it go once its historical moment had passed.

6.4 Two Concepts of Organization: Marx versus Lassalle on the Party

Marx's organizational contributions in the 1860s and 70s also extended to debates over party formation in the German movement. Indeed, some of his most distinctive organizational conceptions were developed in the course of disputes over the influence of Ferdinand Lassalle (1825–64) in the German socialist movement.

Lassalle may not be widely discussed today, but that was not the case in the second half of the nineteenth and the early twentieth centuries. Even such a firm supporter of spontaneous self-activity as Rosa Luxemburg proclaimed,

---

[38] For a fuller discussion of this, see M. Musto, ed., *Workers Unite! The International 150 Years Later* (New York: Bloomsbury, 2014), pp. 36–51. The volume brings together many of the resolutions presented at the London Conference.

[39] See Paris section, 'On the Importance of Having a Central Organization of the Working Class', in Musto, ed., *Workers Unite!*, p. 291.

Lassalle transformed into deed the most important historical consequence of the March [1848] revolution in finally liberating the German working class, fifteen years later, from the levy-in-arms of the bourgeoisie and organizing it as an independent class party ... His immortal work does not diminish but grows more and more with the historical perspective from which we view it.[40]

Innumerable figures in the second (and later the third) IWMA presumed that 'to Lassalle, even more than to Marx, modern socialists are deeply indebted; Marx set the world of culture and arguing, Lassalle set the people organizing'.[41] More was at issue than the fact that Lassalle founded, in May 1863, the first independent German working-class party – the General Union of German Workers. No less influential was his concept that intellectuals are the vehicles of 'science' that *brings* socialist consciousness *to* the workers who cannot attain it by their own endeavour.[42] Karl Kautsky (1854–1938) and others in the second IWMA directly appropriated this notion and then passed it on to Lenin,[43] who famously proclaimed, 'Modern socialist consciousness can arise only on the basis of profound scientific knowledge ... The vehicles of science are not the proletariat, but the bourgeois intelligentsia.'[44] It is no exaggeration that what has come to be considered the 'Marxist' approach to organization largely owes its provenance to Lassalle.[45]

Marx himself, however, was far less impressed with Lassalle's 'immortal work' than his followers. In July 1862, he called Lassalle's statist-

---

[40] R. Luxemburg, 'Lassalle und die Revolution', in *Gesammelte Werke*, vol. 1.2 (Berlin: Dietz Verlag, 2000), p. 418.

[41] B. Villiers, *The Socialist Movement in England* (London: T. Fisher Unwin, 1908), p. 86.

[42] As Lassalle put it, 'The great destiny of our age is precisely this ... the dissemination of scientific knowledge among the body of the people' – the vehicle of which was intellectuals like himself. See F. Lassalle, *Science and the Workingmen* (New York: International Library, 1900), p. 44. See also L. T. Lih, *Lenin Rediscovered: 'What Is to Be Done?' in Context* (Chicago: Haymarket Books, 2006), pp. 57–61.

[43] Lih acknowledged that Lenin was a Lassallean on organizational matters: 'His current absence from historical memory must distort our view of Social-Democratic activists such as Lenin, for whom Lassalle was a hero even after all the criticisms were accepted' (*Lenin Rediscovered*, p. 60). Lih saw this not as a defect, but as the proper continuation of a tradition. He did not engage Marx's critique of Lassalle.

[44] V. I. Lenin, *What Is to Be Done? Collected Works*, vol. 2 (Moscow: International Publishers, 1943), p. 61.

[45] See R. Dunayevskaya, *Rosa Luxemburg, Women's Liberation, and Marx's Philosophy of Revolution* (Atlantic Highlands, NJ: Humanities Press, 1981), p. 154: 'Long after his death, Lassalle remained a pervasive force not only for reformists but for revolutionaries, and specifically on the point of organization ... everyone from Luxemburg to Trotsky extolled Lassalle, not only very nearly on the same level as Marx, but in fact "when it comes to organization," admitted or otherwise, he stood on a higher, that is, more concrete level.'

socialist ideas reactionary and Bonapartist.[46] When his party was formed, he made it clear to his colleagues that he would have nothing to do with it – even though Marx refrained from issuing a public condemnation.[47] A month later, he warned Wilhelm Liebknecht (1826–1900) and others in Germany not to identify with 'the Lassallean sect', as he often referred to the General Union of German Workers. And, by 1865, Marx concluded, 'There is nothing to be done with it as bequeathed by Baron Izzy. The sooner it is disbanded, the better.'[48]

To be sure, Marx bitterly opposed Lassalle's group because of its compromising efforts to obtain German government funding for its 'workers' cooperatives'. But he no less opposed Lassalle's *organizational* conception that intellectuals (like himself) were best equipped to 'lead' the workers via the consciousness that *they* instilled in them. As Marx put it, 'workers are to agitate for *general suffrage*, after which they are to send people like himself into the Chamber of Deputies, armed "with the naked sword of science"'. Lassalle, he argued, 'gives himself airs of a future workers' dictator'.[49]

Unfortunately, Marx's objections to Lassalleanism did not carry much weight with his German 'Marxist' followers. When they formed their own party (the Social Democratic Workers' Party) in 1869, Marx took issue with what he called 'the Lassalle cult' infecting it. In the next several years, he and Engels often complained that Lassalleanism was compromising the party. This became evident in late 1874, when the Social-Democratic Workers' Party began unity negotiations with the General Union of German Workers – without informing Marx or Engels.

In May 1875, Marx responded to the unification of the two groups with his *Critique of the Gotha Programme* – perhaps his most important organizational document. It ruthlessly criticizes the capitulation to Lassallean notions of the state, the peasantry, the 'iron law of wages', and its impoverished conception of communism. In attacking the program's exclusive focus on distribution at the expense of relations of production, Marx issued his fullest-ever discussion of the two phases of communism that will follow capitalism. As much as Marx refrained from speculating about the future, the failure of his followers to grasp the centrality of abolishing value production compelled him to enter into a far-more detailed

---

[46] See 'K. Marx to E. Engels, 30 July 1862', MECW, vol. 41, p. 390. Marx did not know at the time of Lassalle's dealings with Bismarck – news of it came out only after the former's death – but he already suspected him of class collaboration.

[47] Part of the reason for this was Marx's position in the IWMA, in which he had to take care not to give the impression of prejudging the relations of national groupings within it.

[48] 'K. Marx to E. Engels, 3 February 1865', MECW, vol. 42, p. 75.

[49] 'K. Marx to F. Engels, 9 April 1863', MECW, vol. 41, p. 467.

discussion.[50] By including this in a critique of a party document, Marx is indicating that what gives a workers' party its right to exist centres on the clarity of its understanding of capitalism and the revolutionary alternative to it.

Why was Marx so sharply opposed to the new party as to threaten to publicly declare he would have nothing to do with it? It certainly was not because he questioned the need for a party (he had been stressing its importance especially since 1871). Nor is it because he thought that the unity congress failed to grasp the need for a party with *independent* class politics (despite Lassalle's flirtation with Bismarck, there was no evidence that Marx's followers were headed in that direction). The divide between Marx and his followers lies elsewhere – over whether organizational unity trumps revolutionary principles. His followers presumed that unity was the overriding consideration, even to the point of uniting with a tendency that had a wrongheaded analysis of capitalism and what constitutes the alternative to it. For Marx, on the other hand, 'there could be no bargaining about principles'.[51] This discloses one of the most important aspects of his concept of political organization – namely, that having an independent proletarian organization does not by itself suffice to establish a party's historical right to exist. What is above all needed is that it be committed to political and philosophic principles that can enable the working class to surmount the ideological horizon of existing society. This is what was missing at the unity congress, and this is what makes his critique of it in the *Critique of the Gotha Programme* a pivotal document in expressing his concept of political organization.

It is one thing, however, to insist that a party possess an adequate understanding of the alternative to capitalism, and quite another to suggest it serve as the embryonic expression of the new society. Whereas Marx affirmed the former, he rejected the latter. He took sharp issue with those who held, as he put it, that 'The Paris Communards would not have failed if they had understood that the Commune was "the embryo of the future human society" and had cast away all discipline and all arms, that is, the things which must disappear when there are no more wars!'[52] Organization, while crucial, is never an end-in-itself for Marx; the ultimate end is the new society, which towers high above it.

---

[50] For more on this, see P. Hudis, *Marx's Concept of the Alternative to Capitalism* (Chicago: Haymarket Books, 2013), pp. 187–206.
[51] 'K. Marx to W. Bracke, 5 May 1875', MECW, vol. 24, p. 78.
[52] K. Marx and F. Engels, 'Fictitious Splits in the International. Private Circular from the General Council of the International Working Men's Association', MECW, vol. 23, p. 115.

Marx decided not to publish the *Critique of the Gotha Programme* – partly because some party leaders (like August Bebel [1840–1913]) were in prison, but mainly because he hoped that the party's development would render the Gotha Programme moot. But this was not to be. In 1877, Marx was compelled to write, 'In Germany a corrupt spirit is asserting itself in our party, not so much among the masses as the leaders (upper class and workers). The compromise with the Lassalleans has led to further compromise with other waverers.'[53] In fact, it was the Gotha Programme, and not Marx's critique of it, that set the ground for German Social Democracy and the second IWMA. Even when it was published – in 1891, at Engels's insistence over his differences with the Erfurt Program – the *Critique of the Gotha Programme* remained largely ignored.

If there is one comment that summarizes Marx's concept of organization, it is the one that he made to Lassallean leader Johann von Schweitzer (1833–75):

A *centralist* organization, suitable as it is for secret societies and sect movements, contradicts the nature of the *trade unions*. Were it possible – I declare it *tout bonnement* to be impossible – it would not be desirable, least of all in Germany. Here where the worker is regulated bureaucratically from childhood onwards, where he believes in authority, in those set over him, the main thing is *to teach him to walk by himself*.[54]

6.5 Marx versus Post-Marx Marxism on Organization

Although Marx made many contributions to organization, most Marxists have followed alternative concepts of organization – such as those deriving from Lassalle, Kautsky, or Lenin. Although it was widely affirmed that Marx was the greater thinker and that Lassalle was wrong to seek an alliance with the German state, Lassallean concepts of organization went largely unchallenged; indeed, they obtained a new lease on life with Leninism. And, as one study proclaimed, 'Only with Lenin was the concept of a broad party that represents, or is, the working class replaced by that of a "minority" party ... which is the vanguard of the working class.'[55]

Lenin certainly earned his place in the annals of Marxism, but his organizational concepts – which were hardly original with him, but derived from German Social Democracy – have done much damage, especially in promoting the model of a single party state that monopolizes

---

[53] 'K. Marx to F. A. Sorge, 19 October 1877', MECW, vol. 45, p. 283.
[54] 'K. Marx to J. B. Schweitzer, 13 October 1868', MECW, vol. 43, p. 134.
[55] Molyneux, *Marxism and the Party*, p. 36.

power *on behalf* of the masses. Such approaches are clearly nonviable in the aftermath of the horrors perpetrated by the Stalinist regimes. The monopolization of power by a single party, led not by the working class, but by an intellectual elite that claimed to rule in its name, paved the way, in the USSR and other Stalinist states, for some of the most repressive regimes in history. In many respects, the Communist party of the USSR represented the antithesis of everything Marx stood for – above all his conception that 'Freedom consists in converting the state from an organ controlling society to one completely controlled by it.'[56]

Meanwhile, those Marxists who opposed Stalinism while upholding social democratic or Leninist conceptions of the party ultimately failed to provide a viable alternative to capitalism in its 'free market' and statist variants. History shows that nothing is more ephemeral than such parties – which tend to devolve into mere sects.

At the same time, it hardly advances matters to ignore Marx's contributions to organization for the sake of focusing on his major theoretical works – as if the 'esoteric' nature of his theoretical works are completely uninformed by his 'exoteric' political activity (and vice versa). This separation of theory and practice was anathema to Marx from the inception of his intellectual career, and we hardly do justice to the internal coherence of his project by imposing such an interpretation upon it.

The socialist and communist movements of old operated on the premise that the party was needed to mobilize masses towards a goal that was so clearly understood as to hardly need further articulation. Today, in the aftermath of 100 years of failed efforts to build 'socialism' and 'communism', it is clear that the goal was *not* well understood. The most unresolved question facing us today is what constitutes a viable alternative to capitalism. The role of organization takes on altogether new meaning in light of this. It is not enough for organizations to represent specific classes or forces, even though they must; and it is not enough for them to develop non-hierarchical and democratic forms of decision-making, even though they must. These are necessary but insufficient conditions for Marxist organization in the twenty-first century. Above all, we need organizations that raise and develop the question of what happens *after* the revolution *before* it occurs.[57]

In many respects, the response of Liebknecht to Marx's *Critique of the Gotha Programme* reflects the attitude of many Marxists when it comes to issues of organization: 'Theory and practice are two different things. As unconditionally as I trust Marx's judgment in theory, so in practice I go

---

[56] K. Marx, *Critique of the Gotha Programme*, MECW, vol. 24, p. 94.
[57] For more on this, see P. Hudis, 'Über die Notwendigkeit einer Vermittlung von Zielen und Wegen sozialistischer Politik', in M. Hawel and S. Kalmring (eds), *Wie lernt das linke Mosaik?* (Hamburg: VSA, 2016), pp. 196–211.

my own way.'[58] Now that a century of hindsight makes plain how much damage has been caused by this separation of theory from practice, it is surely time to re-examine Marx's 'political': contributions to political organization.

References

Cunliffe, John (1981), 'Marx, Engels and the Party', *History of Political Thought*, 2 (2): 349–67.

Dunayevskaya, Raya (1981), *Rosa Luxemburg, Women's Liberation, and Marx's Philosophy of Revolution*, Atlantic Highlands, NJ: Humanities Press.

Hudis, Peter (2013), *Marx's Concept of the Alternative to Capitalism*, Chicago: Haymarket Books.

(2016), 'Über die Notwendigkeit einer Vermittlung von Zielen und Wegen sozialistischer Politik', in Marcus Hawel and Stefans Kalmring (eds), *Wie lernt das linke Mosaik?* Hamburg: VSA, pp. 196–211.

Lassalle, Ferdinand (1900), *Science and the Workingmen*, New York: International Library.

Lenin, Vladimir Ilyich (1943), *What Is to Be Done? Collected Works*, vol. 2, Moscow: International Publishers.

Lih, Lars T. (2006), *Lenin Rediscovered: 'What Is to Be Done?' in Context*, Chicago: Haymarket Books.

Luxemburg, Rosa (2000), 'Lassalle und die Revolution', in *Gesammelte Werke*, vol. 1.2, Berlin: Dietz Verlag, pp. 417–21.

Marx, Karl (1975), 'Letters from Deutsch-Französische Jahrbücher', MECW, vol. 3, pp. 133–45.

(1975), 'Contribution to the Critique of Hegel's Philosophy of Right: Introduction', MECW, vol. 3, pp. 175–87.

(1975), 'Letters, October 1843–August 1844', MECW, vol. 3, pp. 349–57.

(1977), 'The Victory of the Counter-Revolution in Vienna', MECW, vol. 7, pp. 503–6.

(1978), 'Address to the Central Authority of the League, March 1850', MECW, vol. 10, pp. 277–87.

(1985), 'Instructions for the Delegates of the Provisional General Council. The Different Questions', MECW, vol. 20, pp. 185–94.

(1986), *The Civil War in France. Address of the General Council of the International Working Men's Association*, MECW, vol. 22, pp. 307–59.

(1986), 'Drafts of The Civil War in France', MECW, vol. 22, pp. 435–551.

(1986), 'Record of Marx's Speech on the Seventh Anniversary of the International', MECW, vol. 22, pp. 633–4.

(1989), *Critique of the Gotha Programme*, MECW, vol. 24, pp. 75–99.

Marx, Karl, and Engels, Frederick (1976), 'Letter from the Brussels Communist Correspondence Committee to G.A. Köttgen', MECW, vol. 6, pp. 54–6.

---

[58] Quoted in G. P. Steenson, *After Marx, Before Lenin: Marxism and Socialist Working Class Parties in Europe, 1884–1914* (Pittsburg, CA: Pittsburg University Press, 1991), p. 279.

(1976), *Manifesto of the Communist Party*, MECW, vol. 6, pp. 477–519.
(1978), *Letters, 1849–1851*, MECW, vol. 10.
(1978), 'Review, May to October 1850', MECW, vol. 10, pp. 490–532.
(1982), *Letters, 1844–1851*, MECW, vol. 38.
(1983), *Letters, 1856–1859*, MECW, vol. 40.
(1984), 'To the Workers of Cologne', MECW, vol. 9, p. 467.
(1985), *Letters, 1860–1864*, MECW, vol. 41.
(1986), 'Resolution of the Conference of Delegates of the of the International Working Men's Association Assembled at London from 17th to 23rd September 1871', MECW, vol. 22, pp. 423–31.
(1987), *Letters, 1864–1868*, MECW, vol. 42.
(1989), *Letters, 1874–1883*, MECW, vol. 24.
(1991), *Letters, 1874–1879*, MECW, vol. 45.

Molyneux, John (1978), *Marxism and the Party*, London: Pluto Press.

Musto, Marcello, ed. (2014), *Workers Unite! The International 150 Years Later*, New York: Bloomsbury.

Nimtz, August H. Jr. (2000), *Marx and Engels: Their Contribution to the Democratic Breakthrough*, Albany: State University of New York Press.

Rubel, Maximilien (1974), 'Le parti proletarian', in *Marx critique du marxisme*, Paris: Payot, pp. 183–92.

Steenson, Gary P. (1991), *After Marx, Before Lenin: Marxism and Socialist Working Class Parties in Europe, 1884–1914*, Pittsburg, CA: Pittsburg University Press.

Villiers, Broughham (1908), *The Socialist Movement in England*, London: T. Fisher Unwin.

7 Revolution

Michael Löwy

7.1   Revolutionary Praxis: The Early Writings

The word 'revolution' was traditionally used to describe the movement of planets around their axis, but, after the sixteenth century, it became a political concept, describing radical upheavals in the social and political order, as well as the overthrowing of a ruling class or group. It is in this modern sense that Karl Marx used it. His main reference for thinking about revolutions was the French Revolution (1789–94): a massive popular uprising that deeply transformed the political institutions and social structure of France and Europe more broadly. Marx's analyses of revolutionary events were always linked to the concept of class struggle. He referred to the Peasant Wars of the sixteenth century in Germany as a 'peasant revolution', to the English and French Revolutions as 'bourgeois revolutions', and to the Paris Commune of 1871 as a 'proletarian revolution'. The revolutions of 1848–9 in France and Germany were perceived as a protracted class confrontation between the monarchist aristocracy, the liberal bourgeoisie, the democratic petty-bourgeoisie, and the proletarian masses.[1]

Marx's theory of proletarian revolution was already developed in his early writings (1843–50), based on dialectical and critical reflections on the growing experience of labour class struggles in Europe in the 1840s, and on the existing communist literature. The first document where the

---

[1] The best work on Marx and revolution is still H. Draper's (1914–90) monumental series of five volumes, *Karl Marx's Theory of Revolution, Volume I: State and Bureaucracy* (New York: Monthly Review Press, 1977), *Karl Marx's Theory of Revolution, Volume II: Politics of Social Classes* (New York: Monthly Review Press, 1978), H. Draper and S. F. Diamond, *Karl Marx's Theory of Revolution, Volume III: The 'Dictatorship of the Proletariat'* (New York: Monthly Review Press, 1986), H. Draper, *Karl Marx's Theory of Revolution, Volume IV: Critique of Other Socialisms* (New York: Monthly Review Press, 1990), and H. Draper and E. Haberkern, *Karl Marx's Theory of Revolution, Volume V: War & Revolution* (Alameda and New York: Center for Socialist History and Monthly Review Press, 2005) written from the standpoint of 'socialism from below' against 'socialism from above'.

idea of a proletarian revolution was suggested is the 'Contribution to the Critique of Hegel's Philosophy of Right' (1844), but this was still a 'Left-Hegelian' essay because it promoted the idea that revolution begins 'in the brain of a philosopher', generating a 'lightning of thought' that strikes the proletarian masses who are conceived as the 'material foundation' or the 'passive element' of human emancipation.[2] It is only after writing this document that Marx established direct contacts with French and German Communist worker's circles in Paris, and got better acquainted with the writings of Wilhelm Weitling (1808–1871), a German communist worker, founder of the League of the Just (forerunner of the Communist League), and with the struggles of the Chartist worker's movement in England.

A decisive event for Marx's early reflexions on revolution was the Silesian weaver's uprising of June 1844, the first proletarian rebellion in German history, which could only be suppressed by the intervention of the Prussian army. Under the modest title 'Critical Marginal Notes [*Randglossen*] on the Article "The King of Prussia and Social Reform"', Marx published a polemical text against Arnold Ruge (1802–1880), which celebrates the superiority of social uprisings over the 'merely political ones'. This article was a turning point in young Marx's philosophical and political evolution. It can be considered a break with the neo-Hegelian presuppositions still present in his first communist writings from 1844. In the Silesian revolt, he discovered 'the excellent capabilities of the German proletariat for socialism' – without the need of the 'lightning of thought' from the philosophers. And, even more important, he discovered that the proletariat was not the 'passive element' of the revolution, but quite the contrary: 'A philosophical people can find its corresponding practice (*Praxis*) only in socialism, hence it is only in the *proletariat* that it can find the dynamic element of its emancipation.'[3] In this single sentence, we can find three new themes: (1) philosophy and the people are no longer presented as two separate terms, the first descending on the second like lightning, but rather should be conceived as 'a philosophical people' revealing that this opposition is superseded; (2) socialism is no longer presented as pure theory, an idea born in the brain of a philosopher, but as *praxis*; and (3) the proletariat now plainly becomes the *active* element in emancipation.

The broader philosophical conclusions from this new approach would be presented in the *Thesis on Feuerbach* (1845), a few pages of notes not

---

[2] K. Marx, 'Contribution to the Critique of Hegel's Philosophy of Right: Introduction', MECW, vol. 3, p. 187.

[3] K. Marx, 'Critical Marginal Notes on the Article "The King of Prussian and Social Reform. By a Prussian"', MECW, vol. 3, p. 202.

intended for publication, but which can be considered, as Friedrich Engels wrote in 1888, 'the brilliant germ of a new world outlook'.[4] This new world view, which one could define – using Antonio Gramsci's (1891–1937) phrase – as 'philosophy of praxis', provides the theoretical foundation for Marx's conception of revolution: the transformation of the social conditions and the self-transformation of the individuals together with the process of revolutionary praxis. The key passage, from this perspective, is Thesis III:

> The materialist doctrine concerning the changing of circumstances and upbringing forgets that circumstances are changed by men and that the educator must himself be educated. This doctrine must, therefore, divide society into two parts, one of which is superior to society. The coincidence of the changing of circumstances and of human activity or self-change can be conceived and rationally understood as *revolutionary practice*.[5]

Revolutionary practice simultaneously changes both material circumstances (i.e., economic, social, or political conditions) and oneself, the 'subject of action [*Selbstveränderung*]'. It is therefore the dialectical superseding (*Aufhebung*) of the antithesis between eighteenth-century French materialism (and its German followers such as Feuerbach) and the (idealist) Young Hegelians. While the former advocated for changing the material conditions primarily, the latter believed that changing people's consciousness as a precondition for social change. The first communists or socialists, who were often materialists, entrusted an individual or a group 'raised above society', an elite of 'virtuous citizens', or, in some cases, a king or emperor with the task of changing circumstances. In other words, the notion of revolutionary praxis is the theoretical foundation of the Marxist *radically democratic* conception of revolution as proletarian self-emancipation.

Soon after, this idea was developed in *The German Ideology* (1845–46), a large manuscript which Marx wrote with Engels, but then abandoned, in Marx's words, to 'the gnawing criticism of the mice'.[6] In a decisive passage, probably written by Marx (as most of the manuscript), the argument of Thesis III on Feuerbach was taken up and developed:

> Both for the production on a mass scale of this communist consciousness, and for the success of the cause itself, the alteration of men on a mass scale is necessary, an alteration which can only take place in a practical movement, a *revolution*; the revolution is necessary, therefore, not only because the *ruling* class cannot be

---

[4] F. Engels, 'Ludwig Feuerbach and the End of Classical German Philosophy', MECW, vol. 26, p. 520
[5] K. Marx, 'Thesis on Feuerbach', MEWC, vol. 5, p. 4.
[6] K. Marx, 'A Contribution to the Critique of Political Economy', MECW, vol. 29, p. 264.

overthrown in any other way, but also because the class *overthrowing* it can only in a revolution succeed in ridding itself of all the muck of ages and become fitted to found society anew ... In *revolutionary activity* the changing of oneself coincides with the changing of circumstances.[7]

In other words, revolution is needed not only to destroy the old system, but also in order to enable the proletariat to overcome, by its own practical action, its 'internal' barriers, change its consciousness, and become capable of creating a new, communist, society. For the Marxian revolutionary theory – in contraposition to most previous conceptions of social change, from the Jacobins to François-Noël Babeuf (1760–1797), and from Claude Henri de Saint Simon (1760–1825) to Robert Owen (1771–1858) – there can be no supreme saviour, the only possible emancipation of labour is democratic revolutionary self-emancipation.

Revolutionary ideas, for Marx, did not originate in the writings of philosophers, but in the experience of a class, the proletariat – which does not mean that individuals from other classes may not join the struggle for communism. The proletariat, as stated in *The German Ideology*,

is a class ... which has to bear all the burdens of society without enjoying its advantages, which is ousted from society ... a class which forms the majority of all members of society, and from whom emanates the consciousness of a fundamental revolution, the communist consciousness, which may, of course, arise among the other classes too through the contemplation of the situation of this class.[8]

This theory of revolution as self-emancipation is an essential dimension of Marx's political writings of the following years. Let us take, for instance, the *Manifesto of the Communist Party* (1848). Its definition of the revolutionary labour movement is clearly opposed to any 'substitutionist' vanguardism:

All previous historical movements were movements of minorities or in the interest of minorities. The proletarian movement is the self-conscious, independent movement of the immense majority, in the interest of the immense majority.[9]

Marx and Engels' confrontation with the utopian socialists derived from this fundamental belief: the latter were praised for their ideas on a future society, but criticized for their attitude towards the proletariat, whom they considered to be 'a class without any historical initiative or any independent political movement': 'only from the point of view of being

---

[7] K. Marx, *The German Ideology*, MECW, vol. 5, pp. 52–3, 214.   [8] Ibid, pp. 60, 52.
[9] K. Marx and F. Engels, *Manifesto of the Communist Party*, MECW, vol. 6, p. 495.

the most suffering class does the proletariat exist for them'. Accordingly, they rejected all political and 'especially all revolutionary action' on the part of the working class.[10]

Marx and Engels participated in the 1848 revolution in Germany but were forced, in 1849, to exile themselves in England.[11] It was therefore in London that they wrote a document, the 'Address of the Central Council to the Communist League' (March 1850), attempting to draw lessons from the German revolutionary movement. At that moment, they still believed that a resurgence of the revolutionary movement was possible and were contemplating what forms the revolutionary and self-liberating struggle of the proletarian mass might assume in Germany. According to this message, the proletarians must establish their own authority in opposition to the bourgeois authorities by forming workers councils:

> Alongside the new official government, they must immediately establish their own revolutionary workers' governments, whether in the form of municipal committees and municipal councils or in the form of workers clubs or workers committees.

Moreover, Marx and Engels believed that the workers should try to arm themselves,

> as a proletarian guard with commanders elected by themselves and with a general staff of their choosing, and to put themselves under the command not of the state authority, but of the revolutionary municipal councils set up by the workers.[12]

This is also the first writing where Marx and Engels raised the strategic perspective of permanent revolution and contemplated how a democratic revolution in a backward, semi-feudal, and absolutist state (Germany in the mid-nineteenth century) could be transformed into a proletarian one:

> while the democratic petty bourgeois wish to bring the revolution to a conclusion as quickly as possible ... it is our interest and our task to make the revolution permanent, until all more or less possessing classes have been forced out of their position of dominance, the proletariat has conquered state power.[13]

As an immediate proposal, the 'Address of the Central Council to the Communist League' was, of course, wrong, since the revolution had already been defeated in Germany; but the document appears, in

---

[10] Ibid, pp. 515–17.
[11] The best essay on Marx's strategy during the revolution of 1848 is by the Spanish Marxist, F. Claudin, *Marx, Engels y la Revolucion de 1848* (Madrid: Siglo XXI, 1975).
[12] K. Marx and F. Engels, 'Address of the Central Council to the Communist League (March 1850)', MECW, vol. 10, pp. 281–2.
[13] Ibid, p. 281.

retrospective, as an almost prophetic forecast of the Paris Commune of 1871, and of the October Revolution in Russia, in 1917.

7.2 Revolution as Self-Emancipation: The First International and the Paris Commune

The European revolutions of 1848–50 were defeated, but they had a sort of peculiar aftermath in Spain. In June 1854, two 'liberal' generals, Don Leopoldo O'Donnell (1809–1867) and Don Joaquín Baldomero Fernández-Espartero (1793–1879), supported by the barricades of the people, staged a military uprising that liberated political prisoners and promised reforms. Two years later, in July 1856, O'Donnell, in complicity with the Spanish king, seized power in a coup d'etat. The bourgeois National Assembly capitulated, and only the working-class districts of Madrid fought, until – after several days of desperate urban guerrilla warfare – they were crushed by the regular army. This episode had some similarities with June 1848 uprising in Paris and Marx, in his articles on the revolution in Spain for the *New-York Tribune,* concluded that 'the proletarians were betrayed and abandoned by the bourgeoisie', and therefore, 'the same divisions in the ranks of the people that existed in the rest of Western Europe'[14] also existed in Spain.

The idea of proletarian self-emancipation is not only present in Marx's early writings, but also in his later work. Marx did not participate in the foundation of the International Working Men's Association (IWMA) in 1864, but was invited to write down some of its basic documents. This was how he defined, in the *Preamble to the Rules of the International Workingmen Association,* the guiding principle of the movement: 'The emancipation of the working classes must be conquered by the working classes themselves.'[15] It was in the name of this simple and strong idea of self-emancipation that he opposed all the tendencies within the IWMA, which sought to create utopian, dogmatic, or conspiratorial sects outside the workers' movement. In *Fictitious splits in the International* (1872), Marx and Engels insisted, 'The sects formed by these initiators are abstentionist by their very nature – that is, alien to all real action, politics, strikes, coalitions, or, in a word, to any united movement' of the proletariat.[16]

---

[14] K. Marx and F. Engels, *Revolution in Spain* (New York: International Publishers, 1939), p. 240.

[15] M. Musto, ed., *Workers Unite! The International 150 years later* (London: Bloomsbury, 2014), p. 265. Resolutions and documents of the IWMA are quoted from the anthology of the most important documents of this organization edited by Musto in 2014.

[16] Ibid, p. 288. In a letter from November 1871, Marx explained to his friend Friedrich Bolte (1896–1959) the historical meaning of the IWMA: 'The International was founded in order to replace the socialist or semi-socialist sects by a real organization

Since the beginning of his exile in England, in 1849, Marx followed the developments of the British labour movement with great interest. He became increasingly persuaded that England, being the most advanced industrial capitalist country, would have been the first to know a proletarian revolution. He also believed that such a revolution would emancipate the Irish people from British colonial oppression. In a letter from 9 April 1870 to Sigfrid Meyer (1840–1872) and August Vogt (1830–1883), two German communists and activists of the IWMA living in the United States, Marx reaffirmed the first belief, but resolutely changed his mind in relation to Ireland:

> England, being the metropolis of capital, the power which hitherto ruled the world market, is for the present the most important country for the worker's revolution, and moreover the *only* country in which the material conditions for this revolution have developed up to a certain degree of maturity. Therefore, to hasten the social revolution in England is the most important object of the International Working Men's Association. The sole means of hastening it is to make Ireland independent.[17]

Worried by the capacity of the English bourgeoisie to 'divide and rule', by opposing English and Irish workers in Britain, Marx now believed that the IWMA had to make all efforts to 'awaken a consciousness in the English working class that *for the national emancipation of Ireland* is no question of abstract justice or humanitarian sentiment but *the first condition of their own social emancipation*'.[18] In this same year, Marx wrote a resolution on Ireland for the IWMA, which drew a famous universal conclusion which is relevant to all forms of imperial or colonial domination:

> Ireland is the only excuse the English government has for keeping a large regular army which can, as we have seen, in case of need attack the English workers after having done its basic training in Ireland ... What ancient Rome demonstrated on a gigantic scale can be seen in the England of today a people which subjugates another people forges its own chains.[19]

The great historical experience of proletarian revolution in Marx's times was, of course, the Paris Commune of 1871, in which the members of the IWMA took an active part. Marx writings on the Paris Commune illustrate the way that he developed and enriched his conception of revolution: not through abstract theoretical arguments, but by learning from the concrete historical experience For him, as one can gather from the *Address on*

---

of the working class for struggle. The original Rules and the Inaugural Address show this at a glance' ('K. Marx to F. Bolte, 23 November 1871', MECW, vol. 44, p. 252).
[17] 'K. Marx to S. Meyer and A. Vogt, 9 April 1870', MECW, vol. 43, pp. 475. [18] Ibid.
[19] Musto, ed., *Workers Unite!*, p. 250.

the Civil War in France 1871 (as well as the rich preparatory notes for this document), which he wrote in the name of the IWMA, the Paris Commune was nothing less than the first real and concrete manifestation of the proletarian revolution that he had defined in his early writings, as the first moment of the great process in which the changing of people's consciousness coincides with the changing of the social conditions:

> The working class did not expect miracles from the Commune. They have no ready-made utopias to introduce *par décret du peuple*. They know that in order to work out their own emancipation, and along with it that higher from to which present society is irresistibly tending by its own economical agencies, they will have to pass through long struggles, through a series of historic processes, transforming circumstances and men.[20]

This passage, like several others in Marx writings, contains an element of economic fatalism: the belief that capitalist society 'tends irresistibly' towards socialism, 'by its own economical agencies'.[21] But the main emphasis of Marx's piece on the commune is on the emancipatory agency of the oppressed class. The commune was neither a conspiracy – as argued by the reactionary press and the police authorities – nor a putsch. It was 'the people acting for itself by itself'.[22] And this was clear from its first decree abolishing the standing army and replacing it with the people in arms.

The authorities installed by this democratic self-emancipatory revolution could not, indeed, be authorities of a Jacobin type. It was and could not be but a 'working-class government', 'a government of the people by the people', 'a resumption by the people for the people of its own social life'.[23] The commune was also a *revolution against the state:* instead of trying to conquer the state machinery – a structure suited for the parasitic domination *over* the people – the Parisian revolution

---

[20] K. Marx, *The Civil War in France. Address of the General Council of the International Working Men's Association*, MECW, vol. 22, p. 335.

[21] This economic 'fatalism' also appears in other of Marx's writings, for instance in *Capital*. A new approach was suggested by Rosa Luxemburg's (1871–1919) famous dictum, socialism or barbarism (*The crisis of social-democracy*, 1915). Inspired by Luxemburg's ideas, the heterodox Marxist, Lucien Goldmann (1913–70), argued, in his book, *The Hidden God: A Study of Tragic Vision in the Pensées of Pascal and the Tragedies of Racine (1955)* (London: Verso, 2016) that the triumph of a socialist revolution cannot be scientifically demonstrated, but is grounded on a *wager* on our collective action. Goldmann's argument has been later taken over by Daniel Bensaïd (1946–2010), in his book, *Le Pari Melancolique* (Paris: Fayard, 1997).

[22] The Paris correspondent of the British *Daily News* found no leader wielding 'supreme authority' – on which Marx comments ironically that 'this shocks the bourgeois who wants political idols and "great men" immensely' (Marx, *Civil War in France*, pp. 464, 478).

[23] Marx, *Civil War in France*, pp. 334, 339, 464.

smashed it and replaced it by institutions adequate to popular self-government.[24]

In September 1871, at the London Conference of the IWMA, Marx and Engels proposed a resolution 'On the Political Action of the Working Class', which defined the revolutionary party as a form of proletarian self-organization: 'The constitution of the working class into a political party is indispensable in order to ensure the triumph of the social revolution and its ultimate end – the abolition of classes.' The same document also emphasized that 'to conquer political power has, therefore, become the great duty of the working class'.[25]

7.3 The Late Marx: Germany and Russia, Centre and Periphery

The issue of revolutionary self-emancipation became a central tenet of Marx (and Engels') struggles during the 1870s inside the new German Social Democratic party (SPD), which they helped to found. They wrote several documents fighting the non-revolutionary tendencies among its leadership: first the Lassalleans, who advocated social change 'from above' through the state – and even, for Ferdinand Lassalle (1825–1864), in alliance with Bismarck! – and, later, the Revisionists.

This last struggle is less known but is a powerful illustration of the continuity in their revolutionary outlook. In 1879, three intellectuals of the SPD – Karl Höchberg (1853–1885), Carl August Schramm (1807–1869), and Eduard Bernstein (1850–1932) – wrote an article in the *Yearbook for Social Science and Social Politics* (*Jahrbuch für Sozialwissenschaft und Sozialpolitik*), calling for a 'revision' of the party's

---

[24] This emerges clearly from Marx's well-known letter to Louis Kugelmann (1829–1902) from 12 April 1871, after the first weeks of the Parisian revolutionary process, where he spoke of the destruction of 'the bureaucratic military machine' as something 'essential for every real people's revolution on the continent' (MECW, vol. 44, p. 131).

[25] Musto, ed., *Workers Unite!* p. 285. John Holloway's (1947–) central argument in his book, *Change the World without Taking Power: The Meaning of Revolution Today* (London: Pluto Press, 2002) is grounded on the distinction between 'power-to', the capacity to do things, and 'power-over', the ability to command others to do what one wishes them to do. Revolutions, according to Holloway, should promote the first, and uproot the second. But can there be any form of collective life and action of human beings without some form of 'power-over'? In one of the few passages where he mentioned some positive historical examples of revolutionary self-emancipation, he referred to the Paris Commune as discussed by Marx. However, in the Paris Commune, according to Marx, a new form of power emerged which was not a state any more in the usual sense, but was still a combination of direct and representative democracy which had power over the population by its decrees and decisions. This power, the democratic power of the Paris Commune, was literally 'seized', beginning with the act of seizing the material instruments of power, the cannons of the National Guard.

policy: abandonment of its 'narrowly working-class character' and its excessive revolutionary tendency. The article also proposed that the SPD should lay more stress on winning 'the so-called upper strata of society', as well as entrusting its mandates to the Reichstag to persons who had the leisure to study, which was not the case of 'the simple working man'.

Irritated by this 'revisionist' enterprise, Marx (and Engels) sent a circular letter to the leaders of the SPD, the so-called Leipzig group – Wilhelm Liebknecht (1826–1900), August Bebel (1840–1913), and Wilhelm Bracke (1842–1880) – who considered themselves Marx and Engels' followers, calling them to dissociate themselves from the reformist line of the *Yearbook for Social Science and Social Politics*. The document strongly emphasizes the principle of proletarian self-emancipation:

> As for ourselves there is, considering our antecedents, only one course open for us. For almost 40 years we have emphasized that the class struggle is the immediate motive force of history, and, in particular, that the class struggle between bourgeoisie and proletariat is the great lever of modern social revolution; hence we cannot possibly cooperate with men who seek to eliminate that class struggle from the movement. At the founding of the IWMA we expressly formulated the battle-cry: 'The emancipation of the working class must be achieved by the working class itself.' Hence, we cannot co-operate with men who say openly that the workers are too uneducated to emancipate themselves, as must first be emancipated from above by philanthropic members of the upper and lower middle classes. If the new party organ is to adopt the policy that corresponds to the opinions of these gentlemen, if it is bourgeois and not proletarian, then all we could do – much as though we regret it – would be publicly to declare ourselves opposed to it and abandon the solidarity with which we have hitherto represented the German party abroad.[26]

As most German socialists, Marx believed that the proletarian revolution would start at the most advanced industrial capitalist countries of Western Europe, but in his last writings, he considered the possibility that it could begin in 'backward' Tsarist Russia. Thus, in a letter from 1881 to the Russian revolutionary Vera Zasulich (1849–1919), he

[26] K. Marx and F. Engels, 'Circular Letters to August Bebel and others 17–18 Sept. 1879' (MECW, vol. 45, p. 394). This message is a remarkable restatement of proletarian revolutionary self-emancipation, a theme that ran through their correspondence from the 1840s onwards. The reference to 'almost 40 years' is somewhat exaggerated, since it only after 1844 that this idea became the guiding star of their political thought and action. As it is well known, Bebel and his friends did not join the revisionists, but after his death and particularly after 1914, the anti-revolutionary tendency became hegemonic in the SPD and in most second IWMA parties. The circular, which is one of the forgotten documents of Marxism, was published only in 1931 in a communist journal and is a remarkably powerful summary of their revolutionary perspective, past and present.

asserted that the Russian rural commune (*obschina*) is the strategic point of social regeneration in Russia.[27] In the drafts of the letter, he was more explicit and suggested that, under certain political conditions – a Russian Revolution – the Russian rural commune could provide the basis for a transition to socialism.[28] The same idea was advanced, this time by both Marx and Engels, in their common preface to the reprint of the Russian translation of the *Manifesto of the Communist Party*, written in 1882, just one year before Marx's death. They believed that if a Russian revolution sounded the signal for a proletarian revolution in the West, the prevailing form of communal ownership of land in Russia might form the starting point for a communist course of development.[29]

Of course, Marx was too optimistic about the role of the Russian village community, but once again a predictive error contained a powerful intuition: that the revolution might break out in a 'backward' country, in the periphery and not the heart of the system; that such a revolution might begin the transition to socialism; and that the success of this monumental enterprise would depend to a very great measure upon the extension of the revolution to the West. From the methodological viewpoint, Marx's late writings on an eventual Russian revolution avoid any sort of economic determinism: socio-economic conditions obviously are essential in defining the field of the possible, but the ultimate decision of history depends upon autonomous political factors: the revolutions in Russia and in Europe.

7.4   After Marx

Many important contributions to the Marxist theory of revolution were developed during the twentieth century. A few examples are Vladimir Lenin's (1870–1924) theory of the vanguard revolutionary party, Leon Trotsky's (1879–1940) theory of permanent revolution, Rosa Luxemburg on socialism and democratic freedoms, Gramsci's strategy of struggle for hegemony, and José Carlos Mariategui's (1894–1930) conception of a socialist revolution rooted in the communitarian indigenous traditions. A renewal of the Marxist theory of revolution in the

---

[27] K. Marx, 'Letter to Vera Zasulich', MECW, vol. 24, p. 370.
[28] K. Marx, 'Drafts of the Letter to Vera Zasulich', MECW, vol. 24, pp. 346–69.
[29] K. Marx and F. Engels, 'Preface to the Second Russian Editions of the *Manifesto of the Communist Party*', MECW, vol. 24, p. 425. On Marx and Russia, see the essay by T. Shanin, *Late Marx and the Russian Road: Marx and the 'Peripheries of Capitalism'* (New York: Monthly Review Press, 1983). For a general discussion of Marx's interest in the 'Non-Western world', see K. B. Anderson, *Marx at the Margins: On Nationalism, Ethnicity and Non-Western Societies* (Chicago: University of Chicago Press, 2010).

twenty-first century has to deal with these contributions, taking into account their insights as well as their limitations.

Do revolutions belong to the past? The dominant discourse after the fall of the Berlin Wall (1989) has been the celebration of the End of History, and above all of revolutionary history. In fact, new revolutions in the twenty-first century are not only possible, but probable. And how could one overcome the world dictatorship of the financial markets without challenging the capitalist system itself through a revolutionary process? Of course, the revolutions of the future will be quite different from the past ones, and entirely unpredictable. But is this invention of new forms not one of the quintessential characteristics of revolutions?

Marx's theory of revolution – the philosophy of praxis, and, dialectically linked to it, the idea of workers self-emancipation – remains a precious compass. Not only has it not been made obsolete by the crumbling of the Berlin Wall, but, on the contrary, it provides us with a decisive key to understand why the attempt to 'build socialism' without the people (or against them) – to 'emancipate' labour from above by an authoritarian bureaucratic power, was inevitably doomed to failure. For Marx, revolutionary democracy – the political equivalent of self-emancipation – was not an optional dimension, but the intrinsic nature of socialism itself, as the free association of individuals who take into their hands the production of their common life. Far from 'falsifying' the Marxian theory of revolution, the historical experience of the Stalinist USSR (and of the other Eastern European countries), is its most astonishing confirmation.

This does not mean that one can find in Marx the answers to all our problems, or that there is nothing to be reconsidered or criticized in the complex body of his economic or political views. Many decisive issues, such as the destruction of the environment by the 'growth of productive forces', other forms of oppression (e.g., on women and ethnic minorities), the importance of universal ethical rules and human rights, or the struggle of non-European nations and cultures against Western domination are either absent or inadequately treated in his writings.

This is why Marx's legacy has to be enriched with the experience of the twentieth century's revolutions – both in their positive and their negative lessons – from October 1917 to the great social upheavals in Europe, Asia, or Latin America: Spain, China, Vietnam, Cuba, or Nicaragua, and, last but not least, it must be reviewed and corrected with the contributions of other socialist traditions (utopian, anarchist, communitarian) as well as of the new social movements that have developed during the last decades, such as black liberation, indigenism, feminism, and ecology. It is precisely because it is not a dogmatic and closed system, but an open and critical tradition of revolutionary theory and praxis, that Marxism is able to grow and develop itself, constantly confronting new issues and new challenges, and learning from other experiences and other emancipatory movements.

The ecological crisis of the twenty-first century is perhaps the greatest challenge for Marxism today because it requires a revision of its concept of revolution.[30] There exists a tension in Marx and Engels' writings, between the understanding of the environmentally destructive character of capitalist 'progress', and the acceptance of the productive forces created by capitalism as the economic basis of the new society.

The ecological/socialist revolution requires a radical break with the whole capitalist paradigm of civilization, with its ecologically destructive forms of production and consumption, and its unsustainable way of life. In other words, the traditional Marxist concept of revolution is indispensable, but it has to be deepened, radicalized, and broadened. It has to include not only a radical change in the relations of production (private property), but also in the structure of the forces of production, in the sources of energy (e.g., solar instead of fossil), and in wasteful patterns of consumption. Revolution now means the establishment of a new civilizational model, beyond the Western capitalist industrial civilization which is leading humanity to an unprecedented catastrophe: global warming.

In a preparatory note for his theses 'On the Concept of History' (1940), Walter Benjamin (1890–1940) suggested a new image for the concept of revolution, different from the one offered in some of Marx's writings:

> Marx said that revolutions are the locomotive of world history. But perhaps things are very different. It may be that revolutions are the act by which the human race traveling in the train applies the emergency brake.[31]

This is very relevant to the twenty-first century. We are all passengers of a suicidal train, the train of modern capitalism, racing at an increasing velocity towards an abyss: climate change. Only a revolution can prevent this before it is too late.

---

[30] See the work of one of the most important eco-Marxists today, J. B. Foster, *The Ecological Revolution: Making Peace with the Planet* (New York: Monthly Review Press, 2009).

[31] W. Benjamin, *Gesammelte Schriften*, vol. I, 3 (Frankfurt am Main: Suhrkamp Verlag, 1977), p. 1232. This note does not appear in the final versions of the document. Benjamin's theses 'On the Concept of History' are a radical attempt to emancipate the Marxist concept of revolution from any links to the positivist ideology of 'Progress'.

References

Anderson, Kevin B. (2010), *Marx at the Margins: On Nationalism, Ethnicity and Non-Western Societies*, Chicago, University of Chicago Press.

Bensaïd, Daniel (1997), *Le Pari Melancolique*, Paris, Fayard.

Claudin, Fernando (1975), *Marx, Engels y la Revolucion de 1848*, Madrid: Siglo XXI.

Draper, Hal (1977), *Karl Marx's Theory of Revolution Volume I: State and Bureaucracy*, New York: Monthly Review Press.

— (1978), *Karl Marx's Theory of Revolution, Volume II: Politics of Social Classes*, New York: Monthly Review Press.

— (1990), *Karl Marx's Theory of Revolution, Volume IV: Critique of Other Socialisms*, New York: Monthly Review Press.

Draper, Hal, and Diamond, Stephen F. (1986), *Karl Marx's Theory of Revolution, Volume III: The 'Dictatorship of the Proletariat'*, New York: Monthly Review Press.

Draper, Hal, and Haberkern, Ernest (2005), *Karl Marx's Theory of Revolution, Volume V: War & Revolution*, Alameda and New York: Center for Socialist History and Monthly Review Press.

Engels, Frederick (1989), 'Ludwig Feuerbach and the End of Classical German Philosophy', MECW, vol. 26, pp. 353–98.

Foster, John Bellamy (2009), *The Ecological Revolution: Making Peace with the Planet*, New York: Monthly Review Press.

Goldmann, Lucien (2016), *The Hidden God: A Study of Tragic Vision in the Pensées of Pascal and the Tragedies of Racine (1955)*, London: Verso.

Holloway, John (2002), *Change the World without Taking Power: The Meaning of Revolution Today*, London: Pluto Press.

Marx, Karl (1975), 'Contribution to the Critique of Hegel's Philosophy of Right: Introduction', MECW, vol. 3, pp. 175–87.

— (1975), 'Critical Marginal Notes on the Article "The King of Prussia and Social Reform. By a Prussian"', MECW, vol. 3, 189–206.

— (1975), 'Theses on Feuerbach', MECW, vol. 5, pp. 6–8.

— (1986), *The Civil War in France. Address of the General Council of the International Working Men's Association*, MECW, vol. 22, pp. 307–59.

— (1987), 'A Contribution to the Critique of Political Economy. Part One', MECW, vol. 29, pp. 257–417.

— (1989), 'Drafts of the Letter to Vera Zasulich', MECW, vol. 24, pp. 346–69.

— (1989), 'Letter to Vera Zasulich', MECW, vol. 24, pp. 370–1.

Marx, Karl, and Engels, Fredrick (1939), *Revolution in Spain*, New York: International Publishers.

— (1975), *The German Ideology*, MECW, vol. 5, pp. 19–539.

— (1976), *Manifesto of the Communist Party*, MECW, vol. 6, pp. 477–519.

— (1978), 'Address of the Central Authority to the League, March 1850', MECW, vol. 10, pp. 277–87.

— (1989), 'Preface to the Second Russian Edition of the *Manifesto of the Communist Party*', MECW, vol. 24, pp. 425–6.

(1989), *Letters, 1870–73*, MECW, vol. 44.
(1991), *Letters, 1874–1879*, MECW, vol. 45.
Musto, Marcello, ed. (2014), *Workers Unite! The International 150 Years Later*, New York: Bloomsbury.
Shanin, Theodor (1983), *Late Marx and the Russian Road: Marx and the 'Peripheries of Capitalism'*, New York: Monthly Review Press.

8 Work

Ricardo Antunes
Translated by Caio Antunes and revised by David Broder

8.1 Work as a Vital Human Activity

When Karl Marx drafted his first dialectical critique, he offered an introductory presentation of work. He here presented work as a category centrally important to the process of producing and reproducing social life. As he moved forwards both in his critique of idealism and in his first critical studies of political economy, Marx took an important step in formulating his conception of work. He observed that private property, standing in opposition to free human development, created the conditions for an enduring state of alienated labour. According to his 'Comments on James Mill, *Elements d'Economie Politique*':

> My work would be a free manifestation of life, hence an enjoyment of life. Presupposing private property, my work is an alienation of life, for I work in order to live, in order to obtain for myself the means of life. My work is not my life ... Presupposing private property, my individuality is alienated to such a degree that this activity is instead hateful to me, a torment, and rather the semblance of an activity. Hence, too, it is only a forced activity and one imposed on me only through an external fortuitous need, not through an inner, essential one.[1]

At the same time as Marx was observing workers' strikes, peasants' struggles over firewood, and people's battles over housing, he used his critical analysis of political economy to provide concrete elements for the newly emerging materialist conception of history. Human activity increasingly represented a fundamental element for this new materialism. In the *Economic and Philosophic Manuscripts of 1844*, Marx proposed his first synthesis of work as a vital activity. He stated that the human being

> makes his life activity itself the object of his will and of his consciousness. He has conscious life activity. It is not a determination with which he directly merges.

The author thanks Espaço da Escrita (UNICAMP) for the support.
[1] K. Marx, 'Comments on James Mill, *Elements d'Economie Politique*', MECW, vol. 3, p. 228.

Conscious life activity distinguishes man immediately from animal life activity. It is just because of this that he is a species-being. Or it is only because he is a species-being that he is a conscious being, i.e., that his own life is an object for him. Only because of that is his activity free activity.[2]

The complex relationships between the social being and nature thus found their effective relational dimension: namely, 'that man's physical and spiritual life is linked to nature means simply that nature is linked to itself, for man is a part of nature'.[3]

The transformation of inorganic nature, made possible by the realization of human activity, found its necessary mediation in work, 'the material, the object, and the instrument of his life activity'.[4] Thus, the production and the reproduction of social life had their foundation in the activity of work.

This argument corresponds to the idea presented by Marx and Friedrich Engels (1820–1895) in *The German Ideology*, where they stated:

The first historical act is thus the production of the means to satisfy these needs, the production of material life itself. And indeed this is an historical act, a fundamental condition of all history, which today, as thousands of years ago, must daily and hourly be fulfilled merely in order to sustain human life.[5]

The production of the means necessary to satisfying human needs was then turned into a fundamental condition of human life itself – that is, the very basis of the humanization process. And work was considered something inherent to the life of those who turned themselves into human and social beings:

Men can be distinguished from animals by consciousness, by religion or anything else you like. They themselves begin to distinguish themselves from animals as soon as they begin to produce their means of subsistence, a step which is conditioned by their physical organization. By producing their means of subsistence men are indirectly producing their material life.[6]

Thus emerged the indispensability of work as a vital activity. This is the case even when the mode of production makes work one-dimensional by reducing its amplitude and comprehensiveness.[7] When work is understood as a vital element, indeed the trait that distinguishes human beings

---

[2] K. Marx, *Economic and Philosophic Manuscripts of 1844*, MECW, vol. 3, p. 276. [3] Ibid.
[4] Ibid. [5] K. Marx and F. Engels, *The German Ideology*, MECW, vol. 5, p. 31. [6] Ibid.
[7] In *The German Ideology*, Marx and Engels offered a metaphor that expressed the fullness of their conception of work. According to this text: 'in communist society, where nobody has one exclusive sphere of activity but each can become accomplished in any branch he wishes, society regulates the general production and thus makes it possible for me to do one thing today and another tomorrow, to hunt in the morning, fish in the afternoon, rear cattle in the evening, criticize after dinner, just as I have a mind, without ever becoming hunter, fisherman, shepherd or critic' (ibid, p. 47).

from animals, it thus becomes a central and inherent element of humanity. It is impossible to conceive of a social life without the daily realization of the productive act. Yet the human and social environment itself transformed the original meanings that had existed within work.

8.2 Labour as an Alienated Activity

Conceptualizing work as an expression of vital activity, Marx's early writings moreover asserted that capitalism has reduced this activity to a mere search for means of subsistence. Building on his wider conception of work, he added a concrete element which resulted from his preliminary analyses of political economy, namely, the consideration of this activity also as a commodity.

This important formulation was clearly presented in the *Economic and Philosophic Manuscripts of 1844*. Marx argued:

The worker becomes all the poorer the more wealth he produces, the more his production increases in power and size. The worker becomes an ever cheaper commodity the more commodities he creates. The devaluation of the world of men is in direct proportion to the increasing value of the world of things. Labour produces not only commodities: it produces itself and the worker as a commodity – and this at the same rate at which it produces commodities in general ... Under these economic conditions this realisation of labour appears as loss of realisation for the workers; objectification as loss of the object and bondage to it; appropriation as estrangement, as alienation.[8]

Marx thus showed that, once commodity production become generalized, capitalism subordinates the vital activity of work to an alienated form, as wage labour.[9] This alienation develops as follows:

the more the worker produces, the less he has to consume; the more values he creates, the more valueless, the more unworthy he becomes; the better formed his product, the more deformed becomes the worker; the more civilized his object, the more barbarous becomes the worker; the more powerful labour becomes, the more powerless becomes the worker; the more ingenious labour becomes, the less ingenious becomes the worker and the more he becomes nature's servant.[10]

---

[8] Marx, *Economic and Philosophic Manuscripts of 1844*, p. 272.
[9] Engels observed that there are two distinct English terms to characterize the dialectical relation between work and labour: 'The English language has the advantage of possessing different words for the two aspects of labour here considered. The labour which creates use value, and counts qualitatively, is work, as distinguished from labour; that which creates Value and counts quantitatively, is labour as distinguished from work' (K. Marx, *Capital*, volume I, MECW, vol. 35, p. 57, footnote 1).
[10] Marx, *Economic and Philosophic Manuscripts of 1844*, p. 273.

Workers do not recognize themselves in their own productive action. Their activity then represents a moment that internalizes the alienation that is present in the very process of wage labour as such.

So, for Marx 'alienation [*Entäusserung*]' and 'estrangement [*Entfremdung*]'[11] initially appeared in connection with the products of labour. And this corresponds to their first manifestation. Nevertheless, this condition of alienation is expressed not only through the *outcome* of the production process, but also in the very act of production – within the productive activity itself.

This double manifestation precludes the vital activity of work, and turns 'man's species-being, both nature and his spiritual species-property, into a being alien to him, into a means of his individual existence'.[12] This led Marx to the conclusion that

> an immediate consequence of the fact that man is estranged from the product of his labour, from his life activity, from his species-being, is the estrangement of man from man. When man confronts himself, he confronts the other man. What applies to a man's relation to his work, to the product of his labour and to himself, also holds of a man's relation to the other man, and to the other man's labour and object of labour.[13]

Marx thus arrived at this critical statement: the worker therefore only feels himself outside his work, and in his work feels outside himself. He feels at home when he is not working, and when he is working he does not feel at home. His labour is therefore not voluntary, but coerced; it is forced labour.[14] Instead of performing a vital activity in order to satisfy human needs and necessities, work is converted into a simple means of satisfying needs that are external to it. As the *Economic and Philosophic Manuscripts of 1844* put it, work's alienated and estranged condition becomes so evident that 'as soon as no physical or other compulsion exists, labour is shunned like the plague'.[15]

In the dialectic of labour, even though labour is essentially oriented towards the production of commodities, it does still to some extent produce socially useful goods. But once labour is directed by this 'second nature' – that is, dominated by capital and its need to valorize itself – this

---

[11] Although 'alienation [*Entäusserung*]' and 'estrangement [*Entfremdung*]' have frequently been understood as synonyms, Marx used these two categories – more often, but not only, in his early writings – to refer to the social complex of alienation, as 'exteriorization [*Entäusserung*]' and as 'estrangement [*Entfremdung*]'. See G. Lukács, *History and Class Consciousness: Studies in Marxist Dialectics* (London: Merlin Press, 1971), pp. IX–XXXIX. See also I. Mészáros, *Marx's Theory of Alienation* (London: Merlin Press, 1970), p. 313 and M. Musto, 'Revisiting Marx's Concept of Alienation', in M. Musto (ed.), *Marx for Today* (London: Routledge, 2012), p. 92.

[12] Marx, *Economic and Philosophic Manuscripts of 1844*, p. 277. [13] Ibid.

[14] Ibid, p. 274. [15] Ibid.

dialectical relation will subordinate the production of socially useful goods to the production of exchange-value.

In *Wage Labour and Capital* (1849), Marx indicated an important nuance that would only be fully developed in *Capital* (1867). Marx here laid down the basic outlines of the idea that not labour itself, but the 'capacity to labour'[16] is a commodity. This proceeded via his particular formulation of labour. Labour would no longer be understood only as an expression of a commodity. Rather, it would be considered as a special commodity, the only one capable of creating value. In that same essay, Marx asserted: 'labour was not always a commodity. Labour was not always wage labour, that is, free labour'.[17]

Having understood labour as a special commodity, he added, a little further on, that:

> The free labourer, on the other hand, sells himself and, indeed, sells himself piecemeal. He sells at auction eight, ten, twelve, fifteen hours of his life, day after day, to the highest bidder, to the owner of the raw materials, instruments of labour and means of subsistence, that is, to the capitalist ... But the worker, whose sole source of livelihood is the sale of his labour cannot leave the whole class of purchasers, that is, the capitalist class, without renouncing his existence.[18]

With this formulation, Marx demonstrated that wages are determined by 'the price of a definite commodity, of labour'.[19] That is the reason why 'Wages are, therefore, determined by the same laws that determine the price of every other commodity.'[20]

In *Value, Price and Profit*, Marx reinforced this conceptualization. But here he presented this commodity as 'labour power'. He made clear: 'what the working man sells is not directly his Labour, but his Labouring Power, the temporary disposal of which he makes over to the capitalist'.[21]

8.3   Labour, Value-Theory, Fetishism, and Associated Work

This deepening and consolidation of the distinction between labour and labour power became vital for the development of his greatest work,

---

[16] Ibid, p. 213.
[17] K. Marx, 'Wage Labour and Capital', MECW, vol. 9, p. 203. Although that represented an important prelude to the formulation of the concept of 'labour power', in the original version, Marx used only 'labour', or at most 'capacity to labour'. In the 1891 edition of *Wage Labour and Capital*, Engels did however introduce the full concept of 'labour power'. As he explained in his preface to this edition, incorporating the concept of 'labour power': 'I therefore tell the reader beforehand: this is not the pamphlet as Marx wrote it in 1849 but approximately as he would have written it in 1891' (F. Engels, 'Introduction to Karl Marx, *Wage Labour and Capital*', MECW vol. 27, p. 195).
[18] Marx, 'Wage Labour and Capital', p. 203.   [19] Ibid, p. 204.   [20] Ibid.
[21] K. Marx *Value, Price and Profit*, MECW, vol. 20, p. 128.

Capital. In this book, Marx devoted extensive focus to refining his concept of labour. He proposed the following precise definition:

Labour is, in the first place, a process in which both man and Nature participate, and in which man of his own accord starts, regulates, and controls the material reactions between himself and Nature. He opposes himself to Nature as one of her own forces, setting in motion arms and legs, head and hands, the natural forces of his body, in order to appropriate Nature's productions in a form adapted to his own wants. By thus acting on the external world and changing it, he at the same time changes his own nature. He develops his slumbering powers and compels them to act in obedience to his sway.[22]

So when individuals transform external nature, they also change their own human nature. This takes place within a reciprocal transformation process that converts social work into a central element for the development of human sociability. It is this kind of human action that makes the history of the social being a complex and rich process of accomplishment. It takes place through advances and retreats, victories and defeats. This is because labour remains, to some extent, the expression of some conscious act. There is always something to be made; the means of humanity's production and reproduction have to be produced; needs and demands have to be met, 'whether, for instance, they spring from the stomach or from the fancy'.[23]

Seeking to emphasize this decisive dimension of human work, Marx made his famous distinction between the worst architect and the best bee. The architect plans the work he is going to do, while the bee acts on instinct.[24] Therefore, unlike organic beings and pre-human animals, the human being – *qua* social being – has an essentially reflective dimension. And this is always an expression of a conscious act. It was on this basis that Marx said that

So far therefore as labour is a creator of use value, is useful labour, it is a necessary condition, independent of all forms of society, for the existence of the human race; it is an eternal nature-imposed necessity, without which there can be no material exchanges between man and Nature, and therefore no life.[25]

Standing apart from any naturalist, evolutionist, or ahistorical reading,[26] this Marxian formulation is deeply historical and social. In any form of

---

[22] Marx, *Capital*, volume I, p. 187.   [23] Ibid, p. 45.   [24] Cf. Ibid, p. 187.
[25] Ibid, p. 53.
[26] Among those who consider work or labour as a creation of the capitalist mode of production and, accordingly, criticize the broad notion of work developed by Marx, see A. Gorz, *The Immaterial: Knowledge, Value, and Capital* (London: Seagull Books, 2010), pp. 1–15 and 34–56. See also M. Postone's critical approach to the 'traditional Marxism', M. Postone, *Time, Labor, and Social Domination: A Reinterpretation of Marx's Critical Theory* (Cambridge: Cambridge University Press, 1996), pp. 3–20.

human sociability, the practice of producing socially useful goods can only be realized through work. In this sense, work is the foundational act of the socio-metabolic mediation between humanity and nature.[27] That is why, for Marx, everyday life could not possibly be reproduced without the mediation provided by work. Yet work is simultaneously a historical and social process with a deeply contradictory basis. So, for Marx, it was evident that the evolution and the unfolding of human life could never be exclusively restricted to work. If that were true, then it would, at best, be the condensation and realization of social imprisonment in a single dimension, in a one-sided fashion, contrary to the multiple dimensions that human activity involves.

Put differently, if social life is unthinkable without work (in its vital sense and in its emancipatory dimension), if one's lifetime were exclusively restricted to labour (as is, sadly, frequently the case for masses of humans) then life itself would be an alienating martyrdom. This poses a decisive social imperative. Namely, that we reject the permanence of a type of sociability restricted to a labour which exhausts human-social forces, alienates them and makes them socially unhappy.

In *Capital*, Marx sought to capture the central importance of a commodity that is deeply embedded in the logic of capital. In order to do this, he had to develop an essential distinction. Here he referred to a differentiation that capitalist society introduces on a large scale, between concrete labour – which produces use-value – and abstract labour – which produces exchange-value:

On the one hand, all labour is, speaking physiologically, an expenditure of human labour power, and in its character of identical abstract human labour, it creates and forms the value of commodities. On the other hand, all labour is expenditure of human labour power in a special form and with a definite aim, and in this, its character of concrete useful labour, it produces use values.[28]

This led Marx to assert that:

Along with the useful qualities of the products themselves, we put out of sight both the useful character forms of the various kinds of labour embodied in them, and the concrete forms of that labour; there is nothing left but what is common to them all; all are reduced to one and the same sort of labour, human labour in the abstract.[29]

---

[27] That is the approach defended by G. Lukács, *The Ontology of Social Being: Labour* (London: Merlin Press, 1980), pp. 1–46. A contrary approach can be found in J. Habermas, *The Theory of Communicative Action, vol. 2: The Critique of Functionalist Reason* (London: Polity Press, 1992), pp. 332–43. Here the sphere of communicative action (and not work) is the central element of the constitution of the social being.
[28] Marx, *Capital*, volume I, p. 56.   [29] Ibid, p. 48.

In the capitalist mode of production, society is oriented towards the creation of exchange-value. The use-value of things is minimized, reduced, and subsumed to their exchange-value. It follows that the concrete scope of labour is also entirely subordinated to its abstract one. Therefore, when speaking about labour in capitalist society, it is absolutely necessary that we specify to which scope we are referring: the abstract or the concrete. Unless we properly incorporate the distinction between abstract and concrete labour, we run the risk of a strong incongruity in our analysis, considering a dual-dimension phenomenon in merely one-dimensional terms.

According to Marx, in the universe of human sociability, it is not plausible to conceive the extinction of social work, when this is understood as the creator of use-value, of useful things, as a form of exchange between social being and nature. If the elimination of society's abstract labour is indeed in view,[30] this is something ontologically distinct from conceiving or supposing the end of work as vital activity, as the foundational element of the social being.

It is one thing to conceive the end of abstract and alienated labour with the elimination of capitalism, and quite another to conceive the elimination of the universe of human sociability, and the concrete labour which creates socially useful things.

Whenever work is understood without a proper grasp on its dual dimension, it can only be identified as synonymous with abstract, alienated labour. The consequence is that we can at most imagine a society of free time, but which coexists with the prevalent forms of wage labour and expropriated labour.

Upon the development of the concept of labour power in *Capital*, Marx pointed out that the work time is, then, divided between the necessary labour time and the surplus labour time. The first is the one in which the worker earns his salary to guarantee his own and his family's reproduction, while the second creates a new value, the surplus-value, which is privately appropriated by capital.

Marx also observed that, when there is an increase in surplus labour time, this raises absolute surplus-value. Nevertheless, when the exceeding labour is extended by the intensification of the labour process, through technological advancement and the consequent increase in productivity, Marx designated this in terms of a raise in relative surplus-value:

The surplus value produced by prolongation of the working day, I call absolute surplus value. On the other hand, the surplus value rising from the curtailment of

---

[30] Such action is necessarily linked to the end of capitalist society.

the necessary labour time, and from the corresponding alteration in the respective lengths of the two components of the working day, I call relative value.[31]

In a social structure based on the extraction of (absolute and relative) surplus-value and on the production of exchange-values, overlapping with the production of use-values, there emerges the social phenomenon that Marx named commodity fetishism. The social relations established among producers assume the form of a relationship between labour products. The social relation previously established between social beings acquires the form of a relationship between things:

> The equality of all sorts of human labour is expressed objectively by their products all being equally values; the measure of the expenditure of labour power by the duration of that expenditure, takes the form of the quantity of value of the products of labour; and finally, the mutual relations of the producers, within which the social character of their labour affirms itself, take the form of a social relation between the products.[32]

With the predominance of the abstract dimension of labour over its concrete dimension, the mysterious or fetishized character of the commodity emerges immediately. It covers the social dimensions of labour itself, showing them to be elements inherent on the products of labour.

When the exchange-value is effective, the social bond between people is transformed into a social relation among things, for the personal capacity is also transfigured into a capacity between commodities, what establishes a complex and reified relation between social beings.[33]

The existing social relations between individual labours and the total labour are masked. They are presented as relations between objectified things. What then appears is fetishism: 'it is nothing more than a certain social relation between men themselves, which, for them, assumes the phantasmagorical shape of a relationship between things'.[34] Under the law of exchange-value, the social bonding between human beings transforms into a relation between things: a personal capacity transforms into the capacity of things. A reified relation between social beings thus emerges.

Again in *Capital*, volume I, but also in *Chapter VI (unpublished)*, Marx presented another important point that completes his wider understanding of labour in capitalist society.[35] He stated that labour does not necessarily have to be executed manually in order for it to be defined as

---

[31] Marx, *Capital*, volume I, p. 320.   [32] Ibid, p. 82.   [33] Ibid, pp. 81–2.
[34] Ibid, pp. 81–2.
[35] Marx, *Capital*, volume I, pp. 509–10, as well as in K. Marx, *Chapter VI (unpublished)*, MECW, vol. 34, pp. 441–52.

productive. Moreover, he held that, while the criterion of the predominance of material production applies to the system of collective production considered as a whole, this is not necessarily true of labour considered in isolation.[36]

Marx also wrote that a worker is considered productive if he produces surplus-value for the capitalist. That is, if he takes part in the process of valourization of capital. Taking the example of the teacher, whose activity he considered to be external to the sphere of production, Marx said that this latter is productive once he is under the command of a capitalist who owns a 'teaching factory'.[37] The teacher's labour is, conversely, unproductive when his teaching activity only produces use-value and not exchange-value. We are in the presence of productive labour only when labour is integrated into a social relationship, which is predominantly aimed at the self-valourization of capital.[38] Thus, we should take from Marx the acknowledgement that there do exist activities which are not predominantly material, but still take part in the valourization of capital.

Another central point present in *Capital* concerns the conceptualization of productive and unproductive labour. According to Marx, productive labour is that which:

(1) creates surplus-value and valourizes capital;
(2) is paid by means of capital-money and not in the form of rent;
(3) is the result of collective, social, and complex forms of labour, as opposed to individual labour. For this reason, he said that it is not the individual worker who is the real agent of the process of work as a whole, but rather a socially combined labour capacity;
(4) valourizes capital, independently of the fact that its products are material or immaterial;
(5) the way it enters into the creation and valourization of capital is dependent on its social relationship and social form. For this reason, labour activities that are identical in their tangible nature may be productive or unproductive depending on their relation to the creation of value;
(6) tends to be salaried – even if the inverse is not true, because not all salaried labour is productive.[39]

On the other hand, labour is unproductive when it only creates useful goods and it is not involved in the production of exchange-value.

If this is Marx's formulation for describing capitalism in the mid-nineteenth century, today we are witnessing the rise of new forms of

---

[36] Marx, *Capital*, volume I, p. 510.   [37] Ibid.   [38] Ibid.
[39] Marx, *Chapter VI (unpublished)*, pp. 444–5.

labour. These latter are capable of creating complex mechanisms of value extraction, in the material and immaterial spheres that characterize the global chains of value which are extending within present-day capitalism. Instead of weakening the law of value, this conjunction has amplified it. It has made it more complex and in the twenty-first century it has further intensified its effects.[40]

This is because immaterial labour has come to play a significant, although not dominant, role in the relational configuration of the different forms of living labour with dead labour. This is because it influences the process of capital valourization by reducing capital circulation time and consequently also capital rotation time. This is especially true of the service sectors (and their intersections, like, for example, agribusiness, the service industry, and the industrial services) increasingly controlled by the logic of capital and the logic of its commodification process. This sector is gradually being integrated into the chains of value production, and so it is abandoning its unproductive form by becoming increasingly part of the process of value creation.[41] These are, then, the central elements that characterize wage labour for capital. In frontal opposition to them, in *Capital*, Marx presented the embryonic elements of his new conception: the freely associated producers.

If work finds itself within what Marx called the 'realm of necessity', it will be through the 'shortening of the working day' that the 'true realm of freedom ... can blossom forth'.[42] In that case, the idea of free and

---

[40] In *Capital*, volume II, MECW, vol. 36, pp. 125–55, Marx provided an important analytical indication for understanding labour in service industries as value productive, because it showed us a productive process inside the transportation industry. Marx had an extended notion of industry, which allowed us to understand why we can speak of a process of production in the transportation sector (and in other sectors, such as storage, the gas industry, railways, navigation, communication, etc.), even if this activity does not result in any material production. It is worth pointing out that, by offering these examples, Marx indicated an idea of industry that transcended the traditional vision that instead limited it to material transformation, and also extending it to what we could call the service industries.

[41] There is an important discussion around this issue today. This debate varies from the prevalence of the law of value in the sphere of digital labour – in particular the formulation regarding the cybertariat presented by U. Huws, *The Making of a Cybertariat: Virtual Work in a Real World* (London: Merlin Press, 2003), pp. 152–76 and the polemics developed by N. Dyer-Whiteford in the *Cyber-proletariat: Global Labour in the Digital Vortex* (London: Pluto Press, 2015), pp. 39–59 – to the argument laid out by E. Fisher and C. Fuchs in *Reconsidering Value and Labour in the Digital Age* (Basingstoke: Palgrave Macmillan, 2015), pp. 3–25, among other authors. This latter debate concerns value and labour in the digital arena, and in particular theses regarding the critique of the political economy of the Internet.

[42] K. Marx, *Capital*, volume III, MECW, vol. 37, p. 807.

associated work, beyond the constraints of capital, constitutes a vital element for his conception of a communist society.

> Freedom in this field can only consist in socialised man, the associated producers, rationally regulating their interchange with Nature.[43]

That is precisely the reason why the reduction of the working day has been one of the most important demands of the working class – the basic prerequisite, as Marx observed, for an emancipated life.[44] This is because a meaningful life outside of work presupposes a meaningful life within work. It is not possible to make alienated labour compatible with free time. A life that is deprived of meaning within work is incompatible with a meaningful life outside of it. In some form, the sphere outside of work will be tarnished by the disaffection present in working life:[45]

> The life-process of society ... does not strip off its mystical veil until it is treated as production by freely associated men, and is consciously regulated by them in accordance with a settled plan.[46]

The problem of the elimination of wage labour as the creator of exchange-values, and the elimination of private ownership over the means of production, is thus socially resolved through 'free and associated labour'.[47] The exploitation of labour and of surplus-value would thus be replaced with the disposable time of each of those participating in this 'social' work. Marx's synthesis, presented in his *Critique of the Gotha Programme*, was enlightening in this regard:

> In a higher phase of communist society, after ... the antithesis between mental and physical labour ... has vanished; after labour has become not only a means of life but life's prime want ... only then can ... society inscribe on its banners: From each according to his abilities, to each according to his needs![48]

Thus, Marx's formulation regarding the free and associated producers frontally clashes with one of the main foundations of capitalist society. Marx here presented a dialectic of work that conceived it both as a vital

---

[43] Ibid, p. 807. See also *The Civil War in France*, MECW, vol. 22, when Marx, inspired by the Paris Commune, indicated the formula of the 'free and associated labour' (p. 335) in counter-position to the exploitation of labour.

[44] Marx, *Capital*, volume III, p. 807. On the working day in contemporary capitalism, see P. Basso, *Modern Times, Ancient Hours: Working Lives in the Twenty-First Century* (London: Verso, 2003), pp. 1–25.

[45] A more detailed discussion of these issues can be found in R. Antunes, *The Meanings of Work: Essay on the Affirmation and Negation of Work* (Chicago: Haymarket Books, 2013), pp. 146–55.

[46] Marx, *Capital*, volume I, p. 90.   [47] Marx, *The Civil War in France*, p. 335.

[48] K. Marx, *Critique of the Gotha Programme*, MECW, vol. 24, p. 87.

activity, producing goods that humanity needs, and as the expression of wage and alienated labour, with the consolidation of capitalism. That is why his broad conception of work cannot be seen one-dimensionally.[49]

Marx's understanding of this dialectical dimension in the conceptualization of work is what makes him an author of our own present. His formulation was not only pertinent to the nineteenth century, but endured throughout the twentieth century. And there are no signs that it has lost its actuality.

8.4 Work Today

While some experts argue that labour has lost its importance in capitalist society,[50] what we are instead witnessing is a quantitative reduction (with qualitative effects) in the productive sphere. Abstract labour continues to play a decisive role in the creation of exchange-value. To express that in classical terms: the commodities that are produced still result from manual and intellectual activity. And this activity derives from human labour, in interaction with the means of production and technology.

The 'diminution of the subjective factor of the labour process as compared with the objective factor'[51] relatively reduces but does not eliminate the role of collective labour in the production of exchange-value. The reduction of living labour, owing to the growth of dead labour, offers the worker the possibility of coming closer to being what Marx called 'overseer and regulator'[52] of the production process. However, the complete achievement of this trend is precluded by the very logic of capital.[53]

The contemporary forms of social labour have become more complex, socially combined, and even more intense in their rhythms and processes. In conceiving these forms it does not seem possible to minimize or even ignore the process of exchange-value creation. On the contrary, capitalist society and its law of value needs less secure labour and more precarious and intermittent labour.

---

[49] Among the authors that offer important updates to Marx's thesis, see H. Braverman, *Labor and Monopoly Capital* (New York: Monthly Review Press, 1998), pp. 203–47 and pp. 279–310, A. Bihr, *Du 'Grand Soir' à 'L'Alternative': le Mouvement Ouvrier Européen en Crise* (Paris: Les Éditions Ouvrières, 1991), pp. 87–108 and I. Mészáros, *Beyond Capital: Towards a Theory of Transition* (London: Merlin Press, 1995), pp. 917–36.
[50] See, for example, C. Offe, 'Work: The Key Sociological Category?', in C. Offe (ed.), *Disorganized Capitalism* (Cambridge: Polity Press, 1985), pp. 129–50.
[51] Marx, *Capital*, volume I, MECW, vol. 35, pp. 617–18.
[52] K. Marx, 'Outlines of the Critique of Political Economy [*Grundrisse*]. First Instalment', MECW, vol. 29, p. 112.
[53] Ibid, pp. 90–1.

Precisely because capital depends on living labour for the process of value-creation, it needs to increase labour productivity in order to intensify the forms of surplus-labour extraction in an ever smaller amount of time. The expansion of multifunctional labour endowed with an intellectual dimension refutes the thesis that capital no longer has an interest in exploiting abstract labour. Indeed, it has been characteristic of capital, ever since its origins, to eliminate living labour as far as possible and to expand dead labour.

The reduction of the 'stable' proletariat that is the heir to Taylorism/Fordism; the expansion of intellectual labour inside modern factories; and the generalized growth of forms of precarious labour – developed intensively in the era of the flexible firm – are examples of new forms of the surplus-value extraction today.[54] The complex interaction established between labour and science does not remove living labour from capital's socio-metabolic order. On the contrary, this process makes use of intellectual labour. Interacting with the automated machine, this later transfers part of the new intellectual and cognitive attributes to the new machine that results from this production. This process demands that capital finds even more complex, multifunctional workers, at least in those branches of production where there is greater technological development.

There is another trend, deriving from the growing overlap between material and immaterial labour, which also highlights the strength of Marx's formulation. On the one hand, the advancement of labour in the areas of research, software-creation, and publicity is also an example of the spread of labour in the immaterial sphere. On the other hand, the growth of labour in service industries (such as call centres, information and communications technologies, the hotel industry, etc.) is another important characteristic of the broader notion of labour in the contemporary world. Material and immaterial labour, in the growing overlap that exists between them, are, however, subordinated to the logic of capitalist production. Thus, a reflection on living labour should revisit the discussion which Marx himself conducted of immaterial labour, as a trend in capitalism today.[55]

---

[54] See the significant example of Foxconn in China.
[55] One important contribution is offered by Vincent: 'the intellectual labour-power produced inside and outside of production is absorbed as a commodity by capital, which incorporates it and thus gives new qualities to dead labour: flexibility, rapid displacement and constant self-transformation. Material production and the production of services increasingly require innovations, becoming as a result more and more subordinated to an increasing production of knowledge that is converted into commodities and capital', J. M. Vincent, 'Les Automatismes Sociaux et le "General Intellect"', Paradigmes du Travail, *Futur Antérieur*, 16 (2): 121 (1993). An approach that privileges immaterial

Some of the formulations Marx offered constitute an important point of departure when we envisage an alternative capable of overcoming capitalist society and its enormous social constraints. For that, at least two claims must be at the heart of labour's struggles today, on a global scale.

(1) the fight for the reduction of the working day, in order to reduce unemployment. That leads us to the following vital questions: producing what, and for whom?

(2) the right to work for all is also a necessary demand. This, not because we place any value on alienated and waged labour. This kind of labour must be eradicated with the end of capitalist society. But it is then that work as a vital activity – free and associated labour – becomes one of the essential elements in the construction of a new society. And here the essence of Marx's formulation on work gains enormous social and political relevance, also in our own time.

The imperative for our times remains a new mode of production, based on self-determined activity. This is a mode of producing socially necessary use-values. It thus stands in radical contrast to labour based on surplus time, which is instead aimed at producing exchange-values.

References

Antunes, Ricardo (2013), *The Meanings of Work: Essay on the Affirmation and Negation of Work*, Chicago: Haymarket Books.

Basso, Pietro (2003), *Modern Times, Ancient Hours: Working Lives in the Twenty-first Century*, London: Verso.

Bihr, Alain (1991), *Du 'Grand Soir' à 'L'Alternative': le Mouvement Ouvrier Européen en Crise*, Paris: Les Éditions Ouvrières.

Braverman, Harry (1998), *Labor and Monopoly Capital*, New York: Monthly Review Press.

Dyer-Whiteford, Nick (2015), *Cyber-proletariat: Global Labour in the Digital Vortex*, London: Pluto Press.

Engels, Frederick (1990), 'Introduction to Karl Marx *Wage Labour and Capital*', MECW, vol. 27, pp. 179–91.

Fischer, Eran, and Fuchs, Christian (2015), *Reconsidering value and Labour in the digital Age*, Basingstoke: Palgrave Macmillan.

Gorz, André (2010), *The Immaterial: Knowledge, Value, and Capital*, London: Seagull Books.

Habermas, Jürgen (1992), *The Theory of Communicative Action, vol. 2: The Critique of Functionalist Reason*, London: Polity Press.

---

labour, and minimizes material production (thus moving away from the Marxian formulation) can be found in M. Lazzarato, 'Le Concept de Travail Immatériel: la Grande Entreprise', *Futur Antérieur*, 10: 54–61 (1992).

Huws, Ursula (2003), *The Making of a Cybertariat: Virtual Work in a Real World*, London: Merlin Press.

Lazzarato, Maurizio (1992), 'Le Concept de Travail Immatériel: la Grande Entreprise', *Futur Antérieur*, 10: 54–61.

Lukács, Georg (1971), *History and Class Consciousness: Studies in Marxist Dialectics*, London: Merlin Press.

—— (1980), *The Ontology of Social Being: Labour*, London: Merlin Press.

Marx, Karl (1975), 'Comments on James Mill, *Elements d'economie politique*', MECW, vol. 3, pp. 211–28.

—— (1975), *Economic and Philosophic Manuscripts of 1844*, MECW, vol. 3, pp. 229–346.

—— (1977), 'Wage Labour and Capital', MECW, vol. 9, pp. 197–228.

—— (1985), *Value, Price and Profit*, MECW, vol. 20, pp. 101–49.

—— (1986), *The Civil War in France: Address of the General Council of the International Working Men's Association*, MECW, vol. 22, pp. 307–59.

—— (1987), 'Outlines of the Critique of Political Economy [*Grundrisse*]. First Instalment', MECW, vol. 29, pp. 5–550.

—— (1989), *Critique of the Gotha Programme*, MECW, vol. 24, pp. 75–99.

—— (1994), 'Chapter VI (unpublished)', MECW, vol. 34, pp. 339–471.

—— (1996), *Capital*, volume I, MECW, vol. 35.

—— (1997), *Capital*, volume II, MECW, vol. 36.

—— (1998), *Capital*, volume III, MECW, vol. 37.

Marx, Karl, and Engels, Fredrick (1975), *The German Ideology*, MECW, vol. 5, pp. 19–539.

Mészáros, István (1970), *Marx's Theory of Alienation*, London: Merlin Press.

—— (1995), *Beyond Capital: Towards a Theory of Transition*, London: Merlin Press.

Musto, Marcello (2012), 'Revisiting Marx's Concept of Alienation', in Marcello Musto (ed.), *Marx for Today*, London: Routledge, pp.92–116.

Offe, Claus (1985), 'Work: The Key Sociological Category?', in Clauss Offe (ed.), *Disorganized Capitalism*, Cambridge: Polity Press.

Postone, Moishe (1996), *Time, Labor, and Social Domination: A Reinterpretation of Marx's Critical Theory*, Cambridge: Cambridge University Press.

Vincent, Jean-Marie (1993), 'Les Automatismes Sociaux et le "General Intellect"', Paradigmes du Travail, *Futur Antérieur*, 16 (2): 121–30.

9 Capital and Temporality

Moishe Postone

9.1 Reconceptualizing Marxism

The far-reaching transformation of the world in recent decades has dramatically indicated that contemporary critical theory must be centrally concerned with questions of historical dynamics and large-scale structural changes if it is to be adequate for our social universe. A critical theory of capitalism based on the Marxian category of capital could significantly illuminate these historical developments, but only if it is fundamentally reconceptualized in ways that distinguish it from various understandings of capital in traditional Marxist interpretations as well as in recent social sciences discourses.

The category of capital, according to the reconceptualization presented in here, has little in common with the uses of the term 'capital' by a wide range of theorists, from Gary Becker (1930–2014) through Pierre Bourdieu (1930–2012).[1] It also differs, however, from the ways it has been used by many Marxist theorists for whom 'capital' generally refers to a social surplus that is privately appropriated.[2] While agreeing that Karl Marx's category of capital refers to the structuring of society as a whole, this chapter argues that it not only delineates a determinate mode of class exploitation, but also, more basically, grasps a unique form of social mediation that structures capitalist modernity as a historically specific form of social life. This form of mediation is socially constituted and, yet, abstract and temporal. As will be elaborated further, it manifests itself in peculiar, abstract forms of domination that cannot sufficiently be understood in terms of the domination of a class or, indeed, of any concrete

---

The author would like to thank Mark Loeffler and Robert Stern for valuable critical feedback.

[1] See G. Becker, *Human Capital: A Theoretical and Empirical Analysis, with Special Reference to Education* (New York: Columbia University Press, 1975) and P. Bourdieu, *Distinction: A Social Critique of the Judgement of Taste* (Cambridge, MA: Harvard University Press, 2000).

[2] See, for example, M. Dobb, *Political Economy and Capitalism: Some Essays in Economic Tradition* (London: Routledge & Kegan Paul, 1940).

social and/or political entity. These forms of domination, expressed by categories such as commodity and capital, are, moreover, not static, but generate a historical dynamic that uniquely characterizes capitalist modernity.

The focus in this chapter on the historically dynamic character of capitalist society responds to the massive transformations of capitalism in the past four decades. This period has been characterized by the demise of the post-Second World War state-centred Fordist synthesis in the West, the collapse or fundamental transformation of party-states and their command economies in the East, and the emergence of a neo-liberal capitalist global order that might, in turn, be undermined by the development of huge competing economic blocs. Because these changes have included the collapse of the Soviet Union and of European communism, they frequently have been taken as marking the end of Marxism and of Marx's theoretical relevance. Yet, these historical transformations also highlight the need to grapple with the problem of historical dynamics and large-scale structural changes.

The central importance of this problematic is underlined when one considers the overarching trajectory in the twentieth century of what retrospectively can be termed state-centric capitalism from its beginnings, which can be located in the First World War and the Russian Revolution, through its apogee in the decades following the Second World War, and its decline after the early 1970s. What is significant about this trajectory is its global character. It encompassed Western capitalist countries and the Soviet Union, as well as colonized lands and decolonized countries. Although differences in historical development have, of course, occurred when viewed from the vantage point of the twenty-first century, they appear more as different inflections of a common pattern than as fundamentally different developments. For example, the welfare state was expanded in all Western industrial countries in the twenty-five years after the end of the Second World War and then limited or partially dismantled in the early 1970s. These developments – paralleled by the post-war success and subsequent rapid decline of the Soviet Union and the massive transformations of China – occurred regardless of whether conservative or social democratic ('liberal') parties were in power.

Such general overarching developments cannot be explained in terms of contingent, local, political decisions. They indicate the existence of a historical dynamic in both the East and the West, and reveal that the notion that the state could control that dynamic was at best temporarily valid. That is, they suggest the existence of dynamic forces not fully subject to political control, and of general structural constraints on political, social, and economic decisions.

9.2 History and Domination

These recent historical transformations suggest the importance of a renewed encounter with Marx's critique of political economy, for the problem of historical dynamics and global structural change is at the very heart of that critique. Nevertheless, the history of the last century also suggests that traditional Marxism is not fully adequate to the contemporary world and that an adequate critical theory must differ in important and basic ways from traditional critiques of capitalism.

The term 'traditional Marxism' refers, here, to a very general interpretive framework in which capitalism is analyzed essentially in terms of class relations rooted in private property relations and mediated by the market.[3] Social domination is understood primarily in terms of class domination and exploitation. Within this general interpretive framework, capitalism is characterized by a growing structural contradiction between that society's basic social relations (interpreted as private property and the market) and the forces of production (interpreted in terms of labour and the industrial mode of producing). Socialism is understood primarily in terms of collective ownership of the means of production and centralized planning in an industrialized context. This general framework is based on a transhistorical understanding of labour as the source of wealth in all societies and as the basis for what is universal and truly social. In capitalism, however, labour is hindered by particularistic and fragmenting relations from becoming fully realized. Emancipation, then, is realized in a social form where transhistorical labour, freed from the distortions of the market and private property, has openly emerged as the regulating principle of society. This notion, of course, is bound to that of socialist revolution as the 'self-realization' of the proletariat. Labour here provides the *standpoint* of the critique of capitalism.

Within the basic framework of 'traditional Marxism' there has been a broad range of very different theoretical, methodological, and political approaches which have generated powerful economic, political, social, historical, and cultural analyses.[4] Nevertheless, the limitations of the general framework itself have become increasingly evident in light of

---

[3] M. Postone, '*Capital* in Light of the *Grundrisse*', in M. Musto (ed.), *Karl Marx's* Grundrisse: *Foundations of the Critique of Political Economy 150 Years Later* (London and New York: Routledge, 2008), pp. 121–2.

[4] This would include structuralism and critical theory – two important strands of more recent critical Marx interpretations – both of which sought to get beyond the traditional paradigm. György Lukács (1885–1971) and members of the Frankfurt School, responding theoretically to the historical transformation of capitalism from a market-centred form to a bureaucratic, statist form, implicitly recognized the inadequacies of a critical theory of modernity that defined capitalism solely in nineteenth-century terms, in terms of the market and private property. As the author has elaborated elsewhere, however, they

twentieth-century historical developments. These developments include the non-emancipatory character of what called itself 'actually existing socialism', the trajectory of its rise and decline, paralleling that of the Western form of state-interventionist capitalism (suggesting they were similarly located historically), the growing importance of scientific knowledge and advanced technology in production (which seemed to call into question the labour theory of value), growing criticisms of technological progress and growth (which opposed the productivism of much traditional Marxism), and the increased importance of non-class-based social identities. Together, they suggest that the traditional framework no longer can serve as an adequate point of departure for an emancipatory critical theory.

Consideration of the general historical patterns that characterize the twentieth century, then, calls into question both traditional Marxism, with its affirmation of labour and history, as well as post-structuralist understandings of history as essentially contingent. Nevertheless, such consideration does not necessarily contravene all attempts to formulate a critical theory based on an analysis of history; nor does it negate the critical insight underlying attempts to deal with history contingently – namely, that history, grasped as the unfolding of an imminent necessity, delineates a form of unfreedom.

Precisely that form of unfreedom is the central object of Marx's critique of political economy, which attempts to explain, in social terms, the imperatives and constraints that give rise to the historical dynamics and structural changes of the modern world. His critique differs fundamentally from traditional Marxism, which criticizes capitalism from the standpoint of history and of labour. Marx's analysis, rather, focuses critically on the historical dynamic of capitalism and the centrality of labour to that form of social life. What had been traditional Marxism's *standpoint*, according to this interpretation, were the *objects* of Marx's critique. On the other hand, unlike post-structuralism, the Marxian critique does not deny the existence of a historical logic and its associated unfreedom by insisting that, in reality, human social life always develops contingently. Rather, Marx's critique regards the existence of a historical logic to be

remained bound to some of the assumptions of that very sort of theory (M. Postone, *Time, Labour, and Social Domination* [Cambridge and New York: Cambridge University Press, 1993], pp. 71–120). On the other hand, although Louis Althusser (1918–90) formulated a sophisticated critique of the 'idealism of labour' and treated social relations as structures that are not reducible to anthropological intersubjectivity, his focus on the question of the surplus in terms of exploitation, as well as on the physical 'material' dimension of production, are related to what ultimately is a traditional understanding of capitalism (L. Althusser and É. Balibar, *Reading* Capital [London: New Left Books, 1970], pp. 145–54, 165–82).

a hallmark of capitalist modernity. It seeks to grasp the nature of that peculiar historical logic, uncover its basis, and elucidate the possibility of its overcoming. It does so by grounding the immanent dynamic of modern, capitalist society in a historically specific form of social mediation that is expressed by the category of capital.

By grounding capitalism's dynamic with reference to categories that are historically specific to that social form, Marx's mature theory implies that History, understood as an immanently driven directional dynamic, is not a universal category of human social life. Rather, it is a historically specific feature of capitalist society (that can be and has been projected by many theorists onto human social life in general, as History). Far from viewing history affirmatively, Marx's theory, by grounding this directional dynamic in the category of capital, grasps it as a form of domination, of heteronomy. Moreover, according to this interpretation, Marx's mature theory itself does not purport to be a transhistorically valid theory of history and social life. On the contrary, it regards itself as historically specific.[5] Neither the object of Marx's critical theory nor the theory itself is transhistorical; rather, they are historically specific. Indeed, the theory calls into question any approach that claims for itself universal, transhistorical validity.

As a historical specific theory of domination, of heteronomy, the critical Marxian position is closer to post-structuralism in its *evaluation* of the historical logic of capitalism than it is to orthodox Second International Marxism. Its *analysis* of that logic, however, is critical of post-structuralism inasmuch as it does not regard heteronomous history as a narrative that simply can be dispelled discursively, but as the expression of a structure of temporal domination. Reappropriating the category of capital as the basis of a historically specific heteronomous dynamic allows, then, for an approach that could be critical both of a transhistorical conception of human history in terms of the unfolding of an intrinsic logic, as well as a transhistorical conception of human history in terms of contingency, That is, it could overcome the classical opposition of necessity and freedom. From this point of view, any attempt to recover human agency by insisting upon contingency in ways that bracket the historically specific structures of domination that characterize capitalism is – ironically – profoundly disempowering.

9.3 Critique and Historical Specificity

What is capital, in Marx's analysis? Elaborating this concept involves briefly considering the most fundamental categories with which Marx

---

[5] Postone, '*Capital* in Light of the *Grundrisse*', pp. 123–8.

begins his investigation in *Capital*, such as commodity and value, for they serve as the theoretical foundation for his categories of surplus-value and capital. Within the traditional framework, Marx's category of value generally has been regarded as an attempt to show that direct human labour always and everywhere creates social wealth, which in capitalism is mediated by the market. His category of surplus-value, according to such views, demonstrates the existence of exploitation in capitalism by showing that, in spite of appearances, the surplus product in capitalism is not constituted by a number of factors of production, such as labour, land, and machinery, but by labour alone. This surplus is appropriated by the capitalist class. Surplus-value, within this traditional framework, is a category of class-based exploitation.[6]

This interpretation is based on a transhistorical understanding of labour as an activity mediating humans and nature and conceptualizes emancipation in terms of the realization of labour, the self-realization of the proletariat. It is, at best, a one-sided interpretation. It focuses on the non-overt form of exploitation in capitalism but does not apprehend the historical dynamic grasped by Marx's categories.[7]

As already suggested, however, a close reading of Marx's mature critique of political economy calls into question the transhistorical presuppositions of the traditional interpretation. In the *Grundrisse*, Marx asserts that his fundamental categories should not be understood in narrow economic terms, but as forms of 'being in the world [*Daseinsformen*]', 'determinations of existence [*Existenzbestimmungen*]' – that is, forms of social being that are at once objective and subjective.[8] Moreover – and this is crucial – those categories should not be understood as transhistorical, but as historically specific to modern, or capitalist, society.[9] Even categories such as money

---

[6] See, for example, G. A. Cohen, *History, Labour and Freedom* (Oxford: Clarendon Press, 1988), pp. 209–38; Dobb, *Political Economy and Capitalism*, pp. 70–8; J. Elster, *Making Sense of Marx* (New York: Cambridge University Press, 1985), p. 127; R. Meeks, *Studies in the Labour Theory of Value* (New York and London: Lawrence and Wishart, 1973); J. Roemer, *Analytical Foundations of Marxian Economic Theory* (Cambridge: Cambridge University Press, 1981), pp. 158–9; I. Steedman, 'Ricardo, Marx, Sraffa', in I. Steedman and P. Sweezy (eds), *The Value Controversy* (London: New Left Books, 1981), pp. 11–19; P. Sweezy, *The Theory of Capitalist Development* (New York: Oxford University Press, 1968), pp. 52–3.

[7] Exploitation in the sense of the appropriation of the surplus produced by subaltern social groupings, antedates capitalism, of course, and has been a feature of all historical forms of social life. What is unique about capitalism is not only that its mode of appropriation is not overt – as opposed to the case of feudal lords and peasants, for example – but that it entails a dynamic, as will be discussed later. Traditional Marxism tends to focus on the former, while overlooking the latter.

[8] K. Marx, 'Outlines of the Critique of Political Economy [*Grundrisse*]. First Instalment', MECW, vol. 28, pp. 105–6.

[9] Ibid, pp. 100–8.

and labour that appear transhistorical because of their abstract and general character, are valid in their abstract generality only for capitalist society, according to Marx.[10] It is because of their peculiarly abstract and general character that categories historically specific to capitalism can appear valid for all societies.[11]

This includes the category of value. In the *Grundrisse*, Marx explicitly treats value as the 'foundation of bourgeois production' and characterizes it as a form of wealth historically specific to capitalism that is constituted by direct human labour time expenditure.[12] He indicates that value underlies a system of production that generates the historical possibility that value itself could be abolished and that production could be organized on a new basis, one not dependent on the expenditure of direct human labour in production. At the same time, however, value remains the necessary condition of capitalism. This contradiction between the potential generated by the system based on value and its actuality indicates that, for Marx, the abolition of capitalism entails the abolition of value and value-creating labour.[13] Far from signifying the self-realization of the proletariat, the abolition of capitalism would entail the self-abolition of the proletariat.

This sketch of capitalism's development in the *Grundrisse* illuminates the structure of Marx's argument in *Capital*. In the first place, the self-understanding of Marx's mature critical theory as historically specific meant that its point of departure had to be historically specific. Its form of presentation could not contravene the historically determinate character of the analysis; it could not, for example, proceed in a Cartesian manner from a putative transhistorically valid point of departure. Rather, the point of departure had to express the historical specificity of its object and, reflexively, of the theory itself.[14] At the very end of the *Grundrisse*, Marx settled on a point of departure that he then retained in *Capital* – the commodity.[15] It is clear, in light of Marx's considerations on the nature of an adequate point of departure for his critical theory, that the category 'commodity' here neither refers to commodities as they might exist in many societies, nor to a hypothetical and spurious pre-capitalist stage of simple commodity production, but to the commodity as the most basic, historically specific, social form of capitalist society. Rather than simply

---

[10] Ibid, p. 103.
[11] It should be noted that, more generally, Marx attempted to ground transhistorical projections of social forms specific to capitalism – even by thinkers such as Adam Smith (1723–90) and G. W. F. Hegel (1770–1831) – with reference to the peculiarities of those forms rather than simply as the wilful imposition of conceptions purportedly 'European' on the rest of the world.
[12] Marx, 'Outlines of the Critique of Political Economy [*Grundrisse*]. First Instalment', pp. 87–8.
[13] Ibid, pp. 90–2.   [14] Ibid, pp. 100–8.   [15] Ibid, p. 252.

referring to objects circulated on the market, Marx's category of the commodity delineates a peculiar form of social relations, a form of social mediation. As a structured form of social practice that, at the same time, is a structuring principle of the actions, worldviews and dispositions of people, the commodity is a form both of social subjectivity and objectivity.[16]

In *Capital*, Marx sought to unfold the nature and underlying dynamic of capitalist modernity from this point of departure. The historically specific character of Marx's exposition imparts to it an unusual, reflexive form. Because the point of departure of such a critical theory cannot be grounded transhistorically, it could only be grounded immanently, in the course of its unfolding, whereby each successive unfolded moment retroactively justifies that which preceded it. This is how *Capital* is structured. The categories of the beginning such as commodity, value, use-value, abstract labour, and concrete labour become retroactively substantiated by the subsequent unfolding of the analysis.[17] What appears as the transhistorical 'grounding' of these categories in the first chapter of *Capital* should be read immanently, as a metacommentary on the transhistorical, ontological forms of appearance of the underlying historically specific social forms and, therefore, on approaches, like René Descartes's (1596–1650), that proceed on the basis of such forms of appearance.

What characterizes the commodity form of social relations, as analyzed by Marx, is that it is constituted by labour. Hence, it exists in objectified form and has a dualistic character – value and use-value.[18] Underlying this analysis is Marx's conception of the historical specificity of labour in capitalism. Marx maintains that labour in capitalism has a 'double character': it is both 'concrete labour' and 'abstract labour'.[19] 'Concrete labour' refers to the fact that some form of what we consider labouring activity mediates the interactions of humans with nature in all societies – that is, transhistorically. If the commodity as a social form is historically specific to capitalism, however, then 'abstract labour' must refer to the historically specific dimension of the commodity. This implies that 'abstract labour' does not simply refer to 'concrete labour' in general, but is a peculiar, historically specific category. Yet, Marx presents it in transhistorical fashion, as labour in general, as the expenditure of brain, muscle, nerve, and so on.[20] An adequate account of this category should not only elucidate the social and historical specificity of 'abstract labour',

---

[16] This understanding of the categories suggests an approach to culture and society quite different from the common base/superstructure model.
[17] Postone, *Time, Labour, and Social Domination*, pp. 128–32.
[18] K. Marx, *Capital*, volume I, MECW, vol. 35, pp. 48, 51.   [19] Ibid, pp. 51–8.
[20] Ibid, pp. 54–5.

but also explain why it appears (and is presented by Marx) as physiological and transhistorical.[21] Although this argument cannot be fully elaborated here, it should be noted that, towards the end of the first chapter of *Capital*, Marx indicates that, when the commodity form is universalized (i.e., in capitalism), labour acquires a unique social function that is not intrinsic to labouring activity as such: in a society structured by the commodity form, labour and its products are not socially distributed by traditional norms or overt relations of power and domination, as is the case in other societies. Instead, labour constitutes a new form of interdependence, where people do not consume what they produce, but where, nevertheless, their own labour or labour products function as quasi-objective means of obtaining the products of others.[22] In serving as such a means, labour and its products in effect pre-empt that function on the part of manifest social relations; they constitute a new form of social interrelatedness, a form of social mediation that is constituted by objectifying activity (labour) and that, therefore, appears to be objective, rather than social.

In Marx's mature works, then, the focus on the centrality of labour to social life should not be taken as a transhistorical proposition. It does not mean that material production is the most essential dimension of social life in general. Rather, it refers to the historically specific constitution by labour in capitalism of a form of social mediation that fundamentally characterizes that society. Because labour in capitalism is not only labour as we transhistorically and commonsensically understand it, but is also a historically specific socially mediating activity, according to Marx, its objectifications (commodity, capital) are both concrete labour products and objectified forms of social relations. Within the framework of this analysis, the social relations that most basically characterize capitalist society are very different from the qualitatively specific, overt social relations, such as kinship relations or relations of personal direct domination, which characterize non-capitalist societies. Although the latter kind of social relations do continue to exist in capitalism, what ultimately structures that society is a new underlying level of social relations constituted by labour. Those relations have a peculiar quasi-objective character, and are dualistic: they are characterized by the opposition of an abstract, general, homogeneous dimension and a concrete particular material dimension, both of which appear to be natural rather than social, and condition social conceptions of natural reality.

---

[21] Postone, *Time, Labour, and Social Domination*, pp. 63–101.
[22] Marx, *Capital*, volume I, pp. 179–81.

The abstract dimension of the social mediation underlying capitalism is expressed by value, the form of wealth dominant in that society. As noted earlier, Marx's 'labour theory of value' has frequently been misunderstood as a labour theory of wealth, one that posits labour, at all times and in all places, as the only social source of wealth. Marx's analysis, however, is not one of wealth in general any more than it is of labour in general. He analyzes value as a historically specific form of wealth that is bound to the historically unique role of labour in capitalism. Marx explicitly distinguishes value from what he calls 'material wealth' and relates these two distinct forms of wealth to the duality of labour in capitalism.[23] Material wealth is measured by the quantity of products produced and is a function of a number of factors in addition to labour, such as knowledge, social organization, and natural conditions.[24] It expresses the use-value dimension of labour in capitalism. Value, according to Marx, is an expression of abstract labour and is constituted solely by labour and time that have been socially normed, that is, by the expenditure of socially necessary labour time. It is the dominant form of wealth in capitalism.[25] Material wealth, when it is the dominant form of wealth, is mediated/distributed by overt social relations such as kinship relations or formal hierarchical relations. Value, however, is not mediated by such overt social relations, but is itself a (peculiar) form of social relations. Hence, it possesses the unusual quality of mediating itself.

9.4 The Dialectic of Temporal Mediation

Within the framework of this interpretation, then, what fundamentally characterizes capitalism is a historically specific form of social mediation – a form of social relations that is unique inasmuch as it is mediated by labour. In the course of Marx's exposition in *Capital*, he shows that, although the commodity form of social relations is constituted by forms of practice, it becomes quasi-independent of the people who constitute it and exerts determinate constraints and imperatives on them. The result is a historically new, abstract, form of social domination.

This abstract form of domination, which is at the heart of *Capital*, is fundamentally temporal. Marx begins to develop this dimension of the basic social forms of capitalism with his initial determination of the magnitude of value in terms of socially necessary labour time.[26] In his preliminary elaboration Marx begins to analyze the peculiarities of value as a social form of wealth whose measure is temporal: '[s]ocially necessary labour time' as a measure is not simply descriptive, but delineates

---

[23] Ibid, pp. 51–4.   [24] Ibid, p. 50.   [25] Ibid, pp. 49, 50, 55.   [26] Ibid, p. 49.

a socially general, compelling, norm. Production *must* conform to this prevailing, abstract, overarching norm if it is to generate the full value of its products. Note that the compulsion is not exerted by any individuals or groups, but is abstract, inherent to the structure of value itself. Within this framework, the time frame (e.g., an hour) is constituted as an independent variable. The amount of value produced per unit time is a function of the time unit alone; it remains the same regardless of individual variations or the level of productivity. This is the first determination of the historically specific abstract form of social domination intrinsic to capitalism's fundamental forms of social mediation: it is *the domination of people by time*. This form of domination is bound to a historically specific form of temporality – abstract Newtonian time – which is constituted historically with the commodity form.[27]

A peculiarity of value as a temporal form of wealth, then, is that, although increased productivity increases the amount of use-values produced per unit time, it results only in short-term increases in the magnitude of value created per unit time. Once the productive increase becomes general, the magnitude of value generated per unit time falls back to its base level.[28] The result is a sort of a treadmill. Higher levels of productivity result in great increases in material wealth, but not in proportional long-term increases in value per unit time. This, in turn, leads to still further increases in productivity. It should be noted that this peculiar treadmill dynamic is rooted in value's temporal dimension. It cannot be fully explained by the way this pattern is generalized, for example, through market competition. Nevertheless, it would be one sided to view temporality in capitalism only in terms of Newtonian time – that is, as empty homogenous time.[29] Although changes in productivity, in the use-value dimension, do not change the amount of value produced per unit time, they do determine *what counts as* the norm – that is, what counts as a given unit of time. Once capitalism is fully developed, ongoing increases in productivity redetermine the unit of (abstract) time; they push it forwards, as it were. This movement is *of* time; it renders the abstract time unit a dependent variable. Hence, it cannot be apprehended within the frame of Newtonian time, but requires a superordinate frame of reference within which the frame of Newtonian time moves. What appears as an independent variable within the one frame is a dependent variable within the other. This movement of time can be termed *historical time*. The redetermination of the abstract, constant time unit

[27] Postone, *Time, Labour, and Social Domination*, pp. 200–16.
[28] Marx, *Capital*, volume I, p. 49.
[29] W. Benjamin, 'Theses on the Philosophy of History', in S. E. Bronner and D. M. Kellner (eds), *Critical Theory and Society* (New York: Routledge, 1989), pp. 257, 260–2.

redetermines the compulsion associated with that unit. In this way, the movement of time acquires a necessary dimension. Abstract time and historical time, then, are dialectically interrelated. Both are constituted historically with the commodity and capital forms as structures of domination.[30]

This historically new, abstract, form of social domination subjects people to increasingly impersonal rationalized imperatives and constraints that cannot adequately be grasped in terms of class domination or, more generally, in terms of the concrete domination of social groupings or institutional agencies of the state and/or of the economy. Like Michel Foucault's (1926–1984) notion of power (although more rigorously grounded), this abstract form of domination has no determinate locus and, although constituted by determinate forms of social practice, appears not to be social at all.[31]

The dynamic generated by the dialectic of these temporalities (abstract and historical) is grasped by the category of capital, which Marx initially introduces as self-valourizing value.[32] Capital, for Marx, is a category of movement; it is value in motion. It has no fixed form and no fixed material embodiment, but appears at different moments of its spiralling path in the form of money and of commodities. Capital, then, is an abstract flux behind the phenomenal realm, a ceaseless process of value's self-expansion, a directional movement with no external *telos* that generates large-scale cycles of production and consumption, creation and destruction.

Significantly, in introducing the category of capital, Marx describes it with the same language that Hegel used in *The Phenomenology of Spirit* with reference to *Geist* – the self-moving *substance* that is the *subject* of its own process.[33] In so doing, Marx suggests that a historical Subject in the Hegelian sense does indeed exist in capitalism: Hegel's notion of history as a dialectical unfolding is valid, but only for the capitalist form of social life. Moreover – and this is crucially important – Marx does not identify that Subject with the proletariat (as does Lukács) or even with humanity. Instead, he identifies it with *capital*, a dynamic structure of abstract domination that, although constituted by humans, becomes independent of their wills.

Marx's mature critique of Hegel, then, no longer entails a 'materialist' anthropological inversion of the latter's idealistic dialectic (as undertaken by Lukács, for example). Rather, it is that dialectic's materialist

---

[30] Postone, *Time, Labour, and Social Domination*, pp. 287–98.
[31] M. Foucault, *Discipline and Punish: The Birth of the Prison* (New York: Vintage, 1995).
[32] Marx, *Capital*, volume I, pp. 164–6.   [33] Ibid.

'justification'. Marx implicitly argues that the 'rational core' of Hegel's dialectic is precisely its idealist character. It is an expression of a mode of domination constituted by alienated relations – that is, relations that acquire a quasi-independent existence vis-à-vis the individuals, exert a form of compulsion on those individuals, and that, because of their peculiar dualistic nature, are dialectical in character. In his mature theory, then, Marx does not posit an anthropological meta-subject of history, such as the proletariat, which will realize itself in a future socialist society. Rather, he provides the basis for a critique of such a notion. This implies a position very different from that of theorists like Lukács, for whom the social totality constituted by labour provides the *standpoint* of the critique of capitalism, and is to be realized in socialism. In *Capital*, the totality and the labour constituting it have become the *objects* of critique. The historical Subject is the alienated structure of social mediation at the heart of the capitalist formation's historical dynamic. The contradictions of capital point to the *abolition*, not the *realization* of the Subject.

In *Capital*, Marx roots capitalism's historical dynamic ultimately in the double character of the commodity and, hence, capital. On the one hand, as a historically specific, temporally determined, form of wealth, value underlies an ongoing drive for increased productivity that is a hallmark of capitalist production. On the other hand, because value is a function of socially necessary labour time alone, higher socially general levels of productivity result in greater amounts of material wealth, but not in higher levels of value per unit time. This, in turn, impels still further increases in productivity. This dialectical dynamic of value and use-value is logically implied by Marx's treatment of socially necessary labour time in his preliminary analysis of the commodity form. It emerges overtly when he begins elaborating his concepts of surplus-value and capital. The dialectic he develops cannot be grasped adequately if the category of surplus-value is understood only as a category of exploitation, as *surplus*-value and not also as surplus-*value* – that is, as a surplus of a temporal form of wealth.

In relating surplus-value to production, Marx analytically distinguishes two aspects of the capitalist process of production: it is a process for the production of use-values (labour process) and a process of generating (surplus-)value (valourization process).[34] Analyzing the latter, Marx distinguishes between the production of absolute surplus-value (where increases in surplus-value are generated by increasing total labour time and, hence, directly increasing the amount of surplus labour time) and relative surplus-value (where increases in surplus-value are effected by

[34] Ibid, pp. 196–7, 207.

increasing productivity, which indirectly increases surplus labour time by lowering the labour time necessary for workers' reproduction).[35]

With the introduction of the category of relative surplus-value, the logic of Marx's exposition now becomes a historical logic, one that is characterized by temporal acceleration. Because, in Marx's account, relative surplus-value is effected by increasing productivity in order to lower the time necessary for workers' reproduction, the higher the socially general level of productivity, the more productivity must be still further increased in order to generate a determinate increase in surplus-value.[36] In other words, the expansion of surplus-value required by capital tends to generate accelerating increases in productivity and, hence, in the masses of goods produced and the material consumed. Yet the ever-increasing amount of material wealth produced does not represent correspondingly high levels of social wealth in the form of value. This suggests that a perplexing feature of modern capitalism – the absence of general prosperity in the midst of material plenty – is not a matter of unequal distribution alone, but is also a function of the value form of wealth at the core of capitalism.

The temporal dialectic briefly outlined earlier also indicates that higher socially general levels of productivity do not proportionately diminish the socially general necessity for labour time expenditure (which would be the case if material wealth were the dominant form of wealth). Instead, that necessity – as the necessity of value – is constantly reconstituted. Consequently, labour remains the necessary means of individual reproduction and labour-time expenditure remains fundamental to the process of production (on the level of society as a whole), regardless of the level of productivity. This results in a very complex, nonlinear, historical dynamic of transformation and reconstitution. On the one hand, this dynamic generates ongoing *transformations* of production, of the division of labour and, more generally, of social life. On the other hand, this historical dynamic entails the ongoing *reconstitution* of its own fundamental condition as an unchanging feature of social life – that social mediation ultimately is effected by labour and that living labour remains integral to the process of production (considered in terms of society as a whole), regardless of the level of productivity.

The historical dynamic of capitalism, then, ceaselessly generates what is *new* while regenerating what is the *same*. It increasingly points beyond the necessity of proletarian labour while reconstituting that very necessity. More generally, this dynamic both generates the possibility of another organization of social life and yet hinders that possibility from being

[35] Ibid, pp. 239ff, 319–25.   [36] Ibid, pp. 521–2.

realized. This understanding of capitalism's complex dynamic is, of course, only a very abstract initial determination. Capital's drive for expansion, for example, need not always entail increasing productivity. It can also be effected by lowering wages, for example, or lengthening the working day. Nevertheless, what has been outlined delineates an overarching logic of capital.

9.5 The Dual Crisis of Capital

The understanding of capitalism's complex dynamic outlined earlier is relevant for the looming contemporary dual crisis – that of environmental degradation and the demise of labouring society. Marx's categories allow for a critical social (rather than technological) analysis of the trajectory of growth and the structure of production in modern society. The temporal dimension of value underlies a determinate pattern of 'growth', which gives rise to increases in material wealth greater than those in surplus-value (which remains the relevant form of the surplus in capitalism). This results in pressures for accelerating increases in productivity and, hence, an accelerating demand for raw materials and energy, which contributes centrally to the accelerating destruction of the natural environment. Within this framework, then, the problem with economic growth in capitalism is not only that it is crisis-ridden, as has been emphasized frequently and correctly by traditional Marxist approaches. Rather, the *form* of growth itself is problematic. The trajectory of growth would be different if the ultimate goal of production were increased quantities of goods, rather than surplus-value. The distinction between material wealth and value, then, allows for a critique of the negative ecological consequences of modern capitalist production within the framework of a critical theory of capitalism. As such, it points beyond the opposition between runaway, ecologically destructive growth as a condition of social wealth and austerity as a condition of an ecologically sound organization of social life.

This approach also provides the basis for a social analysis of the structure of social labour and of production in capitalism. It does not treat the capitalist process of production as a technical process that is used by private capitalists for their own individual ends. Instead, it constitutes the basis for a critique of production on the basis of Marx's analysis of the two dimensions of the capitalist process of production – the labour process and the valourization process. At first, according to Marx, production is not yet intrinsically capitalist; capitalism appears to be only a matter of ownership and control. In his terms, the valourization process remains extrinsic to the labour process (what he calls the 'formal subsumption of labour under capital').[37] Then, however, the valourization process begins to mould the nature of the labour process itself (the 'real subsumption of labour under capital').[38] Marx is arguing, then, that the process of production in capitalism cannot adequately be understood in material, technical terms. Rather, his analysis seeks to show that the material form of production itself becomes socially moulded by capital, that production becomes intrinsically capitalist.[39] This implies that production in a post-capitalist social order should not be conceived of as the same process as in capitalism under new, different auspices. Rather, such a social order would entail a different structure of producing.

The process of the real subsumption of labour also entails a transformation in the nature of capital. As we have seen, Marx first introduces the category of capital in terms of the value dimension of labour alone, as self-valourizing value. In the course of his presentation of the development of production in *Capital*, however, Marx argues that the use-value dimension of labour – which includes science, technology, and other general forms of social knowledge – becomes an attribute of capital. Initially, in Marx's treatment, this appropriation of concrete labour's productive powers by capital seems to be simply a matter of private ownership inasmuch as these productive powers are still constituted by direct human labour in production. In manufacture, although the labour of each worker becomes stunted, the productivity of the whole still remains a function of the labour directly involved in the process of production.[40] One could still conceive of the social powers of capital in terms of the social powers of the aggregated workers.

This is no longer the case once large-scale industry is developed, according to Marx. Production now becomes increasingly based on science and technology. In such a situation, capital becomes less and less the mystified form of powers that 'actually' are those of the workers. Instead, the productive powers of capital increasingly become socially general productive powers that no longer can be understood as those of the immediate producers alone. This knowledge and these powers do not simply emerge as a result of an evolutionary development. Rather, the condition of their coming into being historically is a function of capital – that they are constituted in alienated form, separate from, and opposed to, the immediate producers.[41] This development is an important aspect of what Marx seeks to grasp with his category of capital. Capital may initially have been the mystified form of powers that 'actually' are those of the workers. However, as it develops, it increasingly becomes the real

---

[37] Ibid, pp. 510–11. [38] Ibid, p. 511. [39] Ibid, pp. 364–70, 374 ff.
[40] Ibid, pp. 326–70. [41] Ibid, pp. 372–89.

form of existence of 'species capacities' that are constituted historically in alienated form.[42]

This analysis of capital contravenes the idea that overcoming capitalism entails the self-realization of the proletariat. Capital's drive for ongoing increases in productivity gives rise to a technologically sophisticated productive apparatus that renders the production of material wealth essentially independent of direct human labour-time expenditure. The constitution and accumulation of socially general knowledge associated with capital's development renders proletarian labour increasingly anachronistic. This, in turn, opens the possibility of large-scale socially general reductions in labour time, and fundamental changes in the nature and social organization of labour. This possibility indicates, on the one hand, that, for Marx, the abolition of capitalism would not entail the self-realization of the proletariat, but its self-abolition. On the other hand, as we have seen, the dialectic of value and use-value is one of transformation and reconstitution. It not only drives productivity forwards, but also reconstitutes the necessity of value and, hence, value-creating labour – that is, proletarian labour. In other words, capital both generates possibilities that point beyond itself, beyond the necessity of proletarian labour, while reconstituting that very necessity, thereby constrains those very possibilities. It simultaneously generates the possibility of another organization of social life while hindering that possibility from being realized.

This tension skews the form in which that possibility emerges. As a result, ultimately, of the ongoing reconstitution of capital's fundamental forms, the historical possibility of the abolition of proletarian labour appears in the form of increases in superfluous labour, in the superfluity of an increasingly large portion of working populations, of increases in the permanently unemployed and the precariat – the underemployed. This development expresses, in inverted form, the growing superfluity of much proletarian labour. Far from appearing as a linear possibility, then, the possibility of emancipation, of the abolition of proletarian labour, and, hence, the emergence of the possibility of a future, in which surplus production no longer must be based on the labour of an exploited class, is, at the same time, the emergence of the possibility of a disastrous development in which the growing superfluity of labour is expressed as the growing superfluity of people.

Capital, therefore, generates the possibility of a future society – but does so in a form that, at the same time, is increasingly destructive of the environment and the working population.

---

[42] Ibid, pp. 326–70.

9.6   An Adequate Critical Theory for Today

According to the reinterpretation outlined here, then, Marx's theory extends far beyond the traditional critique of the bourgeois relations of distribution (the market and private property). It is not only a critique of exploitation and the unequal distribution of wealth and power. Rather, it grasps modern industrial and post-industrial society itself as capitalist, and critically analyzes capitalism primarily in terms of abstract structures of domination, increasing fragmentation of individual labour and individual existence, and blind runaway developmental logic. It treats the working class as a basic element of capitalism rather than as the embodiment of its negation, and implicitly conceptualizes socialism in terms of the possible abolition of the proletariat and of the organization of production based on proletarian labour, as well as the abolition of the capitalism's dynamic system of abstract compulsions. At the same time, this approach could elucidate the gap between the actual organization of social life and the way it could be organized, especially given the increasing importance of science and technology. This gap has been growing for forty years. It has become expressed socially in the division of the population into a global post-industrial sector and one of increasing social, economic, and political marginalization.

By shifting the focus of the critique away from an exclusive concern with the market and private property, this approach could provide the basis for a critical theory of the so-called actually-existing socialist countries as alternative (and failed) forms of capital accumulation, rather than as social modes that represented the historical negation of capital, in however imperfect a form.

Here, we have not elaborated on Marx's description of his categories as not merely economic, but as *Daseinsformen, Existenzbestimmungen* – that is, also as cultural categories entailing determinate views of the world and concepts of personhood, for example. Nevertheless, by relating the overcoming of capital to the overcoming of proletarian labour, this interpretation could begin to approach the historical emergence of post-proletarian self-understandings and subjectivities. It opens the possibility for a theory that could reflect historically on the new social movements of recent decades and the sorts of historically constituted world views they embody and express. It might also be able to approach the global rise of forms of 'fundamentalisms' as populist, fetishized forms of oppositions to the differential effects of neo-liberal global capitalism, new forms that misrecognize themselves as ancient and authentic.

Note that, within this framework, the idea of another possible form of social life, beyond capitalism, is immanent to capitalist modernity itself. It is not derived from cultural contact or the ethnographic study of fundamentally different forms of social life; nor is it based on the experience of a previous social order with its own moral economy that is being destroyed by capitalism – although that experience certainly has been generative of opposition. Opposition to capitalism, however, does not necessarily point beyond it. It can be – and often has been – subsumed by capital itself or swept aside as inadequate to the exigencies of the larger historical context. Marx's analysis is directed less towards the emergence of *'resistance'* (which is politically and historically indeterminate) than towards the possibility of *transformation*. It seeks to delineate the emergence of a form of life that, as a result of capitalism's dynamic, is constituted as a historical possibility, and yet is constrained by that very dynamic from being realized. This gap between what is and what could be, allows for a future possibility that, increasingly, has become real historically. It is this gap that constitutes the basis for a historical critique of what is. It reveals the historically specific character of the fundamental social forms of capitalism – not only with reference to the past, or another society, or a presumed 'natural' social organization, but also with reference to a possible future.

In constituting a framework for addressing such issues, the interpretation of *Capital* presented here indicates its ongoing significance for an adequate understanding of the far-reaching transformations of our social universe. These historical transformations have not only revealed the weaknesses of much traditional Marxism as well as of various forms of critical post-Marxism, but also suggest the central significance of a critique of capitalism for an adequate critical theory today.

References

Althusser, Louis, and Balibar, Étienne (1970), *Reading* Capital, London: New Left Books.
Becker, Gary (1975), *Human Capital: A Theoretical and Empirical Analysis, with Special Reference to Education*, New York: Columbia University Press.
Benjamin, Walter (1989), 'Theses on the Philosophy of History', in Steven E. Bronner, Douglas M. Kellner (eds), *Critical Theory and Society*, New York: Routledge, pp. 255–63.
Bourdieu, Pierre (2000), *Distinction: A Social Critique of the Judgement of Taste*, Cambridge, MA: Harvard University Press.
Cohen G. A. (1988), *History, Labour and Freedom*, Oxford: Clarendon Press.
Dobb, Maurice (1940), *Political Economy and Capitalism: Some Essays in Economic Tradition*, London: Routledge & Kegan Paul.

Elster, Jon (1985), *Making Sense of Marx*, New York: Cambridge University Press.
Foucault, Michel (1995), *Discipline and Punish: The Birth of the Prison*, New York: Vintage.
Marx, Karl (1986), 'Outlines of the Critique of Political Economy [*Grundrisse*]. First Instalment', MECW, vol. 28.
   (1996), *Capital*, volume I, MECW, vol. 35.
Meeks, Ronald (1973), *Studies in the Labour Theory of Value*, New York and London: Lawrence and Wishart.
Postone, Moishe (1993), *Time, Labour, and Social Domination*, Cambridge and New York: Cambridge University Press.
   (2008), '*Capital* in Light of the *Grundrisse*', in Marcello Musto (ed.), *Karl Marx's* Grundrisse*: Foundations of the Critique of Political 150 Years Later*. London and New York: Routledge, pp. 120–37.
Roemer, John (1981), *Analytical Foundations of Marxian Economic Theory*, Cambridge: Cambridge University Press.
Steedman, Ian (1981), 'Ricardo, Marx, Sraffa', in Ian Steedman and Paul Sweezy (eds), *The Value Controversy*, London: New Left Books, pp. 11–19.
Sweezy, Paul (1968), *The Theory of Capitalist Development*, New York: Oxford University Press.

10 Ecology

John Bellamy Foster

10.1 Marx and the Earth

The widespread recognition of Karl Marx as a leading, classical contributor to ecological thought is a fairly recent historical occurrence. The revival of Marx's ecology since the 1960s, and especially since the 1990s, occurred in a number of stages. The dominant interpretation on the left up through the 1980s faulted Marx for his supposedly instrumentalist, 'Promethean', conception of nature and alleged lack of an ecological sensibility. This view resulted in what has come to be known as 'first-stage ecosocialism', characterized by the grafting of Green thought onto Marxism (or in some cases Marxism onto Green thought) based on the presumption that Marx's entire critique was ecologically flawed.[1]

In his 1982 essay 'Socialism and Ecology', Raymond Williams (1921–1988) introduced a major dissent against the 'running together' in this way 'of two kinds of thinking' related to socialism and Green theory, without doing the hard work of reconsidering the Marxian tradition from its inception – that is, going back to Marx's own writings.[2] Hence, there arose, beginning in the 1990s, a second-stage of ecosocialist analysis that sought to determine, by going to the very foundations of Marx's historical materialism, the extent to which he had incorporated fundamental ecological considerations into his analysis. This second-stage of ecosocialism shifted the focus to the connections between Marx's materialist conception of history and his materialist conception of nature. Marx's entire intellectual corpus – from his doctoral thesis on Epicurus' (341 BC–270 BC) philosophy of nature – up through his final writings in the 1880s – was to be the subject of a vast archaeological dig in an attempt to recover the deep ecological structure of his thought. This led to three major methodological

---

[1] On the first, second, and third stages of ecosocialist analysis, see J. B. Foster, 'Foreword', in P. Burkett, *Marx and Nature: A Red Green Perspective* (Chicago: Haymarket, 2014), pp. vii–xiii.
[2] R. Williams, *Resources of Hope* (London: Verso, 1989), p. 210. Williams saw the need not only to go back to Marx, but also to Engels and William Morris.

discoveries: (1) the ecological value-form theory underpinning Marx's entire critique; (2) the theory of metabolic rift (and with it his concepts of the 'universal metabolism of nature' and the 'social metabolism'); and (3) the two ecological crisis theories (scarcity crises and ecological crises proper) embedded in Marx's analysis. Armed with these new critical tools, radical analysts began to apply them to contemporary ecological and social conditions, generating a third stage of ecosocialism (or ecological Marxism) directly connected to contemporary praxis – in movements like System Change Not Climate Change. In this way, Marx's ecological critique re-emerged as a material force in the global environmental struggle in the opening decades of this century.

This process of unearthing Marx's ecological thought constituted an essential self-critique within the Marxian tradition. But it was equally a response to the unprecedented challenge confronting humanity (and the socialist movement) in the face of today's planetary emergency. Marxian thinkers were compelled, as a practical, revolutionary necessity, to seek methodological answers in the very foundations of classical historical materialism, so as to address more effectively the global ecological crisis. This was consistent with Rosa Luxemburg's (1871–1919) prediction that only with the further development of the Marxism and its confrontation with new historical problems would the movement recognize that 'Marx, in his scientific creation, has outstripped us as a party of fighters'. As conditions changed and new challenges emerged it would be necessary to 'dip once more into the treasury of Marx's thought, in order to extract and utilize therefrom new fragments of his doctrine'.[3]

10.2   Western Marxist Criticisms of Marx on Nature

The overall understanding of Marx's conception of nature and society that predominated in the first three-quarters of a century after his death was associated with Friedrich Engels's *Dialectics of Nature*, and with the dialectical progress of science, to which Marx and Engels' 'scientific socialism' was seen as organically related. This view was sharply challenged by Western Marxists in the early post-Second World War era, as part of a conscious process of distancing Marx from soviet dialectical materialism. Western Marxism thus came to be defined primarily by its rejection of the dialectics of nature. The dialectical method, and hence the Marxian critique in general, was seen as applicable only to the realm of human history, and excluded questions of external nature and natural

---

[3] R. Luxemburg, 'Stagnation and Progress of Marxism', in *Rosa Luxemburg Speaks* (New York: Pathfinder, 1920), p. 111.

processes, which were left to the natural sciences. As Russell Jacoby (1945–) summed up the schism within Marxism, 'Soviet Marxism was regularly sustained by a scientific Hegel, and European Marxism was regularly sustained by a historical Hegel'.[4]

The classic work conveying the Western Marxist interpretation of Marx on nature was Alfred Schmidt's (1931–2012) *The Concept of Nature in Marx*, described by Paul Burkett (1956–) as 'perhaps the most influential study ever written on Marx's view of nature'.[5] It was published in 1962, the same year as the publication of Rachel Carson's (1907–1964) *Silent Spring* in the United States. It thus antedated the modern environmental movement, which arose following the publication of Carson's book. Nevertheless, Schmidt's work, carrying with it the imprimatur of the Frankfurt School, was to have enormous influence on how Marx was viewed by many New Left theorists in the context of the developing environmental movement of the 1960s–80s.

The Concept of Nature in Marx was deeply affected by the general pessimism of the Frankfurt School, which viewed the 'domination of nature' as an intrinsic characteristic of modernity or 'the dialectic of the Enlightenment'.[6] Although a sophisticated work that contained positive contributions (especially with respect to Marx's metabolism concept), it was its conclusions with regard to the mature Marx's alleged Promethean views that proved most influential. 'The mature Marx', Schmidt proclaimed,

withdrew from the [ecologically-sensitive] theses expounded in his early writings. In later life he no longer wrote of a 'resurrection' of the whole of nature. The new society is to benefit man alone, and there is no doubt that this is to be at the expense of external nature. Nature is to be mastered with gigantic technological aids, and the smallest possible expenditure of time and labour. It is to serve all men as the material substratum for all conceivable consumption goods. When Marx and Engels complain about the unholy plundering of nature, they are not concerned with nature itself but with considerations of economic utility ... The exploitation of nature will not cease in the future, but man's encroachments into nature will be rationalized, so that their remoter consequences will remain capable of control. In this way, nature will be robbed step by step of the possibility of revenging itself on men for their victories over it.[7]

---

[4] R. Jacoby, *Dialectic of Defeat* (Cambridge: Cambridge University Press, 1981), pp. 57–8; 'Western Marxism', in T. Bottomore (ed.), *A Dictionary of Marxist Thought* (Oxford: Blackwell, 1983), pp. 523–6.
[5] P. Burkett, 'Nature in Marx Reconsidered', *Organization & Environment*, 10 (2): 164 (1997).
[6] M. Horkheimer and T. W. Adorno, *The Dialectic of Enlightenment* (New York: Continuum, 1972).
[7] A. Schmidt, *The Concept of Nature in Marx* (London: New Left Books, 1971), pp. 154–5.

The last phrase was a reference to Engels, whose views on the need for human beings to control their social relation to nature under socialism, in order to prevent ecological crises, were interpreted by Schmidt, along general Frankfurt School lines, as a case for the extreme 'rationalization' and external control of nature.[8] There was no room in Engels, any more than Marx, Schmidt insisted, for anything but a one-sided conqueror's approach to nature – despite his criticisms of precisely this. Here Engels was reinterpreted in line with a crude domination of nature conception, in order to foist such views more fully on Marx himself.

'The attitude of the mature Marx', Schmidt pronounced, 'has in it nothing of the exuberance and unlimited optimism to be found in the idea of the future society prescribed in the Paris Manuscripts. It should rather be called skeptical. Men cannot in the last resort be emancipated from the necessities imposed by nature.'[9] Marx was thus transformed into a forerunner to the scepticism, world-weariness, and dualistic division between natural science and social science – and between nature and society – that characterized Schmidt's own mentors, Max Horkheimer (1895–1973) and Theodor W. Adorno (1903–1969).[10] 'We should ask', Schmidt queried, 'whether the future society [of socialism] will not be a mammoth machine, whether the prophesy of [Horkheimer and Adorno's] *Dialectic of Enlightenment* that "human society will be a massive racket in nature" will not be fulfilled rather than the young Marx's dream of a humanization of nature, which would at the same time include the naturalization of man.'[11]

This negative assessment of Marx's concept of nature was reinforced in the first-stage ecosocialism that arose in 1970s and 1980s. Early ecosocialist thinkers criticized Marx (and Marxism) for downplaying natural limits, and thus ecological constraints. They therefore sought to promote 'the greening of Marxism' by uncritically running together Marx's

---

[8] Ibid., pp. 155–6, 160; F. Engels, *The Dialectics of Nature*, MECW, vol. 25, pp. 460–4.
[9] Schmidt, *The Concept of Nature in Marx*, p. 139.
[10] For Horkheimer, 'raw nature', in 'revolt against reason' represented animality, primitiveness, and crude Darwinism. 'Whenever man deliberately makes nature his principle', he wrote, 'he regresses to primitive usages ... Animals ... do not reason ... In summary, we are the heirs, for better or worse, of the Enlightenment and technological progress.' M. Horkheimer, *The Eclipse of Reason* (New York: Continuum, 1947), pp. 123–7.
[11] Schmidt, *The Concept of Nature in Marx*, p. 156. See also M. Jay, *The Dialectical Imagination* (Berkeley: University of California Press, 1996), pp. 259, 347. The most profound part of Schmidt's analysis of Marx's concept of nature was his treatment of Marx's theory of metabolism, in which he contended that Marx had 'introduced a completely new understanding of nature', allowing one to speak 'meaningfully of a "dialectic of nature"'. But Schmidt was to marginalize this in his analysis, describing it as a 'pre-bourgeois' conception of a 'rigid cyclical form of nature' that was 'anterior to man'. Schmidt, *The Concept of Nature in Marx*, pp. 11, 76–90, 176.

historical materialism with Malthusian notions of environmental limits and with the abstract ethical views of 'ecologism' (or Green theory).[12] This point of view generally avoided any close scrutiny of the foundations of historical materialism. As Perry Anderson (1938–) wrote, in his *In the Tracks of Historical Materialism*, 'problems of the interaction of the human species with its terrestrial environmental [were] essentially absent from classical Marxism'.[13]

For Ted Benton (1942–), perhaps the most articulate early spokesperson for first-stage ecosocialism, Marx had gone overboard in his critique of Malthus, as shown in his 'reluctance to recognize "nature-imposed limits" to human development'.[14] Elements of Marx's critique of political economy, such as: (1) his political hostility to 'Malthusian "natural limits"' arguments, (2) the priority given to value theory, (3) his neglect of ecological processes, and (4) his alleged 'Prometheanism' or extreme productivism all 'obstructed the development of historical materialism as an explanatory theory of ecological crisis'.[15] Such alleged blind spots in Marx's analysis were often attributed to intrinsic flaws in the labour theory of value. Since 'all value [according to Marx] was derived from labor power', environmental sociologist Michael Redclift (1946–) declared, 'it was impossible [for Marx] to conceive of a "natural" limit to the material productive forces of society'.[16]

10.3   The Rediscovery of Marx's Ecology

Nevertheless, for those with a firm grasp of Marx's critique of political economy, it was obvious that most of the criticisms directed against Marx with respect to ecology were erroneous. It was not difficult to point to numerous cases where Marx (and Engels) had taken natural limits seriously. Marx's work was dotted with criticisms of pollution, deforestation, desertification, the town–country divide, and overpopulated cities. 'The development of civilization and industry in general', he observed in *Capital*, 'has always shown itself to be so active in the destruction of forests that everything that has been done for their conservation and production is quite insignificant in comparison.' Likewise, he observed in a letter to Engels that 'cultivation – when it proceeds in natural growth

---

[12] See T. Benton (ed.), *The Greening of Marxism* (New York: Guilford Press, 1996); M. J. Smith, *Ecologism* (Minneapolis: University of Minnesota Press, 1998), pp. 71–3; A. Dobson, *Green Political Thought* (London: Routledge, 1995).
[13] P. Anderson, *In the Tracks of Historical Materialism* (London: Verso, 1983), p. 83.
[14] T. Benton, 'Marxism and Natural Limits', *New Left Review*, 178: 55, 60, 64 (1989).
[15] T. Benton, 'Introduction to Part Two', in Benton (ed.), *The Greening of Marxism*, pp. 103–10.
[16] M. Redclift, *Development and the Environmental Crisis* (New York: Methuen, 1984), p. 7.

and is not *consciously controlled* ... leaves deserts behind it'.[17] Already in 1977, Howard Parsons had produced an edited collection of excerpts entitled *Marx and Engels on Ecology* that demonstrated, although unsystematically, a wide concern for ecological issues, pervading Marx and Engels's thought as a whole. Italian geographer Massimo Quaini (1914–2017) noted that 'Marx ... denounced the spoliation of nature before a modern bourgeois ecological conscience was born'.[18] All of this suggested the possibility of constructing an ecosocialist analysis starting from classical Marxian foundations.

Yet no systematic exploration of the role of nature-ecology in Marx's thought was possible without a critique of the prevailing understanding of Marx's political economy – one that would serve to clarify the connection between Marx's value theory and an ecological world view. The breakthrough in this respect was made by Paul Burkett in his *Marx and Nature* in 1999, followed in 2006 by his *Marxism and Ecological Economics*.[19] Burkett uncovered what could be called Marx's 'ecological value-form analysis', based on the distinction between *wealth* (which for Marx includes nature as well as labour) and *value* (based on labour alone).[20] Not only did Marx recognize capitalism's tendency to externalize costs on society and nature, but this tendency, he argued, was integral to the logic of capitalist valourization. Nature, he explained in *Capital*, was viewed by classical-liberal political economy as a 'free gift of Nature to capital', with the result that nature's limits were made invisible to the commodity system.[21] What first-stage ecosocialist critics of Marx, in pointing to the supposedly anti-ecological implications of his labour theory of value, had failed to notice was that it was the very one-sidedness of the value form under capitalism, in Marx's conception, that was crucial to understanding the systematic 'robbing' of nature. Once it was recognized that nature – constituting, in Marx's analysis, one of the two sources of wealth – was not included in the capitalist value calculus, but was treated as a free gift to capital, it was impossible *not* to perceive capital's destructive tendency to override all natural limits in its unending drive to accumulation.

---

[17] K. Marx, *Capital*, volume II, MECW, vol. 36, p. 245; translation according to *Capital*, volume II (London: Penguin, 1978), p. 322; 'K. Marx to F. Engels, 25 March 1868', MECW, vol. 42, pp. 558–9.

[18] H. L. Parsons, *Marx and Engels on Ecology* (Westport, CT: Greenwood Press, 1977); M. Quaini, *Geography and Marxism* (Totowa, NJ: Barnes and Noble, 1982), p. 136.

[19] Burkett, *Marx and Nature*, pp. xv–xxi, 79–98; *Marxism and Ecological Economics: Toward and Red and Green Political Economy* (Boston: Brill, 2006).

[20] K. Marx, *Critique of the Gotha Programme*, MECW, vol. 24, p. 81.

[21] K. Marx, *Capital*, volume III, MECW, vol. 37, pp. 732–3. Marx states that nature in production in general is a 'free gift of Nature's productive power to labour, which, however, appears as the productive power of capital'. Ibid.

Marx's notion of capitalism as a necessarily disruptive, degrading force with respect to the nature's processes could be seen not only in his arguments on how capitalism robbed nature, but also how it robbed human beings of their natural-physical (as well as intellectual) essence, using them up prematurely to be thrown away, without cost to capital. 'For all its stinginess', Marx wrote in *Capital*,

> capitalist production is thoroughly wasteful with human material, just as its way of distributing its products through trade, and its manner of competition, make it very wasteful of material resources, so that it loses for society what it gains for the individual capitalist ... It squanders human beings, living labour, more readily than does any other mode of production, squandering not only flesh and blood, but nerves and brain as well.[22]

Burkett's analysis also led to the unearthing of two conceptions of ecological crisis in Marx's critique: (1) environmentally induced economic crises caused by increased scarcity of natural resources, raising costs on the supply-side of the economy; and (2) ecological crises proper (or crises of sustainable human development) in which the effects of accumulation on ecological conditions of human development are not registered by the capitalist economy due to its externalizing properties.

In a resource-scarcity crisis, increasing costs of natural resources generate economic constraints and contradictions for individual capitals and capital as a whole. This was famously explained by Marx in his discussions of the British cotton crisis during the Civil War in the United States, his treatment of the role of rising organic composition in his theory of the falling rate of profit, and his discussions of the conservation of constant capital on the part of individual firms. In such supply-side crises capital can be expected to intervene in various ways to contain costs in order to protect its bottom line.

In ecological crisis proper (or a crisis of sustainable human development), the logic is different. Here the problem is one of capital's degradation of natural conditions in ways that are *not* internalized within its value calculus, but nonetheless represent social and environmental costs. As a result, capital, in Marx's theory, fails to respond to such crises, which are outside its bottom line, leading to what has been called 'the absolute general law of environmental degradation under capitalism'.[23] Marx thus pointed to 'the squandering and exploitation of the earth' as an inexorable tendency of the system

---

[22] Marx, *Capital*, volume III, pp. 90, 92; translation according to K. Marx, *Capital*, volume III (London: Penguin, 1981), pp. 180, 182.
[23] J. B. Foster, 'The Absolute General Law of Environmental Degradation under Capitalism', *Capitalism Nature Socialism* 3 (3): 77–81 (1992).

of capital accumulation.[24] This represented the most startling feature of Marx's approach to ecological crisis. In Burkett's words,

> Many ecological economists and even some eco-Marxists tend to reduce the question of environmental crisis to one of capital accumulation crisis; that is, they treat environmental crises mainly in terms of their impact on capitalist profitability and sustainability of the profit-making system. For Marx, however, capital accumulation can maintain itself through environmental crises. In fact, this is one thing that makes capitalism different from previous societies.[25]

The breakthrough in the reconstruction of Marx's ecological value-form theory opened the way to a much wider reconstruction of Marx's ecology, focusing on the relation between Marx's materialist conception of nature and his materialist conception of history.[26] Second-stage eco-socialist research demonstrated that as early as his 1840–1 doctoral thesis on Epicurus (entitled *Difference between the Democritean and Epicurean Philosophy of Nature*), Marx was already wrestling with the question of a materialist dialectic and the alienation of nature.[27] What he developed out of his confrontation with Epicurus was a powerful, anti-teleological, materialist approach to the dialectic of nature and society. In *The German Ideology*, he wrote: 'Epicurus ... was the true radical Enlightener of antiquity', whose influence carried over into the (modern) Enlightenment itself. The Epicureans argued that 'the world must be *disillusioned*, and especially freed from fear of gods, for the world is my *friend*.'[28] This same materialist outlook, if in more alienated form, was to animate the scientific revolution, beginning in the seventeenth century, and extending into Marx's time.

Marx was to make this broad materialist conception of nature his own, viewing it as the basis for his critical-dialectical development of the materialist conception of history. Drawing on Epicurus' famous statement that 'death is nothing to us', he stated in the *Economic and Philosophical Manuscripts of 1844* that '*Nature* ... taken abstractly, for itself, and fixed in its separation from man, is *nothing* for man.' It was because human beings, as sensual beings, were part of nature and existed in its midst – and because they actively transformed nature and the human relation to nature through their production – that they were able

---

[24] Marx, *Capital*, volume III, pp. 799–800; translation according to Marx, *Capital*, volume III (London: Penguin, 1981), p. 949.
[25] Burkett, *Marx and Nature*, p. xx.
[26] See J. B. Foster, 'Marx's Theory of Metabolic Rift', *American Journal of Sociology*, 105 (2): 366–405 (1999), *Marx's Ecology: Materialism and Nature* (New York: Monthly Review, 2000).
[27] Foster, *Marx's Ecology*, pp. 21–65.
[28] K. Marx and F. Engels, *The German Ideology*, MECW, vol. 5, pp. 141–2.

to alienate nature from themselves. Indeed, the alienation of labour under capitalism had its precondition in the alienation of nature – the severance of human beings form the land, and from their natural environment. Marx thus attributed the 'universal pollution' of the large cities to a world where 'dead matter' in the form of money had come to dominate over both social needs and individual human development. This pointed to the revolutionary necessity of creating a new society as 'the realized naturalism of man and the realized humanism of nature'.[29]

Marx's early materialist ecological perspective was to be carried over into his critique of bourgeois political economy. In contrast to Thomas Malthus (1766–1834), who had carefully avoided use of the term over-population in his famous *Essay on Population*, since this would have contradicted his equilibrium perspective, Marx, in his critique of Malthus in the *Grundrisse*, referred explicitly to 'overpopulation'. But in doing so he considered it not as an invariant natural law, but as the expression of definite historical relations. Each mode of production had its distinctive laws of population. One of the principal goals of socialism, Marx and Engels argued in *the Manifesto of the Communist Party*, must be 'the gradual abolition of the distinction of town and country, by a more equable distribution of population'. This analysis was later coupled with Marx's emphasis in *Capital* on the industrial reserve army (or the relative surplus population) and on sustainable agricultural production as a means of maintaining the conditions for future generations.[30]

In what was to be the most penetrating passage ever written on the dialectic of natural limits under capitalism, Marx stated in the *Grundrisse*:

Just as production founded on capital creates universal industriousness on one side ... so does it create on the other side a system of general exploitation of the natural and human qualities, a system of general utility, utilizing science itself just as much as all the physical and mental qualities, while there appears nothing *higher in itself*, nothing legitimate for itself, outside this circle of social production and exchange. Thus capital creates the bourgeois society, and the universal appropriation of nature as well as of the social bond itself by the members of society. Hence the great civilizing influence of capital; its production of a stage of society in comparison to which all earlier ones appear as mere *local developments* of humanity

---

[29] Epicurus, 'Principle Doctrines', in B. Inwood and L. P. Gerson (eds), *The Epicurus Reader* (Indianapolis: Hackett, 1994), p. 32; K. Marx, *Economic and Philosophical Manuscripts of 1844*, MECW, vol. 3, pp. 277, 296–8, 345–6; translation according to K. Marx, *Early Writings* (London: Penguin, 1992), pp. 329, 348–50, 398–9; Marx, *Capital*, volume I, MECW, vol. 35, p. 704.

[30] K. Marx, 'Outlines of the Critique of Political Economy [*Grundrisse*]. First Instalment', MECW, vol. 28, pp. 522–8; Foster, *Marx's Ecology*, pp. 81–104, 142–4; K. Marx and F. Engels, *Manifesto of the Communist Party*, MECW, vol. 6, p. 505; Marx, *Capital*, volume I, p. 628.

and as *nature-idolatry*. For the first time, nature becomes purely an object for humankind ... and the theoretical discovery of its autonomous laws appears merely as a ruse so as to subjugate it under human needs, whether as an object of consumption or as a means of production. In accord with this tendency, capital drives beyond national barriers and prejudices as much as beyond nature worship, as well as all traditional, confined, complacent encrusted satisfactions of present needs, and reproductions of old ways of life. It is destructive towards all of this, and constantly revolutionizes it, tearing down all the barriers which hem in the development of the forces of production, the expansion of needs, the all-sided development of production, and the exploitation and exchange of natural and mental forces. But from the fact that capital posits every such limit as a barrier and hence gets *ideally* beyond it, it does not by any means follow that it has *really* overcome it, and since every such barrier contradicts its character, its production moves in contradictions which are constantly overcome but just as constantly posited.[31]

Here Marx provided a powerful critique of the famous Baconian ruse, according to which science was enjoined to obey nature's laws as a means to the domination of nature and the expansion of bourgeois society.[32] Hence, all natural boundaries are viewed as mere barriers to be surmounted – resulting in growing contradictions between capital accumulation and natural processes.[33]

It was the mature Marx's integration of the concept of metabolism into his critique of capitalist development, in all of his major works from the late 1850s on, that allowed him to develop most fully his analysis of the material relation between nature and society. In this way, he integrated his class-based critique of the capitalist mode of production with developments in science, particularly the first and second laws of thermodynamics.

At the centre of Marx's material-ecological critique was his theory of metabolic rift. For Marx, the human relation to what he called 'the universal metabolism of nature' took the form of a 'social metabolism' represented by the labour process. As he stated in his *Economic Manuscript of 1861–63*, 'In so far as actual labour creates use values, is appropriation of the natural world for human needs ... it is the universal condition for the metabolic interaction between nature and man.' Marx viewed the metabolism between humanity and nature in similar terms to that of the metabolism *between* a given species or organism and its environment (the part and the whole). In human-historical terms, though, this took the

---

[31] K. Marx, *Grundrisse: Foundation of the Critique of Political Economy*, pp. 336–7; translated according to *Grundrisse* (London: Penguin, 1973), pp. 409–10.
[32] F. Bacon, *Novum Organum* (Chicago: Open Court, 1994), pp. 29, 43.
[33] J. B. Foster, 'Marx's *Grundrisse* and the Ecological Contradictions of Capitalism'; M. Musto (ed.), *Karl Marx's* Grundrisse: *Foundations of the Critique of Political Economy 150 Years Later* (London: Routledge, 2008), pp. 100–2.

form of a distinct *social metabolism* associated with changing historical modes of production. None of this denied that society existed *within* nature or that the relationship via human production was a complex, interdependent relation – what he referred to as a system of 'mutual natural dependence'.[34]

Human beings in the act of obtaining their means of subsistence extracted nature's products and transformed them, utilizing tools that were themselves the product of the combined action of nature and labour. 'Labour', Marx observed in *Capital*, 'is, first of all, a process between man and nature, a process by which man, through his own actions, mediates, regulates and controls the metabolism between himself and nature.'[35] Yet, in the capitalist commodity economy the labour process was transformed into a mere means to the expansion of capital, thereby running roughshod over all natural and human limits, as well as the requirements of individual human and social development.

The resulting ecological devastation was most evident in Marx's day in the soil crisis arising from industrialized agriculture. In the 1850s and 1860s, the German chemist, Justus von Liebig (1803–1873), developed a powerful critique of British 'high farming', arguing that the new industrialized capitalist agriculture was in effect a 'robbery' system that despoiled the soil of its essential nutrients, including nitrogen, phosphorus, and potassium, which were sent in the form of food and fibre hundreds and even thousands of miles to densely populated cities. In the new urban-industrial centres, these soil nutrients ended up as pollution. In the 1862 introduction to his great work on agricultural chemistry, Liebig argued that British industrial agriculture was not only leaching the soil of its nutrients, but, in its attempt to make up for this, was imperialistically importing bones from the Napoleonic battlefields and the catacombs of Europe, along with guano from Peru.[36]

Based on Liebig's critique of capitalist agriculture, Marx developed his theory of metabolic rift, whereby the capital's systematic disruption of the earth's metabolic cycle, undermined the nature-imposed conditions of human development itself, pointing to the need for a 'restoration' of this metabolism within a higher social synthesis. 'Capitalist production', he wrote, 'only develops the techniques and the degree of combination of the social process of production by simultaneously undermining the original

---

[34] K. Marx, *Economic Manuscript of 1861–63*, MECW, vol. 30, pp. 54–66; Marx, *Capital*, volume I, p. 949.
[35] Marx, *Capital*, volume I, pp. 187–8; translation according to Marx, *Capital*, volume I (London: Penguin, 1976), p. 283.
[36] Foster, *Marx's Ecology*, pp. 147–54.

sources of all wealth – the soil and the worker.'[37] As he explained in *Capital*,

> Instead of a conscious and rational treatment of the land as permanent communal property, as the inalienable condition for the existence and reproduction of the chain of human generations, we have the exploitation and plundering of the resources of the powers of the earth ... Large landed property reduces the agricultural population to an ever decreasing minimum and confronts it with an ever growing industrial population crammed together in the large towns; in this way it produces conditions that provoke an irreparable rift in the interdependent process of social metabolism, a metabolism prescribed by the natural laws of life itself. The result of this is a squandering of the vitality of the soil which is carried by trade, far beyond the bounds of a single country (Liebig).[38]

It was this nineteenth-century conception of nutrient cycling and metabolism, raised by thinkers like Liebig and Marx, and integrated with discoveries in thermodynamics, that was eventually to give rise to twentieth-century ecosystem theory – a process in which socialist thinkers played leading roles.

Marx was led by his theory of the metabolic rift to a wider conception of socialism as a process of 'sustainable human development'. This meant the continual reproduction on a sustainable – and necessarily egalitarian – basis, not only of human society itself, but also of those natural-environmental relations that constituted what he called in *Capital* the 'eternal natural condition' for the existence and perpetuation of humanity.[39] 'From the standpoint of a higher socio-economic formation', Marx declared in this same work,

> the private property of particular individuals in the earth will appear just as absurd as the private property of one man in other men. Even an entire society, a nation, or all simultaneously existing societies taken together, are not the owners of the earth. They are simply its possessors, its beneficiaries, and have to bequeath it in an improved state to succeeding generations as *boni patres familias* [good heads of the household].[40]

It was this that led to Marx's most all-encompassing vision of the future society of socialism/communism, in which 'socialized man, the associated

---

[37] Marx, *Capital*, volume I, pp. 505–8; translation according to Marx, *Capital*, volume I (London: Penguin, 1976), pp. 637–8. On metabolic rifts and shifts, see J. B. Foster, B. Clark, and R. York, *The Ecological Rift Capitalism's War on the Planet* (New York: Monthly Review, 2011), pp. 73–87.
[38] Marx, *Capital*, volume III, pp. 799–800; translation according to Marx, *Capital*, volume III (London: Penguin, 1981), p. 949. See also K. Saito, *Karl Marx's Ecosocialism* (New York: Monthly Review Press, 2017).
[39] Marx, *Capital*, volume I, pp. 505–8; translation according to Marx, *Capital*, volume I (London: Penguin, 1976), pp. 637–9.
[40] Marx, *Capital*, volume III, p. 763; translation according to Marx, *Capital*, volume III (London: Penguin, 1981), p. 911.

producers, govern the human metabolism with nature in a rational way ... accomplishing it with the least expenditure of energy and in conditions most worthy and appropriate for their human nature'.[41]

Today, the break in the cycling of nutrients constitutes only one of the many rifts in biogeochemical cycles now occurring on a planetary scale. In the Anthropocene epoch, it is the alteration of the (social) metabolism between a particular animal – *Homo sapiens* – and the rest of the Earth system, including other species, that is at the heart of the ecological problem on a planetary scale.[42] Behind this emerging planetary contradiction is the expansive process of capitalism, which, in the search of ever-greater accumulation transgresses daily the dictates of science and the requirements of human survival alike.[43] Hence, today's climate scientists, faced with a planetary ecological emergency, are increasingly focused on what is called 'the earth metabolism' and on the global 'carbon metabolism'.[44] As Del Weston (1950–2012) observed in *The Political Economy of Global Warming*, Marx's concept of 'the metabolic rift' has proven useful in this respect since it 'neatly captures the lack of balance between "expenditure and income" in the Earth's metabolism under the global capitalist system'.[45]

The rediscovery of Marx's concept of social metabolism has led to an intense debate over the last decade or so within ecological economics with regards to the role that thermodynamics played in Marx and Engels's analysis. First-stage ecosocialist analysts, like J. Martinez-Alier (1939–) and James O'Connor (1930–), claimed that the early formative attempts to merge economics with thermodynamics to develop a genuine ecological economics had originated with Marx's younger follower, the Ukrainian socialist Sergei Podolinsky (1850–1891) – while Marx and Engels were to be faulted for turning 'a deaf ear' to Podolinksy and thus ecological analysis.[46] Subsequent investigations into Podolinsky's work and its relation to that of Marx and Engels by Burkett and the present author were to prove this charge false. In 1880, Marx took very extensive notes from the first unpublished draft of

---

[41] Marx, *Capital*, volume III, p. 807; translation according to Marx, *Capital*, volume III (London: Penguin, 1981), p. 959.
[42] On the Anthropocene, see I. Angus, 'When Did the Anthropocene Begin ... and Why Does It Matter?', *Monthly Review*, 67 (4): 1–11 (2015).
[43] Marx, *Capital*, volume I, p. 591.
[44] J. G. Canadell et al., 'Carbon Metabolism of the Terrestrial Biopshere', *Ecosystems*, 3: 115–30 (2000); NASA Earth Observatory, 'NASA Satellite Measures Earth's Metabolism', 22 April 2003, http://earthobservatory.nasa.gov.
[45] D. Weston, *The Political Economy of Global Warming* (London: Routledge, 2014), p. 66.
[46] J. Martinez-Alier, *Ecological Economics* (Oxford: Blackwell, 1987), pp. 46–64, 61–3; J. O'Connor, *Natural Causes* (New York: Guilford Press, 1997), p. 3.

Podolinsky's manuscript.[47] Two years later, in a letter to Marx at Marx's request, Engels was to comment on Podolinsky's article 'Socialism and the Unity of Physical Forces'. Engels acknowledged the importance of Podolinsky's research into energetics and labour. However, he proceeded to point to errors in Podolinsky's analysis. These included seeking to reduce value relations under capitalism to energetics and failing to incorporate fertilizer and fossil fuels into his overall energy calculations. Here Engels laid heavy emphasis, in contradistinction to Podolinsky, on capital's 'squandering' of coal, viewed as 'past solar energy'. This research led to a much deeper understanding of how Marx had embedded his entire critique of political economy in material science via thermodynamics. The concept of labour power itself, it was discovered, was consciously developed by Marx in a manner consistent with thermodynamics.[48]

Second-stage ecosocialist research also demonstrated the close affinity of historical materialist analysis with the broad evolutionary theory arising out of Charles Darwin (1809–1882), which Marx called 'the basis in natural history' for the development of the overall materialist view, to be integrated with the class conception of society.[49] Not only did Marx and Engels point on numerous occasions to the positive contributions of Darwin's theory – confining their criticisms to Darwin's connection to Malthus population theory and to the social Darwinism already emerging in their time – but some of the leading figures in the development of evolutionary theory were strongly influenced by Marxian ideas. Indeed, Engels and Marx themselves contributed in significant ways to the theorizing of human evolution. As Stephen Jay Gould (1941–2002) noted, Engels' account of the evolutionary origins of the human species in *The Dialectics of Nature* was the 'the best nineteenth-century case for gene-culture coevolution' – that is, the overall theory of the human evolution.[50]

Exploration into Marx's ecological value-form theory and his theory of metabolic rift also led to the discovery of his conception of unequal ecological exchange. This was evident in his references to the guano trade and in his famous observation that for more than a century England had 'indirectly

---

[47] Marx's 1880 extract notes on Podolinsky's unpublished 'Le Travail humain et la Conservation de l'Energie' (Human Labour and the Conservation of Energy), an early draft of Podolinsky's works sent to Marx for comment are to be published in MEGA², vol. IV/27.

[48] 'F. Engels to K. Marx, 19 December 1882', MECW, vol. 46, p. 411. Foster and Burkett, *Marx on Earth*, chs 2–4: A. E. Wendling, *Karl Marx on Technology and Alienation* (London: Palgrave, 2009).

[49] 'K. Marx to F. Lassalle, 16 January 1861', MECW, vol. 41, pp. 246–7.

[50] S. J. Gould, *An Urchin in the Storm: Essays about Books and Ideas* (New York: W. W. Norton, 1987), p. 111.

exported the soil of Ireland', undermining the long-term fertility of Irish agriculture.[51] Marx's understanding of the phenomenon of unequal ecological exchange was derived from his ecological value-form theory, in which natural-material (or use-value) circuits were seen as interconnected in complex, contradictory fashion with value (exchange-value) circuits, allowing one country ecologically to exploit another country by obtaining more natural-material use-values (real wealth) than it provided in exchange. This conception of unequal ecological exchange was further enhanced by his theory of metabolic rift. It is not surprising, therefore, that in constructing a theory of unequal ecological exchange in the late twentieth century, leading systems ecologist Howard Odum (1924–2002) was to draw on these aspects of Marx's analysis, focusing on wealth versus value, use value versus exchange-value, and metabolism (as well as the transformation problem).[52]

10.4 The Emergence of Marxian Ecological Praxis

The rediscovery of Marx's theory of the metabolic rift has led in the last decade and a half to a multitude of historical and empirical investigations, associated with rifts in the carbon metabolism (climate change); the ocean metabolism; aquaculture; depleted fisheries; fertilizer use; wildfires; mountain-top removal; tropical deforestation; 'animal husbandry'; droughts; unequal ecological exchange; toxic wastes; agrofuels, the metabolism of cities; deteriorating public health; and gender and 'metabolic value'.[53] It has been used by movements from *Via Campesina* in the global South to System Change Climate Change in the United States to organize struggles of ecological change and resistance.

Although it is widely recognized that the world needs an ecological and social revolution, the question remains: from whence and by what agency will such a revolution arise? Ecological Marxists suggest that we may already be seeing signs of the rise of what could be called a nascent 'environmental proletariat'. Degraded material conditions associated with intermingled economic and ecological crises are now being encountered on a daily basis by the great majority of the world's population and affecting all aspects of their lives. At the ground level, economic and ecological crises are becoming increasingly indistinguishable. Food crises,

---

[51] Marx, *Capital*, volume I, p. 694; translation according to Marx, *Capital*, volume I (London: Penguin, 1976), p. 860; Foster, Clark, and York, *The Ecological Rift*, pp. 345–72; J. B. Foster and H. Holleman, 'The Theory of Unequal Ecological Exchange', *The Journal of Peasant Studies*, 41 (1–2): 199–233 (2014).
[52] See Foster and Holleman, 'The Theory of Unequal Ecological Exchange', pp. 213–18.
[53] For a select bibliography of research on the metabolic rift and ecological analysis, see R. Wishart, R. J. Jonna, and J. Besek, 'The Metabolic Rift: A Selected Bibliography', http://monthlyreview.org/commentary/metabolic-rift/.

land seizures, electricity shutdowns, water privatization, heightened pollution, deteriorating cities, declining public health, and increasing violence against oppressed populations are all converging with growing inequality, economic stagnation, and rising unemployment and underemployment. The logical result is a coming together of material revolts against the system. This is best exemplified by the global environmental/climate justice movement. As stressed by Bill Gallegos – a Marxist activist and leader in the climate justice and revolutionary Chicano nationalist movements in the United States – the climate justice movement 'has a decidedly revolutionary character'.[54]

Traditional working-class politics are thus co-evolving and combining with environmental struggles, and with the movements of people of colour, of women, and all those fighting basic, reproductive battles throughout society. Such an ecological and social struggle will be revolutionary to the extent that it draws its force from those layers of society where people's lives are most precarious: Third-World workers, working-class women, oppressed people of colour in the imperial core, indigenous populations, peasants/landless agricultural workers, and those fighting for fundamentally new relations of sexuality, gender, family, and community – as well as highly exploited and dispossessed workers everywhere. The most concerted revolutionary response can be expected to arise first in the Global South, where the conditions of the vast multitude of people most closely approximate those that Marx and Engels depicted in their famous existential definition of the revolutionary proletariat in *The Holy Family*:

> When socialist writers ascribe this world-historical role to the proletariat, this is not at all ... because they take the proletarians for gods. Quite the contrary. Because the absence of all humanity, even the appearance of humanity, is practically complete in the fully developed proletariat, because the living conditions of the proletariat represent the focal point of all inhuman conditions in contemporary society, because the human being is lost in the proletariat, but has won a theoretical consciousness of loss and is compelled by unavoidable and absolutely compulsory need (the practical expression of necessity) to revolt against this inhumanity – all these are the reasons why the proletariat can and must emancipate itself. However, it cannot emancipate itself without abolishing the conditions which give it life, and it cannot abolish these conditions without abolishing all those inhuman conditions of social life which are summed up in its own situation.[55]

---

[54] E. Leary and A. Lewis, 'Interview with Bill Gallegos', *Monthly Review*, 67 (5): 32 (2015). On the environmental proletariat, see Foster, Clark, and York, *The Ecological Rift*, pp. 438–40.

[55] K. Marx and F. Engels, 'The Holy Family', MECW, vol. 4, pp. 36–7. Translation according to P. M. Sweezy, *Modern Capitalism and Other Essays* (New York: Monthly Review Press, 1972), p. 149.

Yet, in the present century, such inhuman conditions, although most severe in the periphery of the capitalist world economy, are being generalized across the entire world system as a result of spiraling economic and ecological crises, coupled with growing destruction and expropriation of the means of life themselves. It is precisely the rise of 'disaster capitalism' on a scale that is now planetary, driven by an increasingly destructive drive to capital accumulation without limit, which is threatening the very existence of human beings as well as innumerable other species on which we depend and to which we are connected.[56] Understanding this and taking the appropriate action represents 'the challenge and burden' of the epochal transition confronting us in our times.[57]

A revolutionary ecological movement adequate to this task will undoubtedly pass through an *ecodemocratic phase*, seeking to build a broad alliance – one in which the vast majority of humanity outside of the ruling interests will be compelled by concrete historical circumstance to demand a world of sustainable human development. Over time this will likely create the conditions for a second, more decisive, *ecosocialist phase* of the revolutionary struggle, directed at the creation of a society dedicated to 'From each according to his abilities, to each according to his needs!' and on a sustainable basis.[58] All of this points to the translation of classical Marx's ecological critique into contemporary revolutionary praxis.

Here the first-stage socialism with its eclectic combination of Green theory and Marxism is being replaced with a deeper, more developed ecological Marxist vision, drawn from theoretical foundations provided by Marx himself, as unearthed by second-stage ecosocialist research. The resulting socialist ecological praxis might be called ecological Marxism (or third-stage ecosocialism). Yet, it also might be seen as constituting *Marxism* in the authentic sense, minus any qualifying adjective. Nothing could be more in line with Marx's classical vision of the associated producers rationally regulating the metabolism between humanity and nature.

For Marx, socialism was a revolutionary new form of social metabolic reproduction aimed at the realization of communal needs, rooted in conditions of substantive equality and ecological sustainability. It was defined as a society in which 'the free development of each is the basis for the free development of all', but in which it was also essential to protect the reproductive power of the earth itself in the interests of what

---

[56] N. Klein, *This Changes Everything* (New York: Simon and Schuster, 2014), p. 51.
[57] I. Mészaros, *The Challenge and Burden of Historical Time: Socialism in the Twenty-First Century* (New York: Monthly Review Press, 2008).
[58] Marx, *Critique of the Gotha Programme*, p. 87.

he called in *Capital* 'the chain of successive generations of the human race'.[59] In this way, Marx can be said to have prefigured in his social and ecological analysis the central aspects of the epochal struggle of our times.

'Well-grubbed old mole!'[60]

References

Anderson, Perry (1983), *In the Tracks of Historical Materialism*, London: Verso.

Angus, Ian (2015), 'When Did the Anthropocene Begin ... and Why Does It Matter?', *Monthly Review*, 67 (4): 1–11.

Ayres, Peter G. (2012), *Shaping Ecology: The Life of Arthur Tansley*, Chichester: Wiley-Blackwell.

Bacon, Francis (1994), *Novum Organum*, Chicago: Open Court.

Benton, Ted (1989), 'Marxism and Natural Limits', *New Left Review*, 178: 51–86.

(1996), 'Introduction to Part III', in Ted Benton (ed.), *The Greening of Marxism*, New York: Guilford Press.

Burkett, Paul (1997), 'Nature in Marx Reconsidered', *Organization & Environment*, 10 (2): 164.

(2006), *Marxism and Ecological Economics: Toward and Red and Green Political Economy*, Boston: Brill.

(2014), *Marx and Nature: A Red Green Perspective*, Chicago: Haymarket.

Canadell, J. G. et al. (2000), 'Carbon Metabolism of the Terrestrial Biosphere', *Ecosystems*, 3: 115–30.

Dobson, Andrew (1995), *Green Political Thought*, London: Routledge.

Engels, Frederick (1987), *The Dialectics of Nature*, MECW, vol. 46.

Epicurus (1994), 'Principle Doctrines', in Bran Inwood and Lloyd P. Gerson (eds), *The Epicurus Reader*, Indianapolis: Hackett.

Foster, John Bellamy (1992), 'The Absolute General Law of Environmental Degradation under Capitalism', *Capitalism Nature Socialism*, 3 (3): 77–81.

(1999), 'Marx's Theory of Metabolic Rift', *American Journal of Sociology*, 105 (2): 366–405.

(2000), *Marx's Ecology: Materialism and Nature*, New York: Monthly Review.

(2008), 'Marx's *Grundrisse* and the Ecological Contradictions of Capitalism', in Marcello Musto (ed.), *Karl Marx's* Grundrisse: *Foundations of the Critique of Political Economy 150 Years Later*, London: Routledge, pp. 93–106.

Foster, John Bellamy, and Burkett, Paul (2015), *Marx on Earth: An Anti-Critique*, Boston: Brill.

Foster, John Bellamy, Clark, Brett, and York, Richard (2011), *The Ecological Rift: Capitalism's War on the Planet*, New York: Monthly Review.

---

[59] Marx and Engels, *Manifesto of the Communist Party*, p. 506; Marx, *Capital*, volume III, pp. 798–9.

[60] K. Marx, *The Eighteenth Brumaire of Louis Bonaparte*, MECW, vol. 11, p. 185. For Marx, the mole digging so industrially away beneath the earth represented the unseen, changing historical conditions, which would give rise to a period of radical change – a metaphor he developed out of Shakespeare's *Hamlet*. In Marxian thought, Marx himself is frequently given the nickname the 'Old Mole'.

Foster, John Bellamy, and Holleman, Hannah (2014), 'The Theory of Unequal Ecological Exchange', *The Journal of Peasant Studies*, 41 (1–2): 199–233.
Gould, Stephen Jay (1987), *An Urchin in the Storm: Essays about Books and Ideas*, New York: W. W. Norton.
Horkheimer, Max (1947), *The Eclipse of Reason*, New York: Continuum.
Horkheimer, Max, and Adorno, T. W. (1972), *The Dialectic of Enlightenment*, New York: Continuum.
Jacoby, Russell (1981), *Dialectic of Defeat*, Cambridge: Cambridge University Press.
 (1983), 'Western Marxism', in Tom Bottomore (ed.), *A Dictionary of Marxist Thought*, Oxford: Blackwell, pp. 523–64.
Jay, Martin (1996), *The Dialectical Imagination*, Berkeley: University of California Press.
Klein, Naomi (2014), *This Changes Everything*, New York: Simon and Schuster.
Leary, Elly, and Lewis, Anne (2015), 'Interview with Bill Gallegos', *Monthly Review*, 67 (5): 18–34.
Luxemburg, Rosa (1920), 'Stagnation and Progress of Marxism', in *Rosa Luxemburg Speaks*, New York: Pathfinder.
Martinez-Alier, Joan (1987), *Ecological Economics*, Oxford: Blackwell.
Marx, Karl (1880), Unpublished Notes from S. Podolinski's Unpublished manuscript, 'La Travail humain et la Conservation de l'Engergie', to be published in MEGA^2, vol. IV/27.
 (1975), *Economic and Philosophic Manuscripts of 1844*, MECW, vol. 3, pp. 229–346.
 (1976), *Capital*, volume I, London: Penguin.
 (1978), *Capital*, volume II, London: Penguin.
 (1979), *The Eighteenth Brumaire of Louis Bonaparte*, MECW, vol. 11, pp. 99–209.
 (1981), *Capital*, volume III, London: Penguin.
 (1986), 'Outlines of the Critique of Political Economy [*Grundrisse*]. First Instalment', MECW, vol. 28.
 (1989), *Critique of the Gotha Programme*, MECW, vol. 24, pp. 75–99.
 (1992), *Early Writings*, London: Penguin.
 (1996), *Capital*, volume I, MECW, vol. 35.
 (1997), *Capital*, volume II, MECW, vol. 36.
 (1998), *Capital*, volume III, MECW, vol. 37.
Marx, Karl, and Engels, Frederick (1975), *The Holy Family, or Critique of Critical Criticism. Against Bruno Bauerand Company*, MECW, vol. 4, pp. 5–211.
 (1975), *The German Ideology*, MECW, vol. 5, pp. 19–539.
 (1976), *Manifesto of the Communist Party*, MECW, vol. 6, pp. 477–519.
 (1985), *Letters, 1860–1864*, MECW, vol. 41.
 (1987), *Letters, 1864–1868*, MECW, vol. 42.
 (1992), *Letters, 1880–1883*, MECW, vol. 46.
Mészaros, Istvan (2008), *The Challenge and Burden of Historical Time: Socialism in the Twenty-First Century*, New York: Monthly Review Press.
NASA Earth Observatory (2003), 'NASA Satellite Measures Earth's Metabolism', 22 April, http://earthobservatory.nasa.gov.
O'Connor, James (1997), *Natural Causes*, New York: Guilford Press.

Parsons, Howard L. (1977), *Marx and Engels on Ecology*, Westport, CT: Greenwood Press.
Quaini, Massimo (1982), *Geography and Marxism*, Totowa, NJ: Barnes and Noble.
Redclift, Michael (1984), *Development and the Environmental Crisis*, New York: Methuen.
Saito, K. (2017), *Karl Marx's Ecosocialism*, New York: Monthly Review Press.
Schmidt, A. (1971), *The Concept of Nature in Marx*, London: New Left Books.
Smith, Mark J. (1998), *Ecologism*, Minneapolis: University of Minnesota Press.
Sweezy, Paul (1972), *Modern Capitalism and Other Essays*, New York: Monthly Review Press.
Wendling, Amy E. (2009), *Karl Marx on Technology and Alienation*, London: Palgrave.
Weston, Del (2014), *The Political Economy of Global Warming*, London: Routledge.
Williams, Raymond (1989), *Resources of Hope*, London: Verso.
Wishart, Ryan, Jamil Jonna, R., and Besek, Jordan Fox (2015), 'The Metabolic Rift: A Selected Bibliography', http://monthlyreview.org/commentary/metabolic-rift/.

11 Gender Equality

Heather A. Brown

11.1 Marx, Gender, and Feminism

The complex relationship between gender and class is one that will need to be addressed in order to improve the situation of women everywhere. After efforts in the 1970s and 1980s to adapt and integrate Karl Marx's economics and methodology into feminist theorizing, feminist critics of Marx seem to have won the debate arguing that Marx has little to nothing to offer. A number of these studies have correctly evaluated many of the limitations of socialist feminism and its attempts to synthesize Marxism and feminism.[1] This is especially true in regards to critiques of essentialism, ethnocentrism, and earlier Marxist feminism's largely uncritical acceptance of economic determinism.

Nevertheless, it is not clear that the debate has been completely exhausted. Post-structuralism and theories of difference have been unable to create an anti-capitalist feminism due to their almost sole focus on the admittedly important areas of culture, ideology, and localized resistance.

Marx's writings on the issue of gender are significantly more substantial and valuable than is usually acknowledged. Albeit with some problematic elements, Marx showed considerable insight into the gender relations of his own time, pointing to the need for a total transformation of society that would necessarily involve new relations between men and women.[2] It is true that Marx's writings on gender and the family are located

---

[1] See, for example, Z. Eisenstein (ed.), *Capitalist Patriarchy and the Case for Socialist Feminism* (New York: Monthly Review Press, 1979); H. Hartmann, 'The Unhappy Marriage of Marxism and Feminism: Towards a More Progressive Union', *Capital & Class*, 3: 1–33 (1979); M. Barrett, *Women's Oppression Today: Problems in Marxist Feminist Analysis* (New York: Verso, 1980).

[2] More recent works that draw on Marx's writings on women include: M. Gimenez, 'Capitalism and the Oppression of Women: Marx Revisited', *Science & Society*, 69: 11–32 (2005); J. Grant, 'Gender and Marx's Radical Humanism in *The Economic and Philosophic Manuscripts of 1844*', *Rethinking Marxism*, 17: 59–77 (2005); L. Vogel and M. Gimenez (eds), *Marxist-Feminist Thought Today, Science & Society*, 65 (2005).

sporadically throughout his work and that he does not provide a fully cohesive theory of gender relations. However, this does not necessarily mean that Marx was not interested in understanding this issue or that he was sexist.

There certainly are some problematic areas in Marx's writings on gender and the family such as his ambivalent position regarding the changing moral status of women as they entered the workforce and faced patriarchal and capitalist exploitation. His categories and analysis lead in the direction of a systematic critique of patriarchy as it manifests itself in capitalism.

Openings occur in his early philosophical and political writings that point to a need for changing gender relationships, his political economy in *Capital* that sought to chart changes in family and gender relations caused by industrialization as well as his later political works for the International Working Men's Association (IWMA) and the *Critique of the Gotha Programme*, and his study of pre-capitalist social relations in his *Ethnological Notebooks* that point to the family as an institution that dialectically interacts with economic forces.

11.2 Marx's Early Writings on Gender Equality and Emancipation

Marx's early writings exhibit concern for the position of women within capitalist society. In fact, in the *Economic and Philosophic Manuscripts of 1844*, Marx possibly made his strongest statement for gender equality anywhere in his work, arguing that humanity's development can be measured by the relationship between men and women:

> The direct, natural, and necessary relation of person to person is the *relation of man [Mann] to woman [Weib]*.[3] In this *natural* species-relationship man's relation to nature is immediately his relation to man [*Menschen*], just as his relation to man [*Menschen*] is immediately his relation to nature – his own *natural* destination. In this relationship, therefore, is *sensuously manifested*, reduced to an observable *fact*, the extent to which the human essence has become nature to man [*Menschen*], or to which nature to him has become the human essence of man [*Menschen*]. From this relationship one can therefore judge man's [*Menschen*] whole level of development. From the character of this relationship follows how much *man* [*Menschen*] as a *species-being*, as *man* [*Menschen*], has come to be himself and to comprehend himself; the relation of man [*Mann*] to woman [*Weib*] is the *most*

---

[3] The original German has been inserted to denote those places where Marx is referring to individual 'men [*Mann*]' or 'women [*Weib*]' and when he is referring to humanity (*Menschen*). This helps to overcome the somewhat sexist language in the translation that Marx does not appear to have intended in the original German.

natural relation of human being to human being. It therefore reveals the extent to which man's [*Menschen*] *natural* behaviour has become *human*, or the extent to which the *human* essence in him has become a *natural* essence – the extent to which his *human nature* has come to be *natural* to him. This relationship also reveals the extent to which man's [*Menschen*] *need* has become a *human* need; the extent to which, therefore, the *other* person as a person has become for him a need – the extent to which he in his individual existence is at the same time a social being.[4]

Of particular note is how Marx moved from the abstract universal – the unmediated, 'natural' human understanding of species being where survival and thus reproduction is the primary link between individuals, to the concrete universal understanding of 'natural' where every human being regardless of gender are both beings for themselves and for others – that is, the individual is valued both in terms of who they are and what they can become as well as being a representative of the species being. Thus, women (and men) become valuable to others not just for instrumental purposes, but also simply because they are human beings with similar needs and wants.

Marx was concerned with repressive relationships for women within the family of his day and called for the family's transformation into a more egalitarian institution. In his 1846 piece for *Mirror of Society [Gesellschaftsspiegel]*, 'Peuchet on Suicide', he took up suicide and its relation to alienation for first and only time in his published work.[5] Marx used the bourgeois Frenchman to illustrate that a simple betterment of the working-class position would not be enough. In fact, all in society faced some level of alienation:

[Peuchet's text] may show what grounds there are for the idea of the philanthropic bourgeois that it is only a question of a little bread and a little education for the proletarians, and that the worker is stunted the present state of society, but otherwise the existing world is the best of all possible worlds.[6]

Marx placed particular emphasis on the bourgeois family as a source of repression where familial tyrannies 'cause crises analogous to revolutions'.[7]

It is important to emphasize that three of the four case studies that he excerpted discussed women's suicide, all in relation to familial and gender oppression. In one instance, for example, a woman was publicly ridiculed for spending the night at her fiancé's house. Here Marx strongly chided

---

[4] K. Marx, *Economic and Philosophic Manuscripts of 1844*, MECW, vol. 3, pp. 295–6.
[5] While largely a translation of a text by retired French policeman Jacques Peuchet (1758–1830) from French to German, Marx surreptitiously added his own comments and deleted some of the more moralistic passages.
[6] K. Marx, 'Peuchet on Suicide', MECW, vol. 4, p. 597.
[7] Ibid, p. 604. Italics here represent Marx's emphasis of Peuchet's text.

the family institution and the seemingly moral authority that supported it, and noted that this abuse of power stemmed from the powerlessness of many in public life: 'The most cowardly, unresisting people become implacable as soon as they *can exercise their absolute parental authority. The abuse of this authority is . . . a crude compensation* for all the submissiveness and dependence to which they abase themselves ... in bourgeois society.'[8]

Looking at the working class, Marx and Friedrich Engels in the *Manifesto of the Communist Party* pointed to their absence of property as a source of the dissolution of the family along with the ideological vacuity that follows: 'The bourgeoisie has torn away from the family its sentimental veil, and has reduced the family relation to a mere money relation.'[9] It is the ideology of the bourgeois family that is being abolished by the material conditions in society which become based increasingly on commodity and monetary relations. For this reason, they called for the 'abolition [*aufhebung*] of the family'.[10]

The material basis of the bourgeois family was private gain and this was becoming the case even for the workers since all members of the family who were able to work had to do so to support the family:

The bourgeois clap-trap about the family and education, about the hallowed co-relation of parent and child, becomes all the more disgusting, the more, by the action of Modern Industry, all family ties among the proletarians are torn asunder, and their children transformed into simple articles of commerce and instruments of labour.[11]

Marx and Engels did not, however, describe what will take its place nor did they describe how this process will occur.

11.3 Political Economy, Gender, and the Transformation of the Family

Marx was especially attentive to the condition of women workers in *Capital*, volume I. In fact, a large portion of the chapters 'The Working Day' and 'Machinery and Modern Industry' discussed the work of women and children. The introduction of machinery had a profound effect on the

---

[8] Ibid, p. 595. This is Marx's emphasis of his own text.
[9] K. Marx and F. Engels, *Manifesto of the Communist Party*, MECW, vol. 6, p. 487.
[10] Ibid, p. 501. There has been a great deal of difficulty in translating *aufhebung* into English since there is no commonly used English equivalent for the term which means to both destroy and preserve. Marx seems to posit a double movement in which the oppressive aspects of the family are dissolved but the positive elements are incorporated into a new type of family structure.
[11] Ibid, p. 502.

structure of capitalism, since it allowed for their inclusion in the workforce. It could give strength to those who could not otherwise do certain strenuous tasks. This created a situation where women and children could now be at least as productive, if not more so, than the men who did physically strenuous work, which, consequently, increased the number of workers involved in industry and significantly affected the lives of women and children. Both were taken out of the home to do these seemingly adult male tasks. This, as Marx noted, would have a profound effect on the structure of the family since it would be more difficult for women to carry out their traditional domestic roles while working in the factory.[12]

Claudia Leeb argues that Marx tended to 'reinforce the male/female (strong/weak) opposition in relation to the working-class woman', since they could only enter the workforce through the introduction of machinery.[13] This is all the more apparent since he did not openly question women's weakness in relation to men. While it is probable that Marx was referring to women's supposedly biologically based physical inferiority, taking a more socially based approach in interpreting the statement may be helpful. The crucial point is not whether Marx viewed women as biologically weaker, but that women's position in industry and in private life had changed as a result of the introduction of machinery. Important barriers to women's entry into the workforce had been overcome. Thus, women are not forced to stay in the domestic sphere. Machinery could enhance the abilities of all workers regardless of gender or age.

In addition to their work in modern, mechanized factories, women and young people also represented a large portion of workers in the domestic industries.[14] These industries, which had often not mechanized and produced on a smaller scale, had to compete with modern large-scale industry. The necessity of making up for the lack of technological productivity meant that the workers were exploited all the more to stay competitive. As indicated in *Capital*, volume I:

The exploitation of cheap and immature labour power is carried out in a more shameless manner in modern manufacture than in the factory proper. This is because the technical foundation of the factory system, namely, the substitution of machines for muscular power, and the light character of the labour, is almost entirely absent in manufacture, and at the same time women and over-young children are subjected, in a most unconscionable way, to the influence of poisonous or injurious substances ... this economy now shows its antagonistic and

---

[12] K. Marx, *Capital*, volume I, MECW, vol. 35, p. 398.
[13] C. Leeb, 'Marx and the Gendered Structure of Capitalism', *Philosophy & Social Criticism*, 33: 848 (2007).
[14] These were usually small cottage-based plants with few employees and little modern technology.

murderous side more and more in a given branch of industry, the less the social productive power of labour and the technical basis for a combination of processes are developed in that branch.[15]

Thus, in a variety of ways, capitalism is able to use existing social inequalities, such as gender, to enhance the extraction of surplus value. This was especially true when capitalism mixed with other less developed social forms.

Moreover, women and children were often paid significantly less than men.[16] While Marx did not provide a detailed explanation for this, he pointed to capitalist efforts to bring the cost of the workers' subsistence to a minimum, especially in relation to women where the cost needed to 'maintain the women of the surplus population is below all calculation. Hence nowhere do we find a more shameful squandering of human labour power for the most despicable purposes than in England, the land of machinery.'[17] This was another case where the capitalist interest in profit results in human beings, especially those at the bottom of the social hierarchy, being treated as commodities, all the better the lower price that they fetch in the market.

Marx was not content with noting the harsh conditions that women faced in the workforce. He also pointed to the potential for positive effects on the working class as a whole in the labour force and, as we shall see later, in family relationships as well. Initially, the introduction of women into the workforce created an impetus to regulate the excesses of capitalism's exploitation of women's labour. With his quotation from the report on the Factory Act of 1844, which regulated adult women's work, Marx noted how '[it] states ironically: "No instances have come to my knowledge of adult women having expressed any regret at their *rights* being thus far interfered with"'.[18] This was one of the first attempts to 'interfere' with the rights of workers to 'freely' negotiate wages with their employers. Thus, the facade of freedom and equality was first torn away with regard to women and children's labour, since they could not legally protect themselves. While designed for women and children because of their historically subordinate social status, this would later set a precedent for regulations for adult male workers who worked in tandem with women and children. Thus, from 1844 to 1847, the twelve-hour day was universal for those under the Factory Act as capitalism acted as a leveller.[19]

This is only one tendency inherent in capitalism. Super-exploitation of groups with less access to power, such as women, children, and ethnic minorities, is compatible with capitalist accumulation. This played a role

---

[15] Marx, *Capital*, volume I, pp. 465–6.   [16] Ibid, p. 464.   [17] Ibid, p. 397.
[18] Ibid, p. 287.   [19] Ibid, p. 288.

Gender Equality

in driving wages down for female workers as many capitalists were willing to exploit women's allegedly more nurturing nature to produce more disciplined and docile workers:

> Mr E., a manufacturer ... informed me that he employed females exclusively at his power-looms ... gives a decided preference to married females, especially those who have families at home dependent on them for support; they are attentive, docile, more so than unmarried females, and are compelled to use their utmost exertions to procure the necessaries of life. Thus are the virtues, the peculiar virtues of the female character to be perverted to her injury – thus all that is most dutiful and tender in her nature is made a means of her bondage and suffering.[20]

Marx quotes Lord Ashley on women's more nurturing 'nature' without questioning whether or not it is truly 'natural' for women to behave in this manner or whether this 'natural' state is socially mediated as well. Later, as he saw an increasing number of women struggling alongside men for greater rights in the workplace, his position on the matter seemed to change significantly to one where women's 'nature' was much less of a factor.

Women would have to play a significant role in the struggle for labour rights. This was something that Marx emphasized in his speeches and writings for the IWMA In his opening remarks on the introduction of women and children into the workforce for the General Council sessions in July 1868, Marx gave a dialectical perspective on the effects of machinery on women, children, and the family:

> The woman has thus become an active agent in our social production. Formerly female and children's labour was carried on within the family circle. I do not say that it is wrong that women and children should participate in our social production ... but the way in which they are made to work under existing circumstances is abominable.[21]

Marx not only gave his support for women entering the workforce, but also pointed to the specifically capitalist nature of the working conditions. Moreover, Marx noted that women engaging in social production is not a new phenomenon; what was new was that production now took place outside of the house. Further, Marx emphasized the positive effects of machinery '[that] leads on one hand to associated organised labour, on the other to the disintegration of all formerly existing social and family relations'.[22]

---

[20] Ibid, pp. 405–6.
[21] K. Marx, 'Record of Marx's Speech on the Consequences of Using Machinery under Capitalism', MECW, vol. 21, p. 383.
[22] Ibid, p. 383.

Towards the end of 1868, a group of silk weavers and ribbon makers went on strike in Lyons, France. In his 'Report of the General Council to the Fourth Annual Congress', Marx highlighted the role played by mostly female workers who went on strike despite economic difficulties and police repression: 'Shortly after the Ricamarie massacres, the dance of the economical revolts was opened at Lyons by the silk-winders, most of them females ... At Lyons, as before at Rouen, the female workers played a noble and prominent part in the movement.'[23]

Moreover, in *Capital*, volume I, Marx returned to his discussion of the transformation of the family. As capitalistic organization of industry spread into the areas previously occupied by domestic industry, it helped to create further ground for the dissolution of the family since it became necessary to regulate 'the so-called "home-labour", [since] it is immediately viewed as a direct attack on the patria potestas, on parental authority'.[24] Marx noted that the barriers that were once in place to separate the public and private spheres were being broken down through the incorporation of women and children's labour into industry, outside of the control of the head of household. The state had to at least take over regulation of some of the economic aspects in order to protect the system from collapse – often doing so quite reluctantly.[25]

Marx argued, however, that this form of exploitation and destruction of the family also had some potentially positive effects:

However terrible and disgusting the dissolution, under the capitalist system, of the old family ties *may appear*, nevertheless, modern industry, by assigning as it does an important part in the process of production, outside the domestic sphere, to women, to young persons, and to children of both sexes, *creates a new economic foundation for a higher form of the family and of the relations between the sexes* ... Moreover, *it is obvious that the fact of the collective working group being composed of individuals of both sexes and all ages, must necessarily, under suitable conditions, become a source of humane development*; although in its spontaneously developed, brutal, capitalistic form, where the labourer exists for the process of production, and not the process of production for the labourer, that fact is a pestiferous source of corruption and slavery.[26]

It appears that Marx was summarizing much of his previous argument regarding capitalism's effects on the family. The old ties based upon an economic system in which most production occurred within the domestic sphere had begun to dissolve as it became more industrially based. Although production does not determine, but only conditions the form

---

[23] K. Marx, 'Report of the General Council to the Fourth Congress of the International Working Men's Association', MECW, vol. 21, p. 77.
[24] Marx, *Capital*, volume I, pp. 491–2.   [25] Ibid, p. 492.
[26] Ibid, pp. 492–3. Emphasis added.

of the family, these changes in the production of the means of life have had significant effects on the ability of the patriarchal family to function and created grounds for both the harsh exploitation of new workers under capitalism as well as a non-exploitative form of the family in the new society.

While this is admittedly a brief and abstract discussion of the potential for changes in the family structure, it is important to note that Marx posited that this change occurred as a result of the cooperation of all workers, including women and children. Marx was not questioning the introduction of women into the workforce, let alone calling for a family wage. Instead he pointed to the ways in which in the 'spontaneously developed, brutal, capitalist form, the system works' against the humane development of workers.[27] Equally significant is his dialectical discussion of how these developments could under the right circumstances be transformed into their opposite, that is, to a new form of the family.

Marx also took up issues of gender in the *Critique of the Gotha Programme*. At the 1875 party platform of the German Social Democratic Party, that was as heavily influenced by Lasallian and reformist ideas, he spoke of the need for 'a fair distribution of the proceeds of labour',[28] Marx noted that mere distribution could only be measured based on the form of society in question and not in terms of abstract concepts of justice. Those in power will always claim that the present distribution is just.[29] One of the examples that Marx used to discuss the problems with using the bourgeois concept of right in any new society involved the distribution of labour in the family and how this could lead to unequal distribution overall:

Besides, one worker is married, another not; one has more children than another, etc., etc. Thus, given an equal amount of work done, and hence an equal share in the social consumption fund, one will in fact receive more than another, one will be richer than another, etc. To avoid all these defects, right would have to be unequal rather than equal.[30]

While it is not fully clear that Marx was discussing the value of domestic labour, there appears to be an opening for a critical angle. Domestic labour does not have an exchange value since it is labour done in the house, but it does have an important use-value. Someone has to be available to do the cooking, cleaning, and raise the children. Those that

---

[27] For a discussion of how Marx is ambivalent on the effect of factory work on women's morality, see H. Brown *Marx on Gender and the Family: A Critical Study* (Boston: Brill, 2012), pp. 84–8.

[28] K. Marx, *Critique of the Gotha Programme*, MECW, vol. 24, p. 83.   [29] Ibid, p. 84.

[30] Ibid, p. 87.

live alone have to do these things in addition to their own labour in the public sphere. Thus, there would be a need to rethink the public/private distinction in a new society.

11.4 The Dialectics of the Pre-capitalist Family

Marx's *Ethnological Notebooks*, written in the 1880s and not intended to be published, provide a wealth of interesting material in relation to gender and the family from late in his life.[31] Like Lewis Henry Morgan (1818–1881), Marx was quite critical of the many ethnologists of the day that held to the notion that the origin of the modern family was in the patriarchal family. Marx read and appropriated much of Morgan's understanding of the more egalitarian clan and the family life of early societies from his text *Ancient Society* (1877).[32] Morgan argued that the Iroquois of his day represented one stage in the unilinear development of the human family. Mother-right, as it existed for the Iroquois, for example, was an earlier stage of clan and social life where women had more rights. The family was not always hierarchical and patriarchal according to Morgan and Marx.

Marx appropriated Morgan in his theoretical disputes with Henry Sumner Maine's (1822–1888) *Lectures on the Early History of Institutions* (1875). Throughout his notes, Marx criticized Maine for his failure to understand the importance of the clan in early societies as well as a general lack of understanding of the modalities of change in these societies. He rebuked Maine's argument that the patriarchal joint family, which existed in certain parts of India at the time, was one of the earliest forms of the family, referring to him at one point as a 'blockheaded Englishman'.[33]

---

[31] D. Smith ('Accumulation and the Clash of Cultures: Marx Ethnology in Context', *Rethinking Marxism*, 14: 75 [2002]) believed that Marx was conducting ethnological study to expand *Capital*, while K. Anderson (*Marx at the Margins: On Nationalism, Ethnicity, and Non-Western Societies* [Chicago: University of Chicago Press, 2010], p. 2) argued that he was looking at new forms of resistance to capital.

[32] Engels *Origin of the Family* also used Morgan's text as a starting point; however, Marx was much more critical and seemingly less determinist in his appropriation of Morgan's work. For more on this argument, see R. Dunayevskaya, *Rosa Luxemburg, Women's Liberation, and Marx's Philosophy of Revolution* (Chicago: University of Illinois Press, 1991), pp. 175–88 and Brown, *Marx on Gender and the Family*, pp. 133–75.

[33] K. Marx, 'Marx's Excerpts from Henry Summer Maine, *Lectures on the Early History of Institutions*', in L. Krader (ed.), *The Ethnological Notebooks of Karl Marx* (Assen: Van Gorcum, 1972), p. 292. The English translation is taken from D. N. Smith, *Marx's World: Global Society and Capital Accumulation in Marx's Late Manuscripts* (New Haven, CT: Yale University Press, forthcoming). The parts of text between quotation marks refer to the excerpts of the books transcribed by Marx, while the rest are his own commentaries and paraphrases. Italics are Marx's emphasis.

The *entirely false representation* of *Maine*, that the *private family*, even in the form in which it exists in India ... can be *regarded as the basis* upon which the *Sept* and *Gens* evolved, etc., is shown in the following passage: After he says that the '*power of distributing inheritances vested in the Celtic Chiefs*' is the same institution reserved to the 'Hindoo father' in the *Mitakshara*, he continues: 'It is part of the *prerogative*' (the idiot misses the relationship between the gens and the tribe) 'belonging to the representative of the purest blood in the joint family; but in proportion as the *Joint Family, Sept*, or *Gens becomes more artificial*, the power of distribution tends more and more to look like mere *administrative authority*.' The matter is quite the reverse. For Maine, who after all is unable to forget the English private family, it appears that this *entirely natural function of the Chief of the gens, later of* [the] *Tribe*, natural just because he is *Chief* (and theoretically always 'elected'), is 'artificial' and 'mere administrative authority,' while in fact the arbitrary power of the modern *pater familias* is just as '*artificial*,' as is the private family itself, from the archaic standpoint.[34]

Marx charged that Maine was generalizing the existence of the private family based on one form of the Indian family that occurred under unique circumstances. There is not enough evidence to make the assertion that the clan evolved from the private family. There is proof even within Maine's work to the contrary in his discussion of inheritance rights in India.[35]

Marx also criticized Maine for his assertion that the clan chief's distribution of property was based upon his power as the paterfamilias. Instead, Marx saw the beginning stages of conflict between the principle of the clan and the private family.[36] Initially, the power to dispose of land belonging to the clan was likely in the hands of a number of people. Later, as the chief became more powerful, he gained this power as an exclusive right. Moreover, Marx noted that this only appeared as 'administrative authority'[37] in the final stages of the transition to a patriarchal class society when the clan principle was already in an advanced state of decay.[38]

As in a number of places, Marx pointed out that 'natural' and 'artificial' conditions could only be determined based upon the specific social relations of production and the development of society. Each economic mode of production contains within it a certain range of possible social relations. The modern family would be an artificial and untenable social structure in this early period, just as the clan appears to be an artificial institution in our own society. Marx argued that the current form of the family is not the only possible one. The family would have to change a great deal in any post-capitalist society.

---

[34] Ibid, p. 309.   [35] For this argument, see, for example, ibid, pp. 324–7.   [36] Ibid.
[37] Ibid.   [38] Ibid.

Marx frequently pointed the socially constructed nature of all historical forms of the family, here in his notes on Morgan:

> Each of the *systems of consanguinity* 'expresses *the actual relationships existing in the family* at the time of its establishment ... The *relations* of *mother & child*, ... *brother & sister*, ... *grandmother & grandchild*, were always ascertainable' (since the establishment of any form of family at all), 'but not *those of father & child*, ... *grandfather & grandchild*'; the latter only (at least officially?) ascertainable in monogamy.[39]

Marx suggested that the family is not something ahistorical and 'natural'. Instead, it is a social construction, based in part on the material conditions at a particular time, where paternity will (at least until recent times) necessarily be uncertain. More important than his critique of the monogamous family and its corollary of hetaerism and infidelity is his parenthetical insert regarding the 'relations of mother & child'.[40] There appears to be some room for non-biological determinations. While Morgan states that relationships between family members through the mother were always certain, Marx adds the phrase 'since the establishment of any form of family at all'.[41] Thus, while there is a biological element to the family, even this is socially mediated through the structures of society in order to determine membership.

Marx did not view the family and its gender relationships as static; instead, these relationships were active and dynamic, defying simple categorization and thus allowing for more subjectivity for women regardless of the time period in question. Marx provided a subtle critique of Morgan's discussion of the egalitarian gender relations among the Iroquois. While he noted that Iroquois women had more power than women in his own time, Marx took from Morgan that their position was far from ideal and was in fact based on a double-standard. The husband demanded chastity from the wife who could face severe punishments for infidelity, while polygamy for the male was allowed.[42]

Marx also took down a passage from Morgan documenting the low position of women in Greece, but instead of simply dwelling on their lack of power, Marx added his own comment on the potential for women's subjectivity: 'But the situation of the *goddesses on Olympus* demonstrates nostalgia for the former more free & influential position of the females. Powerhungry Juno, the goddess of wisdom springs from the head of Zeus etc.'[43]

The position of Greek goddesses pointed both to a past in which women were less oppressed and, at the same time, pointed to a possible

---

[39] Marx, 'Marx's Excerpts from Henry Morgan *Ancient Society*', p. 104.   [40] Ibid.
[41] Ibid.   [42] Ibid, p. 117.   [43] Ibid, p. 121.

future in which women would again have a higher status. However, as imbued as certain Greek myths were with patriarchal assumptions, Greek women would need to do more than simply emulate Juno (Hera) and Athena. Nostalgia for the past would not be enough to fundamentally change their position. Nevertheless, these figures did offer some starting points. To begin with, both of these goddesses lived among men rather than in exclusion and played a significant role in society, albeit not always a positive one.

More importantly, both maintained a great deal of control over their sexuality despite the limits imposed both by the primitive state of contraception and by the social forces at the time. Hera was able to decide on her own that she would not raise her son Hephaestus while Athena likely chose to remain a virgin given the difficulties of remaining in a position of authority while raising a family. Certainly, in both cases, these were choices based on imperfect options, but it could have provided a starting point for a critique of Greek patriarchy.

11.5 The Importance of Dialectical Intersectionality

Marx showed considerable insight into the gender relations of his own time, pointing to the need for a total transformation of society that would necessarily involve new relations between men and women. Nonetheless, Marx's work is not without problems. He was not always able to overcome the Victorianism of his own era and at times reverted to a naturalistic understanding of gender. Regardless, Marx's innovative theory of gender was already quite evident in *Economic and Philosophic Manuscripts of 1844*, where he provided an incipient philosophy of gender and society that has much potential for overcoming hierarchical dualisms that have impeded gender equality.

Later, as he moved to political economy, this earlier philosophical grounding remained. Marx seemed to point in the direction of a fully dialectical understanding of the entry of women into the workforce as well as the contractions and opportunities that this provided. His sensitivity to the plight of all women illustrated the need to surpass the boundaries of liberalism. Marx's *Ethnological Notebooks* led to new and theoretically stimulating directions in his thinking on family relations and gender equality, pointing to these areas as not static categories that simply change with new economic circumstances, but as dynamic and dialectical factors that interact with economic forces.

One of the most important factors for understanding the relationship between gender and class is Marxian dialectical interaction. In most cases, Marx's categories came from a dialectical analysis of the empirical world, whether that be the factory, the family, or the pre-capitalist clan. These categories are dynamic and are based on social relationships rather than static and ahistorical formulations. Moreover, they are subject to change as society changes. This could potentially be valuable to feminism today as a tool for analyzing gender relations in their various manifestations globally where both identity and difference are manifest.

The issue of economic determinism in Marx requires more careful examination. Economic factors play a very significant role because they condition other social behaviour; however, Marx was often careful to note the reciprocal and dialectical relation between economic and social factors in so far as they are moments of a particular mode of production. In the last analysis, the two cannot be separated out completely as Marx illustrated in many of his works. He pointed to the unique ways in which economics and the specifically capitalist form of patriarchy interact to oppress women. Thus, Marx, at least tentatively, began to discuss the interdependent relationship between class and gender without fundamentally privileging either in his analysis.

Certainly not all aspects of Marx's writings on women are relevant today, and some carry the limitations of nineteenth-century thought. However, Marx's discussion of gender and the family extended far beyond merely including women as factory workers. He noted the persistence of oppression within the modern family and the need to work out a new form of the family. Additionally, Marx became increasingly supportive of women's demands for equality in the workplace, in unions, and in the IWMA. Despite their unpolished and fragmentary character, Marx's notes on ethnology are particularly significant since he pointed directly to the historical character of the family.

While Marx's theory remains underdeveloped in terms of providing an account that includes gender as important to understanding present-day capitalism, his categories and emphasis on dialectical change nonetheless lead in the direction of a systematic critique of contemporary forms of patriarchy. Therefore, he is able to separate out the historically specific elements of patriarchy from a more general form of women's oppression as it has existed throughout much of human history. In this sense, his categories provide resources for feminist theory or at least areas for new dialogue between Marxists and feminists at a time when Marx's critique of capital is coming to the fore once again.

References

Anderson, Kevin (2010), *Marx at the Margins: On Nationalism, Ethnicity, and Non-Western Societies*, Chicago: University of Chicago Press.

Barrett, Michele (1980), *Women's Oppression Today: Problems in Marxist Feminist Analysis*, New York: Verso.
Brown, Heather (2012), *Marx on Gender and the Family: A Critical Study*, Boston: Brill.
Di Stefano, Christine (1991), *Configurations of Masculinity: A Feminist Perspective on Modern Political Theory*, Ithaca, NY: Cornell University Press.
Dunayevskaya, Raya (1991), *Rosa Luxemburg, Women's Liberation, and Marx's Philosophy of Revolution*, Chicago: University of Illinois Press.
Engels, Friedrich (1990), *Origin of the Family, Private Property and the State*, MECW, vol. 26, pp. 129–276.
Eisenstein, Zillah (ed.) (1979), *Capitalist Patriarchy and the Case for Socialist Feminism*, New York: Monthly Review Press.
Gimenez, Martha (2005), 'Capitalism and the Oppression of Women: Marx Revisited', *Science & Society*, 69: 11–32.
Grant, Judith (2005), 'Gender and Marx's Radical Humanism in *The Economic and Philosophic Manuscripts of 1844*', *Rethinking Marxism*, 17: 59–77.
Hartmann, Heidi (1979), 'The Unhappy Marriage of Marxism and Feminism: Towards a More Progressive Union', *Capital & Class*, 3: 1–33.
Leeb, Claudia (2007), 'Marx and the Gendered Structure of Capitalism', *Philosophy & Social Criticism*, 33: 833–59.
Maine, Henry (1875), *Lectures on the Early History of Institutions*, New York: Henry Holt and Company.
Marx, Karl (1972), 'Ethnological Notebooks', in Lawrence Krader (ed.), *The Ethnological Notebooks of Karl Marx*, Assen: Van Gorcum.
(1975), *Economic and Philosophic Manuscripts of 1844*, MECW, vol. 3, pp. 229–346.
(1975), 'Peuchet on Suicide', MECW, vol. 4, pp. 597–612.
(1985), 'Record of Marx's Speech on the Consequences of Using Machinery under Capitalism', MECW, vol. 21, pp. 382–4.
(1985), 'Report of the General Council to the Fourth Congress of the International Working Men's Association', MECW, vol. 21, pp. 68–82.
(1989), *Critique of the Gotha Programme*, MECW, vol. 24, pp. 75–99.
(1996), *Capital*, volume I, MECW, vol. 35.
Marx, Karl, and Engels, Frederick (1976), *Manifesto of the Communist Party*, MECW, vol. 6, pp. 477–519.
Morgan, Lewis Henry (1877), *Ancient Society or Researches in the Lines of Human Progress from Savagery through Barbarism to Civilization*, Chicago: Charles H. Kerr & Company.
Smith, David Norman (forthcoming), *Marx's World: Global Society and Capital Accumulation in Marx's Late Manuscripts*, New Haven, CT: Yale University Press.
(2002), 'Accumulation and the Clash of Cultures: Marx Ethnology in Context', *Rethinking Marxism*, 14: 73–83.
Vogel, Lise, and Gimenez, Martha (eds) (2005), *Marxist-Feminist Thought Today*, *Science and Society* (Special Issue), 65.

12 Nationalism and Ethnicity

Kevin B. Anderson

12.1 Refuting a Legend

The legend that Karl Marx either said almost nothing on nationalism, race, and ethnicity, or that on these issues he was woefully mistaken and reductionist, has been maintained in axiomatic fashion for decades, despite numerous scholarly refutations.[1] Of course, not everything Marx wrote on nationalism, ethnicity, and race holds up well today. One prominent example concerned the Russians and some of the other Slavic peoples of Eastern and Southern Europe. As will be discussed, Marx strongly supported Polish national emancipation as an important progressive force in European politics. But, in his early writings, he portrayed Russia as an utterly reactionary society, and described most of the other Slavic peoples as dominated by Russian Pan-Slavist propaganda. This has led to extended – and sometimes unfair – attacks on Marx on nationalism *tout court*. To a great extent, Marx's views were connected to Russia's counter-revolutionary role during the democratic revolutionary wave of 1848–9, but this is not a full explanation. For one can find in Marx's writings on Russia before the 1870s not only violent denunciations of the Tsarist Empire as a malevolent force, but also a number of very problematic, even racist statements about the Russian people

---

[1] W. E. B. Du Bois (*Black Reconstruction in America: An Essay toward a History of the Part Which Black Folk Played in the Attempt to Reconstruct Democracy in America, 1860–1880* [New York: Atheneum, 1973]) showed Marx's subtle grasp of the dialectics of race and class, a point demonstrated more recently by A. Nimtz (*Marx, Tocqueville, and Race in America: The 'Absolute Democracy' or 'Defiled Republic'* [Lanham, MD: Lexington Books, 2003]) and R. Blackburn (*An Unfinished Revolution: Karl Marx and Abraham Lincoln* [London: Verso, 2011]). S. F. Bloom (*The World of Nations: A Study of the National Implications of the Work of Marx* [New York: Columbia University Press, 1941]) did so with respect to Marx on nationalism, as have more recent studies of Marx by E. Benner, *Really Existing Nationalisms: A Post-Communist View of Marx and Engels* (New York: Oxford University Press, 1995), M. Löwy, *Fatherland or Mother Earth? Essays on the National Question* (London: Pluto Press, 1998), and A. Walicki, 'Marx, Engels, and the Polish Question', in: *Philosophy and Romantic Nationalism: The Case of Poland* (Oxford: Oxford University Press, 1982).

themselves. As to other Slavic groups, most of the vitriol was expressed by Friedrich Engels (1820–1895) in a series of articles on Pan-Slavism.[2] Both Marx and Engels shifted their positions by the 1870s and the 1880s, however, when one can find Marx – who had learned Russian by this time – extolling the Russian peasant commune as a possible starting point for a global insurrection against the capitalist system.[3]

At the same time, many other writings by Marx offer a far better basis from which to construct a contemporary theory of the relationship of nationalism, ethnicity, and race to class and to the struggle against capital. The following discussion focuses on three sets of Marx's writings, all of them quite substantial: those on Polish national emancipation and the wider European revolution, those on the Civil War in the United States and the dialectics of race and class, and those on Irish national emancipation and the Irish minority inside Britain. The first of these, on Poland, was about national emancipation. The second of these, concerning the United States, was about ethnic and racial minorities and the struggle for democracy and human emancipation. Both of these concerns – national emancipation and ethnic movements in relation to class – come together in Marx's writings on Ireland, where they are also theorized at a more general level.

12.2 Poland and the European Democratic Revolution

Marx's writings on Poland are little discussed today, but during his lifetime that country's struggle for its very existence as an independent nation loomed very large as an issue for leftist and democratic movements. It would not be an exaggeration to say that Polish national emancipation was an even more important reference point in Marx's period than is Palestinian national emancipation today. And, like Palestinians today, Poles were a people without a country, subject to the partition of their homeland among Russia, Austria, and Prussia, with many living in exile in Western Europe and the Americas. Marx underlined the importance of

---

[2] R. Rosdolsky, *Engels and the 'Nonhistoric' Peoples: The National Question in the Revolution of 1848* (Glasgow: Critique Books, 1986).

[3] In concentrating on nationalism, race, and ethnicity in Europe and North America, the present chapter leaves aside another well-known group of sometimes ethnocentric and Eurocentric assessments, which can be found in Marx's discussions of India in the *New-York Tribune* during the early 1850s. More detailed treatments of these writings can be found in A. Ahmad, 'Marx on India: A Clarification', in: *In Theory: Classes, Nations, Literature* (London: Verso, 1992), K. Anderson, *Marx at the Margins: On Ethnicity, Nationalism, and Non-Western Societies* (Chicago: University of Chicago Press, 2010), pp. 11–24, 37–41, and I. Habib, 'Introduction: Marx's Perception of India', in: I. Husain (ed.), *Karl Marx on India* (New Delhi: Tulika Books, 2006).

Poland to the left in a letter to Engels of 2 December 1856, 'the intensity and viability of all revolutions since 1789 may be gauged with fair accuracy by their attitude towards Poland. Poland is their "external" thermometer'.[4]

If Poland was a sort of litmus test for the left, and one that was not always fulfilled by the left, Polish revolutionaries had for their part been more consistent and principled, as Marx saw it. No people had made a more important contribution to the wider democratic and socialist revolutions of the eighteenth and nineteenth centuries, both through the Polish insurrections – of 1794, 1830,[5] 1846, and 1863 – and through the participation of Polish exiles in so many other revolutionary causes. For example, in an 1875 speech to an international gathering in support of Poland, Marx and Engels stressed the 'cosmopolitan' character of Polish revolutionaries:

> Poland ... is the only European people that has fought and is fighting as the *cosmopolitan soldier of the revolution*. Poland shed its blood during the American War of Independence; its legions fought under the banner of the first French Republic; by its revolution of 1830 it prevented the invasion of France that had been decided by the partitioners of Poland; in 1846 in Cracow it was the first in Europe to plant the banner of social revolution; in 1848 it played an outstanding part in the revolutionary struggle in Hungary, Germany, and Italy; finally, in 1871 it supplied the Paris Commune with its best generals and most heroic soldiers.[6]

The language about the 1846 Kraków uprising as the 'first in Europe to plant the banner of a social revolution' harked back to the *Manifesto of the Communist Party*.

This points to a more general issue in terms of Marx and nationalism. It is true that the *Manifesto of the Communist Party* contains the famous language about the workers having no country, and about national antagonisms receding. This has often been interpreted – especially by critics whose study of Marx has not gone much beyond the opening pages of the *Manifesto of the Communist Party* – to buttress erroneous claims that Marx had little time for national movements and underestimated their importance. Yet, in the concluding section of the *Manifesto of the Communist Party*,

---

[4] 'K. Marx to F. Engels, 2 December 1856', MECW, vol. 40, p. 85.
[5] Marx gave particular emphasis to 1830, when a Polish uprising kept Russian troops occupied for several months, preventing them from sending their forces into France to repress the anti-monarchical revolution there. Poland was crushed and the Russian occupation harshened considerably, but France ended up with a less authoritarian system, after which it failed to render reciprocal support to Poland.
[6] K. Marx and F. Engels, 'For Poland', in MECW, vol. 24, pp. 57–8. Here and elsewhere, the *Collected Works* of Marx and Engels and other standard English translations are cited, but the translations have sometimes been altered after consulting the German or French originals of Marx's texts.

entitled 'Position of the Communists in Relation to the Various Existing Opposition Parties', there was a prominent reference to the Polish national cause. There, one could read that communists were to support the left wing of the democratic movement in France, the Chartist labour movement in Britain, and agrarian reformers in the United States. Among these democratic and progressive movements deserving of support could also be found the struggle for the restoration of Poland as a nation, within which communists were to support the left wing of the nationalist movement: 'In Poland they support the party that insists on an agrarian revolution as the prime condition for national emancipation, that party which fomented the insurrection in Cracow in 1846.'[7]

Marx developed a more expansive analysis of 1846 Kraków in a speech at a meeting on 22 February 1848, around the time that the *Manifesto of the Communist Party* was published:

> The men at the head of the revolutionary movement of Cracow shared the deep conviction that only a democratic Poland could be independent, and a democratic Poland was impossible without the abolition of feudal rights, without the agrarian revolution that would transform the dependent peasantry into free proprietors, modern proprietors... The Cracow revolution has given a glorious example to the whole of Europe, by identifying the national cause with the democratic cause and the emancipation of the oppressed class.[8]

The general criteria Marx used when supporting nationalist movements like Poland's has been elucidated well by Erica Benner (1962–): 'To be eligible for support, he argued, a nationalist movement should demonstrate that it is authentically "national" in his democratic sense: it should, that is, positively address the concerns of a broad section of a nation's people by improving social conditions and expanding the bases of political participation.'[9]

If Poland was central to Marx's notion of the kinds of struggles communists needed to support in 1848, it was even more crucial to the founding of the International Working Men's Association (IWMA) in London in 1864. As will be discussed, the European labour, socialist, and democratic tendencies that united in 1864 in the IWMA initially came together across national boundaries to support the United States during the early years of the Civil War, 1861–62. The following year, a major insurrection broke out once again in Poland, which was brutally repressed by Russian troops. The same networks of labour, socialist, and democratic groups now came together to support Poland. Even Bonapartist France, a police state that had muzzled the labour movement but which ostensibly sided with Poland against Russia, allowed a French labour

---

[7] K. Marx and F. Engels, *Manifesto of the Communist Party*, MECW, vol. 6, p. 518.
[8] Ibid, p. 549.   [9] Benner, *Really Existing Nationalisms*, pp. 154–5.

delegation to travel to London to network with other groups supporting Poland. It was out of these meetings that the IWMA was born.

Marx's Inaugural Address of the IWMA of 1864 dealt mainly with class and economic questions, but it also singled out Ireland, Poland, and the Civil War in the United States. On Ireland, Marx wrote of 'the people of Ireland, gradually replaced by machinery in the north and by sheep-walks in the south, though even the sheep in that unhappy country are decreasing, it is true, not at so rapid a rate as the men'.[10] The conclusion to the address maintained that the working classes needed to create their own 'foreign policy', here singling out the Civil War in the United States and Russia's suppression of Poland and of the Chechens of the Caucasus, as well as the Russian government's generally reactionary role in international politics:

> It was not the wisdom of the ruling classes, but the heroic resistance to their criminal folly by the working classes of England that saved the West of Europe from plunging headlong into an infamous crusade for the perpetuation and propagation of slavery on the other side of the Atlantic. The shameless approval, mock sympathy, or idiotic indifference, with which the upper classes of Europe have witnessed the mountain fortress of the Caucasus falling a prey to, and heroic Poland being assassinated by, Russia; the immense and unresisted encroachments of that barbarous power, whose head is in St. Petersburg, and whose hands are in every Cabinet of Europe, have taught the working classes the duty to master themselves the mysteries of international politics ... The fight for such a foreign policy forms part of the general struggle for the emancipation of the working classes. Proletarians of all countries, Unite![11]

Not only were such formulations accepted readily by the newly constituted IWMA; these kinds of ideas had been crucial to its very formation, shared by a wide network of socialist and labour activists across Europe and North America.

In debates within the IWMA in 1864–65, Marx held that, unless democratic and class struggles in Western Europe could link up with those of oppressed nationalities like the Poles, both would fail to realize fully their aims, if not go down in defeat. Thus, support for Poland was more than a moral issue, for, without a liberated Poland, Tsarist Russia would retain its stranglehold over Europe, dooming future revolutions to defeat, just as in 1848. At the same time, he suggested, revolutionary ferment emerging from Poland could, under the right circumstances, ignite a wider European democratic upheaval. He had written to Engels in a similar vein two years earlier concerning the outbreak of the recent

---

[10] K. Marx, 'Inaugural Address of the Working Men's International', MECW, vol. 20, p. 5.
[11] Ibid, p. 13.

Polish insurrection, this in a letter of 13 February 1863: 'What do you think of the Polish business? This much is certain; the era of revolution has now fairly opened in Europe once more . . . This time, let us hope, the lava will flow from East to West.'[12]

An acrimonious debate broke out within the IWMA in late 1865, during which a group of Proudhonists adopted a workerist position, characterizing involvement with the Polish cause as a political distraction that had nothing to do with the struggle of the working class. In reality, their disagreement ran deeper, since Pierre-Joseph Proudhon (1809–1865) had been one of the few socialist leaders to sympathize with Russia rather than with Poland. In response to a request from Marx, Engels responded with a series of articles entitled 'What Have the Working Classes to Do with Poland?' in which he connected the Polish cause to the history of the European working-class movement:

> Whenever the working classes have taken a part of their own in political movements, there, from the very beginning, their foreign policy was expressed in the few words – *Restoration of Poland*. This was the case with the Chartist movement so long as it existed; this was the case with the French working men long before 1848, as well as during that memorable year, when on the 15th of May they marched on to the National Assembly to the cry of '*Vive la Pologne!*' – Poland for ever! This was the case in Germany, when, in 1848 and '49, the organs of the working class[13] demanded war with Russia and the restoration of Poland. It is the case even now.[14]

These articles met with success in terms of staving off the Proudhonist challenge, but this was not hard given the wide sympathy for Poland among labour and socialist activists.

Overall, Marx did not write at great length about Poland's internal social structure or class composition, although he consistently mentioned the progressive character of those forms of Polish nationalism that upheld not only the liberation of their country from foreign domination, but also a radical change in agrarian relations that would free the peasant from landlord oppression. Most often, he discussed Poland as a 'foreign policy' issue for the democratic, labour, and socialist movements. As he saw it, Poland's importance lay in the fact that it was the prime victim of Russian oppression and that, with its long revolutionary tradition, which included leftist elements in favour of agrarian reform, the Poles could be counted upon to fight alongside the Western European democratic and socialist movements. With most of its territory and people trapped inside the

---

[12] 'K. Marx to F. Engels, 13 February 1863', MECW, vol. 41, p. 453.
[13] A reference to the *New Rhenish Newspaper [Neue Rheinische Zeitung]*, edited by Marx.
[14] Marx, 'Inaugural Address of the Working Men's International', p. 152.

Russian Empire, Poland represented a deep contradiction within that empire, a nation that Russia had never succeeded in totally dominating. At the same time, Western revolutionaries damaged not only Poland, but also their own cause, when they betrayed Poland.

12.3 Race, Class, and Slavery during the American Civil War

If Poland was the focus of some of Marx's most important writings on nationalism, the Civil War in the United States brought forth some of his most significant ones on race and class.[15] Marx considered the Civil War to have been a second American revolution, with a socio-economic as well as a political dimension. He expressed these sentiments in the 1867 preface to *Capital*, volume I: 'Just as the in the eighteenth century the American War of Independence sounded the tocsin for the European middle class, so in the nineteenth century the American Civil War did the same for the European working class.'[16] To be sure, he saw it as a bourgeois democratic rather than a communist revolution. As Robin Blackburn (1940–) noted, in Marx's view, 'Defeating the slave power and freeing the slaves would not destroy capitalism, but it would create conditions far more favorable to organizing and elevating labour, whether white or black.'[17]

The Civil War had important economic as well as political implications for Marx. A Northern victory would consolidate what was then the largest democratic republic in the world, partially fulfilling its democratic claims by the abolition of slavery, through which a substantial part of the US population would receive formal freedom. But also given the size of the US economy and of the portion of it based upon slave labour, the emancipation of four million slaves without compensation to their 'owners' constituted in economic terms the greatest expropriation of private property in history up to that time. Moreover, as the war ended, he shared the hope of many progressive liberals and socialists that reconstruction would bring about a real agrarian reform in South that granted the former slaves not only full political rights, but also land. Thus, in the 1867 preface to *Capital*, Marx referred to the program of the Radical Republicans of granting forty acres and a mule to the freed slaves:

---

[15] Although these writings have received attention in the United States ever since Du Bois (*Black Reconstruction in America*) discussed them, followed soon after by a translation of most of them (K. Marx and Friedrich Engels, *The Civil War in the United States* (New York: International Publishers, 1937), they have received far less discussion in international Marx scholarship until very recently.

[16] K. Marx, *Capital*, volume I (New York: Penguin, 1976), p. 91.

[17] Blackburn, *An Unfinished Revolution*, p. 13.

'Mr. Wade, Vice-President of the United States, has declared in public meetings that, after the abolition of slavery, a radical transformation in the existing relations of capital and landed property is on the agenda.'[18] This programme was sidelined the following year by the failure to impeach the virulently racist President Andrew Johnson (1808–1875).

Marx strongly supported the Union cause, even at the beginning of the war when US President Abraham Lincoln (1809–1865) had yet to come out against slavery. Marx argued that the South was utterly reactionary, having placed the 'right' to own slaves as a basic principle of its constitution. But this did not prevent him from making strong criticisms of Lincoln. In an 30 August 1862 article for *Die Presse*, Marx lashed out at Lincoln's failure to come out for emancipation by quoting at length a speech by radical abolitionist Wendell Phillips (1811–1884) that characterized Lincoln as 'first-rate second rate man' who had failed to recognize that the United States would 'never see peace ... until slavery is destroyed'.[19]

As already mentioned, the IWMA was founded in large part on the basis of labour and socialist networks that had supported the North, this during the crucial early years of the war when Britain and France seemed to threaten intervention on the side of the South. In January 1865, the IWMA sent an address to Lincoln drafted by Marx, congratulating him on his solid victory in the 1864 election. After receiving a forty-member delegation from the IWMA and transmitting the address to Lincoln, US minister to Britain Charles Francis Adams (1807–1886) issued a remarkably warm public reply on behalf of Lincoln, which stated that 'the United States ... derive new encouragement to persevere from the testimony of the workingmen of Europe that the national attitude is favored with their enlightened approval and earnest sympathies'.[20] The following year though, after Lincoln had been assassinated, his successor Johnson started to block citizenship rights for former slaves. In response, the IWMA issued a very strong address to the American people that unfortunately has received very little attention, containing a prescient warning about future racial conflict:

Permit us also to add a word of counsel for the future. As injustice to a section of your people has produced such direful results, let that cease. Let your citizens of to-day be declared free and equal, without reserve. *If you fail to give them citizens' rights, while you demand citizens' duties, there will yet remain a struggle for the future which may again stain your country with your people's blood.* The eyes of Europe and

---

[18] Marx, *Capital*, volume I, p. 93.
[19] K. Marx, 'English Public Opinion', MECW, vol. 19, p. 34.
[20] Marx and Engels, *The Civil War in the United States*, pp. 100–5.

the world are fixed upon your efforts at re-construction, and enemies are ever ready to sound the knell of the downfall of republican institutions when the slightest chance is given. We warn you then, as brothers in the common cause, to remove every shackle from freedom's limb, and your victory will be complete.[21]

Although Marx did not author this address, there was no indication that he disagreed with this statement of the IWMA, in which his political influence was paramount.

The theme of race and class in the United States emerged again and again in Marx's Civil War writings, as well as in a passage in *Capital* that has also been frequently overlooked:

In the United States of America, every independent workers' movement was paralyzed as long as slavery disfigured a part of the republic. *Labor in a white skin cannot emancipate itself where it is branded in a black skin.* However, a new life immediately arose from the death of slavery. The first fruit of the American Civil War was the eight hours agitation, which ran from the Atlantic to the Pacific, from New England to California, with the seven-league boots of a locomotive. The General Congress of Labor held at Baltimore in August 1866 declared: 'The first and great necessity of the present, to free the labor of this country from capitalistic slavery, is the passing of a law by which eight hours shall be the normal working day in all the states of the American Union. We are resolved to put forth all our strength until this glorious result is attained.'[22]

This passage was central to the chapter on the 'Working Day', where Marx more than anywhere else in *Capital* took up working-class resistance. Moreover, as Raya Dunayevskaya (1910–1987) has argued, Marx added this chapter in a rather late draft of *Capital*, under the impact of the Civil War in the United States and the massive and principled support movement for the North on the part of British labour. In this sense, Dunayevskaya wrote, Marx 'as a theoretician' was 'attuned to the new impulses from the workers', as a result of which he created some new theoretical 'categories'.[23]

Marx also discussed race, class, and resistance inside the South. One example could be found in a letter to Engels of 11 January 1860, in the aftermath of the abolitionist John Brown's (1800–1859) attack on Harper's Ferry, Virginia:

In my view, the most momentous thing happening in the world today is, on the one hand, the movement among the slaves in America, started by the death of

---

[21] Institute of Marxism-Leninism of the CC, CPSU (ed.), *General Council of the First International: Minutes, 1864–1866* (Moscow: Foreign Languages Publishing House, 1962), pp. 311–12; emphasis added.
[22] Marx, *Capital*, volume I, p. 414; emphasis added.
[23] R. Dunayevskaya, *Marxism and Freedom: From 1776 until Today* (Amherst, NY: Humanity Books, 2000), p. 89.

Brown, and the movement among the slaves in Russia, on the other ... I have just seen in the *Tribune* that there was a new slave uprising in Missouri, naturally suppressed. But the signal has now been given.[24]

Brown's forces, which included black as well as white abolitionists, had attempted to touch off a slave uprising in the area.

Marx took up as well the consciousness of what he termed the 'poor whites' of the South, noting that only 300,000 out of five million Southern whites actually owned slaves. In 1861, as the Southern states voted to secede and the Civil War began, he stressed how the votes at secession conventions showed that large numbers of poor whites did not initially support secession. In his 25 October 1861 article, 'The North American Civil War', Marx alluded to the South's drive for expansion into new territories where slave labour would predominate, here comparing the poor whites to the Roman plebeians, who had received land and slaves from conquered peoples:

The number of actual slaveholders in the South of the Union does not amount to more than three hundred thousand, a narrow oligarchy that is confronted with many millions of so-called poor whites, whose numbers have been constantly growing through concentration of landed property and whose condition is only to be compared with that of the Roman plebeians in the period of Rome's extreme decline. Only by acquisition and the prospect of acquisition of new Territories, as well as by filibustering expeditions, is it possible to square the interests of these poor whites with those of the slaveholders, to give their restless thirst for action a harmless direction and to tame them with the prospect of one day becoming slaveholders themselves.[25]

As August Nimtz suggested, 'The forcible incorporation of Northern Mexico into the United States was clearly on Marx's mind. He sought to explain the material basis for what would later be called the false consciousness of poor antebellum Southern whites, thus offering insights into the establishment and maintenance of ideological hegemony.'[26] This need to create new slave states was what drove the South to secession in 1861, Marx argued, even though at that point the Lincoln administration opposed only the creation of new slave states, not abolition of slavery as such.

As Marx saw it, deep within the Southern social structure lay the possibility of an alliance between poor whites and enslaved blacks. The war itself could burst apart the old Southern society and allow these contradictions to come to the surface. The war held revolutionary

---

[24] 'K. Marx to F. Engels, 11 January 1860', MECW, vol. 41, p. 4.
[25] K. Marx, 'The North American Civil War', MECW, vol. 19, pp. 40–1.
[26] Nimtz, *Marx, Tocqueville, and Race in America*, p. 94.

possibilities for the North as well. Early on, Marx wrote presciently that the war's unfolding would eventually force the North to support not only abolition of slavery, but also black troops in its army, and full civil rights for the former slaves. Engels, for his part, seems to have shared to some extent the views of European socialists like Ferdinand Lassalle (1825–1864) that the North was both insufficiently radical and that the South might well triumph in the war, due to the North's indecision as contrasted with the South's clear will to fight. In his argument with Marx, Engels also pointed to the Southern officer corps' greater military experience, given the fact that most of the national officer corps had defected to the South.[27] It was during one of his arguments with Engels that Marx predicted, in a letter of 7 August 1862, that 'the North will finally wage war seriously, adopt revolutionary methods' and that this would include the use of black troops, which 'would have a remarkable effect on Southern nerves'.[28]

A large portion of Marx's Civil War writings concerned the 'foreign policy' of the working class. From the beginning of the war, there was fear that Britain and France would intervene on the side of the South, thus assuring a Southern victory. Conservative forces in Britain sought to whip up popular sentiment against the North by noting that its blockade of Southern ports, which prevented cotton exports, was causing huge economic hardship among the textile workers of Manchester and other industrial centres. In 'English Public Opinion', a *New-York Tribune* article published on 11 January 1862, Marx discussed how the working classes were resisting the war cries of the British establishment, even after the US Navy had forcibly boarded a British ship and arrested two Confederate representatives on their way to London:

> Even at Manchester, the temper of the working classes was so well understood that an insulated attempt at the convocation of a war meeting was almost as soon abandoned as thought of ... Wherever public meetings took place in England, Scotland, or Ireland, they protested against the rabid war-cries of the press, against the sinister designs of the Government, and declared for a pacific settlement of the pending question ... When a great portion of the British working classes directly and severely suffers under the consequences of the Southern

---

[27] This debate, which continued for several years in their correspondence, may well have been the most explicit political difference in their forty-year relationship.

[28] 'K. Marx to F. Engels, 7 August 1862', MECW, vol. 41, p. 400. In this letter, Marx referred to the need for a 'nigger-regiment', writing the phrase in English in a letter composed in German. This was an example of the use of a very racist term to make an anti-racist point. Such language cropped up a few other times in Marx's writings, including in published articles. In only one instance, however, does he seem to have used the n-word as a term of abuse. He did so in an attack on Lassalle in a letter to Engels of 30 July 1862. In this letter, Marx was denouncing Lassalle's condescending attitude towards the Northern cause ('K. Marx to F. Engels, 30 July 1862', MECW, vol. 41, pp. 389–90).

blockade; when another part is indirectly smitten by the curtailment of the American commerce, owing, as they are told, to the selfish 'protective policy' of the Republicans ... under such circumstances, simple justice requires to pay a tribute to the sound attitude of the British working classes, the more so when contrasted with the hypocritical, bullying, cowardly, and stupid conduct of the official and well-to-do John Bull.[29]

Again and again, Marx reported on large public meetings held by British workers to support the Northern cause, which constituted one of the finest examples to date of proletarian internationalism.

As mentioned, these meetings were crucial in forming the networks out of which the IWMA emerged, as Marx recounted in a letter of 29 November 1864 to his uncle Lion Philips:

In September the Parisian workers sent a delegation to the London workers to demonstrate support for Poland. On that occasion, an international Workers' Committee was formed. The matter is not without importance because ... in London the same people are at the head who ... by their monster meeting with [British Liberal leader John] Bright in St. James's Hall, *prevented war with the United States.*[30]

It was therefore quite natural that, aside from the 'Inaugural Address' drafted by Marx outlining its general principles, the newly formed IWMA's first public declaration was an open letter congratulating Lincoln on his re-election. That letter of January 1865, already mentioned, stressed the internationalist principles that had motivated British workers to support the North in the face of economic hardship:

From the commencement of the titanic American strife the workingmen of Europe felt instinctively that the star-spangled banner carried the destiny of their class ... Everywhere they bore therefore patiently the hardships imposed upon them by the cotton crisis, opposed enthusiastically the proslavery intervention of their betters – and, from most parts of Europe, contributed their quota of blood to the good cause.[31]

The surprisingly warm response of the US government, quoted earlier, gave the IWMA its first substantial publicity in the British press.

In Marx's discussions on Ireland, the national liberation themes of the writings on Poland came together with those on race and ethnicity in the analyses on the Civil War in the United States. This is related to the fact that Ireland was both a British colony fighting for its independence and

---

[29] Marx, 'The North American Civil War', pp. 137–8.
[30] 'K. Marx to L. Philips, 29 November 1864', MECW, vol. 42, p. 47.
[31] K. Marx, 23 December 1864, 'To Abram Lincoln, President of the USA', MECW, vol. 20, pp. 19–20.

the origin of an important ethnic minority within the working class of Britain.

12.4 Ireland: Struggling against both National and Ethnic Oppression

Both Marx and Engels devoted themselves to Irish national emancipation from the 1840s onwards. They were also concerned from early on with the Irish as an ethnic group inside Britain. Engels, for example, devoted considerable attention to the oppressive conditions of Irish immigrant labour in his 1845 study of Manchester, *The Condition of the Working Class in England*. It was in 1867, however, the year he published *Capital*, volume I, that Marx's writings on Ireland began to reach their full development. That same year, the socially progressive Fenian movement staged an abortive uprising inside Ireland that the British government quickly crushed. As against the more conservative forms of Irish nationalism that had predominated in the 1840s, the Fenians advocated an Irish republic based upon the peasantry that would free the country not only from British colonialism, but also from Catholic landlord and clerical domination. From 1867 to 1870, Marx made a number of significant theoretical contributions on the national and ethnic oppression of the Irish in both Ireland and Britain, on the Irish struggle for freedom, and on that struggle's relationship to the revolutionary labour movement in Europe and North America. These years were those of the greatest success of the IWMA, which under Marx's influence offered some strong support to the Irish cause.

One theme in Marx's writings was the persistence of the Irish freedom struggle inside Ireland itself, notwithstanding centuries of British oppression. Despite the fact that the English language had come to dominate Ireland after 700 years of British rule, and the fact that in many other ways the Irish people had been assimilated into British culture, both Marx and Engels stressed repeatedly that the Irish had nonetheless held onto their own national identity. Michael Löwy (1938–) has noted astutely that for Marx, 'In this case, the concept of the nation was not defined according to *objective* criteria (economy, language, territory, etc.), but rather was founded on a *subjective* element, the will of the Irish to liberate themselves from British rule.'[32] The birth of the Fenian movement, a new type of Irish political movement that expressed class as well as national aspirations, was conditioned on the one hand by the new ideas that had emerged from the 1848 revolutions in Europe, and, on the other, by the genocidal

---

[32] Löwy, *Fatherland or Mother Earth?*, p. 21.

Irish famine of 1845–49, in which 1.5 million died and another million was forced to emigrate, this out of a population of only about eight million people.

As the Fenian movement reached the height of its influence during the late 1860s, some of its leaders faced execution by the British government. Inside the IWMA, Marx campaigned relentlessly – and with a remarkable degree of success – to get the British trade unionists who dominated its general council to support the Irish cause, including participation in large demonstrations supporting Irish political prisoners. Given the intense ethnic hostility towards the Irish on the part of the dominant British culture, this was no mean achievement, and it constituted a significant example of both proletarian internationalism and inter-ethnic solidarity.

During this period, Marx also analyzed the transformations being undergone by the Irish colonial economy, most notably in *Capital*, where Ireland occupied a substantial part of the long chapter on 'The General Law of Capitalist Accumulation'. Marx wrote that the famine of the 1840s had led to a tremendous economic restructuring, which involved a radical centralization in which food production plummeted as large commercial agricultural holdings came to predominate. Marx portrayed a dependent economy that had been used up and nearly destroyed: 'Ireland is at present merely an agricultural district of England which happens to be divided by a wide stretch of water from the country for which it provides corn, wool, cattle, and industrial and military recruits.'[33] It was 'her true destiny, to be an English sheep-walk and cattle pasture'.[34] The remaining Irish population continued to suffer terrible poverty, he concluded, noting that according to British officialdom, 'a somber discontent runs through the ranks of this class, that they long for the return of the past, loathe the present, despair of the future, give themselves up "to the evil influence of agitators," and have only one fixed idea, to emigrate to America'.[35] This kind of discussion of British rule over Ireland as a process of capital accumulation also found its way into some of Marx's speeches to the general council of the IWMA and other groups, where he gave it a sharper political twist, charging that British economic policies amounted to the annihilation of the Irish people.

In these years, Marx also made a detailed study of Irish history, from the earliest British incursions through the period of the French Revolution, and then the most recent one of capital accumulation through centralization of the agrarian economy. In notes for a December 1867 speech to the German Workers' Educational Society

---

[33] Marx, *Capital*, volume I, p. 860.   [34] Ibid, p. 869.   [35] Ibid, p. 865.

of London, he compared early English colonialism to similar policies of extermination of the native population carried out in the Americas. The fact that these policies were continued and even intensified by Oliver Cromwell had two results, Marx argued. First, Cromwell's brutal invasion of Ireland marked the end of radical revolution in England. Second, this episode drove a deep wedge between the Irish and the English republicans and progressives, resulting in a particular 'Irish mistrust of the English people's party'.[36]

In the late 1860s, Marx also acknowledged explicitly that he had changed his position on Ireland, this in a letter to Engels of 10 December 1869:

For a long time, I believed it would be possible to overthrow the Irish regime by English working class ascendancy. I always took this viewpoint in the *New-York Tribune*. Deeper study has now convinced me of the opposite. The English working class will never accomplish anything before it has got rid of Ireland. The lever must be applied in Ireland. This is why the Irish question is so important for the social movement in general.[37]

This evolution in his thinking foreshadowed other changes in Marx's last years, not always acknowledged, when he increasingly came to consider the possibility that revolutionary upheaval might begin outside the most industrially developed countries of Europe and North America.[38]

But it was a dispute in early 1870 with the Russian anarchist Mikhail Bakunin (1814–1876) – by then a member of the IWMA – that caused Marx to theorize more comprehensively the connections among the peasant-based movement for Irish independence, the Irish minority within the British working class, the British working class as a whole, and the possibilities of a wider European socialist revolution. The dispute broke out when Bakunin attacked the IWMA's involvement in campaigns on behalf of Irish political prisoners. As with the Proudhonists three years earlier during the controversy over Poland, the Bakuninists wrote that they rejected 'any political action that does not have as is immediate and direct aim the triumph of the workers' cause against capital'.[39] In

---

[36] K. Marx, 'Outline of a Report on the Irish Question Delivered to the German Workers' Educational Society in London on December 16', MECW, vol. 21, p. 196.

[37] 'K. Marx to F. Engels, 10 December 1869', MECW, vol. 43, p. 398.

[38] This was seen most notably in his preface to the 1882 Russian edition of the *Manifesto of the Communist Party*, where he and Engels pointed to resistance to capitalist development in agrarian Russia's communal villages as a 'possible point of departure for a communist development', provided that it could link up to a 'proletarian revolution in the West' (T. Shanin, *Late Marx and the Russian Road: Marx and the 'Peripheries' of Capitalism* [New York: Monthly Review Press, 1983], p. 139).

[39] K. Marx, 'Remarks on the Programme and Rules of the International alliance of Socialist Democracy', MECW, vol. 21, p. 208. Among the few to have commented on the Irish

response, Marx drafted a 'Confidential Communication' on behalf of the general council of the IWMA, part of which argued that an Irish revolution could touch off a British and European one:

> Although revolutionary initiative will probably come from France, England alone can serve as the lever for a serious economic Revolution. It is the only country where there are no more peasants and where landed property is concentrated in a few hands. It is the only country where *the capitalist form*, that is to say, combined labor on a large scale under the authority of capitalists, has seized hold of almost the whole of production. It is the only country where the *vast majority of the population consists of wage laborers* ... The English have all the *material* conditions for social revolution. What they lack is *a sense of generalization and revolutionary passion*. It is only the General Council that can provide them with this, that can thus accelerate the truly revolutionary movement in this country, and consequently *everywhere* ... If England is the bulwark of landlordism and European capitalism, the only point where official England can be struck a great blow *is Ireland*.[40]

Marx's second point concerned contradictions within the British working class, where the dominant ethnic group's ethnocentrism amounted to a form of false consciousness that he compared to that of the 'poor whites' of the US South towards African Americans:

> In the second place, the English bourgeoisie has ... divided the proletariat into two hostile camps ... *In all the big industrial centers in England*, there is profound antagonism between the Irish proletarian and the English proletarian. The common English worker hates the Irish worker as a competitor who lowers wages and the *standard of life*. He feels national and religious antipathies for him. He views him similarly to how the poor whites of the Southern states of North America viewed black slaves. This antagonism among the proletarians of England is artificially nourished and kept up by the bourgeoisie. It knows that this split is the true secret of the preservation of its power.[41]

The confidential communication comments on the Irish in America, before concluding: 'Thus, the position of the International Association with regard to the Irish question is very clear. Its first concern is to advance the social revolution in England. To this end the great blow must be struck in Ireland.'[42]

---

aspect of this early dispute with Bakunin, C. Mathur and D. Dix, 'The Irish Question in Karl Marx's and Friedrich Engels's Writings on Capitalism and Empire', in: S. O Siochain (ed.), *Social Thought on Ireland in the Nineteenth Century* (University College Dublin Press, 2009), note that 'in this interchange it is Bakunin who sticks to what some might see as a "rigid Marxian position" that keeps nationalist struggles strictly at arm's length, and Marx who shows himself to be the more flexible thinker' (p. 105).

[40] K. Marx, 'Confidential Communication', MECW, vol. 21, pp. 118–19.
[41] Ibid, p. 120.   [42] Ibid, p. 120.

Thus, Marx's writings on Ireland brought together the two strands of his thought that have been the subject of this essay: (1) race and ethnicity within the working classes of a large industrialized society, both as source of false consciousness and of new revolutionary subjectivity; (2) the dialectical interaction between struggles for national emancipation and the broader global fight for democracy and ultimately, a socialist transformation. Not only does Marx show a deep intellectual involvement with these kinds of issues at the very time that he was completing *Capital*, volume I; these writings also show a unique and original perspective on ethnicity, race, and nationalism, one that has been too often dismissed or ignored, even by Marx's intellectual heirs.

12.5 Reflections for the Twenty-First Century

What are some of the wider implications for today of Marx's writings on nationalism, ethnicity, and non-Western societies? Over the past decade, a new interest in Marx has emerged in tandem with the rise of the global justice movement, sometimes characterized simplistically as one of 'anti-globalization'. This new interest has centred on his critique of capital, and his notion of a globalizing world system that conquers, commodifies, exploits, and homogenizes. New fields of academic inquiry like critical globalization studies have come to the fore, fields in which Marx's work figures prominently. Especially in the English-speaking world, the new emphasis on globalization has existed in an uneasy relationship with somewhat older concerns with race, ethnicity, gender, and sexuality, which were sometimes couched in terms of a politics of difference rooted in post-structuralist thought. Some of these post-structuralist studies had explicitly criticized Marx as a Eurocentric, even ethnocentric thinker, most notably in the case of Edward Said's (1935–2003) *Orientalism* (1978).[43]

Some more recent theoretical writings have attempted to bridge this gap, most notably Michael Hardt (1960–) and Antonio Negri's (1933–) *Empire* (2000), which relied upon 'difference' philosophers like Michel Foucault (1926–84) and Gilles Deleuze (1925–1995), but also upon Marx's concept of capitalism – especially in the *Grundrisse* – as a globalized order that subsumed nearly everything under its sway. However, Hardt and Negri's attempt, while ambitious and interesting, probably conceded too much to the politics of difference. They tended to regard global struggles against capital and other forms of domination

---

[43] E. Said, *Orientalism* (New York: Random House, 1978).

as operating in something like a parallel fashion, but without really coming together.[44]

Viewing the issues discussed in the present chapter in these terms, one could say that, for Marx, the rise of capitalism as a globalizing system was bringing about an internal contradiction, an increasingly international force of resistance to capital, the working class. This kind of thinking could be found in the ringing language of the *Manifesto of the Communist Party* about barriers being broken down across the globe and within particular societies, whether East versus West, rural versus urban, and so on. But in the very same *Manifesto of the Communist Party*, Marx and Engels sometimes went against the grain of this global narrative. For as discussed earlier, they also noted the importance of more local issues, particularly the national resistance of Poland to the large European empires that had emerged in the eighteenth century. In this sense, Marx's notion of the global was deeply dialectical, in that it took account of the totality of capitalism, while also leaving room for some consideration of what is today often couched in terms of the politics of difference.

Marx's proletariat was never a totally unified group when examined concretely. For example, as noted in the present chapter, he saw both the United States and the English working classes as riven with contradictions based upon ethnicity and race. On the one hand, these contradictions helped to create a false consciousness based upon ethnocentric and racist ideologies that buttressed the capitalist order. On the other hand, the interaction of class with racial and ethnic oppression created a new contradiction within the capitalist order, fostering the emergence of new revolutionary subjects fired with a determination to uproot the entire system: the African American slave, the Irish peasant in Ireland, or the newly immigrated Irish worker in Britain.

For Marx, issues like the Polish struggle for national emancipation, the intertwining of race and class in America, and the Irish national struggle as a 'lever' that could pry open the British and European proletarian struggle were part of the core agenda of the working classes, not side or subordinate issues. This was demonstrated not only in his theoretical writings, but also in his practical activity during the prime years of the IWMA.

---

[44] Marx's concept of global capital lay within the tradition of dialectical thinking, a tradition Hardt and Negri explicitly rejected. Because of this, Marx's work took account not only of difference, but also identity. It was rooted in Hegelian concepts such as the dialectic of identity-difference-contradiction elaborated in the *Science of Logic*, where Hegel had argued that every identity contained a difference, just as every difference contained an identity. This antimony led Hegel to contradiction, a core concept that Marx and later Marxists so often appropriated. See G. W. F. Hegel, 'The Essentialities and Determinations of Reflection', in: *The Science of Logic* (Cambridge: Cambridge University Press, 2010), pp. 354–85.

References

Ahmad, Aijaz (1992), 'Marx on India: A Clarification', in: *In Theory: Classes, Nations, Literature*, London: Verso, pp. 221–42.

Anderson, Kevin (2010), *Marx at the Margins: On Ethnicity, Nationalism, and Non-Western Societies*, Chicago: University of Chicago Press.

Benner, Erica (1995), *Really Existing Nationalisms: A Post-Communist View of Marx and Engels*, New York: Oxford University Press.

Blackburn, Robin (2011), *An Unfinished Revolution: Karl Marx and Abraham Lincoln*, London: Verso.

Bloom, Solomon F. (1941), *The World of Nations: A Study of the National Implications of the Work of Marx*, New York: Columbia University Press.

Du Bois, W. E. B. (1973), *Black Reconstruction in America: An Essay toward a History of the Part Which Black Folk Played in the Attempt to Reconstruct Democracy in America, 1860–1880*, New York: Atheneum.

Dunayevskaya, Raya (2000), *Marxism and Freedom: From 1776 until Today*. With a Preface by Herbert Marcuse and a new Foreword by Joel Kovel, Amherst, NY: Humanity Books.

Engels, Frederick (1985), 'What Have the Working Classes to Do with Poland?', MECW, vol. 20, pp. 152–61.

Institute of Marxism-Leninism of the CC, CPSU (1962), *General Council of the First International: Minutes, 1864–1866*, Moscow: Progress Publishers.

Habib, Irfan (2006), 'Introduction: Marx's Perception of India', in: Iqbal Husain (ed.), *Karl Marx on India*, New Delhi: Tulika Books, pp. xix–liv.

Hardt, Michael, and Negri, Antonio (2001), *Empire*, Cambridge, MA: Harvard University Press.

Hegel, George Wilhelm Friedrich (2010), 'The Essentialities and Determinations of Reflection', in: *The Science of Logic*, Cambridge: Cambridge University Press, pp. 354–85.

Löwy, Michael (1998), *Fatherland or Mother Earth? Essays on the National Question*, London: Pluto Press.

Marx, Karl (1976), '[On the Polish Question] Speeches in Brussels on February 22, 1848 on the Occasion of the Second Anniversary of the Cracow Insurrection. Speech by Dr. Karl Marx', MECW, vol. 6, pp. 545–52.

—— (1976), *Capital*, volume I, New York: Penguin.

—— (1984), 'The North American Civil War', MECW, vol. 19, pp. 32–42.

—— (1984), 'English Public Opinion', MECW, vol. 19, pp. 137–42.

—— (1985), 'Confidential Communication', MECW, vol. 21, pp. 112–24.

—— (1985), 'Inaugural Address of the Working Men's International', MECW, vol. 20, pp. 5–13.

—— (1985), '[Outline of a Report on the Irish Question Delivered to the German Workers Educational Society in London on December 16, 1867]', MECW, vol. 21, pp. 194–206.

—— (1985), 'Remarks on the Programme and Rules of the International Alliance of Socialist Democracy', MECW, vol. 21, pp. 207–11.

Marx, Karl and Engels, Frederick (1937), *The Civil War in the United States*, New York: International Publishers.

(1976), *Manifesto of the Communist Party*, MECW, vol. 6, pp. 477–519.
(1983), *Letters, 1856–1859*, MECW, vol. 40.
(1985), *Letters, 1860–1864*, MECW, vol. 41.
(1987), *Letters, 1864–1868*, MECW, vol. 42.
(1987), *Letters, 1868–1870*, MECW, vol. 43.
(1989), 'For Poland', MECW, vol. 24, pp. 55–8.
Mathur, Chandana, and Dix, Dermot (2009), 'The Irish Question in Karl Marx's and Friedrich Engels's Writings on Capitalism and Empire', in: Seamus O Siochain (ed.), *Social Thought on Ireland in the Nineteenth Century*, Dublin: University College Dublin Press, pp. 97–107.
Nimtz, August (2003), *Marx, Tocqueville, and Race in America: The 'Absolute Democracy' or 'Defiled Republic'*, Lanham, MD: Lexington Books.
Rosdolsky, Roman (1986), *Engels and the 'Nonhistoric' Peoples: The National Question in the Revolution of 1848*, Glasgow: Critique Books.
Said, Edward (1978), *Orientalism*, New York: Random House.
Shanin, Teodor (ed.) (1983), *Late Marx and the Russian Road: Marx and the 'Peripheries' of Capitalism*, New York: Monthly Review Press.
Walicki, Andrzej (1982), 'Marx, Engels, and the Polish Question', in: *Philosophy and Romantic Nationalism: The Case of Poland*, Oxford: Oxford University Press, pp. 359–91.

13 Migration

Pietro Basso
Translated by Patrick Camiller

13.1 The Forced Emigration of Rural Producers

On the question of migration – and it was not the only one – Friedrich Engels got there before Karl Marx. In *The Condition of the Working Class in England* he dealt widely with the Irish immigration in Britain (over one million by 1845). He presented it there as an essential reserve of labour power for the take-off of British industry and the permanent existence of a 'surplus population' of unemployed workers. Borrowing from Thomas Carlyle (1795–1881) a frankly ethnicist characterization of Irish immigrants ('but little above the savage'[1]), Engels highlighted the downward moral and material spiral of competition into which they forced English workers. At the same time, however, as Eric Hobsbawm (1917–2012) noted, he described the political radicalization that developed in the Irish immigration, as well as the ardour and generosity that the Irish brought to the 'cold, rational' English workers through the mixing of temperaments and 'races'.[2] Engels thus also anticipated the key theoretical issue of the industrial reserve army, which Marx would later expound in *Capital*, and the key political issue of the relationship between Irish and English workers (or, more generally, between immigrant and indigenous workers), which would confront the International Working Men's Association (IWMA).

Marx himself treated both these questions, frequently addressing many aspects of mass migration in the capitalist epoch. He did this in his journalistic pieces, in his polemic with supporters of the 'theory of population', in *Capital*, and in his activity for the IWMA. It emerges that, for Marx, forced mass migrations are *an integral part of the formative process of the capitalist mode of production* and of its expanded reproduction on a world scale. They face the labour movement with the unavoidable

---

[1] F. Engels, *The Condition of the Working Class in England*, MECW, vol. 4, p. 391. On the effects of competition, see esp. pp. 390–2.
[2] Ibid, p. 419.

task of combatting attempts to drive a wedge between workers in the dominant countries and workers in the dominated countries, between indigenous workers and immigrant workers, since 'labour cannot emancipate itself in the white skin where in the black it is branded'.[3]

The first aspect of the migratory phenomenon that Marx addressed was the mass expulsion of rural producers from the countryside, which he termed 'the basis of the capitalist mode of production'.[4] He already spoke of this in January 1853, in the article 'The Duchess of Sutherland and Slavery' that he wrote for the *New-York Daily Tribune*; between 1815 and 1820 the lady in question, seeking to transform her county into pastureland, had driven out its entire population (3,000 families) through all manner of violence, up to and including extermination. Marx returned to the theme shortly afterwards, taking in an area from the Scottish Highlands to the whole of England and Ireland. In a piece entitled 'Forced Emigration', he contrasted the rural exodus of the capitalist epoch with the migration of barbarian peoples to pre-medieval Europe:

Here it is not the want of productive power which creates a surplus population; it is the increase of productive power which demands a diminution of population, and drives away the surplus by famine or emigration. It is not population that presses on productive power; it is productive power that presses on population.[5]

The new productive power brutally pressing on agricultural workers and small tenant farmers was the power of the *capitalist agrarian revolution* (although sometimes activated by the big landowners). With the concentration of landholdings, the introduction of modern farming methods, the systematic application of science to agricultural production, and the deployment of new labour-saving machinery, this revolution dealt a severe blow to numerous rural producers, who, in the words of *Capital*, were '*compelled* to seek shelter in villages and towns. There they were thrown like refuse into garrets, holes, cellars and corners, in the worst back slums'.[6] 'The facts are simple', Marx tersely noted. 'The revolution in agriculture has kept pace with emigration.'[7]

In the memorable chapters XXVII–XXX of *Capital*, volume I, Marx analyzed and lambasted the expropriation *en masse* of the rural producers and their expulsion to the industrial cities (or foreign countries), as well as

---

[3] K. Marx, *Capital*, volume I, MECW, vol. 35, p. 305. Marx was referring here to the United States, but his argument extended far beyond antebellum America.
[4] Ibid, p. 755.
[5] K. Marx, 'Forced Migration [etc.]', MECW, vol. 11, p. 531. For the article against the duchess of Sutherland, see K. Marx, 'Elections – Financial Clouds – The Duchess of Sutherland and Slavery', MECW, vol. 11, pp. 486–94. (Marx referred to this article in *Capital*, volume I, p. 720.)
[6] Marx, *Capital*, volume I, p. 698. Emphasis added. [7] Ibid, p. 696.

the 'bloody legislation' used to force them to submit to wage labour. This process advanced quite slowly during the period of manufacture, but then it sharply accelerated and expanded with the advent of large-scale industry, which wiped out forever the domestic spinning and weaving industries. In this way, capital incorporated not only the land, but the agricultural producers themselves, largely converting them into workers and a reserve of wage-earners, and created the foundations of the internal market. Marx mainly described the 'classic form' of this phenomenon in England, but warned that, with 'different aspects', 'at different periods', and in 'different orders of succession' it had a more general character.[8] Today this is completely evident: the birth and worldwide spread of capitalism is *based* on gigantic forced emigration from the countryside – a process that is anything but finished.

13.2 The Slave Trade and the Super-Exploitation of Black Slaves in the Colonies

Another key factor in primitive accumulation, the birth of the world market and a global labour market, was, as Marx put it, 'the turning of Africa into a warren for the commercial hunting of negroes',[9] the violent uprooting and enslavement of more than 100 million young Africans[10] and the transplanting of those who survived to parts of the Americas far from their homelands. Whereas in Europe the birth of capitalism presupposed the overcoming of slavery and serfdom, in the colonies British and continental capital used slave labour for many centuries and on a large scale; in some countries, such as Mexico, it actually introduced it for the first time. The slave trade, managed from Liverpool, contributed decisively to the rise and primacy of British industry and to the 'progress' that derived from it. The lifeblood of this industry and 'progress' came both from British and Irish wage labourers and from African slaves and their descendants in the Americas. In an article entitled 'The British Cotton Trade', which appeared in October 1861 in the *New-York Daily Tribune*, Marx rashly asserted:

English modern industry, in general, relied upon two pivots equally monstrous. The one was the potato as the only means of feeding Ireland and a great part of the English working class ... The second ... was the slave-grown cotton of the United

---

[8] Ibid, p. 707.　[9] Ibid, p. 739.
[10] The total estimates diverge sharply between European (15 million) and African (150–200 million) historians. See B. Davidson, *Black Mother. Africa: The Years of Trial* (London: Gollancz, 1961), H. Jaffe, *Africa. Movimenti e lotte di liberazione* (Milan: Mondadori, 1978), and W. Rodney, *How Europe Underdeveloped Africa* (London: Bogle-L'Ouverture, 1972).

Migration   235

States ... As long as the English cotton manufactures depended on slave-grown cotton, it could be truthfully asserted that they rested on a *twofold slavery*, the *indirect* slavery of the white man in England and the *direct* slavery of the black man on the other side of the Atlantic.[11]

For centuries the 'infamous traffic',[12] which was still alive in the mid-nineteenth century, supplied the agriculture of the West Indies with 'human chattle' to be super-exploited, so that slaves were loaded with colossal burdens of surplus labour. This agriculture, which 'engulfed millions of the African race'[13] as well as countless coolies from Asia[14] (another figure of forced transnational migration), provided raw material for the industry of the metropolitan heartlands; it also functioned, and continues to function, as a source of surplus profits, since

capital invested in colonies ... may yield higher rates of profit for the simple reason that the rate of profit is higher there due to backward development, and likewise the exploitation of labour, because of the use of slaves, coolies, etc.[15]

It is well known that only some of the labour power employed by European capital in the colonies consisted of emigrants/immigrants. But after the holocaust[16] of the indigenous peoples – which took place between 1493 and 1650 in the centre and south, and between the second half of the seventeenth century and the second half of the nineteenth in the north – the repopulation of the Americas and their full integration into the international division of labour created by capital from European countries were possible *entirely* thanks to the forced migration of tens and tens of millions of Africans, Europeans, and Asians. The formation of the world market (as an uneven and combined system) is inexplicable if the role of colonialism is not taken into account. And it is beyond doubt that the forced migrations of black African slaves and of Chinese, Indian, Indonesian, and Japanese (as

---

[11] K. Marx, 'The British Cotton Trade', MECW, vol. 19, pp. 19–20. Emphases added. In a passage in *Grundrisse*, Marx defined the slavery of blacks as 'a purely industrial form of slavery': K. Marx, 'Outlines of the Critique of Political Economy [*Grundrisse*]. First Instalment', MECW, vol. 28, p. 157.

[12] See K. Marx, 'The British Government and the Slave-Trade', MECW, vol. 15, pp. 570–4 f, where Marx denounced the hypocrisy of the British government in hoisting the flag of abolition of the slave trade purely for the purposes of its contest with other states, and the substantial British complicity with Napoleon III, 'the patron of slavery in all its forms'.

[13] See the lengthy quotation from a work by John Elliot Cairnes, in K. Marx, *Capital*, volume I, p. 272.

[14] See L. Potts, *The World Labour Market: A History of Migration* (London: Zed Books, 1990), ch. 3.

[15] K. Marx, *Capital*, volume III, MECW, vol. 37, p. 237.

[16] See D. Stannard, *American Holocaust: Columbus and the Conquest of the New World* (Oxford: Oxford University Press, 1992).

coolies) semi-slaves/semi-wage labourers were two major chapters in the history of colonialism.

13.3 Migration in and from Europe

But the advent of capitalist social relations produced sizeable migratory movements within Europe too – not only from country to city, but also between European nations and from Europe to the colonized continents. Marx studied the 'Irish question' for decades, on the assumption that over the centuries England had reduced Ireland to a colony,[17] 'an agricultural district of England', imposing such a massive haemmorhage of population that, had England suffered it instead, it would have been condemned to death. But the British bourgeoisie knew how to extract great profits from Irish labour power, while the Irish landowning class knew how to convert the emigration of its fellow-countrymen (left penniless by the expropriation of their means of production) into 'one of the most lucrative branches of its export trade'.[18]

It was an export trade in human beings to neighbouring England – where the Irish were 'compelled to seek shelter' in villages and towns that treated them 'like refuse', in degrading living conditions and in an exhausting search for the most precarious jobs as day labourers[19] – but also to faraway North America, where, quite astonishingly, the Irishman 'banished by sheep and ox, reappears on the other side of the ocean as a Fenian'.[20]

England itself by no means remained immune from the transoceanic emigration. But it had different characteristics from the Irish emigration, as well as from the migration within England caused by expropriation and impoverishment of the rural producers. For it was organized by British capitalists for colonial purposes:

---

[17] In a letter to Marx dated 23 May 1856, Engels wrote that 'the English wars of conquest from 1100 to 1850 ... utterly ruined' Ireland (MECW, vol. 40, p. 50). After the war of 1641–52, between 6,000 and 100,000 Irish (the estimates vary hugely) were deported to the West Indies as slaves. See F. Engels, 'Varia on the History of the Irish Confiscations', MECW, vol. 21, p. 303.
[18] Marx, *Capital*, volume I, p. 695. In 'Outline of a Report on the Irish Question Delivered to the German Workers' Educational Society in London on December 16, 1867' (MECW, vol. 21, pp. 194–206) Marx noted: 'Families clubbed together to send away the youngest and most enterprising' (p. 201). The same happens today in nearly all the countries of emigration, especially the poorest ones.
[19] Marx, *Capital*, volume I, p. 698. In Marx's writings on the Irish emigration, we do not find the same disagreeably ethnicist tone and content as in the young Engels.
[20] Ibid, p. 703.

Migration

It might be said that not only capital, but also labourers, in the shape of emigrants, are annually exported from England. ... [These emigrants] are in great part not labourers. The sons of farmers make up a great part of them. The additional capital annually transported abroad to be put out at interest is in much greater proportion to the annual accumulation than the yearly emigration is to the yearly increase of population.[21]

This mixed emigration of non-labourers (the great majority) and have-nothing labourers to North America, Australia, and South Africa contributed to the global primacy of English capital, both strengthening and extending the British Empire. And, in doing this, it contributed to the formation of the global labour market, a discrete and crucial section of the world market.

13.4 Global Labour Market and Industrial Reserve Army

The formation of a global labour market went hand in hand with the formation of the world market. For a long time, it was therefore dominated by commercial capital and the colonial powers. During this historical period, which stretched into the mid-nineteenth century, the main factor in the utilization of the labour of 'coloured people' was *physical compulsion*, as distinct from economic pressure. The enslavement of the American Indians and their subjection to forced labour, the traffic in African slaves, the international trade in tens of millions of coolies, the various forms of compulsory labour imposed in the colonies: all this developed under the aegis of the organized violence of governments and private property-owners. Physical violence also played a fundamental role in the migration from country to city within Europe.

This means that, for a long historical period, the process of capital accumulation, especially in the colonies, involved wage labour only as an exceptional form of labour relation; the most prevalent forms, controlled by the highly civilized capital of the home countries, were slave labour, forced labour, and various hybrids of semi-servile, semi-free labour often performed by immigrants. In Europe, on the other hand, although these forms of labour continued to be present for centuries, the situation changed with the coming of the Industrial Revolution. What now took root, amid the veritable multitudes of paupers and vagabonds, was the modern form of slavery: wage slavery, which nevertheless stood

---

[21] Ibid, p. 607. Marx wrote of this emigration, composed of small English tenant farmers, in the article cited in footnote 5 of this chapter: 'Forced Migration [etc.]' (MECW, vol. 11): they 'have no other alternative but to cross the sea in search of a new country and of new lands' (p. 530).

on the 'pedestal' of 'slavery pure and simple in the new world'.[22] However, as the expropriation of the direct (rural and urban) producers acquired gigantic proportions in Europe and other continents, producing a dizzying decline in the value of available labour power as well as an exponential increase in its quantity, wage labour became for capital – especially industrial capital – the cheapest and most convenient form of labour. It wore away the space for other kinds of labour relation used by capital on a large scale, even though it never caused them to vanish completely.

The great migrations within Europe, and above all the great international migrations already mentioned, played a decisive role in the formation of the global labour market and in the constitution/reconstitution of the industrial reserve army. It would be too schematic to argue that emigrants, forced or 'free', always and in every circumstance formed the lowest, most exploited, and most precarious layer of the global labour market. For a long period that was not the case in the United States – on the contrary. The forced expropriation and extermination of the native peoples, together with the gold rush, enabled many European immigrants to make their fortune there, to become landowning farmers, and small (sometimes more than small) accumulators of capital, making the United States 'the promised land for emigrant labourers'.[23] Nevertheless, even those times of abundance for immigrants came to an end, as Marx noted in *Capital*.

> On the one hand, the enormous and ceaseless stream of men, year after year driven upon America, leaves behind a stationary sediment in the east of the United States, the wave of immigration from Europe throwing men on the labour market there more rapidly than the wave of emigration westwards can wash them away. On the other hand, the American Civil War brought in its train a colossal national debt, and, with it, pressure of taxes, the rise of the vilest financial aristocracy, the squandering of a huge part of the public land on speculative companies for the exploitation of railways, mines, &c, in brief, the most rapid centralization of capital. The great republic has, therefore, ceased to be the promised land for emigrant labourers. Capitalistic production advances there with giant strides, even though the lowering of wages and the dependence of the wage worker are yet far from being brought down to the normal European level.[24]

This is the fundamental reason why, *as a general rule*,[25] capital pushes for increased emigration of workers to the most dynamic growth economies

---

[22] Marx, *Capital*, volume I, p. 747.   [23] Ibid, p. 760.
[24] Ibid. This point had already been made, in slightly different terms, in Marx, 'Outlines of the Critique of the Political Economy [*Grundrisse*]. First Instalment', pp. 499–503, in the pages on Carey's *Principles*.
[25] There is no lack of periods or special cases when industrialists have opposed emigration, or even imposed an actual ban on it, either to assure themselves of specialized manpower in short supply or to avoid the danger of draining the reserve army.

and sectors. It does so in order to be sure of having the labour power for direct use, as well as the surplus necessary to contain and push down the wages of the employed workforce, and to increase the dependence on capital of the employed, unemployed, and semi-employed workforce. Marx demonstrated this masterfully in the chapter entitled 'The General Law of Capitalist Accumulation'. Capital is not satisfied with 'natural' population growth; it needs 'an industrial reserve army independent of these natural limits'. It has neither the capacity nor the interest to employ the entire workforce that it makes available: its way of proceeding, by antithesis, is to condemn one part of the workforce to forced inactivity through 'the overwork of the other part'. And, far from there being any possibility of self-correction, this proletarian reserve army grows ever larger 'with the advance of social accumulation'[26] – today we have an extraordinary confirmation of this thesis before our eyes! In the past, and even more in our own day, emigrants/immigrants have as a rule been a major part of this reserve army, of this 'mass of human material always ready for exploitation',[27] of this last circle of the inferno of wage labour. Yet capital claims that this quota increases and decreases purely in accordance with the different phases of the business cycle.

13.5 A Process That Is Not Natural but Social-Historical

For Marx, then, both the great forced migrations of the pre-industrial epoch and the great 'free' migrations of the industrial age, both the migrations of dispossessed 'coloured people' and those of expropriated European 'whites', were social-historical not natural phenomena. All were inseparably bound up with the rise of capitalist social relations of production on a world scale, and with the violence and coercion that despotic capital has exercised over all forms of living labour since its mode of production came into being. At this level too, Marx polemicized against the viewpoint of political economy, which tended to naturalize every aspect of capitalist society and market functions, including population movements and migratory flows.

Adam Smith (1723–1790), David Ricardo (1772–1823), and the other classical economists generally ignored the fundamental role of colonialism and forced migration, and above all of the African slave trade, in the birth of large-scale industry in England and Europe; and they also ignored the pauperization, expropriation, and forced migration of the Highlanders in Britain. Ricardo, for example, fell into the monumental 'error' of considering the colonies as independent countries, and on this

---

[26] See Marx, *Capital*, volume I, pp. 630–1. [27] Ibid, p. 626.

basis proceeded to naturalize the effects of colonial oppression along with the spread of capitalist mercantile relations.[28]

Another major influence on Ricardo was Thomas Robert Malthus's (1766–1834) axiomatic thesis that population increases geometrically in a simple natural process, whereas the production of foodstuffs increases only arithmetically. For Marx, on the contrary, there is no natural eternal law of population and overpopulation. There are only different laws governing their increase that correspond to different modes of production; population levels ultimately reflect and give concentrated expression to the development of the productive forces of society. In the *Grundrisse*, he showed that the production of a surplus of workers is a phenomenon specific to the capitalist era; it depends on the extraordinary growth of the productive power of labour that occurred under the spur of unlimited accumulation of value and surplus-value. This same factor accounts for the impoverishment of the mass of workers, the spread of pauperism and the migrations from country to city.[29]

Once again Marx's vision was not shaped by national boundaries. He did not consider individual nations in isolation from one another. Nor did he analyze the capitalist heartlands without the colonies, or treat the latter as if they were independent of the former. In his eyes, the history of capitalism opened in the sixteenth century, precisely with 'a world-embracing commerce and a world-embracing market',[30] and 'the tendency to create the world market is inherent directly in the concept of capital itself'.[31] His approach to migrations was similar: he saw them as *forced*, even in the case of the formally 'free' migrations of the era of industrial capitalism, since the force of economic coercion (expropriation of the means of production, poverty, etc.) was no less potent than extra-economic compulsion.

---

[28] 'In the *Principles* he argues that the wage depends essentially on people's customs and habits. In comparing the condition of British and Irish workers, he says nothing about Ireland's colonial status and the historical roots of its underdevelopment. He does not even mention the processes of land concentration, depopulation and emigration resulting from the British rule in Ireland or the central importance of Irish immigration for British industry': see L. Pradella, *Globalisation and the Critique of Political Economy. New Insights from Marx's Writings* (London: Routledge, 2015), p. 31.

[29] See the pages on Malthus's theory of population and overpopulation in Marx, *Economic Manuscripts of 1857–58*, pp. 524–9. For Marx, 'the greatest possible growth of population' is essential for the development of capitalism, since only that permits a combination of 'the greatest absolute quantity of necessary labour with the greatest relative quantity of surplus labour' (p. 527). Capitalist production is not simply production of surplus-value; it is production *for* surplus-value, the result of surplus labour.

[30] Marx, *Capital*, volume I, vol. 35, p. 157.

[31] Marx, 'Outlines of the Critique of Political Economy [*Grundrisse*]. First Instalment', p. 335.

But we would be making a serious mistake if the only distinction we drew between Marx and the leading exponents of political economy was that he provided a scientific analysis of 'internal' and international migrations from the sixteenth to the nineteenth century. For his scientific labours were inseparable from his political position, from his existence as a revolutionary communist and internationalist. This is fully apparent also in his writings on migration, where he was always, unfailingly, *on the side of* the expropriated farmers driven to mutate into workers in the industrial cities at the four corners of the world market; *on the side of* the black slaves and coolies brutally set to work on the plantations, in the mines and in railway construction; *on the side of* the Irish workers, oppressed twice over as proletarians and Irish; *on the side of* Chinese insurgents, Indian sepoys, Javanese, and 'coloured' workers weighed down by the system of colonial super-exploitation and incorporated from birth into the international reserve army of capital; and *on the side of* their resistance, their struggles, rebellions, and insurrections against colonialism and European capital. In this commitment, Marx's aim was not to preserve bygone forms of production, but to further the revolutionary emancipation of the proletariat – a perspective he thought possible only on the basis of the appropriation and radical transformation of the productive forces developed by capital.

13.6 British Proletarians and Irish Proletarians

This militant stance, which marked the whole of Marx's life, came to a climax in his intensive (and influential) participation in the activity of the IWMA. It was then that he tackled the question of migration in its political aspects, with special reference to the 'Irish case'. Paradigmatic in this respect is the famous 'Confidential Communication' of the general council, sent to Kugelmann on 28 March 1870, in which he expressed a *new* viewpoint (overturning his previous one) on the solution to the 'Irish question'. Here, in stark contrast to the political use that the English, Irish, and US bourgeoisies made of the Irish emigration, Marx set out once and for all, in the clearest manner, the internationalist proletarian position on relations between workers belonging to countries linked by ties of domination. After denouncing England's oppression of Ireland, and the objective complicity of the English proletariat in that oppression, he vigorously drove the point home:

the *English bourgeoisie* has not only exploited Irish poverty to keep down the working class in England by *forced immigration* of poor Irishmen, but it has also divided the proletariat into two hostile camps. The revolutionary fire of the Celtic worker does not go well with the solid but slow nature of the Anglo-Saxon worker. On the contrary, in *all the big industrial centres* in England there is profound antagonism between the Irish proletarian and the English proletarian. The average English worker hates the Irish worker as a competitor who lowers wages and the STANDARD OF LIFE. He feels national and religious antipathies for him. He regards him somewhat like the POOR WHITES of the Southern States of North America regarded black slaves. This antagonism among the proletarians of England is artificially nourished and kept up by the bourgeoisie. It knows that this scission is *the true secret of maintaining its power*.

Moreover, this antagonism is reproduced on the other side of the Atlantic. The Irish, chased from their native soil by the bulls and the sheep, reassemble in the United States where they constitute a huge, ever-growing section of the population. Their only thought, their only passion, is hatred for England. The English and American governments – that is to say, the classes they represent – play on these feelings in order to perpetuate the *international struggle* which prevents any serious and sincere alliance between the working classes on both sides of the Atlantic, and, consequently, their common emancipation.

Ireland is the only pretext the English Government has for retaining a *big standing army*, which, if need be, as has happened before, can be used against the English workers after having done its military training in Ireland ...

The position of the International Association with regard to the Irish question is very clear. Its first concern is to advance the social revolution in England. To this end a great blow must be struck in Ireland. The General Council's resolutions on the Irish amnesty serve only as an introduction to other resolutions which will affirm that, quite apart from international justice, it is *a precondition to the emancipation of the English working class* to transform the present *forced Union* – i. e., the enslavement of Ireland – into *equal and free confederation* if possible, into *complete separation* if need be.[32]

This passage outlines the internationalist position on the relationship between the English nation (the 'metropolis of capital') and the Irish nation, and between Irish and English proletarians. The latter are called upon to work for an end to the enslavement of Ireland and an amnesty for fighters in the Irish cause; to break their unnatural alliance with the English bourgeoisie and landlords, and to forge, on a free and equal basis, a sincere and serious alliance between the working classes of Ireland and England and between the two sides of the Atlantic. The 'profound antagonism' between these working classes can be overcome only if the English workers take up the struggle against Ireland's enslavement as their own cause, because only such an alliance can make English proletarians appear in the eyes of Irish

---

[32] K. Marx, 'Confidential Communication', MECW, vol. 21, pp. 120–1. Emphases in the original.

proletarians as *their* allies, instead of allies of their own enemy as deserving of hatred as their bourgeois rulers. And only the victory of Ireland in this struggle and the end of the antagonism between English and Irish proletarians can truly dig the grave of the English bourgeoisie and pave the way for the common emancipation of the proletarians of both countries.[33]

This militant position on the relationship between proletarians of the dominant countries and proletarians of the dominated countries, and between indigenous proletarians and immigrants, was restated in various forms over the subsequent decades: implicitly in the *Report of the General Council to the Fifth Annual Congress of the International Working Men's Association* (1872), where Marx defined the goal of the association as 'the emancipation of labour and the extinction of national feuds',[34] or in the *Critique of the Gotha Programme*, which contains a strong polemic against 'the narrowest national standpoint';[35] explicitly in the Programme of the French Workers' Party, for example – drafted by Marx in May 1880 in London together with Jules Guesde (1845–1922) and Paul Lafargue (1842–1911) – which calls for the 'legal prohibition of bosses employing foreign workers at a wage less than that of French workers'.[36]

This watchword of solidarity, fraternization, and strict equality of rights among proletarians of different nationalities was a challenge to the dominant ideology, to nationalism (especially chauvinism), and to the spread of reactionary racist sentiments and behaviour within the working class; it became of central importance for the workers' movement[37] and has retained its force to this day.

---

[33] Unfortunately the British Federal Council did *not* adopt this perspective, so that two years later Engels had to intervene vigorously against some English members of the general council who were denying to the Irish the right to form an independent organization of their own within the IWMA. In a speech to the general council meeting of 14 May 1872, having attacked 'the belief, only too common among the English working men, that they were superior being compared to the Irish', he spelled out what he thought needed to be done: 'In a case like that of the Irish, *true Internationalism* must necessarily be based upon a distinctly national organisation; the Irish, as well as other oppressed nationalities, could enter the Association *only as equals* with the members of the conquering nation, and under protest against the conquest. The Irish sections, therefore, not only were justified, but even *under the necessity* to state in the preamble to their rules that their *first and most pressing duty*, as Irishmen, was to establish their own national independence.' F. Engels, 'Relations between the Irish Sections and the British Federal Council', MECW, vol. 23, p. 155. Emphases added.
[34] 'Report of the General Council to the Fifth Annual Congress of the International Working Men's Association, Held at the Hague, from the 2nd to the 7th of September 1872', MECW, vol. 23, p. 226.
[35] K. Marx, *Critique of the Gotha Programme*, MECW, vol. 24, p. 89.
[36] J. Guesde and P. Lafargue, 'Le Programme du Parti ouvrier', in: *Textes Choisis, 1867–1882* (Paris: Editions sociales, 1959), 118.
[37] At the height of the imperialist epoch, struck by the persistence of the great Russian spirit inside the Bolshevik Party, Lenin went so far as to argue that 'internationalism on the part

13.7 Yesterday, Today, Tomorrow

The challenge issued a century and a half ago by Marx and the IWMA is reasserting itself today on a global scale. Never before, in the history of capitalism, has migration had such amplitude and depth. The international migratory movements now taking place involve the entire planet, with no exceptions, and they look set to nearly double over the coming decades to a level above 400 million persons. The most powerful cause of this epochal population movement is the uneven development of continents and countries that today's neo-colonialism has inherited and reproduced from historical colonialism. Once again, but in extreme forms that are without precedent, the late-capitalist 'agricultural revolution' under way in the Asian, African, and South American countryside is each year throwing tens of millions of expropriated peasants onto the world market. And, if that were not enough, an uninterrupted series of wars that are local only in appearance, involving the Arab-Islamic world in particular, as well as the new scourge of ecological disasters, are giving another huge spur to migratory movements.

The machinery of global capitalism churns out, and will continue to churn out in the coming decades, huge numbers of emigrants who are compelled by these coercive factors to sell themselves for the lowest price. Along with super-exploitation of their labour, they will face every kind of discrimination and harassment, and often their dream of a life worthy of human beings will end with death at sea, in the desert, or on one of the fortified walls that are being built around the world. But, like the Irish proletarians, or the African slaves before them, the emigrants-immigrants of our own day are not going to play the role of sacrificial victims in the non-stop war that the global markets, national governments, and media industries wage against them. After all, the 'free' migrations of the age of industrial and financial capitalism produced a long history of collective social and political action on the part of emigrant workers, ranging from the decisive role of German, Polish, and Italian proletarians in the United States in the international struggle for the eight-hour day, through the vanguard position of emigrants in the cycle of workers' struggles that shook Europe between 1968 and 1973, to the great revolt of the children of immigrants in the Parisian

of oppressors or "great" nations, as they are called (though they are great only in their violence, only great as bullies), must consist not only in the observance of the formal equality of nations but even in an *inequality* of the oppressor nation, the great nation, that must make up for the inequality which obtains in actual practice'; 'The Question of Nationalities or "Autonomisation"', *Collected Works*, vol. 36 (Moscow: Foreign Languages Publishing House, 1964 [1922]), p. 608. Emphasis added.

banlieues in 2005, the magnificent nationwide strike of millions of Chicanos on 1 May 2006 in the USA, and the resistance of immigrant communities in Europe to racist and discriminatory government policies. Nor should we forget the proliferation of strikes organized by internal migrants in China, that vanguard of the 740 million internal igrants who have made their (mostly female) voices heard in Bangladesh, Vietnam, Mexico and elsewhere.[38]

The self-organization of immigrant workers remains the first and most essential force opposing market and government oppression. But it is crucially important that the proletarians of the destination countries should support their resistance unconditionally, and that they should campaign for the fully equal treatment of immigrant workers and the abolition of all mechanisms liable to produce and reproduce inequality between workers of different nationalities. Only this will cut the ground from under capitalist policies designed to divide workers by nationality and to set them at each other's throats. And, in all this, the position taken by Marx and the IWMA on the 'Irish case' retains all its topicality in today's world.

References

Basso, Pietro and Perocco, Fabio (2014), *Gli immigrati in Europa. Disuguaglianze, razzismo, lotte*, Milan: Angeli.
Davidson, Basil (1961), *Black Mother. Africa: The Years of Trial*, London: Gollancz.
Engels, Fredrick (1975), *The Condition of the Working Class in England*, MECW, vol. 4, pp. 295–583.
    (1985), 'Varia on the History of the Irish Confiscations', MECW, vol. 21, pp. 297–306.
    (1988), 'Relations between the Irish Sections and the British Federal Council', MECW, vol. 23, pp. 154–6.
Guesde, Jules, and Lafargue, Paul (1959), 'Le Programme du Parti ouvrier', in: *Textes Choisis, 1867–1882*, Paris: Editions sociales, pp. 116–19.
Jaffe, Hosea (1978), *Africa. Movimenti e lotte di liberazione*, Milan: Mondadori.
Lenin, Vladimir Ilich (1966 [1922]), 'The Question of Nationalities or "Autonomisation"', in: *Collected Works*, vol. 36, Moscow: Foreign Languages Publishing House, pp. 607–11.
Marx, Karl (1979), 'The Duchess of Sutherland and Slavery', MECW, vol. 11, pp. 486–94.
    (1979), 'Forced Emigration', MECW, vol. 11, pp. 528–34.
    (1984), 'The British Cotton Trade', MECW, vol. 19, pp. 19–20.
    (1985), 'Confidential Communication', MECW, vol. 21, pp. 112–24.

---

[38] P. Basso and F. Perocco, *Gli immigrati in Europa. Disuguaglianze, razzismo lotte* (Milan: Angeli, 2014), p. 42 ff.

(1985), 'Outline of a Report on the Irish Question Delivered to the German Workers' Educational Society in London on December 16, 1867', MECW, vol. 21, pp. 194–206.

(1986), 'The British Government and the Slave Trade', MECW, vol. 15, pp. 570–4.

(1986), 'Outlines of the Critique of Political Economy [*Grundrisse*]. First Instalment', MECW, vol. 28.

(1988), 'Report of the General Council to the Fifth Annual Congress of the International Working Men's Association, Held at the Hague, from the 2nd to the 7th of September 1872', MECW, vol. 23, pp. 219–27.

(1989), *Critique of the Gotha Programme*, MECW, vol. 24, pp. 75–99.

(1996), *Capital*, volume I, MECW, vol. 35.

(1998), *Capital*, volume III, MECW, vol. 37.

Marx, Karl, and Engels, Frederick (1983), *Letters, 1856–59*, MECW, vol. 40.

Marx, Karl, and Guesde, Jules (1880), *The Programme of the Parti Ouvrier*.

Potts, Lydia (1990), *The World Labour Market: A History of Migration*, London: Zed Books.

Pradella, Lucia (2015), *Globalisation and the Critique of Political Economy: New Insights from Marx's Writings*, London: Routledge.

Rodney, Walter (1972), *How Europe Underdeveloped Africa*, London: Bogle-L'Ouverture.

Stannard, David (1992), *American Holocaust: Columbus and the Conquest of the New World*, Oxford: Oxford University Press.

14 Colonialism

Sandro Mezzadra and Ranabir Samaddar

14.1 Capitalism as a World Force and Colonialism

Gerhard Hauck (1939–) wrote that Karl Marx never devoted to the topic of colonialism a 'theoretical-systematic' treatment, and he 'always dealt with colonialism aphoristically and in marginal notes'.[1] Such an assessment of Marx's engagement with colonialism reflects more the scant interest and substantial marginalization of the topic in Western Marxism than the reality of the diverse sites of Marx's deliberations of colonialism, and the diverse occasions when Marx had to engage with colonialism in the course of his theoretical, political, and historical writings. It is well known that *Capital*, volume I, ends with a chapter on 'The modern theory of colonization' and colonialism plays an important role in Marx's investigation of the 'so-called primitive accumulation' in part VIII of the book. In his journalistic writings, in particular in the articles he wrote in the 1850s in the *New-York Tribune*, the question of colonialism in India and China figured prominently. In the following decade a specific manifestation of modern colonialism (Atlantic slavery) and an important instance of internal colonization in Europe (British rule in Ireland) became for Marx important terrains of political intervention. Moreover, in his late years, Marx became increasingly interested in the study of non-European societies, and particularly forms of property prevailing before the colonial encounter.

In the last decades, Marx's writings on colonialism became an issue of debates and controversies outside Marx scholarship. The development of postcolonial studies led to the emergence of new problematic and theoretical approaches, which were often centred upon the question of 'Eurocentrism'. In particular, Marx's article 'British Rule in India' of 1853 was taken as emblematic of his Eurocentric vision of history and capitalism by scholars like Edward Said (1935–2003) in his book

---

[1] G. Hauck, 'Kolonialismus', in: W. F. Haug, F. Haug, P. Jehle, and W. Küttler (eds), *Historisch-Kritisches Wörterbuch des Marxismus*, vol. 7/II (Hamburg: Berliner Institut für Kritische Theorie, 2010), p. 1160.

Orientalism.[2] While these debates are definitely relevant, the focus on Marx's 'Eurocentrism' tends to freeze his interpretation of colonialism around some sentences extrapolated from the 1853 aforementioned article on India, notwithstanding the fact that his evaluation of colonial rule in India – and more generally of colonialism – evolved significantly over the following three decades.[3]

To begin with, it is important to see the role of the question of world market in Marx's analysis of colonialism. 'The tendency to create the *world market*', Marx wrote in the *Grundrisse*, 'is inherent directly in the concept of capital itself. Every limit appears as a barrier to be overcome'.[4] Like no other 'classical economist' of his age, Marx was acutely aware of the relevance of these global geographical coordinates for the very definition of the capitalist mode of production. In the critique of political economy, the 'world market' is something more than an empirical designation of capital's scale of operation. It is a full-fledged concept, which allows grasping the 'general relations of bourgeois society – the concentration of capital, division of labor, wage labor, etc.' in 'their most developed form', since it is on the world market that 'production is posited as a totality and all its moments also, but in which simultaneously all contradictions are set in motion'.[5] Characterized by an 'increasing autonomy', the world market is distinguished by Marx in the *Grundrisse* from the 'international' relationship of production and it is presented as 'both the presupposition of the totality and its bearer'.[6] 'State frontiers disappear' in the world market, he wrote in his discussion of theories of standards of money.[7]

The concept of world market was already present in Marx's early writings, foreshadowing a thrilling combination of a geographical and historical materialism and laying the basis for proletarian internationalism.[8] It was also a crucial entry point into the analysis of colonialism. While in *Capital*, volume I, Marx stressed the importance of

---

[2] See E. Said, *Orientalism* (London: Penguin, 1978), pp. 153–6. For a reply to Said, see A. Ahmad, *In Theory: Classes, Nations, Literatures* (London: Verso, 1992), chapter 6 ('Marx on India: A Clarification'), pp. 221–42.

[3] For a balanced assessment of the whole question, see K. Lindner, 'Marx's Eurocentrism: Postcolonial Studies, and Marx Scholarship', *Radical Philosophy*, 161 (2010).

[4] K. Marx, 'Outlines of the Critique of Political Economy [*Grundrisse*]. First Instalment', MECW, vol. 28, p. 335.

[5] K. Marx, *Bastiat and Carey*, MECW, vol. 28, p. 8.

[6] Marx, 'Outlines of the Critique of Political Economy [*Grundrisse*]. First Instalment', p. 97.

[7] K. Marx, 'A Contribution to the Critique of Political Economy. Part One', MECW, vol. 29, p. 311. On the concept of 'world market', see S. Mezzadra and B. Neilson, *Border as Method, or, the Multiplication of Labor* (Durham, NC: Duke University Press, 2013), pp. 66–75.

[8] See S. Mezzadra, *In the Marxian Workshops: Producing Subjects* (London: Rowman & Littlefield, 2018), pp. 86–8.

'the great discoveries of the end of the 15th century' for the creation of the world market,[9] in a letter to Friedrich Engels (1820–95) in 1858 he repeated that 'the specific task of bourgeois society is the establishment of the world market, at least in outline, and of production based on this world market'. And he added that, '[s]ince the world is round, the colonisation of California and Australia and the opening up of China and Japan would seem to have completed this process'.[10] In this way, the 'colonial system' began figuring as one of the founding moments in Marx's investigation of the 'so-called primitive accumulation'. The violence (the 'brute force') that characterized colonialism was therefore inscribed into the conditions that enabled the existence of the capitalist mode of production.[11] It is important to add that, through his emphasis on the world market – connected with an interest in power relations and in the dominant position of England on that market[12] – Marx laid the basis for later Marxist debates on imperialism, involving such important thinkers as Lenin (1870–1924) and Rosa Luxemburg (1871–1919).[13]

The 'brute force' of colonial conquest and domination works as a kind of blueprint for Marx's analysis of primitive accumulation. Extra-economic violence (i.e., violence conceptually distinguished from 'the dull compulsion of economic relations' that seals the 'subjugation of the laborer to the capitalist' in the standard working of the capitalist mode of production[14]) dominates the scene of capital's coming into being, setting the pace for the enclosures of common lands, the related processes of dispossession of poor peasants in the countryside, the 'bloody legislation against the expropriated', and proletarianization. The role of the state ('the concentrated and organized force of society') is prominent in all the procedures that prompt the 'transformation of the feudal mode of production into the capitalist mode' and work to 'shorten the transition'. Again, one can note the geographical sensitiveness of Marx's analysis,

---

[9] K. Marx, *Capital*, volume I, MECW, vol. 35, p. 738.
[10] 'K. Marx to F. Engels, 8 October 1858', MECW, vol. 40, p. 347.
[11] See Marx, *Capital*, volume I, p. 739. Marx's analysis of the 'so-called primitive accumulation' has been at the centre of lively debates in recent years. For a discussion, see R. Samaddar, 'Primitive Accumulation and Some Aspects of Life and Work in India', *Economic and Political Weekly*, 44 (18): 33–42 (2009), and Mezzadra, *In the Marxian Workshops*, 'Appendix', pp. 101–19.
[12] See, for instance, Marx, *Bastiat and Carey*, MECW, vol. 28, pp. 8–9, and *Capital*, Volume I, p. 642.
[13] See L. Ferrari Bravo, 'Old and New Questions in the Theory of Imperialism', *Viewpoint Magazine* (2018), www.viewpointmag.com/2018/02/01/old-new-questions-theory-imperialism-1975/. The Marxian notion of 'world market' is also foundational for 'world system theory': see I. Wallerstein, *World System Analysis: An Introduction* (Durham, NC: Duke University Press, 2004), pp. 1–22.
[14] Marx, *Capital*, volume I, p. 726.

which emphasizes the distribution of the 'different moments of primitive accumulation' over Spain, Portugal, Holland, and France before arriving at 'a systematical combination' in England towards the end of the seventeenth century.[15] This European geography of primitive accumulation is however complicated and displaced through Marx's emphasis on the role of colonialism, which opens up – as noted by anti-colonial intellectuals[16] – a truly global gaze on the capitalist mode of production. In a well-known passage of *Capital*, volume I, Marx wrote:

> The discovery of gold and silver in America, the extirpation, enslavement and entombment in mines of the aboriginal population, the beginning of the conquest and looting of the East Indies, the turning of Africa into a warren for the commercial hunting of black-skins, signaled the rosy dawn of the era of capitalist production. These idyllic proceedings are the chief moments of primitive accumulation. On their heels treads the commercial war of the European nations, with the globe for a theatre.[17]

It is important to note therefore that investigation of the global geography of primitive accumulation helped Marx to understand the panoply of forms of separation of producers from the means of production. Such an investigation also had important implications for the theoretical foundation of the critique of political economy. The possibility to discover in the colonies something crucially important for the understanding of the capitalist mode of production looms large in the last chapter of *Capital*, dedicated to 'The modern theory of colonization' instantiated by the work of Edward Gibbon Wakefield (1796–1862). It is the great merit of the latter, Marx ironically wrote, 'to have discovered, not anything new about the Colonies, but to have discovered in the Colonies the truth as to the conditions of capitalist production in the mother country' – that is, in England.[18]

As we study Marx's writings on India, China, and Ireland, we shall see that the interface of the process of the primitive accumulation, at the heart of which was the forcible separation of producers from the means of production, and the process of colonial annexation of lands was linked in his presentation of capitalism as a world force and a continuous creator of world market.

---

[15] Marx, *Capital*, volume I, p. 739.
[16] See, for instance, W. E. B. Du Bois, *The World and Africa* (New York: International Publishers, 1946), pp. IX and 56–7.
[17] Marx, *Capital*, volume I, p. 739.
[18] Marx, *Capital*, volume I, p. 752; Marx's engagement with Wakefield's theory of 'systematic colonization' has been recently received attention by scholars of settler colonialism. See, for instance, G. Piterberg and L. Veracini, 'Wakefield, Marx, and the World Turned Inside Out', *Journal of Global History*, 10: 457–78 (2015). See also M. Neocleous, 'International Law as Primitive Accumulation; Or, the Secret of Systematic Colonization', *The European Journal of International Law*, 23 (4): 941–62 (2012).

14.2 Capitalism, Colonialism, Transition

Marx did not write any systematic treatise on India, or specifically colonialism in India, or its pre-colonial past. However, in the course of his vast theoretical and political reflections, as well as in his journalistic writings, he repeatedly touched on and dealt with the British colonial rule over India, the Indian mutiny against British rule, and her pre-colonial past. These analyses – also in form of comments, notes, or letters to Engels – were interrelated, and taken together they may be considered as constituting a body of thought, and as a body of thought it had all the traces of evolving. But, as to the question if by the 'pre-colonial' he always meant the 'pre-capitalist' or 'Asiatic' or 'feudal', different answers are possible. Marx increasingly espoused a heterogeneous view of the pre-capitalist past and the origin of capitalism, and also his views on the relation between capitalism and colonialism also developed over time. The question of transition from pre-capitalism to capitalism therefore involved enormously nuanced discussions in Marx's writings. The possibility of transition to capitalism through colonialism was only one such route of transition. In this context, we have to keep in mind that Marx paid attention to colonial aggrandizement on China also. But China was never fully colonized. It was 'semi-colonial'. So the discussion took a slightly different tenor. Or, in discussions of British colonial control of Ireland, Marx viewed Irish economy as a peasant economy ruthlessly exploited by big landlords and England – a situation that would possibly be today called as 'semi-feudalism'.

Yet the more significant point is that Marx's attention to British rule in India, including in his despatches to the *New-York Tribune*, was mostly a kind of site where interrelations were being explored. India was, as if the alternative scenario, the *foil*, which served the purpose of clarifying what was happening in Europe, or, more fundamentally, which would make a revolutionary think of the varying prospects of revolutions in Europe and elsewhere, for instance the relation between a revolution in the occupied or annexed or colonized country and revolution in the occupying country. In short, reflections on colonialism were part of his reflections on revolution and socialism. In this lay the insights and paradoxes in his analyses of colonialism. The analysis of colonialism was made in the perspective of analysis of capitalism, its global domination, and its ever expanding conquest of territories, economies, and societies. Marx was almost saying, without colonialism there was no capitalism.[19]

---

[19] Perhaps this is the reason as to why Marx's writings on India were studied again and again by political activists and political thinkers in India and other colonized and postcolonial countries. In India, in particular, the question of transition (not only from a pre-colonial order to colonial rule and economy, but also the possibilities of transition from

Resonances between different colonial settings abound in Marx's writings and have shaped their reception, as was for instance the case with his discussion of the Irish Famine in the nineteenth century, which provided an analytic framework for the persistence of famines until the end of British colonial rule in India. Marx's observations in *Capital*, volume I, on the transformation of Ireland into an impoverished agricultural dependency of British capitalism belong to the legacy of socialist anti-colonial thought. Speculating on the prospect of an Irish revolution – an agrarian revolution – and its telling effect on European capitalism was a matter of his relentless speculation and perhaps optimism. Lenin must have noted Marx's analysis of Ireland in relation to England, as he developed his theory of the 'weakest link'.[20] With regard to China too, in his articles for the *New-York Tribune*, occasioned by the Taiping Rebellion and the Second Opium war and written between 1853 and 1860, he discussed the possibility and limits of a radical uprising in China. In any case, this much we can say, revolution in the colonies was a significant theme in Marx's reflections on colonialism. Marx's analysis of colonialism through a global perspective helps to deepen an analysis of the contradictions and complexity of capitalism.

14.3 Colonial Relations, Class Question, and the Peasantry

Two famous articles by Marx in 1853 on India, 'British Rule in India' and 'The Future Results of British Rule in India' presented the problem of analyzing colonial rule in the perspective of the need for social transformation and a political revolution in the colony. We can also name the problem in the familiar term of today, 'nation and class'. The interlinked questions of colony and radical transformation in the colony that independence will bring and the question of class may seem obvious today, but the relation was not so obvious 170 years ago. Marx's concern about social transformation brought him to the issue of pre-colonial order, which he named as 'Asiatic', and which had been overrun by colonialism. He had to focus on the question: wherefrom would the new forces of revolution and transformation come? Expounding his ideas of an 'Asiatic mode of production' based on the political framework of 'oriental despotism', Marx wrote in 'British Rule in India' that the 'Asiatic government' in the form of despotic rule was needed to perform

---

colonialism to an indigenous future) figure prominently in Marxist debates on Marx's writings on India. For a summary, see S. Baru, 'Karl Marx and Analysis of Indian Society', *Economic and Political Weekly*, 18 (50): 2102–8 (1983).

[20] See J. Rodden, '"The Lever Must Be Applied in Ireland": Marx, Engels, and the Irish Question', *The Review of Politics*, 70: 610 (2008).

an economical function ... the function of providing public works. This artificial fertilization of the soil, dependent on a Central Government, and immediately decaying with the neglect of irrigation and drainage, explains the otherwise strange fact that we now find whole territories barren and desert that were once brilliantly cultivated ... it also explains how a single war of devastation has been able to depopulate a country for centuries, and to strip it of all its civilization. [And, while] England, it is true, in causing a social revolution in Hindostan, was actuated only by the vilest interests, and was stupid in her manner of enforcing them ... The question is, can mankind fulfill its destiny without a fundamental revolution in the social state of Asia? If not, whatever may have been the crimes of England she was the unconscious tool of history in bringing about that revolution.[21]

India thus, as Marx saw, had a structure of village communities as 'the solid foundation of oriental despotism' and of the country's 'stagnation'. As a result, the urban centres stood isolated and contributed little to the social life of the country. In this kind of 'Asiatic' system, British rule had the potential to lay the material foundations of a dynamic society. Introduction of railways could facilitate further development of the over-taxed irrigation system, and that of the steam-driven machinery could induce the separation of agriculture and manufacturing. Above all, introduction of private land ownership would bring an end to the old village system. All these modes of colonial intervention would lead to the 'the only *social* revolution ever heard of in Asia'.[22]

Here it is necessary to recognize that Marx did not have any absolute and simplistic notion of the 'Asiatic' system or mode of production. For an appropriate analysis of classes in the colonial society, he had to have a grasp over nature of the 'pre-colonial', and thus the relations between despotism, surplus, commodity production, and exchange. The despot as the 'father of the many communities thus realizing the common unity of all' and the surplus belonged to highest unity.[23] And, further, Marx considered different subjects entitled to landed property in India – focusing in particular on the 'class known as zemindars and talookdars, who have been considered to occupy a position similar to that of the landed nobility and gentry of Europe'. He wrote in his article 'Lord Canning's Proclamation and Land Tenure in India' (1858):

The exclusive proprietary rights claimed by the talookdars and zemindars have been regarded as originating in usurpations at once against the Government and the Cultivators, and every effort has been made to get rid of them as an incubus on

---

[21] K. Marx, 'The British Rule in India' (10 June 1853), MECW, vol. 12, p. 132.
[22] Ibid.
[23] Marx, 'Outlines of the Critique of Political Economy [*Grundrisse*]. First Instalment', p. 401.

the real cultivators of the soil and the general improvement of the country. As, however, these middlemen, whatever the origin of their rights might be, could claim prescription in their favour, it was impossible not to recognize their claims as to a certain extent legal, however inconvenient, arbitrary and oppressive to the people.[24]

The famous historian of the agrarian system in Mughal India, Irfan Habib (1931–), has noted the crucial implication of these observations, namely that, 'the Asiatic state did not represent simply a single person or even only a simple "higher community"; it implied the existence of a definite social class, which appropriated the surplus through the mechanism of the tax-rent. Only out of such a class, in the process of a territorial dispersal of the claims to surplus, could develop local magnates' who formed part of the anti-colonial rebellion in 1857.[25]

Furthermore, Marx's idea of the inner passivity of the Indian society also drew from his ideas of Hindu religion.[26] On one hand, he knew that the nation engaged in conquest, annexation, and colonization was officially 'Christian' – Protestant, and Anglican. The colonial rulers were also driven by the fact that they would civilize a 'barbaric' land, and evangelism along with new missionary sects were always present to lend a hand in this mission. All early colonial rulers, probably Lord Wellesley most clearly, had to conjure something called 'Hinduism' analogous to Protestantism or Catholicism in order to hone a social strategy of colonization. Yet the idea was not purely one of proselytization of the colonized, but reaping also benefits out of the extant practices of the 'Hindu' religion. Thus, Marx noted how the colonial authority protected the priests of the Jagannath temple in Puri who extracted immense profit from mass pilgrimage, and at the same time encouraged temple prostitution and fabulous festivities that would be accompanied by suicide and self-torture of fanatic believers. 'Hindu' religion was thus unable to provide resistance to colonial rule, and Marx argued that, as the village communities crumbled in face of the colonial rule, the potent force of religion in reinvigorating the colonial society was lost forever.[27] Once again, his

---

[24] K. Marx, 'Lord Canning's Proclamation and Land Tenure in India' (6 May 1858), MECW, vol. 15, p. 547.

[25] I. Habib, 'Introduction: Marx's Perception of India', in: I. Husain (ed.), *Karl Marx on India* (New Delhi: Tulika Books, 2006), p. XXVII.

[26] Marx, 'The British Rule in India', pp. 125–6.

[27] Cf. T. Ling, *Karl Marx and Religion in Europe and India* (London: MacMillan, 1980), pp. 68–80. Marx noted in 1857 that 'the old principle of *divide and impera*', according to which 'the Sepoy army served as a safety-valve to absorb the turbulent spirits of the country', had been substituted 'of late years' by a new principle, 'the principle of destroying nationality. The principle has been realized by the forcible destruction of native princes, the disturbance of the settlement of property, and the tampering with the religion

insights into the negotiation of the religious question by the emerging nation were valuable. Not only did religious reform movements begin from the first part of the nineteenth century, but popular sects at times with millenarian ideas also had a say in giving birth to the contradictory nation form, in which Dalits in particular would claim justice and their place in the nation, not as part of the Hindu society and under Hindu religious umbrella, but as a distinct society deserving just recognition.

Of course, passages like the ones cited carry traces of Hegelian world history, yet and at the same time they present to us the first symptoms of the problem of analyzing colonialism in the matrix of social transformation. And, as we shall see, Marx, having set the agenda of social transformation, now had to face the question of class analysis in social transformation. So even in 1853 he did not fail to notice the rapacious nature of colonial rule.[28]

Perhaps we find in commentaries like these and other articles of 1853 on India a faint theory of decolonization – a theory which would imply not only a transformation in the colony, but that a transformation that would perhaps have positive implications for social relations within the imperial country too.[29] On one hand, he would say, as Victor Kiernan (1913–2009) pointed out in his discussion on Marx on India, that 'to be free at home, John Bull must enslave abroad'.[30] On the other hand, his theory of capitalism would also change gradually with issues of race, brutality, violence, and oppression being now incorporated in the history of capitalism. If a ruling class often recapitulated in its colonies its own history of bloody suppressions of peasant revolts, as the mass executions after the Mutiny had reminded him of the Cromwellian reprisals after the Irish Rebellion, then independence of the colony must be achieved to effect social transformation in the oppressor nation. But, while we find decolonization in this formulation still anchored to the fate of bourgeois rule in Europe, the concern soon shifts to the future of the colony itself as Marx had to increasingly discuss the pre-capitalist past of the colony and its transformation. This is not to suggest that there was an exclusively logical link between what he wrote in 1853 and 1857. Indeed the steps were unsure, and even then he declared that 'by and large there will ooze out other facts able to convince even John Bull himself that what he

---

of the people.' See K. Marx, 'The Indian Question' (28 July 1857), MECW, vol. 15, p. 311.

[28] See, for instance, K. Marx, 'The War Question, Doings of Parliament, India' (19 July 1853), MECW, vol. 12, pp. 209–16.

[29] However, some postcolonial scholars think that Marx did not leave behind any clear idea of the possible course of the way the colonial rule would end: see, for instance, A. Kumar, 'Marx and Engels on India', *The Indian Journal of Political Science*, 53 (4): 501 (1992).

[30] V. G. Kiernan, 'Marx and India', *Socialist Register*, 4: 179 (1967).

considers a military mutiny is in truth a national revolt'.[31] But clearly his views on capitalism developed, and he became increasingly scathing in his critique of capitalism, discarding the regenerative role of capitalism that he and Engels had granted in 1848 in the *Manifesto of the Communist Party* or in his writings in 1853 on India.

In order to describe the 1857 mutiny as a national revolt, Marx had to note various factors in the colony, such as discontent of the taluqdars, impoverishment of the peasantry, mutiny in the army, religious discontent, destructive tax burdens, and rapacious nature of colonial administration. To see the colony through the prism of social relations, class terms, which is to say bourgeois power in the imperial country, and the power of proletarians, semi-proletarians, peasants, nascent bourgeoisie, in the colony, was a difficult exercise, not only because the analytical tools were still not fully developed by Marx and Engels, but because the social relations also were unclear at that time with unclarified lines of production relations.[32] Ultimately, Marx found by 1857 with the anti-colonial uprising in India, rebellions in China, and the Fenian revolt in Ireland that the question of transition in the colonial country and its social transformation could not be delinked from the issue of independence – irrespective of the fact as to whether there would be native bourgeois rule after independence or rule of the people. Marx was fully aware of the possible different trajectories of such transition in Ireland, China, India, and even Russia. But to recognize transition in the colony as the subject of history required long and arduous labour, and, to a greater extent imagination, to visualize the colony emerging in its own right as a political actor on the global stage, producing sovereignties, territories, economies, and forms of rule. Indeed, conjuring that future irreducible to given European history and yet a future that would be informed by class analysis and class angle was an immensely difficult exercise.

Marx's writings on colonialism in India therefore not only served the purpose of clarifying his ideas of capitalism or say colonialism in China or Ireland, or the economic system in Russia. As Kevin Anderson (1948–) has averred,[33] these writings also grounded finally his views on capitalism as a world force with manifold varieties, possibilities, and contradictions. His own perspective on capitalism also evolved with his writings on India and other colonies. The articles in the *New-York Tribune* may seem to be

---

[31] K. Marx, 'Indian News' (31 July 1857), MECW, vol. 15, p. 316.

[32] To have that clarity, Marxist thought had to wait for about another forty to fifty years when Mao Tse Tung wrote *Analysis of the Classes in Chinese Society* (Peking: Foreign Language Press, 1926).

[33] K. Anderson, *Marx at the Margins: On Nationalism, Ethnicity, and Non-Western Societies* (Chicago: University of Chicago Press, 2010), pp. 237–45.

occasional pieces where imagination and style of writings play a great role, and where Marx and Engels would get the chance to reflect on 'world history' away from their microscopic interrogation of economic processes in Europe. But these articles, with their continuity and changes, tell us of a 'history's double', playing on each other. If it was capitalism which seemed progressive in relation to the economic and social situation in the colony, in view of the persistence of pre-capitalist forms of property (communal forms) and repeated attempts to destroy or at least undermine them by Western colonialism, Marx found that the anti-colonial resistance was often linked to these many non-colonial and pre-capitalist forms. Capitalism was bringing in only endless misery. Study of the problematic of transition led Marx to throw away earlier notions of the progressiveness of colonialism. Marx had now only harsh and unremitting condemnation of capitalism and colonialism. Capitalism and colonialism, workers and the colonial peasantry, expropriation of property by the process of accumulation and the persistence of small property, rule of law and colonial plunder, the political economy of the 'old' world and colonial economy in the 'new' world – these continuously shifting sites of global capitalist order, and the range of displacements they cause occupied Marx's attention. It was also history's double in another sense. Perhaps only with these occasional reflections Marx could theorize capital, or the other way: only with insights into the dynamics of accumulation Marx could reflect on colonial history, and 'world' history.

As we know, Marx and Engels used the term 'rural proletariat' occasionally, by which they meant small peasants and small tenant farmers, and agricultural labourers.[34] It would perhaps cover all farmers and farm workers who were not prosperous farmers and landed aristocrats or 'middlemen' in the tenant system. But they had never distinguished explicitly the rural classes. Only towards the end of their respective lives with socialist movements making progress in France and Germany did Marx and Engels start thinking concretely of the peasants, of their relationship with the proletariat and proletarian politics, and the stand a proletarian state should take towards them. How would one think of the villages in colonial India with its own specific history and relationship of the mass of rural population to the means of production, land, and other instruments of production, precisely at a time when colonial destruction was proceeding at a furious pace and a new type of land ownership had been recently introduced? Will the peasant class be

[34] For a summary, see T. J. Byres, 'The Agrarian Question and the Peasantry', in: *The Elgar Companion to Marxist Economics* (Cheltenham, Northampton, MA: Edward Eglar, 2012), pp. 10–15.

identified more with poverty, working for wages, experiencing distance from the state, and famines and death, and less with a particular mode of production? Marx's focus on the Indian land systems is noticeable, for nowhere Marx refers to the lowest tier of peasantry as 'rural proletarians'. So was there a difference between the 'Eastern peasant' and the 'Western rural proletarian' in the outlook of Marx and Engels through much of their life? Yet it is also true that by the 1860s Marx became more attentive to the general issue of class differentiation within the peasantry.

Ireland was important in the evolution of their views, because it was from the 1840s that Marx and Engels began paying attention to the 'great clearances' and the birth of the Irish proletarians often through migration. We must repeat at this point that, although Ireland was a nation of peasants during the lifetimes of Marx and Engels, they never discussed Ireland at length in any of their writings on the peasant question, until the Fenian Uprising of 1867, when Marx revised his thinking and acknowledged as much. Marx wrote to Engels in December 1869: 'For a long time I believed that it would be possible to overthrow the English regime by English working-class ascendancy. Deeper study has now convinced me of the opposite ... The lever must be applied in Ireland. That is why the Irish Question is so important for the social movement in general.'[35] As John Rodden (1956–) has noted, 'Elevating Ireland to the status of the crucial nation inciting the revolution was consistent with Marx's conclusion concerning historical materialism in Chapter 25 of *Capital*, Volume I, which is titled "The General Law of Capitalist Accumulation". In this light, the case of agrarian Ireland might be referred to as "the special law of capitalist accumulation."'[36] As Marx wrote of primitive accumulation,

all revolutions are epoch-making that act as levers for the capitalist class in the course of formation; but, above all, those moments when great masses of men are suddenly and forcibly torn from their means of subsistence, and hurled as free and 'unattached' proletarians on the labour market. The expropriation of the agricultural producer or the peasant is the basis of the whole process.[37]

14.4 Slavery

The English colonization of Ireland was more generally a laboratory for the forging of systems of racial oppression. According to Theodore W. Allen (1919–2005), there is a clear 'analogy' between the working of racial domination in Ireland and in 'Anglo-American colonialism' on the

---

[35] 'K. Marx to F. Engels, 10 December 1869', MECW, vol. 43, p. 398.
[36] Rodden, 'The Lever Must Be Applied in Ireland', p. 629.
[37] Marx, *Capital*, volume I, p. 707.

base of Atlantic slavery. While Marx, as we saw, was referring to Ireland in order to understand the social condition of India, Allen invites us to use the 'Irish mirror' to understand the 'invention of the white race' and the connection between race, racism, and slavery in North America.[38] Indeed, in a letter of April 1870, Marx compared the hatred of the 'ordinary English worker' towards the 'Irish worker' with the attitude of 'poor whites' to the 'niggers'.[39] With a terse statement in *Wage Labor and Capital* – 'a Negro is a Negro. He becomes a slave in certain relations'[40] – he anticipated the tradition of black radical scholarship, including the works of W. E. B. Du Bois (1868–1963), C. L. R. James (1901–1989), and Eric Williams (1911–1981), that connected race, racism, and slavery.[41]

In *Capital*, volume I, Marx underscored the relevance of modern colonialism, in particular Atlantic slavery – predicated upon the 'commercial hunting of black-skins'[42] – as a 'moment' of primitive accumulation. Atlantic slavery, along with the many forms of indenture historically intertwined with its development in and beyond the Atlantic world, is bonded labour under capitalism. One can say that it is the colonial other of 'free' wage labour, which was, according to Marx, the standard regulation of the relation between capital and labour. While he carefully distinguished 'free' wage labour from slavery, for instance in chapter 6 of *Capital*, volume I, his occasional use of the phrase 'wage slavery' (which played an outstanding role in the early history of the labour movement in many parts of the world[43]) can be taken as a symptom of the fact that the (colonial) ghost of slavery continued and still continues to haunt 'free' wage labour.

It is well known that Marx had a pronounced interest in the United States and that he had passionately committed himself and the International Working Men's Association to the support of the Union during the civil war.[44] Although Marx has been criticized for his portrayal of the United States as the country where abstract labour, labour in

---

[38] See T. W. Allen, *The Invention of the White Race, Volume 1: Racial Oppression and Social Control* (London, New York: Verso, 1994), pp. 1–24.
[39] 'K. Marx to S. Meyer and A. Vogt' (9 April 1870), MECW, vol. 43, pp. 474–5.
[40] K. Marx, *Wage Labor and Capital*, MECW, vol. 9, p. 212.
[41] 'Slavery was not born of racism: rather, racism was the consequence of slavery', Eric Williams wrote in his *Capitalism and Slavery* (Chapel Hill: The University of North Carolina Press, 1944), p. 7.
[42] Marx, *Capital*, volume I, p. 739.
[43] For an analysis of the ambiguities of this phrase (and particularly of the related phrase 'white slavery') in the United States, see D. Roediger, *The Wages of Whiteness. Race and the Making of American Working Class* (London, New York: Verso, 1999).
[44] See, for instance, R. Blackburn, *Marx and Lincoln: An Unfinished Revolution* (London, New York: Verso, 2011), pp. 1–100.

general, had become a reality in the 1857 'Introduction' to the *Grundrisse*, he was acutely aware of the relevance of the race divide in foreclosing the very possibility of working-class politics in North America.[45] As he wrote in *Capital*, volume I, 'labor cannot emancipate itself in the white skin where in the black it is branded'.[46] Marx's analysis of slavery in the South of the United States is indeed acute and original, both in the journalistic articles he wrote during the war and in scattered references in the *Grundrisse* and in *Capital*. He never doubted the capitalist character of the plantation system and he correctly grasped the expansionist tendency of slavery. As he wrote in October 1861, 'continual expansion of territory and continual spread of slavery beyond its old limits is a law of life for the slave states of the Union'.[47]

In the *Grundrisse*, Marx had already written that 'Negro slavery' is definitely a 'purely industrial form of slavery', adding, however, that 'in any case it is incompatible with and disappears as a result of the development of bourgeois society'.[48] Strictly linked to the colonial origin of the United States – and to primitive accumulation of capital – slavery was captured by Marx in what he thought as the moment of its vanishing, giving way to the full deployment of 'free' wage labour and to working-class struggles and politics. The history of capital and labour in the United States has been quite different from what Marx had forecast and hoped, characterized by a multiplication of the colonial ghosts of slavery that continue to haunt the labour movement in that country – and in a way Marx's work.[49]

Marx's belief that the industrial slavery would disappear with the development of bourgeois society reminds of his similar hope in his early articles on India in 1853, namely that colonialism would usher in social revolution. Yet Marx's focus on Atlantic slavery had neglected at the same time the ongoing extermination of the indigenous population of America – the true process of colonization. Also, his comments on the 'new world' showed that he was struggling with two distinct forms of colonialism – settler colonialism and colonialism based on pure conquest (India). But at least we should note that the issue of 'pre-capitalist

---

[45] 'In the history of the United States', writes, for instance, Lisa Lowe, 'capital has maximized its profits not by rendering labor "abstract" but precisely through the social production of "difference" . . . marked by race, nation, geographical origin, and gender.' See L. Lowe, *Immigrant Acts: On Asian American Cultural Politics* (Durham, NC: Duke University Press, 1996), pp. 28–9.
[46] Marx, *Capital*, volume I, MECW, vol. 35, p. 305.
[47] K. Marx, 'The North American Civil War' (20 October 1861), MECW, vol. 19, p. 39.
[48] Marx, 'Outlines of the Critique of the Political Economy [*Grundrisse*]. First Instalment,', p. 157.
[49] For a summary, see D. Roediger, *Race, Class and Marxism* (London, New York: Verso, 2017), pp. 1–29.

formations' became more acute for him in reflections on India or China than on say United States or Australia.

14.5 The Colonized as the Political Subject

Towards the end of his life it became crucial for Marx to get over the aporia presented before him by issues of property ownership of land and other instruments of agrarian production. And he could do this only by negotiating the supposed difference between the 'Eastern peasant' and the 'proletarian and the semi-proletarian of the West'. The Russian question and the colonial question both became moments in new thinking. The supposed absence of landed private property had distinguished the Asiatic form from the Western form. But, if that absence had made no effect on the mission or the role of colonial power to regenerate social forces in the colony, and if, meanwhile, as Marx recorded, only destruction was to be seen in the colonies, an eastern anti-colonial revolution must be recognized as the moment to break the aporia. The Indian Mutiny of 1857 and the rebellions in China were turning points in Marx's views of colonialism. In the series of essays in *New-York Tribune* on India and China concerning the Sepoy Mutiny and the Taiping Rebellion, he lampooned the colonial army in the Indian mutiny and openly supported the cause of the Chinese rebels. In the mid-1850s, roughly when he began to compose the *Grundrisse*, the impact of the colonial question was evident. For instance, in the critique of political economy Marx was drafting, he tried to lay out a multilinear idea on historical development, while, in the following years, as we saw, race and slavery became important topics for him. And, on the top of all these issues, he was increasingly concerned with Poland, which helped him clarifying the question of *revolution*.

The question around the possibility of the emergence of a native bourgeoisie in the colony, or the transformation of the colonial peasantry into a bourgeois class gradually lost importance in Marx's mind. There was no more 'double mission' of the colonial rule.[50] As an Indian Marxist has observed, Marx less and less spoke of the 'Asiatic mode', but more of anti-colonial uprisings and revolutions.[51] If this was with India, China, or Ireland, it was even more with Poland. Revolution would, as if, redefine the class question. From 1848 onwards, the Polish issue had engaged Marx and Engels. Polish struggles for independence had periodically

[50] K. Marx, 'The Future Results of British Rule in India' (22 July 1853), MECW, vol. 12, p. 217.
[51] S. Ghosh, 'Marx on India', *Monthly Review*, 35 (8): 39–53 (1984).

renewed their attention to the question of revolution as the defining motor of society.[52] If revolution was a clarifying event of history, so was the case with anti-colonial uprisings and revolutions.

We may say then the following things: (a) Marx's first examination of the colonial question was from the angle of world trade and world history; (b) however, the question of world trade led him to look deeper into the colonial society. And the examination of the impact of world trade on colonial economy and the colonized people led him to the recognition that the colonial rule – far from playing a revolutionary role – had thrown the people of the colony into backwardness and ruin. The colonial economy therefore became an appendage to the economy of the colonial power; (c) third, an anti-colonial revolution was a prerequisite for the destruction of the colonial order. The regeneration of the society could be possible by internal forces, the rebellious people in the colony, who must smash the colonial rule to achieve social transformation and social regeneration; (d) finally, Marx's engagements with precisely 'world history' had definitely led him to some erroneous views. But they also led him to analyze events in China, India, Ireland, Poland, the United States, and, to lesser extent, Algeria and elsewhere. Through these analyses, he came to view colonialism as a mode of capitalism and not an accidental adjunct, which an enlightened liberal bourgeois civilization could discard in course of time.

We cannot say that capitalism's course is over in the one-time colonies of the world, now called the postcolonial world. Many of Marx's hesitations over predicting any mandatory future course of countries through capitalism are being resolved by history, as increasingly more nations and regions are entangled in capitalist trade and global capitalist relations. We may have still something to learn from Marx's engagement with colonialism in our present, when the history of anti-colonialism has boiled down to purely one of nationalism and the postcolonial order now exhibits itself in a stark right-wing nationalist frame. Opening up the nation form to discover within it the persistence of the class question in revolutionary terms is the enduring lesson we can draw from Marx's engagement with colonialism and capitalism. Strangely then, or perhaps not, in precisely the numerous and often scattered reflections on colonialism, Marx appears as a strategic thinker. While studying these reflections, we may find this or that formulation wrong, but the strategic thinking was unmistakable and is instructive for us.

---

[52] On Marx's longstanding reflections on Poland, see Anderson, *Marx at the Margins*, pp. 63–78.

Colonialism

The way in which the colony features in Marx's thoughts as an object of knowledge also makes the colony a part of the global history of capital, and goes beyond the usual binary of colonialism/nationalism or colony/nation, compelling us to think of associated questions of primitive accumulation, borders, universalism, concrete, and so on. Colonies were founded not merely by nations; they emerged in the time of empires in whose history the given history of the nation form was scripted. Marx repeatedly raised the problem of capitalist expansion in the time of colonialism and in that context raised the issue of colonial governance. In this way his writings on colonialism, for instance those on British colonialism in India, suggest the need to study the history of modern governance that combines coercion and management of conditions of accumulation. In the telos of globalization, we have not only world trade and free trade, but also a time when, besides the fact of nation-states reigning supreme, there is a present characterized by flows, fuzzy, permeable, and shifting borders, and footloose capitalism. This is the milieu, when empire as a concept is once again returning as a historico-theoretical concept as the other of the nation that had emerged from the colony.

Marx's writings on colonialism furthermore anticipate a theory of the colonized as the political subject. In his writings, he was not only going beyond the colonial state, but was also reflecting on the representation of the political subject in the modern colonial age. From a politics of class struggle he had to shift to a definition of political struggle, in which not the class but the colony emerges as a gesture towards the new subject.[53] This was the point at which he started thinking about religion in the colony, the problem of passivity, faith in the 'celestial' state or the *mai-baap Sarkar* (mother-father government), the hard consideration as to which class would lead the 'national' revolt, and a harder realization that as yet no class was ready, the nation was not ready, and yet the war for independence must begin sooner or later. There was no place of immanence in the search for an answer. The closure would be opened up only by the way the colonized as political subject would develop.[54] This was the exasperating dilemma that gnawed at him. It was the dilemma of class and the nation that

---

[53] Prabhat Patnaik notes in his study of Marx's writings on colonialism in India: 'It is remarkable that the notion of twin revolutions had already been in Marx's mind as early as in 1853, *even before the Indian Mutiny could have possibly brought it to his consciousness*. And it is equally remarkable that Marx had favored the idea of advanced country workers supporting the national liberation struggles even at that stage.' P. Patnaik, 'The Other Marx', in: Husain, *Karl Marx on India*, p. lvii.

[54] This was possible because, as some historians argue, the colonial rule, though dominant, was unable to establish hegemony over the subjects. See, for instance, R. Guha, *Dominance without Hegemony: History and Power in Colonial India* (Cambridge, MA: Harvard University Press, 1997), pp. 1–99.

still afflicts the postcolonial world. Like Marx, we too shall keep on battling the closure knowing that it will be a perpetual struggle of life and death.

References

Ahmad, Aijaz (1992), *In Theory: Classes, Nations, Literatures*, London: Verso.
Allen, Theodore W. (1994), *The Invention of the White Race, Volume 1: Racial Oppression and Social Control*, London, New York: Verso.
Anderson, Kevin (2010), *Marx at the Margins: On Nationalism, Ethnicity, and Non-Western Societies*, Chicago: University of Chicago Press.
Baru, Sanjay (1983), 'Karl Marx and Analysis of Indian Society', *Economic and Political Weekly*, 18 (50): 2102–8.
Blackburn, Robin (2011), *Marx and Lincoln: An Unfinished Revolution*, London, New York: Verso.
Byres, Terence J. (2012), 'The Agrarian Question and the Peasantry', in: E. Elgar (ed.), *The Elgar Companion to Marxist Economics*, Cheltenham, Northampton, MA: Edward Elgar, pp. 10–15.
Du Bois, W. E. B. (1946), *The World and Africa*, New York: International Publishers.
Ferrari Bravo, Luciano (2018), 'Old and New Questions in the Theory of Imperialism', *Viewpoint Magazine*, www.viewpointmag.com/2018/02/01/old-new-questions-theory-imperialism-1975/.
Ghosh, Suniti (1984), 'Marx on India', *Monthly Review*, 35 (8): 39–53.
Guha, Ranajit (1997), *Dominance without Hegemony: History and Power in Colonial India*, Cambridge, MA: Harvard University Press.
Habib, Irfan (2006), 'Introduction: Marx's Perception of India', in: I. Husain (ed.), *Karl Marx on India*, New Delhi: Tulika Books, pp. XIX–LIV.
Hauck, Gerhard (2010), 'Kolonialismus', in: W. F. Haug, F. Haug, P. Jehle, and W. Küttler (eds), *Historisch-Kritisches Wörterbuch des Marxismus*, vol. 7/II (Hamburg: Berliner Institut für Kritische Theorie), pp. 1159–66.
Kiernan, Victor G. (1967), 'Marx and India', *Socialist Register*, 4: 159–89.
Kumar, Ashutosh (1992), 'Marx and Engels on India', *The Indian Journal of Political Science*, 53 (4): 493–504.
Lindner, Kolja (2010), 'Marx's Eurocentrism: Postcolonial Studies, and Marx Scholarship', *Radical Philosophy*, 161: 27–41.
Ling, Trevor (1980), *Karl Marx and Religion in Europe and India*, London: MacMillan.
Lowe, Lisa (1996), *Immigrant Acts: On Asian American Cultural Politics*, Durham, NC: Duke University Press.
Mao Tse Tung (1926), *Analysis of the Classes in Chinese Society*, Peking: Foreign Language Press.
Marx, Karl (1977), *Wage Labor and Capital*, MECW, vol. 9, pp. 197–228.
—— (1984), 'The North American Civil War' (25 October 1861), MECW, vol. 19, pp. 32–42.
—— (1986), 'Indian News' (31 July 1857), MECW, vol. 15, pp. 314–17.
—— (1986), 'The Indian Question' (14 August 1857), MECW, vol. 15, pp. 309–13.

(1986), 'Lord Canning's Proclamation and Land Tenure in India' (6 May 1858), MECW, vol. 15, pp. 546–9.
(1986), *Bastiat and Carey*, MECW, vol. 28, p. 8.
(1986), 'Outlines of the Critique of Political Economy (*Grundrisse*). First Instalment', MECW, vol. 28.
(1987), 'Outlines of the Critique of Political Economy (*Grundrisse*). Second Instalment', MECW, vol. 29.
(1987), 'A Contribution to the Critique of Political Economy. Part One', MECW, vol. 29, pp. 257–417.
(1996), *Capital*, Volume I, MECW, vol. 35.
(2010), 'The British Rule in India' (10 June 1853), MECW, vol. 12, pp. 125–33.
(2010), 'The War Question, Doings of Parliament, India' (19 July 1853), MECW, vol. 12, pp. 209–16.
(2010), 'The Future Results of British Rule in India' (22 July 1853), MECW, vol. 12, pp. 217–22.

Mezzadra, Sandro (2018), *In the Marxian Workshops: Producing Subjects*, London: Rowman & Littlefield.

Mezzadra, Sandro, and Neilson, Brett (2013), *Border as Method, or, the Multiplication of Labor*, Durham, NC: Duke University Press.

Neocleous, Mark (2012), 'International Law as Primitive Accumulation; Or, the Secret of Systematic Colonization', *The European Journal of International Law*, 23 (4): 941–62.

Patnaik, Prabhat (2006), 'The Other Marx', in I. Husain (ed.), *Karl Marx on India*, New Delhi: Tulika Books, pp. lv–lxviii.

Piterberg, Gabriel, and Veracini, Lorenzo (2015), 'Wakefield, Marx, and the World Turned Inside Out', *Journal of Global History*, 10: 457–78.

Rodden, John (2008), '"The Lever Must Be Applied in Ireland": Marx, Engels, and the Irish Question', *The Review of Politics*, 70, pp. 609–40.

Roediger, David (1999), *The Wages of Whiteness: Race and the Making of American Working Class*, London, New York: Verso.
(2017), *Race, Class and Marxism*, London, New York: Verso.

Said, Edward (1978), *Orientalism*, London: Penguin.

Samaddar, Ranabir (2009), 'Primitive Accumulation and Some Aspects of Life and Work in India', *Economic and Political Weekly*, 44 (18): 33–42.

Wallerstein, Immanuel (2004), *World System Analysis: An Introduction*, Durham, NC: Duke University Press.

Williams, Eric (1944), *Capitalism and Slavery*, Chapel Hill: The University of North Carolina Press.

15 State

Bob Jessop

15.1 Are There Essential, Permanent, Stable Elements?

An often-remarked absence in Karl Marx's legacy is the failure to write a comprehensive critique of the state as a medium of class domination. A book on the state was part of his six-book plan for *Capital*, which guided his work between 1857 and 1863.[1] According to this plan, a text on the state would have followed books on capital, wage labour, and landed property. This corresponds to the method of political economy, namely, a movement 'from the simple [concepts], such as labour, division of labour, need, exchange-value ... to the State, international exchange, and world market'.[2] The state is a concrete-complex relational ensemble that can be comprehended theoretically only through prior, more abstract-simple conceptual analysis. Marx's efforts to explore the topics of the first three books (albeit with a different organization) meant that he focused more on the economic than political dynamic of accumulation in his unfinished critique of political economy. Moreover, given the virtual absence of the proposed book on labour,[3] he focused more on capital, neglecting the working class as an active economic, let alone, political subject.[4] Relatedly, although their project was as much political as theoretical, neither he nor Friedrich Engels provided coherent analyses of political parties, nations, nationalism, and nation-states; the strategy and tactics of revolution (especially whether it must be violent or could take a parliamentary form); and the transitional form of the 'dictatorship of the proletariat' that would supersede the

---

[1] On the six-book plan, see K. Marx, 'Outlines of the Critique of Political Economy [*Grundrisse*]. First Instalment', MECW, vol. 28, p. 45; on its fate, see M. Heinrich, '"Capital" after MEGA: Discontinuities, Interruptions and New Beginnings', *Crisis & Critique*, 3 (3): 93–138 (2016).
[2] Marx, 'Outlines of the Critique of the Political Economy [*Grundrisse*]. First Instalment', pp. 37–8.
[3] On this missing book, see M. Lebowitz, *Beyond Capital: Marx's Political Economy of the Working Class* (Basingstoke: Palgrave-Macmillan, 2003), pp. 27–50.
[4] Ibid, pp. 66–75.

capitalist type of state and abolish the separation between the state and the community. These are major omissions.

This does not mean that Marx and his lifelong collaborator, Engels, ignored such issues. Individually and together, they penned a rich body of published and unpublished reflections on the state and state power. Marx offered critiques of political theory analogous to his critique of economic categories in classical and vulgar political economy. He analyzed the capitalist type of state – albeit mainly from the viewpoint of its formal adequacy to – or fit with – the distinctive logic of capital accumulation. He and Engels presented historical analyses of the state (or analogous forms of domination) in pre-capitalist but class-based modes of production and/or contemporary societies outside Europe and the United States. They also studied the development, changing architecture, and class nature of specific states. Both undertook more specific conjunctural analyses of different political periods and/or significant events as well as more strategically oriented accounts of concrete situations that were intended to influence political debates in the labour movement. Their studies also extended to inter-state relations, colonialism, the international balance of forces, the politics of war and peace, and, in addition, the genealogy of some key categories of political analysis.

The diversity of approaches partly reflects a need to simplify the complexities of state power by choosing different entry points for specific purposes at the risk that Marx's work on the state and politics remained fragmented, incomplete, ambiguous, and inconsistent. It could also represent, as Antonio Gramsci (1891–1937) remarked more generally on the oeuvre of Marx and Engels, an unfinished search to develop a materialist approach to history. This process involved selecting 'elements which were to become stable and "permanent"' but had not yet been integrated into a considered theoretical position. These elements must be distinguished from various thought experiments that were later dropped. These comprise 'partial doctrines and theories for which the thinker [here Marx] may have had a certain sympathy, at certain times, even to the extent of having accepted them provisionally and of having availed himself of them for his work of criticism and of historical and scientific creation'.[5] Gramsci's remarks invite the question: what aspects of this heterogeneous set of analyses on the state and state power are essential, which contingent, accidental, discards?

This said, one cannot distil a single essential, general theory of the state or state power from Marx's reflections on at least two grounds. First, textually, they are heterogenous, fragmented, ambiguous, and inconsistent. 'Hence, as long as Marx's writings remain a key reference for the development of state

---

[5] A. Gramsci, *Selections from the Prison Notebooks* (London: Lawrence & Wishart, 1971), pp. 382–6.

theory, it will be necessary to recognize that a range of positions is defensible from within the intellectual canon and that the canon itself provides no basis for arbitrating among the competing theories.'[6] Second, more importantly, there is no 'state in general'[7] that could provide the object of a transhistorical general theory. At most, there would be some general class-theoretical principles that hold for all class-dominated societies, regardless of their dominant mode of production or the more general articulation of diverse modes of production and forms of social and private labour. In this regard, Marx often remarked that the state is a system of political domination that advances the interests of the ruling classes. However, these remarks were primarily descriptive – that is, pre-theoretical[8] – and focused on the class *content* of state power rather than specific *forms* of state considered as a social relation. Marx's theoretical contributions concern the latter topic.

15.2 Three Essential Theories of the State and State Power

In broad terms, three essential accounts of the state can be identified in Marx's work. Each had a specific place in Marx's political, historical, and theoretical analyses. They overlapped in some respects and would be rearticulated in his eventual account of the present-day state.

Some descriptive accounts saw the state as an instrument of class rule wielded with varying success by the economically dominant class or class fraction to maintain its economic exploitation and political control. This theme was first advanced in Marx's articles for the *New Rhenish Newspaper* [*Neue Rheinische Zeitung*] in 1842–43, which presented a moral critique of the use of legal and administrative power to advance propertied interests or to defend the state itself.[9] It was expressed famously (or notoriously) in the *Manifesto of the Communist Party*. This posits that '[t]he history of all hitherto existing society is the history of class struggles' and, against this background, claims that '[t]he executive of the modern state is but a committee for managing the common affairs of the whole bourgeoisie'.[10] Apart from its rhetorical value at a time when revolution seemed feasible, this claim also made sense given the then limited franchise in Europe and North America.

---

[6] C. W. Barrow, 'The Marx Problem in Marxian State Theory', *Science & Society* 64 (1): 88 (2001).

[7] Cf. the remarks in Marx's 1857 'Introduction' that there is no production in general or general production (ibid, p. 23).

[8] On the inherent instability of Marx's 'descriptive theory', not fully theorized, work on the state, see L. Althusser, *On the Reproduction of Capitalism: Ideology and Ideological State Apparatuses* (London: Verso, 2014), pp. 71–3.

[9] For example, K. Marx, 'Debates on the Law on the Thefts of Wood', MECW, vol. 1, pp. 224–63; 'Justification of the Correspondent from the Mosel', MECW, vol. 1, pp. 332–58.

[10] K. Marx and F. Engels, *Manifesto of the Communist Party*, MECW, vol. 6, pp. 482, 486.

Its subsequent extension in many capitalist regimes, which put a parliamentary road to socialism on the agenda, did not modify Marx's views on the *class content* of state power. Thus, from the 1840s to the end of his life, he advanced similar arguments in many press articles and historical studies, describing the dominant class fractions and classes that directly or indirectly controlled the state apparatus.

In other historical accounts, however, Marx saw the state as an autonomous authority that can win significant freedom for manoeuvre when an unstable balance of class forces threatened disorder.[11] The incumbent government (or its successor) could then exercise its exceptional authority to impose social order or to pursue its own interests in a parasitic fashion. Examples included Caesarism, absolutism, and Bismarckism. But this view appeared most famously in Marx's analyses of France in the 1850s and 1860s under Louis Bonaparte (1778–1848). The latter staged a coup d'état in 1851 in a time of economic, political, and social disequilibrium and replaced the Second Republic with an empire that appeared to operate above the main contending classes. Nonetheless, Marx argued, it had a secure class basis in the conservative smallholding peasantry. Unable to organize as an effective class force in its own name, this isolated rural mass did respond to the emperor's rhetorical appeal to their values and Napoleon Bonaparte's memory, even as his economic policies betrayed their long-term interests.[12] Marx even suggested on one occasion that Louis Bonaparte, recognizing 'the general aversion to his rule',[13] was trying to establish a pretorian state, in which the army, led by the emperor himself, had begun to represent itself against the entire society.[14]

Both approaches have been developed one-sidedly by Marxist theorists. Some treat the state as a passive instrument that can be used to advance the interests of whichever class or class fraction happens to control it.[15] Others highlight the necessary 'relative autonomy' of the

---

[11] For a detailed account of Marx on autonomization, see H. Draper and E. Haberkern, *Karl Marx's Theory of Revolution: State and Bureaucracy, Vol. 1* (New York: Monthly Review Press, 1977), pp. 311–590.

[12] K. Marx, *The Eighteenth Brumaire of Louis Bonaparte*, MECW, vol. 11.

[13] K. Marx, 'The Rule of the Pretorians', MECW, vol. 15, p. 466.

[14] Marx wrote: 'the rule of the naked sword is proclaimed in most unmistakable terms, and Bonaparte wants France to clearly understand that the imperial rule does rest not on her will but on 600,000 bayonets... Under the second Empire the interest of the army itself is to predominate. The army is no longer to maintain the rule of one part of the people over another part of the people. The army is to maintain its own rule, personated by its own dynasty, over the French people in general... It is to represent the *State* in antagonism to the *society*' (ibid, p. 465).

[15] For early surveys, see V. I. Lenin, 'The State and Revolution', in: *Lenin: Collected Works* (Moscow: Progress Publishers, 1964), and S. W. Moore, *The Critique of Capitalist Democracy: An Introduction to the Theory of the State in Marx, Engels and Lenin*

state and its officials, who need autonomy in order to better serve the economic and political interests of the dominant class.[16] Yet others suggest the first account holds for more normal periods of class struggle, the latter for 'exceptional' periods when class struggle is stalemated or threatens a social catastrophe.[17]

A third account of the state offers a useful framework to locate and relativize the other two. This was first developed in Marx's *Critique of Hegel's Philosophy of Right* and *Introduction to the Critique of Hegel's Philosophy of Right*. This essential, permanent, and stable account regarded the state as an alienated form of political organization that it is based on the separation of rulers and ruled.[18] This separation takes different forms in different class-based modes of production. Marx reworked this account throughout his life, discarding some arguments, developing others, and presenting it in ever more materialist rather than philosophical terms. It is most clearly restated in his remarks on the 1871 Paris Commune as a radically new form of political organization that sought to overcome this separation of rulers and ruled. The second draft of *The Civil War in France* claimed that state power 'had always been the power for the maintenance of order, i.e., the existing order of society, and, therefore, of the subordination and exploitation of the producing class by the appropriating class'.[19] This said, in his writings on the modern state (or bourgeois state), Marx stressed that this separation assumed a novel form. Evgeny Pashukanis (1891–1937) summarized this as the impersonal domination of a sovereign constitutional state. In other words, class is absent as an explicit organizing principle of the capitalist type of state because the bourgeoisie does not – and does not need to – hold a legal monopoly of power.[20] It must compete for power on formally equal terms with subordinate classes. Substantively, of course, matters are quite different. For, 'where exploitation takes the form of exchange, dictatorship *may* take the form of democracy'.[21] Marx grounded this possibility

---

(New York: Paine-Whitman, 1957); see also B. Jessop, *The Capitalist State: Marxist Theories and Methods* (Oxford: Martin Robertson, 1982).

[16] See especially N. Poulantzas, *Political Power and Social Classes* (London: NLB, 1973), pp. 115–17, 132–4, 255–79, 283–9.

[17] See, for example, R. N. Hunt, 1974, *The Political Ideas of Marx and Engels*, vol. 1 (London: Macmillan, 1974), pp. 121–30; J. Maguire, *Marx's Theory of Politics* (Cambridge: Cambridge University Press, 1978), pp. 24–7; R. Miliband, 'Marx and the State', in: *Socialist Register* (London: Merlin Press, 1965).

[18] An extended account of this approach is presented in P. Thomas, *Alien Politics: Marxist State Theory Retrieved* (London: Routledge, 1994), pp. 27–84.

[19] K. Marx, 'Second Draft Plan of *The Civil War in France*', MECW, vol. 22, p. 534.

[20] E. B. Pashukanis, *Law and Marxism: A General Theory* (London: Ink Links, 1978), p. 185.

[21] Moore, *The Critique of Capitalist Democracy*, p. 59 (italics in original).

on the specific separation-in-unity of the economic and political moments of exploitation and domination in capitalism. This analysis became the distinctive permanent, stable, and essential basis for his analysis of the historical specificity of the capitalist state. It also takes us beyond the tendency (or temptation) noted by Engels in historical materialist analyses of ideology and other matters: 'form is always neglected at first for substance'.[22] In short, form analysis is the key to reading Marx's work on the state and state power from the 1840s to 1880s.

In 1843, after leaving the *New Rhenish Newspaper*, Marx studied the history of states and their relation to societal development in France, Italy, Poland, England, Germany, Sweden, and the United States; the English and French revolutions; and related texts on political and constitutional theory.[23] These intensive studies informed his critique of G. W. F. Hegel's (1770–1831) doctrine of the state and his further work on state (trans)formation and state power. Against Hegel, Marx argued that the emerging bourgeois social formation was characterized by the institutional separation of (a) the 'public sphere', with the state at its centre, in which politics is oriented to the collective interest; and (b) 'civil society', in which private property and individual self-interest are dominant. To Hegel's claim that the modern state could and would represent the common, organic interests of all members of society, Marx replied that it could represent only an 'illusory' community of interest beneath which would lie the continuing antagonisms, crass materialism, and egoistic conflicts of a society based on private property ownership and wage labour. Hegel did not recognize that the real world was contradictory and that this would undermine attempts to secure political unification and social cohesion. For Marx, true emancipation and a true community of interests required the abolition of private property. He refined these views over forty years but never presented them in a single, comprehensive text.

In November 1844, following his critique of Hegel's *Philosophy of Right*, Marx sketched 'A Draft Plan for a Work on the Modern State'.[24] Reflecting his work at the time, its themes would be: first, the history of the origin of the modern state or the French Revolution; second, the proclamation of the rights of man and the constitution of the state, to include freedom, equality, unity, and the popular sovereignty; third, the state and civil society (here understood to bourgeois society based on private property and market relations); fourth, the constitutional representative state and the democratic representative state; fifth, the division

---

[22] 'F. Engels to Franz Mehring, 14 July 1893', MECW, vol. 50, p. 165.
[23] These notes comprise the 'Kreuznacher Hefte 1–5', MEGA², vol. IV/2, pp. 9–278.
[24] K. Marx, 'Draft Plan for a Work on the Modern State', MECW, vol. 4, p. 534.

between the legislature and executive powers; sixth, legislative power, legislative bodies, and political clubs; seventh, the centralization and hierarchy of the executive power, including administrate and local government; eighth, judicial power and the law; ninth, nationality and the people; tenth, political parties; and eleventh, the fight to abolish the state and bourgeois society. While this plan was never realized, these themes are pursued consistently throughout Marx's writings on the state. Indeed, Marx retained a strong interest in the French Revolution and the lessons of the subsequent development of the French state concerning the role of the bourgeois democratic regime (and its crises) in capitalist economic and political development. In key respects, while England was his model for the first stages of capitalist industrial development (with the United States attracting his interest in the 1870s–80s),[25] France provided the main reference point for his analysis of the capitalist type of state.

While Marx's draft plan began with the formal institutional structure of modern state and its implications for the forms of political struggle, he also hinted that this must be understood in terms of the articulation between bourgeois (civil) society and the state. This was a central theme in the materialist conception of history, outlined in *The German Ideology*. Here Marx and Engels highlighted the role of political institutions and specialized political actors in the social division of labour but also argued that, historically, the state has played a crucial role in securing property relations and class domination[26] as well as in maintaining the manual–mental division of labour and its role in ideological domination.[27]

In *Capital*, volume III, Marx encapsulated this concern with the form of the state as follows:

> The specific economic form, in which unpaid surplus-labour is pumped out of direct producers, determines the relationship of rulers and ruled, as it grows directly out of production itself and, in turn, reacts upon it as a determining element. Upon this, however, is founded the entire formation of the economic community which grows up out of the production relations themselves, thereby simultaneously its specific political form. It is always the direct relationship of the owners of the conditions of production to the direct producers ... which reveals the innermost secret, the hidden basis of the entire social structure and with it the political form of the relation of sovereignty and dependence, in short, the corresponding specific form of the state.[28]

This 'formal' analysis of the relation of sovereignty and dependency in the capitalist mode of production implies that the social relations of

---

[25] K. Marx, 'Preface to the First German Edition', MECW, vol. 35, p. 8.
[26] K. Marx and F. Engels, *The German Ideology*, MECW, vol. 5, pp. 32, 45–8, 89–92.
[27] Ibid, pp. 59–60.   [28] K. Marx, *Capital*, volume III, MECW, vol. 37, pp. 777–8.

production shape the social relations of domination and servitude. Note that Marx argued that the dominant political *form* corresponds to the prevailing economic *form*. This does not mean that specific state policies can be read off directly from current economic conditions. Thus, a political order based on the rule of law, equality before the law, and a unified sovereign state naturally 'fits' or 'corresponds with' an economic order based on private property, the wage relation, and profit-oriented, market-mediated exchange. This highlights the 'formal adequacy' of bourgeois democracy to a consolidated, profit-oriented, market-mediated mode of production. Only in the capitalist mode of production are classes defined through relations of production that are disembedded from broader institutional forms (such as the family or kinship, political bonds, or religion). Market forces can then dominate. Capital can then insist on its right to manage the labour process, to appropriate surplus labour and to enforce contracts with other capitals.

There is a dual relation at work here. In the *labour market*, we find 'a very Eden of the innate rights of man. There alone rule Freedom, Equality, Property and Bentham'.[29] In the *labour process*, however, we find economic exploitation and the despotism of capital. A similar duality occurs in the constitutional state based on the rule of law. Marx had indicated this in the 'Draft Plan for a Work on the Modern State', writing that '[a]ll elements exist in duplicate form, as civic elements and [those of] the state'.[30] Thus, on the one hand, the constitutional state guarantees the innate rights of men, whatever their class position, based on ending feudal and guild privileges; on the other hand, it defends the interests of capital in general when these are threatened even as it claims to maintain order in the national interest. In this sense, class conflicts may be transposed from the economic into the political sphere but, reflecting the institutional separation of the two spheres, they normally take different forms in each. This point is elaborated upon in the next section.

It took many centuries of political class struggle before the bourgeoisie, 'with the establishment of modern [large-scale] industry and of the world market, finally conquered for itself, in the modern representative State, exclusive political sway'.[31] Political alienation will only disappear when the separation between civil society and the state is abolished through the self-organization of society. Marx was unclear how this would occur until 1871, the year of the Paris Commune. He then discovered that one could not use existing forms of state (especially one as concentrated, centralized, and

---

[29] K. Marx, *Capital*, volume I, MECW, vol. 35, p. 186.
[30] Marx, 'Draft Plan for a Work on the Modern State', p. 666.
[31] Marx and Engels, *Manifesto of the Communist Party*, p. 486.

authoritarian as the Bonapartist state), which were organs of domination, for the purposes of emancipation. Thus, in the 'Second Draft of *The Civil War in France*', he wrote that the commune showed that 'the working class cannot simply lay hold of the ready-made state machinery and wield it for its own purposes. The political instrument of their enslavement cannot serve as the political instrument of their emancipation.'[32] Thus enlightened, he declared that he had at last discovered the form of the dictatorship of the proletariat – of the exceptional, transitional form of state towards a classless society and form of self-rule that would defend the interests of the 'entire community [*Gemeinwesen*]'. However, the bloody repression of the Commune after just two months ended this experiment before any firm political conclusions could be drawn.

These remarks indicate that a formal analysis is not 'merely formal' or superficial: it focuses on 'social forms' and their material effects – form makes a difference! While political society may be 'the official expression' of civil society,[33] it is a mediated, refracted expression. The fundamental – and fundamentally contradictory – separation-in-unity of the economic and political moments of class domination means that the political sphere does not directly reflect the antagonisms in civil society. Thus, as well as referring to changing economic circumstances, conflicts, contradictions, and crises, Marx considered how policies, politics, and political regimes were shaped by the motley diversity of state forms, political regimes, political discourses, the changing balance of political forces, and so on.

15.3 The State as a Social Relation

Writing in *Capital*, volume I, Marx observed that capital is not a thing but 'a social relation between persons, established by the instrumentality of things'.[34] This implies that capital accumulation depended on struggles to secure this relation as well as struggles that occur within its limits.[35] Marx might also have claimed that the state is a social relation[36] – a relation between class forces mediated through the material instrumentality of

---

[32] K. Marx, 'Second Draft of *The Civil War in France*', MECW, vol. 22, p. 533. The first sentence is repeated in *The Civil War in France* (MECW, vol. 22, p. 328) and in the 'Preface to the 1872 German Edition of the *Manifesto of the Communist Party*' (MECW, vol. 23, p. 175).

[33] 'K. Marx to P. Annenkov, 28 December 1846', MECW, 38, p. 96.

[34] Marx, *Capital*, volume I, p. 753.

[35] For a class agency reading of this, see H. Cleaver, *Reading Capital Politically* (Austin: University of Texas Press, 1979), pp. 57–80; see also Lebowitz, *Beyond Capital*, pp. 178–96.

[36] This claim was elaborated by Poulantzas. He wrote that, like capital, the state is not a thing or rational subject. Rather, it is 'a relationship of forces, or more precisely the material condensation of such a relationship among classes and class fractions [as]

juridico-political institutions and powers. This is implicit in his approach to the state. In both cases, Marx noted the tendency to fetishize social relations – whether in the form of commodity fetishism and eternalization of capital's contingent laws of motion or in the form of statolatry and the treatment of the bourgeois constitution and rule of law as permanent features of modern societies. He subjected both tendencies to scathing criticism, emphasizing the historical contingencies of the economic and political categories of capitalist social formations, their grounding in transient social relations of production, and the scope for class struggle to undermine and overturn these seemingly enduring features of contemporary society. It is always possible for class struggles and other social conflicts to overflow and escape the confines of fetishized institutional frameworks.[37]

Thus, even if the modern representative state is formally adequate, its inherently contradictory nature makes it vulnerable to destabilization or crisis if an institutionalized class compromise cannot be secured via normal political means. For, as Marx wrote in *The Class Struggles in France, 1848 to 1850*, there is a fundamental contradiction at the heart of a democratic constitution. Whereas it gives political power through universal suffrage to the proletariat, peasantry, and petty bourgeoisie, whose social slavery the constitution is to perpetuate, it sustains the social power of the bourgeoisie by guaranteeing private property rights: 'From the ones [the subordinate classes] it demands that they should not go forward from political to social emancipation; from the others that they should not go back from social to political restoration.'[38] This raises the important question of how the antagonisms and conflicts between capital, landlords, and workers (and other classes, such as peasants) are held within the political unity formed by the state. A possible answer, given these features, is that the impersonal form of domination in capitalist social formations depends on the separation of the economic and political in terms both of institutional dynamics and the modalities of class struggle. For class domination can be maintained on two conditions. First, economic class struggles must be confined within logic of the market (i.e., over wages, hours, working conditions, prices) and moderated or suspended if this threatens capital accumulation. And, second, political class struggles must be confined within the logic of a struggle for electoral

---

expressed within the State in a necessarily specific form' (*State, Power, Socialism* [London: NLB, 1978], pp. 128–9, italics removed).

[37] John Holloway critiques the fetishistic reproduction of the capital relation and state power. Open refusal to work within these fetishistic forms can break capitalist domination. See *Change the World without Taking Power* (London: Pluto, 2010), pp. 43–117.

[38] K. Marx, *The Class Struggles in France, 1848 to 1850*, MECW, vol. 10, p. 79.

majorities to influence policies legitimated to the (illusory) general or national interest of the state's citizens. However, when workers use their economic power to challenge political authority (e.g., through a general strike) and/or workers use political power to challenge market relations (e.g., through expropriation of property rights without compensation), bourgeois class domination is fundamentally threatened. This may trigger an open war of class struggle through which the dominant classes seek to suspend the democratic constitution or concentrate power in an executive that escapes democratic control. Marx discussed this in various cases but especially in relation to France.

The Eighteenth Brumaire of Louis Bonaparte is the most famous such analysis. It studied the 'specificity of political struggles' on the terrain of the modern state. There is no class that is directly and unambiguously represented as such on the political scene and Marx took great pains to decipher the 'class bases' and/or 'class relevance' of different political forces, for example, political factions, political parties, the army, paramilitary forces, political mobs, intellectuals, journalists, and so on. Marx did not regard these linkages as transparent or straightforward, but as deeply problematic and highly mediated. Different regimes had different effects on class struggle, privileging different interests and making it easier, or harder, to build economic stability, political order, and social cohesion.

Louis Bonaparte's coup occurred when the fundamental contradiction was no longer containable and decisive action was needed to block a potential majoritarian coalition of proletariat, peasants, and petty bourgeoisie. Bonaparte's coup d'état on 2 December 1851 was an opportunistic effort to seize power that was accepted because of a growing 'political' crisis (only loosely rooted in economic crisis) and widespread fears about the collapse of social order in a period when the dominated classes were politically paralyzed and/or inclined to support a strong leader. The coup led to the suspension of the democratic constitution, the temporary suspension of the universal franchise, and established the personal rule of Louis Bonaparte. It prefigured other exceptional regimes that suspended liberal bourgeois democracies in the face of a shift of the balance of class forces towards subordinate classes seeking to move from political to social emancipation or, more catastrophically, a situation that threatens 'the common ruin of the contending classes'.[39] Louis Bonaparte reintroduced the universal franchise and won a plebiscitary referendum in 1852 to become emperor. As his regime faced losing its legitimacy, Bonaparte attempted to reinforce his power by strengthening

---

[39] Marx and Engels, *Manifesto of the Communist Party*, p. 482.

the military. Yet this threatened the economic interests of the dominant classes and, within a short period, state power was once more tied to capitalist interests through the growth of state debt and the Bonapartist state performed a key role in promoting economic expansion, expropriating the peasantry, and engaging in overseas economic adventures.

A puzzle for Marx, given his materialist approach to history, was to understand whether Bonapartism was a personal dictatorship, a bureaucratic or military dictatorship, or a class dictatorship. Marx's answer in general terms was that Louis Bonaparte represented rhetorically, if not materially, the largest social class in France at the time: smallholding conservative peasantry. He represented them in terms of a demagogic poetry of the past – *idées napoléoniennes*, illusions, the revival of Napoleon's glories – and cheap material concessions, such as providing jobs for their children in the state apparatus, especially the army. But he did not defend them against further parcellization of their land-holdings, mortgage debt, tax burdens, or the speculative depredations of the modern financial aristocracy.[40] Thus, while his dictatorship was not suspended in mid-air, it was relatively unconstrained by the smallholding conservative peasantry which, because of their rural isolation, familial relations of production, and dependence on usurious capital and local political figures, form a class 'much as potatoes in a sack form a sack of potatoes' and therefore need to be represented by others rather than doing this themselves.[41] Another supporting class was the *Lumpenproletariat*, declassed elements, that are inherently disorganised, tend to side opportunistically with one camp or another, and hence prove unreliable allies. In the same text, he argued that the proletariat must abandon 'the tradition of all the dead generations', 'superstition about the past', and 'an entire superstructure of different and distinctly formed sentiments, illusions, modes of thought and views of life'.[42] It had to abandon the 'poetry of the past' and find new words to express its class interests and mobilize other forces for a new social revolution.[43]

Marx also analyzed or commented in greater or lesser detail on many aspects of economic and social policy. He described how the Spanish, Portuguese, Dutch, French, and English states intervened forcefully and forcibly to promote and shorten the transition from the feudal to the capitalist mode of production. He noted how, by the end of the seventeenth century, 'England had perfected this approach to primitive accumulation through a systematical combination, embracing the colonies, the national debt, the modern mode of taxation, and the

---

[40] See Marx's comments in *The Eighteenth Brumaire* and *Civil War in France*.
[41] Marx, *The Eighteenth Brumaire*, p. 187.   [42] Ibid, pp. 103, 106, 128.   [43] Ibid, p. 106.

protectionist system'.[44] These comments also indicate how Marx's analysis of the state was related to the development of the world market. Marx and Engels wrote that '[t]he relations of different nations among themselves depend on the extent to which each has developed its productive forces, the division of labour and internal commerce'.[45] Thus, the international order is not the mechanical sum of different nations, but typically has an informal hierarchy, with a leading state dominated by a particular (national) class. Writing in 1849, for example, Marx claimed that 'the world market is dominated by England and England is dominated by the bourgeoisie'.[46] This could also be linked to the relations among great, middle, and small powers in the world order and the role of world money.[47]

Another example of his remarks on economic policy concern taxes. These 'are the existence of the state expressed in economic terms'.[48] While this is a general proposition, capitalist states have refined taxes as a specific instrument of bourgeois rule. In brief, the constitutional state, which accompanied capitalist development, transformed taxes: (1) from payments linked to precisely circumscribed tasks into general contributions to government revenue that could be applied freely to any legitimate task; (2) from extraordinary, irregular, and overwhelmingly short-term imposts into regular and permanently levied taxes; and (3) from payments that the monarch had to secure through negotiation to payments that effectively became compulsory.[49] The state's monopoly of taxation is backed by its constitutionalized monopoly of organized coercion. For the modern state, 'purchased gradually by the owners of property by means of taxation, has fallen entirely into their hands through the national debt, and its existence has become wholly dependent on the commercial credit which the owners of property, the bourgeois, extend to it, as reflected in the rise and fall of government securities on the stock exchange'.[50] Unsurprisingly, then, taxes, fiat money, state credit, and public debt would have been important themes in the missing book on

---

[44] Marx, *Capital*, volume I, p. 739. [45] Marx and Engels, *The German Ideology*, p. 32.
[46] K. Marx, 'The Revolutionary Movement', MECW, vol. 8, p. 215.
[47] On different aspects of Marx's work on these issues, see K. B. Anderson, *Marx at the Margins: On Nationalism, Ethnicity, and Non-Western Nations* (Chicago: University of Chicago Press, 2010); Draper and Haberkern, *Karl Marx's Theory of Revolution*; M. Krätke, *Die Kritik der Staatsfinanzen: Zur politischen Ökonomie des Steuerstaats* (Hamburg: VSA Verlag, 1987); M. Molnár, *Marx, Engels et la politique internationale* (Paris: Gallimard, 1975).
[48] K. Marx, 'Moralising Criticism and Critical Morality', MECW, vol. 6, p. 328.
[49] Cf. W. Gerloff, *Die Öffentliche Finanzwissenschaft, Vol. 1 – Allgemeiner Teil* (Frankfurt: Klostermann, 1948), pp. 152–4.
[50] Marx and Engels, *The German Ideology*, p. 90.

the state – along with the 'unproductive' classes employed by the state or financed through taxes and debt.[51]

In another context, Marx famously analyzed both the repeal of the Corn Laws and the development of factory legislation. The latter analysis strongly influenced subsequent Marxist state theory. It concerned legislation on the length of the working day and the employment of women and children as instances of the need for state intervention in the organization of labour markets and working conditions in the interests of capital itself as well as working-class families. Competition between capitals (in a period when absolute rather than relative surplus-value was the dominant axis of competition) prevented any individual capitalist from being the first to cut hours, reduce female and child labour, and improve working conditions. Yet, cut-throat competition produced growing infant and adult mortality, demographic decline, and declining productivity – all of this reported by factory inspectors and other state officials.[52] Thus, trade unions, 'bourgeois socialists',[53] philanthropists, and progressive capitalists (who could make profits through relative surplus-value) allied to press the state to pass legislation against the will of many individual capitalists – legislation that was nonetheless beneficial to the most productive capitals and eventually boosted English manufacturing competitiveness. This illustrated what Engels would later call the role of the state as the 'ideal total capitalist'.[54]

15.4 Marx and State Theory Today

Marx's work on the state is consistent with his general materialist approach to the interpretation of history, reflecting the claim of Marx and Engels that 'we know only a single science, the science of history'.[55] Marx's methods of research and presentation in this regard generally follow those of his critique of political economy. He regularly studied history and relevant theoretical literature, making excerpts and comments, regularly updating these. In presenting his results, he sometimes advanced general trans-historical, class-theoretical claims about the state's *function* in securing class domination, regardless of the prevailing forms of economic exploitation. But his more focused work on the modern state addressed its *form*. He asked whether and, if so, how this might

---

[51] Marx, 'Introduction', p. 45. Other topics proposed for the book were population, emigration, and colonies (ibid).
[52] See Marx, *Capital*, volume I, pp. 283–307, 483–505.
[53] See Marx and Engels, *Manifesto of the Communist Party*, pp. 513–14.
[54] F. Engels, *Socialism: Utopian and Scientific*, MECW, vol. 24, p. 319, describes the state as 'the ideal personification of the total national capital'. The French (1880) and German (1891) editions have the 'ideal total capitalist' (p. 319n).
[55] Marx and Engels, *The German Ideology*, p. 28.

be understood as adequate to social formations in which the capitalist mode of production prevails. Deriving the necessary form and/or functions of the capitalist type of state from the commodity form and the capital relation became a major theoretical growth industry in the 1970s–80s in Northern Europe.[56] But Marx himself was more interested in how the distinctive features of the modern state emerged historically, how the modern state and interstate relations are shaped by changes in the world market, how they influenced the forms and stakes of political conflict, and how came to be reproduced in and through social discourses and practices.

His answers emphasized how the institutional separation of the economic and political in capitalist social formations creates considerable scope for disjunctions between the forms of economic, juridico-political, and ideological struggle. In *The Eighteenth Brumaire*, for example, Marx studied not only the specificities of political contestation and struggle, but also the semantics and pragmatics of political language. This can be read as a 'contribution to the critique of semiotic political economy' but Marx combined this, of course, with analyses of the 'social content of politics' acted out on the political stage. More generally, Marx developed a rich vocabulary for analyzing political class relations, for example, class in charge of state, supporting classes, literary representatives, political parties, the class relevance of political discourses, and so on. This conceptual lexicon is politically specific and not reducible to issues of economic class relations. The economic 'base', broadly construed, remained the ultimate source of the *social* or *material* conditioning of political struggles. But social transformation is necessarily mediated through political imaginaries and political practice. This explains why the proletariat must develop its own, novel political language to express its aspirations for a new form of political as well as economic organization.

This issue was central to the work of Antonio Gramsci, especially in his *Prison Notebooks*. Gramsci drew on the published work of Marx, Engels, and Lenin, the histories of the French and Bolshevik Revolutions, and his experience of fascism in Italy and the wider economic, political, and societal crises affecting interwar Europe and the United States. In a comment that could provide a good summary of Marx's own analyses of the modern state, Gramsci suggested that the state is 'the entire complex of practical and theoretical activities with which the ruling class not

---

[56] The best example is the German 'state derivation debate'. For some key contributions, see J. Holloway and S. Picciotto (eds), *State and Capital: A Marxist Debate* (London: Edward Arnold, 1978). For an extended critique, see Jessop, *Capitalist State*, pp. 78–141.

only justifies and maintains its domination, but manages to win the active consent of those over whom it rules'.[57] Above all, he emphasized that, with the entry of the popular masses into politics during the 1870s, politics became focused on a struggle for national-popular hegemony, to make the interests of the ruling class into the illusory general interest of society.[58] Where hegemonic struggles could not secure the institutionalized class compromise necessary to reconcile the 'fundamental contradiction' in the democratic constitution, the dominant classes would seek to secure their power through force, fraud, corruption, police-military action, or an open war of class struggle against the subordinate classes.[59] These comments elaborate and update Marx's insights and analyses for the early twentieth century. They must be further revised in the light of developments after Gramsci's death in 1937, especially the further integration of the world market, the development of new forms of communication, and the expanded scope for surveillance of everyday life.

This said, while Marx's more theoretical analyses focused on the formally adequate type of capitalist state (the constitutional representative state), his more descriptive and historical analyses fully recognized that not all states – even in consolidated capitalist social formations – conformed to this configuration. In short, not all states in capitalist societies were capitalist types of state. This would have had implications in turn for the missing books on international trade and the world market and crisis. The world market was both the presupposition and the posit (result) of capital accumulation. It would be the final book because it is where 'production is posited as a totality and all its moments also, but in which simultaneously all contradictions are set in motion'.[60] Further, through their 'motley diversity of form', historically specific types of state would transform and modify the more general 'laws of motion' of individual capitals and the total social capital.

Debates over the state and state power are not purely academic matters. Errors in theoretical analysis have practical consequences. For, as Marx himself argued in his 1875 *Critique of the Gotha Programme*, errors of analysis concerning the 'present state' are linked to errors in political practice.[61]

---

[57] Gramsci, *Selections*, p. 244.
[58] The Feuerbach chapter in *The German Ideology*, relevant for an analysis of hegemony, was published in Russian 1924 and German in 1926. Gramsci was probably unaware of it. But he did discuss *The Eighteenth Brumaire* (e.g., *Selections*, pp. 166, 190, 211, 219–22, 264, 407).
[59] Gramsci, *Selections*, pp. 80–2, 95, 105–20, 230–2.
[60] Marx, 'Outlines of the Critique of Political Economy [*Grundrisse*]. First Instalment', p. 160.
[61] K. Marx, *Critique of the Gotha Programme*, MECW, vol. 24, pp. 94–6.

Such problems were even more disastrous in the misreading of the political conjuncture in the rise of Italian fascism and German Nazism.[62] It follows that no one can afford to ignore the specificity of the state apparatus and state power in the pursuit of objectives that are politically mediated and/or conditioned. This is where work to build on Marx's critiques of capital and the state as social relations and their significance in specific conjunctures demands much additional serious work.

References

Althusser, Louis (2014), *On the Reproduction of Capitalism: Ideology and Ideological State Apparatuses*, London: Verso.

Anderson, Kevin B. (2010), *Marx at the Margins: On Nationalism, Ethnicity, and Non-Western Nations*, Chicago: University of Chicago Press.

Barrow, Clyde W. (2000), 'The Marx Problem in Marxian State Theory', *Science & Society* 64 (1): 87–118.

Cleaver, Harry (1979), *Reading Capital Politically*, Austin: University of Texas Press.

Draper, Hal (1977), *Karl Marx's Theory of Revolution: State and Bureaucracy, Part I, in 2 vols*, New York: Monthly Review Press.

Draper, Hal, and Haberkern, Ernest (2005), *Karl Marx's Theory of Revolution, Vol. V: War and Revolution*, New York: Monthly Review Press.

Engels, Friedrich (1989), *Socialism: Utopian and Scientific*, MECW, vol. 24, pp. 281–325.

(2004), *Letters, 1892–95*, MECW, vol. 50.

Gerloff, Wilhelm (1948), *Die Öffentliche Finanzwissenschaft, Vol. 1 – Allgemeiner Teil*, Frankfurt: V. Klostermann.

Gramsci, Antonio (1971), *Selections from the Prison Notebooks*, London: Lawrence & Wishart.

Heinrich, Michael (2016), '"Capital" after MEGA: Discontinuities, Interruptions and New Beginnings', *Crisis & Critique* 3 (3): 93–138.

Holloway, John (2010), *Change the World without Taking Power*, third edition, London: Pluto.

Holloway, John, and Picciotto, Sol (eds) (1978), *State and Capital: A Marxist Debate*, London: Edward Arnold.

Hunt, Richard N. (1974), *The Political Ideas of Marx and Engels*, vol. 1, London: Macmillan.

Jessop, Bob (1982), *The Capitalist State: Marxist Theories and Methods*, Oxford: Martin Robertson.

(2007), *State Power: A Strategic-Relational Approach*, Cambridge: Polity.

Krätke, Michael R. (1987), *Die Kritik der Staatsfinanzen: Zur politischen Ökonomie des Steuerstaats*, Hamburg: VSA Verlag.

---

[62] On which, see N. Poulantzas, *Fascism and Dictatorship* (London: NLB, 1974), pp. 36–67.

Lebowitz, Michael A. (2003), *Beyond Capital: Marx's Political Economy of the Working Class*, second edition, Basingstoke: Palgrave-Macmillan.
Lenin, Vladimir Illich (1964), 'The State and Revolution', in: *Lenin: Collected Works*, vol. 25, Moscow: Progress Publishers, pp. 381–492.
Maguire, John (1978), *Marx's Theory of Politics*, Cambridge: Cambridge University Press.
Marx, Karl (1975), 'Contribution to the Critique of Hegel's Philosophy of Right', MECW, vol. 3, pp. 3–129.
—— (1975), *Contribution to the Critique of Hegel's* Philosophy of Right, Introduction. MECW, vol. 3, pp. 175–87.
—— (1975), 'Draft Plan for a Work on the Modern State', MECW, vol. 4, p. 666.
—— (1976), 'Moralising Criticism and Critical Morality. Contribution to German Cultural History. Contra Karl Heinzen', MECW, vol. 6, pp. 312–40.
—— (1977), 'The Revolutionary Movement', MECW, vol. 8, pp. 213–16.
—— (1978), *The Class Struggles in France, 1848 to 1850*, MECW, vol. 6, pp. 45–145.
—— (1979), *The Eighteenth Brumaire of Louis Bonaparte*, MECW, vol. 11, pp. 99–209.
—— (1981), 'Kreuznacher Hefte 1–5', MEGA^2, vol. IV/2, pp. 9–278.
—— (1986), 'The Rule of the Pretorians', MECW, vol. 15, pp. 464–67.
—— (1986), *The Civil War in France. Address of the General Council of the International Working Men's Association*, MECW, vol. 22, pp. 307–59.
—— (1986), 'Drafts of The Civil War in France', MECW, vol. 22, pp. 435–551.
—— (1986), 'Outlines of the Critique of Political Economy [*Grundrisse*]. First Instalment', MECW, vol. 28.
—— (1987), 'A Contribution to the Critique of Political Economy. Part One', MECW, vol. 29, pp. 257–417.
—— (1989), *Critique of the Gotha Programme*, MECW, vol. 24, pp. 75–99.
—— (1996), 'Preface to the First German Edition', MECW, vol. 35, pp. 7–11.
—— (1996), *Capital*, volume I, MECW, vol. 35.
—— (1998), *Capital*, volume III, MECW, vol. 37.
Marx, Karl, and Engels, Friedrich (1975), *The German Ideology*, MECW, vol. 5, pp. 21–93.
—— (1976), *Manifesto of the Communist Party*, MECW, vol. 6, pp. 477–519.
—— (1982), *Letters, 1844–1851*, MECW, vol. 38.
—— (1988), 'Preface to the 1872 German Edition of the *Manifesto of the Communist Party*', MECW, vol. 23, pp. 174–75.
Miliband, Ralph (1965), 'Marx and the State', in: *Socialist Register*, London: Merlin Press, pp. 278–96.
Molnár, Miklós (1975), *Marx, Engels et la politique internationale*, Paris: Gallimard.
Moore, Stanley W. (1957), *The Critique of Capitalist Democracy: An Introduction to the Theory of the State in Marx, Engels and Lenin*, New York: Paine-Whitman.
Pashukanis, Evgeny B. (1978), *Law and Marxism: A General Theory*, London: Ink Links.

Poulantzas, Nicos (1973), *Political Power and Social Classes*, London: NLB.
  (1974), *Fascism and Dictatorship: The Third International and the Problem of Fascism*, London: NLB.
  (1978), *State, Power, Socialism*, London: NLB.
Thomas, Paul (1994), *Alien Politics: Marxist State Theory Retrieved*, London: Routledge.

16   Globalization

Seongjin Jeong

16.1   Globalization in Marx's Words

Despite its retreat after the economic crisis of 2008, there is no denying that globalization continues to be one of the central tendencies of capitalism's law of motion. Indeed, exactly 150 years ago, Marx recognized the phenomenon now understood as globalization as the 'world market [*Weltmarkt*]', although he did not use the former term, because it was coined about a century after his death. However, what Marx meant by 'intercourse with foreign nations … the expeditions of adventurers, colonization … the extension of markets into a world market … a new phase of historical development'[1] in *The German Ideology*, co-authored with Friedrick Engels (1820–1895), was nothing else than today's globalization. They rephrased the same thing in *Manifesto of the Communist Party*:

The need of a constantly expanding market for its products chases the bourgeoisie over the whole surface of the globe. It must nestle everywhere, settle everywhere, establish connections everywhere. The bourgeoisie has through its exploitation of the world market given a cosmopolitan character to production and consumption in every country.[2]

The world market was one of the most frequently used terms of the young Marx, besides humanism or alienation. Indeed, Marx was an authentic globalist throughout his life. However, it is sometimes asserted that the mature Marx took a state-centred or 'one-nation model', while distancing himself from his earlier globalist approach.[3] The following footnote in *Capital*, volume I, seems to support such an assertion:

This chapter was supported by the Ministry of Education of the Republic of Korea and the National Research Foundation of Korea (NRF-2018S1A3A2075204). The author is thankful to Marcello Musto and Greg Sharzer for their comments and editorial suggestions.
[1] K. Marx and F. Engels, *The German Ideology*, MECW, vol. 5, pp. 67, 69.
[2] K. Marx and F. Engels, *Manifesto of the Communist Party*, MECW, vol. 6, pp. 487–8.
[3] Unoists used to regard Marx's *Capital* as a 'theory of a purely capitalist society', abstracting from the state as well as foreign trade and world market. See T. Sekine, 'An Essay on

> In order to examine the object of our investigation in its integrity, free from all disturbing subsidiary circumstances, we must treat the whole world of trade as one-nation, and assume that capitalist production is established everywhere and has taken possession of every branch of industry.[4]

However, a text-based reading of Marx's key writings attempted in this chapter shows that he sustained and developed the globalist perspective of his early days, epitomized in the thesis of 'world market-world market crisis-world revolution' throughout his lifetime.

With the acceleration of globalization since the late twentieth century, Marx's thought on the world market has become more relevant today than during his time. Even some mainstream publications like *The Economist* appreciate him anticipating today's globalization.[5] In contrast, most Marxist theories of world economy after Marx rejected his thought and replaced it with various sorts of stageist or statist theories, such as the Stalinist thesis of state monopoly capitalism.[6] The price was high. After the 1990s, the latter were incapable of explaining the 'new' phenomenon of globalization and became totally disarmed. Reappropriating Marx's original thought on the world market is essential for the revival of a left alternative to global capitalism.

16.2 The Dialectics of Progress

Like earlier thinkers of the Enlightenment, Marx welcomed the world market as a form of great historical progress. In *The German Ideology*, Marx and Engels wrote as follows:

> large-scale industry ... established means of communication and the modern world market ... It produced world history for the first time, insofar as it made all civilized nations and every individual member of them dependent for the satisfaction of their wants on the whole world, thus destroying the former natural exclusiveness of separate nations.[7]

In *Manifesto of the Communist Party*, Marx and Engels admitted the progressive nature of the bourgeoisie in their creation and extension of the world market:

Uno's Dialectic of *Capital*', in K. Uno (ed.), *Principles of Political Economy: Theory of a Purely Capitalist Society* (Sussex: Harvester Press, 1980), p. 153.

[4] K. Marx, *Capital*, volume I (London: Penguin, 1976), p. 727.
[5] Cf. *The Economist*, 'Reconsidering Marx: Second Time, Farce', 427 (9090): 79–80 (2018).
[6] Cf. A. Kozlov (ed.), *Political Economy: Capitalism* (Moscow: Progress Publishers, 1977), pp. 395–420.
[7] Marx and Engels, *The German Ideology*, p. 73.

The bourgeoisie, by the rapid improvement of all instruments of production, by the immensely facilitated means of communication, draws all, even the most barbarian, nations into civilization ... National differences and antagonisms between peoples are daily more and more vanishing, owing to the development of the bourgeoisie, to freedom of commerce, to the world market, to uniformity in the mode of production and in the conditions of life corresponding thereto.[8]

Marx was especially impressed by the economic and cultural unification brought about by the extension of the world market. In the *Grundrisse*, he emphasized the 'propagandistic (civilizing) tendency' of the world market: 'The tendency to create the *world market* is inherent directly in the concept of capital itself.... *Hence the great civilizing influence*... unique to capital.'[9] He also argued that capital created the real basis for a higher social formation, whose basic principle is the universal development of individuals without personal or material dependencies. Up to the end of the 1850s, Marx not only believed in the thoroughness with which the extension of the world market would destroy non-capitalist societies, but also its beneficial consequences for the people living in them.

Marx's emphasis on 'the great civilizing influence' of the world market seems to anticipate current discourses on cultural globalization. Fascinated by the Great Exhibition in London in 1851, he seemed to believe that the cultures of the world would be homogenized and the 'barbarians' would be 'civilized' by the globalization of European culture. However, unlike contemporary Eurocentrists, he was cynical of Europe's 'bourgeois megalomania', while marvelling at its 'cosmopolitan-philanthropic-commercial hymns of peace'.[10] He criticized that the fact that the exhibition was used by the bourgeoisie of the industrialized nations to encourage and celebrate their exploitation and domination of weaker global communities.[11] Marx recognized the imperialist essence of globalization as well as the seeds of its dialectical *aufhebung* in the exhibition:

This exhibition is a striking demonstration of the concentrated power with which modern large-scale industry is breaking down national barriers everywhere and increasingly blurring ... the character of each individual nation ... The bourgeoisie is celebrating this, its greatest festival, at a moment when the collapse of all its glory is at hand, a collapse which will demonstrate more conclusively than ever to it that the powers it has brought into being have grown beyond its control.[12]

[8] Marx and Engels, *Manifesto of the Communist Party*, pp. 488, 503.
[9] K. Marx, 'Outlines of the Critique of Political Economy [*Grundrisse*]. First Instalment', MECW, vol. 28, pp. 335–6, 466.
[10] 'K. Marx to F. Engels, 24 January 1852', MECW, vol. 39, p. 21.
[11] For more discussion of Marx on the Great Exhibition, cf P. Young, *Globalization and the Great Exhibition: The Victorian New World Order* (New York: Palgrave, 2009), pp. 89–93.
[12] K. Marx and F. Engels, 'Review', MECW, vol. 10, p. 500.

Marx recognized the insights of Adam Smith (1723–1790) and David Ricardo (1772–1823) into the world market when he said that they 'know more about the future than about the present'.[13] Exactly the same words can be applied to Marx himself. However, unlike his contemporaries, and earlier thinkers of Enlightenment who one-sidedly applauded the advance of the world market, Marx recognized its dialectics from the beginning. He was never a prisoner of the progressiveness of the world market. In 'Speech on the Question of Free Trade', he emphasized its contradictions while admitting its progressive effects:

> To call cosmopolitan exploitation universal brotherhood is an idea that could only be engendered in the brain of the bourgeoisie ... It [the Free Trade system] breaks up old nationalities and carries antagonism of proletariat and bourgeoisie to the uttermost point. In a word, the Free Trade system hastens the Social Revolution. In this revolutionary sense alone, gentlemen, I am in favor of Free Trade.[14]

In this speech, Marx described the destruction of the old regimes by the extension of the free-trade system as 'revolutionary'. However, he admitted the positive or 'revolutionary' potential of the world market to the extent that it hastened its own supersession through 'Social Revolution'. It is only in this context that he supported free trade against protectionism. In the article 'The British Rule in India', he regarded free trade as a progressive 'unconscious tool of history' that brought social revolution.[15] In another article, 'The Future Results of British Rule in India', Marx wrote that English free trade played a 'double mission' in contemporary India: 'one destructive, the other regenerating – the annihilation of old Asiatic society, and the laying of the material foundations of Western society in Asia'.[16] In his letter to Engels, Marx described the destruction of Indian industry by English industry as 'revolutionary'.[17]

However, after the publication of *Capital*, volume I, Marx seldom talked about the 'double mission', or revolutionary potential of the world market. Instead, he severely criticized the consequences of the extension of the world market into non-capitalist areas. In his 'Third Draft of the Letter to Vera Zasulich', he described them as 'vandalism': 'As for the East Indies, for example, everyone except Sir Henry Maine and others of his ilk realizes that the suppression of communal landownership out there was nothing but an act of English *vandalism*, pushing the native people not forwards but backwards.'[18]

---

[13] K. Marx, 'Speech of Dr. Marx', MECW, vol. 6, p. 289.
[14] K. Marx, 'Speech', MECW, vol. 6, pp. 464–5.
[15] K. Marx, 'British Rule', MECW, vol. 12, p. 132.
[16] K. Marx, 'Future Results', MECW, vol. 12, p. 218.
[17] 'K. Marx to F. Engels, 14 June 1853', MECW, vol. 39, p. 346.
[18] K. Marx, 'Third Draft', MECW, vol. 24, p. 365.

16.3 The World Market and Critique of Political Economy

During the 1840s, Marx used to think about the world market in terms of philosophy. However, based on a ten-year intensive study of classical political economy during the 1850s, Marx came to conceptualize the world market within his specific paradigm: the 'critique of political economy'. Marx adopted the concept of the world market from classical political economy and Enlightenment thinkers. For them, the world market was already a noble but familiar phenomenon. Indeed, in their works they mentioned increased trade and capital flows, frequent crossing of borders, and navigational and communications technologies that drew the world closer together. For example, Smith's account of global commerce in *Wealth of Nations* could be read very much like a theory of globalization. However, contrary to neo-liberal myth, Smith was keen to highlight the gross imbalances of power, destructive economic inefficiencies, and horrific cruelties of global commerce.[19] Compared with Smith, Ricardo was closer to a twenty-first century globaloney. Indeed, he one-sidedly emphasized the positive aspects of foreign trade and tried to justify it with the thesis of competitive advantage. After critically appropriating classical political economics, Marx could compose his six-book plan of critique of political economy, in which the last or culminating book was reserved for the topic of the world market. In the *Grundrisse*, he wrote:

The arrangement has evidently to be made as follows ... Capital, wage labor, landed property ... (3) Concentration of bourgeois society in the form of the state. Viewed in relation to itself ... (4) The international relation of production. International division of labor. International exchange. Export and import. Rate of Exchange. (5) The world market and crises ... the world market the conclusion ... but in which simultaneously all contradictions are set in motion. Hence the world market is likewise both the presupposition of the totality and its bearer. Crises are then the general pointer to beyond the presupposition, and the urge to adopt a new historic form ... Finally the world market. Encroachment of bourgeois society on the State. Crises. Dissolution of the mode of production and form of society based on exchange value.[20]

In *A Contribution to the Critique of Political Economy*, he repeated his plan: 'I examine the system of bourgeois economy in the following order: capital, landed property, wage labour; the State, foreign trade, world market.'[21] For Marx, the world market is not equivalent to a foreign one, because the 'World

---

[19] For more discussion of Smith's view on globalization, cf. S. Muthu, 'Adam Smith's Critique of International Trading Companies: Theorizing "Globalization" in the Age of Enlightenment', *Political Theory*, 36: 185–212 (2008).
[20] Marx, 'Outlines of the Critique of Political Economy [*Grundrisse*]. First Instalment', p. 45, 160, 195.
[21] K. Marx, *A Contribution to the Critique of Political Economy*, MECW, vol. 29, p. 261.

market... is not only the domestic market in relation to all the *foreign markets* existing outside it, but at the same time the domestic market of all *foreign markets* as, in turn, components of the *home market*.'[22] Marx conceived the world market as a separate and higher-level totality, subsuming national economies within it, rather than as an aggregate of distinct national economies, bound together by external relations of trade and investment. In *Capital*, volume I, Marx wrote: 'It is otherwise on the world market, whose integral parts are the individual countries ... the entanglement of all people in the net of the world market, and with this, the growth of the international character of the capitalist regime.'[23] Conceiving capitalism as a single global system was central to Marx's thought. He assumed that the logic of capital operated on a world scale since its inception. For him, the world market is the result as well as the living atmosphere of capitalism. In other words, the world market is not only 'the basis of the capitalist production in its infancy', but also 'the specific product of the capitalist mode of production'. In short, the world market is 'the very basis and living atmosphere of the capitalist mode of production'.[24] Marx wrote that 'the establishment of the world market' is one of the 'three cardinal facts about capitalist production'.[25]

16.4 The World Market and the State

Although a global perspective is paramount in Marx's thoughts from the start, he never conceived of the world market abstracted from the nation-state. In this respect, Marx's approach is critically different from some of the recent discourses on globalization, like Michael Hardt (1960–) and Antonio Negri (1933–)'s *Empire*.[26] The state is always crucial for Marx.[27] For example, even in the *Manifesto of the Communist Party*, which is regarded as the representative globalist text of Marx and Engels, they emphasized very much the role of the state in the formation of the world market and the significance of the 'national struggle' against global capitalism: 'the struggle of the proletariat with the bourgeoisie is at first a national struggle. The proletariat of each country must, of course, first of all settle matters with its

---

[22] Marx, 'Outlines of the Critique of Political Economy [*Grundrisse*]. First Instalment', p. 210.
[23] Marx, *Capital*, volume I, pp. 702, 929.
[24] K. Marx, *Capital*, volume III (London: Penguin, 1981), pp. 344, 205.
[25] Marx, *Capital*, volume III, p. 375.
[26] M. Hardt and A. Negri, *Empire* (Cambridge, MA: Harvard University Press, 2000), pp. 333, 336, 349.
[27] Cf W. Bonefeld, 'The Spectre of Globalization: On the Form and Content of the World Market', in: W. Bonefeld and K. Psychopedi (eds), *The Politics of Change: Globalization, Ideology and Critique* (Basingstoke: Palgrave, 2000), pp. 31–68; R. Desai, 'Marx and Engels' Geopolitical Economy', in: A. Kumar and B. A. Chatterjee (eds), *Marxism: With and Beyond Marx* (New York: Routledge, 2014), pp. 71–91.

own bourgeoisie ... centralize all instruments of production in the hands of the State.'[28] Imagining the emergence of the world market as a by-product of a self-regulating free market was alien to Marx. Instead, Marx conceived the world market as the arena of zero-sum struggle between nations, rather than as a positive-sum game or a homogenous conflict-free world, as was often argued by contemporary free-traders. He never accepted the Ricardian cosmopolitan view of the world market: '[i]f the Free-traders cannot understand how one nation can grow rich at the expense of another, we need not wonder, these same gentlemen also refuse to understand how within one country one class can enrich itself at the expense of another'.[29]

According to Marx's critique of political economy, the topics of foreign trade and the world market are to be presented after the state as 'a synthesis of many determinations', or a 'rich totality of many definitions and relations' by 'advancing from the abstract to the concrete'.[30] Among the 'many determinations' or 'relations', the state is crucial, for it mediates the former three more abstract categories of capital, landed property, and wage labour using the latter two more concrete categories of foreign trade and the world market. He viewed the nation-state and the interstate system as essential conditions for the existence of the world market. The formation and extension of the world market are inconceivable without extra-economic preconditions and events such as law, ideologies, war and diplomacy, and so on.[31] The nation-state played the key role in securing the conditions for the primitive accumulation of capital through the conquest and plunder of colonies, the development of foreign trade, the creation of world money and the global division of labour, and so on. In *Critique of the Gotha Programme*, Marx noted that 'the framework of the present-day national state ... is politically within the framework of the system of states', which took 'motley diversity of form', while emphasizing that it 'is itself in its turn economically within the framework of the world market'.[32] Unlike some of the recent discourses on globalization which project a flat global village,[33] the contradictory coexistence of the one world market with conflictual 'many-states' is central to Marx's conception of global capitalism.[34]

---

[28] Marx and Engels, *Manifesto of the Communist Party*, pp. 495, 504.
[29] Marx, 'Speech', pp. 464–5.
[30] Marx, 'Outlines of the Critique of Political Economy [*Grundrisse*]. First Instalment', pp. 37–8.
[31] B. Jessop, 'World Market, World State, World Society: Marxian Insights and Scientific Realist Interrogations', in: J. Joseph and C. Wight (eds), *Scientific Realism and International Relations* (New York: Palgrave, 2010), p. 191.
[32] K. Marx, *Critique of the Gotha Programme*, MECW, vol. 24, pp. 90, 95.
[33] T. Friedman, *The World Is Flat: A Brief History of the Twenty-first Century* (New York: Farrar, Straus and Giroux, 2005).
[34] Cf A. Callinicos, *Imperialism and Global Political Economy* (Cambridge: Polity, 2009), pp. 73–92.

16.5 Uneven and Combined Development on a World Scale

Marx's critical appropriation of classical political economy in the 1850s was reflected in his view of the world market. Above all, he reconceptualized the world market as the arena of uneven and combined development – a concept later coined by Leon Trotsky[35] – rather than a flat world composed of the universal civilizing movement of capital. Witnessing the effects of British capital on Ireland was critical in changing his views on the world market. In 'Outline of a Report on the Irish Question Delivered to the German Workers' Educational Society' (1867), he emphasized that 'the [oppression] since 1846, though less barbarian in form, has been in effect destructive, leaving no alternative but Ireland's voluntary emancipation by England or life-and-death struggle'. He based this conclusion on the observation that 'Every time Ireland was about to develop industrially, she was *crushed* and reconverted into a purely *agricultural land*.'[36] Previously, he regarded the destruction of the native industry of India by British capital as 'revolutionary'. But now he saw the destruction of Ireland's native industry by the same British capital as reactionary. He explicitly disavowed his original premise of capitalist globalization's 'double mission'. Previously, he imagined that British free trade would destroy the framework of the old society, like India, and generate the development that would lay the basis for a new society. But now he broke with this view and recognized that the destruction of an old society would not necessarily give rise to the material conditions for a new one. Instead, he thought that the forcible integration of an old society into global capitalism would result in a complete dependency and degeneracy. Indeed, the reality of capitalist globalization's 'double mission' was the destruction of the old society and the suppression of the essential conditions for the new one's regeneration.[37]

Based on this new understanding, Marx conceived the world market movement of capital as the process of uneven and combined development on a global scale, rather than a simple geographical extension of European capitalism. In *Capital*, volume I, he formulated the 'general law of capitalist accumulation' on a world scale, characterized by the articulation of different modes of exploitation:

> By ruining handicraft production of finished articles in other countries, machinery forcibly converts them into fields for the production of its raw material. Thus India was compelled to produce cotton, wool, hemp, jute and indigo for Great Britain ... A new and international division of labor springs up, one suited to the

---

[35] L. Trotsky, *The History of the Russian Revolution* (London: Pluto Press, 1977), p. 27.

[36] K. Marx, 'Outline of a Report on the Irish Question Delivered to the German Workers' Educational Society in London on December 16, 1867', MECW, vol. 21, pp. 194, 200.

[37] Cf. K. Mohri, 'Marx and "Underdevelopment"', *Monthly Review*, 30: pp. 32–42 (1979).

requirements of the main industrial countries, and it converts one part of the globe into a chiefly agricultural field of production for supplying the other part, which remains pre-eminently industrial field ... In fact the veiled slavery of the wage-laborers in Europe needed the unqualified slavery of the New World as its pedestal.[38]

Marx conceived contemporary global capitalism as a hierarchically structured international division of labour, in which some regions were subordinated to others. He confirmed that accumulation constantly generated a hierarchy of forms of labour exploitation within the highly integrated British colonial system.[39] In *Capital*, volume II, Marx described the contemporary world market underpinned by uneven and combined development:

Within its circulation process, in which industrial capital ... cuts across the commodity circulation of the most varied modes of social production ... Whether the commodities are the product of production based on slavery, the product of peasants (Chinese, Indian riots), of a community (Dutch East Indies), of state production (such as existed in earlier epochs of Russian history, based on serfdom) or of half-savage hunting peoples, etc. ... they function on the market as commodities ... Thus the circulation process of industrial capital is characterized by the many-sided character of its origins, and the existence of the market as a world market.[40]

Marx's description seems to prefigure today's global value chains, organized by global companies like Apple. Indeed, Marx expected that the extension of the world market would result in 'varieties of capitalism each with their own logics that coexist in a heterogeneous global economy',[41] which is far from a global homogenization. This does not mean that Marx came to support the methodological nationalism. On the contrary, Marx tried to explain the uneven and combined development of global capitalism by applying his labour theory of value on a world scale.

16.6 International Value and Exploitation

What distinguished late Marx from early Marx, as well as from other contemporary thinkers, is that he not only conceived of the world market dialectically, but also theorized it through the rigorous application of value categories. Based on more than ten years of intensive study of classical political economy, he succeeded in constructing his own labour

---

[38] Marx, *Capital*, volume I, pp. 579–80, 925.
[39] For further discussion, refer to L. Pradella, 'Marx and the Global South: Connecting History and Value Theory', *Sociology*, 51: 146–61 (2017).
[40] K. Marx, *Capital*, volume II (London: Penguin, 1978), pp. 189–90.
[41] Jessop, 'World Market, World State, World Society', p. 194.

theory of value and used it to explain the contradictory dynamics of the world market. In the *Grundrisse*, he broke with the Ricardian comparative advantage thesis and theorized the exchange of unequal quantities of labour in the world market: 'Two nations may exchange according to the law of profit so that both gain, but one is always short-changed ... One nation may continuously appropriate part of surplus labor of the other and give nothing in exchange for it, except that here the measure is not as in the exchange between capitalist and worker.'[42] In the *Economic Manuscript of 1861–63*, Marx wrote that the basic categories of the capitalist mode of production, such as value and abstract labour, could only get their full meaning on the basis of the world market. For him, a commodity has an international or world value from the outset, determined as the internationally necessary average social labour: 'it is only *foreign trade*, the development of the market to a world market, which causes money to develop into world money and *abstract labor* into social labor ... the measure of the value, e.g. of cotton, is determined not by the English hour of labor, but by the *average necessary time of labor* on the world market'.[43] In the *Economic Manuscript of 1861–63*, Marx created the concept of international exploitation or international unequal exchange, that is, the exchange of unequal quantities of labour between countries. Poor countries with lower productivity took greater labour time in producing a same commodity traded in world market, while rich countries with higher productivity took lesser labour time in producing it, even though its value is determined as the internationally necessary labour time to produce it. The result will be the exchange of unequal amount of labour time between rich and poor countries:

> Say, in his notes to Ricardo's book ... makes only *one* correct remark about *foreign trade*. Profit can also be made by cheating, one person gaining what the other loses. Loss and gain within a single country cancel each other out. But not so with trade between different countries. And even according to Ricardo's theory, three days of labor of one country can be exchanged against one of another country – a point not noted by Say. Here the law of value undergoes essential modification [*wesentliche Modifikation*] ... In this case, the richer country exploits the poorer one, even where the latter gains by the exchange, as John Stuart Mill explains in his *Some Unsettled Questions*.[44]

In *Capital*, volume I, Marx argued that:

> the law of value is ... modified in its international application by the fact that, on the world market, national labor which is more productive also counts as more

---

[42] Marx, 'Outlines of the Critique of Political Economy [*Grundrisse*]. First Instalment', pp. 532, 244.
[43] K. Marx, *Economic Manuscript of 1861–63*, MECW, vol. 32, p. 388; K. Marx, *Economic Manuscript of 1861–63*, MECW, vol. 33, p. 384.
[44] Marx, *Economic Manuscript of 1861–63*, vol. 32, p. 294.

intensive, as long as the more productive nation is not compelled by competition to lower the selling price of its commodities to the level of their value.[45]

What Marx meant by 'modification' of the law of value in this passage is not its nullification, but its full operation on the world market. In the *Economic Manuscript of 1861–63*, Marx implied that prices of production tended to form on a world scale, based on the tendency of profit rates to equalize internationally: 'The industrial capitalist faces the world market; [he] therefore compares and must constantly compare his own cost-prices [prices of production] with market prices not only *at home*, but also *on the whole market of the world*. He always produces taking this account.'[46] In *Capital*, volume III, Marx also wrote that '[t]he industrial capitalist is constantly faced with the world market; he compares and must compare his own cost-prices [prices of production] not only with domestic market prices, but with those of the whole world'.[47] Marx thought that differences in national profit rates would necessitate the international movement of national capitals from states with low rates of profit to those with higher rates of profit, resulting in the tendency of international profit rate equalization and the related formation of international production prices.[48] Marx also implied that the international value of the commodity – determined as the internationally socially necessary labour time needed to produce it – tended to transform itself into the international price of production due to the tendency of international profit rate equalization, according to the progress of capitalist globalization.[49] Marx also made it clear that the formation of international value and price of production are accompanied by the transfer of surplus-value from capitals with low productivity and low organic composition, mostly located in poor countries, to capitals with high productivity of labour and high organic composition, which are mostly located in rich countries. This results in the exacerbation of global inequality between rich and poor countries.[50] The reason why Marx treated the capitalist mode of production as one nation in the footnote to *Capital*, volume I is now clear. It is because he chose an integrated capitalist global unity, rather than a set of national capitalisms, as his unit of analysis, and formulated his labour theory of value on this basis.

---

[45] Marx, *Capital*, volume I, pp. 702.
[46] Marx, *Economic Manuscript of 1861–63*, vol. 32, p. 467.
[47] Marx, *Capital*, volume III, p. 455.
[48] For the first formulation of Marxian theory of international prices of production based on the international equalization of rates of profit, cf. H. Grossmann, *The Law of Accumulation and Breakdown of the Capitalist System* (London: Pluto Press, 1992), pp. 169–73.
[49] Cf. S. Jeong, 'Marx's Crisis Theory as a Theory of World Market Crisis', in: *Beitrage zur Marx-Engels-Forschung Neue Folge 2013* (Hamburg: Argument, 2014), pp. 47–9.
[50] Cf. G. Carchedi, *Frontiers of Political Economy* (London: Verso, 1991), pp. 217–73.

16.7 World Market Crisis

Marx always conceived of the globalization of capitalism as a process full of contradictions that would eventually explode in a global crisis. In the *Manifesto of the Communist Party*, Marx and Engels clearly noted that that the result of the globalization of capitalism is nothing else than global crisis:

> the commercial crises by their periodical return put on its trial, each time more threateningly, the existence of the entire bourgeois society ... bourgeoisie get over these crises ... on the one hand by enforced destruction of a mass of productive forces; on the other, by the conquest of new markets, and by the more thorough exploitation of the old ones.[51]

In the *Grundrisse*, the perspective of world market crisis was paramount from the start. Indeed, in its introductory notes on 'Bastiat and Carey', Marx noted that 'world-market disharmonies' are nothing else than the culmination of the 'disharmonies' of all local and abstract relations. He emphasized that the disharmonious relations of bourgeois society appeared in their most developed form on the world market, because that was the arena where the contradictions of capitalism operated on their fullest scale:

> All the relations which appear harmonious to him [Carey] within particular national boundaries ... appear to him as disharmonious where they show themselves in their most developed form – in their world market form ... these world-market disharmonies are only the ultimate adequate expression of the disharmonies which have become fixed in the economic categories as abstract relations or have a local existence on the smallest scale.[52]

In a passage inserted in the French edition of *Capital*, volume I, published in 1872–75, Marx highlighted the intimate relations between the world market, industrial cycle, and crisis:

> [O]nly after foreign trade began to predominate over internal trade, thanks to mechanical industry; only after the world market had successively annexed extensive areas of the New World, Asia and Australia; and finally, only after a sufficient number of industrial nations had entered the arena – only after all this had happened can one date the repeated self-perpetuating cycles, whose successive phases embrace years, and always culminate in a general crisis, which is the end of one cycle and the starting-point of another.[53]

In *Capital*, volume I, Marx emphasized that the characteristic elasticity of the capitalist machinery factory system was behind the cyclical world market crisis:

---

[51] Marx and Engels, *Manifesto of the Communist Party*, pp. 489–90.
[52] Marx, 'Outlines of the Critique of Political Economy [*Grundrisse*]. First Instalment', pp. 8–9.
[53] Marx, *Capital*, volume I, p. 787.

as soon as the technical basis peculiar to it, machinery, is itself produced by machinery ... this mode of production acquires an elasticity, a capacity for sudden extension by leaps and bounds, which come up against no barrier but those presented by the availability of raw materials and the extent of sales outlets ... The factory system's tremendous capacity for expanding with sudden immense leaps, and its dependence on the world market, necessarily give rise to the following cycle ... moderate activity, prosperity, over-production, crisis and stagnation.[54]

In the *Economic Manuscript of 1861–63*, Marx argued that:

In the crises of the world market, the contradictions and antagonisms of bourgeois production are strikingly revealed ... the most complicated phenomenon of capitalist production – the world market crisis ... The world trade crises must be regarded as the real concentration and forcible adjustment of all the contradictions of bourgeois economy.[55]

In *Capital*, volume III, Marx presented the 1857 crisis as a world market crisis *par excellence*, anticipating the main aspects of the global economic crisis of 2008:

In 1857 the crisis broke out in the United States. This led to a drain of gold from England to America. But as soon as the American bubble burst, the crisis reached England, with a drain of gold from America to England ... In times of general crisis the balance of payments is against every country, at least against every commercially developed country, but always against each of these in succession – like volley firing – as soon as the sequence of payments reaches it; and once the crisis has broken out in England, for example, this sequence of dates is condensed into a fairly short period. It is then evident that all these countries have simultaneously over-exported (i.e. over-produced) and over-imported (i.e. over-traded) and that in all of them prices were inflated and credit overstretched.[56]

However, for Marx, the world market was not only the condition of the crisis, but its fix as well. In the *Grundrisse*, he emphasized that the extension of the world market, supported by innovation in transportation, accelerated the circulation, and valourization of capital through the 'annihilation of space by means of time'.[57] In *Capital*, volume III, Marx also emphasized that the world market acted as a powerful countervailing force to the crisis tendency of the falling rate of profit:

In so far as foreign trade cheapens on the one hand the elements of constant capital and on the other the necessary means of subsistence into which variable capital is converted, it acts to raise the rate of profit by raising the rate of surplus-value and

---

[54] Marx, *Capital*, volume I, pp. 561, 579–80.
[55] Marx, *Economic Manuscript of 1861–63*, vol. 32, pp. 131, 132, 140.
[56] Marx, *Capital*, volume III, pp. 623–4.
[57] Marx, 'Outlines of the Critique of Political Economy [*Grundrisse*]. First Instalment', p. 463.

reducing the value of constant capital ... As far as capital invested in colonies, etc. is concerned, however, the reason why this can yield higher rates of profit is that the profit rate is generally higher there on account of the lower degree of development, and so too is the exploitation of labor, through the use of slaves and coolies, etc.[58]

For Marx, the extension of the world market pursued by capital and state is not the cause of crisis, but a counteractive force to stem it. Thus, the regulation of globalization[59] cannot be an effective measure to cope with crisis. However, the unregulated pursuit of globalization advocated by neo-liberals cannot work either, because it will only temporarily postpone the day of reckoning, preparing the explosion of a bigger crisis in the future, by extending and deepening the contradictions of capital accumulation on a global scale.

16.8 From World Market to World Revolution

World revolution is a necessary political consequence of Marx's globalist perspective. It is natural for Marx, who conceived of the laws of movement of capitalism on a world scale, to project anti-capitalist revolution on the same scale. So-called socialism in one country is alien to Marx. Marx and Engels wrote in *The German Ideology*:

> Empirically, communism is only possible as the act of the dominant peoples 'all at once' and simultaneously, which presupposes the universal development of productive forces and the world intercourse bound up with communism ... The proletariat can thus only exist *world-historically*, just as communism, its activity, can only have a 'world-historical' existence.[60]

Marx based the prospect of a successful communist revolution on the existence of an integrated world economy. He thought that global capitalism could only be transcended by the world-historical action of its victims, the proletariat and allied classes.[61] In 'Draft of an Article on Friedrich List's book: *Das Nationale System der Politischen Oekonomie*', he argued that workers have no nationality: 'The nationality of the worker is neither French, nor English, nor German, it is *labor, free slavery, self-huckstering*. His government is neither French, nor English, nor German, it is capital. His native air is neither French, nor German, nor English, it is factory air.'[62]

---

[58] Marx, *Capital*, volume III, pp. 344–5.
[59] J. Stiglitz, *Making Globalization Work* (New York: W. W. Norton, 2007), pp. 13–19.
[60] Marx and Engels, *The German Ideology*, p. 49.
[61] For Marx's struggle to build the First International, cf. M. Musto 'Introduction' in M. Musto (ed.), *Workers Unite! The International 150 Years Later* (New York: Bloomsbury Publishing, 2014), pp. 1–68.
[62] K. Marx, 'Herr List and Ferner', MECW, vol. 4, p. 280.

Marx discerned many of the characteristics which have appeared in a magnified form in today's globalization. However, he is far from a naïve cosmopolitan, regarding the growth of the world market as the result of pure economic process. Remember that he situated the state as the starting category among the second half of his six-book plan of critique of political economy. Marx always paid keen attention to the systematic interaction between the state and the world market. It did not occur to Marx that the creation and extension of the world market is possible without the help of the visible hands of the state. He never imagined that the ultimate destination of the globalization would be the end of sovereignty or the supersession of the nation-state by a transnational global economy. His global perspective has nothing to do with so-called globaloney or hyperglobalism. He always analyzed the world market dialectically, focusing on its contradictions and eventual supersession. However, without the benefit of Marx's thoughts on the world market, such as the thesis of uneven and combined development, theory of international value and the world market crisis, existing Marxist theories of world economy have oscillated undialectically between two opposite conceptions of the world economy: statism versus transnationalism.[63] In this situation, reviving Marx's thoughts on the world economy is necessary for any progressive project that aims to understand and transcend global capitalism.

References

Bonefeld, Werner (2000), 'The Spectre of Globalization: On the Form and Content of the World Market', in: W. Bonefeld and K. Psychopedi (eds), *The Politics of Change: Globalization, Ideology and Critique*, Basingstoke: Palgrave, pp. 31–68.

Callinicos, Alex (2009), *Imperialism and Global Political Economy*, Cambridge: Polity.

Carchedi, Guglielmo (1991), *Frontiers of Political Economy*, London: Verso.

Desai, Radhika (2014), 'Marx and Engels' Geopolitical Economy', in: A. Kumar and B. Chatterjee (eds), *Marxism: With and Beyond Marx*, New York: Routledge, pp. 71–91.

Friedman, Thomas (2005), *The World Is Flat: A Brief History of the Twenty-first Century*, New York: Farrar, Straus and Giroux.

Grossmann, Henryk (1992), *The Law of Accumulation and Breakdown of the Capitalist System*, London: Pluto Press.

---

[63] For the statist position, cf. L. Panitch and S. Gindin, *The Making of Global Capitalism: The Political Economy of American Empire* (London: Verso, 2012), pp. 1–5. For transnationalist position, refer to Hardt and Negri, *Empire*, pp. 206–7, 353 and W. Robinson, 'Debate on the Global Capitalism: Transnational Capitalist Class, Transnational State Apparatus, and Global Crisis', *International Critical Thought*, 7 (2) (2017), pp. 171–89.

Hardt, Michael, and Negri, Antonio (2000), *Empire*, Cambridge, MA: Harvard University Press.
Jeong, Seongjin (2014), 'Marx's Crisis Theory as a Theory of World Market Crisis', in: *Beitrage zur Marx-Engels-Forschung Neue Folge 2013*, Hamburg: Argument, pp. 37–77.
Jessop, Bob (2010), 'World Market, World State, World Society: Marxian Insights and Scientific Realist Interrogations', in: J. Joseph and C. Wight (eds), *Scientific Realism and International Relations*, New York: Palgrave, pp. 186–202.
Kozlov, Genrikh A. (ed.) (1977), *Political Economy: Capitalism*, Moscow: Progress Publishers.
Marx, Karl (1975), 'Draft of an Article on Friedrich List's Book Das Nationale System Der Politischen Oekonomie', MECW, vol. 4, pp. 265–93.
—— (1976a), *Capital*, volume I, London: Penguin.
—— (1976b), 'Speech of Dr. Marx on Protection, Free Trade, and the Working Classes', MECW, vol. 6, pp. 287–90.
—— (1976c), 'Speech on the Question of Free Trade delivered to the Democratic Association of Brussels at Its Public Meeting of January 9, 1848', MECW, vol. 6, pp. 450–65.
—— (1978), *Capital*, volume II, London: Penguin.
—— (1979a), 'The British Rule in India', MECW, vol. 12, pp. 125–33.
—— (1979b), 'The Future Results of British Rule in India', MECW, vol. 12, pp. 217–22.
—— (1981), *Capital*, volume III, London: Penguin.
—— (1983a), *Letters 1852–55*, MECW, vol. 39.
—— (1983b), *Letters 1856–59*, MECW, vol. 40.
—— (1985), 'Outline of a Report on the Irish Question Delivered to the German Workers' Educational Society in London on December 16, 1867', MECW, vol. 21, pp. 194–206.
—— (1986), 'Outlines of the Critique of Political Economy [*Grundrisse*]. First Instalment', MECW, vol. 28.
—— (1987a), 'Outlines of the Critique of Political Economy [*Grundrisse*]. Second Instalment', MECW, vol. 29, pp. 1–256.
—— (1987b), *A Contribution to the Critique of Political Economy*, MECW, vol. 29, pp. 257–417.
—— (1989a), *Critique of the Gotha Programme*, MECW, vol. 24, pp. 75–99.
—— (1989b), 'Drafts of the Letter to Vera Zasulich', MECW, vol. 24, pp. 346–69.
—— (1989c), *Economic Manuscript of 1861–63*, MECW, vol. 32.
—— (1991), *Economic Manuscript of 1861–63*, MECW, vol. 33.
Marx, Karl, and Engels, Frederich (1976a), *The German Ideology*, MECW, vol. 5.
—— (1976b), *Manifesto of the Communist Party*, MECW, vol. 6, pp. 477–519.
—— (1978), 'Review: May to October 1850', MECW, vol. 10, pp. 490–532.
Mohri, Kenzo (1979), 'Marx and "Underdevelopment"', *Monthly Review*, 30 (11): 32–42.
Musto, Marcello (2014), 'Introduction', in: M. Musto (ed.), *Workers Unite! The International 150 Years Later*, New York: Bloomsbury Publishing, pp. 1–68.

Muthu, Sankar (2008), 'Adam Smith's Critique of International Trading Companies: Theorizing "Globalization" in the Age of Enlightenment', *Political Theory*, 362: 185–212.

Panitch, Leo, and Gindin, Sam (2012), *The Making of Global Capitalism: The Political Economy of American Empire*, London: Verso.

Pradella, Lucia (2017), 'Marx and the Global South: Connecting History and Value Theory', *Sociology*, 51: 146–61.

Robinson, William (2017), 'Debate on the New Global Capitalism: Transnational Capitalist Class, Transnational State Apparatus, and Global Crisis', *International Critical Thought*, 72: 171–89.

Sekine, Thomas (1980), 'An Essay on Uno's Dialectic of *Capital*', in: K. Uno (ed.), *Principles of Political Economy: Theory of a Purely Capitalist Society*, Sussex: Harvester Press, pp. 127–68.

Stiglitz, Joseph E. (2007), *Making Globalization Work*, New York: W. W. Norton.

The Economist (2018), 'Reconsidering Marx: Second Time, Farce', 427 (9090): 79–80.

Trotsky, Leon (1977), *The History of the Russian Revolution*, London: Pluto Press.

Young, Paul (2009), *Globalization and the Great Exhibition: The Victorian New World Order*, New York: Palgrave.

17 War and International Relations

Benno Teschke

17.1 A Belated Discovery

In his 1846 letter to Pavel Annenkov (1813–1887), Karl Marx asked whether 'the whole organization of nations, and all their international relations' was 'anything else than the expression of a particular division of labour. And must not these change when the division of labour changes?'[1] Commenting on the Crimean War a few years later, he noted in a 1853 letter to Friedrich Engels that 'we had given the issue of foreign policy insufficient attention'.[2] And in his 1877 letter to editor of the *Otecestvenniye Zapisky*, Marx objected to reading his historical account of the genesis of capitalism in Western Europe as a supra-historical philosophical theory, 'fatally imposed upon all peoples, whatever the historical circumstances in which they find themselves placed'.[3] This brief selection of quotes indicates an evolution, however unsystematic, in Marx's thought on international relations that led from schematic formalizations, via concessions of omission, to agnostic open-endedness.

Marx's work is replete with similar suggestive references to the problematique of international relations, war, and foreign policy, including – especially towards the later part of his work – open admissions of their under-problematized nature. This raises fundamental questions for the analytical premises of the conception of historical materialism as a theory of history. For this belated recognition of the efficacy of the sphere of international relations for the course of history, as even sympathetic commentators have repeatedly noted,[4] did never advance beyond

---

The author would like to acknowledge the superb editorial comments of Marcello Musto, Samuel Knafo, Steffan Wyn-Jones, and Clemens Hoffmann on various drafts of this chapter.

[1] 'K. Marx to P. V. Annenkov, 28 December 1846', MECW, vol. 38, p. 95.
[2] 'K. Marx to F. Engels, 2 November 1853', MECW, vol. 39, p. 395.
[3] K. Marx, 'Letter to Editors of *Otechestvenniye Zapiski*', in: D. Sayer (ed.), *Readings from Karl Marx* (London: Routledge, 1989), p. 34.
[4] R. N. Berki, 'On Marxian Thought and the Problem of International Relations', *World Politics*, 24 (1) (1971); F. Halliday, *Rethinking International Relations* (London: Macmillan,

fragmentary and miscellaneous insights. It failed to engender a more systematic reflection on the geopolitical dimensions of social processes over time on a universal scale – a reflection that would have to be reconciled with the basic premises of historical materialism. This absence of an explicit historicization and theorization of relations between spatio-temporally, differentially developing political communities exposes a deficiency that pervades Marx's conceptions of history in general and his theory of capitalism in particular. This deficiency underwent several permutations in his intellectual trajectory without ever receiving a definitive resolution.

This problem has generated three broad responses in the literature. Most commentators have concluded that the magnitude of the challenge of an internationally expanded historical materialism may constitute an insuperable obstacle, which pushes the whole exercise beyond recovery for the tradition.[5] Others suggest that this absence requires a substantial reformulation of the entire conception of Marx's theory of history.[6] Marxological studies, in turn, argue that Marx and Engels's writings provide rich and sufficient resources, including under-appreciated anti-Eurocentric insights, for an exegetic reconstruction of the role of international relations in history that may not require substantial further revision.[7] This chapter shows how Marx's thought on international relations developed over time and argues that attempts within the fields of International Relations (IR) and International Political Economy (IPE) to reconstruct a Marxist theory of international relations – by drawing either from the wider Marxist tradition or from the body of his writings – have remained unsatisfactory. They remain problematic because they tend to subscribe to a conception of theory (with the partial exception of Robert Cox's [1926–] historicism) that

---

1994); D. Harvey, *Spaces of Capital: Towards a Critical Geography* (New York: Routledge, 2001), pp. 312–44; H. Soell, 'Weltmarkt – Revolution – Staatenwelt', *Archiv für Sozialgeschichte*, 12 (1972).

[5] A. Giddens, *The Nation-State and Violence: Volume 2 of the Contemporary Critique of Historical Materialism* (Cambridge: Polity Press, 1985); T. Skocpol, *States and Social Revolutions: A Comparative Analysis of France, Russia, and China* (Cambridge: Cambridge University Press, 1979).

[6] R. Cox, *Production, Power, and World Order: Social Forces in the Making of History* (New York: Columbia University Press, 1987); D. Harvey, *The New Imperialism* (Oxford: Oxford University Press, 2003); J. Rosenberg, 'Why Is There No International Historical Sociology?', *European Journal of International Relations*, 12 (3) (2006); I. Wallerstein, 'The Rise and Future Demise of the Capitalist World-System: Concepts for Comparative Analysis', *Comparative Studies in Society and History*, 16 (1974).

[7] K. Anderson, *Marx at the Margins: On Nationalism, Ethnicity, and Non-Western Societies* (Chicago: Chicago University Press, 2010); T. R. Kandal, 'Marx and Engels on International Relations, Revolution and Counterrevolution', in: M. T. Martin and T. R. Kandal (eds), *Studies of Development and Change in the Modern World* (New York: Oxford University Press, 1989).

privileges abstract theory-building, whether for world history in general or capitalist history in particular. Consequently, history is demoted to a secondary instance that merely validates a preconceived set of general theoretical axioms. General theory-building, especially when construed under the rubric of 'general abstraction', objectifies the course of history, rendering agents as passive personifications of pre-established laws and categories. Marxological reconstructions, even when showcasing Marx's impressive grasp of contemporaneous international politics, remain tied to his nineteenth-century evidentiary context. In contrast, a turn to a radical historicism, which reincorporates foreign policy, diplomacy, and international politics in line with Marx's early philosophy of praxis, can escape the reificatory tendencies of structuralist and nomological Marxist re-theorizations of international relations.[8]

17.2 The General Problem of International Relations in Marx's Thought

Marx's geopolitical deficit can be traced back to biographical, programmatic, and theory-immanent causes. His engagement with the phenomena of international relations and war falls into the middle and later parts of his intellectual preoccupations after the conception of history and the core categories of the critique of political economy were already articulated in advanced form. Programmatically, the 1857 "Introduction" to the *Grundrisse* projects the coverage of international relations and war, even if only implicitly, for the never completed volumes on the state, colonies, international exchange, and the world market.[9] International politics, as opposed to the 'international relations of production', does not appear as a research desideratum. Analytically, the more direct incorporation of international relations into his research agenda was precluded by the axiomatic research-organizing presupposition to accord explanatory primacy to the vertical social conflicts within political communities,

---

[8] This suggests different epistemological foundations for the research agenda of geopolitical Marxism. B. Teschke, *The Myth of 1648: Class, Geopolitics and the Making of Modern International Relations* (London: Verso, 2003). World Systems Theory, the 'universal law' of uneven and combined development, and arguments about two generic and analytically dissociated modes of power accumulation – the capitalist and the territorial logics of competition – with two invariant rationalities assigned to firms and states exemplify these trends towards structuralism, nomology, and reification. For critiques, see B. Teschke, 'Marxism', in: C. Reus-Smit and D. Snidal (eds), *The Oxford Handbook of International Relations* (Oxford: Oxford University Press, 2008), pp. 163–87; B. Teschke, 'IR Theory, Historical Materialism, and the False Promise of International Historical Sociology', *Spectrum: Journal of Global Studies*, 6 (1) (2014).

[9] K. Marx, 'Outlines of the Critique of Political Economy [*Grundrisse*]. First Instalment', MECW, vol. 28, p. 45.

which generated periodic crises, civil wars, and revolutions, as the central dynamic of historical development. This vertical and endogenous social antagonism was never sufficiently related to the horizontal and exogenous conflicts between political communities. Inter-polity forms of conflict and co-operation, which can neither be derived *in toto* from social contradictions, nor comprehended immediately as secondary or epiphenomenal, are consigned to the margins of analysis.

This omission of inter-polity relations – and the wider issue of changing political geographies – is compounded, in striking contrast to Vladimir Lenin's (1870–1924) concept of imperialism, by the absence of a concept of war as a category of the critique of political economy. Notwithstanding a utopian understanding of the abolition of war consequent upon the abolition of states in a universal classless society, Marx co-founded an understanding of history removed from the requirements of a social interpretation of war and peace in their consequences for historical development. Both phenomena were primarily conceptualized instrumentally from the perspective of their significance for the (sometimes rapidly changing) strategic calculations of national and international working-class movements, rather than as historically efficacious objects of inquiry that permanently transgress and intervene into the bounds of singular political communities. While this instrumental perspective should have led to a closer examination of the causes and consequences of war, it did not translate into a more serious reflection on conflict and co-operation as central historical phenomena in their implications for the Marxist conception of history. In spite of these shortcomings, Marx entertained throughout his work a historical-sociological reading of war as a form of violent conflict between political communities grounded in differential social relations. This axiomatic premise – the socialization of war and international relations – distinguishes his approach *a priori* from conventional diplomatic history or the abstractions of power-political theories of Realist provenance. In this specific sense, it has proven productive for a historical, if static, typology of forms of war – medieval feuds, peasant wars, colonial-mercantilist trade wars, dynastic-absolutist wars of succession, revolutionary wars, anti-colonial wars of liberation, and guerilla wars – and for aspects of military sociology and military strategy, especially in Engels's work.[10]

Still, the absence of inter-polity relations as a dimension of world history presents a more acute challenge to Marxism's most ambitious project – the historical-materialist theory of history – since it collides sharply with the unreconstructed theoretical presuppositions of Marx's early works. For the

---

[10] B. Semmel, *Marxism and the Science of War* (Oxford: Oxford University Press, 1981).

orthodox model of a sequence of modes of production posits 'national' trajectories of development in which singular political communities function as units of analysis in abstraction from their wider geopolitical contexts. This position leads directly to the aporias of comparative history, which elides the incorporation of interstate conflict and co-operation into the analyses of the spatio-temporal variations of regional developmental trajectories (and vice versa). Comparative history, premised on the idea of a 'methodological nationalism', restricts historical sociology to the diachronous, but essentially 'national' and unilinear analyses of long-term and large-scale developments within discrete, self-contained and self-referential units of analysis – states. This optic generates either a historical sociology of singular societies or a comparative, but non-international, historical sociology, which contrasts the dissimilar trajectories of distinct state/society complexes without developing a methodological perspective on their relationality, especially in terms of the causes and consequences of multiple foreign policy encounters.

Next to this a-spatial stadial model, Marx also envisaged in *The German Ideology* (1845–46) and, in the *Manifesto of the Communist Party* (1848), the idea of a universalizing bourgeois society, which would progressively inflate itself towards a 'world society [*Weltgesellschaft*]', geographically commensurate with the establishment of the capitalist world market. But this extrapolation repressed the question why capitalist 'world society' should exist within the territorial framework of a system of sovereign states and how states actively construct and resist diverse political geographies of capital accumulation. The problematique of (capitalist) international relations, conceived as the mediating instance that activates difference, disappears between these two analytical poles – methodological nationalism versus totalizing universality.

This dilemma generates a specific question. Which consequences have to be drawn for a type of theory, which suggests in essence a spaceless ideal-type of successive, necessary, irreversible, and ascending modes of production as a periodizing model of history, whose abstractions (primitive society [*Urgemeinschaft*], slave society, feudalism, capitalism, and socialism), in spite of their geographically and temporally specific historical manifestations, are nevertheless pressed into a supra-historical schema, which privileges time over space? This reduction of history to a uni-linear teleology, Marx's protestations notwithstanding, requires a reconstruction of Marx scattered ideas on war and international relations in order to demonstrate the extent of the problem and to provide resources to expand and redefine historical materialism by reflecting on the theoretical adjustments necessary to capture the geopolitical dimensions of history. These research desiderata constitute a task which points beyond the classical corpus of Marxism. They also presuppose a paradigm shift from teleology and structural determinisms towards a radically historicized and praxis-oriented critical social science of interpolity relations, revolving around the social construction of geopolitics and political geography.

17.3 The Early Wager: The Universalization of Capitalism

Marx's initial position was influenced by liberal cosmopolitanism and premised on the transnationalizing power of capitalism and the pacifying consequences of 'universal interdependence',[11] as noted in the 1848 *Manifesto of the Communist Party*, based on international commerce. Commerce, in turn, was conceived as the expression of the international division of labour governed by the regionally uneven development of the forces of production. These assumptions ultimately implied a world-historical convergence towards a 'world after capitalism's own image'.[12] Here, the mega-subject of modern history was capitalism that would expand geographically to perfect a world market, creating first a transnational bourgeoisie and then a communist *cosmopolis*. This perspective was first sketched in *The German Ideology*: 'The relations of different nations among themselves depend upon the extent to which each has developed its productive forces, the division of labour and internal intercourse.'[13] It received its canonical definition in the *Manifesto of the Communist Party*:

National differences and antagonism between peoples are daily more and more vanishing, owing to the development of the bourgeoisie, to freedom of commerce, to the world market, to uniformity in the mode of production and in the conditions of life corresponding thereto.[14]

This process was driven by the progressive universalization of capitalism, which was inconclusively and equivocally defined as synonymous with free trade based on an advanced form of the division of labour. The commercial opportunities offered by long-distance trade gave production and consumption over time a cosmopolitan character whose cumulative result was the creation of the capitalist world market. While this perspective retained the role of states as guarantors of exploitative and antagonistic class-divided societies, national antagonisms and war – among capitalist and between capitalist and non-capitalist states – would decline due to the 'universal interdependence of nations'. Militarized interstate conflicts were gradually replaced by the consolidation and polarization of classes, leading to the

---

[11] K. Marx and F. Engels, *Manifesto of the Communist Party*, MECW, vol. 6, p. 488.
[12] Ibid, cf. n. 12.
[13] K. Marx and F. Engels, *The German Ideology*, MECW, vol. 5, p. 32.
[14] Marx and Engels, *Manifesto of the Communist Party*, p. 503.

intensification of class struggle on a global scale. The dialectical outcome was envisaged in terms of the formation of a world proletariat as a universal class – 'workers have no fatherland'[15] – and the collective subject that precipitated a single and synchronized world revolution on a planetary scale. As *The German Ideology* stated:

> Empirically, communism is only possible as the act of the dominant peoples 'all at once' and simultaneously, which presupposes the universal development of productive forces and the world intercourse bound up with communism ... The proletariat can thus only exist *world-historically*, just as communism, its activity, can only have a 'world-historical' existence. World-historical existence of individuals means existence of individuals which is directly linked up with world history.[16]

Here, the notion of a 'simultaneous development on a world scale'[17] prevails. This original conception provides a singular analytic revolving around the vertical deepening and horizontal widening of capitalism progressively unifying the world geographically, homogenizing national differences socio-politically, while polarizing class relations universally. This narrative would eventuate in the abolition of national histories, hitherto understood as a series of particular and self-referential histories, and prepare the terrain for world history proper, even though the term 'world history [*Weltgeschichte*]' as a consciously planned collective enterprise was reserved for the post-capitalist age.

Yet, Marx never clarified how exactly the trade-mediated expansion of capitalism, based on the international division of labour, would transform prevailing regional non-capitalist class relations and pre-capitalist polities in a capitalist direction. The crux was that this early conceptionalization of capitalism-qua-trade imputed an automaticity to a transnationalizing and homogenizing process that discounted how the expansion of capitalist practices was refracted through a pre-existing interstate system that generated resistance and differences through geopolitics, war, and class conflict in the contested and regionally highly differentiated (non-)transitions from pre-capitalist to capitalist state-society complexes. *Ex hypothesis*, countries were to be absorbed into the world market and conceived – logically, deductively – as passive recipients of transnational imperatives, which rendered their political institutions and social relations compatible with the demands of capitalist commerce. Spatio-temporally diachronic and differential regional trajectories of socio-political development are temporally synchronized and geographically assimilated. The temporal dimension of simultaneity and the spatial dimension of immediacy indicate the

---

[15] Ibid. [16] Marx and Engels, *The German Ideology*, p. 49.
[17] Soell, 'Weltmarkt – Revolution – Staatenwelt', p. 112.

formation of a uniform and de-politicized world market as an internally undifferentiated totality. Nations, ethnies, and polities, within the advancing world market and at the geographical limits of its expansionary dynamic, were conceived as non-agential objects subject to a superior reified logic. Social, political, and geopolitical agency was written out of the metaphysical entity of the world market. The integration of the mediating impact of the interstate system on the expansion and reproduction of capitalism appeared not only as a non-problem for Marx, but could not even be captured by these early economistic, cosmopolitan, and universalizing assumptions, since the territorial fragmentation of the interstate system could not be derived from the formation of a transnationalizing capitalist bourgeoisie. This pristine conception extrapolated directly from the national to the universal, eliding interstate relations as the decisive instance that frames national specificities and fractures and disables any universality to this day. Here, the unit of analysis appeared as a self-universalizing capitalist world market freed of all international politics or, alternatively, as a bourgeois world society. In this version of historical materialism, methodological nationalism was dissolved into a teleological methodological universalism. Capitalist geopolitics appeared as a non-problem.

17.4 From Logic to History: The Impact of 1848 and the Crimean War

These early supra-historical abstractions, based on logical deductions unchecked against the historical record, received several qualifications after the failed 1848 revolutions and, in particular, in reaction to the Crimean War (1853–56), which transformed Marx's perspective on the nexus between capitalist development, foreign policy, revolutions, and war. In fact, foreign policy became for the first time an object of dedicated interest.[18]

---

[18] This turn to foreign affairs generated the voluminous material compiled in eight large tomes – mainly notes, excerpts, articles, and correspondences, although also including substantial books – which Marx (and Engels) wrote between 1853 and 1864. Much of this material centers on diplomatic and military history, comprising reflections on the Crimean War, British and Russian foreign policy, the Italian Risorgimento, Revolutionary Spain, and the American Civil War, including the series of polemical articles on *Lord Palmerston* written in 1853 and the 1856–7 *Revelations of the Diplomatic History of the 18th Century*. These writings are full of insights and show Marx to be a keen and perceptive observer and critic of contemporary European and world affairs. Still, they tend to carry the character of situative interventions on specific conjunctures governed by the overriding concern to draw lessons for revolutionary strategy. This turn to international affairs in the 1850s and 1860s failed to generate a deeper reflection on how war and international politics needs to be thought in relation to domestic socio-economic

Prior to 1848, Marx expected progress from a successful German bourgeois revolution, which would position a democratic and united German Republic against late-absolutist states (Denmark, Russia, and Austria). The German Revolution would end the Holy Alliance and shift the European balance of power towards the progressive Western countries. This would lead to a division of Europe into a revolutionary and counter-revolutionary camp. The new constellation was depicted as a struggle between freedom and despotism carried out by world war between two ideological blocs. After the failed 1848 revolution, the expectation of the internationalization of revolutions by means of interstate wars, which can be formalized as 'domestic revolution plus war equals international progress', was now reformulated as 'war plus revolution equals domestic progress'. The world-historical march towards communism came now to be derived less from the radicalization of domestic class dynamics, spilling over into the international sphere, as from defeat in interstate wars. The consequent legitimation crises of the defeated European Old Regimes would facilitate revolutionary change in the affected countries or engender the import of new socio-political regimes from the outside.

But even this conceptual adjustment did not suffice to capture the complexity of the diplomatic crises and wars in the revolutionary period – American War of Independence, French Revolutionary Wars, German Wars of Liberation, the First and Second Opium Wars, the First and Second Italian Wars of Independence, the Crimean War, and the German Wars of Unification – in a theoretically controlled way. While pre-1848 Congress Europe and the Holy Alliance had already focused the problem of the international dimension of a pan-European counter-revolutionary conservatism that arrested even liberal-national movements, Marx turned his attention post-1848 to the foreign policies of the Western Powers.[19] In this respect, the advances and limits in Marx's thought on international relations can be exemplified in relation to the complicated problem of the 'Eastern Question', sharply illuminated by the Crimean War, which he could not resolve in line with his own theoretical premise of world-historical progress driven by the most advanced capitalist nations. For it proved impossible to derive from the 'objective' interests of the British (and French) bourgeoisie a definitive and unambiguously liberal-progressive foreign policy, either in intentions or outcomes. It also proved impossible to identify a transnational bourgeois class interest – Marx's

---

dynamics. Centrally, they failed to revise Marx's theory of history and, perhaps more demandingly, to clarify his conception of the relation between history and theory.

[19] E. Benner, *Really Existing Nationalisms: A Post-Communist View from Marx and Engels* (Oxford: Oxford University Press, 1995), pp. 114–22.

earlier bourgeois and cosmopolitan 'world society' of the *Manifesto of the Communist Party* – that somehow dispensed with interstate conflicts.

During the Crimean War, the alliance between the liberal Western powers (and 'reactionary' Austria) with the 'backward' Ottoman Empire against Tsarist Russia revised the European Concert of Powers – the pentarchy – that was orchestrated by Britain and institutionalized at the 1815 Vienna Congress. While the anti-Russian and pro-Ottoman alliance during the Crimean War protected British trading routes in the Mediterranean to their overseas colonies from Russian interference and while it undermined the Holy Alliance between the three dynastic Eastern Powers and the pentarchical 'European Concert', it also consolidated the late-absolutist Ottoman Empire (itself a polity that cannot be decoded through the notion of an 'Asiatic mode of production') and gave the national-liberal movements on the continent and in the Ottoman parts of the Balkans, no decisive support.[20] Security interests – geopolitical stability – (even if these can be decoded as economically shaped) and geo-economic calculations – open sea lanes – remained tightly connected and could not be directly read off domestic class positions or classified in their consequences as either reactionary or progressive. Recognizing these difficulties, Marx lamented that 'it goes without saying that, in foreign policy, there's little to be gained by using such catchwords as "reactionary" and "revolutionary"'.[21]

In fact, Marx's attacks on Lord Palmerston's (1784–1865) foreign policy revealed that while British mid-nineteenth-century foreign policy was broadly consonant with 'bourgeois' domestic class interests – showing in the process that the 'national interest' is not a class-neutral category – he concluded that British foreign policy support for constitutionalism and liberalism on the continent was highly circumscribed – in fact, prevented. Marx suggested that this was partly due to fears of fomenting social demands at home, and partly due to the fact that British security concerns on the continent trumped economic and ideological interests. British foreign policy differentially and opportunistically stabilized and destabilized various European polities from the vantage point of national security first.[22] This revealed a strategic pattern that could not be aligned with a general narrative of world-historical progress. Quite the contrary, Marx stumbled in the process on the balance of power as the key British foreign policy technique. This volatile and situation-bound strategic opportunism – combining

---

[20] C. Hoffmann, 'The Balkanization of Ottoman Rule: Premodern Origins of the Modern International System in Southeastern Europe', *Cooperation and Conflict*, 43 (4): 380–4 (2008).
[21] 'K. Marx to F. Lassalle, 2 June 1860', MECW, vol. 41, p. 150.
[22] K. Marx, 'Lord Palmerston', MECW, vol. 12, pp. 344–6.

selective verbal support for pro-constitutional interventionism with material support for smaller reactionary powers against greater reactionary powers – was expressed with candid clarity in Palmerston's famous dictum that 'we have no eternal allies, and we have no perpetual enemies. Our interests are eternal and perpetual, and those interests it is our duty to follow'.[23] The idea of the balance of power as a principled non-principle was eloquently captured by Marx's acerbic character profile of Palmerston as the personification of 'perfidious Albion'.[24]

Even though Marx's sojourns into diplomatic history resulted in a sharpened awareness of the problematique of regionally dissimilar developmental trajectories, which was now conjoined to a consciousness of unevenness and backwardness among the various polities that composed the system of states, no clear-cut results could be derived from this in abstraction from the study of the actual processes of foreign policymaking – the social construction of geopolitics.

And a third complication came into view. In contrast to earlier pre-1848 confident assumptions of international working-class formation, which was even referred to as 'the sixth European Great Power',[25] Marx started to envisage the prospect of the renationalization of different working classes into their respective nation states. The concept of social imperialism tried to capture the idea of the pacification of domestic class conflicts by means of a chauvinist and aggressive foreign policy in order to cleave the European working-class movement and to replace international working-class solidarity with national loyalty through warfare. Social imperialism found its foreign policy correlate in the 1870s in the ideology of a geopolitical Social Darwinism, first articulated by Friedrich Ratzel (1844–1904) in political geography, in the context of the sharpening of the colonial question and the new imperialism, which biologized international politics as a power-political *survival of the fittest* in the struggle for living space [*Lebensraum*] and exclusive spheres of influence. This tension between working-class nationalism and internationalism anticipated the debates of the Second International of the European Socialist parties prior to the First World War, and the later controversies in the Third International. This was expressed in Leon Trotsky's (1879–1940) theory of permanent revolution and Joseph Stalin's (1878–1953) idea of socialism in one country.[26] These debates were still suffused with the basic and unresolved problem of the asymmetrical development of the socio-political structures of nationally differential

---

[23] Benner, *Really Existing Nationalisms*, p. 122.   [24] Marx, 'Lord Palmerston', p. 345.
[25] K. Marx and F. Engels, 'The European War', MECW, vol. 13, p. 129.
[26] P. Anderson, 'Internationalism: A Breviary', *New Left Review*, 2 (14): 14–16 (2002).

industrial proletariats and their party-political forms of organization and theoretical programmes, which proved difficult to co-ordinate and synchronize on a Pan-European level.

Overall, the general insight into the variability of country-specific resolutions of particular social and geopolitical conflicts, which retarded or accelerated national developmental tempos within the spectrum of progress and reaction, led during the 1850s to a shift from the notion of 'simultaneous development on a world scale' to the empirical recognition of different national trajectories, encapsulated in the notion of 'unevenness'.[27] In spite of the empirical recognition of the geographical multi-linearity of developmental trajectories and their interactive nature – secured by the conceptual transition from spatial immediacy to inter-spatial mediation – the uni-linear conception of history as a sequence of modes of production was not subjected to a fundamental revision and remained largely intact. The growing recognition of international unevenness and of strategy, diplomacy, and war as integral components of an expanding capitalist world market (Russia, India, China, the United States, and the Ottoman Empire) generated only a series of partial tergiversations that never resulted in a self-conscious revision of Marx's concept of history that accounted for the relation between world-market formation, class conflict, states, revolution, and geopolitics.

Furthermore, the problem as to *why* political power constitutes itself territorially in the shape of multiple sovereign states and *how* the dynamics between these political jurisdictions relate to the national and transnational reproduction of capitalism was not dramatized as a research desideratum. More fundamentally, the move towards international unevenness relied on a taken-for-granted prior determination: the existence of a system of states that was the precondition for regionally multiple differential developments; hence, the precondition for unevenness. However, as this spatial fragmentation of the total historical process was captured only in its results – differences between separately existing entities – unevenness as a central category of analysis discounted both, an explanation of this geopolitical pluriverse and the efficacy of geopolitical dynamics. In this respect, the statement of *The German Ideology* that 'civil society ... embraces the whole commercial and industrial life of a given stage and, insofar, transcends the state and the nation, though, on the other hand again, must assert itself in its foreign relations as nationality, and inwardly must organise itself as state'[28] raises precisely the question in what exactly this requirement consists, insofar as the territorial fragmentation of the states system cannot be derived from the formation of a transnationalizing capitalist civil society.

---

[27] Soell, 'Weltmarkt – Revolution – Staatenwelt', pp. 113–15.
[28] Marx and Engels, *The German Ideology*, p. 89.

While this geopolitical deficiency received intermittent attention in Marx's journalistic and historical writings, its full challenge surfaces most dramatically where Marx's thought turns most theoretical: the three volumes of *Capital*. Here, the central object of investigation was capital in the abstract, unfolding according to its inner contradictions (the 'laws of motion of capitalist accumulation'), conceived as a dialectical self-movement that relegates agency and history to the margins as mere exemplifications and personifications of 'economic categories'. Although *Capital* is adorned with illustrative references to Victorian Britain, it was essentially conceptualized in ideal typical fashion in a political and geopolitical vacuum – beyond history. While the working plan for the 1857 introduction to the *Grundrisse* envisaged a theory of the state and international relations[29] (that would remain eventually unfinished), the tension between a conception of capital as a self-developing category and capitalism as a historical and contested social relation remained submerged.

Overall, Marx's interest in geopolitics remained primarily tied to the tactical consequences of alterations in world politics for communist strategy and, hence, limited to very perceptive but primarily ad hoc interventions, rather than governed by a sustained reflection on the implications of geopolitical and trans-societal relations for the general course of history. In the end, the intellectual problem of the tension in the relation between theory and international history remained unaddressed and unresolved.

17.5 Historicism as Theory

Marx's work remains an indispensable resource for the conceptualization of international relations for past and present analytical purposes. It provides multiple theoretical pointers that reject – *avant la lettre* – the Anglo-American mainstream conception in the discipline of IR/IPE of the interstate system as a reified, autonomous, and invariant sphere abstracted from domestic social conflicts and the attendant conception of the state as a power-maximizing, rational, and unitary actor governed by the singular logic of interstate anarchy. Still, no ready-made, coherent, or convincing approach to international relations and war can be directly derived from an exegesis of Marx's writings. This left a problematic intellectual legacy that persists in the historical-materialist literature on the subject.[30] Marx oscillated between foregrounding theoretical abstractions held to impose their deep logics and functional requirements on the course of history – notably, a single world-historical pattern of sequences of modes-of-production, the mega-subject of

---

[29] Marx, 'Outlines of the Critique of the Political Economy [*Grundrisse*]. First Instalment', p. 44.
[30] Teschke, 'Marxism', pp. 163–87.

a transnationalizing, homogenizing, and unifying capitalist world market, or the spaceless self-expansion of the concept of capital – and delving into historical concretions – a series of case studies on specific geopolitical conjunctures. Both modes of inquiry were expressed in the use of different analytical registers: theoretical-logical tracts versus journalistic, political, and historical narratives.

This centres the wider question of the relation between theory and history, which continues to plague the contemporary Marxist IR discourse. Here, the perceived need towards social-scientific formalization has recreated the opposition between the objectification of social and political (including diplomatic) praxes subject to higher laws and logics, veering towards a nomological positivism in which history merely exemplifies preconceived logics, and the turn towards history for concrete analyses. The puzzle as to how to square the explanatory emphasis accorded to impersonal developmental tendencies, logics, or laws of motion with the conscious activity of historical actors, their subjectivities and inter-subjectivities, remains an enduring one. But, if Marx had a persistent methodological *leitmotif*, then this could be conceived as a rebellion against modes of theorising *sub specie aeternitatis* (generalizations). For this was the charge that he raised consistently against the naturalizing obfuscations of liberal political economy, replacing transhistorical abstractions with a commitment to thinking in terms of identifying *differentiae specificae* (specificities), even if he relapsed into his own generalizations of capitalism's laws of motion.[31]

This chapter suggests that escaping the reifications inherent in grand IR model-building, whether Marxist or non-Marxist, requires rejecting a nomological conception of theory that posits generic logics and laws – general abstractions – that govern the course of history supra-individually, be they grounded in capitalist (or any other) structural imperatives. In contrast, recalling Marx's epistemological *a priori* of human praxis developed in his early philosophical writings, including the *Thesis on Feuerbach*, the *Contribution to the Critique of Hegel's Philosophy of Right*, the *Economic and Philosophic Manuscripts of 1844*, and his critique of the bourgeois method of 'general abstraction' in the *Grundrisse,* suggests a move towards a historicizing perspective. At the centre of this historicism for a Marxist approach to international relations stands a recovery of the situated agency of socio-political communities and their foreign policy encounters to comprehend the historicity and variability of (capitalist) geopolitics and world orders. This is not to deny that 'the logic of inter-state anarchy' and 'the logic of capital' exercise certain structural pressures, but to insist that the

---

[31] Marx, 'Outlines of the Critique of the Political Economy [*Grundrisse*]. First Instalment', p. 21–4.

ways in which agents (states, firms, or classes) react to these pressures cannot simply be read off these contexts. They have to be historically established. This shifts the burden of explanation away from imperatives to an assessment of how agents interpret, navigate, and creatively alter these constraints and innovate in the process, drawing on a variety of resources, including the balance of class forces, the degree of self-organization, the setting of hegemonic discourses, the mobilization of institutions, and other sources of power. This is not simply an exercise in moving to lower levels of abstraction that keep general abstractions intact as 'theory', but implies a more comprehensive move to an agency-centred and dialectical approach to history. This accords explanatory primacy to the widely varying and fundamentally contested construction, contestation, and implementation of foreign-policy strategies by historically situated actors – historically situated within historically specific strategic force fields of domestic and international conflicts.

This turn towards a relational and agency-centred historicism can answer some of Marx's questions, reject extant Marxist IR theories, and point indicatively towards an alternative research agenda. For there is no straight causal line from an expanding world market to a border-cancelling cosmopolitan world state, nor did capitalism or a transnational bourgeois society generate the interstate system, nor is the interstate system a functional requirement for capitalist reproduction. Rather, historically very specific pre-capitalist processes, driven by very specific social conflicts, shaped over time an interstate territorial pluriverse within which capitalism developed *ex post factum*.[32] This also implies that the category of the 'interstate system' is too crude and ahistorical a concept to generate any purchase on concrete political geographies. Any further reflections on the relation between capitalism, political geography, and international relations should thus not be conceived in terms of the functional requirements derived from the deep logic of capitalism (or any other logic). Capitalism and 'the interstate system' stand neither in a relation of 'logical determinacy' nor 'absolute contingency', but in a relation of historical construction, since political geography became itself the object of grand strategy from the early modern period onwards. As both phenomena did not remain identical with themselves over time, the reconstruction of the history of

---

[32] For the historicist promise of political Marxism, see R. Brenner, 'The Agrarian Roots of European Capitalism', in: T. H. Aston and C. Philpin (eds), *The Brenner Debate: Agrarian Class Structure and Economic Development in Pre-Industrial Europe* (Cambridge: Cambridge University Press, 1985), pp. 213–327; H. Lacher, *Beyond Globalization: Capitalism, Territoriality, and the International Relations of Modernity* (London: Routledge, 2006); B. Teschke, 'Bourgeois Revolution, State-Formation and the Absence of International Relations', *Historical Materialism*, 13 (2) (2005).

capitalism in relation to the construction of political geographies requires a radically historicist approach that centres the efficacy of agency, articulated ultimately as foreign policy and diplomacy. This points to a research programme that revolves around the historically specific and variable foreign policy strategies – including strategies of territorialization – of multiple polities, whose encounters appear as geopolitical relations: international politics.

For the relations between capitalism, political geography, and international relations are infinitely malleable: from Britain's grand blue-water strategy and continental balancing enacted at the Peace of Utrecht (1713), via its orchestration of the post-Napoleonic Vienna Congress System (1815), its (neo-)mercantilist and free-trade policies of the *Pax Britannica*, and its flexible handling of the formal and informal empires, to the US Monroe-Doctrine and the New Imperialism of the pre-First World War period; from the national-socialist conception of a German 'greater territorial order [*Grossraum*]', the Italian *Mare Nostrum* strategy, and the Japanese idea of a 'Greater East Asia Co-Prosperity Sphere', via the multilateral hegemony of the *Pax Americana* and decolonization within the Cold War context, and the project of European integration, to the efforts towards global governance or American neo-imperialism: the historical record of international relations and political geographies, capitalist or otherwise, is too diverse for its subsumption under any 'covering law'. They are historically unique.[33]

A historicist approach posits consequently a more radical break with forms of structuralism. It reconceives a Marxist approach to international relations in terms of the socio-political construction of geopolitical encounters to capture the historically varying configurations of political spatiality and geopolitical relations as contested practices in non-reductionist and non-deterministic ways. These brief reflections point to a further problematization and, ultimately, rejection of abstract theory-building and model formation. For, if, as Marx suggested, 'success will never come with the master-key of a general historico-philosophical theory, whose supreme virtue consists in being supra-historical',[34] then this implies that we cannot reason from axiomatic premises to history, but need to conceive of history itself as the primary terrain on which people construct their own reality. The history of international relations is, in short, what people make of it.

---

[33] B. Teschke, 'Imperial Doxa from the Berlin Republic', *New Left Review*, 2 (40): 133–4 (2006).
[34] Marx, 'Letter to Editors of *Otechestvenniye Zapiski*', p. 34.

References

Anderson, Kevin (2015), *Marx at the Margins: On Nationalism, Ethnicity, and Non-Western Societies*, Chicago: University of Chicago Press.
Anderson, Perry (2002), 'Internationalism: A Breviary', *New Left Review*, 2 (14): 5–25.
Benner, Erica (1995), *Really Existing Nationalisms: A Post-Communist View from Marx and Engels*, Oxford: Oxford University Press.
Berki, Robert N. (1971), 'On Marxian Thought and the Problem of International Relations', *World Politics*, 24 (1): 80–105.
Brenner, Robert (1985), 'The Agrarian Roots of European Capitalism', in: Trevor H. Aston and Charles Philpin (eds), *The Brenner Debate: Agrarian Class Structure and Economic Development in Pre-Industrial Europe*, Cambridge: Cambridge University Press, pp. 213–327.
Cox, Robert (1987), *Production, Power, and World Order: Social Forces in the Making of World History*, New York: Columbia University Press.
Giddens, Anthony (1985), *The Nation-State and Violence: Volume 2 of the Contemporary Critique of Historical Materialism*, Cambridge: Polity Press.
Halliday, Fred (1994), *Rethinking International Relations*, London: Macmillan.
Harvey, David (2001), *Spaces of Capital: Towards a Critical Geography*, New York: Routledge.
(2003), *The New Imperialism*, Oxford: Oxford University Press.
Hoffmann, Clemens (2008), 'The Balkanization of Ottoman Rule: Premodern Origins of the Modern International System in Southeastern Europe', *Cooperation and Conflict*, 43 (4): 373–96.
Kandal, Terry R. (1989), 'Marx and Engels on International Relations, Revolution and Counterrevolution', in: Michael T. Martin and Terry R. Kandal (eds), *Studies of Development and Change in the Modern World*, New York: Oxford University Press, pp. 25–76.
Lacher, Hannes (2006), *Beyond Globalization: Capitalism, Territoriality, and the International Relations of Modernity*, London: Routledge.
Marx, Karl (1975), 'A Contribution to the Critique of Hegel's Philosophy of Law. Introduction', MECW, vol. 3, pp. 175–87.
(1975), *Economic and Philosophic Manuscripts of 1844*, MECW, vol. 3, pp. 229–346.
(1979), 'Lord Palmerston', MECW, vol. 12, pp. 345–406.
(1986), 'Revelations of the Diplomatic History of the 18th Century', MECW, vol. 15, pp. 25–96.
(1986), 'Outlines of the Critique of Political Economy [*Grundrisse*]. First Instalment', MECW, vol. 28.
(1989), 'Letter to Editors of *Otechestvenniye Zapiski*', in: Derek Sayer (ed.), *Readings from Karl Marx*, London: Routledge, pp. 32–4.
Marx, Karl, and Engels, Frederick (1975), *The German Ideology*, MECW, vol. 5, pp. 19–539.
(1976), *Manifesto of the Communist Party*, MECW, vol. 6, pp. 477–519.
(1980), 'The European War', MECW, vol. 13, pp. 129–31.
(1982), *Letters, 1844–1851*, MECW, vol. 38.
(1983), *Letters, 1852–55*, MECW, vol. 39.

(1985), *Letters, 1860–1864*, MECW, vol. 41.
Rosenberg, Justin (2006), 'Why is There no International Historical Sociology?', *European Journal of International Relations*, 12 (3): 307–40.
Semmel, Bernard (1981), *Marxism and the Science of War*, Oxford: Oxford University Press.
Skocpol, Theda (1979), *States and Social Revolutions: A Comparative Analysis of France, Russia, and China*, Cambridge: Cambridge University Press.
Soell, Hartmut (1972), 'Weltmarkt – Revolution – Staatenwelt', *Archiv für Sozialgeschichte*, 12: 109–84.
Teschke, Benno (2003), *Class, Geopolitics and the Making of Modern International Relations*, London: Verso.
　(2005), 'Bourgeois Revolution, State-Formation and the Absence of International Relations', *Historical Materialism: Research in Critical Marxist Theory*, 13 (2): 3–26.
　(2006), 'Imperial Doxa from the Berlin Republic', *New Left Review*, 2 (40): 128–40.
　(2008), 'Marxism', in: Christian Reus-Smit and Duncan Snidal (eds), *The Oxford Handbook of International Relations*, Oxford: Oxford University Press, pp. 163–87.
　(2014), 'IR Theory, Historical Materialism, and the False Promise of International Historical Sociology', *Spectrum: Journal of Global Studies*, 6 (1): 1–66.
Wallerstein, Immanuel (1974), 'The Rise and Future Demise of the Capitalist World-System: Concepts for Comparative Analysis', *Comparative Studies in Society and History*, 16: 387–415.

18   Religion

Gilbert Achcar

18.1   Marx's Engagement with Religion

Religion is one of the issues on which the Marxian corpus – the writings authored or co-authored by Karl Marx himself – is deficient. Although there are plenty of references to religion in Marx's oeuvre, his most quoted statements on the topic belong to the initial transitional phase in his intellectual trajectory during which his break with the Young Hegelians unfolded.

Thus, there is no *Marxian* theory of religion – a theoretical lacuna that contributed to the fact that, to this day, there is no reference work or body of work that can be regarded as providing a comprehensive *Marxist* theory of religion.[1] The major reason for that, of course, is the high complexity of religion compared to plainly political ideologies. The theoretical tools developed by Marx cannot account alone for the multidimensional aspect of the question. Historical materialism is a necessary but insufficient explanans of religion, a topic that requires the input of all major human sciences such as anthropology, sociology, or psychoanalysis. Moreover, Marx wrote quite a bit less than Friedrich Engels about religion, probably because of a more limited interest in the topic determined by the limits of his personal religious experience compared to his friend's.

Yet, there are, of course, numerous analytical comments on religious matters in Marx's writings beyond the famous statements of his youth. They can be classified under two categories: on the one hand, elements of a materialist interpretation of religion – scattered theoretical insights more than a full-fledged theory; on the other hand, religious metaphors

---

[1] In her *Le Statut de la Religion chez Marx et Engels* (Paris: Editions sociales, 1979), pp. 76–7, Michèle Bertrand rightly asserted that 'Marx's and Engels's analysis of religion does not take the form of a full-fledged and complete theory of religion in general.' A Marxist herself, she found in Marxism no valid answer to the question of 'the permanence of religion' (p. 184). For a wide-angle overview of Western Marxist and para-Marxist engagements with religion, see R. Boer's five-volume *On Marxism and Theology* (Leiden: Brill, 2007–14).

and analogies – the most famous is that of 'fetishism',[2] but there are several others – with which Marx's economic writings are ridden and which are of little use for a study of religion per se.[3]

Besides, Marx's writings include several political statements that constitute a coherent Marxian political attitude towards religion. Much less attention has been paid to this dimension of Marx's thinking, largely subsumed under the Bolsheviks' political stances on religion.[4]

18.2 Marx' Left-Hegelian Critique of Religion

The young Marx set most clearly the Left-Hegelian atheistic and antireligious tenor of his doctoral dissertation (1840–41) in its foreword, where, after quoting 'the cry of Epicurus' – 'Not the man who denies the gods worshipped by the multitude, but he who affirms of the gods what the multitude believes about them, is truly impious' – he presented the 'confession of Prometheus' – 'I hate the pack of gods' – as philosophy's 'own aphorism against all heavenly and earthly gods who do not acknowledge human self-consciousness as the highest divinity'.[5]

However, it is only after finishing his dissertation – judging from the notebooks he wrote during his 1842 sojourn in Bonn[6] – that Marx read some major works on religion, taking extensive notes. Two works had an outstanding impact on him: Charles de Brosses's (1709–1777) *On the Worship of Fetish Gods* (1760), which Marx read in German translation, and Benjamin Constant's (1767–1830) *On Religion Considered in Its Source, Its Forms, and Its Developments* (1824–31).

---

[2] With commodities, 'it is a definite social relation between men, that assumes, in their eyes, the fantastic form of a relation between things. In order, therefore, to find an analogy, we must have recourse to the mist-enveloped regions of the religious world. In that world, the productions of the human brain appear as independent beings endowed with life, and entering into relation both with one another and the human race. So it is in the world of commodities with the products of men's hands. This I call the Fetishism which attaches itself to the products of labour, so soon as they are produced as commodities', K. Marx, *Capital*, volume I, MECW, vol. 35, p. 83.

[3] See F. Bellue, 'Typologie des métaphores religieuses dans *Le Capital* de K. Marx', in: G. Labica and J. Robelin (eds), *Politique et Religion* (Paris: L'Harmattan, 1994), pp. 61–91. This study will not deal with the religious metaphors used by Marx, but only retrace the development of his historical materialist perspective on religion itself.

[4] Two recent works on the Bolsheviks and religion are R. Boer, *Lenin, Religion and Theology* (New York: Palgrave Macmillan, 2013) and P. Gabel, *And God Created Lenin: Marxism vs. Religion in Russia, 1917–1929* (New York: Prometheus Books, 2005).

[5] K. Marx, *Difference between the Democritean and Epicurean Philosophy of Nature*, MECW, vol. 1, p. 30. Marx ended his dissertation likewise with a pugnaciously antireligious quote of Lucretius praising Epicurus, whom the young doctorand described as 'the greatest representative of Greek Enlightenment' (ibid., p. 73).

[6] The *Bonner Hefte* are published in the MEGA², vol. IV/1.

From de Brosses, Marx borrowed the notion of fetishism (also discussed in Constant's work, albeit in different terms).[7] His earliest use of this notion – a recurrent theme in his writings thereafter – appeared in a July 1842 article in the *New Rhenish Newspaper [Rheinische Zeitung]*,[8] which is Marx's first extensive public comment on religion. It includes his first materialist inversion of the idealist interpretation of the role of religion in history: 'It was not the downfall of the old religions that caused the downfall of the ancient states, but the downfall of the ancient states that caused the downfall of the old religions.'[9] A few months later, in a letter to Arnold Ruge (1802–1880), Marx displayed a rather simplistic conception of religion along with the conviction that it will eventually fade away: 'religion in itself is without content, it owes its being not to heaven but to the earth, and with the abolition of distorted reality, of which it is the *theory*, it will collapse of itself'.[10]

The materialist inversion lies at the heart of Marx's 1843 essays criticizing two writings by the Young Hegelian Bruno Bauer (1809–1882) on the 'Jewish question'. In that two-fold rebuttal entitled 'On *The Jewish Question*', Marx had not completely broken yet with an essentialist appraisal of religion – Judaism and Christianity in that case – in the vein of Ludwig Feuerbach's (1804–1872) half-baked assessment of the Christian religion, characteristically titled *The Essence of Christianity*.[11] Thus, Marx was still discussing the 'essence' of each of Judaism and Christianity in idealizations called 'the Jew' and 'the Christian'. He saw the essence of 'the Jew' and 'Judaism' as defined by monetary relations and contended that this essence is the result not of the Jewish religion per se, but of the Jews' actual historical insertion 'in the interstices' of medieval European societies, as he put it in his economic manuscripts of later years.[12]

---

[7] For a discussion of Marx's borrowing from de Brosses, see R. Boer, *On Marxism and Theology: Vol. IV, Criticism of Earth* (Leiden: Brill, 2012), pp. 177–206 and *On Marxism and Theology: Vol. V, In the Vale of Tears* (Leiden: Brill, 2014), pp. 289–309. For a comparison between Constant's and Marx's notion of fetishism, see B. Garsten, 'Religion and the Case against Ancient Liberty: Benjamin Constant's Other Lectures', *Political Theory*, 38 (1): 4–33 (2010).

[8] K. Marx, 'The Leading Article in No. 179 of the *Kölnische Zeitung*', MECW, vol. 1, p. 189.

[9] Ibid.   [10] 'K. Marx to A. Ruge, 30 November 1842', MECW, vol. 1, p. 395.

[11] See L. Althusser's critical discussion of Feuerbach and his influence on the early Marx in his *For Marx* (Harmondsworth: Penguin, 1969).

[12] Here are three statements from Marx's *Grundrisse* (K. Marx, 'Outlines of the Critique of Political Economy [*Grundrisse*]. First and Second Instalment', MECW, vols 28 and 29) on the economic role of Jews in history: 'Special trading peoples could play this mediating role between peoples whose mode of production did not yet presuppose exchange value as its basis. Thus, in antiquity, and later the Lombards, thus the Jews within the old Polish society or in medieval society in general' (vol. 28, p. 184). 'Wealth as an end-in-itself appears only among a few trading peoples – monopolists of the carrying trade – who live in the pores of the ancient world like the Jews in medieval society' (vol. 28, p. 411). '[T]he

Let us not look for the secret of the Jew in his religion, but let us look for the secret of his religion in the real Jew ... The Jew has emancipated himself in a Jewish manner, not only because he has acquired financial power, but also because, through him and also apart from him, *money* has become a world power and the practical Jewish spirit has become the practical spirit of the Christian nations. The Jews have emancipated themselves insofar as the Christians have become Jews. ... Judaism continues to exist not in spite of history, but owing to history. ... The god of the Jews has become secularized and has become the god of the world.[13]

It is in the wake of these essays that Marx wrote the much-quoted and very lyrical 'Contribution to the Critique of Hegel's Philosophy of Right. Introduction', published in 1844 in the *German–French Annals* [*Deutsch–Französische Jahrbücher*].

The basis of irreligious criticism is: The *human being makes religion*; religion does not make the human being. Religion is the self-consciousness and self-esteem of the human who has either not yet found himself or has already lost himself again. But the *human* is no abstract being encamped outside the world. The human is *the world of the human* – state, society. This state, this society, produce religion, an *inverted world-consciousness*, because they are an *inverted world*. Religion is the general theory of that world, its encyclopaedic compendium, its logic in a popular form, its spiritualistic *point d'honneur*, its enthusiasm, its moral sanction, its solemn complement, its universal source of consolation and justification. It is the *fantastic realisation* of the human essence because the *human essence* has no true reality. The struggle against religion is therefore indirectly a fight against *the world* of which religion is the spiritual *aroma*.[14]

Restating in this passage a central idea of Feuerbach's critique of religion ('The human being makes religion'), Marx went one step further in his materialist critique. The statement that 'the human is no abstract being' is a direct rebuff to Feuerbach. Like the latter, however, and with Christianity mainly in mind, the young Marx fully acknowledged the spiritual role played by religion, alongside its essence as a vulgar 'false consciousness'. He formulated this insight in admirable terms:

Religious distress is at the same time the *expression* of real distress and also the *protest* against real distress. Religion is the sigh of the oppressed creature, the heart

---

Semites in the interstices of the ancient world, and the Jews, Lombards and Normans in the interstices of the medieval society, alternately represent ... the different moments of circulation – money and commodity. They are the mediators of the social exchange of matter' (vol. 29, p. 481). On Marxist discussions of 'the Jewish question' from Marx to Abram Leon, see E. Traverso, *The Marxists and the Jewish Question: The History of a Debate (1843–1943)* (Atlantic Highlands, NJ: Humanities Press, 1993).

[13] K. Marx, 'On the Jewish Question', MECW, vol. 3, pp. 169–72. Here and in all subsequent quotes; emphasis is in the original.

[14] K. Marx, 'Contribution to the Critique of Hegel's Philosophy of Right. Introduction', MECW, vol. 3, p. 175. Here and in further quotations, 'man' has been replaced with 'human' in translating the German *Mensch*.

of a heartless world, just as it is the spirit of spiritless conditions. It is the *opium* of the people.

To sublate religion as the *illusory* happiness of the people is to demand their *real* happiness. The demand to give up illusions about the existing state of affairs is the *demand to give up a state of affairs which needs illusions*. The criticism of religion is therefore *in embryo the criticism of the vale of tears*, the *halo* of which is religion.[15]

To describe religion as both a sublimated 'expression' of 'real distress' and a 'protest' against it was a very perceptive statement, but Marx did unfortunately not pursue the 'protest' dimension. He did not give thought to the fact that Christianity – as Engels would later acknowledge in his 1850 *The Peasant War in Germany*, albeit in a limited way[16] – had proven 'its ability to shoulder the aspirations of the oppressed and the poor' in the words of Michèle Bertrand.[17] Hence, Marx's unqualified diatribe in 1847 against 'the social principles of Christianity' which he presented as completely antithetic with communism.[18]

The opium metaphor is widely regarded as epitomizing Marx's view of religion. It became one of his most quoted phrases, although he was merely resorting to an analogy used by several authors before him, from Immanuel Kant (1724–1804) to Heinrich Heine (1797–1856), to illustrate a view that is 'not at all specifically Marxist' as Michael Löwy (1938–) emphasized.[19] Marx's description of the consoling virtue of religion was also in tune with the first chapter of Constant's *On Religion Considered in Its Source, Its Forms, and Its Developments*.[20]

In the context of the battle waged by twentieth century's communism against religion, this famous statement came to be interpreted as more pejorative than intended. This was also related to a negative shift in the perception of opium compared to the nineteenth century, when it was still commonly used medically as sedative and tranquillizer.[21] Yet, the pendulum of historical interpretations shifted again in recent years towards overemphasis on the seemingly positive connotation of Marx's description of religion as 'the sigh of the oppressed', seen as denoting empathy.

---

[15] Marx, 'Contribution to the Critique of Hegel's Philosophy of Right. Introduction', pp. 175–6. Here and in one more quotation, 'abolition' has been replaced with 'sublation' in translating the German *Aufhebung* after verification of the original in the *Marx Engels Werke*.

[16] F. Engels, *The Peasant War in Germany*, MECW, vol. 10. For a critique of Engels's views, see G. Achcar, *Marxism, Orientalism, Cosmopolitanism* (London: Saqi; Chicago: Haymarket, 2013), pp. 10–39.

[17] Bertrand, *Le Statut de la Religion*, p. 34.

[18] K. Marx, 'The Communism of the *Rheinischer Beobachter*', MECW, vol. 6, p. 231.

[19] M. Löwy, *The War of Gods: Religion and Politics in Latin America* (London: Verso, 1996), p. 5.

[20] B. Constant, *De la Religion* (Arles: Actes Sud), 1999, 'Du sentiment religieux', pp. 39–52.

[21] See A. McKinnon, 'Reading "Opium of the People": Expression, Protest and the Dialectics of Religion', *Critical Sociology*, 31 (1–2): 15–38 (2005).

The young Marx, however, was only stating the obvious: religion acts as a tranquillizer against the deep anxiety provoked by the modern world. It provides an 'illusory happiness' that, he believed, could be superseded by the realization of 'real happiness', which would make illusions superfluous. The criticism of religion should therefore lead to the criticism of the down-to-earth world.

> The immediate *task of philosophy*, which is at the service of history, once the *holy form* of human self-estrangement has been unmasked, is to unmask self-estrangement in its *unholy forms*. Thus the criticism of heaven turns into the criticism of the earth, the *criticism of religion* into the *criticism of law* and the *criticism of theology* into the *criticism of politics*.[22]

Marx went on for a while pursuing the philosophic task of unmasking 'unholy' alienation as a necessary complement to his former comrades' unmasking of religious alienation. In this endeavour, he made an analogy between both types of alienation, thus providing a clue to the later mutation of his philosophical critique into a political-economic critique of capitalism and highlighting the methodological continuity between them.

> [T]he more the worker spends himself, the more powerful becomes the alien world of objects which he creates over and against himself, the poorer he himself – his inner world – becomes, the less belongs to him as his own. It is the same in religion. The more humans put into God, the less they retain in themselves ...
>
> Religious estrangement as such occurs only in the realm of *consciousness*, of the human's inner life, but economic estrangement is that of *real life*; its transcendence therefore embraces both aspects.[23]

This led Marx to supersede the atheistic critique of religion as a foregone moment. He no longer felt the need to engage in it, thus distancing himself from his former Young Hegelian comrades.

> [A]theism is a *negation of God*, and postulates the *existence of the human being* through this negation; but socialism as socialism no longer stands in any need of such a mediation. It proceeds from the *theoretically and practically sensuous consciousness* of the human being and of nature as the *essence*. Socialism is man's *positive self-consciousness*, no longer mediated through the sublation of religion.[24]

---

[22] Marx, 'Contribution to the Critique of Hegel's Philosophy of Right. Introduction', p. 176. In the German original, *Selbstentfremdung*, here translated as 'self-estrangement', refers to the concept of alienation, *Entfremdung*.

[23] K. Marx, *Economic and Philosophic Manuscripts of 1844*, MECW, vol. 3, pp. 272, 297.

[24] Ibid, p. 306. Compared to Engels's much later assertion about 'German Social Democratic workers' that 'atheism has already outlived its usefulness for them; this pure negation does not apply to them, since they no longer stand in theoretical, but only in practical opposition to all belief in God: they are *simply through with God*, they live and think in the real world and are, therefore, materialists' (F. Engels, 'Programme of the Blanquist Commune Refugees', MECW, vol. 24, pp. 15–16).

In *The Holy Family*, the first work that Marx co-wrote with Engels, Bauer was attacked for keeping the debate on the terrain of religion. The book constitutes a useful complement to Marx's essays 'On *The Jewish Question*' in that it clarifies the latter's arguments and sheds a useful light on the issue of its alleged antisemitism. Bauer shared Hegel's brand of anti-Judaism combined with no hostility to the Jews as citizens, and Hegel's view of Christianity as the absolute religion. He dealt with the 'Jewish question' in such religious-philosophical terms, while Marx and Engels strived to bring the issue down to the earth of material determinants.

> Herr Bauer has no inkling that real *secular* Jewry, and hence *religious* Jewry *too*, is being continually produced by the *present-day civil life* and finds its final development in the *money system* ... For Herr Bauer, as a theologian of the *Christian faith*, the *world-historic* significance of Jewry had to cease the *moment* Christianity was *born*. Hence he had to repeat the old orthodox view that it has maintained itself *in spite* of history.[25]

The Holy Family reinstated in clearer form the key theses of Marx's essays. Rather than targeting the Jews singled out by Bauer's 'theological' approach, which it characterized as 'theological fanaticism', the book asserted that the material basis of the Jews' historical specificity within Christian society, that is, their function as agents of the monetary economy, has become universal.

> The existence of the *present-day* Jew was not explained by his religion – as though this religion were something apart, independently existing – but the tenacious survival of the Jewish religion was explained by practical features of civil society which are *fantastically* reflected in that religion. The emancipation of the Jews into human beings, or the human emancipation of Jewry, was therefore not conceived, as by Herr Bauer, as the special task of the Jews, but as a general practical task of the present-day world, which is *Jewish* to the core. It was proved that the task of abolishing the essence of Jewry is actually the task of abolishing the *Jewish character of civil society*, abolishing the inhumanity of the present-day practice of life, the most extreme expression of which is the *money system*.[26]

Marx distanced himself further from the Young Hegelians as his political radicalization progressed. His 1845 *Thesis on Feuerbach*, with their conclusion on revolutionary praxis – 'revolutionary, practical-critical, activity' – represented a new step towards overcoming the essentialism inherent in Feuerbach's 'contemplative materialism':

---

[25] K. Marx and F. Engels, *The Holy Family*, MECW, vol. 4, p. 109.
[26] Ibid, pp. 109–10.

Feuerbach starts out from the fact of religious self-estrangement, of the duplication of the world into a religious world and a secular one. His work consists in resolving the religious world into its secular basis. But that the secular basis lifts off from itself and establishes itself as an independent realm in the clouds can only be explained by the inner strife and intrinsic contradictoriness of this secular basis. The latter must, therefore, itself be both understood in its contradiction and revolutionised in practice.[27]

18.3 Towards a Materialist Interpretation of Religion

Marx and Engels completed their break with the Young Hegelians and expounded main tenets of their new materialist conception of history in *The German Ideology*, which they drafted in 1845–6 and ended renouncing to publish. The issue of religion was still central to that final engagement with their former companions:

The Young Hegelians *criticised* everything by ascribing religious conceptions to it or by declaring that it is a theological matter. The Young Hegelians are in agreement with the Old Hegelians in their belief in the rule of religion, of concepts, of a universal principle in the existing world. Except that the one party attacks this rule as usurpation, while the other extols it as legitimate.[28]

This time, however, the two co-thinkers went beyond their philosophical 'critique of critical criticism', as they had called it ironically, into laying out the foundations of their new conception of history with a radical inversion of perspective leading to the elaboration of historical materialism.

The phantoms formed in the brains of the humans are ... necessarily, sublimates of their material life-process, which is empirically verifiable and bound to material premises. Morality, religion, metaphysics, and all the rest of ideology as well as the forms of consciousness corresponding to these, thus no longer retain the semblance of independence.[29]

The *materialist conception of history* was thus born along with its dialectical dimension:

This conception of history thus relies on expounding the real process of production – starting from the material production of life itself – and comprehending the form of intercourse connected with and created by this mode of production, i.e., civil society in its various stages, as the basis of all history; describing it in its action as the state, and also explaining how all the different theoretical products and forms of consciousness, religion, philosophy, morality, etc., etc., arise from it, and

---

[27] K. Marx, *Thesis on Feuerbach*, MECW, vol. 5, p. 4.
[28] K. Marx and F. Engels, *The German Ideology*, MECW, vol. 5, p. 30.
[29] Ibid, pp. 36–7.

328 *Gilbert Achcar*

tracing the process of their formation from that basis; thus the whole thing can, of course, be depicted in its totality (and therefore, too, the reciprocal action of these various sides on one another).[30]

The manuscript included an interesting insight on religion – 'Religion is from the outset *consciousness of the transcendental* arising from *actually existing* forces' – which the authors did unfortunately not develop 'more popularly' as they intended to do.[31] What they provided about the materialist explanation of religion were essentially leads into a research programme.

[D]efinite relations of industry and intercourse are necessarily connected with a definite form of society, hence, with a definite form of state and hence with a definite form of religious consciousness. If [Max] Stirner had looked at the real history of the Middle Ages, he could have found why the Christian's notion of the world took precisely this form in the Middle Ages, and how it happened that it subsequently passed into a different one; he could have found that *'Christianity' has no history whatever* and that all the different forms in which it was visualised at various times were not 'self-determinations' and 'further developments' 'of the religious spirit', but were brought about by wholly empirical causes in no way dependent on any influence of the religious spirit.[32]

In their *Manifesto of the Communist Party*, Marx and Engels further discussed the view of the intimate connection of religion, as a form of consciousness, and the material conditions of society. They formulated a heuristic, albeit rather crude, explanation of the historical persistence of religions and other ideological forms, attributing it to the permanence of class division. 'Undoubtedly', it will be said:

religious, moral, philosophical and juridical ideas have been modified in the course of historical development. But religion, morality, philosophy, political science, and law, constantly survived this change ... The history of all past society has consisted in the development of class antagonisms, antagonisms that assumed different forms at different epochs.

But whatever form they may have taken, one fact is common to all past ages, *viz.*, the exploitation of one part of society by the other. No wonder, then, that the social consciousness of past ages, despite all the multiplicity and variety it displays, moves within certain common forms, or general ideas, which cannot completely vanish except with the total disappearance of class antagonisms.[33]

The dialectics of religious permanence and change – the transmutation of religions along with the historical change of material conditions while retaining some forms, which is the key to religions' historical persistence – is a theme that is recurrent in the two co-thinkers' comments on Christianity

---

[30] Ibid, p. 53.   [31] Ibid, p. 93.   [32] Ibid, p. 154.
[33] K. Marx and F. Engels, *Manifesto of the Communist Party*, MECW, vol. 6, p. 504.

in particular. Thus, in the sharp critique of Georg Friedrich Daumer's (1800–1875) *The Religion of the New Age* (1850) that they published in 1850, they stressed 'that after the Germanic invasion the "new world conditions" did not adapt themselves to Christianity but that Christianity itself changed with every new phase of these world conditions'.[34]

In Marx's later economic writings, Christianity is portrayed as the religion of capital *par excellence*. As he put it ironically in his 1861–63 economic manuscripts, capitalism is

> as truly cosmopolitan as Christianity. This is why Christianity is likewise the special religion of capital. In both it is only humans who count. One human in the abstract is worth just as much or as little as the next human. In the one case, all depends on whether or not the human has faith, in the other, on whether or not the human has credit. In addition, however, in the one case, predestination has to be added, and in the other case, the accident of whether or not a human is born with a silver spoon in mouth.[35]

Marx expanded upon this idea in *Capital* in the famous section on 'The Fetishism of Commodities':

> The religious world is but the reflex of the real world. And for a society based upon the production of commodities, in which the producers in general enter into social relations with one another by treating their products as commodities and values, whereby they reduce their individual private labour to the standard of homogeneous human labour – for such a society, Christianity with its *cultus* of abstract man, more especially in its bourgeois developments, Protestantism, Deism, &c, is the most fitting form of religion.[36]

A footnote in *Capital* also includes a brief methodological statement that Marx did alas not elaborate:

> Technology discloses the human's mode of dealing with Nature, the process of production by which, the human sustains the human's life, and thereby also lays bare the mode of formation of the human's social relations, and of the mental conceptions that flow from them. Every history of religion, even, that fails to take account of this material basis, is uncritical. It is, in reality, much easier to discover by analysis the earthly core of the misty creations of religion, than, conversely, it is, to develop from the actual relations of life the corresponding celestialised forms of those relations. The latter method is the only materialistic, and therefore the only scientific one.[37]

There are scattered insights informed by this perspective in Marx's economic writings. They mostly deal with Protestantism as the version of

---

[34] K. Marx and F. Engels, 'Reviews from the Neue Rheinische Zeitung. Politisch-Ökonomische Revue No. 2', MECW, vol. 10, p. 244.
[35] K. Marx, *Economic Manuscript of 1861–63*, MECW, vol. 33, p. 369.
[36] Marx, *Capital*, volume I, p. 90.   [37] Ibid, p. 375, note 2.

Christianity that is correlative with capitalism, in the historical materialist vein that Max Weber (1864–1920) famously discussed in his *The Protestant Ethic and the Spirit of Capitalism*. Here are two such comments:

> The cult of money has its corresponding asceticism, its renunciation, its self-sacrifice – thrift and frugality, contempt for the worldly, temporary and transient pleasures; the pursuit of *eternal* treasure. Hence the connection of English Puritanism or also Dutch Protestantism with money-making.[38]
>
> The monetary system is essentially a Catholic institution, the credit system essentially Protestant. 'The Scotch hate gold.' In the form of paper the monetary existence of commodities is only a social one. It is *Faith* that brings salvation. Faith in money value as the immanent spirit of commodities, faith in the mode of production and its predestined order, faith in the individual agents of production as mere personifications of self-expanding capital. But the credit system does not emancipate itself from the basis of the monetary system any more than Protestantism has emancipated itself from the foundations of Catholicism.[39]

One aspect of the capitalist function of Protestantism is that it *'was also a means for increasing surplus labour'*:[40] 'Protestantism, by changing almost all the traditional holidays into workdays, plays an important part in the genesis of capital.'[41] Marx also emphasized the correlation between Malthusianism and Protestantism: 'It is characteristic that the economic fall of man, the Adam's apple, the urgent appetite ... that this delicate question was and is monopolised by the Reverends of Protestant Theology, or rather of the Protestant Church.'[42] He mocked Protestantism's lack of empathy for the poor: 'If the Venetian monk found in the fatal destiny that makes misery eternal, the *raison d'être* of Christian charity ... the Protestant prebendary finds in it a pretext for condemning the laws in virtue of which the poor possessed a right to a miserable public relief.'[43] This, Marx called 'the "spirit" of Protestantism'.[44]

Much less, and much less interesting, comments on other religions are found among Marx's writings.[45] His most apposite observation in this regard is the not so 'easily answerable' question that he formulated about the Orient in a 1853 letter to Engels: 'So far as religion is concerned, the question may be reduced to a general and hence easily answerable one: Why does the history of the East *appear* as a history of religions?'[46] Marx's

---

[38] Marx, 'Outlines of the Critique of Political Economy [*Grundrisse*]. First Instalment', p. 164.
[39] K. Marx, *Capital*, volume III, MECW, vol. 37, p. 587.
[40] Marx, *Economic Manuscript of 1861–63*, p. 300.
[41] Marx, *Capital*, volume I, p. 281, note 2.   [42] Ibid, p. 612.   [43] Ibid, p. 641.
[44] Ibid, p. 712, note 2.
[45] See K. Anderson, *Marx at the Margins: On Nationalism, Ethnicity, and Non-Western Societies*, second edition (Chicago: Chicago University Press, 2016).
[46] 'K. Marx to F. Engels, 2 June 1853', MECW, vol. 39, p. 332.

emphasis on 'appear' here sounds as a clue to the fact that the problem lies primarily in the Western perception of the East, that is, the problem of Orientalism in the sense popularized by Edward Said (1935–2003). It is highly unlikely though that this was Marx's intent.[47]

18.4 The Marxian Political Attitude on Religion

Marx's political attitude towards religion took shape at the confluence of two influences: the anticlerical atheism that he inherited from his time with the Young Hegelians was tempered with the liberal-secular attitude that he found in Constant, whose influence on Marx is generally underrated if mentioned at all.[48] That the young Marx, in his 1842 article on censorship, should defend the freedom to criticize religion, Christianity included, is not surprising.[49] He construed this freedom as part of the general freedom of opinion in the liberal-secular vein, as he did in his first long engagement with the topic of religion where he rejected any privilege to any dogma or creed.[50]

Marx went on to develop a strong argument for a strict separation of religion and state, vigorously denouncing those who want to 'make religion into a theory of constitutional law':[51]

The truly religious state is the theocratic state; the head of such states must be either the God of religion, Jehovah himself, as in the Jewish state, or God's representative, the Dalai Lama, as in Tibet, or finally ... all the Christian states must subordinate themselves to a church which is an 'infallible church'. For where, as under Protestantism, there is no supreme head of the church, the rule of religion is nothing but the religion of rule, the cult of the government's will.

Once a state includes several creeds having equal rights, it can no longer be a religious state without being a violation of the rights of the particular creeds, a church which condemns all adherents of a different creed as heretics, which makes every morsel of bread depend on one's faith, and which makes dogma the link between individuals and their existence as citizens of the state.[52]

Yet, by the end of 1842, Marx, whose communist political views were maturing, was also clearly taking his distance from the fixation with religion of some of the Young Hegelians.[53] He reported to Ruge his

---

[47] See Achcar, *Marxism, Orientalism, Cosmopolitanism*, pp. 68–102.
[48] One almost confidential exception is P. Higonnet, 'Marx, disciple de Constant?', *Annales Benjamin Constant*, 6: 11–16 (1986).
[49] K. Marx, 'Comments on the Latest Prussian Censorship Instruction', MECW, vol. 1, especially pp. 116–19.
[50] K. Marx, 'The Leading Article in No. 179 of the *Kölnische Zeitung*', MECW, vol. 1, p. 191.
[51] Ibid, p. 198.   [52] Ibid, p. 199.
[53] See A. Toscano, 'Beyond Abstraction: Marx and the Critique of the Critique of Religion', *Historical Materialism*, 18: 3–29 (2010).

reply to a query from Eduard Meyen (1812–1870), a prominent member of the Berlin circle of 'The Free':

> I replied at once and frankly expressed my opinion about the defects of their writings, which find freedom in a licentious, sans-culotte-like, and at the same time convenient, form, rather than in a *free*, i.e., independent and profound, content ... I requested further that religion should be criticised in the framework of criticism of political conditions rather than that political conditions should be criticised in the framework of religion ... Finally, I desired that, if there is to be talk about philosophy, there should be less trifling with the *label* 'atheism' (which reminds one of children, assuring everyone who is ready to listen to them that they are not afraid of the bogy man), and that instead the content of philosophy should be brought to the people.[54]

Constant's impassionate defence of the freedom of religion, unrestricted individual religious freedom, as being the most effective guarantee against the power of any single religion, had left its mark on the young Marx.[55] The clarification of his polemics with Bauer in *The Holy Family* confirmed this inspiration, including a repudiation of the 'terroristic attitude' that emerged during the French Revolution:

> Herr Bauer was shown that when the Jew demands freedom and nevertheless refuses to renounce his religion, he *'is engaging in politics'* and sets no condition that is contrary to *political* freedom. Herr Bauer was shown that it is by no means contrary to political emancipation to *divide* the human into the non-religious *citizen* and the religious *private individual*. He was shown that just as the state emancipates itself from religion by emancipating itself from *state religion* and leaving religion to itself within civil society, so the individual emancipates himself *politically* from religion by regarding it no longer as a *public* matter but as a *private matter*. Finally, it was shown that the *terroristic* attitude of the French *Revolution* to *religion*, far from refuting this conception, bears it out.[56]

Thus, Marx and Engels emphasized that 'the *right* to believe what one wishes, the right to practise any religion, is explicitly recognised as a *universal human right*' and reminded Bauer that Jacques Hébert's (1757–1794) faction was defeated during the French Revolution under the accusation that 'it attacked human rights by attacking *freedom of religion*'.[57] Furthermore, in their *The German Ideology*, the two friends ridiculed Bauer with mordant irony for his pretence to have 'smashed' religion and the state.[58]

---

[54] 'K. Marx to A. Ruge, 30 November 1842', MECW, vol. 1, pp. 394–5.
[55] This was the powerful conclusion of Constant's *De la Religion*: 'In every epoch then, we should demand religious freedom, unlimited, infinite, individual ... It will multiply religious forms ... A single sect is always a fearsome rival ... Divide the torrent or, more accurately, let it split into a thousand streams. They will fertilise the soil that the torrent would have devastated' (pp. 576–7).
[56] Marx and Engels, *The Holy Family*, p. 111.   [57] Ibid, p. 114.
[58] Marx and Engels, *The German Ideology*, p. 94.

Yet Marx and Engels kept advocating within the communist movement a relentless struggle to debunk bourgeois ideology under all its guises, religion included. 'Law, morality, religion, are to [the proletarian] so many bourgeois prejudices, behind which lurk in ambush just as many bourgeois interests.'[59] However, Marx must have bitterly regretted the blunder he made in November 1847, in his report to the London German Workers' Educational Society, when he praised Daumer's book *The Secrets of Christian Antiquity* (1847). Daumer, the same author whom Marx and Engels harshly criticized three years later,[60] had tried to give new currency to the ancient Roman legend according to which the persecuted early Christians practised anthropophagic rites. 'This story', explained Marx to his audience, 'as presented in Daumer's work, deals Christianity the last blow ... It gives us the certainty that the old society is coming to an end and that the edifice of fraud and prejudice is collapsing.'[61]

Marx's and Engels's attitude towards religion remained fundamentally dual: defence of unhindered individual freedom of belief against state interference, combined with emancipatory fight by the workers' party against religious beliefs. It is this same position that Marx forcefully reiterated in his 1875 *Critique of the Gotha Programme*:

'*Freedom of conscience*'! If one desired at this time of the *Kulturkampf* to remind liberalism of its old catchwords, it surely could have been done only in the following form: Everyone should be able to attend to his religious as well as his bodily needs without the police sticking their noses in. But the workers' party ought at any rate in this connection to have expressed its awareness of the fact that bourgeois 'freedom of conscience' is nothing but the toleration of all possible kinds of *religious unfreedom of conscience*, and that for its part it endeavours rather to liberate the conscience from the witchery of religion.[62]

And yet, Marx and Engels firmly and consistently upheld the liberal rejection of state coercion of religious belief and practice in the private sphere. This came out most clearly in their critique of other radical left currents advocating the suppression of religion. In 1868, Marx commented on the margin of the Bakuninist programme, promising 'abolition of cults, substitution of science for faith and human justice for divine justice': 'As if one could declare – by decree – the abolition of faith!'[63] He reiterated this opinion in the interview he gave in 1879 to the *Chicago*

---

[59] Marx and Engels, *Manifesto of the Communist Party*, pp. 494–5.   [60] Ibid.
[61] 'Minutes of Marx's Report to the London German Workers' Educational Society on November 30, 1847', MECW, vol. 6, p. 631.
[62] K. Marx, *Critique of the Gotha Programme*, MECW, vol. 24, pp. 97–8.
[63] K. Marx, 'Remarks on the Programme and Rules of the International Alliance of Socialist Democracy', MECW, vol. 21, p. 208. Engels expressed the same view in 1874 in his

Tribune: 'We know... that violent measures against religion are nonsense; but this is an opinion: as Socialism grows, religion will disappear. Its disappearance must be done by social development, in which education must play a great part.'[64]

Socialism, as envisaged by Marx, did not grow in the twentieth century; the regimes that claimed that label and invoked his name across the world did much disservice to both, and most have ended up crumbling miserably. Far from disappearing, religion witnessed a spectacular surge in the century's final decades, most strikingly in fundamentalist versions. To understand this 'revenge of God', as one observer called it,[65] Marx's reflections on religion provide indispensable clues, along with other key inputs in social sciences such as Emile Durkheim's (1857–1917) notion of anomie.[66] The materialist conception of history leads us to explore the socio-economic background upon which the 'return of the religious', as the phenomenon has been widely designated, did occur. Indeed, its concomitance with the massive degradation of social conditions that resulted from both the neoliberal turn in global capitalism and the terminal crisis of 'really existing socialism' followed by its collapse is certainly not a sheer coincidence. In this regard, even the young Marx's Left-Hegelian conceptualization and formulation of the correspondence between socio-economic alienation and religious alienation are useful.

The ongoing religious surge lends renewed importance to the Marxian political attitude towards religion. The European heartlands of Enlightenment themselves are confronted anew with this problem, complicated in their case by the fact that the religion in question is Islam, the creed of downtrodden populations of migrant origin. Marx's attitude towards religion should become again a source of inspiration to those who adhere to his general theory. Religious freedom must be defended

---

critique of the programme of the Blanquist Commune Refugees, which stipulated that 'every religious service, every religious organisation must be banned'. He emphasized that 'persecution is the best way of strengthening undesirable convictions' and that 'the only service that can still be rendered to God today is to make atheism a compulsory dogma' (Engels, 'Programme of the Blanquist Commune Refugees', p. 16).

[64] 'Account of Karl Marx's Interview with the *Chicago Tribune* Correspondent', MECW, vol. 24, p. 576.
[65] G. Kepel, *The Revenge of God: The Resurgence of Islam, Christianity, and Judaism in the Modern World* (London: Polity, 1994).
[66] For a use of both Marx and Durkheim in understanding the surge of religious fundamentalism in the late twentieth century, see G. Achcar, *The Clash of Barbarisms: The Making of the New World Disorder*, second edition (Boulder, CO: Paradigm; London: Saqi, 2006).

even more vigorously when it is curtailed out of racist hatred for the holders of a minority religion. Under such conditions, the defence of this freedom becomes a necessary component of the struggle against racism in addition to being a component of the fight for political freedom in general.

However, as Marx reminded his German comrades, the defence of religious freedom of conscience must not eclipse the struggle against religious unfreedom of conscience, as well as religious unfreedom to attend to one's bodily needs, whether it is a matter of state-imposed unfreedom, as is still the case in many countries, or one of religious chains self-imposed in a desperate attempt to soothe the anxiety generated by high degrees of patriarchy and gender oppression or the precariousness of social conditions in the neo-liberal age. The struggle for the secular separation of religion and state, and in defence of this separation where it is accomplished, remains of immediate relevance in the twenty-first century, as is the struggle against the broad range of uses of religion for reactionary political purposes.

References

Achcar, Gilbert (2006), *The Clash of Barbarisms: The Making of the New World Disorder*, second edition, Boulder, CO: Paradigm; London: Saqi.
   (2013), *Marxism, Orientalism, Cosmopolitanism*, London: Saqi; Chicago: Haymarket.
Althusser, Louis (1969), *For Marx*, Harmondsworth: Penguin.
Anderson, Kevin (2016), *Marx at the Margins: On Nationalism, Ethnicity, and Non-Western Societies*, second edition, Chicago: Chicago University Press.
Bellue, Françoise (1994), 'Typologie des métaphores religieuses dans *Le Capital* de K. Marx', in: Georges Labica and Jean Robelin (eds), *Politique et Religion*, Paris: L'Harmattan, pp. 61–91.
Bertrand, Michèle (1979), *Le Statut de la Religion chez Marx et Engels*, Paris: Editions sociales.
Boer, Roland (2007–14), *On Marxism and Theology*, five vols, Leiden: Brill.
   (2012), *On Marxism and Theology: Vol. IV, Criticism of Earth*, Leiden: Brill.
   (2013), *Lenin, Religion and Theology*, New York: Palgrave Macmillan.
   (2014), *On Marxism and Theology: Vol. V, In the Vale of Tears*, Leiden: Brill.
Constant, Benjamin (1999), *De la Religion considérée dans sa source, ses formes et ses développements*, Arles: Actes Sud.
Engels, Frederick (1978), *The Peasant War in Germany*, MECW, vol. 10, pp. 397–482.
   (1989), 'Programme of the Blanquist Commune Refugees', MECW, vol. 24, pp. 12–18.

Gabel, Paul (2005), *And God Created Lenin: Marxism vs. Religion in Russia, 1917–1929*, New York: Prometheus Books.
Garsten, Bryan (2010), 'Religion and the Case against Ancient Liberty: Benjamin Constant's Other Lectures', *Political Theory*, 38 (1): 4–33.
Higonnet, Patrice (1986), 'Marx, disciple de Constant?', *Annales Benjamin Constant*, 6: 11–16.
Internationalen Marx-Engels-Stiftung (eds) (1976), *Marx-Engels-Gesamtausgabe, IV/1M/E: Exzerpte und Notizen. Bis 1842*, Berlin: Walter de Gruyter.
Kepel, Gilles (1994), *The Revenge of God: The Resurgence of Islam, Christianity, and Judaism in the Modern World*, London: Polity.
Löwy, Michael (1996), *The War of Gods: Religion and Politics in Latin America*, London: Verso.
Marx, Karl (1975), *Difference between the Democritean and Epicurean Philosophy of Nature*, MECW, vol. 1, pp. 25–108.
 (1975), 'Comments on the Latest Prussian Censorship Instruction', MECW, vol. 1, pp. 109–31.
 (1975), 'The Leading Article in No. 179 of the Kölnische Zeitung', MECW, vol. 1, pp. 184–202.
 (1975), 'To Arnold Ruge. November 30, 1842', MECW, vol. 1, pp. 393–5.
 (1975), 'On The Jewish Question', MECW, vol. 3, pp. 146–74.
 (1975), *Economic and Philosophic Manuscripts of 1844*, MECW, vol. 3, pp. 229–346.
 (1975), *Thesis on Feuerbach*, MECW, vol. 5, pp. 6–8.
 (1976), 'The Communism of the Rheinischer Beobachter', MECW, vol. 6, pp. 220–34.
 (1985), 'Remarks on the Programme and Rules of the International Alliance of Socialist Democracy', MECW, vol. 21, pp. 207–82.
 (1986), 'Outlines of the Critique of Political Economy [*Grundrisse*]. First Instalment', MECW, vol. 28.
 (1987), 'Outlines of the Critique of Political Economy [*Grundrisse*]. Second Instalment', MECW, vol. 29.
 (1989), *Critique of the Gotha Programme*, MECW, vol. 24, pp. 75–99.
 (1989), 'Account of Karl Marx's Interview with the Chicago Tribune Correspondent', MECW, vol. 24, pp. 568–79.
 (1991), *Economic Manuscript of 1861–63*, MECW, vol. 33.
 (1996), *Capital*, volume I, MECW, vol. 35.
 (1998), *Capital*, volume III, MECW, vol. 37.
Marx, Karl, and Engels, Frederick (1975), *The German Ideology*, MECW, vol. 5, pp. 19–539.
 (1975), *The Holy Family, or Critique of Critical Criticism. Against Bruno Bauer and Company*, MECW, vol. 4, pp. 5–211.
 (1976), *Manifesto of the Communist Party*, MECW, vol. 6, pp. 477–519.
 (1983), *Letters, 1852–55*, MECW, vol. 39.
 (1987), 'Reviews from the Neue Rheinische Zeitung. Politisch-Ökonomische Revue No. 2', MECW, vol. 10, pp. 241–56.

McKinnon, Andrew (2005), 'Reading "Opium of the People": Expression, Protest and the Dialectics of Religion', *Critical Sociology*, 31 (1–2): 15–38.

Toscano, Alberto (2010), 'Beyond Abstraction: Marx and the Critique of the Critique of Religion', *Historical Materialism*, 18: 3–29.

Traverso, Enzo (1993), *The Marxists and the Jewish Question: The History of a Debate (1843–1943)*, Atlantic Highlands, NJ: Humanities Press.

19 Education

Robin Small

19.1 Marx's Contribution on Education

The end of the twentieth century saw the collapse of communist state systems and a brief moment of Western triumphalism that has given way to new uncertainties as deep-seated economic and political problems re-emerge. Even so, there are areas of social life where capital's drive to create a society after its own image is hard at work, despite the wider issues. One of these is education. Now that Karl Marx is back on reading lists as a source of insight into today's world, we want to know if he makes a useful contribution to debates over our schools and universities. The evidence for Marx's views on education comes from texts throughout his career. They include not only well-known passages from the *Manifesto of the Communist Party*, written with Friedrich Engels (1820–1895), and the first volume of *Capital*, but also documents of the International Working Men's Association (IWMA) that are known to be his work.[1]

Marx was working before the introduction of state school systems in economically advanced societies, and many of his ideas were overtaken by that historic change. An example is his carefully thought out plan for combining work with schooling for children. It is based on the assumption, as stated in his *Critique of the Gotha Programme*, that an abolition of child labour is 'incompatible with the existence of large-scale industry and hence an empty, pious wish'.[2] That turned out not to be the case. Yet Marx's approach is always instructive. It shows us how his big ideas – the

---

[1] Of special interest are two 'speeches' on education. In fact, these are just Marx's interventions at meetings of the IWMA's general council, recorded in the secretary's minutes. They make intriguing reading, since they show him as a working political activist, engaged in down-to-earth interaction with an assorted group of trade unionists and social reformers, many under the influence of other radical thinkers. In this setting, Marx is quite forbearing with opinions that are dealt with far more roughly in his published works. By the same token, what he says at general council meetings is not to be taken as his last word on schooling.

[2] K. Marx, *Critique of the Gotha Programme*, MECW, vol. 24, p. 98.

analysis of class society, the tensions between means and social relations of production, and so on – bear on particular questions about education.

The following discussion will look at three areas where Marx's ideas resonate with today's concerns: first, his view of the economic role of education and its implications for public policy; second, his conception of a schooling for the working class; and, finally, his view of teachers as a social group and of teaching as work.

19.2 The Political Economy of Education

In Marx's *Theories of Surplus Value* the school's economic role is defined succinctly: 'education produces labour capacity'.[3] One might prefer to call this process 'training'. Still, it is something that schools and colleges do see themselves as doing, among other activities. Like medicine, education is one of those services that 'train labour capacity, maintain or modify it, etc., in a word, give it a specialised form or even only maintain it'.[4] Modern production requires workers with general knowledge and practical skills, as well as a versatility that assists technological innovation. In the twentieth century, successive increases in the school leaving age in advanced societies have been justified by appealing to the needs of the national economy.

This point applies beyond manufacture and industry. In discussing the position of commercial occupations in *Capital*, volume III, Marx noted that 'the necessary training, knowledge of commercial practices, languages, etc., is more and more rapidly, easily, universally and cheaply reproduced with the progress of science and public education the more the capitalist mode of production directs teaching methods, etc., towards practical purposes'.[5] In effect, the training of these workers is contracted out to the public school and paid for by the community as a whole. Marx noted that this motivation becomes a determining influence on the curriculum and even on methods of teaching. 'Practical purposes' is a loaded expression, though: whose interests are served by the practices?[6]

As well as the passing on of knowledge, the production of new knowledge is crucial to capitalism. Marx asserts in the *Grundrisse* that the modern technology on which it depends is just 'the application of science to production'.[7] He had been impressed by the Scottish writer Andrew

---

[3] K. Marx, *The Economic Manuscript of 1861–63*, MECW, vol. 31, p. 104.
[4] Ibid, pp. 22–3.   [5] K. Marx, *Capital*, volume III, p. 299.
[6] Today's debates over changes in teachers' work, involving reduced autonomy and demands to satisfy testable standards, are driven by the same outside pressures, dressed up in the language of 'accountability'.
[7] K. Marx, 'Outlines of the Critique of Political Economy [*Grundrisse*]. Second Instalment', MECW, vol. 29, p. 90.

Ure's (1778–1857) claim that the Industrial Revolution was made possible by advances in machine design based on scientific principles. Conversely, Ure thought, a great deal of science could be learned from technology. The properties of heat, for example, 'may all be better studied in a week's residence in Lancashire, than in a session of any university in Europe'.[8] On this view, scientific knowledge is a force of production in its own right, and an essential element in modern economies.

But where does this knowledge come from, and whom does it belong to? In the *Grundrisse*, Marx used the expression 'general intellect'.[9] This English phrase of uncertain origin refers to the body of useful knowledge that belongs to a given society. In effect, this asset is privatized by capitalism in something like the way that the common land of the Middle Ages was enclosed and became the economic basis for the social domination of private ownership. Marx wrote: 'At this point, invention becomes a business, and the application of science to immediate production itself becomes a factor determining and soliciting science.'[10]

Another persistent feature of capitalist society is the tension between its need for public education and its drive to treat this as an overhead expense that should be minimized as far as possible.[11] Apart from that, education appears as a private good to be allocated on the 'user pays' principle, taking the 'user' to be the individual or family, not the community. Even Adam Smith (1723–1790) drew back from this conclusion. He recognized the public benefits of a modest amount of schooling: it made people 'more decent and orderly' and less liable to 'wanton or unnecessary opposition to the measures of government'.[12] Marx's remark that 'by moral education the bourgeois understands indoctrination with bourgeois principles'[13] might be taken as a comment. In later political engagement, Marx advocated a school curriculum stripped down to basics such as grammar and arithmetic along with physical education, and leaving out 'subjects that admitted of different conclusions' or which 'admitted of party and class interpretation'.[14] This may have been a tactical move in the face of well-meant demands for teaching children 'the value of labour', or it could

---

[8] A. Ure, *The Philosophy of Manufactures* (London: Charles Knight, 1835), p. 25.
[9] K. Marx, 'Outlines of the Critique of Political Economy [*Grundrisse*]. First Instalment', MECW, vol. 28, pp. 92, 84.
[10] Ibid, p. 90. Nobody who works in today's universities, forced into increased dependence on contract research income by successive governments, can fail to recognize a familiar pattern of behaviour here.
[11] R. Small, *Karl Marx: The Revolutionary as Educator* (Dordrecht: Springer, 2014), pp. 77–80.
[12] A. Smith, *The Wealth of Nations* (New York: Modern Library, 1937), p. 740.
[13] K. Marx, 'Wages', MECW, vol. 6, pp. 427–8.
[14] K. Marx, 'Record of Marx's Speeches on General Education. From the Minutes of the General Council Meetings of August 10 and 17, 1869', MECW, vol. 21, pp. 399–400.

express suspicion of a teaching workforce acting as one of the 'ideological castes'[15] of the capitalist system.

Marx did support mass schooling, but without the separation of children from adult working life that has been taken for granted since compulsory education came in towards the end of the nineteenth century. One reason is a practical one. Many of his comments on education refer to the Factory Acts, which required part-time schooling to be provided by employers of children. Marx drew attention to flaws in the policy's implementation, but endorsed the combination of work and schooling. His reasons included an answer to demands for teaching children 'the value of labour'.[16] He believed that this learning cannot be done in the classroom, but only through experience of actual work.

A noticeable work ethic runs through Marx's thought. He regarded the establishment of 'general industriousness' as one of the achievements of capitalism, and a gain for future generations.[17] This bias also comes through when he turned to education. He had some sympathy with the utopian Charles Fourier's (1772–1837) fanciful pictures of future childhood[18] but criticizes the educators of his day whom we would see as the pioneers of modern progressive or 'child-centred' education.[19] Marx believes in the value of work for children, in the classroom as well as in the factory. Genuine attainment of any kind, he believed, means dealing successfully with the givenness and resistance of a real, material world, including the limitations of our own mental abilities, as one can see with artistic and intellectual creativity.

Marx's disagreement with educational progressivism had another aspect. He was concerned above all with the needs of a social class that had in the past been deprived of educational opportunity and, even then, was given only the minimum amount that the social status quo required. He was unconcerned about the schooling of middle-class children, and briskly dismisses their problems: 'If the middle and higher classes neglect their duties towards their offspring, it is their own fault. Sharing the privileges of these classes, the child is condemned to suffer from their prejudices.'[20]

---

[15] Marx, *The Economic Manuscript of 1861–63*, p. 197.
[16] Marx, 'Record of Marx's Speeches on General Education', p. 399.
[17] Marx, 'Outlines of the Critique of Political Economy [*Grundrisse*]. First Instalment', p. 250.
[18] K. Marx and F. Engels, *The German Ideology*, MECW, vol. 5, p. 512.
[19] K. Marx, *Capital*, volume I, MECW, vol. 35, p. 491n.
[20] K. Marx, 'Instructions for the Delegates of the Provisional General Council. The Different Questions', MECW, vol. 20, pp. 188–9. If we are set on defending Marx, this might be read as a response to the economist Nassau Senior's (1790–1864) 1863 public

19.3 Education, the State, and Society

Public education was part of the German intellectual tradition from which Marx came. In his *Philosophy of Right*, G. W. F. Hegel (1770–1831) had defended the right of civil society to take over the family's control of children's upbringing, given that they were to become its members. 'Society's right here is paramount over the arbitrary and contingent preferences of parents, particularly in cases where education is to be completed not by the parents but by others.'[21] Hegel had been a school principal for eight years and knew something about dealing with parents:

> Parents usually suppose that in the matter of education they have complete freedom and may arrange everything as they like. The chief opposition to any form of public education usually comes from parents and it is they who talk and make an outcry about teachers and schools because they have a faddish dislike of them. Nonetheless, society has a right to act on principles tested by its experience and to compel parents to send their children to school, to have them vaccinated, and so forth.[22]

Marx may well agree with these views, even if his view of civil society was very different from Hegel's. He rejects any reconciliation of opposed class interests through a higher form of social life in the 'State'. On the contrary, it is civil society that determines the form of state power and its ideological expressions. The implications for the politics of education are spelled out in a polemical passage of the *Manifesto of the Communist Party*:

> But, you say, we destroy the most hallowed of relations, when we replace home education by social. And your education! Is not that also social, and determined by the social conditions under which you educate, by the intervention direct or indirect, of society, by means of schools, &c.? The Communists have not invented the intervention of society in education; they do but seek to alter the character of that intervention, and to rescue education from the influence of the ruling class.[23]

Two decades later, Marx repeated the last point when he defended the use of existing state authority to bring about social reforms including compulsory school attendance for children. 'In enforcing such laws, the working class do not fortify governmental power. On the contrary, they transform that power, now used against them, into their own agency.'[24]

---

speech in defence of middle-class education, from which Marx nevertheless borrowed a suggestion for shorter classroom hours. Marx, *Capital*, volume I, p. 486.

[21] G. W. F. Hegel, *Philosophy of Right* (Oxford: Clarendon Press, 1952), p. 148.
[22] Hegel, *Philosophy of Right*, p. 277.
[23] K. Marx and F. Engels, *Manifesto of the Communist Party*, MECW, vol. 6, pp. 501–2.
[24] Marx, 'Instructions for the Delegates of the Provisional General Council', p. 189.

Education   343

The logic of Marx's argument is clear enough. The modern school has arisen within capitalist societies for reasons more to do with the needs of capital than with the interests of children. Yet something like his distinction between means and social relations of production applies here as well. Like the factory, the modern school is a resource that a future society can use for its own purposes. In the meantime, it is a place where competing interests encounter one another, especially when they compete to drive public policy. Again, the *Manifesto of the Communist Party* spelt this out: 'The bourgeoisie itself, therefore, supplies the proletariat with its own elements of political and general education, in other words, it furnishes the proletariat with weapons for fighting the bourgeoisie.'[25]

However, Marx's thinking about the state's role in education evolved in later years. On several occasions, he expressed an opinion that locally based school systems of the kind existing in several parts of the United States were preferable to a school operated by the central state, the model best known in its Prussian version. Under the American system, public schools were financed by local taxation and run by locally elected school boards. The only role of government was to prevent excessive variation between districts by appointing inspectors similar to the British factory inspectors whose work Marx admired. In his view, this showed that education might be 'national' without being 'governmental'.[26]

This reluctance simply to endorse government schooling became sharper in the 1870s. The experience of the Paris Commune had a big impact on Marx's thinking about state power and, in consequence, about education. During its brief life, the commune had put in place a democratic administration which included a new kind of school. 'The whole of the educational institutions were opened to the people gratuitously, and at the same time cleared of all interference of church and state.'[27] As these words show, Marx was more than ever against reliance on the state to carry out social reforms. That comes through in his comments on the education policy of the newly formed German Socialist Workers' (later, Social Democratic) Party. In the 1875 text known as his *Critique of the Gotha Programme*, Marx wrote:

'*Education of the people by the state*' is altogether objectionable. Defining by a general law the expenditures on the elementary schools, the qualifications of the teaching staff, the subjects of instruction, etc., and, as is done in the United States, supervising the fulfilment of these legal specifications by state inspectors, is a very different thing from appointing the state as the educator of the people!

---

[25] Marx and Engels, *Manifesto of the Communist Party*, p. 493.
[26] Marx, 'Record of Marx's Speeches on General Education', p. 398.
[27] K. Marx, *The Civil War in France. Address of the General Council of the International Working Men's Association*, MECW, vol. 22, p. 332.

Government and Church should rather be equally excluded from any influence on the school. Particularly, indeed, in the Prusso-German Empire (and one should not take refuge in the rotten subterfuge that one is speaking of a 'state of the future'; we have seen how matters stand in this respect) the state has need, on the contrary, of a very stern education by the people.[28]

In fact, Marx's position on the state's role is still something of a middle way between opposed tendencies within the socialist movement, represented by the supporters of Ferdinand Lassalle (1825–1864) and Mikhail Bakunin (1814–1876) whom, at different times, he was forced to confront.[29] Despite its rhetorical attack on the state, the policy he was advocating here retained centralized control of several key aspects of education: budgeting, the school curriculum, and the composition of the teaching workforce. These are topics in which Marx has a particular interest, and about which he offered ideas worth closer examination.

19.4 Marx's Curriculum

Marx's continuing affinity with Hegel is evident when he appealed to the humanistic ideal of a balanced and many-sided personality as a goal for education. In many ways, he was a typical product of that tradition, founded on the German conception of *Bildung* (a word often translated as 'education' or 'culture', but with connotations of formation of personality).[30] The continuity between his ideas on education and this model is disguised by a shift of conceptual vocabulary to the context of class society. Like Smith, Marx wants public schools to counteract the effects of the intensified division of labour in modern workshops and factories. A worker who has to carry out a few simplified tasks throughout the working day, Smith said, 'generally becomes as stupid and ignorant as it is possible for a human creature to become'.[31] Smith did not explain just how this can be avoided, but Marx drew on a French writer, Claude-Anthime Corbon (1808–1891), whose book on technical education he read with interest.[32] Corbon argued for a training that promotes flexible work skills in place of vocational specialization.[33] Marx added a theoretical dimension, consistent with his linking of science and technology and, one

---

[28] Marx, *Critique of the Gotha Programme*, p. 97.
[29] R. Small, *Marx and Education* (Aldershot: Ashgate, 2005), pp. 148–52.
[30] Marx never refers to his experience in the Trier Gymnasium, and disparages Prussian education as 'only calculated to make good soldiers'. Marx, 'Record of Marx's Speeches on General Education', p. 399.
[31] Smith, *The Wealth of Nations*, pp. 734–5; see also Marx, *Capital*, volume I, p. 367.
[32] Small, *Marx and Education*, pp. 116–18.
[33] C. A. Corbon, *De l'enseignement professionnel* (Paris: Imprimerie de Dubuisson et cie, 1859), p. 145.

might add, with his philosophical conception of a unity of theory and practice. Hence, his insistence in *Capital* that, with the ending of class society 'technical instruction [*technologischen Unterricht*], both theoretical and practical, will take its proper place in the working-class schools'.[34]

A key passage in *Capital* brings together these ideas in a vision of the school within a future society:

> From the factory system budded, as Robert Owen has shown us in detail, the germ of the education of the future, an education that will, in the case of every child over a given age, combine productive labour with instruction and gymnastics, not only as one of the methods of adding to the efficiency of production, but as the only method of producing fully developed human beings.[35]

As he was writing these passages, Marx returned to political activity, becoming a member of the London-based general council of the IWMA. In 1866, an opportunity arose to give these ideas on 'the education of the future' a practical form. The first congress of the IWMA, held in Geneva, passed a resolution on 'Juvenile and Children's Labour (Both Sexes)' which is also a policy for children's schooling. Written in English (with the odd German turn of phrase) this is apparently Marx's work.[36] It starts out with an endorsement of child labour.

> We consider the tendency of modern industry to make children and juvenile persons of both sexes co-operate in the great work of social production, as a progressive, sound and legitimate tendency, although under capital it was distorted into an abomination. In a rational state of society *every child whatever*, from the age of 9 years, ought to become a productive labourer in the same way that no able-bodied adult person ought to be exempted from the general law of nature, viz.: to work in order to be able to eat, and work not only with the brain but with the hands too.[37]

The resolution outlines a version of the British system of 'factory schools' attended by working children for part of each day, and goes on to specify a school curriculum consisting of three elements. The first two are familiar enough: 'mental education', apparently centring on basic literacy and numeracy, and 'bodily education', involving gymnastics and (perhaps more surprisingly) 'military exercise'.

The third part of the proposed curriculum is Marx's most original contribution to educational thinking: 'Technological training, which imparts the general principles of all processes of production, and, simultaneously initiates the child and young person in the practical use and handling of the elementary instruments of all trades.'[38] Later writers used

---

[34] Marx, *Capital*, volume I, p. 491.   [35] Ibid, p. 486.
[36] Small, *Marx and Education*, pp. 106.
[37] Marx, 'Instructions for the Delegates of the Provisional General Council', p. 188.
[38] Ibid, p. 189.

an equally apt label: 'polytechnical education'. The concept is a bold transposition of the humanistic ideal of *Bildung* into the reality of modern industry and its working class. Marx gave full credit to Hegel, who, he remarked in *Capital*, 'held very heretical views on division of labour'.[39] But he identified two key issues – the increased division of labour in the factory, and the separation of knowledge and work in the use of machinery – as made far worse by the capitalist social relations of production. Part at least of the solution, he concluded, could come from a model of schooling that addressed both divisions at the same time.

When the Geneva education policy was discussed at a later meeting of the general council, Marx took the trouble to emphasize the socialist character of his polytechnical principle.

> The technological training advocated by proletarian writers was meant to compensate for the deficiencies occasioned by the division of labour which prevented apprentices from acquiring a thorough knowledge of their business. This had been taken hold of and misconstructed [sic] into what the middle class understood by technical education.[40]

In the resolution itself, he was even more optimistic in his predictions for the benefits of this new model of education: 'The combination of paid productive labour, mental education, bodily exercise and polytechnic training, will raise the working class far above the level of the higher and middle classes.'[41]

19.5 Teachers and Their Work

Marx's ideas on education were not limited to the children of the working class. He also had things to say about the adults whose working life occurs in schools. What sort of occupation is teaching? Its claim to be a profession is recent, insecure, and contested. Compared with older professions, there are certainly similarities. Teaching requires specialized knowledge and expertise that, in modern societies, is acquired through formal training and confirmed by certification. Nowadays, this is done at universities, which are also where the knowledge base is increased through academic research. Teaching displays typical professional features in the way practitioners make decisions in their daily work. With this autonomy comes a sense of responsibility to a community that places its trust in the profession as a whole, and an insistence on ethical standards and on collegiality among teachers.

---

[39] Marx, *Capital*, volume I, p. 368.
[40] Marx, 'Record of Marx's Speeches on General Education', p. 399.
[41] Marx, 'Instructions for the Delegates of the Provisional General Council', p. 189.

What was Marx's attitude towards the professional work model? The *Manifesto of the Communist Party* draws attention to capitalism's hostility to this tradition. 'The bourgeoisie has stripped of its halo every occupation hitherto honoured and looked up to with reverent awe. It has converted the physician, the lawyer, the priest, the poet, the man of science, into its paid wage-labourers.'[42] It is startling to read the authors' apparent approval of this and related social changes, which they treat as sweeping away sentimentalism and superstition. In fact, things are not so simple. This is a rhetorical passage, provocatively pretending to celebrate the loss of old values and ideals in fully developed modernity. The opening pages of the *Manifesto of the Communist Party* praise not only capitalism's material achievements, but also its radical simplification and rationalization of social life. But this sets up what follows: a darker side of the picture, where the price paid by some for benefits enjoyed by others is set out in detail. In that context, the earlier dismissal of 'sentimentalism' need not be taken at face value.

If teaching is a professional occupation, it is one whose practitioners do not come, by and large, from the most privileged social classes. Their becoming teachers often means a negotiation of upward social mobility. Marx made a similar point about office workers who, with mass education, are drawn 'from classes that formerly had no access to such trades'.[43] C. Wright Mills (1916–1962) defined the social position of mid-century teachers in acerbic language: 'Schoolteachers, especially those in grammar and high schools, are the economic proletarians of the professions.'[44] He pointed out that teachers are numerous – the biggest single group within the professions – and, more to the point, they are salary earners who remain under relatively close employer control compared with the older, fee-charging professions.

Later Marxists such as Magali Sarfatti Larson (?–) have emphasized the ideological function of the concept of professional work.[45] When Larson's analysis was published, critiques of the role of professions in modern society had become common. The same year saw the appearance of Ivan Illich's 'Disabling Professions'.[46] In this essay, Illich applied the analysis of formal education in his influential *Deschooling Society*[47] more broadly. He identified professionalism with a monopoly of practice, dismissing any rationale as an excuse for oppressive paternalism. Forty years

---

[42] Marx and Engels, *Manifesto of the Communist Party*, p. 487.
[43] Marx, *Capital*, volume III, p. 299.
[44] C. W. Mills, *White Collar: The American Middle Classes* (New York: Oxford University Press, 1956), p. 129.
[45] M. S. Larson, *The Rise of Professionalism: A Sociological Analysis* (Berkeley: University of California Press, 1977).
[46] I. Illich, 'Disabling Professions', in: I. Illich, I. K. Zola, J. McKnight, J. Caplan, and H. Shaiken (eds), *Disabling Professions* (London: Marion Boyars, 1977), pp. 11–39.
[47] Ivan Illich, *Deschooling Society* (Harmondsworth: Penguin Books, 1971).

later, we see that things are not so simple. Teacher resistance to managerial pressures on their work in the classroom has often appealed to aspects of the professional model to good effect. The old-school Marxism of Larson's analysis plays down these possibilities, and risks leaving teachers without a useful resource in their unavoidable confrontation with attempts to turn them into submissive employees.

In their book, *Schooling in Capitalist America*, Samuel Bowles (1939–) and Herbert Gintis (1940–) argue that one effect of research into education may be to legitimize a shift of power away from practitioners to managers and administrators. They suggest that this occurred with teachers' work in the twentieth century.

> In the interests of scientific management, control of curriculum, evaluation, counselling, selection of texts, and methods of teaching was placed in the hands of experts. A host of specialists arose to deal with minute fragments of the teacher's job. The tasks of thinking, making decisions, and understanding the goals of education were placed in the hands of high-level administrators.[48]

This is a rationalization of the teaching process along the lines of previous changes in the division of labour: in particular, the de-skilling associated with the introduction of machinery, where specialized knowledge became, so to speak, locked up within the machine. Something similar occurs where systems embody the knowledge that no longer belongs to those who work within them. Just as the problem with machinery was not technology as such, so too the issue for teachers is not about educational research itself, but about its misuse as a lever of power.

Another neo-liberal initiative, resisted by teachers as an organized group, is the privatization of schooling. Milton Friedman's (1912–2006) proposed voucher scheme, designed to give public funding to private providers as well as state schools[49] proved too radical in its pure form for a public alarmed by any perceived undermining of 'its' schools, but the more recent charter school movement has pursued essentially the same goal. Again, the impact of such programmes on teaching as an occupation, as well as on teachers' daily work, is a hotly debated issue.

19.6 Marx and Education Today

Reading Marx on education is valuable for noting aspects of his thought that are set aside when the focus on the central themes of his critique of

---

[48] S. Bowles and H. Gintis, *Schooling in Capitalist America* (London: Routledge and Kegan Paul, 1976), pp. 204–5.
[49] M. Friedman, 'The Role of Government in Education', in: R. A. Solo (ed.), *Economics and the Public Interest* (New Brunswick, NJ: Rutgers University Press, 1955), pp. 123–44.

political economy. On the one hand, his political agenda for schooling is quite pragmatic and firmly based on existing practices in the factory schools of Great Britain. On the other hand, his hard-headedness does not exclude moments of utopian vision, looking beyond the break between class society and a future condition of humanity. Between these extremes, Marx's class analysis of capitalist society provides a powerful framework for approaching the problems of education in the modern world.[50]

What does Marx have to contribute to our understanding of these current issues? In education as elsewhere, his strategy is to look at the bigger picture of society as a totality of social relations, and at the ongoing maintenance and reproduction of this structure. He approaches political policy by identifying power relations with the conflicting interests of social classes.[51] Of course, the world is very different. Yet – to take just one example – the globalization of capitalism described by Marx and Engels in 1848 is still in progress in the twenty-first century, along with the social and political turmoil that goes with capital's restless search for new markets. Education is itself an international business, especially at university level, and marked by the same competitive rivalries, fluctuating fortunes, and shifts in location as other forms of industry and commerce. Within nation-states, the situation of schools and the teachers who work in them is under renewed pressure from policies that promote the maintenance and reproduction of the established system of production. All this is recognized in Marx's work. His vision for schooling has been aptly summarized by Brian Simon (1915–2002) as 'popular, local and democratic'.[52] It remains a vision, but one that is capable of driving a forceful analysis and critique of today's educational realities.

References

Bowles, Samuel, and Gintis, Herbert (1976), *Schooling in Capitalist America*, London: Routledge and Kegan Paul.
Corbon, Claude-Anthime (1859), *De l'enseignement professionnel*, Paris: Imprimerie de Dubuisson et cie.
Friedman, Milton (1955), 'The Role of Government in Education', in: Robert A. Solo (ed.), *Economics and the Public Interest*, New Brunswick, NJ: Rutgers University Press, pp. 123–44.
Hegel, G. W. F. (1952), *Philosophy of Right*, Oxford: Clarendon Press.

---

[50] Small, *Karl Marx*, pp. 69–85.
[51] We can see this approach on display in Marx's journalism, often overlooked by later readers, and imagine corresponding comments on today's events.
[52] B. Simon, 'Popular, Local and Democratic: Karl Marx's Formula', *Education*, 11 (March: 186–7 (1983)).

Illich, Ivan (1971), *Deschooling Society*, Harmondsworth: Penguin Books.
   (1977), 'Disabling Professions', in: Ivan Illich, Irving K. Zola, John McKnight, Jonathan Caplan, and Harlan Shaiken (eds), *Disabling Professions*, London: Marion Boyars, pp. 11–39.
Larson, Magali Sarfatti (1977), *The Rise of Professionalism: A Sociological Analysis*, Berkeley: University of California Press.
Marx, Karl (1976), 'Wages', MECW, vol. 6, pp. 415–37.
   (1985), 'Instructions for the Delegates of the Provisional General Council. The Different Questions', MECW, vol. 20, pp. 185–94.
   (1985), 'Record of Marx's Speeches on General Education. From the Minutes of the General Council Meetings of August 10 and 17, 1869', MECW, vol. 21, pp. 398–400.
   (1986), *The Civil War in France. Address of the General Council of the International Working Men's Association*, MECW, vol. 22, pp. 307–59.
   (1986), 'Outlines of the Critique of Political Economy [*Grundrisse*]. First and Second Instalment', MECW, vols 28 and 29.
   (1989), *Critique of the Gotha Programme*, MECW, vol. 24, pp. 75–99.
   (1989), *The Economic Manuscript of 1861–63*, MECW, vol. 31.
   (1996), *Capital*, volume I, MECW, vol. 35.
   (1998), *Capital*, volume III, MECW, vol. 37.
Marx, Karl, and Engels, Frederick (1975), *The German Ideology*, MECW, vol. 5, pp. 19–539.
   (1976), *Manifesto of the Communist Party*, MECW, vol. 6, pp. 477–519.
Mills, C. Wright (1956), *White Collar: The American Middle Classes*, New York: Oxford University Press.
Simon, Brian (1983), 'Popular, Local and Democratic: Karl Marx's Formula', *Education*, 11 (March): 186–7.
Small, Robin (2005), *Marx and Education*, Aldershot: Ashgate.
   (2014), *Karl Marx: The Revolutionary as Educator*, Dordrecht: Springer.
Smith, Adam (1937), *The Wealth of Nations*, New York: Modern Library.
Ure, Andrew (1835), *The Philosophy of Manufactures*, London: Charles Knight.

20 Art

Isabelle Garo

20.1 Art and Alienation

Karl Marx never wrote a work specifically on art. Yet one of his very first projects – even if it did not come to fruition – was an essay on Christian art, and the question of art never entirely disappeared from his view. Indeed, it made regular appearances, from the first to the last of his writings, with angles of approach that changed in the course of time. It was mainly art as a social activity that held his attention: in so far as this allows one to measure the development of individuals, and on the other hand the degree of their alienation, within a given historical formation, the level of artistic capacities may be considered the index of a historical process of emancipation. We may say therefore that art was a constant preoccupation for Marx.[1]

Two axes of analyses may be broadly distinguished in Marx's thinking on art; these are not separated by a sharp break, however, but add to and influence each other's contributions. In a first period, stretching from 1842 to the *Economic and Philosophic Manuscripts of 1844*, the young Marx began to reflect on art in the context of the lively aesthetic debate that developed in Prussia in the 1830s and 1840s. In a second period, from the second half of the 1840s until the end of his life, he addressed the question of artistic activity in the framework of his analysis of capitalism and the critique of political economy, thereby evoking the perspective of an overcoming of alienation and exploitation.

In the early 1840s, Marx belonged to the Young Hegelian movement, of which Bruno Bauer (1809–1882) was a leading member. Having attended Bauer's course of lectures in Bonn, he agreed to collaborate with him on a work entitled 'The Hegelian Doctrine of Religion and Art

---

[1] We should add that, after a few forays into literature that he did not follow through, Marx punctuated his texts with numerous quotes from poems, plays, and novels that served to strengthen his analyses. These testify to his vast culture and, above all, to his interest in the pictures of the world drawn by various writers. See S. S. Prawer, *Karl Marx and World Literature* (London: Verso, 2011), chs 7, 9, and 11.

Considered from the Point of View of Faith' (1842). The article on art that this was to be included never saw the light of day, but Marx worked on it enthusiastically and took copious notes on scholarly works in the history of art and religions.[2] Moreover, although he did not complete it, this preparatory work played a not insignificant role in the broader intellectual and political itinerary of the young Marx. Whereas Bauer's priority was the critique of Christianity, in order to achieve an intellectual revolution that would make the political revolution possible, the fate of Marx's scheduled article proves that his perspective was quite different; he began by expanding its theme, so that it became 'On Religion and Art, with Special Reference to Christian Art'.[3]

In the *Economic and Philosophic Manuscripts of 1844*, artistic activity is directly associated with the analysis of human alienation, which is conceived as a relinquishment and loss of man's essence. But Marx's perspective was not that of Ludwig Feuerbach (1804–1872), the first philosopher to develop the concept of alienation within the Young Hegelian school. In Marx's view, Feuerbach's denunciation of religious alienation could not but be one-sided and misleading, since it did not tackle the causes of what permits or blocks the development of man's faculties, including his artistic creativity. For his own part, Marx dwelled on the development and education of the human senses, underlining the capacity of individuals to constitute the human world, even in their sense activity, which, although seemingly the least mediated of all, was in reality a socially mediated and mediating activity. In the pages relating to the eye as a 'social organ' and to vision as an activity that humanizes its object, he wrote: 'The sense caught up in crude practical need has only a restricted sense.'[4] And, in a terminology he would never cease to employ, he counterposed the market wealth of utility to real human wealth – that is, the active capacity to develop rich and complex social perceptions and the education required to cultivate 'a musical ear, an eye for beauty of form'.[5]

Within the framework of a broader theoretical project, artistic activity – seen from the viewpoint of the person exercising it – gave Marx the opportunity to theorize, in a move away from Feuerbach, a socially defined human essence consisting of capacities and potentialities. Artistic creation was one of the forms in which this historical human essence manifested itself, making it possible to measure *a contrario* the degree of ordinary alienation of exploited labour. For Marx, this held true

---

[2] See M. A. Rose, *Marx's Lost Aesthetic: Karl Marx and the Visual Arts* (Cambridge: Cambridge University Press, 1984), part one, ch. 3.
[3] K. Marx, 'Letter to Arnold Ruge, 20 March 1842', MECW, vol. 1, p. 385.
[4] K. Marx, *Economic and Philosophic Manuscripts of 1844*, MECW, vol. 3, p. 302.
[5] Ibid., p. 301.

both for artists and for their public: anyone can buy a work of art, of course, but 'if you want to enjoy art, you must be an artistically cultivated person'.[6] Consequently, the reciprocal determination of subject and object was at the centre of the critique of political economy; Marx never lost sight of the question of individual development. This is why we can say that the new approach to art that Marx achieved at the end of his early years of reflection left its stamp on the whole of his later work. His reposing of the question of art involved abandoning any Kantian-inspired aesthetic of the beautiful or judgement of taste, but also any Hegelian-style philosophy of art bound up with an idealist philosophy of history. For these he substituted a materialist theory of artistic creation as a social activity enabling the development of individual faculties, as well as a dialectical analysis of the function of (socially produced and received) representations.

This new orientation gained further depth with the radical critique of Feuerbach that Marx began to develop in 1845. Whereas Feuerbach reduced activity to sensation, Marx aimed to rethink sensation as one social practice among others. The fifth of the *Thesis on Feuerbach* (1845) spelt out the new direction he sought to give to a critique that he considered far too narrow, since it remained locked into a vindication of sensuousness without perceiving its social-historical dimension: Feuerbach 'does not conceive sensuousness as practical, human-sensuous activity'.[7] Hence, in *The German Ideology* (1845–46), art no longer had the exceptional character of a fully emancipatory activity; it was resituated within the division of labour, having ceased to be a model of liberation and become, more modestly, one object of the historical understanding that Marx was attempting to develop. He included art in the sphere of the superstructures, thereby breaking from the thesis of the absolute autonomy of thought dear to the Young Hegelians. Indeed, he now argued: 'There is no history of politics, law, science, etc., of art, religion, etc.'[8]

At that time, Marx was looking for what specifically defined a mode of production, and his analysis of the division of labour in relation to class structure was a major stepping stone in this direction. Significantly, he wrote in the middle of a polemical chapter against Max Stirner (1806–1856): 'Whether an individual like Raphael succeeds in developing his talent depends on the division of labour and the conditions of culture resulting from it.'[9] If we bear in mind that the German school of the Nazarenes worshipped Raphael as the most inspired of painters, it will be

---

[6] Ibid, p. 326.   [7] K. Marx, *Thesis on Feuerbach*, MECW, vol. 5, p. 7.
[8] K. Marx and F. Engels, *The German Ideology*, MECW, vol. 5, p. 92.   [9] Ibid, p. 393.

clear that Marx's criticism was aimed not only at Stirner, but at the dominant aesthetic that he had already engaged in combat. Quite simply, what he now targeted was not a certain type of artistic production, but a conception of artistic production in which genius was defined as an absolute exception. If art now became more of a side issue for Marx, it was because he thought it should be placed in its particular historical and social context and linked to a revolutionary, emancipatory practice in which artists were neither the prime actors nor the main bearers (precisely because of the relative protection they enjoy from the human damage that results from capitalist production). On the other hand, he did think that artists had a place in that practice.

It is here that the paradox of Marx's aesthetic takes clear shape: art is conditioned by its epoch but is also partly alien to the prevailing relations of production. A few lines after stressing the collective character of the work of such a renowned painter as Horace Vernet (1789–1863), and after noting the cooperative endeavour behind the production of vaudevilles and novels as well as astronomical observation, Marx denounced 'the exclusive concentration of artistic talent in particular individuals, and its suppression in the broad mass which is bound up with this'.[10] Two themes are thus superimposed, in a relative tension with each other. On the one hand, the labour of artists is dependent, like any other, upon the organization of production as a whole; in that respect, they enjoy no special privilege. But at the same time Marx did see the artist as an exception – as one of the very few who develop their creative powers – and his critique therefore bore only on the narrow, specialized character of the artist's talent, which concerned only one part of man's faculties and, above all, only one fraction of humanity.

Nevertheless, the two arguments are by no means equal in kind: in the first, the artist is a worker like any other; in the second, he represents, at least in outline, the complete individual who begins to feature in Marx's work from *The German Ideology* on.[11] 'In a communist society there are no painters but only people who engage in painting among other activities.'[12] Marx could not have better expressed the contradictory nature of a social practice that suffers alienation while helping to clear a path to its abolition. In sum, then, art presents itself at the end of this second period as both determined and autonomous, alienated and liberatory – an echo of the contradictions in reality and a yearning for their transcendence. Clearly this paradox refers mainly to a real dialectic, which can be clarified only within the more general framework of the critique of political economy.

[10] Ibid, p. 394.   [11] Ibid, p. 46.   [12] Ibid, p. 394.

20.2 Art and the Critique of Political Economy

Following this first approach centred on the development and alienation of human capacities, Marx tackled the question of art in relation to the more precise analysis of capitalism that he undertook from 1857 on. Although the link between art and labour became closer, it never became one of identity: on the contrary, the tension between the two components of artistic activity seemed to impel him to clarify what the abolition of alienation and exploitation might look like, by basing himself on the concrete immanent critique of alienation represented by the exceptional individuality of the artist. Two texts may be cited here: the *Grundrisse* (1857–58) and *Theories of Surplus-Value* (1861–63). The reflections on art contained in them are extremely brief, but the frequent analytic references to the question, amidst passages concerning production and the nature of the commodity, prove that they had a real importance for Marx, being linked in his mind with the general problem of representations as social realities endowed with specific functions and beset with their own peculiar contradictions.

Beginning in 1857, Marx's systematic development of the critique of political economy and his concern with superstructures led him to analyze the capitalist socio-economic formation as a differentiated contradictory totality, whose various strata occupied particular functions in reproducing class relations and ensuring the accumulation of capital. By virtue of this underlying unity of the capitalist formation, he thought it conceivable that artistic activity might in some cases produce a conscious recovery of its world, and that certain works might thereby acquire a real critical import.

Furthermore, the reception of art from past epochs as the expression of a lost harmony echoes a fundamentally dialectical understanding of history and its various yearnings. This is how we should understand the famous passage in the 'Introduction' of 1857 on the interest we still feel with regard to Greek art from many centuries ago: 'But the difficulty lies not in understanding that Greek art and epic poetry are bound up with certain forms of social development. The difficulty is that they still give us aesthetic pleasure and are in certain respects regarded as a standard and unattainable model.'[13] After mentioning the 'unequal development of material production and e.g. art',[14] Marx emphasized that the Greeks were 'normal children', who blossomed in an era and social conditions that 'can never recur'.[15] The goal of building a post-capitalist mode of

---

[13] K. Marx, 'Outlines of the Critique of Political Economy [*Grundrisse*]. First Instalment', MECW, vol. 28, p. 47.
[14] Ibid, p. 46. [15] Ibid, p. 48.

production may feed on such nostalgia for a vanished world, in the sense, and up to the point, that this is a prefiguration of the future. Marx's analysis here may be thought to anticipate his later study of traditional social forms peculiar to pre-capitalist societies, as well as his analysis of the resources these offer to build communism without going through the stage of capitalism and its social and colonial barbarities.[16]

Whenever Marx addressed the question of art, his aim was not to promote an aesthetic model of any kind, but to theorize artistic activity as formative of the human individual; in this respect, it was the same as labour, although with a special character of its own. Marx tried to include in his analysis the impact of artworks on those who behold them, in so far as these are sensitive creatures open to a developed sense of the beautiful: 'An *objet d'art* – just like any other product – creates a public that has artistic taste and is capable of enjoying beauty. Production therefore produces not only an object for the subject, but also a subject for the object.'[17] This amounts to saying that art is not an inert reflection, but a social function, both expressive and structuring in its own way, like any representation in the broad sense of the term. A work of art helps to shape the eye, ear, and intellect of its audience, placing it in the situation of actors and subjects. But Marx also emphasized the uneven development of the different social spheres, as well as the distinctive temporality of artistic creation:

> As regards art, it is known that certain periods of its florescence by no means correspond to the general development of society, or, therefore, to the material basis, the skeleton as it were of its organization. For example, the Greeks compared with the moderns, or else Shakespeare. It is even acknowledged that certain forms of art, e.g. epos, can no longer be produced in their epoch-making, classic form after artistic production as such has begun; in other words, that certain important creations within the compass of art are only possible at an early stage of its development. If this is the case with regard to the different arts within the sphere of art itself, it is not so remarkable that this should also be the case with regard to the entire sphere of art in its relation to the general development of society.[18]

It thus became possible for Marx to affirm the exceptional character of the artist and the relative social 'extra-territoriality' of his or her activity, while also maintaining the idea of the essential (contradictory) cohesion of every socio-economic formation. The artist simply looks ahead to the future, building on the potential for individual and collective development that prefigures the necessary overcoming of contradictions at work

---

[16] See K. B. Anderson, *Marx at the Margins: On Nationalism, Ethnicity and Non-Western Societies* (Chicago: University of Chicago Press, 2010).
[17] Marx, 'Outlines of the Critique of Political Economy [*Grundrisse*]. First Instalment', p. 30.
[18] Ibid, p. 46.

in the present. Here we find again the question of labour and the development of human faculties that Marx already addressed in his early writings. Against Charles Fourier's (1772–1837) praise of 'relaxation', and in contrast to his own theses in *The German Ideology*, he now wrote that 'really free work, e.g. the composition of music, is also the most damnably difficult, demanding the most intensive effort'.[19] By this token, art should be likened to work free from exploitation and alienation, 'the exertion of the worker as a subject', not as 'a natural force drilled in a particular way'.[20]

Art, like labour, transforms the external world and fashions its material in accordance with techniques that have evolved over time. But, unlike in production, technical development is not here driven by the demand for greater productivity and economies of socially necessary labour time, nor by the tendency to intensify and mechanize work tasks. In a sense, therefore, art is fully and truly labour, which marks human emancipation from nature: the idea was not new. What was original, however, was Marx's notion that the artist's labour lastingly escapes the process of real subsumption[21] that subjects an older practice to capitalist reconfiguration. In this sense, the artist is not a worker – or rather, offers to workers the paradoxical figure of a worker spared the loss of self that characterizes the world of work ruled by the law of value.

This raised two questions. First, how should one conceive the modern status of bought and sold artworks, which for their owners tend to be no more than reserves of value irrespective of their content or real artistic importance? Does not the process of formal subsumption lead to ever greater capitalist colonization of an activity that was selectively spared by the dominant relations of production? And second, what should we make of a purely relative emancipation that is at best a local privilege, a vestige of the ancient status of the liberal arts that makes even more patent the mass alienation in which it is now encased – an emancipation that does not result from an emancipatory struggle and does not constitute a social class (like the proletariat) bearing a perspective of revolutionary transformation?

The first question highlights the problematic character of the definition of the artist as a productive worker. This definition, Marx stressed, provides the only justification of his existence in the eyes of bourgeois economists: 'These people are so dominated by their fixed bourgeois

---

[19] Marx, 'Outlines of the Critique of Political Economy [*Grundrisse*]. First Instalment', p. 530.
[20] Ibid.
[21] The term 'subsumption' allows us to distinguish the stages through which capitalism takes over inherited forms of production, first by annexing them (formal subsumption), then by profoundly restructuring them (real subsumption). See K. Marx, *Capital*, volume I, MECW, vol. 35, p. 511.

ideas that they would think they were insulting Aristotle (384 BC–322 BC) or Julius Caesar (100 BC–44 BC) if they called them "unproductive labourers".[22] In fact, artistic production may, like any other, be creative of surplus-value. But that is not its function, and, without vanishing altogether, artistic activity at least partly resists integration into the productive forces. This intrinsic resistance to its real (sometimes even formal) subsumption by the capitalist mode of production is precisely what explains the suspicion directed against artistic activity and, *a contrario*, the importance it had in Marx's eyes. As he noted, 'capitalist production is hostile to certain branches of intellectual production, for example, art and poetry'.[23] It is not that art is always revolutionary in content, but as a basically free activity it opposes its complete annexation by the world of the commodity. In Marx's time, the art market was still limited in extent and the culture industry did not exist. Moreover, the quantity of abstract labour crystallized in the artwork is not what defines its value; David Ricardo (1772–1823) already pointed out this peculiarity of 'non-reproducible' goods, whereby they escape the law of value[24] without escaping the market.

It is worth noting that, in order to account for this peculiarity, Marx had recourse to the concepts of *praxis* and *poiesis*, and that he was then referring not to Greek art, but to the Aristotelian categories of activity.[25] Aristotle's actual terms do not appear in this context, but we read that 'some services or use values, the results of certain activities or kinds of labour, are incorporated in commodities; others, however, leave behind no tangible result as distinct from the persons themselves: or they do not result in a saleable commodity'.[26] The assertion that there exist 'pure' activities without a material result to be hijacked by the market – the example Marx gives is singing – allows him to insist once more on the free development of man's faculties as an end in itself.

The term 'wealth' then changes its meaning, in accordance with its fundamental ambiguity. Its non-commodity definition allows us to perceive a world emancipated from the law of value. For,

> if the narrow bourgeois form is peeled off, what is wealth if not the universality of the individual's needs, capacities, enjoyments, productive forces, etc., produced in universal exchange; what is it if not the full development of human control over the forces of nature – over the forces of so-called Nature, as well as those of his own nature? What is wealth if not the absolute unfolding of man's creative

---

[22] K. Marx, *The Economic Manuscript of 1861–63*, MECW, vol. 31, p. 184.
[23] Ibid, p. 182.
[24] D. Ricardo, *On the Principles of Political Economy and Taxation* (New York: Dover Publications Inc., 2004), section 1, ch. 1.
[25] See Aristotle, *Nicomachean Ethics* (Oxford: Oxford University Press, 2009), book 1, ch. 1.
[26] Marx, *Economic Manuscript of 1861–63*, p. 139.

abilities, without any precondition other than the preceding historical development, which makes the totality of this development – i.e. the development of all human powers as such, not measured by any previously given yardstick – an end-in-itself, through which he does not reproduce himself in any specific character, but produces his totality, and does not seek to remain something he has already become, but is in the absolute movement of becoming?[27]

In sum, Marx's strange aesthetics – which was never systematized, but kept bubbling up to the surface – turned away from analysis of artworks and the social conditions of their reception, and concentrated instead on the social-anthropological process bound up with their production and the associated formation of free individuals. It prioritized the insight that the liberation of work can already base itself on some of its (partially or potentially) non-alienated forms, which as such are bearers of an active critique of alienation. Art thus became a limiting case through which Marx could test and, without lapsing into utopianism, suggest actual roots for the future liberation of labour and the worker. Seen from this angle, the attention he gave to art was certainly sporadic but not at all secondary. For it enabled Marx to corroborate his definition of communism in terms of 'the free development of each' as the 'condition for the free development of all',[28] and the claim that 'the social history of man is never anything but the history of his individual development'.[29] This was also consistent with his idea that a historical base conditioned the totality of a socio-economic formation and delimited the historical development of individuality.

The conclusion one can draw from this is in a sense surprising. In so far as it synthesized a conviction that labour is 'life's prime want'[30] with the programme that work should simply be abolished,[31] artistic activity was for Marx inseparable from the perspective of the abolition of capitalism; it rooted this in the present, providing the criterion and the point of reference for a free praxis at once non-paid and disinterested. But this virtue was at the same time its defect: it inevitably left open, and even evaded, the question of the social and political construction of a non-capitalist mode of production; it bypassed the centrality of the class struggle, the necessity of a reorganization of production and a confrontation with the power of the state. For it is the peculiarity of artistic activity that it places itself on the margins of social conflict, which is the only motive force for the abolition of relations of domination and exploitation.

---

[27] Marx, 'Outlines of the Critique of Political Economy [*Grundrisse*]. First Instalment', pp. 411–12.
[28] K. Marx and F. Engels, *Manifesto of the Communist Party*, MECW, vol. 6, p. 506.
[29] K. Marx, 'Letter to P. V. Annenkov, 28 December 1846', MECW, vol. 38, p. 96.
[30] K. Marx, *Critique of the Gotha Programme*, MECW, vol. 24, p. 87.
[31] Marx and Engels, *The German Ideology*, p. 77.

20.3 The Contemporary Relevance of Marx's Analysis of Art

Marx's thinking on art had an important legacy, as many Marxist theorists developed ideas on the subject in highly varied directions. At the same time, the political regimes issuing from the popular revolutions of the twentieth century set out aesthetic prescriptions that laid claim to Marxism. But, although art theories and practices looked for sources in his work – which was not necessarily illegitimate – Marx's analysis was fundamentally alien to such developments. This is precisely why it may prove fruitful again today, at several levels. Let us mention three of these.

The first level is the development of individual capacities. Not only does Marx's analysis not lead to a normative aesthetic; it implicitly frees artistic activity from any political injunction concerning its content or tasks, beyond the circle of art professionals. The only function of artistic activity lies precisely in its not being enslaved, and in knowing how to remain so. This function is certainly not fulfilled in 'socialist realism', but rather in the appeal of art to the sensory faculties, in the pure pleasure of the eye and ear, which give material roots to the development of individuality. In fact, Marx saw the creation and reception of art as the dimension of play and dream, the recapturing of childhood, the liberation of time as opposed to the 'theft of human time' that was the essence of capitalism. Paradoxically, Marx came close to the Kantian 'free play of the faculties'[32] – and, more paradoxically still, to the aesthetics of Friedrich Schiller (1759–1805)[33] – while totally rejecting the idea of an aesthetic road to liberty and communism. Convinced that the way out of capitalism could only be political, in the form of a revolution, Marx saw artistic activity as evidence that such an exit was possible, but not as the instrument through which it could be achieved. It may be thought that artistic activities today preserve this implicit critical thrust, as one potential form of resistance to the capitalist logic of ever greater annexation of individual lifetime.

Second, art and culture have become a fully fledged sector of capitalism, to a degree that Marx only barely glimpsed. Yet his analysis of the logic of capitalism and of its capacity to take over activities originally alien to it remains highly relevant. Although artistic and cultural activities are becoming closer than before to other activities that are subject to the law of value, they continue to escape that law in part even as they also submit to it in part: this contradiction relates directly to one of the fundamental contradictions of capitalism, namely, its drive to incorporate labour

---

[32] I. Kant, *Critique of Judgement*, trans. J. C. Meredith (Oxford: Oxford University Press, 2008), part one, first book, §9.
[33] F. Schiller, *On the Aesthetic Education of Man* (New York: Dover Publications Inc., 2004).

power as fully as possible, even if the labour power is never produced as a commodity. In fact, analysis of the complex proximity between art and labour – which Marx studied in his time – is today more pertinent than ever.[34] It opens up political space for various forms of resistance to capitalist logic, by highlighting the critical awareness that is characteristic of all political intervention.

The third level concerns the complexities of critical art that is *engagé* in its very content, produced by artists participating in the social and political process of human emancipation. Such art existed all through the twentieth century. And today the question of what it can do and what it can produce is being explored along many different paths, in which the problem of combining its specific autonomy with its partisan commitment is continually addressed. It is up to creative artists themselves to keep rethinking and reinventing the terms of this commitment, while at the same time renewing its creative fertility. But the need for renewal also concerns their audience as well as the theoretical critics of capitalism. Marx did not explore these paths as such, but here as elsewhere inventive strength is more faithful to his approach than is a repetition of the letter of his work.

References

Anderson, Kevin B. (2010), *Marx at the Margins: On Nationalism, Ethnicity and Non-Western Societies*, Chicago: University of Chicago Press.
Aristotle (2009), *Nicomachean Ethics*, Oxford: Oxford University Press.
Beech, Dave (2015), *Art and Value: Art's Economic Exceptionalism in Classical, Neoclassical and Marxist Economics*, Leiden: Brill.
Garo, Isabelle (2013), *L'or des images: art, monnaie, capital*, Montreuil, La Ville Brûle.
Kant, Immanuel (2008), *Critique of Judgement*, trans. J. C. Meredith, Oxford: Oxford University Press.
Marx, Karl (1975), 'To Arnold Ruge, 20 March 1842', MECW, vol. 1, pp. 383–6.
  (1975), *Economic and Philosophic Manuscripts of 1844*, MECW, vol. 3, pp. 229–346.
  (1975), *Thesis on Feuerbach*, MECW, vol. 5, pp. 6–8.
  (1986), 'Outlines of the Critique of Political Economy [*Grundrisse*]. First Instalment', MECW, vol. 28.
  (1989), *Critique of the Gotha Programme*, MECW, vol. 24, pp. 75–99.
  (1989), *The Economic Manuscript of 1861–63*, MECW, vol. 31.
  (1994), *The Economic Manuscript of 1861–63*, MECW, vol. 34.

---

[34] See D. Beech, *Art and Value: Art's Economic Exceptionalism in Classical, Neoclassical and Marxist Economics* (Leiden: Brill, 2015), part 2; I. Garo, *L'or des images: art, monnaie, capital* (Montreuil: La Ville Brûle, 2013), part 4.

(1996), *Capital*, volume I, MECW, vol. 35.
Marx, Karl, and Engels, Frederick (1975), *The German Ideology*, MECW, vol. 5, pp. 19–539.
(1976), *Manifesto of the Communist Party*, MECW, vol. 6, pp. 477–519.
(1982), *Letters, 1844–1851*, MECW, vol. 38.
Prawer, Siegbert Salomon (2011), *Karl Marx and World Literature*, London: Verso.
Ricardo, David (2004), *On the Principles of Political Economy and Taxation*, New York: Dover Publications Inc.
Rose, Margaret A. (1984), *Marx's Lost Aesthetic: Karl Marx and the Visual Arts*, Cambridge: Cambridge University Press.
Schiller, Friedrich (2004), *On the Aesthetic Education of Man*, New York: Dover Publications Inc.

21 Technology and Science

Amy E. Wendling

21.1 Science and Technology in Marx's Research

Karl Marx synthesized a new critical concept of technology. As with the legal and political norms purporting to be universal and neutral that Marx exposed as bourgeois, Marx also showed how technology was capitalist. In *Capital*, volume I, Marx argued that capitalism does not work to develop technology, in general; instead, it develops only those kinds of machines that abet its economic, social, and political interests. It even inhibits the development of technologies that do not. However, capitalism also claims that it is developing technology, in general, and so reigns in our ability to imagine non-capitalist technologies.

When Marx began work on the topic of technology in late 1845 and early 1846, he was not yet using this critical concept. In fact, he began with a naïve idea of technology in which machines themselves can be separated from their use. This is very clear in the letter of 28 December 1846 to Pavel Annenkov (1813–1887), where Marx wrote, 'Machinery is no more an economic category than the ox who draws the plow. The present use of machinery is one of the relations of our present economic system, but the way in which machinery is exploited is quite distinct from the machinery itself. Powder is still powder, whether you use it to wound a man or to dress his wounds.'[1] Although a division between technologies and their employment is already visible in the passage, this division is pre-critical because Marx has not yet understood that the capitalist mode of developing and using technologies will condition which technologies themselves are built and used.

By contrast, in *Capital*, volume I, Marx wrote, 'It would be possible to write quite a history of inventions, made since 1830, for the sole purpose of supplying capital with weapons against the revolts of the working-class. At the head of these in importance, stands the self-acting mule, because it opened up a new epoch in the automatic system.'[2] In light of this critical

---
[1] 'K. Marx to P. Annenkov, 28 December 1846', MECW, vol. 38, p. 99.
[2] K. Marx, *Capital*, volume I, MECW, vol. 35, p. 439.

concept of technological invention, Marx might have rewritten the last sentence of his 1846 letter to read, 'powder will most often be required to dress wounds after, and because, it has been used to wound'.

Marx's transition from a pre-critical to a critical concept of technology came about as he studied how science and technology developed in tandem with capital's quest for surplus-value.

Science [*Wissenschaft*] was a broader term for Marx than it is in its English usage, where it carries with it an empirical epistemology and a positivist methodology, both of which Marx rejected. For Marx, science was, above all, the very thing that made his materialist presentation true. The contrasting term for science was ideology: Hegelian ideology in Marx's early works and capitalist ideology in his later works. Again, unlike in English, where elegance is a value of scientific presentation, to be *wissenschaftlich* requires a degree of complexity and conceptual density. Thus, Marx issued his famous warning, in the preface to the 1872 French edition of *Capital*, that '[t]here is no royal road to science'.[3]

Beginning as early as the year 1845, with a concentration on the topic in 1851 and continued interest in it through the 1860s, Marx studied the history of technological development in considerable detail.[4] From the German-language sources, Marx studied, in particular, the works of Johann Heinrich Moritz von Poppe (1776–1854).[5] Poppe was Johann Beckmann's (1739–1811) student in Göttingen.[6]

As Guido Frison explained, the concept of technology that Marx inherited from Poppe and Beckmann mimicked the methodology of the natural sciences, especially that of Linnaeus, who studied the adaptation of natural objects to social uses.[7] The histories of inventions that resulted appeared as catalogues of objects, only some of which might be recognized as technological today: in Beckmann's *A Concise History of Ancient Institutions, Inventions, and Discoveries in Science and Mechanic Art* there

---

[3] Marx, *Capital*, volume I, p. 23.
[4] Two historians, Rainer Winkelmann and Hans-Peter Müller have transcribed portions of this material (in 1982 and 1981, respectively), which does not yet appear in the MEGA², but is slated for inclusion in volume 10 of the fourth series. Müller's account, in particular, treats the notebook that contains the Poppe extracts comprehensively (>H. Müller, *Karl Marx: Die Technologisch-Historischen Exzerpt* [Frankfurt: Ullstein Materialien, 1981], p. 3–148).
[5] Ibid, p. 47.
[6] F. Yoshida, 'J. H. M. Poppe's History of Technology and Karl Marx', *Hokudai Economic Papers*, 13: 25 (1983).
[7] G. Frison, 'Linnaeus, Beckmann, Marx and the Foundation of Technology. Between Natural and Social Sciences: A Hypothesis of an Ideal Type', *History and Technology*, 10: 152 (1993).

were entries for the sewing machine and ribbon loom, but also for pineapple and bees.[8]

In 1851, Marx studied Beckmann's mature work, where Beckmann had categorized these entries, ordering the material by the identity or similarity of the procedures employed in the various crafts he surveyed, and working, within the rubrics established by similarity of procedure, from the simple to the complex.[9] This was how technology became a more general inquiry, and how technologies came to be both isolated from particular arts, and also transferred between and among them. Beckmann and those working after him, including Marx, called this 'general technology'. General technology was identified with a new branch of science: the applied industrial arts, or what was subsequently called engineering. In the nineteenth century, general technology was also identified with an object that assimilated mechanical discoveries to a centralized engine: the machine.

As Fumikazu Yoshida (1950–) documented, Marx drew at least four important ideas from Poppe: (1) the notion of general technology; (2) specific details about mills, weaving, and watchmaking; (3) the discussions of transition in tool use from the handcraft to the factory stage; and (4) the importance of chemistry in relationship to mechanics.[10] All four of these ideas are in evidence in the discussions of technology that Marx offered in *Capital* and the manuscripts leading up to it, where they have been merged with the studies of the steam engine that Marx made from English-language sources of Peter Gaskell, Andrew Ure (1778–1857), and Charles Babbage (1791–1871).

But Marx absorbed something else from his studies of Poppe and Beckmann, something far more relevant to his critical concept of technology. According to Frison, the Prussian state had funded the university positions that generated the idea of general technology, and it demanded that the discoveries of general technology work to advance its interests.[11] The connections between the Prussian state and technological development were thus overt, unlike in the English-language environment, where technology appeared – although was not actually – more politically neutral. If Marx was able to spot the politics of technological development at work in England's Industrial Revolution, this was partly because he had been trained to look for a politics of technology.

---

[8] J. Beckmann, *A Concise History of Ancient Institutions, Inventions, and Discoveries in Science and Mechanic Art* (London: G. and W. B. Whittaker, 1823), pp. xi–xvi.
[9] Frison, 'Linnaeus, Beckmann, Marx and the Foundation of Technology', p. 163.
[10] Yoshida, 'J. H. M. Poppe's History of Technology and Karl Marx', pp. 24–6.
[11] Frison, 'Linnaeus, Beckmann, Marx and the Foundation of Technology', pp. 144–5.

Marx's critique of particular states developed into a critique of the capitalist shaping of all modern states. It was but a short step to the insight that capitalism had shaped the development of general technology. Capitalism's norms of profit extraction, rather than the desires of a particular state, were the new politics of technological development.

This worry was something different from the pre-critical idea that a technology, neutral in itself can become deployed in violent ways: the powder used to maim instead of heal. Instead, Marx realized that certain features of capitalism's regime of profit extraction had been built into technologies themselves, influencing their form. In Andrew Feenberg's (1943–) example, machines built to fit children's bodies were used to argue that only children could work machines,[12] since child labour was a key element of profit extraction.

And the regime of profit extraction not only influenced which technologies were developed, but also those that were not. In *Capital*, Marx wrote,

So soon as it shall happen that the children of the manufacturers themselves have to go through a course of schooling as helpers in the mill, [some] unexplored territory of mechanics will soon make remarkable progress. 'Of machinery, perhaps self-acting mules are as dangerous as any other kind. Most of the accidents from them happen to little children, from their creeping under the mules to sweep the floor whilst the mules are in motion ... If machine makers would only invent a self-sweeper, by whose use the necessity for these little children to creep under the machinery might be prevented, it would be a happy addition to our protective measures.' ('Reports of Insp. of Fact.' for 31st Oct., 1866, p. 63.)[13]

Marx also realized that if technology, precisely as one the disciplines of statecraft, were to be employed by the very fine political aims of communism, it would be developed in ways that benefit and ameliorate both the working class and humanity as a whole. We glimpse this positive picture of technology most powerfully in the texts on technology from Marx's *Grundrisse* known as the 'fragment on machines'.[14]

21.2 Communist Machines in the *Grundrisse*

The comparison between capitalist technology and communist technology is, in fact, characteristic of the *Grundrisse*. While Marx continued to

[12] A. Feenberg, *Questioning Technology* (New York: Routledge, 1999), pp. 86–7.
[13] Marx, *Capital*, volume I, pp. 424–5.
[14] K. Marx, 'Outlines of the Critique of Political Economy [*Grundrisse*]. Second Instalment', MECW, vol. 29, pp. 79–98. A. Negri, *Marx beyond Marx: Lessons on the Grundrisse* (New York: Autonomedia, 1992), pp. 139–47; and M. Postone, *Time, Labor, and Social Domination: A Reinterpretation of Marx's Critical Theory* (Cambridge: Cambridge University Press, 1993), pp. 24–36 have offered compelling readings of this text.

develop his critical account of capitalist science and technology, he was still disposed to highlight the pathways along which science and technology could develop to undermine capital. In the *Grundrisse*, Marx thus moved back and forth between negative and potentially positive aspects of technological development.

For example, Marx wrote that 'all the sciences have been forced into the service of capital ... At this point, invention becomes a business, and the application of science to immediate production itself becomes a factor determining and soliciting science.'[15] This new motivation for science, however, contrasted with both the origins of science in the histories Marx had studied and with what Marx claimed should be its proper motivations. Mechanical science had studied, and then replaced, the detailed motions of the labourer, and so properly belonged to her rather than to the capitalist. In addition, the motivation for science ought not to be the norms of production, including profit extraction, but the dignifying of the human species. Marx showed that technologies were immersed in a system of values, and necessarily so. Were this system to have, as its goal, such dignity, technology would look very different.

As Marx showed in the *Grundrisse*, under capitalism, machinery forces longer worker hours in order to drive up the accumulation of surplus labour, and because machinery must be worn out as quickly as possible before the capital fixed in it becomes obsolete and unprofitable.[16] So, while it is true that one worker can make as much linen as ten did previously, this does not mean that he is working 1/10 of the time. Instead, mass production for all workers means they work longer than before, producing in 'enormous mass quantities'.[17]

The problem with these long hours is that, as Marx put it, 'the whole time of an individual is posited as labour time, and he is consequently degraded to a mere labourer, subsumed under labour'.[18] Because capitalist machinery also deprives the worker of both skill and physical power,[19] it reduces her to 'overseer and regulator'[20] during these long hours. For this reason, the worker is not even subsumed under a kind of labour that would have some kind of interest. Instead, she is subject to a production process, one that has, as Marx wrote, 'ceased to be a labour process in the sense that it is no longer embraced by labour as the unity which dominates it'.[21]

Communist machinery would finally make good on the general ability of machinery to reduce necessary labour to a minimum.[22] The result of not having to produce any surplus value would be free time for all: Marx

---

[15] K. Marx, 'Outlines of the Critique of Political Economy [*Grundrisse*]. First Instalment', MECW, vol. 28, p. 90.
[16] Ibid, p. 89. [17] Ibid, p. 84. [18] Ibid, p. 94. [19] Ibid, p. 82. [20] Ibid, p. 91.
[21] Ibid, p. 83. [22] Ibid, p. 91.

claimed that wealth itself would come to be defined as disposable time.[23] Marx sketched the results of this beautifully when he wrote:

> The saving of labour time is equivalent to the increase of free time ... From the standpoint of the immediate production process it can be considered as the production of *fixed capital*, this fixed capital being man himself ... Free time – which is both leisure and time for higher activity – has naturally transformed its possessor into another subject; and it is then as this other subject that he enters into the immediate production process ... [a subject] whose mind is the repository of the accumulated knowledge of society'.[24]

The kind of knowledge Marx had in mind was especially the scientific and technological knowledge that workers are systematically excluded from by capitalism.[25]

And so, in the *Grundrisse*, Marx was hopeful about the future of communist technology. Even if machinery is the most adequate form of fixed capital, as he acknowledged,[26] 'it in no way follows that its subsuming under the social relation of capital is the most appropriate and best social production relation for the application of machinery'.[27] Confidently, Marx concluded that 'machines will not cease to be agents of social production when they become, e.g., the property of the associated workers'.[28] These workers will be newly skilled in owning, operating, and developing such machines in line with a communist system of values.

This hope was still alive in *The Economic Manuscript of 1861–63*, where Marx even wrote about 'the extraordinarily beneficial consequences [of the development of production] for the physical, moral and intellectual amelioration of the working classes in England'.[29] However, in *Capital*, volume I, there are very few speculations about the use of machines in a liberated society. This idea was retained only as a single footnote in the 'Machinery and Modern Industry' chapter, where Marx wrote, 'in a communistic society there would be a very different scope for the employment of machinery than there can be in a bourgeois society'.[30]

21.3 Technology and Contradiction in *Capital*

The change of tone in *Capital* happened because Marx had refined his understanding of surplus-value and the role of machines in producing it.

---

[23] Ibid, p. 94. [24] Ibid, p. 97.
[25] The demand for universal public education at the end of the *Manifesto of the Communist Party*, and especially its provision for a 'combination of education with industrial production' (MECW, vol. 6, p. 505), is best understood in light of these observations.
[26] Marx, 'Outlines of the Critique of Political Economy [*Grundrisse*]. First Instalment', p. 84.
[27] Ibid, p. 85. [28] Ibid, p. 211.
[29] K. Marx, *The Economic Manuscript of 1861–63*, MECW, vol. 33, p. 386.
[30] Marx, *Capital*, volume I, p. 396.

The emphasis on the relationship between machines and surplus-value meant that in *Capital* Marx was not talking about machinery as it could be developed and deployed in some possible mode of production. He was talking about machinery as it was developed and deployed in the capitalist mode of production, specifically. And, while a pre-critical theory of technology could assert that existing machines were used in ways inimical to the interests of the working class, a critical theory of technology argues for something stronger: that capitalism only develops machines that advance its social and political interests. All machines are capitalist machines: all technology is capitalist technology.

Recall that by surplus-value Marx meant the labour that could be extracted from the worker over and above that which was required to meet her daily needs. The extension of the working day contributed to what he called absolute surplus-value. For example, the worker had to work three hours to create enough value to supply her with food, shelter, and other necessities for the day. However, she would work a twelve-hour shift. The value that she had created in the remaining nine hours was profit to the capitalist enterprise in which she worked, since this enterprise only compensated for her total time with just enough value to meet her minimal daily needs.

Marx complicated this picture by adding the category of relative surplus-value. Relative surplus-value shortens the portion of the day devoted to recouping the value of minimal daily needs still further. It does so by increasing the productivity of the labour process, such that this value is produced more quickly. Now, the same worker can, in two hours, produce the same amount of value that he used to produce in three hours, leaving ten hours of similarly intensified value output as profit for the capitalist. The division of labour is a simple example of the means through which productivity is increased.

Drawing on the material from his research studies, Marx understood the use of machinery in factory labour as a culmination of the history of the division of labour. This culmination drove the increase in the productive power of labour to new heights, and amplified the production of relative surplus-value in tandem. Marx defined the machinery that accomplished this as follows:

All fully developed machinery consists of three essentially different parts, the motor mechanism, the transmitting mechanism, and finally the tool or working machine. The motor mechanism is that which puts the whole in motion. It either generates its own motive power, like the steam-engine, the caloric engine, the electromagnetic machine, &c., or it receives its impulse from some already existing natural force, like the water-wheel from the head of water, the wind-mill from wind, &c. The transmitting mechanism, composed of fly-wheels, shafting, toothed wheels, pulleys, straps, ropes, bands, pinions, and gearing of the most varied kinds, regulates the motion ... and divides and distributes it among the working machines. These two first parts of the whole mechanism are there, solely, for putting the working machines in motion, by means of which motion the subject of labour is seized upon and modified as desired. The tool or working machine is that part of the machinery with which the industrial revolution of the 18th century started. And to this day it constantly serves as such a starting point, whenever a handicraft, or a manufacture, is turned into an industry carried on by machinery.[31]

Marx was particularly concerned to describe the new innovations in the motor mechanism, and the steam engine in particular. Its use removed the need to rely on wind or waterpower, and so removed any natural obstacles that might stand in the way of constant productive activity. For this reason, capitalist machinery as such was defined by the new motor mechanisms – or, more precisely, by the amplification of power in the new motor mechanisms once they were attached to the working machines.

In the passage, Marx also emphasized the transition from handicraft to manufacture. The machine's absorption of functions and processes previously performed by human labour becomes the basis for Marx's famous discussions of labour's deskilling. And, indeed, the tone of the chapter rapidly shifts from descriptive to normative, emphasizing the debilitating effects of work with machinery on labourers:

As soon as the machine executes, without man's help, all the movements requisite to elaborate the raw material, needing only attendance from him, we have an automatic system of machinery, and one that is susceptible of constant improvement in all of its details ... a mechanical monster whose body fills whole factories, and whose demon power, at first veiled under the slow and measured motions of his giant limbs, at length breaks into the fast and furious whirl of his countless organs.[32]

To work at a machine, the workman should be taught from childhood, in order that he may learn to adapt his own movements to the uniform and unceasing motion of an automaton.[33]

It is not the workman that employs the instruments of labour, but the instruments of labour that employ the workman, and it is only in the factory system that this inversion for the first time acquires technical and palpable reality. By means of its conversion into an automaton, the instrument of labour confronts the labourer, during the labour process, in the shape of capital, of dead labour, that dominates, and pumps dry, living labour-power. The separation of the intellectual powers of production from the manual labour, and the conversion of those powers into the might of capital over labour, is, as we have already shown, finally completed by modern industry erected on the foundation of machinery.[34]

---

[31] Marx, *Capital*, volume I, p. 376.   [32] Ibid, p. 384.   [33] Ibid, p. 423.   [34] Ibid, p. 426.

The third passage, in particular, links the issue of deskilling to the debilitating effects of machinery not simply on the labourer's work process, but also on her ability to contest for political and social power.

In fact, devices designed to keep workers in their place will become an explicit goal of capitalist technological development. Examples include both the internalized time discipline that E. P. Thompson (1924–1993) movingly described[35] and the panoptical systems of surveillance that Foucault chillingly chronicled.[36] Increasing absolute surplus-value may be the ostensible reason for introducing machinery into the production process. But there is another reason, without which the increase of surplus value would be meaningless or impossible: machinery is introduced to discipline the industrial work force, to weaken its bargaining position, and to entice it to engage in self-surveillance. Without a work force willing to take the kinds of jobs most likely to produce relative surplus-value, capitalism would simply be impossible.

Now, ideally, capitalist technologies can meet the two goals of efficiency and domination simultaneously: machines can both increase productive efficiencies and discipline workers. However, the two goals are perhaps most interesting when they come into conflict with one another. When this happens, efficiency often gives way to the political domination that conditions it.

Here Marx's training to pay particular attention to the political dimensions and implications of technological infrastructures bore fruit. Following Marx in this, theorist of automation Georges Friedmann (1902–1977) offered the insight that capitalism does not always develop technology, as is sometimes presupposed by philosophers of technology, but also hinders its development in sites where changes might improve conditions of comfort or safety for workers. This fettering of development – Friedmann calls it the 'hidebound' aspect of certain industries – occurs even when instituting conditions of greater comfort and safety would ultimately also increase profit margins.[37] For this same reason, technologies developed under capitalism do not necessarily render the system of production more efficient, as they claim. They are, rather, direct political mechanisms for the consolidation and control of capitalist power.

---

[35] E. P. Thompson, 'Time, Work-Discipline, and Industrial Capitalism', *Past & Present*, 38: 56–97 (1967).

[36] M. Foucault, *Discipline and Punish: The Birth of the Prison* (New York: Random House, 1977), pp. 195–228.

[37] G. Friedmann, *Industrial Society: The Emergence of the Human Problems of Automation* (Toronto: Collier-Macmillan, 1955), pp. 173–90.

In addition to the contest that can erupt between efficiency and domination, there is one other very important contradiction inherent to capitalist technology. Capitalism has a very ambivalent relationship with machinery's tendency to cancel the need for human labour. While machines can certainly increase relative surplus-value, they do not produce relative surplus-value by themselves. They require, instead, human intermediaries whose subsistence commodities they have cheapened. However, the nature of machinery is to reduce the need for human labourers, and so to cancel the very intermediaries from whom capitalism derives its profits. Thus, even as it has compelling internal reasons to develop and use technology, capitalism also has compelling internal reasons to fetter both its development and its use.

Citing some of the excesses that this contradiction produces, Marx wrote:

> In the older countries, machinery, when employed in some branches of industry, creates such a redundancy of labour in other branches that in these latter the fall of wages below the value of labour-power impedes the use of machinery, and, from the standpoint of the capitalist, whose profit comes, not from a diminution of the labour employed, but from a diminution of the labour paid for, renders that use superfluous or often impossible ... In England women are still occasionally used instead of horses for hauling canal boats, because the labour required to produce horses and machines is an accurately known quantity, while that required to maintain the women of the surplus-population is below all calculation. Hence nowhere do we find a more shameful squandering of human labour power for the most despicable purposes than in England, the land of machinery.[38]

Compared with the term 'machinery', Marx used the term 'technology' only very sparingly in *Capital*, volume I. However, when it does appear, it is always very relevant to our understanding of Marx's critical concept of technology. Emblematic, in this regard, is the passage where Marx wrote:

> The principle which [Modern Industry] pursued, of resolving each process into its constituent movements, without any regard to their possible execution by the hand of man, created the new modern science of technology. The varied, apparently unconnected, and petrified forms of the industrial processes now resolved themselves into so many conscious and systematic applications of natural science to the attainment of given useful effects. Technology also discovered the few main fundamental forms of motion, which, despite the diversity of the instruments used, are necessarily taken by every productive action of the human body; just as the science of mechanics sees in the most complicated machinery nothing but the continual repetition of the simple mechanical powers.[39]

---

[38] Marx, *Capital*, volume I, p. 397.   [39] Ibid, p. 489.

Note that in the passage Marx spoke not simply about technology, but about 'the new modern science of technology'. This is a sign that he was talking specifically about the discipline developed by Beckmann and Poppe. The passage then bears this out, since the discovery of what Marx has called 'the main fundamental forms of motion' belonged to what Beckmann, and Poppe following him, called 'general technology'.

The shadow of a critique also falls across the passage in Marx's assertion that the science of technology operates 'without any regard to [its] possible execution by the hand of man'. In inventing machines to mimic the productive actions of the human body, the science of technology views the productive actions of human bodily labour as if they were simply or merely the actions of a machine. In this observation, Marx's critical theory of technology reaches its fullest development. Marx has shown that technological science, precisely as capitalist, demands the assimilation of human labour to the mechanical model. Marx rejected this assimilation, since it enables a severely reductionist view of human labour.

21.4 The Use of Marx's Account of Technology

In his famous essay 'The Question Concerning Technology', Martin Heidegger (1889–1976) argued that technology had a singular essence: one that 'enframes' objects or processes and sees them only as 'standing reserve' for other objects or processes.[40] No substantive properties are left in the object: it is simply a means to other ends, which are a means in turn. This instrumental treatment of everything escalates, and its values remain unexamined, until a kind of habitual efficiency in use is the order of the day. There is no regard to long-range consequences, and no substantive goal behind the efficiencies enabled.

These arguments have a predecessor and a parallel in Marx's own arguments about the subjugation of use-value to exchange-value, and the tandem move from the formal to the real subsumption of capital. Marx also, already in *Capital*, had a sense for the hyper-exploitation that worried Heidegger: making reference to Justus Liebig's discoveries in agricultural chemistry, Marx closed the chapter on machinery in *Capital*, volume I, with the observation that 'Capitalist production ... develops technology ... only by sapping the original sources of all wealth – the soil and the labourer.'[41]

---

[40] M. Heidegger, 'The Question Concerning Technology', in: D. Krell (ed.), *Martin Heidegger Basic Writings* (New York: Harper & Row, 1977), pp. 307–41.
[41] Marx, *Capital*, volume I, pp. 507–8.

Heidegger's analysis diverged from Marx's, however, on a crucial point. If Marx is right, there is no development of technology, in general: there is only the development of technology in the context of a given political, economic, and social environment. For this reason, technology *per se* has no essence. From a Marxist perspective, Heidegger's analysis is not a very accurate assessment of the development of technology, in general, but it does aptly character the capitalist development of technology, in particular.

Starting from this insight, Marx can be used to explain how Heidegger came to think that technology had a singular, alienating essence. Marx showed that capital works to erase its own markings, so that we accept its results as inevitable. Heidegger has interpreted enframing to be the essence of technology, rather than the essence of capitalist technology. In doing so, he has colluded with the capitalist mode of production by making its historicity disappear.

Herbert Marcuse (1898–1979) understood this lesson from Marx very well. In *Technology, War, and Fascism*, he wrote, 'Technics hampers individual development only insofar as they are tied to a social apparatus which perpetuates scarcity, and this same apparatus has realized forces which may shatter the specialized historical form in which technics is utilized ... All programs of an anti-technological character ... serve only those who regard human needs as a by-product of the [current] utilization of technics.'[42]

In this warning, Marcuse expressed Marx's critical concept of technology. But, which technologies, in particular, have been tied to the capitalist social apparatus that Marcuse highlights?

Perhaps the best example has been the overdevelopment of fossil fuel technologies. Because fossil fuel technologies enable huge rate of profit extractions, they have been disproportionately developed in comparison to other technologies with less potential for exploitation.[43] Not only have fossil fuel technologies, such as drilling and the automobile, been overdeveloped in comparison to other energy technologies, such as biofuels, they have produced the profound ecological crises and helped precipitate the cyclical economic crises Marx also predicted.

---

[42] H. Marcuse, *Technology, War, and Fascism, Collected Papers of Herbert Marcuse*, vol. 1 (New York: Routledge, 1998), p. 63.

[43] J. B. Foster, B. Clark, and R. York, *The Ecological Rift: Capitalism's War on the Earth* (New York: Monthly Review, 2010), pp. 121–50 examined the consequences of this. In the twentieth century, the internal combustion engine superseded the steam engine as the capitalist motor mechanism *par excellence*. It would be wildly successful both as a production and as a consumption technology.

As in the visionary passages of the *Grundrisse*, to image a technology that does differently is to imagine technology differently, and to enable it to be developed in light of a different set of values: communist in the very basic sense of protecting the earth and all of the human beings in it – not just the rich ones, and then only in the very short term.

References

Beckmann, Johann (1823), *A Concise History of Ancient Institutions, Inventions, and Discoveries in Science and Mechanic Art*, London: G. and W. B. Whittaker.

Feenberg, Andrew (1999), *Questioning Technology*, New York: Routledge.

Foster, John, Clark, Brett, and York, Richard (2010), *The Ecological Rift: Capitalism's War on the Earth*, New York: Monthly Review.

Foucault, Michel (1977), *Discipline and Punish: The Birth of the Prison*, New York: Random House.

Friedmann, Georges (1955), *Industrial Society: The Emergence of the Human Problems of Automation*, Toronto: Collier-Macmillan.

Frison, Guido (1993), 'Linnaeus, Beckmann, Marx and the Foundation of Technology. Between Natural and Social Sciences: A Hypothesis of an Ideal Type', *History and Technology*, 10: 139–73.

Heidegger, Martin (1977), 'The Question Concerning Technology', in: David Krell (ed.), *Martin Heidegger Basic Writings*, New York: Harper & Row, pp. 307–41.

Marcuse, Herbert (1998), *Technology, War, and Fascism, Collected Papers of Herbert Marcuse*, vol. 1, New York: Routledge.

Marx, Karl (1976), *Marx Engels Collected Works Volume 6: Marx and Engels 1845–1848*, London: Lawrence & Wishart.

(1982), *Letters, 1844–1851*, MECW, vol. 38.

(1986), 'Outlines of the Critique of Political Economy [*Grundrisse*]. First Instalment', MECW, vol. 28.

(1989), *The Economic Manuscript of 1861–63*, MECW, vol. 32.

(1996), *Capital*, volume I, MECW, vol. 35.

Müller, Hans-Peter (ed.) (1981), *Karl Marx: Die technologisch-historischen Exzerpte*, Frankfurt: Ullstein Materialien.

Negri, Antonio (1992), *Marx beyond Marx: Lessons on the* Grundrisse, New York: Autonomedia.

Postone, Moishe (1993), *Time, Labor, and Social Domination: A Reinterpretation of Marx's Critical Theory*, Cambridge: Cambridge University Press.

Thompson, E. P. (1967), 'Time, Work-Discipline, and Industrial Capitalism', *Past & Present*, 38: 56–97.

Winkelmann, Rainer (1982), *Exzerpte über Arbeitsteilung, Machinerie, und Industrie: Historisch kritische Ausgabe*, Frankfurt: Ullstein Materialien.

Yoshida, Fumikazu (1983), 'J. H. M. Poppe's History of Technology and Karl Marx', *Hokudai Economic Papers*, 13: 23–38.

22 Marxisms

Immanuel Wallerstein

22.1 Different Versions of Marxism

All important thinkers tend to have followers and disciples as well as intellectual opponents, both of whom try to define the thinker's thought in particular ways. In itself, this is normal, neither to be deplored nor applauded. Any thinker who produces writings is like someone on a ship who throws overboard a glass bottle with some text inside. Once he has thrown it overboard, he can no longer control where the seas will take it, who will claim to own it, who will pick it up and change it, who will try to destroy it or hide it. It is well known, and often repeated, that Karl Marx, referring to the so-called Legal Marxists, said 'what is certain is that I'm not a Marxist!'[1]

Furthermore, any thinker who produces multiple writings over a lifetime almost inevitably exhibits an evolution in his point of view. Some persons are relatively consistent in their output, some less so. But there are surely always some differences between the writings at different periods of the thinker's life. And Marx is no exception to these simple banal observations.

In the case of some thinkers, their writings become encrusted by the emergence of movements – intellectual movements, social movements – which try to propagate their ideas or use them to achieve intellectual or social objectives. Generally speaking, in Indo-European languages, this leads to adding the suffix 'ism' (in its multiple linguistic variations) to their names. This was the fate of Marx. The need today is to try to historicize the meaning of 'Marxism'.[2]

Any review of the literature shows that there are many different versions of Marxism. Even more than different, they are often quite in contradiction

---

[1] This statement of Marx to Lafargue is reported in Engels's letter of 2–3 November 1882 to Eduard Bernstein, in MECW, vol. 46, p. 356.

[2] This chapter is not trying to give one more version of what Marx intended to argue. The aim, rather, is to elucidate what 'Marxism' has meant, or has been used to mean, to different groups over the last 150 years.

with each other. Many versions of Marxism have added a connecting word or modifying adjective – Revisionist Marxism, Marxism-Leninism, Marxist feminism, and so on. It also seems to be the case that Marxism has been interpreted in different ways in different zones of the world-system, and consequently the term 'Marxism' is sometimes preceded by a geographic adjective. This chapter shall seek to analyze what was intended by keeping 'Marxism' in the compound descriptive name.

In addition, descriptions of others as Marxists or as not being Marxists have been meant by some to be praise and by some to be condemnation. But what is being praised or being condemned? If, in these compound names, one includes 'Marxism' rather than using a descriptive name without that label, it indicates that the users believe there is some significant advantage in doing so. Or sometimes, it may indicate that the users think there is some negative tonality in doing so – a form of generalized condemnation. Obviously, in both cases, it is presumed that the label 'Marxist' evokes some particular imagery, some particular arguments about the world. This imagery, these arguments may or may not be directly derived from the writings of Marx.

Furthermore, it seems clear that the concept of Marxism has evolved historically. One can notice several key break points in the usage of the term: the death of Marx in 1883, the Russian Revolution, 1945 and the onset of the Cold War, the world revolution of 1968, and the collapse of the communisms, especially that of the USSR in 1989–91. With the exception of Marx's death, these are all major political turning points. Thus, it seems to be the case that the evolving definition of Marxism has been closely linked to changing geopolitical realities. It may well be that the intellectual definitions of Marxism are more consequence than cause, as may also be the 'discovery' of previously unknown texts by Marx.

22.2 Engels' Marxism

As long as Marx was alive, he obviously could react to the use of his name by others. Hence his famous statement about not being a Marxist. Marx was a prodigious author. He was also a voracious reader. In that sense, he was a true intellectual, devoted to an effort to understand the world in general, the social world in particular, and capitalism most particularly. Of course, his views evolved, or matured if you prefer. Whether there was a moment of real caesura, such that one can talk of a young Marx and a late Marx has been much debated.[3] There did occur a normal evolution

---

[3] Cf. L. Althusser, *For Marx* (Harmondsworth: Penguin, 1976), pp. 51, 53, and I. Fetscher, *Marx and Marxism* (New York: Herder and Herder, 1971), p. 314.

of a person's thought in the light both of more reading and reflection and of observing the realities of the world. However, since Marx himself never asserted the existence of such a caesura whereas other thinkers often do so about themselves, the fact that Marx did not do so is at the very least something one should take into account.

Marx was more than an academic intellectual. He was a political activist, in many ways the model of what Antonio Gramsci (1891–1937) would later call an organic intellectual.[4] The *Manifesto of the Communist Party* was written as a statement of a political organization. Marx was a major figure in the creation of the International Working Men's Association. He was a frequent commentator on the positions of organizations that considered themselves 'Marxist' or at least 'socialist', as in the *Critique of the Gotha Programme*. In short, Marx never claimed any kind of separation between his role as an analyst and his role as a political activist. It is not sure, nonetheless, that all those who subsequently called themselves Marxists took the same position about the inseparability of analysis and commitment.

Finally, it is important to note that Marx himself did not speak of 'Marxism' nor did he insist on any other abstract label for his thinking. He did think of himself as a communist, although not with a capital letter. For him, to be a communist was to be someone who, by his thinking and his activism, sought to advance the likelihood, which for Marx was virtually inevitable, of arriving at a communist world. Therefore, it seems reasonable to argue that 'Marxism' – as an ideology and as a movement – came into existence only with the death of Marx in 1883.

From this point on, it was widely recognized that Friedrich Engels was the spiritual heir of Karl Marx and the one who had the moral right to claim the legacy. Engels had been the companion-in-arms of Marx for almost forty years. He had been as well the co-author of Marx's single most widely read text. Engels assumed the heritage with panache. He wrote widely. He intervened regularly in party debates. He unquestionably established the first public version of Marxism. Some subsequent authors have argued that Engels's version of Marxism was different, even significantly different, from Marx's own thought. This may or may not be true. Nonetheless, Engels's version is what became the first version of Marxism – a version that has remained influential ever since.

Engels's version served as the foundation stone of what would become the most important 'Marxist' political party in the late nineteenth

---

[4] Cf. A. Gramsci, *Selections from the Prison Notebooks* (London: Lawrence & Wishart, 1971), pp. 131–61.

century – the German Social-Democratic Party (SPD). The SPD may be so considered for a number of reasons: (1) it achieved the greatest relative political success of any socialist movement in this period, and this despite very severe repression; (2) it was able to sponsor a number of attached and subordinate movements in Germany, thereby creating a powerful network of structures in the larger 'civil society'; and (3) it became the locus over some thirty to forty years of the most important debates about Marxist political strategy in the world.

Because of its strength, the SPD was the first Marxist or socialist party to confront seriously the issue of how to deal with participation in the existing parliamentary system. There ensued, as we know, a vigorous debate in the SPD between Eduard Bernstein (1850–1932) and Karl Kautsky (1854–1938). Bernstein's position was reasonably clear-cut. He called for a 'revision' of the theoretical position that had implied that only by some kind of insurrection could the existing order be overthrown and a socialist society created.[5] Bernstein argued instead that, since workers were the numerical majority of the population, they could simply vote themselves into power, once universal (manhood) suffrage was achieved.

There are many reasons to doubt the plausibility of Bernstein's analysis. Did 'workers' in fact constitute the numerical majority of those with suffrage, even if it were universal? Even if they did, would they all without significant exception vote for a socialist party? We know now all the reasons why the original Bernstein arguments do not hold up. But one can understand their appeal to the political base of the SPD. The party was composed of very many who had more to lose than their chains, and who did not relish the idea of becoming revolutionary outlaws rather than upwardly mobile participants in a thriving and growing industrial country in the late nineteenth-century world.

The alternative position – that of Kautsky – was in fact much less clear. Kautsky utilized more traditional revolutionary verbiage in the texts. But the Kautsky faction in the party did nothing to create a revolutionary avant-garde.[6] They argued forcefully and in sophisticated language against the Bernstein position. However, in practice the Kautsky faction ultimately yielded to the revisionist views, as was to be seen when the crunch came, with the outbreak of the First World War. Revisionist Marxism continued to dominate the SPD in the post-1918 period – through Weimar, the Nazi period, and the post-1945 period – until the

---

[5] See E. Bernstein, *Evolutionary Socialism* (New York: Schocken, 1961).
[6] See K. Kautsky, *The Road to Power* (Atlantic Highlands: Humanities Press, 1996); cf. E. Matthias, 'Kautsky und der Kautskyanismus', *Marxismusstudien*, II: 151–97 (1957).

party dropped any pretence that it was 'Marxist' in Bad Godesberg in 1959.

Parallel debates consumed most of the other European socialist parties in the same period, with more or less the same outcome as in Germany. It was the First World War that forced the issue. Quite famously, the day before the war broke out, all the socialist parties in the Second International pledged to oppose a war that was not the concern of the workers. And a day or two after, the very same parties voted almost unanimously in their respective parliaments to support their country's side in the war.[7]

It was clear at this point that the 'Marxist' parties in Europe were nationalist, not internationalist, parties. What they meant by Marxism was not to achieve a communist world, or at least this was in no sense their priority. They sought primarily to improve the political, economic, and social position within their countries of the 'workers'. In practice, they essentially meant by 'workers' male workers who were employed in industry, commerce, and the civil service, and who were primarily of the dominant ethnic group within the country. Marxism in this sense was strongly 'reformist' – seeking the material improvement of the party's clientele. The label 'Marxist' signified primarily therefore an emphasis on 'economism' and 'statism' – a position they were able easily to base on Engels's version of Marxism.

There were two major exceptions in Europe to this revisionist scenario – Great Britain and Russia. The British Labour Party never adopted the Marxist label at all. In a sense, their integration into the parliamentary processes was so early that the Labour Party's equivalent of the Bernstein position, Fabianism, dominated its outlook from the outset.

Russia represented the other extreme in Europe. Russia's industrial working class was relatively so small and its parliamentary system so undeveloped that the logic of the Bernstein position seemed quite implausible. Already in 1902, the majority position within the party – the Bolsheviks – rejected such 'reformism' and insisted on the creation of an avant-garde disciplined party that would seize power – that is, be 'revolutionary' and not 'reformist'.

22.3 Soviet Marxism

Until 1917, this revolutionary position of the Bolsheviks seemed just as implausible as a strategy to obtain power as the would-be revisionist

---

[7] W. Abendroth, *A Short History of the European Working Class* (New York and London: Monthly Review Press, 1972).

position of the Mensheviks. Suddenly, however, something largely unanticipated and undiscussed in the Russian theoretical debates before 1914 intervened – the First World War. Russia fared poorly in that war, and the regime was faced with popular calls for peace, bread, and land.[8] The Tsarist regime collapsed. It was followed for nine months by the Alexander Kerensky (1881–1970) provisional government, which opted to continue the war.

The Kerensky regime was never able to establish firm authority in the country. As Vladimir Lenin (1870–1924) famously said, by October, power was lying in the streets and the Bolsheviks simply picked it up. They would remain in power from this point until 1991. The seizure of state power by the Bolsheviks led to important rethinking about what one meant by Marxism. One might even talk of a redefinition of Marxism.

There were four important moments in this early period of Bolshevik power (1917–25). Initially, the Bolsheviks felt that somehow the first such revolution should not have occurred in Russia. They were still adhering to the analysis of the Engels version that the first socialist revolution should occur in the economically most advanced country. This had come to be interpreted as meaning Germany rather than Great Britain, largely because of the political strength of the SPD. At first, therefore, the Bolsheviks in power were waiting for the German revolution to occur. This turned out to be waiting for Godot.

The second was the political decision to found the Third International (or Comintern) in 1919.[9] It was to be composed only of 'revolutionary parties' ready to commit themselves to the defined objective of insurrections leading to the ascension of an international soviet republic as the transition to a self-abolishing state. The immediate result was the split of most of the world's Marxist parties into those parties or segments of parties ready to commit themselves in this way and those which declined to do so.

When, however, it turned out that there were no insurrections in other European countries, or the putative insurrections failed, the Bolshevik Party turned eastwards geographically, and convened in Baku in 1920 the Congress of the Peoples of the East. They invited to this meeting not only communist parties, but various national-revolutionary movements from Asia that were not explicitly or necessarily Marxist. The central theme of this meeting was not the national class struggle, but anti-imperialism in

---

[8] E. H. Carr, *The Bolshevik Revolution 1917–1923*, vol. 1 (New York: W. W. Norton & Company Inc., 1985).
[9] On the way in which the Comintern was increasingly reduced to the policy of Moscow, see H. Gruber, *Soviet Russia Masters the Comintern: International Communism in the Era of Stalin's Ascendancy* (Garden City: Anchor Press, 1974).

colonial and 'semicolonial' countries. This marked in fact a striking difference from the emphasis just the year before on worker-led insurrections in advanced industrial countries.

This third moment was confirmed by a fourth in 1925. The Bolsheviks, now called the Communist Party of the Soviet Union (CPSU), proclaimed the doctrine of 'socialism in one country'. All talk of an 'international Soviet republic' had disappeared, and in practice talk of worker-led insurrections in Europe slipped into the background.

We then had a new version of Marxism. It was centred on the protection of the Soviet Union as a 'socialist' state, indeed, at this point the only socialist state in the world. The Soviet Union was defined as a 'dictatorship of the proletariat' and it was governed by a centralized, hierarchical, and disciplined party. This party not only governed the Soviet Union, but in effect governed the policies and practices of all parties affiliated to the Comintern, whose headquarters were located in Moscow.

Between 1919 and 1945, there were now at least two competing versions of Marxism – that espoused by the Second International and that espoused by the Comintern. The language both groups used to describe their difference was that between 'reformist' and 'revolutionary' paths to socialism. However, the reality was rather different. Increasingly, the difference really turned around the acceptance by the Second International parties of centrist liberal norms concerning national politics and the acceptance by parties affiliated to the Comintern of unquestioning loyalty to the one-party system in the Soviet Union.

The Marxisms of both internationals did have something important in common, nonetheless. They were both basically committed to national economic development. The radically opposing political consequences each drew from this common objective derived from the different possibilities for such development between those in core zones of the world economy and those in peripheral and semiperipheral zones. In the core zones, the conclusion of the social-democratic parties was the need for a welfare state. In the non-core zones, the conclusion of the communist parties was the need for a strong state push for an accelerated capital investment programme and an important dose of protectionism.

The focus on national development led to a further concern. Who constituted the nation? There had been an early discussion of this question by Marx, for example in his reflections on Irish nationalism and in his famous letter to Vera Zasulich (1849–1919).[10] But there

---

[10] K. Marx to V. Zasulich, 8 March 1881. There were three previous drafts of this letter, which may be found in MECW, vol. 24, pp. 346–69. There were important changes

were quite different emphases in his writings about India. Marx's views were not totally consistent, or, to be fairer, were not completely thought through. As time went on, however, and as the socialist/Marxist parties became stronger, the issue became ever more pressing.

Most European states were strongly Jacobin in their national cultures. They wished to create a single nation and integrate and/or assimilate 'minority' groups of different language, ethnicity, or even religion. The Marxist/socialist parties on the whole tended to accept this political/cultural premise, and saw all assertions of collective 'minority' rights (even 'cultural' rights) as divisive of the working class and of the priority of the class struggle of the proletariat against the bourgeoisie. The two European states where it was most difficult to sustain this kind of Jacobin position were Austria-Hungary and Russia. They were both 'empires' that were patently 'multi-national'.

In Austria-Hungary, the so-called Austro-Marxists began to discuss this problem openly and sought ways to reconcile the class struggle and collective cultural rights by vesting the latter in individual non-geographical choice. Their discussion was intense and important.[11] However, Austria-Hungary was dismantled after its defeat in the First World War. And once the empire was no more, the movements in all the successor states began to pursue the Jacobin model. In Russia, the most important theoretical attempt to deal with this issue was that of Stalin in his paper written shortly before the revolution.[12] The Stalin solution was to permit the creation of a complex network of national and sub-national structures within the Soviet Union, while relying on the CPSU to impose a de facto Jacobin solution via its unquestioned centralized authority.

Despite the fact that neither the Austro-Marxist nor the Stalinist 'solutions' resolved in any serious way what began to be called the 'national question', the genie had escaped the box in which it had been held throughout the nineteenth century. The debate on this issue within the multiple Marxisms continued to go on, ever more passionately, and remains unabated up to now.

---

between the drafts, which show how difficult Marx found the correct formulation to be. The actual letter is the briefest.

[11] The literature by and about the Austro-Marxists is voluminous. There is an excellent summary by T. Bottomore, *A Dictionary of Marxist Thought*, second edition (Oxford: Blackwell, 1991), pp. 39–42.

[12] J. V. Stalin, *Marxism and the National Question* (New York: International Publishers, 1942).

22.4 US Hegemony and the Cold War

The end of the Second World War changed the world geopolitical situation and had a great impact on definitions of Marxism. The most important consequence of the war's outcome was the assumption of unquestioned hegemony in the world system by the United States. At the same time, the end of the war left the USSR's Red Army in occupation of half of Europe along what came to be called the Oder-Neisse line. There ensued the so-called Cold War between the United States and the Soviet Union.

The metaphorical Yalta arrangement between the United States and the Soviet Union provided for three things. The first was a de facto division of spheres of influence – one-third of the world for the Soviet Union, the other two-thirds for the United States. There was an underlying *sotto voce* understanding that neither side was to try to change the boundaries of this division, an agreement that basically was observed (despite multiple 'crises') until the dissolution of the USSR in 1991.

The second provision was for strict economic separation between the two camps, a provision that lasted until the 1970s. And the third provision was unremitting (but essentially meaningless) mutual ideological denunciation. The function of this ideological clamour was not to transform the other, but to maintain the unremitting loyalty to the leaders of each camp of their allies/satellites.

The impact of this new geopolitical situation on the definition of Marxism cannot be underestimated. The first sign was the dissolution of the Comintern in 1943, which signalled the final abandonment by the world's communist parties of any pretence of engaging in revolutionary insurrection in the core zones as a political strategy.[13] This meant that the essential distinction between the political strategy of the Second and Third Internationals had been dissolved, something that permitted the SPD and other social-democratic parties to abandon the label 'Marxist' altogether. This meant in addition that the communist parties in the core zones were pushed in the direction of assuming the historic role of 'revisionist Marxism' – in a version that would later be called Eurocommunism. They suffered, however, as a consequence the serious reduction of their electoral strength in European countries.

The communist parties in the East-Central European satellite states had not come to power in either the classic parliamentary or the classic insurrectionary fashion. They were essentially installed in power by the

---

[13] The changing dynamics of the international communist movement from the beginning of the soviet era to the cold war are discussed at length in F. Claudin, *Communist Movement: From Comintern to Cominform* (New York and London: Monthly Review Press, 1975).

strength of the soviet military. To explain their curious status, they invented a new stage of theoretical evolution – 'popular democracy' – to define the nature of their regimes. The formulations of Marxist doctrine became ever more contorted. Like the West European parties, they also moved in a 'revisionist' direction, beginning to talk of 'market socialism', as did theorists within the Soviet Union itself.

The political process of 'de-Stalinization' inaugurated by Nikita Khrushchev (1894–1971) in 1956 at the 20th Party Congress of the CPSU exploded the legitimacy of the previous theoretical constructions without replacing them with a coherent alternative. The result was the worldwide reopening of the question, what is Marxism? This occurred in two forms. One was the discussion, never since ended, of the relation of 'socialism' and the market. The other was the much more arcane discussion about the 'Asiatic mode of production'.

The Asiatic mode of production had always been one of the most curious and obscure concepts in the Marxist armoury. Stalin did not like its political implications and banned its discussion – the most overt rewriting of Marx's writings that he undertook.[14] After 1956, it became possible to reopen the discussion, which began to happen in the Soviet Union, in the East-Central European states, and in Western communist parties.

Giving credence in whatever form to the concept of the Asiatic mode of production had two theoretical consequences. It raised into question the automaticity of the sequence of modes of production that presumably led from primitive communism to the communist world of the future. It thereby made possible discussing the validity of the Enlightenment concept of inevitable, uni-linear 'progress'. In the long run, this might be the most important consequence.

The second consequence was more immediate, and provided a link to the discussion of the 'national question'. If some countries (or societies or social formations), but not all, passed through an Asiatic mode of production (or something equivalent), this meant that there was no longer a single path along which all countries passed. This implied that 'Marxist' social analyses of particular parts of the world had to be based

---

[14] While it is clear that Stalin was opposed to the concept, the question of when and how it was 'banned' is a complicated one. According to Anatoly Khazanov (1937–), writing in 1992, he was told by S. L. Utchenko (1908–1976), who had been at the time editor-in-chief of *Herald of Ancient History*, that 'there was no official ban', but that 'it had not been and never would be mentioned in his journal because this subject had never received official blessing' (A. Khazanov, 'Soviet Social Thought in the Period of Stagnation', *Philosophy of the Social Sciences*, XXII (2): 232 [1992]); in chapter 3 of his book, *State and Society in Soviet Thought* (Oxford: Basil Blackwell, 1988), E. Gellner (1925–95) traced the complex history in soviet thought of what he called the 'Asiatic trauma' (p. 232).

on the historical particularities of that part of the world. Classical Marxism was essentially nomothetic. This discussion led one in the direction of an idiographic epistemology.

At the same time that this was going on, another geopolitical reality affected the debate on what the term Marxism represented. The Yalta arrangements were not at all to the taste of the national liberation movements in what was then being called the Third World. Some of these movements called themselves Marxist and some did not. Even those that did not however seemed to have a 'Marxisant' component in several senses. They took from Marxism (or at least credited to Marxism) three things: anti-imperialism, as defined by Lenin, and directed both against United States hegemony in the world system and their immediate colonial rulers (if they had them); national developmentalism, as found in the 'orthodox' Marxisms of both the SPD and the CPSU varieties; and a Leninist conception of the role of the avant-garde party and its relations with other social movements.

The theoretical consequences of this Marxisant quality of the movements took two forms – one in the 'semicolonial' countries and one in those that were still, after 1945, colonial territories. The Chinese Communist Party (CCP) is the best, and most important, example of the situation in 'semicolonial' countries. The CCP kept the label Marxist, but broke from the link to soviet central decision-making for the world's communist parties. They explicitly elaborated a new version of Marxism, which was officially labelled Marxism-Leninism-Mao Zedong thought.

Mao's writings espoused a new version of the class struggle, with considerably more emphasis on rural zones. In practice, however, the internal class struggle was less important in the ideology than national developmentalism ('the great leap forward'). It is only with the Cultural Revolution that Mao returned to emphasis on an internal class struggle. However, this internal class struggle seemed less linked to location in the forces of production than to political objectives ('capitalist roaders' vs 'socialist roaders') within the ranks of the CCP, indeed, within the top leadership. In any case, after the death of Mao, 'Mao Zedong thought' evolved rapidly and radically into 'market socialism', eliminating thereby the specificity of Mao Zedong thought.

What happened in the national liberation movements of the 'colonial' countries involved a further redefinition of Marxism. The policies of the Soviet Union accorded a political devolution of decision-making about colonial territories to the parties of the colonial power. These parties tended to view the concept of independence for the colonies as somehow violating the spirit of the class struggle. And this led to a rebellion of the Marxist or Marxisant cadres in the colonial territories, most notably in the cases of France and Portugal.

In the case of France, Aimé Césaire (1913–2008), Martinican poet and political leader, wrote his *Letter to Maurice Thorez* (1956), resigning from the French Communist Party.[15] He specifically cited his dismay with the Khrushchev revelations, but then proceeded to display his grievances about the positions the French Communist Party had taken on colonial issues, notably in the case of Algeria. He said that he could not accept the idea that the political and cultural rights of the colonized peoples took second place theoretically to metropolitan France's internal class struggle. Césaire's position became widely emulated by other Marxist and Marxisant cadres in the colonies.

The situation in Portugal was basically similar. The parallel group of Marxist and Marxisant intellectuals resigned at approximately the same time from the Portuguese Communist Party and threw in their lot uniquely with the movements of national liberation in the various colonies. In the British colonies, the role of the British Communist Party had always been so small that there were fewer affiliated intellectuals from the colonies. But the basic itinerary of Kwame Nkrumah (1909–72) and the Convention People's Party in the Gold Coast/Ghana reflected the same break with British movements. Finally, in South Africa, the long-existing South African Communist Party did not break officially with the CPSU. But it did enter into a formal alliance with the African National Congress, according it the prime role in the national liberation struggle for a 'non-racial' South Africa with universal suffrage.

In effect, in the period following 1945, and especially following 1956, the national liberation movements in the Third World all insisted on the priority of national liberation over any putative internal class struggle. To the extent that they remained Marxist, or at least Marxisant, they insisted that this was the meaning of Marxism. One way to describe this might be to say that these parties were Leninist without being Marxist in the classical Engels version.

22.5   The World Revolution of 1968

If these developments were not confusing enough in terms of the meaning of Marxism, the world revolution of 1968 added considerable fuel to the fire.[16] This world revolution actually went on from 1966 to 1970. It was a world revolution in that it occurred in all three political zones of the world system: the pan-European 'North', the 'socialist' countries, and the 'Third World'.

---

[15] A. Césaire, *Lettre à Maurice Thorez* (Paris: Présence Africaine, 1956).
[16] D. Singer, *Prelude to Revolution: France in May 1968* (London: Cape, 1970).

While the national political situations varied, and therefore the expression of this world revolution took on a somewhat different face in different countries, there emerged two underlying themes that seemed to resonate everywhere. The first was the universal condemnation of US imperialism/hegemony and the 'collusion' of the USSR with it. The most striking assertion of this theme was that expressed during the Chinese Cultural Revolution. The argument was that there were two 'superpowers' against whom stood all the other countries and their movements in the world.

If this were not provocative enough, the second theme that seemed to occur everywhere was the condemnation of the Old Left (by which was meant the trio of communist parties, social-democratic parties or their equivalents, and national liberation movements). What the activists in the 1968 uprisings asserted about the Old Left was that they had indeed come to state power in one form or another almost everywhere but that they had not 'changed the world', as they had promised. Instead they had become themselves not the solution to the world's ills, but part of the problem.

Both themes had a profound impact on what was meant by Marxism. There were two different results. One was the immediate flourishing of a series of 'Maoist' parties, which seemed to reassert the pre-1917 Bolshevik call for revolutionary insurrections. There were two problems with this. In the first place, outside of China itself, not only did none of these parties achieve much strength, but also in most countries there were multiple competing 'Maoist' movements. But the second problem was greater. With the death of Mao Zedong, the Chinese Cultural Revolution itself came to an end, and the Chinese no longer proclaimed this doctrine. The various Maoist parties in the rest of the world tended thereupon to wither on the vine.

There was a second, different impact on the definition of Marxism. It came to be rejected by a variety of different New Left movements and parties because, it was argued, it espoused the themes of the Engels version – economism and statism. There were different versions of this rejection. One was to 'add' other concerns to the classic ones of Marxism – for example, feminism, ecology, and the legitimacy of multiple sexualities. A second version – that of post-modernism – was more radical. It was to insist that both economism and statism reflected 'metanarratives' and that all metanarratives had to be rejected in the name of multiple different readings of reality.

Both varieties of reaction – that of the New Left movements and that of the post-modernists – found organizational expression in movements of the 'forgotten peoples' – those of women, those of 'minority' peoples, and those of 'minority' sexualities. Their complaint about classical Marxism in all its varieties (and about national liberation movements as well) is that the Old Left as a whole had imposed on these 'forgotten peoples' a secondary status. The Old Left had in effect told them that the satisfaction of their concerns had to await the outcome of the 'primary' struggle – either the class struggle or the national struggle.

The movements of these oppressed people insisted that their struggles were just as urgent as the class and national struggles, and it was illegitimate to try to push them into the background. As these movements became stronger, their arguments had great impact both on the remaining Marxist parties and on the post-modernist movements. These arguments began to have internal debates of the following variety: are the interests of all women the same, or is there a difference/conflict between the interests of white women and women of colour? There were parallel kinds of debates within all the movements. The result after a decade or so of these debates was to create a trinity called 'race-gender-class' that was supposed to govern intellectual and political analysis. The inclusion of class was a way of reintroducing some version of Marxism into the analytic and political concerns of these groups, and to create distance between the proponents of this trinity from those post-modernists who were not willing to accept its legitimacy.

At the same time, the pressures of these movements, and their emerging trinity of concerns, affected the Marxism of those political movements that continued to use the label Marxist to describe themselves. They began to define Marxism as having a concern (even an equal concern) with the whole trinity of race-gender-class, and not with class alone.

22.6 Collapse of the Communisms

Then came the collapse of the communisms – the dissolution of the links between the erstwhile communist regimes of East-Central Europe and the CPSU, followed by the disintegration of the USSR and the dissolution of the CPSU in 1991. The idea that a 'socialist' regime, once established, could be reversed and overthrown made hash of the once firm assumption of historic irreversibility, ensconced in the Marxism of the CPSU and those parties that followed its lead.

The initial dismay of Marxist parties and Marxisant intellectuals led to severe doubts about Marxism as a mode of analysis. Persons and parties that still called themselves Marxist began to adopt openly neo-liberal arguments, or at best post-Marxist social-democratic positions. But once again reality caught up. The magic of the market began to pale as a politico-economic mode of national development by the mid-1990s. The neo-Zapatista movement launched its dramatic action in Chiapas in 1994, and created a worldwide discussion about how Marxism related to the 500-year-long struggle of Mayan peoples/peasants in one of the poorest parts of a country located in the South.

From that point forward, there emerged on the world stage what is now being called a global justice movement, which took concrete form in the creation of the World Social Forum (WSF). The WSF became a meeting ground of multiple kinds of movements, including movements of the 'forgotten peoples' and Marxist parties of multiple descriptions.

At this point, Marx and Marxism began to be rediscovered, especially by the younger persons who began to be active in the different movements – movements devoted to 'global justice' but not calling themselves Marxist. It was a paradoxical situation where the few still officially Marxist parties scarcely mentioned Marxism any more while the social movements that did not call themselves Marxist seemed willing to read, discuss, and debate Marx's views and their relevance to their struggles.

In the first decade of the twenty-first century, left or left-of-centre parties came to power in a series of Latin American countries. Hugo Chávez in Venezuela launched what he called a struggle for a twenty-first-century version of socialism and sought to constitute a Fifth International. How this related to Marxism is still an open question after his death.

When the world economy was more or less officially defined as being in a 'financial crisis' in 2008–9, Marxist ideas suddenly became again a major focus of discussion, even in mainstream circles.[17] Marxism, which had been proclaimed dead so many times, seemed once more to be alive – both analytically and politically.

The question now is, what is this Marxism that is once more alive? There seem to be several unclear aspects to the present debate. Marx sought to explain in his writings how capitalism as a historical system functioned and why, in his view, its internal contradictions meant that it would inevitably come to an end. In the era of the Engels version, it was always assumed that the end of capitalism meant inevitably the coming of something better and more socially rational.

Today, there are some Marxists who still believe this, but many Marxists have resuscitated and reinvigorated the ancient formula of 'socialism or barbarism'. This formula is quite different from the Engels version because of the little word 'or'. Using the 'or' suggests that 'progress' is not inevitable, but only possible. And, if it is only possible, then what strategy, and with which actors, will it become more possible rather than less possible?

---

[17] Cf. E. Hobsbawm, *How to Change the World: Tales of Marx and Marxism* (New Haven, CT and London: Yale University Press, 2011), pp. 5–15.

Neoclassical economists always preached an economics of growth, made possible by ever more efficient technology. The Marxism of the parties (the SPD and the CPSU) embraced this same economics of growth. Many of those parties that still call themselves Marxist still embrace the economics of growth. However, the world environmental crisis has led to placing growth as an objective into question, including among Marxists. The 'indigenist' movements in Latin America and elsewhere have put forwards an alternative economics – that of *buen vivir*, which means a rational calculation of egalitarian allocation of resources that are not only limited, but that should be limited, in order to preserve the planet for the well-being of future generations. These groups are exploring those aspects of Marx's writings that seem to encourage this objective.

The relationship of the trinity of race, gender, and class is a central issue in the redefinition of Marxism. The implicit world Jacobinism of the Marxisms of a century ago seems to have faded among all but a tiny handful of persons. But this does not solve the issue; it only permits its debate. How to reconcile the universal and the particular in the socialist societies of the future is not at all self-evident. Nonetheless, it has enormous impact on the political strategies of today.

The writings of Marx continue to provide an enormously rich treasure of analytic and political insight. But Marx died in 1883. The world has begun to pose additional questions to those with which Marx himself wrestled and we must add to his theories subsequent writings of others, written in the same analytic, moral, and political spirit. The Marxism of tomorrow will be the product of further analysis and further praxis, but one of its basic requirements will be to read Marx intelligently, carefully, and critically. His *oeuvre* still provides the most ample source of historical social science, a resource we cannot afford to ignore or distort.

References

Abendroth, Wolfgang (1972), *A Short History of the European Working Class*, New York and London: Monthly Review Press.
Althusser, Louis (1976), *For Marx*, Harmondsworth: Penguin.
Bernstein, Eduard (1961), *Evolutionary Socialism*, New York: Schocken.
Bottomore, Tom (1991), A Dictionary of Marxist Thought, second edition, Oxford: Blackwell.
Carr, Edward Hallett (1985), *The Bolshevik Revolution 1917–1923*, vol. 1, New York: W. W. Norton & Company Inc.
Césaire, Aimé (1956), *Lettre à Maurice Thorez*. Paris: Présence Africaine.
Claudin, Fernando (1975), *Communist Movement: From Comintern to Cominform*, New York and London: Monthly Review Press.

Fetscher, Iring (1971), *Marx and Marxism*, New York: Herder and Herder.
Gellner, Erenst (1988), State and Society in Soviet Thought, Oxford: Basil Blackwell.
Gramsci, Antonio (1971), *Selections from the Prison Notebooks*, London: Lawrence & Wishart.
Gruber, Helmut (1974), *Soviet Russia Masters the Comintern: International Communism in the Era of Stalin's Ascendancy*, Garden City: Anchor Press.
Hobsbawm, Eric (2011), *How to Change the World: Tales of Marx and Marxism*, New Heaven, CT and London: Yale University Press.
Kautsky, Karl (1996), *The Road to Power*, Atlantic Highlands: Humanities Press.
Khazanov, Anatoly (1992), 'Soviet Social Thought in the Period of Stagnation', *Philosophy of the Social Sciences*, XXII (2): 231–7.
Marx, Karl (1989), *Critique of the Gotha Programme*, MECW, vol. 24, pp. 75–99.
  (1989), 'Drafts of the Letter to Vera Zasulich', MECW, vol. 24, pp. 346–69.
  (1989), 'Letter to Vera Zasulich', MECW, vol. 24, pp. 370–1.
Marx, Karl, and Engels, Frederick (1976), *Manifesto of the Communist Party*, MECW, vol. 6, pp. 477–519.
Matthias, Erich (1957), 'Kautsky und der Kautskyanismus', *Marxismusstudien*, II: 151–97.
Singer, Daniel (1970), *Prelude to Revolution: France in May 1968*, London: Cape.
Stalin, Joseph V. (1942), *Marxism and the National Question*, New York: International Publishers.

Index

accumulation
   capital, 2, 8, 11–16, 21, 57, 65, 67, 75, 83, 96, 97, 174, 183–4, 193, 225–6, 237, 267, 274, 275, 281, 298, 355
   capitalist, 18–19, 202, 258, 292–3, 314
   of misery, 19
   over-, 15
   primitive, 2, 17, 234, 247–50, 258–60, 263, 277, 291
   rate of, 13, 15, 21, 97
   social, 239
   theory of, 19
Adams, Charles Francis, 219
Adorno, Theodor W., 180
   Dialectic of Enlightenment (1944) (with Horkheimer), 180
adventurism, 111
African National Congress, 387
agriculture, 12, 17–20, 40, 187–8, 191, 233, 235, 253
alienation, 42, 47, 54, 143, 184–5, 199, 273, 285, 325, 334, 351–9
Allen, Theodore W., 258–9
Allen, Vic, 79
Althusser, Louis, 95
American bourgeoisie, 241
American Civil War, 79, 115, 183, 213, 215–16, 218–24, 238, 259
   as second American revolution, 218
American hegemony, 384–7
American War of Independence, 214, 218, 310
anarchism, 32
Ancient Greece, 52–6, 208–9, 355–6, 358
Ancient Roman Empire, 72, 75, 132, 221, 333
Anderson, Kevin B., 256
Anderson, Perry, 181
   In the Tracks of Historical Materialism (1983), 181
Annenkov, Pavel, 302, 363
anomie, 334

Arab-Islamic world, 244
Aristotle, 53, 357–8
art, 40, 351–61
   and alienation, 351–4
   and critique political economy, 355–9
   as a social function, 356
   as unproductive labour, 358
   Marx's analysis of, 360–1
   theory of, 353
Asiatic, 251, 252–4, 385–6
atheism, 321, 325, 331, 332
attack on Harper's Ferry, Virginia, 220
Australia, 237, 249, 261, 296
Austria, 213, 310–11
Austria-Hungary, 383
automation, 12, 19, 371

Babbage, Charles, 365
Babeuf, François-Noël, 27, 129
Bakunin, Mikhail, 99, 118, 226–7, 344
Bakuninism, 226, 333
Banaji, Jairus, 87
banking, 4–5, 18, 72
   national bank, 36
barbarism, 390
Bauer, Bruno, 322, 326, 332, 351
Bebel, August, 94, 122, 135
Becker, Gary, 157
Beckmann, Johann, 364–5, 373
   Concise History of Ancient Institutions, Inventions, and Discoveries in Science and Mechanic Art (1823), 364
Benner, Erica, 215
Bensen, Heinrich Wilhelm, 73
Benton, Ted, 181
Berlin Wall, xvii, xviii, 137
Bernstein, Eduard, 134, 379–80
Bertrand, Michèle, 324
Bhandari, Rakesh, 87
Bismarck, Otto von, 121, 134, 269
Blackburn, Robin, 72, 218

393

Blanc, Louis, 1
  The Organization of Work (1850), 1
Blanqui, Jérôme-Adolphe, 92
Blanqui, Louis August, 117
Bolshevik Party, 321, 380–2, 388
Bolte, Friedrich, 99
Bonaparte, Louis, 62, 76, 269, 276–7
Bonaparte, Napoleon, 269, 277
Bonapartism, 61–3, 120, 215, 274, 276–7
Bonapartist dictatorship, 61, 277
Bourdieu, Pierre, 157
bourgeoisie, 3–4, 19, 25, 31, 37, 38, 39, 40, 42, 43, 46–7, 51–3, 58–62, 66, 68, 70, 72, 74, 76, 83, 92, 94, 99–100, 110–11, 112–15, 119, 126, 130–1, 132, 135, 163, 174, 185–6, 199–200, 205, 218, 227, 236, 241–3, 248–9, 255–6, 260–2, 268, 270–3, 274–7, 278–9, 285, 286–91, 296, 297, 306, 307, 309, 310–11, 315–16, 329, 333, 340–1, 343, 347, 357–9, 363, 368, 383
  distribution of, 174
  domination of, 276
  family, 199–200
  freedom of, 58, 60
  freedom of conscience, 333
  ideology of, 37, 333
  liberal, 113, 126, 262, 276
  production, 3–4, 42, 163, 297
  progressive, 110
  property, 36
  republic, 59, 61, 62
  revolution. See revolution, bourgeois
  social power, 275
  state, 270
Bowles, Samuel, 348
  Schooling in Capitalist America (1976), 348
Bracke, Wilhelm, 135
Bright, John, 223
Britain, 18, 70–1, 74, 85, 86, 96, 99, 102–4, 115, 118, 132, 183, 187, 209, 213, 215, 219, 220, 222–7, 229, 232, 234, 236–7, 239, 241–3, 247–8, 251–3, 263, 288, 292, 293, 310–12, 314, 317, 343, 345, 380, 387
British bourgeoisie, 236
British Communist Party, 387
British cotton crisis, 183, 223
British Labour Party, 380
British Museum, 115
Brosses, Charles de, 321–2
  On the Worship of Fetish Gods (1760), 321

Brown, John, 220
Brussels Democratic Association, 111
Brussels Workers' Society, 113
Burkett, Paul, 179, 182
  Marx and Nature (1999), 182
  Marxism and Ecological Economics (2006), 182

Cabet, Étienne, 27, 29
  The Voyage to Icaria (1840), 27
Caesarism, 269
capital, xviii, 1, 2, 5, 6–8, 9–14, 16–19, 21–2, 37, 39, 40, 41–2, 45, 56, 62, 64–7, 75, 81–3, 84, 87, 93, 96–7, 99, 100–1, 105, 144, 150–1, 154, 157–8, 161, 168, 169, 170, 172–3, 174–5, 183–4, 185–6, 193, 210, 225–6, 228, 234, 235–6, 237–9, 240, 248, 259, 260, 267, 272–3, 274–5, 277, 279, 280, 281–2, 287, 289, 290, 291–3, 297–8, 306, 314–15, 329, 343, 345, 363, 367, 368, 370, 374, 382
  as a social relation, 10, 13
  circuit, 9–10, 14
  concentration of, 19, 98, 221, 248
  constant, 57, 65, 82, 183, 297–8
  double character of, 169
  fetish, 16
  industrial, 12
  labour and, xviii, 59, 87, 100, 101, 154, 259
  metropolis of, 132, 242
  relations of, 219
  rotation time, 151
  rule of, 7
  variable, 81–3, 88, 297
capitalism, xvii–xxi, 30, 32, 33, 34, 36, 37–44, 47, 51–3, 55–7, 61–8, 70, 74–5, 79, 81, 82–8, 94, 95–100, 101–3, 105–6, 116, 120–1, 123, 132, 133, 135, 137, 138, 143, 145, 147–8, 149–51, 152–5, 157–75, 182–8, 189–90, 197–8, 200–10, 213, 218, 220, 227, 228–9, 232–7, 238–40, 244–5, 247–52, 255–7, 258–61, 262–3, 266–7, 269, 270–1, 272–3, 275, 276–81, 285–6, 287, 288, 289–99, 302–4, 306–11, 313–17, 325, 329–30, 334, 339–41, 343, 345–7, 348–9, 351, 354, 355–6, 357–8, 359–61, 363–4, 366–9, 370–5, 377, 386, 390
  as a system of social relations, 63, 65–6
  dictatorship of, 62
  disaster of, 193

Index

double character of, 164, 169
economy, 4, 10, 17, 66, 183
exploitation, 198, 202
features of modern, 6–8
general laws of, 6
global, 286, 290–3, 298–9, 334
globalization of, 296, 349
hegemony of, 1
history of, 1–3, 17, 87, 240, 244, 255, 260, 263, 317
ideal total, 279
industrial, 12–13, 15, 18, 56, 105, 240
Marx's usage of, 2
mode of production. See mode of production, capitalist
modern, 5–11, 14, 16–18, 63, 138, 161, 164, 170, 171, 174
precapitalism, 251
production, 2, 3, 7, 11, 18, 20, 75, 97, 98, 103, 154, 169, 171, 183, 187, 250, 286, 289–90, 297, 354, 358, 373
progressive, 279
relations of production, 3, 8, 239, 346
state-centric, 158
state-interventionist, 160
state-monopoly, 286
structure of, 201
theory of, 3–6, 8, 13, 16–19, 61, 157, 171, 255, 303
universalization of, 307–9
carbon metabolism, 189, 191
Caribbean, 74, 82–3
Carlyle, Thomas, 232
Carson, Rachel, 179
Cassagnac, Adolphe Granier de, 73
Césaire, Aimé, 387
  Letter to Maurice Thorez (1956), 387
Chartism, 54–6, 99, 109–10, 127, 215, 217
Chauvinism, 243, 312
Chávez, Hugo, 390
Chicago Tribune, 334
China, 105, 137, 158, 235, 241, 245, 247–9, 250–2, 256–7, 260–2, 293, 313, 386–8
Chinese Communist Party, 386
Chinese Cultural Revolution, 386–8
Christianity, 254, 322–33, 351–2
  Anglicanism, 254
  Catholicism, 102, 224, 254, 330
  Protestantism, 102, 254, 329
Civil society, 58–9, 63–4, 70, 86, 271, 273–4, 313, 326–8, 332, 342, 379
class
  abolition of, 36
  antagonism, 94, 96, 104, 328

capitalist, 12, 13, 44, 145, 162, 258, 308
compromise, 275, 281
conflict, 273, 308, 312–13
content, 268–9
dictatorship, 277
middle, 74–5, 135, 218, 341, 346
of modern society, 4
organization, 25
power, 51–2
rule, 45, 117, 268
ruling, 22, 64, 86, 99, 116, 126, 128, 216, 255, 268, 280–1, 342
structure, 4, 59, 60, 353
theory of, 71
war, 102
class struggle, 5, 53, 59, 70, 72, 74, 92–106, 112, 118, 126–7, 135, 216, 260, 263, 268, 269–70, 274–6, 281, 308, 359, 381, 383, 386–7, 389
  theory of, 103–6
Cold War, 317, 377, 384–7
colonialism, xviii, 87, 132, 158, 224–6, 234–8, 239–41, 244, 247–64, 267, 277, 285, 291, 293, 298, 304, 305, 311, 312, 317, 356, 357, 381–2, 386–7
  anti-, 249–57, 261–2, 305
  as superexploitation, 241
  decolonization, 158, 255, 317
  neo-, 244
  oppression, 132, 240
  postcolonial studies, 247
  semi-, 251, 382, 386
  settler, 260
  theory of, 247, 250, 255, 263
combined development, 292–3
Comintern, 381–4
commodification, 67, 87–8, 151
  decommodification, 67, 68
commodity
  circulation, 9, 293
  fetishism, 16, 149, 275
  saleable, 358
Commune, 27, 29
communism, xix, 24–47, 60, 73, 85, 100, 102–3, 108, 109–12, 114, 116, 120–1, 123, 126–9, 132, 136, 151–2, 188, 214–16, 298, 307–8, 310, 314, 324, 331, 333, 338, 342, 354, 356, 359, 360, 366–8, 375, 377, 378, 380, 381, 382, 384–7, 388, 389–91
  as free association, 37–41
  as negation of the negation, 34
  collapse of, 338, 389–91
  definition of, xix

communism (cont.)
  dictatorship, 26
  economy of, 114
  machinery. See machinery, communist
  revolution. See revolution, communist
  theory of, 36
Communist Correspondence Committees, 109–10
Communist League, 85, 100, 103, 110, 111–14, 127, 130–1
Communist Party of Great Britain, 104
Communist Party of the Soviet Union, 123, 382, 383, 385–6, 387, 389–91
communitarianism, 136, 137
conscious association, 41
Constant, Benjamin, 321–2, 324, 331–2
  On Religion Considered in Its Source, Its Forms, and Its Developments (1824–31), 321, 324
constitutionalism, 51, 53–5, 110, 134, 165, 219, 270, 271–2, 273–6, 278–9, 281, 311–12, 331
  democratic, 53, 275–6, 281
  rights, 54
  theory of, 271, 331
consumption goods, 41, 179
Corbon, Claude Anthime, 344–5
cost-price, 295
Cox, Robert, 303
credit, 5, 9–10, 15, 17, 36, 278–9, 297, 329
  commercial, 278
  system, 9, 15, 19, 330
Crimean War, 302, 309–14
crisis, xvii, 14–15, 138, 171–3, 177–8, 180, 181, 183–4, 187, 193, 223, 244, 275, 276, 281, 285, 286, 296–8, 334, 374, 390
  climate change, 138, 177–8, 191–2
  cycle, 15
  dual crisis of capital, 171–3
  ecological, 138, 178, 180, 183–4, 189, 191, 193, 244, 374, 391
  economic, 276
  global, 296–8
  global economic crisis of 2008, xvii, 285, 297, 390
  industrial soil, 187
  of capital accumulation, 184
  of capitalism, xvii, 15, 171
  political, 276
  resource scarcity, 183
  world market, 15, 286, 296–9
Cromwell, Oliver, 226, 255

Darwin, Charles, 190
Daumer, Georg Friedrich, 329, 333
  The Religion of the New Age (1850), 329
  The Secrets of Christian Antiquity (1847), 333
debt, 55, 119, 238, 276–9
  bondage, 55
  national, 238, 277, 278
  public, 278
deforestation, 181, 191
Deleuze, Gilles, 228
democracy, xix, 24, 39, 51–68, 110–14, 116, 117, 118, 123, 126, 128, 130, 133, 136–7, 158, 212, 213–19, 270, 271–2, 273, 275–6, 281, 310, 343, 349, 385
  ancient Greek, 52, 54, 55
  Aristotle's definition of, 53
  bourgeois, 51–3, 58–62, 66, 68, 218, 272, 273, 276
  capitalism, 61, 62
  commodification, 67–8
  liberal, 51, 52–3, 55, 58, 63, 66, 68
  Marx's critique of, 51–3
  popular, 385
  representative, 54
  revolution. See revolution, democratic
  social, 52, 66, 123, 158, 382, 388, 389
  socialism, 60, 61
Denmark, 310
Descartes, René, 164
  Cartesianism, 163
determinism
  economic, 136, 197, 210
  structural, 307
  technological, 95
Dézamy, Théodore, 27
  Community Code (1842), 27
dialectic, 34, 93–4, 109, 126, 128, 137, 141, 144–5, 152–3, 166–71, 173, 178–80, 184–5, 198, 203, 205, 206–10, 213, 228, 229, 286–8, 293, 299, 308, 314, 316, 327, 328, 353, 354, 355
  of class, 213
  of class struggle, 126
  of intersectionality, 209–10
  of labour, 144
  of materialism, 184
  of natural limits, 185
  of nature, 178, 184
  of progress, 286–8
  of race, 213
  of religious permanence and change, 328
  of society, 184
  of temporal mediation, 166–71

of temporalities, 168, 170
of the Enlightenment, 179
of the precapitalist family, 206–9
of value, 173
of work, 152–3
dialectical movement, 93
disposable time, 44, 152, 368
Dmitrieff, Elisabeth, 117
Durkheim, Emile, 334

Eastern Question, 310
ecological crisis theory, 178, 181
ecology, xviii, 40, 65, 137–8, 171, 177–94, 388
  ecological value form theory, 178, 182, 190–1
  Marxist, 178, 184, 191, 193
  materialist, 185
  sustainability, 65, 193
economics, xviii, 3–6, 8–10, 13, 14–16, 17–19, 20, 21, 27, 30–1, 33–4, 43, 44, 55–9, 62–8, 72, 92–3, 97, 100, 162, 197, 210, 239, 248, 309, 357, 391
  bourgeois, 92, 100, 297, 357
  capitalist, 5, 21, 272
  classical, 4, 6, 8, 17, 239, 248
  ecological, 184, 189–90
  exploitation, 55
  geo-, 311
  laws of, 27
  Marxist, 197, 329
  modern, 14, 65
  natural economic order, 6
  neoclassical, 6, 391
  science of, 57, 63
economism, 380, 388–89
ecosocialism, 177–84, 189–93
ecosystem theory, 188
education, 26, 36, 44, 45–6, 199, 200, 334, 338–49, 352, 366
  collective satisfaction of needs, 45
  economic role of, 339
  factory school, 345, 349
  free education, 36
  mass schooling, 341
  political economy of, 339–41
  producing labour capacity, 339
  public, 37, 339–41, 342–4
  state school, 338, 348
  teachers, 150, 339, 342, 346–9
  teaching as a profession, 346–8
emancipation
  full, 45
  of women, xviii, 198–200

  political, 58, 118, 332
  self-, 70, 103, 128–9, 131–7
employment, 14–15, 29, 77–9, 84–7, 97, 155, 173, 191–2, 232, 239, 279, 363, 368
  self-, 77, 84–7
  un-, 14–15, 77–9, 155, 173, 192, 232, 239
  under-, 15, 173, 192
end of history, 137
Engels, Friedrich, 2–3, 4, 21, 24–5, 34–5, 36, 45, 59, 72, 73, 75, 81, 85–6, 94–5, 99–100, 104, 109–10, 120, 122, 127–31, 134, 135–6, 138, 142, 178–80, 181–2, 185, 189–90, 200, 212–14, 216–17, 220, 221–2, 224–5, 226, 229, 232, 249, 251, 255–8, 261, 266–7, 271, 272, 278, 279–81, 285, 286–7, 288, 290, 296, 298, 302, 303, 305, 320, 324–6, 327, 328, 330, 332–4, 338, 349, 377–80, 381, 387, 388, 390
  The Condition of the Working Class in England (1845), 72, 99, 224, 232
  The Dialectics of Nature (1883), 178, 190
  The Peasant War in Germany (1850), 324
engineering, 365
England, 17–18, 55, 56, 71, 74, 85, 102, 109–10, 126, 127, 130, 132, 190, 202, 206–7, 216, 222, 225–7, 229, 232–7, 239, 241–3, 248–53, 258–9, 271, 272, 277–9, 288, 292, 294, 297, 298, 330, 365, 368, 372
English bourgeoisie, 132, 227, 241–3
English Revolution, 126, 271
Enlightenment, 179, 180, 184, 286, 288, 289, 334, 385
Epicurus, 177, 184–5, 321
epistemology, 315, 364, 386
essential modification, 294
essentialism, 197, 322, 326
ethnocentrism, 197, 227, 228–9
Eurocentrism, xviii, 87, 228, 247–8, 287, 303
Eurocommunism-, 384
European communism, 158
evolution, 146–7, 190
exploitation, 11–16, 43, 55–6, 64, 79, 82–3, 88, 96, 98, 104–6, 159, 161–2, 169, 174, 179, 183, 185–6, 188, 198, 201, 202–3, 204–5, 234–6, 238–9, 241, 244, 268, 270–1, 273, 279, 285, 287–8, 292–5, 296, 298, 328, 351, 355, 357, 359, 373–4

exploitation (cont.)
  economic, 55, 268, 273, 279
  environmental, 40, 179, 183
  hyper-, 373
  labour, 11, 40, 59, 152, 202, 293, 298
  labour power, 12, 14
  mode of, 64, 79, 82–3, 157, 292
  rate of, 96
  slavery as, 55
  super-, 202, 234–6, 241, 244
expropriation, 148, 193, 218, 233, 236–41, 244, 249, 257, 258, 276, 277
extra-economic violence, 249

factory legislation, 279
Factory Acts, 202, 341
false consciousness, 221, 227, 228, 229
family, 27, 148, 192, 197–8, 199–210, 273, 340, 342
  as a social construction, 208
  monogamous, 208
  precapitalist, 206–9
  structure, 205
  transformation of, 200–6
  wage, 205
fascism, 280–2
Feenberg, Andrew, 366
feminism, 137, 197–8, 209–10, 377, 388
  anti-capitalist, 197
  Marxist, 197, 377
  socialism, 197
  theory, 210
Fenian movement, 224–5, 236, 256, 258
Ferguson, Adam, 70
Fernández-Espartero, Don Joaquín Baldomero, 131
fetishism, 15–16, 149, 275, 321, 322
feudalism, 25, 43, 56, 58, 64–5, 113, 130, 215, 249–51, 273, 277, 306
  semi-, 130, 251
Feuerbach, Ludwig, 34, 109, 128, 322, 323, 326–7, 352–3
First and Second Italian Wars of Independence, 310
First Vienna Workers' Association, 113
Fordism, 154, 158
foreign policy, 216–18, 222, 302–4, 306, 309–13, 315–17
Foucault, Michel, 104–5, 168, 228, 371
  notion of power, 168
  panopticon, 371
Founding Fathers, 54
Fourier, Charles, 25–6, 28–9, 35, 341, 357
  The New Industrial and Societal World (1829), 29

Theory of the Four Movements (1808), 28
France, 1, 2–3, 24, 26–7, 46, 62, 70–2, 73, 75–6, 78, 85, 92, 103, 109–10, 112–13, 115, 126–8, 133, 199, 204, 214–15, 217, 219, 222, 227, 243, 250, 257, 269–77, 280, 296, 298, 310, 332, 344, 364, 386–7
Frankel, Léo, 117
Frankfurt school, 179–80
free development, xix, 38, 43, 47, 193–4, 358–9
free time, 39, 41–4, 148, 152, 367–8
free trade, 263, 288, 292, 307
freedom, xviii, xix, 34, 37, 39, 45–7, 55, 57–8, 60–2, 64–5, 66–8, 71, 109, 110, 113, 123, 136, 151–2, 160–1, 202, 218, 220, 224–5, 269, 271, 273, 287, 307, 310, 331–5, 342
  democratic, 57, 61, 62, 65, 67, 68, 136
  from exploitation, 55
  individual, xviii, 46–7, 66, 333
  of association, 52
  of commerce, 287, 307
  of conscience, 333–5
  of religion, 332, 334–5
  of speech, 52
  of the economy, 68
  of the press, 51, 52, 58, 110
  of the state, 45, 60, 68
  political, 332
  to criticize religion, 331
  unfreedom, 71, 160–1, 333–5
freely associated producers, 151
French bourgeoisie, 199, 310
French Civil War, 274
French communism, 27
French materialism, 128
French Restoration, 92
French Revolution, 24, 27, 70, 76, 112, 126, 133, 225, 271, 272, 280, 310, 332
French Revolutionary Wars, 310
French socialism, 1, 46
Friedman, Milton, 348
Friedmann, Georges, 371
Frison, Guido, 364, 365
fundamentalism, 174, 334

Gallegos, Bill, 192
Gaskell, Peter, 365
gender, xviii, 104, 105, 191, 192, 197–210, 228, 389, 391
  equality, 197–210
  relations, 197–8, 209
  theory of, 198, 209, 210

Index

general abstractions, 304, 315–16
General Association of German Workers, 47
general intellect, 340
General Union of German Workers, 119–20
Geneva Congress of 1866, 116
Geneva education policy, 346
German bourgeoisie, 113, 310
German communism, 73
German Republic, 310
German Revolution, 72, 119, 126, 130, 310, 381
German Social Democracy, 85, 122
German Social Democratic Party, 134, 205, 343
German socialism, 25, 110, 118, 135
German Socialist Workers' Party, 343
German Wars of Liberation, 310
German Wars of Unification, 310
German Workers' Party, 60
German Workers' Educational Society, 111, 113, 225, 292, 333
German Workers' Society of Brussels, 111
Germany, 1, 3, 5, 27, 47, 60, 73, 85, 110, 112–14, 115, 118–20, 122–3, 126–8, 130–1, 132, 134–6, 214, 217, 244, 257, 271, 282, 298, 317, 329, 335, 342, 353, 379, 380, 381
Gigot, Philippe, 110
Gintis, Herbert, 348
  Schooling in Capitalist America (1976), 348
global
  anti-globalization, 228
  cultural globalization, 287
  globalism, 285–6, 290, 298
  globalization, 19, 20, 228–9, 263, 285–99, 349
  globalization theory, 289
  globaloney, 289, 299
  hyperglobalism, 299
  South, 79, 191–2
  village, 291
Glorious Revolution of 1688, 55
Gotha Programme, 122
Gould, Stephen Jay, 190
government, 26–7, 29, 31, 38, 45–6, 54, 67, 114, 116–17, 120, 130, 132, 133–4, 216, 222–5, 237, 242, 244–5, 252–3, 263, 269, 272, 278–9, 298, 331, 340, 342, 343–4, 381
  class representation in, 242
  democratic, 54
  force, 46

function, 45
  of the working class, 133
  oppression, 245
  organized violence, 237
  power, 342
  role of the, 343
  self-, 38, 117, 134
governmentality, 105
Gramsci, Antonio, 95, 103, 128, 136, 267, 280–1, 378
  Prison Notebooks (1929–35), 95, 280
Great Britain, 292, 349, 380–1
Great Exhibition, 287
green theory, 177, 181, 193
Grossman, Henryk, 98
Guesde, Jules, 243
Guizot, François, 92

Habib, Irfan, 254
Hague Congress 1872, 118
Hamilton, Alexander, 54
Hardt, Michael, 228–9, 290
Harney, Julian, 110
Hauck, Gerhard, 247
health, 43, 45, 191, 192
  collective satisfaction of needs, 45
  healthcare, 45
  public, 191–2
Hébert, Jacques, 332
Hegel, Georg Wilhelm Friedrich, 34, 93, 114, 127, 168–9, 178–9, 271, 326, 342, 344, 346
  Geist, 168
  notion of contradiction as constitutive, 93
  notion of history, 168
  Philosophy of Right (1820), 342
  The Phenomenology of Spirit (1807), 168
Hegelian dialectics, 34, 109
Hegelianism, 58, 255, 353, 364
  Left, 35, 127, 321–7, 334
  neo-, 127
  Old, 327
  Young, 128, 320, 322, 325, 326, 327, 331, 351, 352, 353
Heidegger, Martin, 373–4
Heine, Heinrich, 324
high farming, 187
Hill, Christopher, 104
Hilton, Rodney, 104
Hinduism, 254–5
historical subject, 168, 169
historical time, 167–8
Hobsbawm, Eric, 104, 232
Höchberg, Karl, 134
Horkheimer, Max, 180

Humanism, 34, 185, 285, 344, 346
Hume, David, 70
Hungary, 214
Icarian Constitution, 29
Illich, Ivan, 347–8
  Deschooling Society (1970), 347
  Disabling Professions (1977), 347
imperialism, 102, 187, 249, 287, 305, 312–13, 381, 386
India, 206–7, 235, 241, 247–8, 250–8, 259, 260–3, 288, 292–3, 313, 383
Indian Mutiny of 1857, 251, 261
indigenism, 137, 391
  movement, 391
indigenous peoples, 136, 192, 226, 235, 237, 250, 260
Indonesia, 235
industrial
  post-, 174
  reserve army, 15, 18, 97, 101, 185, 232, 237
Industrial Revolution, 24, 104, 237, 340, 365, 370
industrialization, 19, 20
inheritance, 37, 207
instrumentalism, 177
international relations, 302–17
International Working Men's Association, 31–2, 42, 99, 101, 103, 114–18, 131–4, 135, 198, 210, 215–17, 219–20, 223–7, 229, 232, 241, 243–5, 259, 338, 345, 378
  statutes of, 47
internationalism, 110, 223, 225, 241–3, 248, 312, 380
internationalization, 310
Ireland, 102, 132, 191, 213, 216, 223–8, 229, 232, 233, 234, 236, 241–3, 244–5, 247, 250–2, 256–9, 261–2, 292
  as a colonial economy, 225
  as immigrant labour, 224
Irish bourgeoisie, 241
Irish Famine, 225, 252
Irish nationalism, 224, 382
Irish Question, 226, 227, 236, 241–2, 258, 292
Irish Rebellion, 255
Irish Revolution, 227, 252
Islam, 334
Italian fascism, 282
Italy, 214, 244, 271, 280, 317

Jacobinism, 129, 133, 383, 391
Jacoby, Russell, 179

Japan, 235, 249, 317
Jewish Question, 58, 322, 326
Johnson, Andrew, 219
Judaism, 322–3, 326, 331

Kant, Immanuel, 324, 353, 360
Kautsky, Karl, 119, 122, 379–80
Kerensky, Alexander, 380–1
Khrushchev, Nikita, 385, 387
Kiernan, Victor, 78, 255
Köttgen, Gustav Adolf, 110
Kugelmann, Ludwig, 102, 241

labour
  abstract, 8–9, 147–8, 153–4, 164–5, 166, 294
  as a conscious act, 146
  as a vital activity, 141, 142, 153, 155
  capacity, 80, 145, 150, 339
  child, 80, 279, 338, 345, 366
  collective, 153
  concrete, 9, 147–8, 164–5, 172
  corvée, 43, 64
  dead, 151, 153–4, 370
  division of, 9, 12, 17, 34, 40, 57, 170, 235, 248, 266, 272, 278, 289, 291–3, 302, 307–9, 344, 345–6, 348, 353–4
  domestic, 204, 205–6
  forced, 144, 202, 237–8
  global market of, 234, 237–8
  immaterial, 151, 154
  immediate, 94
  living, 82, 96, 151, 153–5, 170, 183, 239, 370
  market, 238, 258, 273, 279
  movement, 74, 85, 86, 129, 132, 215, 224, 232, 259, 260, 267
  multifunctional, 154
  power, 6, 7, 11–16, 37, 41, 42, 66, 75, 77, 79–83, 87, 96–7, 145, 147, 148–9, 201–2, 232, 236, 238, 239, 360–1, 372
  productive, 44–5, 150, 345–6
  semi-free, 237
  social, 8–11, 38, 40, 41, 153, 171, 293–4
  superfluous, 173
  surplus, 38–9, 42–4, 56, 63–4, 83, 148, 169–70, 235, 294, 330
  unpaid, 63, 82, 272
  wage, 79–83, 95, 113–14, 143–5, 148, 151, 152, 227, 234, 237–8, 239, 248, 258–60, 289, 291
Lafargue, Paul, 102

Index

landed property, 5, 17–18, 188, 219, 221, 227, 253, 266, 289–90, 291
landlord, 80, 81, 217, 224, 242, 251, 275
landlordism, 227
Larson, Magali Sarfatti, 347
Lassalle, Ferdinand, 31–2, 118–22, 134, 205, 222, 344
Latin America, 86, 137, 390, 391
law of communal production, 44
laws of motion, 3, 17, 30, 275, 281, 285, 314–15
laws of movement, 298
League of the Just, 111, 127
Lenin, Vladimir, 102–3, 108, 119, 136, 249, 252, 280, 305, 381
Leninism, 108, 122–3, 386–7
Leopardi, Giacomo, 46
Leroux, Pierre, 1
  Malthus and the Economists, or Will There Always Be Poor People (1848), 1
leveller, 55
liberalism, 1, 46–7, 51–5, 57, 58, 65, 66, 68, 92, 94, 102, 113, 126, 131, 158, 182, 209, 218, 223, 262, 276, 289, 298, 307, 310–12, 315, 331, 333–5, 348, 357, 382, 389
  democracy, 51–5, 58, 63, 66, 68
  neo-, 53, 105, 158, 174, 289, 298, 334, 335, 348, 389
  political philosophy of, 57, 65
Liebig, Justus, 187–8, 373
Liebknecht, Wilhelm, 120, 123, 135
Lincoln, Abraham, 219–23
List, Friedrich, 298
  The National System of Political Economy (1841), 298
London Conference 1871, 117, 118, 134
London Congress of June 1847, 111
London Corresponding Society, 74
Lord Palmerston, Henry James Temple, 311–12
Löwy, Michael, 224, 324
Ludwig, Feuerbach
  The Essence of Christianity (1841), 322
Lukács, Georg, 168–9
Lumpenproletariat, 73, 75–9, 84, 277
Luxemburg, Rosa, 98, 103, 118, 136, 178, 249

machinery, 12, 13, 38, 41, 62, 71, 77, 81, 93, 96, 117, 133, 154, 162, 180, 200–2, 203, 216, 233, 244, 253, 274, 292, 296–7, 340, 346, 348, 363, 364–75
  capitalist, 41

communist, 366–8
reducing labour to a minimum, 367
Madison, James, 54
Magna Carta, 55
Maine, Henry Sumner, 206–7, 288
  Lectures on the Early History of Institutions (1875), 206
Malthus, Thomas Robert, 100, 180–1, 185, 190, 240, 330
  Essay on Population (1798), 185
Mandel, Ernest, 51
Maoism, 386–8
Marcuse, Hubert, 374
  Technology, War, and Fascism (1998), 374
Maréchal, Sylvain, 26
  Manifesto of the Equals (1795), 26
Mariategui, José Carlos, 136
market
  global, 244
  home, 290
  laws of, 22
  regime, 22
  socialism, 385, 386
  world, 14–16, 18, 84, 105, 132, 234, 235, 237, 240–1, 244, 247–50, 266, 273, 278, 280–2, 285–99, 304, 307–8
Martinez-Alier, Joan, 189
Marx, Karl, works by
  'A Draft Plan for a Work on the Modern State' (1844), 271
  'Address of the Central Council to the Communist League' (1850), 130
  'Circular Letter to August Bebel and Others' (1879), 94, 135
  'Comments on James Mill, Elements d'Economie Politique' (1844), 141
  'Conspectus of Bakunin's Statism and Anarchy' (1875), 2, 26, 38, 45
  'Draft Plan for a Work on the Modern State' (1844), 273
  'English Public Opinion' (1862), 222
  'Future Results of British Rule in India' (1853), 252, 288
  'Inaugural Address of the Working Men's International' (1864), 115–16, 216, 223
  'Instructions for the Delegates of the Provisional General Council' (1866), 43
  'Marginal Notes on Wagner's Treatise on Political Economy' (1879–80), 31, 41
  'On the Jewish Question' (1844), 58, 322, 326
  'On the Political Action of the Working Class' (1871), 134

Marx, Karl, works by (cont.)
'Peuchet on Suicide' (1846), 199
'Programme of the French Workers' Party' (1880), 32, 42, 243
'Report of the General Council to the Fourth Annual Congres', 204
'Speech on the Question of Free Trade' (1848), 288
'The British Cotton Trade' (1861), 234
'The British Rule in India' (1853), 247, 252, 288
'Draft of an Article on Friedrich List's book The National System of Political Economy' (1845), 298
A Contribution to the Critique of Hegel's Philosophy of Right (1844), 70, 127, 270, 271, 323
Capital (1867–94), xvii–xviii, 2–10, 13–16, 17–19, 20–1, 30, 32, 35, 37, 38, 39, 40–1, 42–3, 59, 63–4, 75, 77, 79, 83–4, 94, 95–8, 101, 103, 114–18, 145, 146, 147, 148, 149–50, 151, 162, 163–5, 166–7, 169, 175, 181, 182–3, 185, 187–9, 194, 198, 200–1, 204, 218–19, 220, 224, 225, 228, 232–4, 238, 247, 249–50, 252, 258–60, 266, 272, 274, 285, 288, 290, 292–3, 294–8, 314, 329, 338, 339, 344–5, 346, 363–6, 368–73
  volume I, 2–3, 7, 9, 10, 13, 15, 16, 17, 18, 30, 37, 38, 39, 40, 42, 43, 75, 79, 83, 96, 97, 98, 101, 103, 149, 200, 201, 204, 218, 224, 228, 233, 247, 248, 250, 252, 258, 259–60, 274, 285, 288, 290, 292, 294, 295, 296, 338, 363, 368, 372, 373
  volume II, 2, 10, 14, 40, 293
  volume III, 4, 6, 15, 41, 42, 63, 83, 97, 272, 295, 297, 339
Contribution to the Critique of Political Economy (1859), 31, 95, 115, 289
Critique of Hegel's Philosophy of Right (1844), 71, 270, 315
Critique of the Gotha Programme (1875), 32, 38, 40, 42, 45, 60, 61, 120–2, 123, 152, 198, 205, 243, 281, 291, 333, 338, 343, 378
Difference between the Domocritean and Epicurean Philosophy of Nature (1840–1), 177, 184, 321
Economic and Philosophic Manuscripts of 1844 (1844), 31, 33–5, 59, 141, 143, 144, 198, 209, 315, 351, 352

Ethnological Notebooks (1880–1), 198, 206, 209
Fictitious Splits in the International (1872) (with Engels), 45, 131
German–French Annals (1844), 323
Grundrisse (1857–8), 3, 14, 16, 21, 31, 32, 37, 38–44, 46, 59, 63, 84, 86, 115, 162–4, 185, 228, 240, 248, 259–61, 287, 289, 294, 296, 297, 304, 314, 315, 339–40, 355, 366–8, 375
London Notebooks (1850–3), 100
Manifesto of the Communist Party (1848), 19, 24, 31, 32, 36–7, 59, 73, 74, 76, 85, 92, 95, 99, 103, 111–13, 116, 129, 136, 185, 200, 214–15, 229, 256, 268, 285, 286, 290, 296, 306, 307, 311, 328, 338, 342–3, 347, 378
The Civil War in France (1871), 31, 32, 38, 45, 46, 116, 133, 270
The Economic Manuscript of 1861–3 (1861–3), 2, 39, 93, 96, 186, 293–5, 297, 329, 368
The Eighteenth Brumaire of Louis Bonaparte (1852), 61–2, 76, 276
The German Ideology (1845–6), xvii, 4, 31, 34–6, 63, 70, 75, 128, 129, 142, 184, 272, 285, 286, 298, 306, 307, 308, 313, 327, 332, 353, 354, 357
The Holy Family (1845), 192, 326, 332
The Poverty of Philosophy (1847), 71, 93–4, 98, 100, 111
Theories of Surplus Value (1863), 44, 339
Theses on Feuerbach (1845), 127, 315, 326, 353
Urtext (1858), 31, 46
Value, Price and Profit (1865), 26, 32, 41, 97, 101, 145
Wage Labour and Capital (1849), 113, 145, 259
Marx-Engels-Gesamtausgabe (MEGA²), xvii
Marxism
  Austro-, 383
  classical, 386, 388
  legal, 376
  revisionist, 379, 384
  traditional, 138, 157, 159–61, 171, 175
Marxism-Leninism, 33, 377, 386
materialism, 4, 63, 71, 109, 128, 141, 168–9, 177–9, 180–1, 184–5, 190, 248, 258, 267, 270–1, 272, 277, 279, 302–4, 305, 306, 309, 314, 320–2, 323, 326–8, 329–30, 334, 353, 364
communism, 109

Index

contemplative, 326
dialectical, 178
historical, 63, 71, 141, 177–8, 180–1, 184, 190, 248, 258, 267, 271, 272, 277, 302–4, 305, 306, 309, 320, 327, 330, 334
religious, 320
materialist interpretation of religion, 327–31
Mensheviks, 381
Meyen, Eduard, 332
Meyer, Sigfrid, 102, 132
migrant self-organization, 245
migration, 232–45
  forced, 232–4, 235–6, 239–40
military, 61, 64–5, 131, 222, 225, 242, 256, 276–7, 281, 305, 307, 345, 385
Mill, John Stuart, 294
  Some Unsettled Questions (1844), 294
Mills, C. Wright, 347
Mirror of Society, 199
mobile guard, 78
mode of distribution, 25
mode of production, xviii, 1–8, 12–15, 19–21, 25, 30–2, 37–8, 40–3, 70, 94–5, 142, 148, 155, 183, 185–6, 207, 210, 232–3, 239, 248–50, 252, 253, 258, 268, 272–3, 280, 287, 289–90, 294, 295, 297, 307, 311, 327, 330, 339, 353, 356, 358, 359, 368–9, 374, 385–6
  Asiatic, 252, 311, 385–6
  capitalist, xviii, 1–7, 14, 19–21, 30, 38, 42, 94, 148, 186, 232–3, 248–50, 272–3, 277, 280, 289–90, 294, 295, 339, 358, 359, 369, 374
  class based, 267, 270
  non-capitalist, 359
modern industry, 3, 13, 14–15, 74–5, 97, 174, 200–1, 204, 234, 345, 346, 370, 372
monarchy, 24, 113, 117
Moorhouse, Bert, 86
Morgan, Henry, 206
  Ancient Society (1877), 206

Napoleon, Louis, 61
Napoleonic Vienna Congress System, 317
national question, 102, 383, 385
nationalism, xviii, 192, 212–29, 243, 262–3, 266, 293, 306, 312, 380, 382
  methodological, 306, 309
natural limits, 180–2, 185, 239
naturalism, 34, 146, 185, 209
Nazism, 282, 379

Negri, Antonio, 228–9, 290
Neo-Zapatista movement, 389
Netherlands, 31, 250, 277, 330
New Left, 179, 388–89
New Rhenish Newspaper, 112–14, 268, 271, 322
New-York Tribune, 131, 222, 226, 233, 234, 247, 251, 252, 256, 261
Nieuwenhuis, Ferdinand Domela, 31
Nimtz, August, 221
Nkrumah, Kwame, 387
nobility, 109, 253

O'Connor, James, 189
O'Donnell, Don Leopoldo, 131
Odum, Howard, 191
Old Left, 388–89
Oligarchy, 53, 102, 221
Opium Wars, 252, 310
organic intellectual, 378
Ottoman Empire, 311, 313
Owen, Robert, 25–6, 29, 129, 345
  Observations on the Effect of the Manufacturing System (1815), 26
  The Book of the New Moral World (1836–44), 29

Palestine, 213–14
Paris Commune, 31, 33, 38, 85, 114–18, 121, 126, 130–3, 214, 270, 273, 343
Parsons, Howard, 182
  Marx and Engels on Ecology (1977), 182
paternalism, 347
patria potestas, 204
patriarchy, 198, 205, 206, 207, 208–10
Patriotic Notes, 2
pax Americana, 317
pax Britannica, 317
Peace of Utrecht, 317
Peasant Wars of Germany, 126
peasantry, 55, 61–5, 74, 75–7, 102, 113, 120, 126, 141, 192, 213, 215, 217, 224, 226–7, 229, 244, 249, 251, 252–8, 261–2, 269, 275–7, 293, 305, 390
peon, 64
Peru, 187
petty bourgeoisie, 25, 74, 112, 114, 126, 130, 275, 276
Philips, Lion, 223
Phillips, Wendell, 219
phraseology, 25
Piketty, Thomas, 105
plebeian, 76, 92–3, 221
Podolinsky, Sergei, 189–90

poiesis, 358
Poland, 115, 213–18, 223–4, 226, 229, 244, 261–2, 271
polis, 53
Polish national liberation, 115, 212–13, 215
Polish Restoration, 217
Polish Revolution, 213–18
political economy, xviii, 1–2, 3–5, 15–16, 20, 57, 59, 62–5, 75, 93, 94, 100, 101, 103–4, 105, 115, 141–2, 143, 159, 160, 162, 181–2, 185, 190, 198, 200–6, 209, 239, 241, 248, 250, 257, 261, 266–7, 279–80, 289–90, 291, 292, 293, 299, 303–5, 315, 339–41, 349, 351, 353, 354–9
  bourgeois, 185
  classical, xviii, 1–2, 5, 57, 63, 65, 93, 100, 182, 267, 289, 292, 293
  critique of, 5, 59, 63, 75, 94, 104, 105, 141–2, 159, 160, 162, 181–2, 190, 248, 250, 261, 266, 279–80, 289–90, 291, 299, 304, 305, 349, 351, 353
  false critique of, 20
  international, 303
  liberal, 315
  Marxist, 104, 105, 182
  of education, 339
  semiotic, 280
  vulgar, 267
political science, 65, 328
pollution, 181, 185, 187, 192
  universal, 185
Poppe, Johann Heinrich Moritz von, 364–5, 373
population, 15, 61, 72, 100, 181, 185, 188, 190, 202, 232–3, 236, 238–40, 244, 372
  laws of, 100, 185, 240
  over-, 181, 185, 240
  surplus, 15, 61, 185, 202, 232, 233, 372
  theory of, 190, 232
Portugal, 250, 277, 386–7
Portuguese Communist Party, 387
positivism, 315, 364
post-capitalism, 33, 36–7, 207, 308, 355
poststructuralism, 104, 105, 160–1, 197, 228
power-knowledge, 105
praxis, 4, 126–31, 137, 178, 191–4, 304, 307, 315, 326, 358, 359, 391
  ecological, 191–4
  philosophy of, 128, 137, 304
  revolutionary, 128, 138, 193, 326

precapitalism, 8, 64, 206–9, 255, 256–7, 260, 267, 308–9, 316, 356
precariat, 173
price inflation, 297
primitive society, 306
private property, 27, 34, 42, 53, 71, 85, 138, 141, 159, 174, 188, 218, 237, 261, 271–3
  abolition of, 36, 271
production
  collective, 38, 150
  cooperative, 26
  mass, 8, 12–13, 18, 367
  over-, 2, 14–15, 297
  relations of, 3–4, 8, 16, 20, 35, 94–5, 97, 98, 120, 138, 207, 239, 256, 272–3, 275, 277, 304, 339, 343, 346, 354, 357, 368
  social, 13, 39–40, 46, 185, 203, 293, 345, 368
productivism, 160, 181
profit
  maximization, 65
  rate of, 14, 21, 97, 297–8
  theory of, 97
proletarianization, 85–6, 249
  full, 85, 86
  semi-, 85
proletariat, xix, 18, 25, 30–1, 37, 42, 43, 47, 56, 60, 62, 70–88, 94, 103, 109, 110–11, 112–13, 114, 115, 117–18, 119, 121, 126–36, 154, 159, 162, 163–4, 168–9, 170, 173–4, 191, 192, 199, 200, 216, 223, 227, 229, 239, 241–5, 248, 249, 256, 257–8, 261, 266, 274, 275, 276, 277, 280, 288, 290–1, 298, 307–8, 313, 333, 342–3, 346, 347, 357, 382, 383
  categories of, 72–5
  dictatorship of, xix, 47, 60, 72, 94, 266, 274, 382
  environmental, 191
  internationalism, 223, 225, 248
  revolution. See Revolution, proletarian
  self-abolition of the, 173
  self-emancipation of the, 70, 128, 131–4, 135
  struggle of the, 42
  theory of, 87
Prometheanism, 181
propaganda, xix, 14, 25, 32, 33, 36, 110, 212, 287
protest, 78, 222, 323–4
Proudhon, Pierre-Joseph, 1, 31, 93, 109, 217

Index

The General Idea of the Revolution in the Nineteenth Century (1851), 1
Proudhonism, 116, 217, 226
Prussia, 127, 213, 343, 344, 351, 365
psychoanalysis, 320
puritanism, 330

Quaini, Massimo, 182
Quesnay, François, 70

Ratzel, Friedrich, 312
real estate, 5
realm of necessity, 151
Redclift, Michael, 181
reification, 16, 149, 304, 309, 314, 315
relative autonomy, 61, 269
religion, 16, 22, 30, 73, 142, 227, 242, 254–5, 256, 263, 273, 320–35, 351–2, 383
   anti-, 321
   of capital, 329
   theory of, 320
religious alienation, 325, 334, 352
revisionism, 134–5, 377, 379–81, 384–5
revolution, 12, 13, 19–20, 24, 26, 27, 30–1, 35–6, 42, 55, 58–62, 63, 70–2, 73–6, 84, 92–3, 94–5, 103–4, 108, 109–15, 116–18, 119, 120–1, 123, 126–38, 178, 184–5, 186, 191–4, 199, 212–19, 221–2, 224–8, 229, 233, 241–2, 244, 251–3, 258, 260–2, 266, 268, 271–2, 286, 288–9, 292, 298, 305, 308, 309–11, 312, 313, 326–7, 332, 351–2, 354, 357–8, 360, 377, 379–82, 383, 384, 386–8
   agrarian, 214–15, 233, 244, 252
   bourgeois, 19, 59, 126, 310
   class, 74, 109
   communist, 218, 241, 298
   democratic, 128, 129, 130, 133, 212, 213–18
   ecological, 138, 191, 193
   government, 31
   of self-emancipation, 129, 131–4
   peasant, 126
   period of, 310
   proletarian, 71–2, 74, 94, 110, 126–7, 132–3, 135, 136, 192
   scientific, 184
   slave, 74
   social, 94–5, 117, 132, 134, 135, 138, 191, 214, 242, 253, 260, 277, 288
   socialist, 103, 136, 159, 226, 381
   subject of, 30
   technological, 19
   theory of, 72, 126, 129, 136–8, 312
   world, 286, 298–9, 308, 377, 387–89
Revolution of July 1830, 27
revolutionary subject, 70–2, 84, 113
Ricamarie massacres, 204
Ricardianism, 97, 291, 294
Ricardo, David, 2, 93–101, 111, 114, 239–40, 288, 289, 294, 358
rights, 45–7, 70, 202–3, 253–4, 271, 273, 330, 331, 332, 342
   bourgeois, 60
   citizenship, 53, 219
   civil, 52, 53, 55, 56, 58, 66, 222
   constitutional, 54
   cultural, 383, 387
   democratic, 54, 62, 65, 67
   economic, 68
   equal, 46, 47, 80, 243, 331
   feudal, 215
   formal, 59
   human, 137
   individual, 66
   inheritance, 37, 207
   innate, 273
   labour, 65, 203
   liberal, 68
   minority, 383
   political, 52, 53, 55–6, 58, 62, 65, 66, 67, 68, 218
   property, 275–6
   to form unions, 67
   to freedom of religion, 332
   to organize, 112, 120
   to own slaves, 219
   to self-determination, 103
   to use a commodity, 81
   to work, 155
Rodbertus-Jagetzow, Carl von, 1
Rodden, John, 258
Ruge, Arnold, 127, 322, 331
rural exodus, 233
Russia, 2–3, 131, 134–6, 158, 212–14, 215–18, 221, 256–7, 293, 310–11, 313, 377, 380–1, 383
Russian Question, 261
Russian Revolution, 131, 135–6, 137, 158, 280, 377, 381
Russian rural commune, 135–6

Said, Edward, 228, 247, 331
   Orientalism (1978), 228, 248
Saint Simon, Claude Henri de, 25–6, 28, 32, 37, 129
   New Christianity (1824), 28

Schäffle, Albert, 1
Capitalism and Socialism (1870), 1
Schapper, Karl, 113
Schiller, Friedrich, 360
Schmidt, Alfred, 179–80
Schramm, Carl August, 134
Schweitzer, Johann von, 122
science, 12, 43, 46, 57, 119–20, 154, 172–3, 174, 178–9, 180, 185, 186, 189, 190, 233, 279–80, 333, 339–40, 344, 347, 353, 363–75
Scotland, 17, 29, 222
Second International, 119, 122, 161, 380, 382, 384
Second International of the European Socialist Parties, 312
sectarianism, 111
secularism, 73, 323, 326, 327, 331, 335
self-determination, 102, 155, 328
Sepoy Mutiny, 261
serfdom, 55, 64, 92, 234, 293
Silesian weavers' rebellion, 71–2, 84, 127
Simon, Brian, 349
slavery, 55, 74, 79–84, 87, 216, 218–24, 234–6, 237–9, 247, 258–64
  abolitionism, 219–21
  as fixed capital, 82, 88, 368
  semi-, 236
Smith, Adam, 2, 239, 288, 340
Social Darwinism, 190, 312
  survival of the fittest, 312
Social Democratic Party of Germany, 134–5, 378–80, 381, 384, 386, 391
social reproduction, 63
Social Democratic League, 31
Social-Democratic Workers Party, 120
socialism, xvii, xviii–xix, 1, 2, 19, 24–6, 28–9, 30–2, 36, 38, 40–2, 44, 46–7, 51, 52–3, 55, 56, 59–61, 66, 78, 94, 99–100, 103, 108, 110, 111–12, 118–20, 123, 127–8, 129, 133, 135–8, 159–60, 168–9, 174, 177–9, 180–2, 184, 185, 188–90, 192, 193–4, 197, 214, 215–19, 222, 226, 228, 251–2, 257, 269, 279, 298, 306, 312–13, 317, 325, 333–4, 344, 346, 360, 378–80, 381–3, 384–5, 386, 387, 389, 390–1
  bourgeois, 279
  reactionary, 25
  revolution. See Revolution, socialism
  scientific, 178
  state, 47
  theory of, 94
  utopian, 24–6, 94, 129, 137
Society of Fraternal Democrats, 110
Sombart, Werner, 3
Modern Capitalism (1902), 3
South Africa, 237, 387
South African Communist Party, 387
sovereign authority, 53
Soviet Red Army, 384
Soviet Union, 123, 137, 158, 377, 380–6, 388, 389
Spain, 131, 137, 250, 277
Spanish Revolution, 131
Stalin, Joseph, 312, 383, 385
Stalinism, 122–3, 137, 286, 383
  de-Stalinization, 385
state, xviii, 36, 45–7, 54–5, 56–9, 60–7, 68, 71, 83, 96, 99, 109, 116–17, 120, 122–3, 130–1, 133–4, 158–9, 160, 168, 204, 215, 221, 248, 249–50, 254, 257–8, 260, 263–4, 266–82, 285–6, 289–91, 293, 295, 298, 299, 304–6, 307–10, 311, 312–17, 322, 323–4, 327–8, 331–4, 338–9, 342–4, 345, 348, 349, 359, 365–6, 381–5, 388
  absolutism, 62, 130, 310
  apparatus, 66, 269, 277, 282
  constitutional, 270, 273, 278
  nation-state, 263, 266, 290–1, 299, 312, 349
  power, 45, 54, 67, 109, 116–17, 130, 267–71, 277, 281–2, 342, 343, 381, 388
  pretorian, 269
  real, 58
  theory of, 58, 267–8, 279–82, 314
statism, 299, 380, 388
Ste Croix, Geoffrey de, 104
  The Class Struggle in the Ancient Greek World (1981), 104
Stein, Lorenz von, 71
  The Socialism and Communism of Contemporary France (1842), 71
Stirner, Max, 328, 353–4
strike, 99–100, 127, 131, 141, 204, 244–5, 276
structuralism, 304, 317
suffragette, 55
suicide, 199, 254
superpower country, 388
superstructure, 63, 95, 103, 277, 353, 355
supra-historical, 6, 302, 306, 309, 317
Sweden, 271
Switzerland, 60

Taiping Rebellion, 252, 261
taxation, 55, 64, 238, 253–6, 277–9, 343
Taylorism, 154

Index

technological
   change, 21, 86
   communication, 289
   determinism, 95
   innovation, 364
   productivity, 201
   progress, 160
   revolution. See revolution, technological
technology, 8, 12–14, 19, 20, 21, 43, 86, 96–7, 101, 148, 153–4, 159–60, 171, 172–3, 174, 179, 201, 289, 329, 339–40, 344, 345–6, 348, 363–75, 391
   capitalist, 371–2, 374
   communist compared to capitalist, 366
   development of, 20, 363
   emancipatory potential of, xviii
   general, 365–6, 373
   history of, 364
   Marx's critique of, 374
   non-capitalist, 363
   philosophy of, 371
   science of, 373
   theory of, 368–9, 373
teleology, 103, 184, 306–7, 309
The Economist, 286
The Organizer, 28
The Source and Remedy of the National Difficulties, Deduced from Principles of Political Economy, in a Letter to Lord John Russell (1821), 44
theological fanaticism, 326
theory of history, 94–5, 98, 104, 161, 302–3, 305, 314–17
theory of metabolic rift, 178, 186, 187–91
thermodynamics, 186, 188, 189
Third International, 119, 312, 381, 384
Thompson, Edward P., 74, 104, 371
   The Making of the English Working Class (1963), 104
time
   abstract, 167–8
   surplus, 155
transformation problem, 191
transnationalism, 299
transnationalization, 307, 308–9, 313, 315
Traugott, Mark, 78
trinity formula, 16
Trotsky, Leon, 136, 292, 312
Tsarist Russia, 135, 212, 216, 311, 381
Turgot, Anne Robert Jacques, 70

Ukraine, 189
unionism, 55, 65, 67, 98–103, 116, 118, 122, 210, 225, 279

United States of America, 18, 29, 54, 60, 79, 83–4, 132, 179, 183, 191–2, 213, 214–16, 218–24, 225, 227, 229, 235, 238, 242, 244–5, 250, 259–61, 262, 267, 271, 272, 280, 297, 313, 317, 343–4, 384–7, 388
universal metabolism of nature, 178, 186
universal suffrage, 55, 56, 275, 387
universalism, 263, 309
Ure, Andrew, 340, 365

Vaillant, Édouard, 117
valorization, 7, 10–13, 144, 150–1, 168, 182, 297
   process of, 169, 171–2
   self-, 150, 168, 172
value, 6, 16, 82–3, 88, 120, 143, 145, 150, 151, 163, 167–8, 169–70, 171, 172, 173, 368–9
   absolute, 11, 96, 148–9, 169, 279, 369, 371
   abstract, 10
   enhancement, 10–11
   exchange, 21, 39, 41, 46, 145, 147–55, 190, 205, 266, 289, 373
   form, 16, 170, 182, 184, 190
   international, 293–5
   labour theory of, 83, 88, 93, 97, 160, 166, 181, 182, 293–4, 295
   law of, 8–9, 22, 151, 294, 357, 358–61
   magnitude of, 166–8
   metabolic, 191
   relative, 11, 96, 148, 149, 169–70, 279, 369–72
   simple form of, 9
   surplus, 6–8, 11–14, 42–4, 81–4, 88, 95–6, 148–50, 154, 161–2, 169–70, 171, 202, 240, 279, 295, 297, 358, 364, 367, 368–72
   theory of, 181
   use, 9, 21, 82, 146, 147–50, 155, 164, 167, 169–70, 186, 190–1, 205, 358, 373
Venezuela, 390
Vernet, Horace, 354
Victorian Britain, 314
Victorianism, 209
Vienna Congress 1815, 311
Vogt, August, 102, 132

wage
   double-free, 84
   labour, 5–6, 11–14, 17, 18, 41, 59, 75
   of rate, 97
   real, 100, 101

wage (cont.)
  relative, 101
  theory of, 101
Wagner, Adolph, 31, 41
Wakefield, Edward Gibbon, 250
Walter, Benjamin, 138
  On the Concept of History (1940), 138
wealth
  abstract, 10
  common, 40
  real, 44, 191
  social, 10, 18, 162, 170, 171
Weber, Max, 22, 104–5, 330
  The Protestant Ethic and the Spirit of Capitalism (1905), 330
Weimar period, 379
Weitling, Wilhelm, 27, 110, 127
  Humanity As It Is and As It Should Be (1838), 27
welfare state, 52–3, 158, 382
Weston, Del, 189
  The Political Economy of Global Warming (2014), 189
Weydemeyer, Joseph, 72, 92–3, 94
Williams, Eric, 259
Williams, Raymond, 177
  'Socialism and Ecology' (1982), 177
Willich, August, 113
Wolff, Wilhelm, 113
women, 53–5, 73, 77, 79, 84, 137, 192, 197–210, 279, 372, 388–9
  oppression of, 137, 199, 210

working class, xix, 12, 24, 26, 30, 31, 43–4, 45, 47, 52–3, 55–6, 59, 67, 71, 72, 73, 79, 84, 96, 98–102, 105, 113, 114, 116–19, 121, 122–3, 130, 131–3, 134–5, 152, 174, 199–200, 202, 216–17, 218, 220, 222–4, 226–8, 229, 234, 242–3, 259–60, 266, 274, 312–13, 339, 342, 345–6, 366, 368–9, 380, 383
  movement, 52, 56, 116
  restriction of development, 43
  theory of, 84
working conditions, 84, 203, 275, 279
working day, 12, 26, 42–4, 95–6, 101, 148–9, 151–2, 155, 220, 279
  eight hour, 99, 220, 244
world history, 46, 138, 192, 255, 257, 262, 286, 298, 304, 305, 307–8, 310–12, 314, 326
World Social Forum, 390
World War I, 158, 312, 380, 381, 383
World War II, 104, 158, 178, 384
Wright, Erik Olin, 103

Yalta arrangement, 384, 386
Yearbook for Social Science and Social Politics, 134
Yoshida, Fumikazu, 365

Zasulich, Vera, 2, 135, 288, 382

Printed in the United States
By Bookmasters